AARON *and* AMANDA SHIRK

of Laurel Hill 1937-2010

How they raised their fifteen children in Lancaster County, PA

LOUISE B. (SHIRK) MARTIN

Aaron *and* Amanda Shirk

of Laurel Hill 1937-2010

International Standard Book Number: 978-1-60126-288-2

ABOUT THE FRONT COVER

Aaron and Amanda's aerial view of the farm in 1971, includes the house and barn they purchased in 1937.The pond and the sheep shed on the right were not yet theirs and neither were the deep woods. Half of their long lane noticeable here, leads North towards the turnpike beyond the left edge of the photo. The farm that had been criss–crossed with stone fences bordering ten small fields, has only one remaining ridge of densely covered rocks showing a bit on the left edge.

Silver Hill lies to the left of this setting and Laurel Hill slopes up steeply towards the top and right. Below the photo and over the next hill, lay Turkey Hill where Aaron grew up. The field lane leading west to Jesse's went left, towards the bottom corner. The power line and the Black Creek cut through the woods along the bottom edge. The white springhouse is downhill from the house and the laundry lines hang between the house and barn.The chicken houses are gone, but the buggy shed/corn shed combination still stands.

The farm changed tremendously! This is where all fifteen children were born and raised at 492 Laurel Road, Narvon, PA.

TABLE OF CONTENTS

PREFACE

Fifty years ago, some talented teachers tried their best to teach me all about English. I had good grades, but promptly forgot, with no desire to diagram another sentence for the rest of my life!

Twenty years later, I saw many family history stories that needed preservation. I started gathering information and made a crude attempt at starting a book. Several children later, I lost all interest in the project and saw that I did not know how and the information I needed, was a thousand miles away. I put family ahead of book writing and I quit.

Daniel's two oldest girls learned typing and had more time. They took up the project and laid out the history, spending many hours gathering vital information. Amanda had a clear memory and they did a wonderful job with the help of Daniel. Thank you Susan and Wilma!

They could not add the details such as a person who lived through the events, and they dropped the project, neatly typed out as, "Lest we forget." The book lay dormant for another decade, until I read the book *Bart and Lydia*, by Elsie Hoover. Barts had lived about three miles from us, along the same Black Creek. Suddenly inspired, I saw how Elsie wrote that book in a common everyday style. Perhaps I could also! Her title idea gave the project a huge push, because I then had the perspective of who Aaron and Amanda were. Until then, Amanda was 'Grandma Shirk', to her growing crowd of descendants.

I opened my Bible for direction and read, "...if there first be a willing mind." With renewed confidence, I found the original copy and started writing. Mom often said, "*Duh Kon-net iss shoont long dote,*" [the cannot is long dead.] I planned to polish the story a bit and have it printed. I got in deeper as Irene dug out more of our parents many diaries.

The pile kept growing. With help from the family, we sifted out some basic facts and much more.

I saw the convenience of a computer, but at the age of 60, I had no desire to tangle with such modern technology. I was sure that no one could decipher all the scribbled notes and I had to do it myself. Ivan bought me a computer and our youngest son Shane, age 16, painstakingly tried to teach me how to use it. Double click here, and right click there...sigh! Every evening Shane had to fix problems. The computer-deleted things I still wanted and the project appeared nearly hopeless.

The Office Word program came up with warnings such as "passive writing-consider revising." I struggled with split infinitives, and prepositions at the end of the sentence. That's just how the people talked and some of that stayed on purpose. The story goes on, even with poor sentence structure and such. Rather than spend the rest of my lifetime revising and correcting, please overlook all the mistakes and find the main story and the thoughts I felt compelled to share, in my very first book.

These stories and collection of memories are as true as we could make them, with the information in our possession. The memories did not stay in chronological order but all tumbled over each other. No names have been changed! Keep in mind that all the characters are imperfect people like ourselves, needing improvement.

Sometimes I wondered why I wanted to write a book with so many mistakes on a beginners level, and then I go on and say, "Why not?" 'There is something important about telling younger children where they are coming from. Our lives revolved around tobacco farming and the next generation never heard of a 'stripping room'. [By the way, it is a room where farmers removed the leaves from dried tobacco plants]. Overlook all the short-comings and savor the importance of family and neighbors.

The Pennsylvania Dutch language has many dialects and different pronunciations for the same words. Berks County Dutch differs from Lancaster County, and Michigan was slightly different from those. No one could prove who was right or wrong. Living next door, Jesse Brubacher's called their beans *buna*, with a long U, and we ate *bone-a*. Our family ate *poshing*, while Jesse's had *pashing*, as we all enjoyed the same peaches. For the sake of simplicity, all Dutch words in this book are spelled as they sounded, and then translated into English.

Aaron died without seeing his book come true and so did Titus. He wrote many helpful letters, from his deathbed. Most of Aaron and Amanda's generation passed on. When I ask an older person, 'Do you remember Aaron Shirk?" Either their face lights up with vivid recall or I get a blank look, never anything in between. Anyone who met him once, usually remembered him. This thirty-year-old letter from my father, A.M. Shirk, inspired me to print what I had.

LAUREL HILL   Pa.

Aug 15th 1979   Dear Louise I do appreciate your plans to write a book about (The Life of Mandie) I think this should be a hit by most story book readers and I think you would be a qualified person for a writer because your heart is in it, starting with mom in the sand box in woodland michigan then carry water to the men folks fencing stoney land for grazing, and a thousand other items should be listed on notes then the notes get sorted into a story, then a good english person should do the proof reading and make corrections. if I get into the picture at dateing time and if my talents are expected to enter the story book I will most gladly let my self be used as the Lord sees fit
                        A M Shirk DAD

INTRODUCTIONS

Most people knew Amanda as Mandie, an humble German variation of the name. In this book, she will be Amanda or Mom and her daughter is Mandy.

Aaron Martin Shirk signed his name as A M Shirk, because another Aaron Shirk lived in the area. Aaron and Amanda raised 15 children:

Daniel born August 16, 1938 married Edna Horst
Sarah Ann born January 19, 1940 married Mahlon Zimmerman
Walter born September 1, 1941 married Marian Martin
Peter (Pete) born April 27, 1943 married Naomi Martin
Aaron (Dick) born July 6, 1944 married Ruth Zimmerman
Rhoda born July 29, 1945 married Mervin Brubaker
Ruth born July 29, 1945 married Carl Weiler
Martha born October 5, 1946 married Mervin High
Mary born January 17, 1948 married Roland Weiler
Louisa born March 7, 1949 married Ivan Martin
Irene born August 27, 1950 married Marlin Brubaker
Wesley born November 4, 1951 married Mary Jane High
Lydia born December 2, 1952 married Carl Hoover
Rose Anna born March 2, 1954 married Lewis Nolt
Amanda born March 13, 1956 married Henry Martin

Aaron came from a close-knit family. His father Benjamin Weaver Shirk was the son of Benjamin Horning Shirk, and therefore he signed his name BW Shirk. He offered $10 for grandsons named Benjamin, and he got five of them. BW Shirk had a son Ben M. Shirk, and made the name more confusing. Benjamin W Shirk married Annie [Martin] and they had nine children:

Aaron, born December 24, 1913 married Amanda B. Brubacher
Samuel, born February 14, 1915 married Lydia Zimmerman
Lydia, born June 11, 1916 married Jesse K. Brubacher
Eva born February 6, 1918
Benjamin born July 11, 1919 married Grace Martin
Elias born October 2, 1920 married Nancy Weaver
Annie born June 26, 1924 married Reuben Weaver
Menno born July 11, 1926 married Martha Kilmer
Titus born February 23, 1930 married Katie Leinbach

Amanda's family ties were dear to her:

Peter and Sarah Ann [Brenneman] Brubacher raised seven children in Michigan;

Silas born July 2, 1910 married Sarah Hawk
Mary born January 19, 1912 married Martin Kilmer
Betsy born September 26, 1913 married Christian Kilmer

Amanda born February 22, 1915 married Aaron Shirk
Lydia born August 1916 married Eli Stauffer
Katie born January 4, 1920 married Dan Martin
Joshua born February 14

If you get lost in the crowd, refer back to this map for the main characters.

1

Amanda's head nodded She knew she may not go to sleep at the train depot, no matter how tired she was. To her right, sat her brother Silas. He was husky and built bigger than their father, who was at home doing the farm chores without their help. The masculine presence of Silas, was a comfort to the three slim girls as they travelled together.

To her left, sat her sister Lydia dozing off as they waited on the rugged depot bench. None of them ever went to a train depot without their parent's. Lena Martin, a friend, travelled with the three Brubacher children.

Amanda watched people come and go. Big ones and small, rich people and poor-looking ones, some in a hurry and some waiting as patiently as they were. The four travelers missed the train! The night stretched before them, as the longest one Amanda ever knew in her twenty-one years. Her head nodded again. While Lydia slept, Amanda knew she must keep Silas from sleeping. They carried cash for travelling and planned to make sure that no one picked their pockets. They needed their hard-earned money and their belongings, for traveling far, in search of lifetime companions!

Life in Michigan had never been easy for the Peter Brubacher family. With the 1930's depression upon them, life became even harder. Furthermore, dissatisfaction among some church members split their group. Some wanted automobiles and joined another Mennonite church in the Brutus area that allowed cars. This was the Indiana-Michigan Conference, commonly known as "Funk" people, similar to the Lancaster Conference in Pennsylvania. Their leader was Clyde Kauffman. These two Mennonite churches alternately used the Maple River Mennonite Church.

Some families sold out and moved from Michigan to Pennsylvania. Amanda's older sisters, Mary and Betsy, married to brothers, Martin and Christian Kilmer, were among those who relocated. The remaining five Brubacher children lived securely among loving parents at home, but God gave them each a deep longing for marriage.

No partners seemed available for them among their dwindling church group. Since Silas, Amanda and Lydia were of age and none of them had a job just then, the three went traveling. In January 1937, they left home for a lengthy excursion. Silas purchased their tickets. He paid his own and Amanda paid for hers and Lydias. They spent six weeks in Canada among many relatives where their father grew up.

When they arrived at Kitchener, Ontario, from Michigan, they waited a long time for Uncle Amos Brubachers to meet them. At the other depot in town, Aunt Lucinda and Cousin Wesley also waited long, until they thought of checking the other depot and found the travelers there. What a rejoicing! Those cousins had never met before and they chatted all the way to Uncle Amos where they received a warm welcome.

Amanda, Lydia, and Silas met their grandfather Jacob Brubacher, [he had a nickname of Notion Jecky, because two men shared the same name]. It was the last time they saw him; he died the following May. They spent time at Uncle Eli Baumans, and at Uncle Christian Brubachers.

While in Ontario, they socialized with the young people every chance they had. They attended three weddings. Cousin Barbara Bauman married Noah Frey, on February 18, on the bride's 21st birthday. They stayed a week longer than first planned, so they could attend that wedding yet.

Amanda and Lydia had the misfortune of spending time in bed with the measles while in Canada. They were laid up at Cousin Leah and Emanuel Martins where their father's single sister,

Aunt Barbara resided. As they traveled from place to place, Amanda and Lydia collected small scraps of print fabric from their friends. Sewing by hand, over several years time, they each made a flower garden quilt. They stitched together a few thousand small six sided pieces with no two prints alike. On one of the last evenings in Canada, they sat around the stove at Uncle Christians and talked until two o'clock in the morning, making happy memories!

Uncle Amos's boys, Wesley and Abner, took them to Niagara Falls in their car, where their friend Lena joined them again, after spending time with her relatives. It was February 22, Amanda's 22nd birthday, a day to remember! In Niagara Falls, at a place called Burning Springs, someone demonstrated a cupful of water that burned.

Amanda, Lena, Lydia and Silas

There they saw the barrel that William Red hill used to go down over the falls. They toured a power plant and the shredded wheat factory, then it was time to get to Buffalo, New York, to take the night train to Sunbury, Pennsylvania. They considered taking the bus out of Niagara Falls to Buffalo, but were told that it would be figuring almost too close. They might not have enough time to meet their train on schedule.

"We could drive you to Buffalo," offered Wesley and Abner. "That might get you there on time." So that is what they did. By that time, it was snow-

ing, and they had trouble reading the road signs. Progress was slow. When they finally reached the Buffalo train station, they were dismayed to find out that they had just missed the 11:20 PM train! The next train was not leaving until nine o'clock in the morning. There was nothing to do but wait. They said," Goodbye, Wesley and Abner and thank you very much for all the trouble." Wesley and Abner headed for home, they really had no permission to come to Buffalo in the first place.

So there they sat, Silas, Amanda, Lydia, and Lena waiting out the night. Amanda's head nodded again. They simply could not trust sleeping among so many strangers. They talked and reminisced many hours about their childhood and about their father's past life.

Their father, Peter Brubacher, was born and raised in Ontario, Canada, the oldest of nine children of Jacob B and Elizabeth Brubacher. When the Stauffer Mennonite or 'Pikers' started a group in Ontario in 1882, the Brubacher's joined that church. Jesse Bauman was ordained as Bishop and Josiah Martin as their preacher. Those Canadians had no church-house yet and desired to move out and start elsewhere. They wanted a glorious church without spot or wrinkle. They would not tolerate pride in any form!

They discovered a large ranch of open prairie land for sale near May City, Iowa. Jesse Bauman bought one square mile, which is 640 acres, at eight dollars an acre. Other farmers bought quarter sections of 160 acres, at $10 per acre in 1888. Mennonite families congregated there from Pennsylvania, Michigan, Indiana, and Canada. They all agreed on ten basic rules. (1.) No public offices may be served whatsoever. (2.) Serving on jury duty is forbidden. (3.) Voting at public elections is forbidden. (4.) No insurance companies allowed, nor attending their worldly meetings and conventions. (5.) Do not arrest or sue anyone. (6.) No lightning rods are allowed–depend upon God. (7.) Do not attend camp meetings or singing schools or suchlike. (8.) Use only a common note to show proof of true debt. (9.) No stylish hairstyles are allowed on men or women. (10.) Decorations, adornment in homes or on clothes are worldly fashion. It is wrong to have double-breasted coats, bold or multi-colored, fringed, gathered and frilled items. All things with a haughty appearance are forbidden by the power of God's Word.

People kept on moving in, working hard and helping one another, breaking the prairie sod and making fences. There were no buildings and very few trees. They faced extreme cold and a lack of firewood. Coal was expensive, so they used corn-cobs and bundled wild hay for cooking and heat-ing. Water in the teakettle froze overnight. The cemetery was started before everyone had houses to live in when the measles epidemic took the lives of four little children in the month of April.

Bishop Jesse Bauman set the rules. He arrived first and wanted simplicity and unity. All buildings should be painted red, because he got a bargain on red paint. A cornice on a building was too fancy. The people measured with rulers to make sure that their hat brims were wide enough.

Those who moved to May City, IA, were mostly people who were dissatisfied where they had been. The basic rules on paper were not a problem, but some men had beards and some did not. Was it plainer to hitch up two horses to the carriage or just use one horse?

People constantly squabbled about minor things. They needed all the quilts they had in the cold hard winter, even the intricate fancy ones. Some people dyed quilts black because nothing may be fancy! They could not agree, and seldom did they have communion, due to the lack of peace. The Weav-ers, Stauffers and Gingrichs shaved their faces, but the Brubachers and Baumans wore beards.

The Bishop was first and he had the most money and the biggest barn. He lost the respect of his followers and he was accused of strong drink at Chicago while driving cattle to market. What start-ed out as an excellent opportunity fell apart.

Someone wrote that the devil caught a ride on the train's cow-catcher and he was there wait-ing for them, before the first people got off the train. In 1900, about 40 families and many chil-dren lived there, and by 1915, the majority had left, moving out by train. Peter Brubacher lived there eleven years; age fourteen to twenty five, with his

parents and siblings. They worked long, hard days helping where they could, building solid buildings and breaking the sod.

When May City dreams fell apart, Peter's brothers and sisters scattered, Amos and Christian moved back to Ontario, Canada and found wives there. Amos married Lucinda Her and Christian married Selina Brox. Peter's sister Catherine or 'Katie' married Daniel Bauman, son of Bishop Jes-se Bauman from May City. After Daniel died, she married his younger brother Eli and with their six children, they moved to Pennsylvania. They were no longer of the Pike Church.

Peter's sister Mary married Eli Stauffer and moved to Pennsylvania and they joined the Pike church there. Barbara was single and stayed with her parents, Jacob Brubachers, as they moved to Michigan. Peter's younger brother Isaac never joined a conservative church. He studied at Moody Bible Institute in Chicago and became a preacher. He married Ruth Hodgson and served as a minister in a Presbyterian church in Seattle, Washington.

Peter's sister Leah died before her 17th birth-day, with complications from an appendix opera-tion. Her death was a shock to her family. In the bloom of youth, her life was gone, and they buried her in the Mc-bride's Cemetery in Montcalm Coun-ty, Michigan. Peter with his wife and five children, traveled to the funeral in a stagecoach. Silas, who was five at that time, sat inside the stagecoach with the women, and did not know his father was along, since father, Uncle Henry and his cousin Joseph sat on the outside seat up front with the driver.

Henry and Peter moved to northern Michi-gan, where lumber and sawmills were big busi-ness. Brutus had a big sawmill and trees were disappearing rapidly. Land agencies offered cheap land in the 1800s. In 1879, the first settlers came to Brutus and by the time Peter and Henry arrived in 1905, a Mennonite church was well es-tablished. The Detweilers, Gehmans, Ebys, Bur-kharts, Brubacher's and Snyders were farmers at heart and ready to clear fields and raise buildings. The land was cheap and the work was hard, but Peter was twenty-five years old with no place of his own. He bought eighty acres of lumbered-off woodland, three and one half miles northeast of Brutus.

Across the road from each other, Peter and Henry worked long days clearing land and erecting buildings. They had practiced building farms in May City. Peter lived with preacher Daniel Brubacher until his new frame house was finished. For quite awhile, Peter thought he might remain a bachelor if the Lord so will, but on October 7, 1906, he married Sarah Ann Brenneman. Preacher Daniel Brubacher married them, even though Daniel was not ordained as a bishop until five years later. Therefore, in one year's time Peter had a new wife and a new house, and dreams of a happy home. He was 26 and she, a teenager, almost 20.

His wife Sarah Ann was only five years old when her mother died. Mary Isura Selner Brenneman died and left Henry Brenneman with three young children needing a mother. He soon remarried to Sarah S. Burkey from Indiana and had three more children. Sarah Ann [Mommy Brubacher] was the oldest of those six, then John Wayne, and Mertie Elnora, plus [aunt] Amanda, Salome, and Joseph from the second wife.

This Brenneman family moved to Central Michigan with Yosiah or 'Yussie' Martin from the May City group for their preacher. The Brenneman's had moved from Indiana to Michigan by wagon and a team of horses, stopping along the way for months at a time, even a whole summer. When Sarah Ann was almost 17, Henry Brenneman's second wife died, leaving Sarah Ann motherless again. She was out of school and old enough to understand, but it was hard.

It was in Central Michigan, where Peter and Sarah Ann first met. Peter had traveled there when he moved from May City, Iowa, to Brutus, Michigan, with some other young fellows. Sarah Ann noticed the group of young men and thought to herself, "If I would want any of them, it would be Peter". Eventually Peter did notice Sarah Ann and they were married. Sarah Ann's father Henry certainly missed his grown daughter as the oldest child, and the one that filled in as a substitute mother. The next year Henry Brenneman married his third wife, Lydia Buehler from Ontario. Amanda remembered her as Grandmother Brenneman even though she was not her mother's mother.

In January of 1908, Peter and Sarah Ann held their first-born son, and named him Henry after his grandfather, Henry Brenneman and his Uncle Henry Brubacher, living close by. However, little Henry only lived two days. With sad hearts, they laid him to rest in the Maple River Church Cemetery.

They had not yet recovered from that devastating blow, when two weeks later; Peter's new home caught fire in the middle of the night and burned to the ground. Since there was no outside door in their bedroom, Peter and Sarah Ann escaped through the window. Peter hurriedly rescued his brother Henry with a ladder, since Henry slept and boarded there. He also rescued Sarah Ann's sister Mertie, the maid for the new baby. They were both sleeping upstairs. The only things they frantically managed to save were some bedding and clothing that they grabbed off the hooks on the bedroom wall and one trunk they got out through the window. Sarah Ann walked stocking footed one-half mile through the snow, over the field lane to her father's house. The fire had started in the adjoining woodshed where they had saved ashes in a barrel for making lye soap.

Happy dreams lay shattered! God took their precious first-born baby and the house they worked so hard to complete. The Lord giveth and the Lord taketh away... blessed be the name of the Lord... somehow life went on, and thankfully, they had each other. They moved in with preacher Daniel Brubachers, until Peter built a new house. They needed a new home as soon as possible and built a small log cabin. In that log cabin, just fifteen months later, their second son, Jacob, arrived in April 1909. They named him after Peter's own father (Notion Jecky).But alas! Little Jacob died also, at the age of three weeks old, and they buried him beside his infant brother. Their hearts overflowed with sorrow but one day at a time, they continued, in deep faith.

After Peter and Sarah Ann moved into their third new house, the log cabin became a stable. In that farmhouse, they had their third son. Silas came to stay on July 2, 1910. Baby Mary arrived on January 19, 1912, and then Betsy joined the family on September 26, 1913.

On February 22, 1915, baby Amanda arrived with the same birthday as her Aunt Amanda, and the former President George Washington. Without a doubt, the new baby was named after her Aunt who was there helping the new mother. 'Aunt Amanda' was Sarah Ann's sister but the new baby did not get to know her aunt she was named after, because that Amanda died in childbirth about a year later and then her husband Amos Gregory married Susanna. In 1918, the flu epidemic hit the community hard and many people died. The bishop said, "That was the easiest flock to lead, because so many people died suddenly and unexpectedly. No one depended on waiting until tomorrow". Amos Gregory's second wife died and so did their new baby, after they had been married about one year. The mother held the baby in her arms in the casket, but nobody could view the touching incident. Due to quarantine, the congregation could not attend the funeral services.

Peter and Sarah Ann [Mommy Brubacher] loved and cared for their precious new baby, never knowing how long they might keep her. They well–knew how frail life was. However, baby Mandie was a healthy child, and the next summer, she had a new sister named Lydia, on August 25, 1916, keeping their parents exceedingly busy.

After Lydia, came another son, Gideon, in October of 1917, but he was not a strong healthy child. He had pneumonia several times and then at the age of thirteen months, he died in that big flu epidemic of 1918. That made the third small

Brubacher grave for Peter and Sarah Ann in the Maple River Cemetery.

When the flu struck, Amanda was only three years old. So many people were sick, that there was a shortage of well people to help the sick. Even Amanda's own mother had the flu. One night she was so low, that Peter was sure she would soon be gone. Amanda remembered how her father asked all the children to come downstairs, and "Give mother one more goodbye!"

Thankfully, Sarah Ann survived! Peter felt the doctor could have tried harder to help baby Gideon, whereas the doctor felt thankful that the mother lived for the sake of their five young children. Amanda's young memory remembered seeing her brother Gideon sitting in a high chair, close to the stove to keep warm. Somehow, the high chair tipped over and baby Gideon's head touched the hot wood stove. She saw it all happen and she was horrified that she could not prevent it. Amanda felt badly about it and remembered how the burn barely healed before Gideon died from the flu. She still noticed the burn wound of her dear little brother in a coffin.

Baby Katherine was a welcome addition to Peter's family on January 4, 1920, making five girls in a row. Then Silas finally got a healthy little brother on Valentine's Day in 1922. They named him Joshua.

The Peter Brubacher family milked cows by hand, and put the milk through a separator. The skim milk helped to fatten the pigs, and they sold the cream. Once a week the horse and wagon, hauled from five to 10 gallons of cream to the Brutus train depot. From there it went by rail to

Grand Rapids, Michigan, and to the Blue Valley creamery. Peter had three cream cans, two 5-gallon sized cans, and one that held 8 gallons. Without refrigeration, the cream cooled in water, and it did not really matter that the cream turned sour before it was sold, for making butter.

Working close to the land with manual labor, Peter found an endless amount of work to keep his children busy. Before he bought his land, all the lumber trees were cut and sold by the former owner. Most of the huge remaining stumps were ten years older than Amanda was. Some of them rotted out. Peter dynamited some of them, where he wanted to farm the land. He removed the last ones with a hand-cranked winch on a tripod. A chain and pulley helped pull the stump straight up when he pumped the handle.

Before Amanda was born, her father felled a tree that came down in an unexpected way. Peter had a scar on his nose for the rest of his life and a crooked little finger.

Amanda was four years old when her father built their big bank barn, with the supervision and help from his brother Henry. Until then Peter made do with the log cabin they had made quickly when their house burned down. After they gathered all the supplies, Peter announced a barn raising. All the neighbors arrived early. Some came in horse and buggies and some came walking. Each man brought a hammer.

Amanda could not help much at the age of four. She remembered the long table set up in the yard, laden with food for the hungry volunteers, especially the sugar cookies. The men worked fast, and by noon, the trusses stood tall. Before the men went home, they finished the roof. Peter had a lot of work remaining, but most of it, he could do with the help of one or two men.

Amanda remembered back to her fourth birthday. She went across the road to Uncle Henry Brubacher's. Uncle Isaac Brubacher sat there on a rocking chair, recovering from pneumonia. He was Peter's youngest brother and still a teenager. As he sat, he kept his hands busy and braided a horsehair watch chain for a pocket watch.

A metal bar at one end slipped into a buttonhole in his broad fall pants. The other end hooked onto the watch. Amanda stared awhile as he made neat one-half inch braided rings about one eighth inch wide. She never figured out just how he did that. Her father owned one of those horsehair watch chains and used it for Sunday. What Amanda remembered best of all; Isaac pulled her ears four times on her fourth birthday.

The entire family worked hard and one-year Peter raised green beans on a contract. When the beans matured, everyone in the family dug in to help. Amanda worked as hard as she was able, right along with the grownups. All the girls put in long hours of hard work. When the check arrived, their parents rewarded the sisters with a tea set, service for four. Amanda was seven years old. Mary, Betsy, Amanda and Lydia shared and enjoyed that aluminum tea set with many fond memories, as they pretended and giggled and sang to their dolls. Katie and Joshua got smaller gifts and Silas helped the most, so he got a bigger gift. He was already thirteen years old.

Amanda remembered when the girls had new dolls that did not stay nice very long. The dolls had heads and arms constructed of a hard composition, somewhat like paper-mache. The bodies and legs were made of cloth and stuffed with shredded wood. Amanda's doll never had a special name. When the dolls stayed outside, the brown painted hair peeled off and the heads got sticky, so their mother bought new tin replacement heads and repaired the dolls.

The clock ticked slowly at the depot, much slower than it did at home, as all four of the travelers continued in childhood memories.

Amanda started to school at the age of six. Woodland School was merely half a mile away and her parents could watch them walk to and from school. Amanda was in the beginners class only six weeks, before her teacher put her into second grade. Six children shared that grade; Leah Kilmer, Hannah Burkhart, Amanda Brubacher, Jesse Brubacher, David Newswenger, and Martin Reed.

Amanda was a teacher's pet in second and third grade when Will Brown was her teacher. She was the smallest in her grade and earned the nickname of 'cricket.' At the end of second grade, the teacher saw that most of the students were not ready to pass to third grade, so he retained them all in second grade for another term. It was not fair to Amanda, because lessons were easy for her. That is just how it was!

Amanda took an apple and some flowers to school for the teacher, before the frost claimed them. Her parents did not come to school often and they trusted the teacher. Her mother came to visit school one time, but her father never! Neither did the other parents. In third or fourth grade, she tasted her first orange, given for Christmas at school.

The non-Mennonite teachers at Woodland School had a higher education. Amanda learned proper English as a major subject. It stayed with her for all her life. The teacher at school had a problem with German speaking students. They could maybe talk behind her back so she made a rule, "No speaking German or Dutch at school." Children forgot themselves at times on the playground, while talking to each other. One winter the boys had fun sliding on a huge snow bank that covered the fence in front of the schoolhouse. They were having a great time when Sydney Brubacher said to Aaron Leinbach."Hey, Aaron, *Des gate vee shmutz!*" {This goes like grease!]At that moment, the teacher happened to be on the porch and heard them. She said, 'Sydney, go take your seat!'"

With public teachers, they had traditional Christmas decorations, including a decorated tree, Santa Claus, balsam or fir boughs with candles at the window and a room criss-crossed with red and green crepe paper. Amanda helped string up popcorn for the tree. She knew the real Christmas story and her parents did not want a decorated tree in their home. Christmas to them, meant church and a big dinner plus a few cherished homemade gifts and always, good homemade candy.

Amanda's mother seldom baked cookies because cookies needed eggs. During the cold weather, their three or four dozen hens did not lay many eggs and her parents needed all of them to trade for groceries. They were too poor to eat the eggs they raised, or perhaps too frugal. Peter and Sarah Ann managed well and the children never knew hunger. They did not buy things they could not afford, and did without many things, and they kept their farm through the 1930's. A hardboiled egg was a special treat, and they did not eat eggs for breakfast, except maybe for Easter Sunday.

When they had more eggs, they traded for more groceries. Beside the usual, flour, sugar, salt, soap, yeast and matches, they might enjoy things such as rice, macaroni, or oatmeal. Mother bought cocoa at Christmas time! They used any cracked egg in baking, but were not supposed to crack any. That was a loss!

Woodland School and Amanda

Most of the children in school carried identical molasses buckets for their lunches. Each one marked his own bucket, with perhaps a piece of colored yarn on the handle. Sometimes they had homemade bologna in a sandwich, but mostly they ate apple butter or jelly on their homemade bread. They did not wrap any of the food in their tin buckets, just neatly laid it in the pail. They ate apples galore, and baked many pies. Way back then already, Amanda learned that people eat to live and should not live to eat!

Peter bought a twenty-five pound bag of roasted corn meal because they lived too far north to raise corn to maturity. The field corn he planted went into his wooden silo with a flat roof. Amanda's mother used most of the cornmeal to make johnnycakes, somewhat like cornbread. They served it hot for supper with milk and fruit. They ate wheat mush for breakfast with no shortage of rich milk and cream. In season, they gathered huge amounts of wild fruit of all kinds. One year they canned one hundred quarts of wild huckleberries. Another year, they collected such an abundance of wild blackberries. They canned twenty-five quarts of wild strawberries. It took many hours to pick and cap them.

Mother had a screened cupboard in the basement where she kept things cool. The screen kept the flies off her pies and off the cured hams. Some people had an icebox, but not Peter Brubachers. In the hottest weather, her mother lowered the milk down into the well with a hoe, after she removed the wooden board from the pump bed. The well had wooden sides and a sand floor, approximately six feet deep. From there on down, it had pipes driven deeper to the water source. They had very little mud in Michigan, mostly sand.

They lived a slower paced life and found time to sit around the stove on a cold winter evening, eating apples and fresh buttered popcorn. The only coffee Amanda knew was roasted grain, ground by hand in their little coffee mill. Their house was not tight and Amanda's parents hung a heavy blanket across the west kitchen door.

The children enjoyed sledding, but their homemade wooden-runner sleds did not go fast and the only hill they had on the farm was the slope on the side of the bank barn. Later they had a sled with metal strips attached to the wooden runners and that went faster. One time Amanda watched some town children on a long toboggan. They gained speed going down a steep grade and across the railroad track. She was not given a ride.

All the children tended cows many hours in a day, in springtime. The cows grazed where no fences confined them. During such a time-consuming job, Peter's girls kept their hands busy with knitting and sewing by hand. At the age of 10, Amanda sewed an entire apron for herself, while sitting on a big stump, watching the cows. Her mother Sarah Ann had carefully cut the pieces and taught her girls how to sew at a young age. She also drilled in them the need to keep their hands busy.

Children climbed to the rafters in the barn, and jumped on heaps of loose hay, with energy to spare. Burt Lake was only two miles away, but seldom did they go there, with not much time or interest in fishing and swimming.

Starting at the age of twelve, the children helped as hired hands, wherever someone needed them. They lived with the people where they worked. While working as a hired girl, Amanda earned $3.50 a week. Ordinary tie shoes cost $2.98, so it took almost a week to earn a pair of new shoes. Parents provided for the children and then the children gave their money home to the parents until they were twenty years old. Many times, pay consisted of fruits and vegetables instead of money, until they were on their own, and then they preferred money.

That seemed oh so long ago, and some of that hard-earned money was in their pockets now. They seldom spent much!

In the fall of 1929, Amanda's parents with Isaac Kilmer's, the parents of Martin and Christian Kilmer, went on a long trip. They left home in the beginning of November, and headed for Indiana, Ohio and Pennsylvania. They had never traveled to these places, and stayed nearly four months. Silas at the age of nineteen took care of the farm chores. Mary turned eighteen while they were gone, and Betsy was sixteen. Amanda still attended school, and so did Lydia, Katie and Joshua. They had no electricity back then, and no telephone to keep in touch.

Peter Brubachers spent Christmas in Snyder County, Pennsylvania, with his brother Henry's family. That was one of the main attractions of going on a trip and so was spending time with his parents again. When Peter's mother was going away for dinner, walking from the buggy to the house, she fainted or fell. They carried her to the house and laid her on the couch, where she died that evening, in Lancaster County. Peter and his wife returned to Lancaster County, where they had just departed. They attended the funeral of his mother Elizabeth Brubacher, at the Pike Mennonite Church. Thankfully they had just spent some time with his parents a week earlier. From there they went to Canada where Peter grew up. He had two brothers and quite a few other relatives there.

Back at home, at Brutus, Michigan, their children worked hard, and even managed to butcher their winter supply of meat without their parents. Dan Horst from Ohio came for a visit, while the parents were gone. He came with other boys, and had his eyes on Betsy. After he left, Dan and Betsy exchanged letters in the mail for about a year. Later he returned in a car and brought along an engagement ring. Betsy kept the ring, but Dan did not stay around long. Peter Brubacher did not approve of his daughter moving to Ohio, because the church was shrinking and they needed everyone of their youth to stay in Michigan. Perhaps Peter did not like the idea of a car, and furthermore, his daughter was only sixteen!

He broke up their courtship, and later when Christian Kilmer asked Betsy for a date, Betsy was determined to keep this young man! Amanda did not know her sister had a hidden engagement ring, and neither did anyone else for another fifty years. The ring remained hidden among old letters until Betsy died, and her children started asking questions. Amanda and Norma Reed filled in some of the details.

Amanda never forgot a tragic event in her childhood when Clement Leinbach and Mary Ann Shantz tipped over in the sleigh on the way to church. Mary Ann was wet from the snow but she did not want to sit beside the stove, because that is where the older women sat. She got very sick with a respiratory infection, and her funeral was before the next Sunday. Amanda had considered Mary Ann as the prettiest girl in church. Clement Leinbach and Mary Ann had plans to get married soon. Clement lost interest in Michigan and with four other boys, Paul Brubacher, Ezra Kilmer, Allen and Sylvester Brubacher, moved to Pennsylvania, a heartbroken man. That was in 1925.

To keep the Michigan community growing, they depended upon the five boys and five girls that joined church that summer. Many hopes and dreams were buried with Mary Ann Shantz, and the church never quite recovered from the blow. Part of the problem was coincidental, when the church was struggling with dissatisfaction and needed all the young people to start new homes there. At one time only two girls remained among the youth group, Salome Brenneman and Amanda Eby [Kulp].

The entire youth group suffered a blow and parents allowed teenagers to join the social gatherings at a younger age, needing new couples to keep the church going. The church was resting on younger shoulders, and not enough of them. Some of Peter's hopes and dreams were buried in Mary Ann's grave, with all the hard work he put into the community and he had hoped his children would stay in Michigan.

Members of their church also disagreed over the use of tractors and rubber tired equipment, and some joined other churches. Hidden among other problems, was a disrespectful 'leadership problem'.

Getting ahead in life meant raising the next generation as decent up- building Christians. The farming, gardening, food preserving and such was all for this common cause, and the church group of fellow believers was the anchor that united them. As a close-knit community, they knew each other well and had many social gatherings to help make a brother's cares their own. He, who does not work, should not eat and they kept busy or they would not survive.

The three travelers stranded at the depot rejoiced to see the first rays of light, as a new day dawned and the long night ended. "Oh look, here comes our train!" Silas cheered.

They boarded the train and caught a nap, before safely arriving at Sunbury, Pennsylvania, where Uncle Henry Brubacher waited for them. Another of Peter's brothers, Henry, had waited there for them the day before until he realized that they missed the train in Buffalo, which was not unusual. At Sunbury, they got on the bus, and rode to Selinsgrove where Uncle Henry had his team. By the time they arrived at Uncle Henry's home, they were exhausted and welcomed a good night's sleep.

They spent two days visiting cousins and others in Snyder County, and then took the train to Lancaster County. Cousins Amos and Aaron Stauffer met them at the Ephrata train station and took them along home to Eli Stauffers, whose wife was their father's sister Mary. They lived on a farm in the Murrell area.

Aunt Mary took them to cousin Dan Stauffer's for dinner, then cousins Aaron, Amos and Lydia took the travelers by team to Goodville, and to their sister Mary and Martin Kilmer. After supper, Martins took them to Churchtown to Christian Kilmers for the night. All four sisters rejoiced to see each other again, two were single and two were married.

After attending Bowmansville Church on Sunday, they went to Christian Leinbachs for dinner, people who had formerly lived in Michigan, and they knew each other well. That afternoon, the Leinbachs had a gathering for anyone wanting to meet the Michigan travelers because they understood the lack of a youth group these young people had in MI. Amanda noticed a certain young man, and his name was Aaron Shirk.

At another young people's gathering, dates were arranged for the evening. Aaron Shirk for Amanda, and his good friend, Christ Shirk, distantly related, would see Lydia. So it was, Amanda and Lydia had special friends during their stay in Pennsylvania, and that is what they wanted.

Amanda and Lydia spent most of their six-week stay with their married sisters, Mary or Betsy. Amanda helped Martin Kilmer's move to a place in Hinkeltown, and helped them plant their garden. About two weeks before leaving Pennsylvania, Amanda offered to work at Dan Goods since their hired girl was sick. Amanda worked there four days, cleaning house at $.75 a day.

All this time, Aaron was coming to see Amanda on Saturday and Sunday evenings. Toward the end of their stay, he came during the week a few times. On a Wednesday evening, when he left home in his buggy, he admired an unusually bright rainbow in the sky. God felt close-by in that rainbow. Aaron and Amanda had been doing some serious thinking. She did not want to spend all her time in Pennsylvania with Aaron if he was just going to let her set when she returned home to Michigan. If he was not serious about this, she had certainly spent too much time with him already! So on that rainbow evening, she asked him, "How long do you expect our friendship will last?" He answered, "Till you quit me!" "What if I don't quit you?" she wondered. "Then we'll just stay together!" he

said. Barely six weeks after they first met, Aaron and Amanda were secretly engaged.

The following week, Amanda and Lydia were both at Christian Kilmer's, when Aaron and Christ came one last time to see their girlfriends. They stayed quite late! All five of Peter Brubacher's children met at Christian Kilmer's and stayed up until midnight, talking and dreading the parting.

Silas was not going along home with Amanda and Lydia, because he had seen so many single girls in Pennsylvania that he was going to stay! Surely, God planned one of them for him. He found a job as a hired man working for Adam Nolt.

The next morning came too soon. They were up at 3:45 AM! After the last goodbyes, a neighbor boy took Amanda, Lena, and Lydia to the Lancaster train station where they headed for Orrville, Ohio. They always sent word ahead, by mailing a postcard, letting people know when to pick them up at the next depot.

In Ohio, they spent a few days visiting their mothers' Brenneman relatives. Then they went on to Indiana, where they spent ten days, visiting more relatives, cousins, aunts and uncles, and Pletcher relatives, on their mothers' side. They also visited other people from their church and spent the weekend with the young people.

Lena's brother Harvey was in Indiana at the time. He took the travelers back home to Michigan.. .the only place Amanda had ever called home. After a three-and-a-half month vacation, Peter Brubacher's farm was alive with springtime and home had never looked so good before. Amanda and Aaron did not forget each other, as both of their lives changed with dreams about marriage.

2

On Christmas Eve in 1913, Benjamin W. Shirk and Annie Z. (Martin) Shirk welcomed their first child, and named him Aaron. They resided at the tenant house on the Joe Weaver farm. When Benjamin wanted to call the doctor to come deliver their first child at home, he had a problem. He needed to use the phone in the big farmhouse and it hung on the wall, behind a table full of company eating dinner. It took them a long time to finish that big meal, while he nervously waited to call the doctor in private.

Benjamin [B.W.] and Annie raised their family of nine children in Lancaster County, Pennsylvania, on a small farm on the south side of Turkey Hill.

When Aaron started first grade, he walked, one-mile to Smoketown Public School. His father asked another student, Abner Brown, "For $.10 a day would you see that Aaron gets to school on time and home again, and also see that he is not bullied at school?" That was a deal and it worked fine, but Aaron soon lost interest in school. His parents and the teacher agreed to let him drop out, and start first grade again the next year, with his younger brother Samuel.

When Aaron and Samuel went to school together, their mother said, "I certainly don't hear much about school. " However, when their sister Lydia started school, she tattled to her mother, "You should just see what Aaron and Sam did today at school!" Aaron and Sam preferred that Lydia kept to the other girls playing dolls. Aaron and all his younger siblings attended Smoketown School for their eight years of formal education. When they came home from school hungry after 3:00, their mother sometimes gave them a lard sandwich...a slice of bread, spread with lard and sprinkled generously with salt and pepper. It was good!

Aaron remembered when the roads closed with an icy crust over deep snowdrifts. He helped neighboring men work hard with picks and shovels, breaking the ice, and scooping away enough snow for one-way traffic. At several places they shoveled a turnout for a passing spot. While old Clarence Brown shoveled the snow halfway up the bank, Aaron stood there and scooped the snow up higher. He tossed it further back, out of the way.

The state paid local farmers $.17 an hour to shovel the roads by hand. Men kept track of their hours and handed them in when spring arrived. Old Mr. Brown said, "I wish it would snow again, because $.17 an hour is good money for winter wages." He did not raise tobacco for a living, which kept most farmers busy all year.

Aaron's father raised steers, and farmed corn and tobacco. For their own use, they had a small orchard, with a few apple, pear and cherry trees. At one time, Aaron had a project raising his own watermelons and cantaloupes for cash. The sandy soil produced a dandy crop of "watter melons" according to Aaron's diary, and his father called them "vassah pickles" (water pickles).

Anytime the Shirks had a social gathering in watermelon season, B W treated his guests or workmen, with nice big, cold watermelons from the springhouse. In season, he kept watermelons floating in the spring water, with a garden rake nearby to reach out and bring one in. Annie set up the wringer washer in that large springhouse, rather than to carry the wash water up-hill to the house. The clear spring water nearly surrounded the spot where the washing machine set, and occasionally a frog plopped into the cool water.

Annie lit a fire beneath a big kettle in the fireplace, and dipped the spring water into the big iron pot, and then she dipped the heated water into the washer. She worked hard, pushing the wooden handle back and forth 100 times, or more, for each load of laundry. The handle and a flywheel agitated four crude wooden paddles inside the washing machine. Annie rinsed the laundry and hung it out to dry without feeling deprived. After all the laundry hung in the breeze, she worked to carry all the dirty water out the door. It was often smoky inside the springhouse from the back -draft coming down the chimney, but she knew she had it easier, than washing by hand on a washboard.

When Annie was young, she had worked for Christ Zimmermans and carried their wash water on Sunday evening, so they could wash before daylight, or before their neighbors did. She cheerfully tackled any dirty work without complaining, even cleaning out the chicken houses.

Aaron's father was a man of action, a commanding type of person, and somewhat demanding. With the help of his gentle wife and able children, they accomplished a lot of work, selling produce and helping others, while managing their farm. BW Shirk and Noah Zimmerman raced to be first to plant, and first to harvest their crops.

Ben might be stripping tobacco at four o'clock in the morning and allow his boys to sleep in, until almost 6 o'clock. He was very particular about his tobacco crop and only cut the ripest stalks, maybe three-fourths of a load one day and three-fourths the next day. His boys preferred to do it all at once. They could rapidly strip tobacco, but their father sorted it into the right length, so he knew it was done right.

Oysters from Elk River, Maryland were a treat, costing one cent each. BW Shirk stored a burlap sack full of oysters in their shells, in the damp, dark tobacco celler. If they covered the sack and kept them moist, the oysters might live a month or two. The family enjoyed oysters and the boys sneaked some, split them open and ate them raw, but they were not supposed to do that!

The entire neighborhood farmed with steel wheels on their farm machinery. Aaron's father was influenced by the opinions of Mexico Aaron Martin and both men strictly forbade modern," fancy"

rubber tires, available on equipment as 'optional.' The growing boys wanted bicycles but could not have any, because they had rubber tires. Some people did not even allow their children to swing in a tire swing.

BW Shirk came from a family of 11 children. His brother Peter, died at the age of one, and Menno died when he was five. Anna was 22 years old when she died from falling down a trap door in the factory where she worked. The remaining seven children did not all marry.

BW Shirk was known as Benny, Israel was" Iss", Joseph was "sleepy Joe" because his eyes drooped and looked sleepy. John was nicknamed "duh gveah Johnny", for the naturally cross look on his face.

Three single sisters, Mary, Lydia and Barbara, lived together. Mary later married a widower by the name of Frank Hoover, leaving Barbara to care for retarded Lydia who had epilepsy in her youth. Lydia had a talent for memorizing many birthdays, but she talked rather loudly and close-up to the person to whom she was talking.

Esther's nickname was Hettie. She married Enos Eby and they had eight children. They dressed poorly and pinched pennies. When Enos bought cattle at the sale barn, the owners did not trust taking a check from such a poor looking man, and called his banker to see if the check would bounce. The banker said, "You can sell him the whole stockyards!"... or so the story goes. Their family worked hard and wore their things out. When they gave outgrown clothes to Aaron and Amanda, some things were already worn out, even by Amanda's frugal standards.

Something was majorly lacking between Aaron's Uncle John and his wife. One Sunday morning she was not quite ready for church, so he went without her. She managed to find a ride to church with neighbors, and as soon as church dismissed, she took the horse and buggy and left without her husband, leaving other people to wonder what that couple understood about the Bible and the sermon that morning.

When Aaron turned 20, he was of age, and he ordered a brand new bike from Sears. Issy Brendle, the mailman brought the "Roll Fast" bike, in a box in the mail. Aaron and his buddies had a party until midnight, assembling the bike in Aaron's saddler shop. The younger boys were forbidden to watch, since it was not favorably accepted to even own a bike.

It was Aaron's job to milk the cow regularly. After he was of age, he milked the cow for his room and board at home. He had a patch of tobacco for his own, on the Eby Sauder farm. When Aaron's younger brothers came home from school, they passed that farm. When they stopped to help strip tobacco, Aaron paid them with clear toy candy. He had the colorful clear candies arranged at the window with the light shining through, making them almost too pretty to eat. Eby was an elderly man of retirement age and Aaron confided in him often. One day Eby said to Aaron "I hear you have a girlfriend".

Eby figured it was a secret, and he was surprised when Aaron said, "Yes that's right!" Aaron then pulled a letter out of his pocket, ready for the mail, showing Amanda's full name and address on the front. Eby was confused! In those days, a young man would normally not freely share his girlfriend interests with just anybody. Eby, not convinced, said, "There is no such place as Brutus, Michigan! That letter will end up in the dead letter office!" Aaron just smiled.

When going with the youth on a weekend, Aaron's brother Titus remembered Aaron playing the Jews' harp better than anyone else did. Aaron liked singing and music, but when he sang "second bass", others said it sounded as if he struck out. Among the youth group, Aaron liked to say, "The prettiest girl has a spot of dirt on her face". Then he grinned as they all wiped their faces.

Aaron had a small dark thoroughbred horse named Sailor that moved fast! One time when Aaron came home, he said "I don't know how many mailboxes the buggy knocked over!" Henry Shirk said "If I could only get my hands on that horse, I would like to race him."

Aaron spent time in Virginia, in the Dayton area, for business related to the harness making trade, and he had an interest in a girlfriend there, before he met Amanda. He traveled on the Greyhound bus, and got sick over the rough roads, because he seldom traveled in a motor vehicle. He quit seeing her, because she did not want to move to Pennsylvania.

He dated a Newswenger girl from Pennsylvania for nearly a year, and she grew up in Brutus, Michigan, therefore Aaron knew a lot about Michigan.

B W. Shirk paid his boys a new pocket watch if they did not smoke before they turned 18. Aaron earned that watch, but still gave in and smoked many years, and so did his brother Sam. Their mother was disappointed and said, "The money you spend for smoking in one year, would buy new shoes for all of our children."

Their mother Annie, never had greenbacks to spend. The coins she had, she spent wisely, and vanilla from a peddler might cost $.35. They bartered for groceries with eggs, butter, and lard, and therefore handled less money. She wore her husband's worn out shoes, trying to save money. When Annie understood her husband still owed the bank $500.00, she did not make a new dress for herself, until they repaid the loan in full. B W and Annie Shirk had been on a trip to Canada and ten years later, Canadians came to Pennsylvania and told Annie, "You are wearing the same dress you wore in Canada!" B W and Annie appreciated their clothes and wore them out completely.

B.W.'s bride was not popular when she was young. She was black around the eyes and called *"de shwatz Annie"*. (Black Annie). She was a steady worker and an anchor for Ben. She spaded her own garden, worked hard and helped others. The Martins, on her side, were a close-knit family and helped each other through many trials. Annie had virtues of kindness and meekness like in Galatians 5… she had them all! She was a big help to Amanda in years to come, and no one could ever wish for a better mother-in-law. Perhaps what she went through in her childhood, helped mellow her heart.

She was a daughter of Elias Martin, who moved to Pennsylvania from Ohio. Elias was the youngest of 14 children, and he was only two years old when his mother died. He grew up and enjoyed working! At the age of 46, he was digging a well on the farm, and inhaled too much toxic gas and he died. Elias's wife Annie was okay when they got married, but then she had mental challenges. She was a very nervous woman before the accident of her husband, and she went crazy when he died. She bought the farm where they resided, and the many hardships forced her daughter Annie to quit school at the age of 13.

She stayed at home and worked hard. She was only twelve years old, when she found her father dead beside the well. This young Annie, with a brilliant mind, grew up to be Aaron's mother. At one time, she wanted to teach school, but her father Elias said, "*Sell iss net fo unsery lite. Sell iss yusht fa weltlichy lite.*" (That is not for our people, just for worldly people.) Due to her mother's mental health problems, Annie preferred to work for other people, rather than stay-at-home. When she wished for time off, to sew herself a new dress, her mother sent her down to the creek, to scrub and polish their pots and pans with sand.

Maria was the oldest of the Elias Martin family, and she worked in the factory to provide for the fatherless family. David "Dafe" was 21 and John was 10, Lizzie 8, and Samuel only two years old. Three more children had died young. The six remaining children had many rough times without their father. As they worked out in the field, and their hunger pangs said dinnertime, they sent a child in to peep into the kitchen window, to see if their mother was in a bad mood. Occasionally they preferred to eat some raw eggs from the chicken house, rather than go to the kitchen.

The children cared for each other and worked hard. They drove a horse that had a "hootch" or foal, and every so often, they stopped to let it drink from its mother. By hand, and without gloves, they husked 90 acres of corn before Christmas time.

With an abundance of grapes, they canned a large amount of grape juice one summer, and discarded the heap of pulp into the garden. Annie looked out and said, "Look out there. . . All the geese are dead! Just what could have happened?" Her mother said, "We will not eat anything that has blood remaining in it, so the only thing we can save are the downy feathers. The children helped pluck all the breast feathers to make pillows, with thoughts of no roast goose that winter.

The plump greedy geese had eagerly gobbled a large amount of fermented grape pulp and were drunk, not dead! The next morning the family stood grinning as they beheld a strange sight of slightly de-feathered geese coming up the lane, very much alive. The geese had time to grow more downy feathers before winter.

David married Fianna, and lived just across the meadow. Things got so bad, that one day Fianna looked out and saw Annie chasing Lizzy with a butcher knife! Maria married Joe Weaver, and they took her mother to live with them for a while. One night her mother was missing, and they searched until they found their deranged mother walking along the Conestoga Creek, wearing a nightgown.

The married children all took their turn caring for their mother, except for Uncle John, because his wife got seizures and was not capable. Annie did not seem to notice, or care, when she stepped on a crawling babies' fingers. She had many mishaps, and talked all the time! Someone counted her repeating the same phrase 200 times in a row, non-stop. Lizzie married David O. Weaver, [brother to Bishop Joseph O Weaver]. Annie's daughter Annie [Aaron's mother] never complained when things were bad, even when she had intense pain from gallstones and rolled on the floor in pain upstairs in her bedroom, without telling her mother, because that would make her fussy.

One night after the family went to bed, they heard strange bumping noises. They froze with fear and thought they heard burglars, but they were all too scared to go and look. It was a long night! When daylight finally arrived, the mother and children looked around to see if anything was missing. With a sigh of relief, they noticed some cow patties on the porch. Upon closer inspection they realized the steers had been on the porch and they rubbed against and unhinged the window shutters that night.

Annie needed much care for eighteen years. She was blind and easier to keep for the last fourteen, because she stayed sitting and rocking much of the time. She asked for her meals and asked for her bed, and someone led her to the outhouse. Her children all grew up and joined the Horning church, except Samuel and his wife, who joined the Pike church in Snyder County.

Aaron had memories of his blind grandmother coming to stay a while at their house when he was a child. She stayed put in her rocking chair and developed a keen sense of hearing. She knew which family member walked in the house by listening to their footsteps. When BW Shirk bought a huge bunch of bananas, they kept them in the cellar, and the schoolboys delighted in sneaking a few between meals. The boys never managed to sneak down the stairway, without their blind grandmother knowing it. She would catch them red-handed and said, "*See sin vid-ah un de bananas!*". ["They are at the bananas again!"] The boys figured a way to outsmart Grandma, by prying apart two of the bars on the window grate of the outside cellar window. Aaron would hand bananas through the bars, to his accomplice outside, and when he came upstairs again, he showed his empty hands to his grandmother, before joining his brother outside to share the treat.

Aaron's sisters Eva and Lydia took the trolley from Terre Hill to Bareville, to visit their mother's cousin. The trolley line, interestingly took them across their Uncle Joe Weaver's property. Lydia pretended she was not afraid, but the trolley swayed and rattled so badly that Eva did not think they would survive. She expected to perish before they arrived at Bareville. Thankfully, she stepped off alive.

⁂

As a teenager, Aaron worked as a hired man a few years, but the last year or two before his wedding, he had his own little harness shop in his dad's tobacco stripping room. Aaron was known for talking a lot. In fact, he was dubbed "Luftich", or "Windy" Aaron Shirk. Amanda did not seem to mind that, and the first time she saw him, she knew he was for her. The letters between Michigan and Pennsylvania kept going steadily back and forth.

Their mailman came in the forenoon, and Aaron answered Amanda's letters the same day he received them. He would quickly write a reply, and send his brother Menno, to give it to the mailman on his afternoon route just north of them. One time Menno was on his way with Aaron's reply, swinging his arm and the letter in a carefree way. All of a sudden, nosey Mrs. Weaver came rushing out across her porch, grabbed the letter in his hand, and looked to see to whom it was addressed."That's just what I figured!" she exclaimed.

That told Menno that this letter was something extra special. He had never given it a thought that he should hide it in his pocket, but from then on, he did and delivered it carefully.

Menno read one of the letters that Aaron received from Amanda, but he never told Aaron. When a letter came with the Brutus, Michigan postmark, Aaron eagerly took it down in front of the barn, sat in a wheelbarrow in the sun, and proceeded to read the contents. Menno sneaked into the barn from the backside, on the upper level, climbed down the hay hole, into the feed alley, and looked over the top edge of the closed lower half-door and read the letter. He did not know what the entire letter said, but one thing he did remember... the last line.. . "I will come to Pennsylvania." Then he knew what was up!

Caring people and close neighbors were quick to help each other, and some were quick to mind each other's business! Perhaps it was the mystery of a romance, why Menno wanted to sneak a look at a letter, and the neighbor lady wanted to see to whom it was addressed. Even the mailman was curious. He put a note in the BW Shirk mailbox for Aaron, and it said, "I counted 43 letters for you from Michigan this summer." (Signed, I W Brendle). He wanted Aaron to know that he was counting!

That summer, Aaron was seriously looking for a property to buy. He considered a small place in Goodville as a business location for a harness shop, but Amanda wanted a farm. So when he heard that Raymond Sweigart wanted to sell his 42 acre farm, (30 acres tillable), Aaron bought it privately for $2000 (about $50 per acre). Raymond Sweigart's sold produce and fresh dressed chickens at Reading. If he needed more chickens, he came across the Turkey Hill to B.W. Shirks for chickens to dress.

That is how they knew this land was for sale. The Sweigart's' lost interest in tending market and they were leaving the farm.

Aaron wrote many letters. "You have a choice, Amanda." I could keep on working with leather in my saddle shop, for our income, or buy that Sweigart farm that's for sale at the edge of Laurel Hill." Amanda read the letter eagerly and knew what she wanted! She had her heart set on a small farm, even if it was out back at the edge of civilization.

Aaron bought the farm before her reply came. He wrote, "I bought the farm because my father thought it was cheap and because we knew someone else considered buying it. Father can help us pay for the farm and several others offered to help."

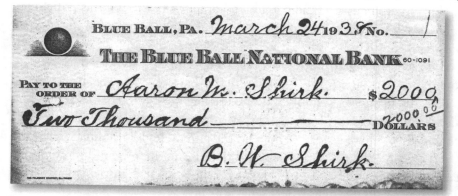

B W Shirk seldom wrote such large amounts on a check as this one to pay a whole farm. He had neat penmanship, even with a crude fountain pen that blotted.

Aaron went on to say, "The frame house is well kept. I will help Sweigart put a new metal roof on this winter. The paint is mostly rained-off the house and it will take a new *perge* [porch] floor. The inside of the house will suit you and the plaster is good with some new wallpaper. The yard fence needs repairs around the awful big garden. Eight apple trees near the house have seen their better days and about twenty young orchard trees are ready to start bearing fruit. The farm has about thirty or thirty-two acres tillable and four acres of grass. It has about four acres of trees for firewood and lumber. Some stone fences surround the farming land.

You can make the wedding when you wish and where you wish, in Pennsylvania or in Michigan. I advertised in the paper to sell most of my harness

making goods. I will need the money and I can't do two things at one time.

To me there is no girl like you! Never in my life have I 'reseaved' [received] a letter that was so dear to me! The most important fact is that you are still thinking of me. I had the cold and wasn't feeling well, but your letter in the mail helped me more than a bottle of cod liver oil.

Eight girls and nineteen boys made application to join church at Weaverland Church. You can see why the girls don't reach around.

Oh, how my heart quivers and longs for the satisfaction of we two living together as one. One thought, one spirit and one God! It is my desire to give you what you want. I am thankful that you want that which is wright according to the scriptures.

Amanda replied," I prefer a frame house rather than a stone house. I just love flowers and a big garden. I don't care if we cannot have chickens the first year. If my parents want the wedding in Michigan, we would quite likely be married before X-mass, but if they don't care, we'll have the wedding in PA after New Year's then.

I'll have to get the courage to talk to mother about the wedding this week, because the next week I'll be at Kulps. I wanted to ask all last week, but I didn't have enough nerve.ha! I know mother can keep a secret, and she won't tell dad without my consent. I hope you can keep it a secret too. Let other people talk!

What color do you plan to paint our house? I prefer white. Everyone knows us girls are back home and we have a lot of job offers. I plan to charge $3.50 per week now. People on Mackinac Island offer $4.00 a week, but that is thirty miles away.. .and so the letters continued...

Laurel Hill was wild and uninhabited, and the small farm edged the hills way back in the sticks. Wayne Steffy lived on the farm west of the Sweigarts, and deep woods surrounded the other three sides. The ten small fields averaged three acres apiece.

People were incredulous when they heard that Aaron had bought such a place. "What!" they said. "That poor looking farm? You'll starve.. .and so the comments ran. Many people called his farm, "God's forsaken country." Some even said the farm was so hidden under Laurel Hill that the morning sun would not shine on it before 11 o'clock.

His single buddies, who were not aware that he was writing with a girl from Michigan, asked, "Who's going to cook for you? Your sister?" "No," Aaron replied, "I am going to have a wife." His friends were sure he was just joking!

It was true that the rocky farm was not the best one. Sweigart was not selling because he was old and retiring. He was a young man with three school-aged children, but he could hardly make a living there. It was in a rather rundown condition, with poor management, and no modern conveniences like running water and electricity.

The road and the long lane leading to the farm had ruts so deep, that a person hardly knew where to drive. Among rocks and boulders, the Sweigart's farmed ten small fields. Heaps of stones bordered the fields, as they cleared the land for farming. Hard work and poverty were nothing new in 1937. Most people farmed tobacco as the main cash crop, and the barn was designed for curing and stripping tobacco. The sturdy house and the bank barn might last many decades.

The lane divided behind the barn; one part led to the house and the other part went back into the woods. Somewhere back there, near a good spring, not too far from the creek, stood an illegal whiskey still. "There are two fellows, Slim and Shorty, who own it," Raymond Sweigart explained. "They use my lane because that's the right of way for anyone with property back there, but they are all right. They've been here for years already. When the weather is really nasty, the bootleggers sleep in the barn."

To the west of the barn stood the three-story farmhouse and between the house and barn grew a large garden surrounded by a fence. Trailing among the weedy patch of tea and perennial flowers, lay a dirt path through the middle, leading to a back porch on the east side of the house. The porch-door opened into the kitchen, a long, nar-row room, with dark green walls, nearly black from years of collecting wood smoke. The floor had no linoleum, only bare wood, and the chimney was in poor condition, so was the porch.

No matter how drab or how much work lay ahead, this was much better than what Amanda's parents started out with, near Brutus, Michigan, in 1905. Peter Brubacher had purchased 80 acres of lumbered-off land, with nothing but huge stumps among the remaining trees there. Getting rid of those stumps created a problem. Some rotted with time, but some needed dynamite to clear the farmland, and that was dangerous work. Blasted roots sailed into the air, especially when Peter lit fifty sticks of dynamite beneath one large stump. One 3-foot long section of wood punctured the house roof! They gathered and dragged the stump pieces into a row, to make a livestock fence. Amanda's father and the entire neighborhood worked just as hard at erecting all the buildings and the windmill on their sandy soil in Michigan.

Now here in Pennsylvania, was a set of buildings ready for Aaron and Amanda to start their first home. Two thousand dollars was a lot of money back when Franklin D. Roosevelt was President. Aaron was uneasy, not knowing if the Depression was over or not, but he had looked long and hard for any small farm.

Connected to the back porch was a summerhouse with a chimney and a fireplace in the far corner. Its folding doors opened into a big old stone oven outside that was not usable. The springhouse stood on the south side of the lane and on the north, side was a small shack where Sweigart butchered chickens for market. A pigsty with three pens, and a narrow corncrib stood east of the chicken house \brooder house combination. The large barn was designed for tobacco farming.

Amanda agreed and only heard the details in letters Aaron wrote. Amanda was happy that they could have their own farm. Since settlement would not be until the following spring, Raymond Sweigart stayed on the farm until then. As part of the deal, Raymond paid for a new tin roof for the house, and Aaron helped to put it on. The old wooden shingles remained scattered on the ground.

After writing many letters back and forth, to "my dear Mandie", Aaron went to the Squire in Ephrata for an agreement on his farm. He went to Lancaster for a new suit and to Ephrata in September for a wedding hat. In October, Aaron was ready to travel to Michigan to claim his bride.

He left home on October 30, and boarded the train at Lancaster. He pulled out a pencil and paper and started writing while driving, sending directions to Amanda. Mailing his letter at Harrisburg train station, she was supposed to get it two days later on a Monday. It said, "My trunk will be in Pellston, on the latter part of Sunday, October 31. I have a check enclosed for you in this letter, which you will have to show to reserve and claim the trunk. So please don't go to Pellston for the trunk without this ticket check. The trunk must be moved in 24 hours, if failed to do so, it will cost $.25. So I am hoping you will find it convenient in every way. I paid $17.45 for my ticket from Lancaster to Pellston, Michigan. Well, I can't write so good on the train. I won't eat breakfast now. I have enough along for one day. I do not know where I will get to tonight. I never was in Ohio and no one knows I am coming. Aaron Shirk, your coming husband, on the train. X

Later: "I am hoping you have already received my wedding clothes as I mailed them to you the other day. Now you have the suit, but no one to put in it yet. Ha! That will be something for Lydia to talk about again. Ha!"

When Aaron stopped in Ohio, William Martin's Dan took him along to the Horning Church and to the funeral of someone he did not know. Aaron helped William husk corn. They went to a singing that evening and Annie Weaver talked to Aaron. She asked, "Are you bringing Mandie along to PA on your way back?" Aaron did not tell her. He said, "There is one thing I forgot... a can of fish worms!" She asked. 'What do you want with them?" Aaron said, "To catch suckers like you!" Ha! Ha!

Aaron arrived at Brutus Michigan, two weeks before the wedding, because a new law stated that people needed a blood test before getting a marriage license. They had no idea how long that might take, so Aaron came earlier than first planned. Af-

ter a blood test, they had to wait four days before applying for a marriage license, and finally, the license arrived in the mail on their wedding day.

They were openly published in church two weeks before the wedding and, as was the custom, did not want to hear their names announced so they went for a buggy ride instead of going to church!

Aaron came to Michigan with everyday clothes along to help work as needed. He split a pile of firewood and helped Peter Brubacher with hauling hay. He also worked at a new barn being built in the neighborhood.

From a mail order catalog, Amanda ordered royal blue "feather sheer" material for her wedding dress. She made it by herself in the same two-piece pattern that she made all her dresses. She sewed the apron and the cape together and wore that over the dress, all in the same color. At $.69 a yard, it was the most expensive dress she had ever worn.

November 16, 1937, dawned sunny, then turned cloudy, with some rain and (snow *stivvers*) or snow showers. Their wedding was a simple affair. They invited all their church friends in Michigan but the group was so small by now that only 18 guests were present. They served cookies and homemade dandelion wine as the guests arrived for the happy occasion.

Aaron and Amanda remained upstairs until their parents had given their marriage consent to the Bishop, then they came downstairs and took their seats as the guests sang. This was the last wedding where Bishop Daniel Brubacher officiated in Michigan among the dwindling group. They had no (*navasitzers*) or attendants, so the Bishop asked Manasseh Kulps to stand up with them, as witnesses for the solemn vows.

Aaron's family was all a long way off in Pennsylvania, and so were Amanda's two married sisters, Mary and Betsy and even her brother Silas. Amanda regretted later that she did not at least invite these Pennsylvania people, even if she knew they could not afford to travel so far to a wedding.

They did not get many wedding gifts. Manasseh Kulps, where Amanda worked, gave a bed blanket. They also still owed her $200, which they paid a year or two later as they were able. [De Tillie mate,] Henry Martin's girls gave a big gift of three aluminum sauce-pans with handles and lids for cooking. Other gifts included two brooms, a new round wooden bushel basket for laundry, two agate buckets, a rolling pin, and pie plates.

Peter Brubacher's had given their daughters, Mary and Betsy each a cow as a wedding gift but Amanda was moving to Pennsylvania in a week. There was no way to send a cow and they were too poor to purchase one for them in Pennsylvania. Amanda's own mother supplied bedding as a gift; an empty straw tick, a pair of feather pillows, two pair pillowcases, sheets and a blanket.

Amanda paid for her own wedding dinner of bread, chicken, mashed potatoes, gravy, macaronis, a vegetable, cornstarch pudding, Jell-O, cake with icing and sour cream raisin pies with meringue on top.

Weddings were in the forenoon and the married folks left before supper. The young people stayed for a supper of leftovers, singing and games all evening. Serenaders came with a lot of noise late on the wedding day. A few church people joined local hometown people. When Aaron finally got a wife, the people wished them luck and he would say, "I already have my luck by finding a wife." Amanda had attended two weddings in Michigan and three in Canada, before her own wedding. Her sister Mary was not at any wedding before her own, and neither was their mother. Amanda and Silas had the honor of being attendants at Betsy and Christian Kilmer's wedding. Elsie Ringler was attendant on the Kilmer side and both her, and Amanda wore maroon dresses for that wedding, even if they were not the same shade.

Aaron and Amanda's wedding was a joyous occasion, and yet deep underneath, Peter was concerned about another daughter leaving Michigan. He had his roots there and he wished to stay, but not without a church group. Amanda was their fourth child leaving Michigan for Pennsylvania, and to make matters worse, Lydia planned to hitch a ride to Pennsylvania with them, to make friends there. She did not want to stay in Michigan with a lack of young people, and how could she part with her closest sister when they had shared everything all their lives?

Aaron and Amanda stayed in Michigan one week. Amanda's brothers-in-law, Martin and Christian Kilmer had a brother named David, and he drove them to Pennsylvania with his car, instead of them taking a train. They drove nearly 12 hours to get to Bishop Joe Martins in Indiana for the night, where they spent three days, and went to Blossers Church on Thanksgiving Day, and heard Bishop John Martin for the last time. Michigan, Ohio, and Indiana had church conference together and John Martin was one Bishop among those districts.

Inferior country roads connected one small town with the next one. It took 27 hours to drive the 600 miles from Indiana, to B. W. Shirks in Pennsylvania. They started at 5 AM and drove all night with just one driver. The roads were not good and one place they drove wrong for one half hour. There was nothing like an interstate highway, as they traveled on many bumpy roads. They arrived at Aaron's parents at 8 AM, dead tired, and spent the day talking, resting and sleeping.

The next day they attended Weaverland Church and went to B.W. Shirk's for Aaron and Amanda's wedding "infare", or reception. Relatives bestowed them with wedding gifts from the Pennsylvania families and they received many Sunday dinner invitations for that entire winter.

On Monday morning, Amanda eagerly anticipated exploring the farm they would call home. She had not seen it yet, only descriptions in letters. Amanda was pleased even when the cleanup looked overwhelming. Shingles all around the house would make good kindling, paint would brighten the dark kitchen and they could destroy the weeds. Aaron's family was eager to help, as soon as they got possession in springtime.

Meanwhile the newlyweds lived with Aaron's parents, the B.W. Shirk family from November until April. This was the customary way to help young people start out on their own. Amanda was so slim that Aaron could reach around her waist with his hands. He playfully buttoned her in his overcoat with him.

Some of the time, Amanda worked away. She lived with Martin Kilmers when baby Emma was born, living with them from Monday morning to Saturday evening. Amanda also helped her sister Betsy and Christian Kilmer when Betsy came down with the flu. In March, she helped Martin Kilmer's move from Martindale to Hahnstown. Martin's Lydia was four, Adin was two, and William was one year old. Mary scrubbed the laundry on a washboard and she had barely enough kettles to heat the water or rinse the wash. Martin worked in a tobacco warehouse but money and food were scarce.

Did Amanda get homesick for Michigan? No indeed! Not with so many interesting things to do, places to explore, and people to visit on the weekends. She didn't even have time to write many letters.

Amanda had some major adjustments! In Michigan, snow covered the ground from Thanksgiving until spring, and here the ground was often bare. Pennsylvania had many different groups of Amish and Mennonites, where in Michigan, Amanda knew everyone who wore a black bonnet. Somehow, she aimed to turn all those strangers into friends.

The hardest adjustment was married life. Aaron and Amanda were completely opposite in nature, and they barely knew each other. They both struggled with the adjustments. Aaron was a visionary person with radical ideas that did not always hold out. He talked too much without thinking, and even his own mother said, "Amanda must have a lot of patience to get along with him". He was 23 years old, and many girls had turned him down, especially since there were more boys than girls among the youth group. Amanda, at the age of 22 was willing to try her best, knowing that divorce was not an option even if they were completely opposite in a major way.

Aaron was a morning person and preferred to retire early, while Amanda was an evening person, and had a way of getting many things done yet, before blowing out the lamp. Aaron slept with his head covered and his feet exposed, while Amanda wanted the covers at her feet and not at her head. Aaron's letter writing had revealed how lacking he was in spelling and penmanship. Amanda could overlook that, but nothing had prepared her for his lack of patience and temperance. Truly, love is blind and marriage is an eye opener!

Aaron's father, BW Shirk, wanted to be the first; be in the fields by 7 AM, dinner at 11 o'clock, and back in the fields by noon, with supper at four o'clock. Amanda inherited a much slower pace from her Brenneman and Brubacher ancestors, while Aaron valued promptness! "Until death do us part, was not just maybe even if he snored loudly and his feet stank."

She had imagined a young man more like her own father, but the two were extreme opposites. He had imagined a wife like his own mother and Amanda was not natured like that at all. She was," a *vennich longsome*," [somewhat slow] by the Shirk family standards. Aaron and Amanda would not recommend a courtship by mail, across many miles. There were too many surprises!

Both had a deep longing for a home of their own. They had a new roof overhead, enough to eat and enough to wear, and each other to love and cherish. They set to work trying to minimize the many faults and maximize the good points. They believed in the Bible and in going to church together. When counting their many blessings, their cups were running over.

By moving in with Aaron's family, Amanda learned to know the Shirk family and how they did things and what they ate. Aaron was the oldest of nine children, so the house was full. Mommy Shirk was known by some to be about as nearly perfect as anyone was. She did not talk about others and was *goot mainich* or good-natured. Amanda got a very warm welcome from such a lively bunch. After Aaron sold his harness shop, Aaron and Amanda put their money into a joint bank account and tried to work together. One thing for sure, they did not marry for money. They had very little!

Since Amanda brought no furniture along from Michigan, shopping for household goods and farm implements occupied some of their time that winter. They acquired hardly anything new; most of it came from auctions.

Amanda had spent $200 traveling the winter before, when she first met Aaron, and Manasseh Kulp still owed her $200 for her work in the past. However, she still had $100, and with that, they furnished their house.

At one auction in Terre Hill, a big glass cupboard came up for sale. Amanda expected it would bring more than they could afford. When the auctioneer came down to one dollar to get a bid, she found enough courage to bid on it, because Aaron had just walked away. Amanda got it for $5.50. It was the first time she ever bid on anything, and she enjoyed auctions the rest of her life!

For seven dollars, Amanda bought a 100-piece china set, service for 12, in perfect condition. She had searched for dishes in several stores that winter but had found none yet and she was delighted with such a bargain.

Along with the quilts, sheets, and pillowcases from Michigan, Amanda had a pieced comfort top. Aaron's folks helped finish that, and another comforter, plus a quilt. They filled three straw-ticks with fresh straw, as mattresses for Aaron and Amanda.

Finally, on April 5, 1938, they moved onto their own farm. It took three two-horse wagons, and two spring wagons to move all the goods they had collected. All of Aaron's family helped, and also a neighbor.

Titus remembered the molasses cookies their mother made, that had a way of going flat and sticking together. He said "they stuck together in Aaron's springhouse until we got hungry enough unloading all that stuff.. .and then!.............."

Amanda's kind helpful mother-in-law supplied them with necessities, and filled the gray Hoosier cabinet with all the basics. They canned fruits, vegetables and pickles for Aaron and Amanda, and gave cornmeal, flour, sugar, salt, soda, baking powder, oatmeal, tapioca, cocoa, vanilla, cornmeal, dried corn and potatoes. They even butchered a pig for them and canned the meat. The only food Amanda brought along from Michigan was one dozen quarts of canned huckleberries and one dozen quarts of blackberries. She knew she wouldn't get them in Pennsylvania.

To start farming, a man first needed land, and secondly, money. Aaron's extended family helped make that possible by loaning the young people money to start farming. Aunt Mary helped what she could. She remained single until the age of fifty-two, and earned money from quilting at one cent a yard for someone from New York City. She shared her money.

The third most important thing to a farmer was a wife and God provided. Aaron and Amanda both grew up on farms and understood the basics. Animals needed tender loving care to thrive, and so did people. Farming was a gamble and hardships were common, yet out-weighed with advantages of living so close to nature and their wonderful creator. They understood that God gives the increase, and they needed his help, every step of the way.

When Aaron and Amanda moved in, the house was not very tight. The walls consisted of two layers of heavy boards and siding, with no storm windows or insulation... On a chilly April morning, draft came in at the windows and Aaron was cold! He wore his overcoat to eat breakfast, and long before the next winter, the windows had new putty.

A patch of clover with tiny red leaves grew in the yard. "This is where a murder supposedly occurred," Raymond Sweigart said. Amanda did not know if she wanted to believe that, because the Sweigarts were superstitious people.

The damp dark cellar beneath the house created ideal storage for potatoes and fruit jars. The upstairs had four bedrooms plus an attic up above. After seeing the property, there was one thing that puzzled Amanda. Nowhere had they seen an outhouse! Had the Sweigart family of five managed to live without one? Amanda's puzzlement about the outhouse was solved, when Aaron found it at a very odd place. In the barn, he walked through the feed aisle, and there at the end was a little outhouse in the pigpen! This location did not please Aaron and Amanda at all, so Aaron partly rebuilt it and moved it beside the summerhouse, against the northwest corner beside the fireplace and oven.

On the back porch stood a pump connected to a no-good well. One of the first things Aaron did was dig a ditch from the spring to the back porch. It was a tedious job, since all the digging was done by hand. He laid a water pipe in the ditch and put a new water pump on the porch, along with a steel pump trough. During the summer, Amanda kept the washbasin out there for the men to wash up before entering the house.

While Aaron was working at the pump, he also laid pipes to the barn. The pump had an elbow that could swing to make the water run into the trough or into the pipe for the barn.

The entire project cost $55.75. They pumped that pump handle up and down many times to pump enough water for the horses and for the laundry.

After this improvement, they no longer carried water from the springhouse about 60 feet away. Now all the water for the house, barn and the tobacco beds came from the back porch pump. Aaron plowed the garden between the house and the barn, and then started tobacco plants in beds under muslin sheets.

Aaron and Amanda still carried food to the springhouse because they had no icebox or refrigerator and this was the only means to keep things cool. Amanda covered the food, because the open springhouse had no roof.

That first summer kept Aaron and Amanda busy. Aaron's 11-year-old brother Menno often came to help them. While Amanda drove the horses, Aaron and Menno planted around 3 acres of tobacco. Brothers Ben and Elias also helped with the fieldwork, such as picking stones off the fields, haying, harvesting, and tobacco farming. They worked hard because everything was done by hand. Aaron paid Menno fifteen cents an hour for some of his help and Titus worked for nothing. He was younger. They all needed the work more than they needed the money.

Aaron had two workhorses, Prince, the lead horse, and Kurt, an old almost worn-out horse from his dad. When he needed a third horse for fieldwork, he used Saylor, the driving horse. Aaron's equipment consisted of a walking plow, harrow, drill, a one-horse shovel harrow, and a riding cultivator. He borrowed a corn planter and a grain binder from neighbors.

Amanda remembered how her father planted corn by hand in Michigan. Two people carried a pole with three or five chains dragging in the prepared soil to mark the rows. Then they dragged the chains the other way across and planted the corn kernels at each corner. What worked so well in the sandy soil in Michigan probably did not work in the rocky soil of Pennsylvania.

B.W. Shirk shunned modern conveniences, and the corn planter was fairly modern. Someone said of the corn planter, 'I did not think the devil would come to Turkey Hill in such a way.' Aaron enjoyed modern technology and bought his own corn planter when he could afford it.

Animals on the farm, other than the horses, consisted of one cow, one pig, and seven chickens. For $5.20, Aaron bought a rifle from Sears. He was not a hunter but his brothers shot many a rabbit for supper when they came to help him work.

Amanda usually did the washing on the back porch. She heated water on the kitchen range and then poured it into the wash machine. She was glad Aaron's brother Menno helped on washday, because he could pump the agitator of the hand-operated machine. The wringer washer was lined with corrugated metal, like a washboard. She set an old "rattler" alarm clock at 10 minutes for every load. Menno liked to work, but this job was so monotonous, that he lay down on the job. That is, until Amanda caught him and said, "Crank that load 10 more minutes because it can't be clean!" Lazy or bored people are smart, and he tried to rig up a way to lie down while cranking the wash machine.

Aaron's mother worked hard and managed well. Her youngest child went to school, so she came over to Aarons, one day each week, while so much work beckoned. Her children came along sometimes, and gathered the wooden shingles they stacked for kindling, while she puttied windows. Annie had many old rags, and together, Amanda and she took them to a carpet weaver on the Turkey Hill, who wove carpet runners one yard wide and Amanda ordered 20 yards.

Aaron and Amanda bought groceries in Bowmansville or Churchtown, but only the basics; flour, sugar, oatmeal, salt, tapioca, yeast, matches and hand soap.

3

To the west of Aarons lived Wayne Steffy. Since Wayne's father passed away, his mother Emmaline lived with him. Wayne was a brother to the Mrs. Sweigart who formerly lived on the farm Aaron bought. Wayne raised produce on his farm and took fruits, vegetables, butter and eggs to market in Reading. He left early in the morning, making that trip by horse and wagon. Wayne also owned a small sawmill and he moved it around cutting trees whenever someone wanted lumber. Aaron paid him to clear a small section of woods at the end of the lane, so he could farm more land, and use the lumber.

Emmaline was in her seventies, but looked older. She was hump-backed, and walked with her head hanging low. Emmaline related some happenings to Aarons from the years gone by. "Half way up Laurel Hill, in that neat little clearing with a stone fence around it, there used to be a cottage," she told them. "It belonged to an old witch-like lady by the name of Sal Weller. The whole neighborhood accused her of practicing witchcraft and other evil things. They even accused her of murder. However, she denied it, declaring, "If I ever murdered anyone, the horses won't carry my body across the creek at the bottom of the hill when I die."

"When my girls were young," continued Emmaline, "they'd go berry picking way back in the bush, but they tried to avoid Sal Weller, because if they came too close to her cottage, she would shriek, I... see... you! She tried to scare the girls away because she wanted all the berries."

"When the day came that Sal Weller died, her coffin was taken down the hill by horse and wagon. When they came to the creek, behind what is now your barn," said Emmaline, "the horses balked. The drivers coaxed them and tried to lead the horses across, but they refused. They could not make them cross the 6 inches of clear water, until they removed the coffin from the wagon and carried it across. Then the horses crossed the creek like normal."

"Sometime later, that land was sold and the cottage was torn down," continued old Emmaline. "And would you know," she paused, "when the walls were torn apart, human skeletons were found among the ruins, mostly of babies."

Amanda shuddered. She was glad that Sal Weller and the cottage were gone.

The Weller lot and the woodland around it belonged to Henry Burkholder. One year Aaron tried to farm the land in the clearing, but the soil was sandy and washed off. Wildlife ate the corn he planted and he could not get manure on it, at that location.

In 1943 and 1944, Henry Burkholder planted more cherry trees, but the cherry production never amounted to much. Big cherry trees on that southeast slope gave some small dark sweet cherries. The trees needed more pruning and spraying. Eventually the woods reclaimed the clearing. Only the legends and stories remain of Sal Weller, plus a rundown, rambling stonewall. The foundation of the cottage hid among vines tangles of underbrush.

⁂

In September, Wayne Steffy, next door to Aaron, sold his farm to Aaron's father, B.W. Shirk. Aaron's sister Lydia planned to marry Jesse Brubacher, also from Michigan, and this place suited them. Some implements and tobacco laths came with the farm, for the sum of $5500. Aaron and Amanda were pleased with this arrangement. It would be wonderful to have such close Mennonite neighbors, and a sister at that!

Spring and summer passed swiftly with work on every side. This wooded area, way out back, made the headlines in July, when Emmaline Steffy turned up missing! When Emmaline went berry picking, and failed to return, her family notified the authorities. Aaron and many others joined the search in the thicket-choked Silver Hill area near her home, 2 1/2 miles southeast of Bowmansville, where she lived with her daughter. Seventy-seven year old Emmaline, roamed the entire area many times, and no one could figure out how she could get lost.

People knew that Emmaline was not a church-going type of person. Not so long ago, she had met neighbors who were coming home from church, and she said, "See what I earned while you sat in church!" Perhaps, someone had now hexed her?

After two days of searching, Emmaline stepped out of the woods at the Silver Hill School, while the posse of 100 people, together with the state motor police, and a bloodhound, still searched the area. At Elmer Groff's, her daughter's place where she lived, a group of people had read a few Bible passages, hoping to overpower any possible hex. She was okay after spending three days and two nights in the woods. Less than five months later, Emmaline died, on December 7, 1939. She was buried at the Center Church cemetery.

Even more exciting, was the arrival of Aaron and Amanda's first-born son! Baby Daniel was born at home at 3:45 AM on August 16, 1938, weighing 10 pounds. Dr. Schnader did not know if Amanda would survive, but her time was not up. God had a lot of work for her to do yet.

Everyone showered Baby Daniel with all the love and attention that a baby could wish for. He was named after Bishop Daniel Brubacher of Michigan. Aaron was a proud new father and Amanda loved babies all her life. Having her own was like a bit of heaven on earth. She counted the fingers and the toes and marveled at the miracle in her arms.

She stayed in bed 10 days while others did her work. Aaron's sister Lydia was their maid for the remainder of the summer, before getting married and moving next door. Mommy Shirk also came over the hills to help what she could in a very kind way. Baby Daniel was her first grandchild! She brought her own baby crib that she no longer needed, because their youngest child turned eight already.

Amanda rocked and sang, as she cuddled and bonded. The soft flannel baby clothes she had lovingly made were already too small. She had no more soft fabric to sew…. but sugar sacks…. that's what she could use! And improvise she did! The fabric was rather coarse for a new baby, but baby Daniel thrived all the same.

Aaron's younger sisters, Eva and Annie, were pleased to help. They thought Daniel was the nicest baby around, and so "*brawf*" (content). They liked to hold him at church, and squabbled about whose turn it was. When baby Daniel was almost seven weeks old, Aaron and Amanda took him to church for the first time. Like all the other little boys in the area, he wore dresses until he was potty trained.

August kept everyone very busy, preserving the great abundance from the garden, while the men worked hard at harvesting tobacco. Their first tobacco crop yielded 4,000 laths [about 20,000 plants], and sold for a total of $894.60. The wrappers sold for fifteen cents a pound and the fillers sold at five cents. The tobacco cost very little to raise, besides labor. With all the help from his extended family, Aaron and Amanda were off to a good start.

The B.W. Shirk family had two weddings in December. Their son Sam Shirk married Lydia Zimmermann on Sunday, December 18, 1938. They married at Martindale, in the church anteroom before the regular services started. One hundred and twenty-five people ate dinner at the bride's parents, Weaver Zimmerman's.

Four days later, Aaron's sister Lydia Shirk married Jesse Brubacher at the home of the bride. Aaron had the job of calling the names of 84 guests to the table for the wedding dinner. His brother Menno wanted a perfect attendance at school so much, that he skipped his own sister's wedding! He returned home from school to a crowd of people still at the house. Some of the younger guests stayed for supper and the evening, so he really did not miss the entire wedding.

The day after the wedding, the new bride went to work for Lem Martins. Lydia had promised her first cousin, to be their maid for the new baby, named Lena. Lydia was pleased when Aunt Fiana offered to help her there. Jesse and his bride moved onto their farm besides Aaron and Amanda on March 28, 1939.

Baby Daniel suddenly had three Aunt Lydias. Amanda's single sister remained as Aunt-Lydia, and Sam's new wife, was Samsy. The third Lydia, Aaron's sister, wife of Jesse Brubacher was Jessesy. This Lydia next door was mostly called Lydi-Jes-sey.

When the young couple moved next to Aarons, one of the first things they did was make a lane to connect both their farms. This connected them and cut off about a mile of driving, coming or going to BW Shirks on Turkey Hill. These two young families, living side-by-side, formed a special bond, sharing and confiding as neighbors, cousins and in-laws for over 70 years. They even shared the mailbox at the end of the new lane, right beside Jesse's house.

With some of the tobacco money, Aaron bought two steers to fatten at six and one half cents a pound. Homemade butter sold at $.20 a pound, and eggs fetched $.18 a dozen. Butter and eggs paid for the groceries, because they raised most of the food they ate.

Aaron purchased 300 Barred Rock chicks at eight and one fourth cents apiece, for a total of $25. They both knew that fragile new chicks needed constant heat and protection. Aaron and Amanda could not afford to lose any of them, so Aaron slept out in the brooder house with the new chicks for several nights, making sure they do not pile on top of each other, suffocating some. He also needed to keep an eye on the temperature of the brooder-house stove.

At J B Zimmerman, Aaron bought a new gas-powered wringer washer for $71.25. Aaron's brother Menno, no longer needed to crank the old worn-out wooden washing machine, with a leaking tub.

By the time Daniel turned 13 months old, he had learned to walk. At nine months, he had his first tooth and Amanda showed it to Aaron saying, "Look, I found a pearl!"

All this time, the bootleggers in the bush were busy too. Aaron and Amanda could hear their trucks in the night, hauling in sugar and grain, and hauling out whiskey. Amanda did not know where the still was, but it made her a little uneasy. Aaron figured it was none of his business, and he did not report them

to the authorities. They were not located on his land and they had the right to use his lane.

When their sugar and grain sacks accumulated, they gave them to Aarons, even as many as 200 at a time. Amanda made many things from these: pillowcases, sheets, diapers, underwear, and some were dyed for shirts and dresses. In fact, Aarons accumulated so many sacks, that seven babies later, they did not run out of sugar sack diapers.

One night the bootleggers tapped on Aaron's bedroom window. "Hey, our truck got stuck," they said. "Could you pull us out?" So, Aaron hitched up the horses in the night and pulled them out. Occasionally Slim and Shorty helped Aaron work for a day.

The rinsings from their still went into the Black Creek. People downstream said that at certain times you could smell and taste whiskey in the water. One time there was even a rumor that pigs got drunk further down the hill. If bootleggers had even half a year at one place, they might move on to hide elsewhere, but they stayed at this secluded spot for years. The still was on the property of deacon Pit Weaver, and he knew nothing about it.

When neighbor Jim, was very sick, Dr. Wenger said it appeared to be from too much moonshine. Since Jim was getting money from welfare, Dr. Wenger was required to report such abuse to the welfare society and that is why the law came looking around.

The days of the moonshine still ended on Saturday, October 21, 1939, when Aaron and Amanda were at church for preparatory services. When they returned home, they discovered the police had destroyed the whiskey still with dynamite.

Slim and Shorty were not arrested. The story goes, that from a distance, they watched the authorities destroy their still, and then they fled. As Aaron and Elias stripped tobacco, the FBI came to question Aaron, but he did not say much, and did not want to get involved. Several years later, one of the bootleggers came back and paid Aaron a visit. Daniel remembered that visit.

Eventually, BW Shirk used some of those left-over pipes from the distillery to make a barnyard fence.

∽

Baby Sarah Ann brought much sunshine into Aaron and Amanda's life in the middle of winter. She arrived on January 19, 1940. Doctor Wenger delivered baby Sarah Ann because Dr. Schnader was busy on another case. Dr. Wenger was a well-liked doctor, at least when he was sober. Amanda had no gardening in January and more time to enjoy her babies, and this she did. She cuddled their wonderful new baby and still enjoyed 17-month-old Daniel.

Baby Sarah Ann wore Daniel's outgrown baby dresses. She was named after Amanda's own mother, who lived in Michigan. Amanda sent a lock of soft baby hair in a latter to her parents, but she could not send them a photo. Aaron nicknamed the petite new baby "Dolly" and he made a play-pen to protect little Sarah Ann from her rough, one year old brother's good intentions. Aaron's sister Eva came to help Amanda.

BW Shirk helped Aaron install new boards on the bedroom floor, spending $11 for the lumber. Eva helped Amanda paint and wallpaper the bedroom.

Lydi-Jess-sey walked across the field lane many times. She helped Amanda lay the carpet Aarons had ordered. The 36-inch wide carpet runners cost $.85 a yard for a total of $16.80. The room-length strips, laid side by side, covered the parlor floor, but one strip cut too long made the next strip too short. Amanda and Lydi-Jess-sey cut and patched! By hand, they sewed a binding edge on the cut ends to keep the woven rug pieces from unraveling. Later, Amanda moved the carpet pieces upstairs and that bedroom was the "carpet room", because it was the only carpeted room in the house. Without a sweeper, they removed and cleaned the carpet strips at house cleaning time.

Another spring and summer came, bringing its planting and growing season. In August 1940, Aaron tore away the big old stone oven behind the summerhouse fireplace. This left a hole in the wall with only the inside fireplace doors to close it. Where the oven had been, he built a woodshed. Now they could go through the fireplace doors to get wood. Aaron had made it his business to have that shed filled with firewood every year before winter. He enjoyed woodcutting.

In December of 1940, Bob Fox and Paul Burkhart helped Aaron install a new water system. It was a Rife hydraulic water ram, from Jake B. Zimmerman. When they completed the waterline, the overflow water from the spring dropped, or flowed, through a pipe, into a dug shaft, which held the ram. The ram, by the power of the trickling waterfall, forced the water up another pipe into a holding tank in the upstairs of the house. By gravity, like a water tower, the overflow from the tank flowed to the barn's water trough and from there flowed away outside, to the swamp. Two pipes from the upstairs water tank came downstairs into the kitchen. One led to the waterfront on the kitchen range, where water heated in the stove reservoir, then led to a spigot in the zinc-lined dry sink. The other, a cold water pipe, also came to the dry sink. They had hot and cold running water in the house, and even made a drain at the dry sink. However, water from the washbasins was still dumped into the slop bucket and carried out. The spring never went dry, so the ram ticked day and night, seldom stopping. The wooden barrel for the ram, submerged in the ground, had to be replaced from time to time over the years. The large water tank behind the bed upstairs, made spooky gurgling noises to concern young children at times. The water was no longer as fresh; in fact, it was room temperature. A cold drink from the springhouse tasted much fresher.

Aaron and Amanda had no lofty goals of achieving honor and fame, nor even riches on earth. They wanted to live in peace and raise a family if the Lord so will. Little by little, their dreams came true. With fair prices in farming, most hard-working people with common sense could make a living on a diversified farm with tobacco as a cash crop. If one thing failed, hopefully something else paid better. Aaron and Amanda received much help in cleaning up their farm and it looked better all the time. With Daniel and Sarah Ann healthy and growing and a third child on the way, what more could they wish for, but only in heaven do people live "happily ever after". Clouds gathered on the horizon as Amanda's parents planned to move in with them.

4

Aunt Lydia's diary

Lydia arrived in Pennsylvania with Aaron and Amanda, right after their wedding. She did not want to part with her closest sister, eighteen months older than her. They shared nearly everything all their young lives. Lydia knew she could find housework, working for others. Everyone in Pennsylvania gave her a warm welcome, and Lydia wrote in her diary, "It was grand!" She had no trouble finding jobs as a maid, and said, "It's a swell place to work!" but that only lasted 10 weeks before she was looking for another job. Then, while at Aarons, Lydia wrote, "Amanda and I are working on her rug and eating candy. Lydi-Jes-sey and Jesse Brubacher came over at noon and we all walked over to explore the place they bought next to Aaron and Amanda. Trash, trash and more trash to clean up."

Lydia went to Christian Kilmer's to stay awhile, and wrote that Christian went to look after a home to buy, and he came home hopeless again. The next week he again went looking for a home, and the next week he was still looking. Small farms for sale were scarce. However, Christian's persistence paid off and by mid-March, Lydia was helping her sister pack up and move to a place where Christian worked. He did not buy the place.

When Betsy was not well, Lydia put in a hard days' work helping her sister get ready for the movers. They canned a sheep and it yielded seventeen quarts of meat. Christian's family moved to Shirktown. Lydia worked hard, helping Martin Kilmers can a large amount of food that summer. She was there for the arrival of a new baby. When baby Nancy was five weeks old, Lydia moved in with Aaron and Amanda for a month. She helped Amanda get ready for Sunday dinner guests, and commented on washing many cloth sacks, from the bootleggers. They had some good times together, but Lydia was hard to please.

Wayne Steffy took Aaron, Amanda and Lydia to Ephrata. Lydia went to Dr. Brenneman. She started a new job at Chester and Esther Groff, where she watched "kiddies" while Esther went to work and Lydia's pains returned. Chester helped her one day, and Esther's mother came when Lydia's heart was too weak to work. She went to the doctor three times in ten days and "not much better" . .. She went to the doctor three times in the next week, and then the doctor advised Lydia to wait two weeks before returning. He simply did not know what to do for her! Chester Groff took Lydia to the doctor for her next appointment, and he even helped Lydia mop the floors when he had time off from work. When Esther took Lydia to her next Dr. appointment, the doctor explained things plainly to Lydia.

Then Esther took Lydia to Aaron's to see the new baby Sarah Ann. Aunt Eva had dinner ready for them there. Back at Groffs, Chester took Lydia to the doctor eight times for a series of eight shots within three weeks time, with no clue as to why. Meanwhile Lydia suffered off and on from fever, side ache, terrible sick headache, and earache and gas pain in the night. Lydia stopped working for Groffs after she helped them move to Farmersville. She was very tired! After two years on her own, she had about enough, and longed for Michigan.

The thought of returning home to her parents intrigued her. After resting a week, Lydia boarded the train at Lancaster, and four connections later, Joshua and Katie picked her up at Brutus, Michigan. Lydia wrote, "Just like a dream. I'm home!" It was nearly springtime in Michigan and she went to sap camp and helped her father cook sap until late. Peter had gathered 20 gallons to cook into maple syrup.

When company arrived, they played a lively game of Jing Hands Up. Joshua netted 900 smelt fish. Ma, Katie and Lydia cleaned them and canned 11 quarts by removing the heads and insides of the tiny fish. Canning them softened the bones. They found time for family fellowship of singing and a taffy pull.

When church was at Peter Brubacher's house, they had a lot of company all day. Church west of Brutus on a rainy day had only nine members show up. Peter struggled to help keep the community going, but the church had fallen apart. After much prayer and many hard decisions, Peter put his farm up for sale. He wanted to stay where he was, but not without a plain church. Katie and Lydia talked until 12:30 at night. They had many concerns about what might happen after they sold the farm.

Lydia's doctor sent her for surgery and this was not her first, she had many problems. Five years earlier, back in June of 1934, Lydia had female problems. At the age of nineteen she ended up with a hysterectomy; much against their wishes, and her life was never the same. At that time, Amanda sent her sister a lengthy letter about all the local happenings, to keep her informed. Amanda, still single, wrote:

In the afternoon, we played ball, then in the evening we had a lively game of run sheep-run and Flying Dutchman. I wore my new stockings and new shoes. One stocking caught while climbing through a fence and I busted a hole in the knee of the other one. Oh dear! I did not have rubbers on, and my shoes are quite badly scuffed. After that, the teenagers cleaned up the barn floor and played big four, Dusty Miller and John John, but I was too tired to help. Well let's hope and pray that you may soon be able to come home again. I sure do hope you will be well and strong again and I hope they will get you cured. I would do most anything in the world for you if I could only help you out. Your well-wishing sister, Amanda.

[Amanda sincerely meant that last sentence and she spent the next sixty-eight years catering to her sister who was unable to have a family of her own.]

∽

Peter had many burdens, beside Lydia's health problems. He was working to get the farm ready for an auction. He put in long hard days filling silo, and planting oats. Sarah Ann made dinner for the potato diggers who came to dig their potatoes.

Lydia, Katie and Joshua, got very tired of hearing the planning, because Peters family planned to move to Pennsylvania, and they were burning bridges behind them. Lydia had a taste of life in Pennsylvania, and knew that her life would never be all roses without thorns. It hurt deeply to say goodbye to the farm they all helped build from scratch…. after blasting many stumps and making fences ….the house Peter built… and rebuilt…. the schoolhouse…the church with their three small graves….and the entire neighborhood… the many friends... the garden, and the trees they planted… the well they dug…. and the windmill, put there with Sarah Ann's inheritance money…. the animals they raised….the young chickens just starting to lay. Peter had recently purchased eighty more acres for a better pasture, and worked long hard days putting up more fences. After the farm auction was over, most of his former possessions belonged to the Vangness family. Joshua showed them how to feed his horses, cows, pigs and chickens. It keenly hurt him to walk away, but he was young.

Peter saw May City, Iowa, fall apart over gritty little church disputes, and Brutus, Michigan had somewhat the same type of disputes, about rubber tires, farming with tractors and owning cars, but for Peter, the problems were much worse, because he was no longer a young man and his youngest son was sixteen years old. His helpers were nearly grown and gone, and who wanted to start over at the age of 60? What next, Lord? Peter needed help to relocate and start over.

He had forbidden his oldest daughter from marrying someone from out-of-state, because Peter wanted to keep his family in Michigan, but he lost. The Brubacher's were not moving for financial reasons. They survived the Great Depression and knew how to live with less. After forty years of hard work, and deep memories, Peter was hard to transplant. His roots lay deep, but he wanted what was best for his family.

These are all earthly possessions, and he wanted to see his children and grandchildren grow up in a conservative church with simplicity. He could stay where he was, and join a more liberal church, or move to a horse and buggy group elsewhere. Peter enjoyed working with horses and he chose to stand fast and hold on to the traditions, which he was taught. They sadly said farewell and moved to Pennsylvania. The bright side was meeting their four children living in Pennsylvania, and seeing several new grandchildren.

God's protecting hand had helped them thus far, and would not forsake them now. Surely, they could find a place to live and make many new friends. The future sounded exciting, and yet they dreaded the unknown.

On Sunday, they spent the last night in their home in Michigan, and on November 25, on a Monday, they tore their beds apart and slept at newlywed Martin Reeds. She, Norma was a niece to Peter and Sarah Ann Brubacher. Three days later, the crating was finished and delivered to the train station. On December 10, 1940, Aaron went to the East Earl train station in Pennsylvania to get the freight of household goods from Michigan. It weighed 4060 pounds, and filled two, two- horse-wagons and two spring wagons, costing $67 for the shipping.

The freight on the train arrived at Aaron Shirks, but Peters were not in a hurry to get there yet. They slowly drifted in that direction for nearly three months, before they settled into place. With no chores to do, Peter enjoyed visiting and traveling, like his father Jacob before him. [Notion Jecky lived many places.] The Sauders invited them for supper, and the Bushkirks had a singing for them. They spent an enjoyable time at Peter's parents for one supper and the night, and went to the schoolhouse the next day for an arithmetic contest and reminiscing. Then grandpa and Uncle Joe Brenneman took them to Pellstontrain station on December 9, 1940.

They spent time at Stanton and Grand Rapids Michigan, and then moved on to Indiana, where they got off the train at three different places: South Bend, Mishawaka, and Elkhart. After attending Aunt Florence's funeral, they spent the next day visiting at eight different places and the next day among six different families. The train that took them to Ohio was "heaping full. Before heading to Lancaster County, Pennsylvania, they had a great time at Uncle Henry's with boat rides and games until after midnight at Snyder County, Pennsylvania.

On New Year's Day, they arrived at Martin Kilmers, and Lydia had a sick headache. They stopped many places and went to Uncle Eli Stauffers for the night. It was January 4 when they arrived at Aaron Shirks. Aaron stayed home babysitting when Amanda went to fetch her parents, because the carriage would not hold them all. While waiting, he decided to try his hand at baking a cake to surprise Amanda and her parents, who planned to move in and stay a while. Aaron mixed up a cake, and baked it just right, but something went wrong, and when the cake cooled, it was rock hard. To surprise Mandie, he nicely hung the pan, cake and all, back on its nail in the cellar-way." Won't she be surprised?" he said. After Amanda returned with her parents, Aaron could not keep his secret, and he simply had to show them his cake. He was never good at secrets! They were a burden to him, because he preferred saying what was on his mind and he did not keep people guessing what he thought. Peter and Sarah Ann had much to learn about this unusual man who was their son-in-law.

Aaron might very well be a bachelor, if Peter Brubacher had not given his daughter's hand in marriage. He was deeply indebted to his father-in-law and agreed to have Amanda's parents stay until they find a place of their own.

Amanda had not seen her parents for three years and her parents had never seen the place their daughter called home. They heard descriptions through the letters they sent back and forth . Eagerly they met their two new grandchildren, including Sarah Ann's namesake, a little dolly learning to walk. Baby Daniel was already two years old.

Amanda moved her yellow sideboard cupboard into the parlor, and set her mother's big Dutch cupboard there, to make her mother feel more at home in a strange new place. Amanda's mother put her own dishes in the top part, the way they had been in Michigan, and Amanda took her good Sunday dishes out of the yellow sideboard and put them in the bottom part of her mother's big cupboard.

After arranging some belongings at Aaron's house, Peter and Sarah Ann kept drifting among relatives, spending time with Martin Kilmers and Christian Kilmers among others. While Peters stayed at Eli Stauffers, his sister Mary's house, Peter's wife Sarah Ann [Mommy Brubacher] got seriously sick with pneumonia. Dr. Shantz from Ephrata came out every day to see Mommy for the first week. It took two weeks until she was well enough to sit up, even for one-half hour.

While Amanda's mother laid deathly sick, the mail was the only way they could communicate. Amanda expected a postcard in the mail, and wondered if her mother was still alive? She wanted to hurry to the mailbox and send a post-card without taking two little children along in the cold weather, slowing her down. "I'll just shut them in the kitchen" she decided, "and I will hurry back." When she saw Aaron and his brother Ben taking down tobacco she told them "I want to go to the mailbox now, would you please check on the children soon?"

Ben soon followed Amanda over to the mailbox at Jesse's, and said, "You should just see what your kitchen looks like. The children threw out most of your dishes from the cupboard!" Oh what a mess to clean up! Amanda felt like crying because two thirds of her "bargain" Sunday dishes lay in shattered ruins. She still had a stack of vegetable dishes, and the big-glass fruit dishes remained. Most of the water- glasses were whole and a few of the jelly dishes.

Aaron spanked the children and shut them in the cupboard for a few minutes. Daniel and Sarah Ann were usually well behaved and had never bothered Amanda's cupboard. Perhaps they could sense the interference of this new cupboard belonging to strangers. Most of all, they could feel the deep stress of their mother with a pre-occupied mind. They missed her undivided attention!

⁓

Peter searched for a small farm or acreage close to their three married daughters in the Bowman-ville area, but he could not find what he wanted. So many people had moved here from Michigan for cheap land that the area had been nicknamed Little Michigan for a while. No longer were Aarons the only Mennonites back this way. Between Laurel Hill and Bowmansville lived Noah Hoovers, Abe Ringlers, Isaac Kulps, Manuel Brubachers, Jesse Brubacher's, and Eli Huber's, among others. Small farms sold rapidly and Dawdy Brubacher had a hard time finding one.

Where Peter had been the steering wheel for 40 years of his life, he was now less than a spare tire and no longer felt needed. Raising tobacco was foreign to him, and that is what every man and boy worked over winter. Aaron's younger brothers enjoyed showing Peter how fast they could pull off the dried leaves from the stalks and sort them in boxes according to their length. That was something Peter had never learned and it made his head go around, just watching them work.

He was still wishing for a place to call his own, but the prices kept going up and the places he wanted were in big demand. Peter wanted a chicken house for Sarah Ann and a shed for a horse and buggy. When facing stark reality, Peter understood what all had been left behind in Michigan.

He stepped outdoors on a late winter day, with the feel of spring in the air. He would enjoy hauling sap from his sugar bush in Michigan, but Lancaster County was farther south and not ideal for sugaring. He might have found a few trees and plugged them, and brought in some sap, if he was fortunate, in their shorter runs, but then came the sticky mess of boiling sap. Amanda's kitchen would not do. The sticky steamy work needed a sugar shack and there was none here. Peter could no longer work as hard as he once did, and eventually he would need a hernia repaired. He could not lift much weight. He was starting to feel his age and he needed an income.

Mommy Brubacher was skilled in housework because she had been in charge of managing a house since the age of 16 when her mother died. She had no problem keeping busy when she was well. There was no end to laundry mending, cooking and cleaning, but her slow recovery left her tired and recuperating at Eli Stauffers.

On Sunday morning, Aaron, Amanda, Daniel and baby Sarah Ann started to church in the top buggy, turning right at the end of their lane, towards Churchtown. That morning they met Mr. Styer, a neighbor, looking at a black charred car, pulled off beside the road. "Look" he said grimly, pointing under the car, towards the body of a young man. "I was on my way through here," said Mr. Styer, "when I saw smoke coming from this car, and I went to call Dr. Wenger. I plan to stay here and wait for him."

Aaron and Amanda waited also, until Dr. Wenger came, and pronounced the young man dead, and identified him as Robert Hackman. Then Aarons went on their way to church. What Aaron had seen, disturbed him greatly. A murder! And so close to home, that he was shaken. In church, his mother wondered, "What's wrong with Aaron?" After church, Amanda told her what they had seen. Later, they learned the whole story and Aaron's picture was among the newspaper write-ups. A murder in Lancaster County was shocking enough, but to have it happen among nonresistant Mennonite people was unthinkable!

Robert Hackman was dating Eva Martin of Union Grove. Eva had been William Redcay's girlfriend, even in school days, but she had broken their friendship. Watching from his house in Union Grove, Redcay could see Hackman's car at the Martin home that Saturday evening. Filled with jealousy and hatred, he laid in wait at the Union Grove crossroad, until Hackman left his girlfriend. When Hackman stopped at the intersection, Redcay jumped in the car and knocked him unconscious. Then he drove north on Reading Rd. (now Route 625), and turned onto Laurel Rd. driving way out back to the woods where civilization nearly ended at Aaron's lane. There he beat Hackman to death, and tried to burn the car and the body.

Dr. Wenger, the coroner, knew of the fight concerning Eva Martin's companionship. Eva was his patient and was doctoring for her nerves. Therefore, Dr. Wenger sent the police directly to the Redcay residence, where Bill was taking a bath. People who heard more details claimed that Eva's parents broke up the friendship of William and Eva after a two-year courtship. A major objection to Bill was that he had a motorcycle, and that was frowned upon in the Lancaster Conference Church.

Some said, "Parents should not wait two years to end an unapproved courtship, because the Pennsylvania law says a two-year courtship was equal to an unspoken engagement." The story goes that Robert Hackman irritated Bill many times, by blowing his car horn, long and loud, at midnight when passing Bill's house on his way home from a date with Eva. Bill knew which car to attack at the intersection when Robert stopped at the Union Grove stop sign.

Headlines in the newspaper were unbelievable! These were Lancaster Conference Mennonite youth, and they refused to fight for their country! Hackman died on his mother's 46th birthday and 3000 people attended the funeral. His father was a preacher in the Old Order German Baptist Church, and he had four brothers and one sister.

Redcay was sent to prison where he stayed for 20 years. He repented and   was a caring, honest person.

In March, Mommy Brubacher had recovered from her pneumonia, and moved in with Aaron and Amanda. Lydia also came to stay with her parents and her closest sister. She wrote, "Amanda is in work head over heels, getting ready for company." They had a family get-together for Martin Kilmer's, Christian Kilmers, Silas, Katie and Lydia and Joshua, together with their parents, at Aaron Shirks.

Silas, Joshua and Katie, lived where they worked and kept busy. Peter struggled to fit in, and Lydia did more so. Her diary was boring, disgusting, and sad. Lydia started a new job at Clarence and Betty Groff. When her nerves got bad, she had a spat with them, and "got old-timer pains." She had a toothache one day and felt bad all over the next day.

Dawdy Brubacher helped Aaron make hay and put away tobacco, the best he could. Lydia stayed upstairs in her bedroom for nine days straight, with her mother attending to her. She made two potholders and knitted a dishrag. She went downstairs for Sunday and the next day Aaron and Amanda welcomed a new baby boy, named Walter. Lydia was disappointed that the baby boy wasn't named Neal; she hardly slept, thinking of a name for him.

This time, Amanda's own sister Katie and her mother helped her with the work of a new baby. While the others worked, Lydia spent most of those ten days on the bed with Amanda... tired... headache... nerves out of order. Dr. Wenger came to check up on Amanda and checked Lydia! She was weak, had a headache and she went to the doctor. He says she is getting along nicely! Maybe he is trying to convince her, because Lydia was back in bed, in her own bedroom again, as soon as Amanda's ten days were up. Joshua came home for Sunday dinner, when baby Walter was six days old, but Amanda did not make the meals, she was still in bed.

Aaron's parents helped Aaron and Amanda by keeping baby Daniel nearly two weeks, when Walter arrived, and Amanda was still in bed. Peter and Sarah Ann gave Amanda a break when they took baby Sarah Ann along to look at a place for sale. It was the 'Good' place.

Aaron had a hard time adjusting to extra people around the house, and finding a chance to discuss what was on his mind, with Amanda alone. When he went to the Lancaster stockyards, he might make it take a little longer on purpose. Other local businesses had places where men lingered to chat such as Benj. F. Weaver at Union Grove, at Blacksmith Eli Martin, or at Smith M. Shirk, who ran the general store in Churchtown.

When Aaron needed another horse, he started pricing some. He went to a horse sale but he didn't buy any. Four days later, he came home with a horse on trial. Paul Z. Martin had a five-year-old carriage horse for $115, but that did not suit Aaron for some reason. Three days later, he bought a horse at Ephrata for $137. He was pleased with the new horse named Barney, but four days later, it died, and Aaron got four dollars from the scavenger at Terre Hill.

Aaron and Amanda gladly welcomed her parents into their home, but company manners disappeared. What started out as a temporary arrangement got

longer, week after week, and month after month, as time dragged on. Mommy Brubacher straightened out children as she thought necessary. When Aaron's brother Titus, was helping Aaron work, he noticed how mommy spanked Daniel until she ran out of breath. Daniel missed his mother's attention and teased Sarah Ann endlessly, until Mommy felt obligated to protect her cute little namesake.

Amanda plainly had her hands full, as she tried to please everyone, her husband, her parents, her dear children and her sister Lydia. Amanda felt sorry for Lydia, and would have done anything she could to help her find happiness, but she did not know how, and neither did anyone else. Her parents also needed help.

The next four weeks, Lydia was sick at Martin Kilmer's and sick at Eli Stauffer. She got her eyes tested at Ephrata and went to Dr. Shantz. In the morning, she rested a bit, and wrote," not good on my feet." Then, "low and behold, cousins Henry and Ruben Reist came at 3; 30, and I took them through the Stauffer's shop. I was with them until 10:00 PM and we had a grand time!"

Dr. Schnader came out two days for sick baby Walter, and he checked Aunt Lydi., The next week she went back to the doctor with a sore throat and a backache, while Amanda helped Aaron strip tobacco. Dr. Schnader was a farmer at heart, and he took time to visit a little when he made house calls. He knew the farmers had rough going in those Depression years of the 30s. Office calls with medicine included, were usually $1 to $3, depending on what kind or how much medicine. Babies delivered at home cost $20 for Daniel, and then on up to the $50 or $60 in the later 1940s.

Aaron's brother Elias Shirk married Nancy Weaver before church services, in the Bowmansville anteroom, on November 30, 1941. One week later, BW Shirk had a reception for them, before Ben Junior left to live in Indiana. He went to serve two years in a CPS camp. Lydia had a nice chat with the guests. Aaron and Amanda stayed home that day and missed the gathering because Daniel had tonsillitis.

Out back in a rural setting, without connections to the outside world, none of them knew that the Japanese bombed Pearl Harbor that day. No matter how remote and secluded, the war affected their lives also. Monday came soon enough and it was a blue one for Lydia and Amanda, because the wash machine motor did not start until noon, on a nice washday. Aaron gathered the butcher tools and cleaned the barnyard, for butchering the next day. In his diary, he recorded on December 8, "Japan started war on USA".

Aaron liked to keep in touch by subscribing to a daily newspaper, the *Lancaster Intelligencer Journal*, when he could afford it. He also talked with every neighbor and feed man that he met.

The Peter Brubacher family gathered for Christmas, at Aaron Shirks. That was like home, or as close to a home as they had, and they all had a good time. The next week when Lydia had a sore throat, Dr. Schnader came in the evening and said, "it is not bad". She wrote, "I don't have much use for him."

January brought a bright spot when Peter Brubacher's spent time measuring rooms in the "Good" place. They finally found a place to live. Lydia still had all sorts of aches and pains. She also had a problem with the thought of her last sister leaving her. Katie was getting things together to move to Indiana. Lydia saw it coming due to the many letters Dan and Katie wrote regularly.

When Amanda married, and suddenly left her parents, they were just too far away. For three years, she wished they were closer, and now they were too close for comfort. However, this too shall pass!

Peter Brubachers bought the place near Churchtown, and three days later, they moved. They spent all day packing things at Aarons, to move out. Joshua gathered his belongings at Stauffer's where he boarded, when he worked at the packinghouse. Joshua and Lydia helped lay linoleum in their new home. They spent time unpacking things they had not seen since they left Michigan, because they had no place to put them. In Terre Hill, Peters bought furniture at Mahlon Zimmerman [Senior's] household auction, and Mahlons moved to Florida for health reasons.

Katie moved to Indiana, and only Lydia and Joshua moved in with their parents. It was a long year, but now they had a home. Peters had help putting up a chicken house, and they ordered baby chicks of their own. Things were looking better for them, but Lydia's health problems remained. Peter took Lydia to Blue Ball and from there on the bus, and the trolley line to Ephrata, where they removed her tonsils at noon.

Aaron and Amanda soon adjusted to the welcome change of privacy. They enjoyed many good times when Peter Brubacher's lived there, and the stories in Lydia's diary, generally showed the pessimistic side. That entire year was one to "forgive and forget" and move on. Amanda barely mentioned the year they spent together, but Lydia's diary did.

A few weeks after Amanda's parents moved out, Aaron had trouble with his appendix. Amanda prepared green beans with bacon for supper, and that night Aaron had serious pain, which then subsided. He blamed the green beans and bacon for causing his problem.

About a month later, Amanda again prepared green beans and bacon for supper just to prove that it does not cause an appendix attack. Aaron had low tolerance for pain, and that night it became so severe that Amanda took the kerosene lantern and walked over to Jesse Brubachers through the darkness, to ask Jesse to go and call the doctor.

Aaron had appendicitis! Dr. Schnader charged five dollars to come out at night and take Aaron to the St. Joseph Hospital in Lancaster, where he stayed for eight days. The total of $138.50 was a lot of money. Amanda's mother-in-law was a tremendous help when Amanda was home alone a whole week, with three little children, and a lot of work.

When Aaron was in the hospital, preacher Henry Horst came in to visit him. Henry shook hands with Aaron and with his roommates, and then Aaron said, "This is my preacher". One patient then said to Henry, "If all your members are like Aaron, it will take an awful lot of praying!" Aaron wrote in his diary, "I got up on the sly, early-morning, it worked!"[Meaning he sneaked out of bed against the doctor's orders, five days after surgery.]

Aaron and Amanda had invited several families for Sunday dinner, so then when Aaron laid in the hospital with appendicitis on a Friday night, Aaron's brothers Menno and Titus got the task of canceling dinner invitations. No one had telephones, and it was too late for postcards, so they biked awhile.

With one in the hospital, the entire neighborhood pitched in to help. On April 29, about 25 men volunteered to help pick up stones, make fence, and plant the corn for Aaron. Lydi-Jes-sey walked across the fields to help Amanda serve food at mealtime. Amanda's mother also showed up and so did Aaron's mother and her daughter Annie. They worked around the house, doing whatever they could.

"Do green beans and bacon really cause appendicitis, asked Aaron? He never wanted to find out and did not want Amanda to cook them together anymore ever, even when he knew he could not get appendicitis a second time.

∞

In June, Aaron went to Lancaster for a blasting permit to use dynamite. He bought 50 pounds of dynamite and used the explosives to dislodge rocks in the fields and a major rock outcropping in the lane causing problems. He used horses to move the loosened rocks.

Aaron and Amanda both grew up on farms, but they had a tremendous amount to learn by error. In his diary, Aaron wrote that Amanda was helping him throw out rotten tobacco. It was not the entire crop, but even a small amount was a loss, after all the work of getting it raised and harvested. Experience was the best teacher, and they learned how much air-space tobacco needed for drying properly in the barn. It may not be crowded! Some sections in the barn had better circulation and damp weather accelerated the problem.

During wartime, rationed sugar cost seven and a half cents a pound. They signed up for their allotment at Silver Hill School. Shoes, gas, and kerosene, were also limited. When it came to blackouts, Aaron and Amanda had no problem, because they lived miles from town, with dim kerosene lights. They did not mind skimping, but alarming war stories concerned them. They were uneasy about German submarines prowling along the coast, not very far from eastern Pennsylvania. Occasional horror stories accompanied the news. Aaron and Amanda opposed war and all its atrocities.

It took a lot of effort from Aaron, to keep his horses healthy, and the horse drawn equipment in working order. In June, Menno smashed the spring wagon! The next week, Aaron wrote," Dick, our driving horse, killed himself in the hayfield at Jesse's". Apparently, Aaron tied his horse a little too high up in the apple tree, with a chain and the $115 horse strangled, creating a problem in the busy June weather, minus one horse. Aaron borrowed a horse from Noah Hoover, and then Aaron helped Noah make hay. Making hay was hard work and not to Aaron's liking. In later years, Aaron said, my back starts hurting when I see hay cut and drying in a field.

On a Sunday morning, Aaron walked part ways to Weaverland Church, without his horse, and then someone took him along. Five days later, he walked half way to Groffdale Church for the funeral of 64 year old Eli Nolt, with Amanda and three children at home.

In the heat of summer, in 100° temperatures, Jesse thrashed 130 bushels from 5 acres at Aarons. Aaron got sick from the dust of thrashing in the heat wave. He borrowed a horse from Jesse for farm work. In August, he borrowed a horse and buggy from Jesse when Dave Martins invited them for Sunday dinner. Aaron bought another horse for $77. Two months later he recorded in his diary "demolished our carriage." Later, when the new horse, Prince, hurt his hind leg at a singletree hook, Aaron borrowed a horse from Noah Hoover again. He wrote, "Sunday… went to brother Sams by trolley." Aaron and Amanda had to drive to Terre Hill to get on the trolley. In November, Aaron broke Jesse's carriage shafts while unhitching the horse. "Stayed home Sunday", his diary said.

Amanda invited company for Thanksgiving dinner, and they stayed home to get ready. With three small children and lots of work, Amanda needed extra help. Aaron wrote, "Looked for hired girl at Ringlers" I had to be it. [Aaron ended up being the hired help around the house!] Nevertheless, they had a wonderful Thanksgiving Day, with many blessings to count.

Aaron replaced the shafts he broke on Jesse's carriage and kept the old ones. He loaded up all the broken carriage and buggy parts, taking them to Amanda's Uncle Eli Stauffer at Murrell, traded them in, and ordered a brand-new carriage. After getting his horse shod at the blacksmith, Aaron and Amanda could go again.

When Freddy, Aaron's next horse, kicked him on the leg, Aaron took it easy awhile. Later when Aaron helped haul Canadian travelers, Daniel Shantz and Osiah Martin, the horses ran off for Dan and smashed through the yard fence.

Aaron planned a new chicken house, and he did not build it alone. Jesse helped cut down suitable trees and he helped with dragging logs out of the woods for the rough lumber, seven months in advance. Jesse, Menno and Aaron cut down trees in Berks County to make boards at Redcay's sawmill, costing two and one half cents per foot, for three thousand feet of boards.

Aaron dug a pipeline to the chicken house and hauled six load of crushed rock for part of the foundation. He went to the train station to pick up the chicken house roof that he had ordered. Concreting took a while, because they did it themselves, with a borrowed cement mixer, powered with a pulley.

The two-story building with a hip roof, stood south of the barn. The overflow from the water trough in the barn, filled the chicken waterers, and from there the water flowed into the swamp along the woods. Daniel remembered losing his pocketknife in the chicken house and he did not find it, until a month later. "There it was, hanging on a nail in the upper part, right where he put it!"

They staked off the new chicken house in October, and by June, they raised the rafters with many volunteers, to make the double- floored chicken house. They lined the inside walls with brown paper feedbags, and the windows had a covering of glass cloth, or "icing glass", instead of windowpanes made of glass. The entire poorly built project, did not last many years. The paper lining was not sufficient, nor were the window coverings, of fiberglass mesh. The outer red siding consisted of gritty, sandy roll- roofing.

The location close to the swamp was not ideal and disease set in. Mites or chicken lice moved in, and made gathering eggs miserable. The interior paper walls harbored mites and diseases. Aaron sometimes paid for feed bills higher than the income. Most farmers in the area sold eggs for an income, besides raising tobacco and steers. The eggs in wartime made good money and they made work to occupy children. They gathered the eggs and washed them on a regular basis before the "Oy-yah huck-shtah"[egg buyer] came. They weighed each egg individually on small scales, to grade the eggs and put them in the proper crate according to size. The egg merchant knew where to find the eggs without asking. At some places, he found the eggs in the springhouse but at Aaron's, he went down in the basement to get them.

⁓

When Jesse Brubacher hurt his foot, it was Jesse's time to accept charity help. The cast on his foot needed a re-cast. In April, a dozen plows and two manure spreaders arrived among many helpers for a plowing party at Jesses, and Aaron was among them.

On April 27, 1943 Aaron and Amanda with Daniel, Sarah Ann, and Walter welcomed baby number four. Baby Peter arrived at 10 AM and was named after Peter Brubacher, who lived close by. With two Peter's in the family, this one was Pete at an early age. Aaron's sister Eva was the maid this time, and a busy one.

In 1943, victory gardens sprang up all over America, and about one out of every five people planted a garden. Americans by the millions, learned how to raise and preserve food, even those that lived in towns and cities. Aaron and Amanda had a head start in experience and frugality. Their parents had taught them gardening as a way of survival, and simply the healthiest food available! Those same parents understood that a garden was a place to heal hurts and to restore the spirit while whacking weeds or sowing hope. A person could emerge from a garden with a fresh perspective on life.

Sometimes Daniel went to Jesse Brubacher's with a message on a note, pinned to the back of his shirt, where he would not lose it. He walked across the field lane, with the dog along, and then Jesses sent him back again. Dawdy Shirks came along in an open buggy, where they found Daniel lying near the stone line fence, sound asleep! They stopped to pick him up and brought him along home.

Cooked macaroni on the table fascinated Daniel, at the age of four. He understood how the drill bit worked; as he watched Aaron crank the handle on a brace and bit. The wood shavings curled out from deep inside the board. Daniel was curious about the curved tunnel. He asked his parents, "How do they drill a hole in the curved elbow macaroni?" Aaron was greatly amused by the question. He told Daniel, "You have to ask the store man."

The next time Aaron and Daniel shopped in Bowmansville, Aaron told James Kern, the storekeeper, "Daniel needs to know how the holes are made in macaroni." The grownups thought it was funny! However, Daniel would have liked a decent answer, and not just to be laughed at. He was through school before he found the answer.

Amanda had trouble baking bread and Harding's bakery was just three miles away, so she quit baking bread. She baked plenty pies and cakes and cookies. For a while Amanda had a lard can setting at the end of the lane, containing a slip of paper with her bread order, and some money. Then the bakery truck stopped and the driver put bread into the can.

Occasionally Aaron went to Bowmansville and came home with a spring wagon full of bakery throw-outs for pig feed. They saved the best pieces for eating, and dried some to use in soup or as breadcrumbs.

Selling eggs during World War II was a profitable major income for Aaron. Those eggs went to a hatchery. When Andy Weber bought hatching eggs, he paid $.58 a dozen. With the help of Aaron's extended family, the farm prospered. Prices were good. Three dozen eggs and half a pound of homemade butter paid a week's groceries with two cents left over. Candy was often listed on the grocery receipts and so was sugar. Amanda did not skimp on cocoa as they did in Michigan.

Cocoa cost $.20. Bread cost $.11 a loaf and Kellogg's corn flakes were $.28 a box. Fifty cigars cost one dollar, and ten pounds of nails cost $.60. Local workers made hand rolled cigars at the factory in Bowmansville.

Income was just as low and hoeing tobacco by hand netted $.25 an hour, while a carpenter earned about one dollar an hour. The tobacco crop boosted the economy. In seven years time, Aaron had his farm nearly paid off, with about 5 acres or more in tobacco. Wrappers, the large choice leaves, sold at $.21 a pound and the fillers ground up at the factory, sold at seven cents a pound. Broken leaves were a big loss for the same amount of work, and every farmer handled tobacco carefully, for better prices. Occasionally a company bought pull-off tobacco and that needed no sorting, just pull it off the stem and bunch it as is.

Daniel remembers:

"I remember boyhood days of tender innocence and not a worry in the world. Dad was not fully bald, and mom had a youthful appearance with a slender figure. While sitting beside mom at the table, she explained to me, and showed me by counting fingers that I was four years old, and also by folding and unfolding both hands with fingers spread, that dad is 29 and she is 27.

I remember when Franklin D. Roosevelt was President, and Second World War was raging in all its fury. Grownups discussing the latest developments of the war, talked about Adolf Hitler and the "Japs" or Japanese. Talks centered on which country invaded where, the bombing of Pearl Harbor, the battles in the South Pacific, involving islands such as Midway, Guam, the Philippines, and others.

Our country used many resources to supply military needs. Things like new cars were scarce. Gasoline was rationed, and so was sugar, and new shoes. Building materials were scarce, and we used to hear about buying things on the black market, which meant buying illegally, and usually selling at a premium price."

I remember warm nights with the windows open and I heard the sounds of nature, like a rooster crowing early in the morning. In the evening, I heard Whippoorwill's, tree frogs, katydid, crickets and the Burr -room Burr- room of bullfrogs at the swamp. I heard clear water trickling into the water trough, in the barnyard. On a still night, I heard Dad coming home, half a mile away. The horse in the meadow, could hear it before I could, and he started calling to the horse pulling the buggy on the way home. Without a sound, winter nights were serenely quiet, unless the wind howled around the corner of the house or sleet tapped against the windowpane and the shutters rattled. Sometimes I heard the ghostly call of an owl in the pear tree, right outside my bedroom window, or fighting tomcats or a barking dog. Children felt secure tucked in cozy, warm beds, in a room so cold that a glass of water froze overnight.

TERMS: WEEKLY IN ADVANCE

Lancaster, Pa., _April 19, 1942_

Mr. _Aaron Shirk_

To SAINT JOSEPH'S HOSPITAL, Dr.

On Account Board and Care	8 da. at $ 3.50 per Day	28	00
Special Nursing	at $ per Day		
Use of Operating Room		15	00
Delivery Room			
Laboratory Fee		5	00
Hospital Ambulance			
Telephone Service in City $1.00 Weekly			
Special Medication			50
From 4-11-42 to 4-19-42 Amount Due		48	50

Received Payment _____

1-42 10M

PER _Sr. M. A. A._

Aaron's Hospital Bill

5

Aunt Lydia went to the doctor often, and the doctors tried to understand, but it is almost a wonder they did not lock the doors when they saw her coming. Lydia's parents had their hands full with Lydia's aches and pains, hardly knowing what to do. Now to make matters worse, Sarah Ann went to Dr. Schnader, who said she has TB. Lydia got up first to make breakfast for her mother, and together they snitzed some apples. Lydia cleaned Josh's suit, hat and shoes, and wrote in her diary "I'm tired to the bones" Peter helped Lydia do laundry, and took her to many doctor appointments, taking Lydia to Dr. Shantz one day, and his wife to Dr. Schnader the next day. How they could afford this, the diary doesn't say. Lydia only earned three or four dollars a week while doing housework for others. They had some happy times and Lydia writes about playing flinch and crokinoles until midnight.

Dr. Schnader decided Sarah Ann does not have TB after all, and Peter could stop worrying about that. He had greater concerns when Joshua received a notice from the draft board, and had to go for a blood test and for a physical.

In January 1943, Peter ended up in the hospital for six whole weeks, and three consecutive surgeries. The only problem mentioned, was hernia repair. The details were skimpy, but he was a lonely man. Lancaster General Hospital was far away, while his wife at home struggled with health problems. Lydia writes, "father is homesick". Neighbors came to help do the work, like pruning the grapevines and cutting firewood. It was wonderful to have Peter home again, and then two weeks later Joshua was admitted to the Lancaster Hospital for a planned surgery. Dr. Shantz operated on who knows what? He stayed there five days. His mother's health was improving and she sat on a chair for the first time in about 12 weeks, at home. After the long winter ended, spring brought more sunshine.

Peters invited 25 young folks for supper. They played games in the yard until almost midnight. Joshua and Lydia had a hard time fitting in among the youth group.

Katie came home from Indiana, planning her wedding. Lydia rejoiced at having her sister at home again, even just for a short while. At the age of 26, Lydia was no doubt envious and felt left over.

Aaron's brother Ben and family came from Indiana for Katie's wedding, and so did the Joe Martin girls. On November 16, 1943, on a Tuesday, Katie married Dan Martin at home, at Peter Brubacher's. It was a simple wedding with 45 guests, on the same day as Aaron and Amanda's sixth wedding anniversary. Sarah Ann (Amanda's mother, and two sisters), Lydia and Katie worked hard getting ready for the wedding and preparing the food... Everyone had a good time all day. The travelers stayed for the weekend and gathered at the Martin Kilmer farm for Sunday dinner. Dan and Katie spent time visiting, and soon moved on to their home in Indiana.

Six weeks later, on January 1, 1944, Aaron's brother Ben married Grace Martin of Indiana. Ben's two years in a CPS camp were nearly completed, before he learned to know Grace. BW Shirks traveled all the way to Indiana, for the wedding of their son, and to see where he would live. Grace was a sister to Dan Martin, Katie's husband. These two couples resided in Indiana and were part of the Wisler Mennonite Church. They farmed with rubber tires on the equipment and bought a car.

At the age of nine months, baby Pete suffered seriously with pneumonia, and it took him long to recover. He didn't walk until he was 15 months old. Aaron wondered if Pete's contentment in the highchair, with a wet diaper, in a drafty house made it worse. The floor was too cold for a baby on a blanket. On January 3, Pete had a fever, and kept getting worse; Dr. Schnader came out and tried to save his life. The fever left three days later and Pete survived.

Dawdy Brubacher's fetched Walter and Sarah Ann, to care for them when Amanda had such a sick baby. BW Shirks fetched Daniel. Lydi-Jes-sey walked over to help. Everyone cared! One month later Aaron and Amanda called Dr. Schnader out on a Sunday, when Pete had bronchitis.

In wheat harvest time, a fourth boy was born to Aaron and Amanda on July 6, 1944. Aaron fetched a maid named Barbara. Amanda chose the name of Clayton, but that didn't suit Aaron. Neither did Aaron have a better name for the baby. When Aaron went over to help Jesse with the wheat harvest, the men asked him every day "what did you name the baby?" Each time Aaron said we just do not know what to name him. "Name him Junior," someone suggested.

Finally, Amanda took slips of paper and wrote a name on each one. The names were Aaron, Clayton, and a few others. Fourteen-month-old Peter chose one slip of paper, and therefore 'the baby' became Aaron Junior. Baby Aaron had problems when Amanda quit nursing, at three-month-old, and put him on boiled cow's milk. What worked for the other babies did not work for Aaron Junior. He became sick and sicker. On a Saturday evening, he lay listless on the couch and Amanda said "we must call the doctor."

The heavy thunderstorm kept Aaron from calling, until Sunday morning. Dr. Schnader promptly put baby Aaron on formula, and told them "this baby cannot handle cows' milk!" On a Sunday morning Dr. Schnader drove to Ephrata and came back with SMA baby formula for little Aaron. Dr. Schnader was a kindhearted and understanding doctor, or Aaron Junior might not have survived.

The formula made a big difference and Aaron Jr's color returned. He gained more than average and became a chubby baby. From there on, Amanda gave SMA to babies that were too small for cow's milk.

The springhouse was Amanda's only refrigeration. A strong clear underground stream surfaced in a deep draw south of the house. A walkway along one side of the deep clear water made a convenient way to set kettles and crocks among the rocky foundation. A tight tin roof made an ideal sliding board, but those nail heads might rip holes in clothes or knock dirt into the drink water. That was not allowed. The springhouse door had a latch to keep out everyone except those sent on a mission.

Daniel became brave, because it was his job to get the food from the springhouse, a dark, drab, spooky place, used instead of a refrigerator. A bullfrog lived there, and every time Daniel stepped inside the door, the frog jumped into the water with a big splash and scared the wits out of him! It got to the point where he was afraid to go into the cool dark springhouse. While eating dinner Amanda said, 'Daniel, go fetch the applesauce", and he dreaded that terrible frog. He went reluctantly after being told several times, and just as he got to the springhouse door, he turned chicken and stopped. He returned to the house empty-handed, but that was a mistake, because he was looking at the wrong end of a yardstick. Aaron gave him some yardstick inspiration and on the second trip to the springhouse, he brought the applesauce.

Daniel asked "why do Dawdy Shirks and other people have an icebox refrigerator and we don't have any?" Aaron and Amanda explained, "No ice truck came so far outback to deliver ice here."

Tools always fascinated Daniel even as a little boy. He was thrilled when Aaron came home from town with a brand-new wooden 6-foot folding rule. Before Aaron unhitched the horse from the spring wagon, Daniel had a good time playing with it, and somehow managed to break it, by folding it wrong. His heart sank in his shoes, as he held the two pieces. It was not a toy, and to Daniel's horror, Aaron used it for the only thing that it was still good for. He grabbed hold of Daniel and gave him a thorough "wompshing", until the new rule lay in many pieces and good for nothing. What a disaster! Not all was lost, because Daniel's education advanced a step further for the rest of life's journey.

6

A Trip to Michigan

Daniel learned his capital letters from the cereal boxes, with Amanda as a teacher. He was curious and wanted to know, while Amanda was pleased and possibly helped him along more than she should have. Daniel wanted to read so much, that Aaron and Amanda sent him to first grade as soon as he turned six. Like everyone else, Daniel needed a smallpox vaccination before starting first grade.

In Michigan, Amanda's mother could see the schoolhouse and she watched the children coming and going as they walked half a mile. Here in Pennsylvania, Daniel walked nearly two miles, and through wooded areas. About a week before school started, Aaron drove to the school to show Daniel where it was. He had never gone that way before and he had no idea a school stood there. The thought of all that overwhelmed Daniel. Aaron and Amanda did not want to send Daniel alone, so Christian Kilmer's Naomi, a second grade cousin, came to live at Aarons to walk with him to school.

On the first day of school, Naomi Kilmer and Daniel thought it was very far. They walked and walked until they finally came to the schoolhouse, and saw the playground deserted! School had already begun without them."Let's go home," said Naomi, as they turned around and headed back the way they came. Someone saw them, and came running out to convince them to come inside the school. Lessons were not a problem for Daniel and he had a nice teacher, Mrs. Frances Weaver. She was an older Mennonite lady from Union Grove. She taught Bible verses, but not the Pledge of Allegiance to the flag, because she opposed that. She believed in pledging her allegiance to God, not a country. Half way through the term, Naomi Kilmer went home.

When Daniel went to school by himself, he was easily distracted along the way. His mind wandered far off the road and sometimes he came to school late, even with plenty of time. One evening he came home and asked Amanda about the neighbor boy, Isaac Weinhold's only child Aaron. "If Aaron Weinhold would marry an only child, and they had children, would those children have any cousins?" Amanda answered her curious six-year-old, with a "no". In later years, that was what happened, as Aaron an only child, married an only child, and their children had no cousins. "No first cousins," was far beyond imagination, for any children from a large family with dozens of cousins.

One morning on the way to Silver Hill, Daniel was sure he saw a bear. He panicked and went back home and told his parents. The "bear" turned out to be a burned corn fodder shock, the work of pranksters at Halloween. It did resemble a bear, from a distance!

The cold winter had plenty of snow. Daniel took a small short, hard to steer sled for recess on the steep sledding hill, behind Silver Hill School. A very tall eighth-grade boy, teased Daniel by picking up his short sled by the runners with one hand and holding it high over Daniel's head. While sledding, Daniel did not make the turn at the bottom of the hill and rammed into a boulder. What a blow! He saw stars for a minute, but he got up and went on. As a loner, he had to fend for himself, and he got tough.

It was nearly dark when Daniel came home from school on those short winter days, all by himself. By the time he came home, he was thoroughly chilled and crying in the bitter cold.

As Amanda worked around the house, her mind drifted to her childhood days in Michigan. She knew many friends moved away, but she dreamed of someday returning to the place where she grew up. The home farm, the school and the church retained many happy carefree memories. Were things still standing the way it was when she left? Amanda knew her place was at Laurel Hill with her own children, and a new baby every year kept her there. With the farm nearly paid off, maybe others could babysit.

Before winter, Aaron and Amanda went on a trip to see again all those things dear to Amanda's childhood. She left Michigan suddenly, after their wedding and seven years was a long time to think back. After careful planning, they took Daniel out of school. Daniel and Sarah Ann went along to Michigan and the three younger children stayed at Dawdy Shirks. When Aaron and Amanda brought the children to BW Shirks for several weeks, they also brought along their wringer washer that had a motor! It was much easier to use than mommy Shirk's washer was with the agitator turned by hand and all three children wore diapers. Three-year-old Walter was not yet potty trained, so BW Shirk took him along out to the stripping room and he tried his best to potty-train Walter, to no avail. They returned him in diapers the way he came.

Aaron and Amanda got up at 2AM and caught the 4; 30 train to Michigan for three days there, and they took a ride on a ferry across the straits before the Mackinac Bridge existed. In Michigan, Aaron and Amanda visited people from the Funk Church, which did not move away. They slept at Eli Gregory's and met the Bushkirks, Shuntzs, Ebys and Burkharts again. It all seemed so strange to Amanda to see the familiar home community so vacant of the familiar Old Order Mennonite families. The old landmarks and buildings had changed very little, but Amanda's friends were nearly all gone.

The sign that said; twenty miles to Petosky, reminded Amanda how she went there with her sisters and her father when Peter took a load of steel there, long ago, by horse and sleigh. When working away the children gave their money home to their parents, but anytime someone gave them small pay or a tip, it was all theirs. How those sister enjoyed shopping in Petosky, with some money in their pockets! They each bought a doll for a quarter! Amanda and Lydia still had theirs, but times had certainly changed.

Aaron and Amanda rode a train to Indiana after their stay at Michigan, the ride thrilled Daniel and Sarah Ann. Daniel, sat at the window, and started pressing on the latches, just as the train whistle blew. Daniel was astonished! He was impressed that he could make the train blow its whistle, so he pressed it again. Sure enough, the whistle blew again! Thoroughly convinced, and eagerly excited he said, "Look mom, I can make the whistle blow!" On the third try, nothing happened and what a letdown? Both Aaron and Amanda laughed and thought it was funny, but Daniel was embarrassed!

In Indiana, Aaron and Amanda saw where Aaron's brother, Ben Shirks lived, and they saw Amanda's sister Katie and Dan Martin's place. Both families lived on farms and had children they had not seen. Aaron helped pick corn from 'big' fields with his brother and Amanda had the wonderful privilege to sit down and quilt with her sister Katie, while talking in person. Letters in the mail, left many things unsaid.

The trip was time well spent, to let Amanda see how much things had changed. Her friends scattered. The church and the schoolhouse still stood, with many happy memories. She saw the graves of her three small brothers, but she could never go back again to childhood. Life kept changing, and even her parents lived in Pennsylvania. Only in her memories would Amanda feel the warmth, of her childhood in Michigan.

Aaron and Amanda returned to Blue Ball, Pennsylvania. Menno picked them up in time for supper at B W Shirks, after they spent a long day riding the train. When Aaron and Amanda returned home, they were overjoyed to meet their three young children and settle down to the farm at Laurel Hill where they belonged.

On Grandmother's lap, baby Aaron Junior got his nickname, when Walter called him "du dickah ding"[you thick thing]. Five-month old baby Dick bounced a lot, nearly jumping off Grandma's lap constantly. He hardly ever cried, and he got a lot of attention as all the aunts and uncles helped to entertain the three youngsters. A baby is a "baby" for only so long, until he gets a name, or another baby arrives in the family, and Aarons were going to have twins.

7

Joshua

Amanda's brother Silas came along to Pennsylvania with Amanda and Lydia, looking for partners in 1937, and he stayed. Joshua was younger and quite the clown among the youth group. He was easy to get along with, and had no problems making friends.

 Peter Brubacher, with his wife and their three youngest children, Lydia, Katie and Joshua, traveled several weeks from Michigan, moving to Pennsylvania, in 1941. They sold their home, and searched for a new one. After many weeks of living out of trunks and boxes, they arrived at Aaron's for a temporary home.

Joshua found work in different places, as a dependable 16-year-old hired hand. Working was not a problem, but his home life was lacking, as he did not feel like he belonged anywhere. He was always welcome at Aarons, but that would never replace the home he knew on their farm in Michigan, with his own chores and his own horse.

Katie and Lydia also came along for the stay at Aarons place. Katie was not troubled, because while coming from Michigan to Pennsylvania she met a charming young man in Indiana, by the name of Dan Martin and her heart stayed in Indiana, as they wrote letters regularly. She happily worked and sang, saving money for future dreams and possibly marriage.

Joshua's brother Silas was twelve years older than Joshua was, and he had a speech problem. Silas had a hard time making friends. He wanted a wife and asked nearly every single girl around. Silas in Dutch was pronounced "see-lus", and after asking so many girls he was jokingly called "seedless" or "she-less". Silas had a hard time making friends at the time when Joshua started running around with the youth group.

Joshua understood and loved his brother Silas, and it hurt him deeply to see others make fun of him. It hurt even more, when people compared Joshua to Silas and made fun of him also. This was a problem not easy to fix! Joshua shrugged off the hurts and tried to make his own name. He tried not to let the pain show, and he kept on going.

Joshua often boarded where he worked at Sauder's and Gehmans among others. At Noah Gehmans Joshua went along to the Philadelphia market, where they sold produce and dressed chicken meat. On the way home from Philadelphia he sat on the back of the truck. It was hard to light a cigarette in all the wind, so after he finally got one lit, he chain smoked a whole pack of Camel cigarettes, using one to light the next one.

Joshua loved to play the mouth organ and was very good at it. He often played at the young people singings and he was a good singer with a bass voice. His cousin Lydia (Stauffer) Bauman remembered Joshua walking over to their house from Eli Stauffer's shop, singing loud enough for the entire neighborhood to hear. "Farther along we'll know all about it... farther along will understand why... cheer up my brother... live in the sunshine... we'll understand it all by and by."

All Joshua really needed, was a girlfriend and then he could ignore all the other boys. When he asked a girl from Weaverland, others looked down on him and thought he was trying to start at the prestigious top, when he was just from Bowmansville. Even this made a mark against his name. There were not enough girls to go around and competition was tough, with each man on his own. Joshua was an outsider and not quite able to crack their code. In Michigan, he was somebody, and in Pennsylvania, he was a nobody and just a face in the crowd. He craved acceptance but he did not find it!

When people moved to a new location, they started over at the bottom. Bowmansville was the tail end, where mostly poor people lived, like those coming from Michigan. One teenager complained to their mother, that others called them, "Dee shimlichy Bowmansvillah" (the moldy Bowmansvillers). That mother kindly told her children that mold would come to the top. Churchtown was not considered much better in the social ladder.

Sam Ringler was one of Josh's good friends, who grew up with him in Michigan. Sam remembered serenading Aaron and Amanda in Michigan, while Sam's parents were gone on a trip, looking for a farm in Pennsylvania. When the boys came into the house for a treat, Peter Brubacher saw 15-year-old Sam and said "Sellah glay shtinkah set da-hame im bet sigh," (that little stinker should be at home in bed). Sam and Joshua remained good friends in Pennsylvania and had some good times together. They took young people sleigh riding in Joshua's box sleigh.

Joshua believed the Bible and wanted to do what was right. On October 11, 1941, he was baptized when he was 19, Bishop Joe Wenger baptized 27 youth at Weaverland church.

Barbara Martin	Noah Leid
Alta Hoover	Christ Fox
Mary Zimmerman	Joshua Brubacher
Emma Horst	Samuel Ringler
Laura Martin	Reuben Weaver
Martha Brubaker	Ammon Shirk
Lydia Stauffer	Eli Newswenger
Emma Martin	George Burkholder
Lizzie Hoover	Harvey Martin
Lena Shirk	John Sauder
Minnie Martin	John Shirk
Esther Shirk	Ivan Martin
Maggie Hoover	David S. Martin
Martha Martin	

Since the Joe Wenger and Mose Horning church split, they shared all five of their church houses alternately between the two groups. The Joe Wenger group had four preachers. Henry Horst was ordained for Bowmansville and Churchtown,

and Isaac Zimmerman for Groffdale. Aaron Burkholder and Aaron Sensenig were for Weaverland and Martindale. The three deacons were Peter Weaver, Isaac Nolt, and Ben Hoover.

Joshua tried hard to fit in, but he had a problem, and didn't find a girlfriend. Eventually he gave up and considered the Pike church. Those teenagers "sowed wild oats" and many had cars, before joining the church and then settled down later. Maybe he could find acceptance among the Pike group, the same church that started the May City, Iowa settlement, where Peter had belonged before he married and moved to Michigan.

Joshua broke his father's heart when he bought a car, and he was no longer a member in good standing with the church. Trying to find a girlfriend one night after midnight, the boys were at Noah Martins, and Josh walked around the house with his flashlight and called for Irene. She did not hear him, or did not wish to respond. Then the boys went to blinky Aaron Martins but couldn't get a response from their daughter either, on that same night. The other boys hid behind Josh's model A Ford, in case her dad would shoot.

Joshua dated Elsie Auker quite a while, and Sam Ringler went there scouting with some boys. The doors were locked, so Sam looked until he found a window he could open, and he climbed in. He was shocked to discover he was in her parents' bedroom, and he left as fast as he could, the same way he came in, through the window! The young couple then opened the door and let them in.

Joshua bought some firecracker bombs that exploded when he put them on the spark plugs of a car. At a singing among the Horning church, at Sam Nolt's of Churchtown, Sam Ringler found these bombs in Josh's car. While Joshua was in the house playing the mouth organ for games, Sam Ringler, plus Joe and Alvin Martin, put two of the bombs on the sparkplugs of Joshua's model A Ford. Then they went to the house and fabricated a story to get Joshua to take them for a drive. "Would you please take as to Morgantown to buy cigarettes?" they asked. When he started the car, a bomb smoked and exploded loudly! The boys had a good laugh over that, and at the end of the lane,

Sam Ringler is on top of the pile. Number two is Will Martins Joe, who was killed by lightening, while working in a tobacco field at the age of 22. His hatband was loose, so he fixed it with a copper wire, and that attracted the lightening. Number three Elvin Brubaker, (a first cousin to Bishop Leonard Brubaker). Number four Alvin Martin from Penn Valley. Joshua is on the bottom right. One of Jess Brubacher's girls of the Pike church had the camera.Sh sh sh (cameras were forbidden).

they told him "we don't want to go to Morgantown after all". Some jokes were practical but many were not.

Gas was rationed during World War II and Joshua had a problem getting gas to go see his girlfriend. Someone told him if he puts mothballs in kerosene, he could use that in his car instead of gasoline. At Aaron Shirks on a Sunday afternoon, his model A Ford was about out of gas, with not enough to go see Elsie. Aaron had 5 gallons of kerosene and Joshua put that in his car, with one box of mothballs added. The car ran nice so they parked it, and ate supper. Then when Sam Ringler and Joshua wanted to leave, it would not start. Josh tried until the battery was dead and then he cranked the starter by hand. Aaron gave them a little gas to pour on the carburetor. He turned up the fuel and

got it started, but it ran wild and smoked. It would not idle, so off they went out the field lane to Jesse's, and they couldn't slow down. A rocky bump remained in the gap of the stone fence, and they ramped it hard, breaking a spring in the model A.

When they shut the car off, to see what broke, it would not start again. They pushed it several hundred feet to the road, and coasted down that hill to the metal bridge, but that did not work either.

Joshua walked back to Aarons, exhausted and disgusted, and changed his soiled clothes. Sam Ringler didn't remember what happened next, but either way, Joshua did not get to Elsie's place on time. Perhaps, he biked all the way to Farmersville. Joshua did not like to be the butt end of every joke!

A good name was rather to be chosen, than great riches. Joshua's name was ruined everywhere he went, and he could not get away from it. When others tarnished his name, they robbed him of a valuable thing that is worth nothing to them, and yet left Joshua very poor. He knew mockery was wrong and he tried to be nice, but he didn't know how to fix the problems he faced. Joshua trusted everyone and did not appreciate the many jokes and pranks. He tried to laugh them off, even when it hurt. His model A Ford was all that he could afford in war times, when vehicles were scarce.

In German, Joshua is pronounced Yuss-vah. When boys saw him coming, they thought, "Here comes Yuss in his flipper, time for another joke!" Joshua could not return to his childhood or the friends that were dear to him there. Those bridges were gone. How could he start all over and where?

He got a draft notice when he owned a car, and he could not get a CO or "conscientious objector" exemption without a church membership. CO camps were set up so that young man worked on roads, forestry crews, and other work, instead of fighting in the war. He was in trouble, not knowing which way to turn. Joshua was a peace-loving person with no desire to fight. His parents loved him dearly, and he was the apple of his father's eye. How did things go wrong?

Hard telling what all went through Joshua's mind, not knowing what to do next. On August 25, 1944, he entered the service, and trained at Fort Blanding, Florida, asking for non-combatant work.

Four months later, he came home over Christmas time, to see his family one more time, before being sent overseas in January. On December 27, Peter and Sarah Ann Brubacher and Joshua came to Aaron and Amanda's house for dinner. Peter was taking Joshua to visit all of his five sisters and his brother Silas one more time. It was the last time Amanda saw him, and neither could they talk with him on the phone.

Daniel had a clear picture in his mind of that visit. It looked unreal and strange to see a soldier in full uniform riding in a buggy with his Old Order Mennonite father and mother.

In the middle of November from Camp Blanding, 300 miles north of Miami, he sent letters home to his parents. "Would you please send me a shoe stamp? I want to buy a pair of dress shoes to wear on weekends, and so far, I only have these heavy work shoes. I would ask you to send my black shoes, but black is not allowed in the Army. Joshua realized that people did not have extra shoe stamps, and he hoped none of the family had to go without shoes if they send him a shoe stamp.

Excerpts from many letters he wrote; the postage was free: I can send about $25 a month home, because I have no use for money here except PX, which does not come very often.

You asked about church…. there is a church to every battalion, just ordinary church.

I was on guard duty from 11 to one on Friday night. I just walked around keeping order and if somebody will not obey, we just call the corporal of the guards.

The hurricane did not hit here, but we had no lights when the electric and telephone lines were down.

I still didn't get those packages.

In January, Joshua was sent overseas and wrote many more letters.

I talked with a sergeant this morning that was from Reading, Pennsylvania. He recognized my talk right away to be Dutch, and we talked together quite a while. He has been here quite a long and he said I am the first Dutchman he met over here. He really enjoyed talking Dutch once again. Well, I guess I will quit for this time. May God be with you and protect you all till we meet again. I remain your son, brother and uncle, Joshua Brubacher

I am really glad I can talk German. The people around here talk some kind of German or Dutch. I get along fine with these people and act as interpreter for our squad.

Tomorrow I will find out what these C- rations taste like when we move 23 miles from camp. I weigh 145 pounds now, and that is ten pounds more than when I came, due to eating cakes and chocolate milk after work.

I have to take the same training as the rest of the people here and then I might get a noncombatant job to drive a truck or ambulance or something.

Joshua dearly wanted to stay away from fighting, and he wrote; let's hope God finds enough of precious grain in my crop.

I saw actual combat now. I did not get hurt, but it sure was not nice. We had some casualties. We also took quite a few prisoners. Yes, parents, when we were out there in the trenches, I really did some praying. I think all of us did.

Joshua died instantly, when shell fragments hit him, six weeks after he went overseas. The two comrades present were Sgt Paul I Mills ASN 3548239 and Robert M Frisell ASN 37771921, both of Company E. 276th Infantry.

He was buried on March 2, 1945 in plot 3 A, row 13, grave number 7189, in Epinal, France, because his parents did not fill out the papers to return the body home. They did not understand, until it was too late.

In the beginning of March, Aarons received the sad news that Joshua was killed in war. Amanda's mother sent them a postcard with the death message. The mailman scribbled the stamp with an ink pen and delivered it that same day. Mommy Brubacher colored the edges of the card with black crayon to announce a death. The oldest children vividly remember that sad day, because it was the first time they ever saw their mother shed tears.

Protestant chaplain, Loren T. Jenks conducted graveside services reading the 23rd Psalm, 121 Psalm, first Thessalonians 5: 1 to 11 and Revelations 14: 13 and Revelations7: 15 to 17. Closing with "we commend into the hands of the loving father who gave it, the soul of this, our comrade departed, trusting in the mercy of our Lord Jesus Christ, insure certain hope of the resurrection unto eternal life. Amen".

Joshua was transferred to other places so often overseas, that his mail never caught up with him. He sent letters home about every week but he never received any of the letters sent overseas to him by his family. After his death, all of his belongings, most letters, and even a box of Christmas goodies from his mother came back in the mail. All their kind admonishments came back like a slap in the face.

His family pondered 'Does that mean our words of encouragement never reached him? Were all our efforts in vain...Did Joshua even know how

much we cared...and how many prayers were sent his way...how many tears we shed. ..Most of all. .. did he remain faithful to the teachings in the Bible? Will we meet him in Heaven... or . ..."

Joshua's heartbroken parents wept bitter tears, and they felt like failures... Did they do their part? Their children meant more to them than anything else on earth. The three small graves in Michigan were nothing, compared to this. They knew where those innocent souls resided in eternity.. . but Joshua, Oh Joshua!. ..They had no funeral... only tears, and many of them... in a torrent of weeping.

A government letter arrived for Peter and Sarah Ann Brubacher, stating that Joshua had a $10,000 life insurance policy. Joshua's parents sadly refused to collect the money, and just wanted their son. Ten grand was more money than Peter ever owned, and he was direly in need of money at the time. Peter did not apply for the insurance, but a government official personally delivered the check to Peter. He refused the money because it was the price of blood. A second check arrived, but Peter refused the money due to the words of the Bible, in Matthew twenty-seven, verse six. The church needed money in the treasury, but they could not accept the small fortune.

Amanda trusted that Joshua was safe in the arms of Jesus and it was not his desire to serve in the army. Perhaps it was God's way of taking him out of the situation he was in. A few months later, the war ended. One day as Daniel walked home from school, he heard sirens going and church bells ringing from far away, just ringing and ringing continuously. He could not figure out why they didn't stop, and later learned the message, that the war was over.

8

Twins

Dr. Schnader had been sick with food poisoning, for several months. He was surprised that Aaron and Amanda were getting twins, because he had not seen her for a while. When Aaron called him on July 29, 1945, the doctor was just returning to work again.

The twins arrived on a Sunday morning around 8:30, when everyone in the neighborhood already left for church. Aarons had no help available, besides five-year-old Sarah Ann and 11-year-old Katie Kilmer, a niece, who helped Aaron and Amanda many times and stayed there for the weekend. The girls changed diapers and fixed water bottles with a little help from Aaron. He made sure that things were sterilized.

At four o'clock in the afternoon, BW Shirks brought Aaron's sister Annie to be the maid for two new babies. When BW Shirks headed for home again, they took along Dick, nearly 13-month-old. He was big and heavy and could not walk by himself. They had enjoyed keeping Dick just eight months earlier when Aaron and Amanda took a trip to Indiana and Michigan.

Twin girls meant two names to choose from the hat. The names Amanda put in the hat were Mary and Martha, Ruth and Rhoda, or Hannah and Harriet. Dick chose a paper with the names of Ruth and Rhoda. Aaron and Amanda suddenly had seven children before the oldest one turned seven.

Right from the start, it was easy to tell the twins apart. Ruth was slim, weighing 7 pounds and had a head full of black hair, while Rhoda was chubby, weighing 6 1/2 pounds, and she was almost bald with a little bit of light hair. Amanda knew which baby was which, even when she only saw a hand or a foot. Both babies slept in the same crib with their heads at either end, and their feet towards the middle.

Daniel remembered hot August nights when the babies took turns crying. As soon as one settled, the other one started crying. Taking care of two babies made for some hectic times, day and night. Three diaper babies made a lot of wash. The twins wore diapers made from the bootleggers' sugar sacks.

Aaron's sister Annie stayed to help for four weeks, then Katie Kilmer stayed till September, then Lydia Kilmer came for a few weeks. At this time, Dan Martin was Aarons hired boy, in his first year out of school. He helped to hang out the wash and so did Aaron.

{Weaver Martins Dan saw many tales untold, about reality among such a family. The story goes, that one time Amanda put him in charge of a small child. The baby cried so much when Amanda was gone, that Weaver took the baby and the diaper bag over the field lane to Jesses. Lydi-Jes-sey helped him out.]

After the maids left, Sarah Ann, age 5 1/2, became her mother's right-hand helper. She changed many diapers and sometimes she quickly tried to hush- up a crying baby, by putting a pacifier in her mouth, after she accidentally jagged her baby sister with a diaper pin. When Amanda noticed the tell-tale marks, she decided that Sarah Ann had better not change diapers anymore.

Amanda quit breast-feeding when the babies were three months old. Every morning she prepared a kettle full of bottles to cool in the springhouse, inside a 5-gallon crock with a lid on top. At feeding time, Sarah Ann went to the springhouse for two bottles at a time. At church, when Amanda stepped out of the carriage, she handed one baby to Sarah Ann. She took the other one. As soon as she opened the church door, a volunteer eagerly took one baby during the services, and sometimes even two, leaving Amanda's arms empty.

BW Shirks kept baby Dick for most of the year, because Aaron & Amanda paid off the farm in 1945 and planned to enlarge their house. Mommy Shirk thought a toddler might fall into a newly dug cellar or get hurt among the carpenters. Amanda was not pleased with that arrangement for her little boy, but she did not have much choice with a baby in each arm.

His grandparents bonded to Dick, and did not want to part with him. When Dick got so much attention, BW Shirk said, "We can't farm until Dick is of age". When they finally did return him to Aaron and Amanda, Mommy Shirk could not bear to come along and see Dick stay there. The house was full of noise, commotion, dirt and flies, and children everywhere. Amanda's lap was so full that she had no room for Dick, and he cried with homesickness, even when he was at home. As he grew older, he leaned against Amanda, and wished to be held.

The new kitchen they planned would have one big bedroom upstairs and a double porch on the south side, with a balcony upstairs and downstairs. They had outgrown the old kitchen, with its limited space that Aaron called the "foodah gong" or feed alley.

Any time people needed a new building, or repairs, they did it themselves. No one called a carpenter, a plumber or a mason. They learned home handyman skills, from each other, by sharing and watching. In August, Aaron had help dragging and rolling logs out of the woods for making beams and rough lumber. One month later, those logs were cut at the sawmill.

In September, Wayne Steffy's D4 Caterpillar moved the heavy pile of lumber to the building site at Aarons. Jesse Brubacher and others helped Aaron dig the new cellar by hand and used a one-horse scoop. The horse pulled the metal scoop full of dirt away from the construction site and a man guiding the handles dumped the dirt on a pile. It was hard work. Aaron tried working alone when the ground was muddy. He ended up with lumbago in his back, and he always rejoiced when a volunteer showed up.

Some people thought a new basement under the house was not necessary, but Dr. Schnader rec-ommended it. He said a basement would keep the house drier and warmer even if they did not use it otherwise.

Aaron had a water trough concreted into the new cellar. He planned to use that as a cooling system with the constantly running spring-water that the ram pumped to the house. The trough in the basement had an overflow pipe to the water trough in the barn. The water was not very cold because it warmed- up, in the holding tank upstairs and they still took the milk to the springhouse, to keep it from spoiling.

The entire neighborhood pitched in to help erect a new house. Amanda cooked for extra men and boys at the table, who came to help concrete. In February, Aaron and Amanda went to New Holland and purchased windows and doors. Jesse Brubacher and his hired man, Phares Shirk did much of the carpentry on the new kitchen, with the help of Aaron and his brother Menno. Noah Hoover lived in this neighborhood and he helped Aaron a lot in many ways. Titus worked for his brother Elias, and they both came to help Aaron, when they could.

Aaron bought a new level to use in carpenter work, and it disappeared. He searched long and hard but he finally gave up, thinking it might have been built into the walls or the floor.

Aaron and Amanda had a raising in March and many people helped put up the rafters. It took several weeks longer until they were finished cutting the asbestos siding shingles, and returned the borrowed cutter. In between the farm work of that spring and summer, Aaron spent every chance he had, on the building project. He was so busy that his diary writing slowed down. He quit writing and Amanda started.

Aaron and Amanda moved into their new kitchen before the floor had any linoleum. The store recommended the floor should dry out and season first. The 9-inch square linoleum tiles from Sears came with a lifetime warranty. It took many years of heavy wear, but eventually the color wore through, on the floor, in front of the kitchen sink. Nobody complained to Sears because the flooring was worth the money.

Daniel was eight years old when he drove the horses for the first time in haymaking. Aaron was pleased to write such a milestone in his diary. Daniel could drive the horses for seven loads of hay at Aaron and Jesse, while the men forked it on the wagon.

In those busy spring months, Ruth and Rhoda came down with the measles, at ten months old. They had a high fever and lay listless. Dr. Schnader did not know if Rhoda would survive and he said, "Give them each 1 teaspoon of water every 15 minutes". Amanda was exhausted and needed a rest, so they got another ladies' maid for a few days. Aaron fetched Alta Zeiset for a day and a half, at $10 a day.

Two weeks later, more of the children had measles. Aaron took a turn tending children while Amanda needed a break, and she went with Jesse Brubachers to the funeral of Mrs. Charlie Weaver.

Aaron was not skilled in holding small babies, let alone care for them. He did his best to provide for the family, taking good care of their small farm. He fattened steers, raised a tobacco crop for cash, milked one or two cows by hand for their own use, and raised chickens to sell the eggs. He worked in the garden too, raising vegetables and helping Amanda. In the evening, when he came into the house after a day's work, he would wash the dishes while Amanda cared for the children. Any time when Amanda needed extra help in the house, Aaron went to look for a maid.

A maid, or hired girl, was usually a single girl from another Mennonite family, often a teenager or a single maiden lady, or even a school age girl. She lived with the family for as long as they needed help, and she worked whatever needed doing. That included just about anything: doing farm chores, milking the cow, laundry, tending children, gardening, cleaning, baking, canning and cooking etc. When a mother was sick, or in bed after a new baby, the maid cared for the entire family, sometimes for a few weeks, and sometimes for an entire summer. They worked hard and earned a hands-on education.

Amanda worked as a hired girl for many years when she was growing up in Michigan. It seemed like oh, so long ago. She recalled memories of working for Manesseh Kulps when she was nineteen years old. They lived double with Manesseh's in-laws, Cyrus Ebys and had planned for Lydia Ann Martin as a helper for their new baby in November. When Lydia Ann came down with scarlet fever, the doctor quarantined their home and she could not help. Amanda went to help instead.

Manesseh Kulps had three children, Paul age six, Rachel age four and Mary Ann age two. Soon after Amanda arrived, Paul got scarlet fever, and the doctor quarantined their farm for three weeks. Mother Eby had a stroke and she was confined in bed. They moved the Eby's out. Manesseh and Amanda worked hard every day, and thankfully, only the six year old got the highly contagious scarlet fever. Amanda tended to the new baby and the mother in bed, plus cooking, baking and canning.

Manesseh used a horse —drawn potato digger to unearth a row of potatoes in the morning and then Amanda helped to pick them up. They could not afford to let them freeze. In four days of hard work; they picked up many pounds of potatoes.

The family could not sell their milk and eggs, due to the quarantine but they milked the cows by hand as usual and gathered the eggs. They used all they could and gave the rest of the milk to the calves, pigs and chickens. They made a lot of butter and packed it in small crocks. With a thin cloth cover and a layer of salt on top they stored extra butter in the cellar. The chickens only laid three dozen eggs a day.

The hard work did not bother Amanda much, but she had her heart set on helping her sister Betsy with their first baby. Christian's cute baby Katherine Kilmer arrived on October 6, 1934 and Amanda missed the privilege of working there. It was hard for Amanda to believe now, but that all happened not much more than ten years ago. So soon the tables had turned, and she needed the help. Seven children close together zapped Amanda's strength. That new baby Katherine Kilmer [Katie Ramer] turned into a wonderful helper. At the age of ten, she helped Amanda often.

One of the first mornings after a new girl started working for Aarons; she wanted to help the three little boys, Walter, Peter, and Dick to get dressed. "Now," she said, "which pants belong to which boy?" Walter said "shake them once, if they rattle, they are mine!"

They were all pleased with the morning light streaming in the sunny new kitchen windows, where they could see everything going on outside. Aarons family of nine, gathered three times a day to eat in their cheerful kitchen. Over summertime Amanda did the cooking and canning in the summerhouse, a room to the north side of the kitchen. That kept the wood burning stove from heating up the entire house. Aaron bought another cook stove at a sale for the new kitchen, a green and tan Kalamazoo that had a warming closet. He moved the old steel Columbian stove to the basement, to heat the wash water on laundry day.

Aaron's sister Annie, married Reuben Weaver on December 23, 1945, in the minister's room at Bowmansville church, before the Sunday morning services started. Bishop Aaron Sensenig was sick that morning and he sent the hired man to tell Henry Horst to perform the wedding. Henry was old and forgetful and "doppich" [feeble] and he did not get all the questions asked properly. Reuben and Annie married anyway! They served the wedding meal at her parents, the BW's Shirk family. "Rubes" moved to a farm south of Bowmansville.

When Ruth and Rhoda outgrew their baby crib, Aaron made a heavy-duty double sized crib. The straw -tick mattress, lay on the crisscrossed ropes. Two preschool children slept without falling out of bed. It was the "green crib" or beddly and Amanda made covers that size.

∽

Aaron still had trouble with his back. The chiropractor only relieved his wallet and not his pain. In 1946, Aaron and Amanda purchased a mattress in hopes that it should be better for a back then the lumpy old straw tick. Daniel treasured the wonderful event when that cotton mattress arrived for Aaron and Amanda's bed. Sarah Ann also marveled at such extravagance and hoped she would see the day when she could

have one for her own bed. They considered a mattress a luxury for fancy people.

Most people in the neighborhood slept on big linen chaff bags, about the size and shape of a mattress. They used them on rope beds, or on bedsprings. Daniel helped Aaron fill the bags with finely cut straw from the "hock bunk", or straw clutter, out on the barn floor. After filling the bag with straw, and sewing it shut by hand, Daniel helped return it to the house, ready for a good nights' sleep. Once a year, he emptied the straw into the chicken house, and freshly re-filled the bags with clean straw. Unless a person fluffed it up a little every now and then, he slept on a bump or in a hole, because the straw did not stay spread out evenly. Everyone enjoyed going to bed on a freshly filled chaff bag.

Aaron and Amanda did not allow children to play with the old-fashioned straw cutter, a narrow wooden trough shaped bench with an open end on the left and a sharp knife blade with a long curved handle on the right, like a heavy-duty paper cutter. It looked like a nice toy, except for the fact that it could swiftly sever a finger or a hand.

On October 5, 1946, they welcomed another 10-pound daughter at 3:30 AM. They recorded in their diary "all well", with the help of Dr. Schnader. Aaron and Amanda had four girls and four boys, with the twins only sixteen- months old. One of the twins chose a name out of the hat, and the name was Martha.

Sarah Ann was a good helper around the house, but she started in first grade four weeks earlier. Daniel was in third grade already, and he was Sarah Ann's guardian and hero. He was big and strong and smart and he could even read! She was small for her age and needed his support all the way. Ivan Brubacher also started in first grade, and looked up to Daniel as a big brother. Ivan was the oldest in Jesse's family.

When Elias Shirk's Lena started to school as the oldest one in Elias's family, she clung tightly to Sarah Ann's hand, while walking to school, and during recess. Being an oldest child was intimidating, even scary at times. Four more cousins joined the crowd: Walter Shirk, Jesse Brubacher's Annie, and Elias Shirk's identical twins, Reuben and Raymond. School became a party, more fun than staying home, when a dozen cousins walked to school together. Aaron's children walked farther than the others, but Jesse's and Elias's children joined them as they kept walking and the crowd swelled.

The new mattress did not end Aaron's backache. He lay around with lumbago, for quite a while. Menno helped cut tobacco and brought his mother along to help cook for the workers, while Aaron spent a week lying around. He helped butcher five barred rock chickens, for a tobacco party. A dozen men arrived and cut three and one half acres of tobacco. The helpers later cut one and three fourths acres the next day and Aaron paid $175, divided among a dozen men, for their help.

The neighboring Kohl boys came to help husk corn, and so did Josie Latshaw, as Aarons back gradually improved.

He had lumbago at butchering time. Jesse and Menno hung up the carcass, while Lydia Ann Martin and Emma Martin helped Amanda for two days of canning meat. Menno helped Aaron finish the butchering and then he helped cut firewood. His brothers hauled seven loads of dung, cleaning the horse stable and the chicken house. Aaron turned 33 years old!

∞

Summer vacation seemed as long as a nine-month school term to Sarah Ann, because summer meant hard work. The summer of 1947 tried her more than usual due to all the regular work plus toddlers to watch. Amanda direly needed seven-year-old Sarah Ann. Dick was three years old, the twins were two, and Martha a year old. Such a combination doubled the trouble with many messes to clean up.

Aaron wished for fresh tender lettuce from the garden, but Amanda was too busy to prepare it. Meal after meal, Aaron still had no lettuce on the table, so he helped himself! When he came in from the tobacco beds, he first walked over and cut lettuce with his pocketknife, and laid the unwashed lettuce beside his plate. At the table, Amanda noticed something on Aaron's lettuce. "Look" she said. "There is a snail on your lettuce!" Aaron replied, "Well the snail better watch it, or I'll eat her too!"

Ruth and Rhoda rocked on the big rocking chair, drinking their bottles. The rocker upset! Ruth landed on broken glass and cut a one and a half inch gash in the side of her forehead. Old Dr. Schnader came out and put in three or four stitches.

The hired girl, Barbara Ringler, worked in the kitchen, and saw something fall down past the window. She went out to look, and saw that Rhoda had landed on Dick, who was innocently playing on the grass below. Both children were upset and crying, but neither one appeared hurt seriously, beyond bruises and bumps on their heads. Dick cried for a long time. The upstairs bedroom window had no screen, but the blind and curtain were closed, where Rhoda climbed onto the cedar chest inside the window, and fell out.

Barbara painted the little crib, and set it on newspaper to dry beside the stove in the long middle room. After dinner, Aaron, Amanda and Barbara remained seated at the table talking, until all of a sudden, Barbara jumped up and said, "Where are the little people?" She found them in the next room, very busy. They tore up the newspaper into small pieces and stuck it all over the wet paint on the crib. What a mess! Amanda and Barbara picked off all the paper, wiping the crib with a rag dipped in kerosene and then Barbara repainted it.

At a young age, the twins knew the perfect time for getting into mischief... when Amanda was doing laundry in the basement. They knew she could not see or hear them.

Before Amanda started the wash she said,"Sarah Ann, Please check up on the little ones. I'll be in the cellar and won't hear them if they cry." After a while, Dick came down in the cellar and said, "Mom, you should see what the twins are doing." Amanda said, "Go tell Sarah Ann, she is supposed to watch them." It did not go long until Dick returned and said, "Mom, you should see what the twins are doing with the butter."

Butter! Amanda did not hesitate, and hurried to the kitchen where she found the twins had plastered the screens and walls around the windows with freshly churned butter. They also had it on the floor, a chair and their dresses. Amanda could salvage a little, but they had wasted three or 4 pounds, and what a mess to clean up!

Another time when Amanda wanted to wash, she waited for Aaron to start the wash machine motor, and meanwhile she filled the dishpan with warm sudsy water, to wash dishes. Leaving the dishes, she followed Aaron to the cellar, to get the first load started washing. By the time she returned to the kitchen, Ruth and Rhoda had dipped the fresh dishwater out on the floor and all over themselves.

The twins watched Amanda fill the reservoir on the kitchen range. Then Aaron and Amanda went to the basement to start the laundry, with the" hard to start" motor. About that time one of Jesse's children walked over with a hurried message," travelers are coming!" Kindhearted Lydi-Jess-sey knew how much a 5-minute notice meant. Aaron and Amanda ignored the wash and went to the kitchen where they found water everywhere! The twins had

opened the spigot on the front of the stove and drained the reservoir. Thankfully, the water was not hot, but the whole floor was flooded and special guests were coming. Aaron and Amanda opened the door and swept the water out! The floor was still wet when the visitors arrived. Amanda enjoyed hearing from Canadian friends and relatives, even at inconvenient times.

After a warm spring rain, the twins walked back to the creek, where Aaron had tobacco beds. With an abundance of mud puddles, they undressed and sat in the mud to play. Amanda said many a time, "it's good we don't live along a road where people can see us."

At tobacco cutting time, someone set an oil-can at the end of the walk and Ruth and Rhoda used it to squirt oil into each other's hair. Another time, they had little Martha's head plastered with axle grease, when she had just enough hair for two little pigtails at the front. Amanda used strong grease cutting laundry detergent to scrub the grease out of Martha's hair.

9

Baby Mary

In the fall of 1947, Dr. Schnader approached Aaron and Amanda with a special request. The doctor had a concern for Joseph Latshaw, a poor man living in a filthy shack along Spook Lane, half a mile west of 625. Josey was a mentally retarded tramp who walked many miles pulling a wagon, looking for food or work. He asked for straw for his dog, corn to feed a few chickens and food to take along. Aaron met Josey for the first time, when Josey came looking for work.

Josey was only a few years older than Aaron, born May 4, 1911. He lived with his mother, older brother, and numerous cats and dogs. He spent four years in school but never learned to read or write. He mastered two languages, English and Pennsylvania Dutch. Dutch was easiest for him. After his older brother left home, Josey and his mother lived on local handouts.

Neighbors helped occasionally, but when his mother lost her eyesight, Dr. Schnader had her admitted into the County home. That was a disaster to Josey, because he was afraid to stay in a shack alone. He had a brother Clarence in Reading, a sister Maria in Adamstown, and a sister Lizzie. None of them wanted to look after Josey.

"Aaron, would you look after Josey and give him work ", asked Dr.Schnader? I do not think he should be put into the County home yet, because he is able to work for a living." Aaron and Amanda decided to take Josey into their home. The poor man could not help it that God made him that way and it was a Christian's duty to help the needy. Aaron knew that Josey had a strong back to help with his farm work.

At first Josey lived in the stripping room, sleeping there on a couch for a few months. Aaron's brother Menno helped move Josey there, and even slept with him a few nights, to help him adjust. A few weeks later, on January 17, 1948 Aaron and Amanda had a new baby girl. Her birthday was just two days near Aunt Mary's and no name out of the hat that time.

Josey got pneumonia and Amanda agreed that after baby Mary's arrival, he may move into the house. Sleeping downstairs in the front parlor all alone was scary for Josey. He worked whatever Aaron asked him to do. For a few weeks that winter, he had a job at the tobacco packinghouse in New Holland. He walked out to route 73 [now 625] and got a ride to New Holland. He talked to himself and he had many strange ways. Josey's stay at Aaron's farm among nine children lasted about one year. That arrangement did not work well, because he became unruly and did not behave with the children. Josey moved back into his shack and Aaron tried to help him there.

Soon after Josey moved back, a woman named Mattie Redcay moved in with him. Mattie chose to live with Josey, in his filthy shack. Over the next twenty years, Josey came to the Shirk family often. He was a regular visitor at their place and Amanda always fixed him food to eat. Aaron shaved him regularly, and when it was time to put tobacco away, Josey came to help. He was strong and could work hard for two dollars a day. Aaron and Amanda treated him as though God were watching, because they knew he was.

Amanda remained slim for the first half of her family. She took after her slim mother, and she worked hard. She wrestled every week with a kick-start Maytag gasoline engine. When she could not start the washer, she had to wait until Aaron came in from the fields. When Aaron could not start the motor, it tried the patience of them both. Amanda wrote in her diary, "Aaron can't start the wash machine." The next day she wrote again, "Aaron can't start the wash machine." The next day after that, "washed by hand."

Nine children soiled piles of laundry even though they wore one outfit for a whole week, and clothing was limited. Was it any wonder that Amanda requested things worn until completely dirty? Amanda made sure the children changed their clothing after coming home from school, so they could wear that outfit again. Two school dresses a week were plenty. Amanda could not complain about the boys changing underwear or stockings too often, because they did not wear any over summertime. The only underwear most men knew was the wintertime one-piece union suits.

Everyone shared the same towels, and the hankies had a tremendous opportunity to spread germs. Only the fittest people survived, but that included all of them, as they developed a healthy immune system.

On laundry day, Amanda gathered dirty clothes upstairs in the semi dark bedrooms. Sometimes she smelled the clothes to decide if they needed laundry or not. Downstairs, she gathered the wash all around, including her apron from the door-knob, the tea towel at the kitchen sink, and the smelly slop rag hanging beside the 'sinkly' [the smaller trough- type wash sink].The all purpose clean-up rag smelled rank and hung stiff with dirt!

Amanda had many helpers, but she preferred to sort the laundry her way. She looked for things to presoak. She emptied all the pockets to make sure no feed or chaff floated in the wash water, for the succeeding loads of wash. She removed any tar or chewing gum with gasoline. She always washed the Sunday shirts and tablecloths in the first load and tried hard to keep the diapers white.

Amanda heated water on the wood stove, scooped it in the washer, and then she filled both of the rinse tubs with cold water. Only then did she start the wash machine motor, or tried to. On a lovely washday, she was disgusted to get thus far, and not be able to finish.

She washed each load and rinsed it twice, putting everything through the wringer three times. She tried to keep the apron strings and the stockings from tangling around the wringer -rollers in a serious knot. She watched her chance to teach any beginner how to run that wringer, all the time remembering how quickly Daniel had his arm caught. Amanda or a helper lugged each load in a soggy heap to the clothesline.

Wooden clothespins came in a one-piece style that split apart as easily as a wishbone from the chicken platter at the table, when any beginner tried to hang bulky garments on the clothesline. On a windy day, Amanda could not keep the wash pinned to the line securely. She kept an eye on the line and sent a child to retrieve a Sunday shirt or a sheet dangling from the line by one clothespin. The invention of snap clothespins was a great improvement in the tedious chore of washing.

The clotheslines sagged seriously beneath the weight of the dripping wash. As the lines sagged lower each year, Amanda added more forked saplings as props to hold the wash off the ground. Children loved to grab hold of the wash line anytime and lift their feet up and Amanda scolded,"Henk net ugh de vesh line! [Hang not on the wash line.]

After completing the last load of laundry, Amanda carefully released the pressure on the two rollers of the wringer part, and lowered the drain hose to the floor. While the thickened dark -colored water swirled down the drain, Amanda lifted out the agitator and automatically ran her nimble fingers through the dirty water, searching for a coin or a button that might clog the drain hose.

If a button got in the hose, Amanda blew in the exit end of the hose to dislodge it backwards. She carefully put any stray button in her pocket, so she could replace it on the proper garment. The wringer rollers had a way of popping buttons off clothes and splitting some buttons in half, making more work. Amanda rinsed the washer and the rinse tubs, and then replaced the lids to keep the tubs clean until next washday.

By then, it was dinnertime, and Aaron would be in the house. When Amanda stepped into the brightly glaring sunshine, she felt like she stepped out of a cave. First thing, she removed her "shlop shotz", or slop apron, and put on a clean dry one. Sometimes Amanda added her dirty wet apron to the last load of laundry.

If all went well, and the wash dried, Amanda folded, mended, ironed and returned each piece to where it belonged. Anytime Amanda finished the laundry, she accomplished something worth recording in her diary. Sometimes they washed one day and hung the laundry on the line the next day due to the weather, and sometimes the wash took several days to dry. Eventually it dried, if not outdoors, then inside draped everywhere.

When baby Mary got pneumonia, Aaron and Amanda knew it was time to call the doctor. "Daniel, on your way to school this morning, please stop at Lem Kiefer's with this note," said Aaron. "We need them to call the doctor for us." When Daniel knocked on the door, no one answered, and he didn't know what to do, so he went on to school.

When he came home that evening, Aaron and Amanda were both sitting there with a very sick baby, wondering why the doctor hadn't come yet. Daniel explained that no one answered the door at Kiefers! Aaron asked, "Why didn't you come home right away and tell us?" Only then, did Daniel realize how seriously sick his baby sister was, and he felt badly about that.

Aaron and Amanda raised a huge patch of strawberries, just north of the house. Using the tobacco planter, they planted 1000 plants. Fifteen-year-old Erla Nolt helped Aaron and the boys pick enough to can 100 quarts, for their own use, with none left over to sell. They also planted asparagus, with intentions of selling some, without much success, and the weeds took over. Daniel and Sarah Ann seldom had time to themselves.

On a lovely Sunday afternoon in June, the family traveled home from visiting at Dawdy Shirks. Aaron, Walter, Pete and Dick drove in the old open buggy ahead of Daniel and Amanda, who drove the carriage with the other children. Daniel had the lines, and Amanda was on the front seat, holding baby Mary. Sarah Ann sat in the back seat with the little ones, Ruth, Rhoda and Martha. A little over half way down

the north side of the Turkey Hill, the horses began to trot. "Watch out, Daniel, there's a car coming towards us!" said Amanda. "Get to the side of the road!"

Then, afraid that Daniel would not get over far enough, she reached over and grabbed the lines from him. The buggy went too far to the side of the road, with one wheel running up over a big rock, jutting out like a low shelf. The carriage flipped over on the side!

The approaching car stopped and offered assistance, while Aaron and the boys came running to help. Baby Mary flew out, but thankfully, no one was hurt, or the harness broken. The carriage was broken and some walked the rest of the way home, thanking God for his protecting hand.

∞

"Guess what? Aunt Lydia is getting married!" Amanda was shocked! Her closest sister was getting married, and she knew nothing about a romance! Such a jolting announcement was enough to make her reach for a chair and sit down in astonishment. Eli Stauffer was twice Lydia's age, her own uncle, and from the Pike church. My, what a surprise! Amanda was happy for them both!

As a widower, Eli visited at Peter Brubacher's and took a liking to Lydia. His first wife Mary was a sister to Peter Brubacher, and she died at the age of 60, from cerebral hemorrhage. Eli was 64 years old and Lydia was almost 32.

Eli's eleven grown children did not approve of their fathers plans. Neither did Peter Brubacher's sister Barbara. She sent her niece, Lydia, a lengthy letter recommending that Lydia think twice before marrying Eli Stauffer. "Are you sure you can handle such a responsibility? Do you want to give up your freedom, to take care of an older man? Do you know all that is required? ", Barbara asked.

About the time that Aaron and Amanda married, in 1937, Aunt Barbara married a widower with a family of grown children, and she did not think that Lydia should try marriage, under such conditions as she did. Perhaps Barbara knew what she was talking about, but Lydia did not want to miss her first chance at marriage.

Eli knew his niece, and all about her aches and pains. If God was for them, who could be against them? Feeling needed was the greatest thing in life, and that was what Lydia wanted. Bishop Jake Stauffer married them on a Sunday morning before church services started at the Pike Church in 1948. Lydia became stepmother to Eli's eleven grown children and they had some step- grandchildren living close by. Lydia's first cousins suddenly became her stepchildren.

Lydia was a queen on her throne, and finally she had a home of her own. She enjoyed housekeeping and could arrange the furniture, plan the meals, and have her very own weed free garden, with Eli's help. He was skilled with an orchard and gardening, and worked in his buggy shop at Murrell, just east of Ephrata. His grown children did the farming.

Lydia knew all about the Pike Mennonite Church that she joined. The Stauffer Mennonite group split off from the Lancaster Conference Church, due to differing beliefs and opinions, all from studying the same Bible.

Many local roads were not blacktopped, and when the Stauffer Church built a new churchhouse in a central location, besides the piked 322, they were the "piker" church, no matter how the dictionary defines the word piker.

The May City, Iowa group was a branch off this church, and they allowed nothing fancy. Lydia's quilts on the beds should not have printed fabric and neither may Lydia's dresses have flowers on them. They used some of her quilts upside down, with a solid color showing on the back. She had a black stove to be as plain and humble as they could be. With black enamel paint, Lydia carefully repainted every scratch or nick that showed white paint below, because no one could buy black appliances back then. No scratches showed on the varnish on Lydia's sewing machine either. A pad of cloth beneath the scissors, kept it from scratching the varnish. Everyone could see that Lydia did not raise a big family as all four of her sisters did.

Lydia said, "I would be ashamed if the sun shone before I got up in the morning!" She was the most proper lady Aaron and Amanda's children

knew, sometimes too proper for their lifestyle. Lydia's pride and joy was a singing canary that received as much attention as a child. She talked to her bird, entertained it, and lovingly covered it each night. [Half a century later, while digging in a flowerbed, a gardener found her pet bird still preserved in a jar of formaldehyde. They understood and tucked it beneath the soil again, long after Lydia died.]

In his later years, Uncle Eli had hardening of the arteries and he was hard to live with, but Lydia was there for him. She kept the house and even the hair in his nose and ears were neatly trimmed. Occasionally, a niece came to help Lydia clean, but they were used to seeing a difference where they cleaned. Lydia expected perfection and if her helper was done too soon, the lintel over the door might get a white glove inspection. One girl remembered sitting upstairs reading a book, while bumping the floor every now and then, pretending to be cleaning, because everything already looked clean, and Lydia did not know the difference.

Lydia still had health problems, but it was good for her to forget about her own self. She was in charge of preserving the fruit from Eli's well-kept orchard, and she enjoyed her flowers, but she never quite got over her longing for a child of her own.

Laundry

Amanda remained slim for the first half of her family. She took after her slim mother, and she worked hard. She wrestled every week with a kick-start Maytag gasoline engine. When she could not start the washer, she had to wait until Aaron came in from the fields. When Aaron could not start the motor, it tried the patience of them both. Amanda wrote in her diary, "Aaron can't start the wash machine." The next day she wrote again, "Aaron can't start the wash machine." The next day after that, "washed by hand."

Nine children soiled piles of laundry even though they wore one outfit for a whole week, and clothing was limited. Was it any wonder that Amanda requested things worn until completely dirty? Amanda made sure the children changed their clothing after coming home from school, so they could wear that outfit again. Two school dresses a week were plenty. Amanda could not complain about the boys changing underwear or stockings too often, because they did not wear any over summertime. The only underwear most men knew was the wintertime one-piece union suits.

Everyone shared the same towels, and the hankies had a tremendous opportunity to spread germs. Only the fittest people survived, but that included all of them, as they developed a healthy immune system.

On laundry day, Amanda gathered dirty clothes upstairs in the semi dark bedrooms. Sometimes she smelled the clothes to decide if they needed laundry or not. Downstairs, she gathered the wash all around, including her apron from the door-knob, the tea towel at the kitchen sink, and the smelly slop rag hanging beside the 'sinkly' [the smaller trough- type wash sink].The all purpose clean-up rag smelled rank and hung stiff with dirt!

Amanda had many helpers, but she preferred to sort the laundry her way. She looked for things to presoak. She emptied all the pockets to make sure no feed or chaff floated in the wash water, for the succeeding loads of wash. She removed any tar or chewing gum with gasoline. She always washed the Sunday shirts and tablecloths in the first load and tried hard to keep the diapers white.

Amanda heated water on the wood stove, scooped it in the washer, and then she filled both of the rinse tubs with cold water. Only then did she start the wash machine motor, or tried to. On a lovely washday, she was disgusted to get thus far, and not be able to finish.

She washed each load and rinsed it twice, putting everything through the wringer three times. She tried to keep the apron strings and the stockings from tangling around the wringer -rollers in a serious knot. She watched her chance to teach any beginner how to run that wringer, all the time remembering how quickly Daniel had his arm caught. Amanda or a helper lugged each load in a soggy heap to the clothesline.

Wooden clothespins came in a one-piece style that split apart as easily as a wishbone from the chicken platter at the table, when any beginner

tried to hang bulky garments on the clothesline. On a windy day, Amanda could not keep the wash pinned to the line securely. She kept an eye on the line and sent a child to retrieve a Sunday shirt or a sheet dangling from the line by one clothespin. The invention of snap clothespins was a great improvement in the tedious chore of washing.

The clotheslines sagged seriously beneath the weight of the dripping wash. As the lines sagged lower each year, Amanda added more forked saplings as props to hold the wash off the ground. Children loved to grab hold of the wash line anytime and lift their feet up and Amanda scolded,"Henk net ugh de vesh line! [Hang not on the wash line.]

After completing the last load of laundry, Amanda carefully released the pressure on the two rollers of the wringer part, and lowered the drain hose to the floor. While the thickened dark -colored water swirled down the drain, Amanda lifted out the agitator and automatically ran her nimble fingers through the dirty water, searching for a coin or a button that might clog the drain hose.

If a button got in the hose, Amanda blew in the exit end of the hose to dislodge it backwards. She carefully put any stray button in her pocket, so she could replace it on the proper garment. The wringer rollers had a way of popping buttons off clothes and splitting some buttons in half, making more work. Amanda rinsed the washer and the rinse tubs, and then replaced the lids to keep the tubs clean until next washday.

By then, it was dinnertime, and Aaron would be in the house. When Amanda stepped into the brightly glaring sunshine, she felt like she stepped out of a cave. First thing, she removed her "shlop shotz", or slop apron, and put on a clean dry one. Sometimes Amanda added her dirty wet apron to the last load of laundry.

If all went well, and the wash dried, Amanda folded, mended, ironed and returned each piece to where it belonged. Anytime Amanda finished the laundry, she accomplished something worth recording in her diary. Sometimes they washed one day and hung the laundry on the line the next day due to the weather, and sometimes the wash took several days to dry. Eventually it dried, if not outdoors, then inside draped everywhere.

When baby Mary got pneumonia, Aaron and Amanda knew it was time to call the doctor. "Daniel, on your way to school this morning, please stop at Lem Kiefer's with this note," said Aaron. "We need them to call the doctor for us." When Daniel knocked on the door, no one answered, and he didn't know what to do, so he went on to school.

When he came home that evening, Aaron and Amanda were both sitting there with a very sick baby, wondering why the doctor hadn't come yet. Daniel explained that no one answered the door at Kiefers! Aaron asked, "Why didn't you come home right away and tell us?" Only then, did Daniel realize how seriously sick his baby sister was, and he felt badly about that.

Aaron and Amanda raised a huge patch of strawberries, just north of the house. Using the tobacco planter, they planted 1000 plants. Fifteen-year-old Erla Nolt helped Aaron and the boys pick enough to can 100 quarts, for their own use, with none left over to sell. They also planted asparagus, with intentions of selling some, without much success, and the weeds took over. Daniel and Sarah Ann seldom had time to themselves.

On a lovely Sunday afternoon in June, the family traveled home from visiting at Dawdy Shirks. Aaron, Walter, Pete and Dick drove in the old open buggy ahead of Daniel and Amanda, who drove the carriage with the other children. Daniel had the lines, and Amanda was on the front seat, holding baby Mary. Sarah Ann sat in the back seat with the little ones, Ruth, Rhoda and Martha. A little over half way down the north side of the Turkey Hill, the horses began to trot. "Watch out, Daniel, there's a car coming towards us!" said Amanda. "Get to the side of the road!"

Then, afraid that Daniel would not get over far enough, she reached over and grabbed the lines from him. The buggy went too far to the side of the road, with one wheel running up over a big rock, jutting out like a low shelf. The carriage flipped over on the side!

The approaching car stopped and offered assistance, while Aaron and the boys came running to help. Baby Mary flew out, but thankfully, no one

was hurt, or the harness broken. The carriage was broken and some walked the rest of the way home, thanking God for his protecting hand.

∞

"Guess what? Aunt Lydia is getting married!" Amanda was shocked! Her closest sister was getting married, and she knew nothing about a romance! Such a jolting announcement was enough to make her reach for a chair and sit down in astonishment. Eli Stauffer was twice Lydia's age, her own uncle, and from the Pike church. My, what a surprise! Amanda was happy for them both!

As a widower, Eli visited at Peter Brubacher's and took a liking to Lydia. His first wife Mary was a sister to Peter Brubacher, and she died at the age of 60, from cerebral hemorrhage. Eli was 64 years old and Lydia was almost 32.

Eli's eleven grown children did not approve of their fathers plans. Neither did Peter Brubacher's sister Barbara. She sent her niece, Lydia, a lengthy letter recommending that Lydia think twice before marrying Eli Stauffer. "Are you sure you can handle such a responsibility? Do you want to give up your freedom, to take care of an older man? Do you know all that is required? ", Barbara asked.

About the time that Aaron and Amanda married, in 1937, Aunt Barbara married a widower with a family of grown children, and she did not think that Lydia should try marriage, under such conditions as she did. Perhaps Barbara knew what she was talking about, but Lydia did not want to miss her first chance at marriage.

Eli knew his niece, and all about her aches and pains. If God was for them, who could be against them? Feeling needed was the greatest thing in life, and that was what Lydia wanted. Bishop Jake Stauffer married them on a Sunday morning before church services started at the Pike Church in 1948. Lydia became stepmother to Eli's eleven grown children and they had some step- grandchildren living close by. Lydia's first cousins suddenly became her stepchildren.

Lydia was a queen on her throne, and finally she had a home of her own. She enjoyed housekeeping and could arrange the furniture, plan the meals, and have her very own weed free garden, with Eli's help. He was skilled with an orchard and gardening, and worked in his buggy shop at Murrell, just east of Ephrata. His grown children did the farming.

Lydia knew all about the Pike Mennonite Church that she joined. The Stauffer Mennonite group split off from the Lancaster Conference Church, due to differing beliefs and opinions, all from studying the same Bible.

Many local roads were not blacktopped, and when the Stauffer Church built a new churchhouse in a central location, besides the piked 322, they were the "piker" church, no matter how the dictionary defines the word piker.

The May City, Iowa group was a branch off this church, and they allowed nothing fancy. Lydia's quilts on the beds should not have printed fabric and neither may Lydia's dresses have flowers on them. They used some of her quilts upside down, with a solid color showing on the back. She had a black stove to be as plain and humble as they could be. With black enamel paint, Lydia carefully repainted every scratch or nick that showed white paint below, because no one could buy black appliances back then. No scratches showed on the varnish on Lydia's sewing machine either. A pad of cloth beneath the scissors, kept it from scratching the varnish. Everyone could see that Lydia did not raise a big family as all four of her sisters did.

Lydia said, "I would be ashamed if the sun shone before I got up in the morning!" She was the most proper lady Aaron and Amanda's children knew, sometimes too proper for their lifestyle. Lydia's pride and joy was a singing canary that received as much attention as a child. She talked to her bird, entertained it, and lovingly covered it each night. [Half a century later, while digging in a flowerbed, a gardener found her pet bird still preserved in a jar of formaldehyde. They understood and tucked it beneath the soil again, long after Lydia died.]

In his later years, Uncle Eli had hardening of the arteries and he was hard to live with, but Lydia was there for him. She kept the house and even the hair in his nose and ears were neatly trimmed.

Occasionally, a niece came to help Lydia clean, but they were used to seeing a difference where they cleaned. Lydia expected perfection and if her helper was done too soon, the lintel over the door might get a white glove inspection. One girl remembered sitting upstairs reading a book, while bumping the floor every now and then, pretending to be cleaning, because everything already looked clean, and Lydia did not know the difference.

Lydia still had health problems, but it was good for her to forget about her own self. She was in charge of preserving the fruit from Eli's well-kept orchard, and she enjoyed her flowers, but she never quite got over her longing for a child of her own.

10

Nine children had a way of taking care of each other. The older ones automatically helped the little ones, and knew where they were, or what they were doing. One evening late in summer, Dick was missing, and no one had a clue where to find him."Where did you see him last," Amanda asked. Aaron's whole family searched everywhere; upstairs, downstairs, the cellar, the barn, the feed alley, the corncrib, the buggy shed, the chicken house and even in the garden, with no sign of Dick. He simply disappeared!

Aaron and Daniel had chopped corn stalks for the evening chores, and Dick could be lost in the cornfield. The sun went down and darkness crept in, while everyone searched in all the likely places and even in unlikely places. At the age of four, Dick usually fell asleep on the couch before bedtime, all tuckered out. Since he did not answer when they called, Amanda thought he might be sleeping somewhere.

The search continued and Aaron was ready to go to the neighbors for help. It was not likely that Dick would roam anywhere all alone and darkness entered into Amanda's thoughts. What would life be like without their lively little question box? Was he still alive...? God trusted them to take care of him.... please help! They kept on searching and after looking in the buggy shed, Amanda found him sleeping on the back seat of the carriage, barely noticeable in the dark shadows. She roused him and hugged him, with tears of relief, and called off the search. His sweet innocence reminded her of the greatest job on earth, raising the next generation fit for the master's use. Thank you God for the privilege!

In the winter of 1948, -49 Aaron and Amanda met serious financial and physical hardships, even with frugal living and their best efforts. Aaron had so much back trouble that he could hardly do his own work anymore. In August, he went to Terre Hill where he received a shot for arthritis backache. Five days later, he was back for another shot, and so it continued during the heat of the summer

Aaron spent his 11th wedding anniversary in the hospital, wishing to be at home, where fifty men showed up to help do his work. He came home, but his back problems came along home.

Dr. Amos B Schnader died in January. Aaron and Amanda's wonderful family doctor rested in peace beside his wife Mary, at the Center Church. His wife had passed away in 1936 and perhaps he was a lonely widower, all the years Aaron and Amanda appreciated his kind help, delivering nine babies for them. Dr. Michael Lauria replaced Dr. Schnader.

Aaron's backache problems did not improve, all winter. Aaron and Amanda had more than they could handle, not knowing which way to go. Baby number ten was due to arrive any day, as Aaron lay helpless. He had so much sciatic pain, especially in one leg, that he could not turn himself in bed anymore. Aaron was hard to care for, and Amanda could do only so much. She was busy waiting on him, heating pillows and using the hot water bottle to keep his legs warm and turning him from side to side. Fifteen year-old Erla Nolt helped Amanda with cooking, cleaning, laundry and taking care of three-year-old twins, two-year-old Martha and one-year-old Mary. Amanda still regularly milked the cow, while ten-year-old Daniel tended the horses and did the other chores. Two whole weeks of that, wore Amanda out. She had barely settled in bed, weary to the bone and desperately needing a good night's sleep, when Aaron writhed in so much pain, that they both knew the night would be long. She did not want to bother others, but Amanda got dressed again because they had to have help.

She found a match and lit the kerosene lantern, and walked alone in the cold winter night for help. Amanda dreaded the thought of waking their neighbors, but she had no choice. Jesse put on his clothes and biked a mile out the road and woke more neighbors to use their phone. He awoke Dr. Lauria, who sent out an ambulance to take Aaron to the hospital.

Amanda, being great with child, was filled with troubling thoughts. She knew all about skimping and doing without things during hard times in her childhood. They were poor people in a way, but Peter managed his money wisely and they did not face the problems Aaron and Amanda did. What might happen to their children? Amanda hurt more for her children than she did for herself as they sank so deep in need of help...in need of money every where she looked...in need of physical labor, she could not see a way through...in need of healing for the pain Aaron suffered...most of all, they needed wisdom to guide their children in the right way. She begged God for help...in the name of Jesus. Amen!

As a young starry-eyed bride in 1937, Amanda had no idea what life might hold in store. She did not imagine things this tough, but none of them could quit now.

The ambulance arrived at one o'clock at night and she was ever so glad! Dr Lauria referred Aaron to Dr. Nutter in Lancaster, who admitted him to the St. Joseph Hospital for surgery to correct a crooked spine. They put 18-pound weights to his legs and raised the foot end of the bed ten inches. He started taking muscle exercises, and had "electric treatment". He spent two weeks in traction. Aaron had some lonely days without visitors, and his roommate died in the bed beside him, but most of the time, Aaron had many callers. The hospital bills kept mounting.

The day after Aaron went to the hospital, Dr. and Mrs. Lauria delivered a slow baby Louisa at home, at 6: 40 PM. Aaron did not see his daughter until she was three weeks old. Dr. Lauria came out to the farm, to check up on Amanda in the morning, and then he went to see Aaron in the Lancaster Hospital in the afternoon. Lydi-Jes-sey walked over to help, knowing Aaron was at the hospital. She saw an urgent need. When she came home, telling her husband how it made, Jesse Brubacher kindly fetched Martha Kilmer as an able worker to help Amanda. Aaron's children always enjoyed Martha, as she worked around the house. She sang sweetly and sometimes relaxed with her knitting in the evening. This time Martha was too busy for knitting anything.

Jesse Brubacher compassionately helped Aaron and Amanda, by taking Pete age five, and Dick age four, to Mary Bauman and Lydia Zimmermann, where the boys stayed several weeks. Those two unmarried women operated a small goat dairy, on a farm near Pennytown, and they enjoyed keeping children. Pete and Dick considered the disciplining more strict than necessary, but they had fun on the goat farm. Dick had a problem pronouncing all the sounds plainly and he tried hard to say black goat in Dutch. "Schwatz gase", [black goat] came out as (fotz-gase) to amuse his older brothers because "fotz" means fart in Dutch. On the same day, Jesse took Ruth and Rhoda, the three-year-old twins, to spend several weeks with Uncle Eli Stauffer and newly married Aunt Lydia, nearly fourteen miles away.

Without a telephone, Amanda could not talk with Aaron in the hospital, so she sent a letter announcing the birth of baby number ten. Aaron was dazed after surgery and he could not read the letter, so his company opened it and read it to him, barely registering. They did not need a name out of the hat, because Aaron and Amanda had agreed on baby names before he left. Amanda liked the name Louisa, from reading Louisa May Alcott books long ago in school.

Amanda 's sisters often helped each other in time of need, but not this time, because Christian Kilmer's had a baby Annetta, just one week old, while Mary, Mrs. Martin Kilmer, had gallstone surgery around the same time.

On Sunday, Daniel biked to Bowmansville Church alone. Aaron and Amanda's hardships stressed the entire family. Aunt Hettie gave money to BW Shirk, and said it is for Aaron and Amanda, but it should remain anonymous. A.M. Shirk asked not a word, but he said 'thank you' and appreciated it. The Eby family that pinched pennies and completely wore out their own clothes, kindly shared with the poor.

When baby Louisa was eight days old, Amanda got out of bed and helped work, even if she stayed in bed ten days for the others. She did the lighter work and had good help, and ten days after Louisa arrived, Amanda was mending and sewing doll clothes, according to her diary. Perhaps the doll dress was a thank you gift to nine-year-old Sarah Ann, for all her hard work and the responsibility on her young shoulders.

After Aunt Lydia kept the twins three weeks, Silas brought them home, as soon as Amanda got out of bed. When baby Louisa was two weeks old, the other children returned, adjusting to a new baby, before Aaron came home from the hospital. Amanda was home alone with her ten children, and five families came in the afternoon to see the twelve -day old baby. Aaron's uncle, David O. Weavers, brought Aaron home on March 27, and three groups of company came to see them that day.

After Aaron's dismissal from the hospital, he had a hard time adjusting to the noise and commotion of seven preschool age children. Daniel was ten, and now they had ten children. Aaron hoped the church would help with more of his hospital bills, because he was up against financially. He seriously tried to sell some woodland because he needed money, but he could not find a buyer. Amanda cut her grocery lists to bare necessities, ordering only flour, sugar, salt, tapioca, cornstarch and soap. Times were hard, and they could not see a way through.

After B W Shirk and his sons all worked together improving Aaron's farm for ten years, they did not wish to see Aaron lose the farm to the bank, or to anyone else. Rather than mortgage the farm to the bank, Aaron's father wanted the mortgage. Therefore Aaron received $2,000.00 from his father, to keep going.

Aaron improved slowly and he could walk again. Life was a struggle. Later that year when things still looked grim, Leonard Keister asked Aaron and Amanda, "Do you have room in your house, to board workers from the Turnpike?" After talking it over, they both agreed, 'there is always room for one more!" God answers prayers in strange ways.

Turnpike

Aaron had heard about plans for a new Pennsylvania Turnpike, or a Superhighway, also called a Dream Highway by others. He noticed right away, that the big road might be crossing through his neighborhood, but when he shared such information with the folks of the area, he was ridiculed and mocked!"Coming through such backwoods? No way! Haw Haw, Haw!"Aaron had a reputation for talking too much, and they naturally doubted his word. Wait and see!

Aaron was right ! The PA turnpike commission sought permission to build a 4-lane toll road across the northern end of his property, for $250. Aaron refused to sell at that price, and thought $1000 might be more reasonable. They tried to compromise for $450, but still Aaron refused and said, "that price is under the market value."

None of the farmers wanted the Turnpike gobbling up their farmland. They at least wanted a fair price for their land, so they took the situation to court. Then the farmers and the Turnpike commission each got the land appraised, and reached a peaceful agreement. The Turnpike commission ended up paying $2000 for Aarons 2 acre slice of land, but that settlement took four years.

Some of the farmers had their farm cut into two sections, making it very unhandy to farm the acreage on the other side. Aaron's remaining land was almost all on the south side of the new highway, as the road cut across his lane. The surveyors arrived first, and carefully marked the new roadway, and the actual work began in September of 1949, as bulldozers toppled trees, moved earth, and blasted rocks with dynamite.

Construction of the Turnpike brought extra activity and workers into the neighborhood. Leonard Keister and his wife, Mary, moved into the parlor, for about half a year or so. Leonard drove a four-wheel-drive willies Jeep. He explained that when the spring thaw sets in, the entire excavation area of the new Turnpike as well as the unfinished township road would be impassable for most vehicles. It was so! That is why local lodging was necessary. Mrs. Keister was a jewel and enjoyed children, or she would not have endured it all, without electric, telephone, or a bathroom, and who needs a TV with ten lively children to watch.

The Keisters had a stove to use, plus a bed and a table in the parlor, where they cooked their own food, and carried water in a bucket. They shared Aaron's outhouse. These strangers became friends and were a help to Amanda and Aaron. Mrs. Keister delighted in giving day old bread to Aarons and a few times, she took Amanda shopping. She had a way of bringing in boxes of food from Green Dragon when she found a bargain. Aaron and Amanda appreciated the rent money and spent it wisely.

Aaron made room for two Belgian horses in his barn. A worker used the big tame, highly- trained and obedient horses to move logs, and to go where the dozer could not. Their master lovingly cared for the horses.

Some neighbors said "no." to taking strangers into a home like that, but these residents compared to angels unaware, and Aarons felt richly blessed, as they struggled to make ends meet. The footprints poem might say, "It was then that I carried you."

Leonard Keister supplied Aaron's boys with inside stories about his job on the Pike. The Turnpike commission had sections contracted to different construction companies. The Lowell Hannah company worked from Black Creek Road east to Morgantown, and the C.W. Good outfit worked west of Black Creek Road. It was easy to see the difference in companies by the brand of equipment they used. Schoolboys lingered on the way

home and did not get home until dark. They were too busy watching construction, because the Turnpike cut across the path to Silver Hill School.

The deep trench they dug for the new highway, needed flares set up at night, to keep motorists from plunging into the trench. They used wick-type flares, with the wick reaching into a small kerosene pot. Aaron and the boys tended the flares for Leonard Keister. Ten-year-old Daniel helped light the flares, every evening and put them out every morning. Leonard offered to pay Aaron and his boys for that work, but Aaron was much more interested in swapping labor instead.

Just three months earlier, Aaron had hired Earl Hurst (Oregon Dairies), to remove a stone fence. When Daniel worked in the small field just northeast of the barn, he could not see the house and he thought he could get lost. It took three days to lay drain tile in part of the field, and move a heap of stones with his bulldozer. Aaron was pleased with draining the swamp and he wished for more cleared spaces. He saw the possibility of hiring Leonard Keister, after hours. They agreed! Therefore, Leonard and others arrived with three bulldozers from the Lowell Hannah company, and cleared off several more stone fences for Aaron in April.

CW Good worked to the west of Black Creek Road, and even made some money, but the Lowell Hannah Company to the east of Aarons, did not bid enough for the problems they faced. They had never worked with ironstone rocks that could not be crushed, nor blasted. They pushed the biggest boulders into the creek bed, and piled some on the east edge of Aaron's field, where they covered them with dirt. Swampland and hard to move rocks, bankrupted the company in the two-mile stretch east of Aaron, where civilization ceased to exist. They bid two and three fourths million dollars to make approximately 6-miles of the Turnpike, and that was not enough.

Workers on the Turnpike could not use the big rocks for backfill, because their rules required them to fill only 8-inch layers at a time, and packing each layer as they go, with strict government inspections. The rocks could not be crushed, because the iron ball of a ball and crane rig bounced off them.

Equipment broke even when they had good quality, some made by Letourneau. There was nothing like a backhoe, and occasionally the heavy off-road trucks rolled over. They set them up again and kept right on going. Every detail was extremely fascinating to growing boys.

The Lowell Hannah company worked on a Sunday, to make up for lost time. A cable snapped and hit dangerously close to a group of spectators, about 20 feet away. A worker said, "all you guys better get back!" The workmen did not appreciate the sarcastic comment, "that's what you get for working on a Sunday."

The turnpike crew detonated lots of dynamite, and several men died among the dangerous work. One piece of blasted rock fragment accidentally hit a box of dynamite, blowing up the entire supply, and throwing a man high. He died right there! Another worker died when he worked on the equipment and he told his friend, "Do not let the blade down!" Among all the noise, the friend just heard "Let the blade down!" and that is what he did, crushing his co-worker.

Aaron and Jesse's children walked up the lane and made some money selling lemonade, and raw chocolate- milk. All the workers quit for a break, and shut down their equipment…all sharing the same germy cup… that was before OSHA, e-coli and salmonella. The children carried the milk bucket and a dipper to fill the cup, at five cents a glass. One girl had the title of "The 1949 chocolate milk cow." When the parents heard about some dirty talk among the men, the girls did not go back.

As more trees toppled, the entire neighborhood had lots of free firewood. Some of them dragged logs home for wintertime. John Leinbach came with a wagon to haul firewood. Jesse Brubacher's D4 Caterpillar had a mounted circular saw, ideal for cutting firewood on the spot. They kept it busy!

Aaron liked to invite company after church whenever he saw someone there from a distance. Ezra Burkholder's happened to be the guests one Sunday and their boys complained about going along to these Aaron Shirks for dinner, and they do not even know them. When it was time to leave again the boys were having so much fun, they

were not quite ready to go home yet. It was not every day they had a chance to play on the unfinished Turnpike and under the bridges, through the arched tunnel, slopping in water and watching the earth moving equipment.

Titus thought the boys should come home from school earlier, because Aaron needed more help putting tobacco away. The boys took a keen interest in watching every detail of the equipment at work. They were plenty close enough and there were no restrictions against it. The arched tunnel beneath the turnpike, close to Aaron's lane was low and rounded for the small stream to pass beneath the road. The next tunnel, between Jesse and Elias had a square shape. The schoolchildren named it, "Kee Pately" [cow path], designed to let the cows to the pasture on the other side of the pike. A small stream ran through that one also, and that was the shortcut to school. The parents laid planks along the one side to keep the children's feet out of the water when the stream rose.

Merv Weaver and his brother hauled sand to the Turnpike for the workers, and then hauled back crushed rocks. With sixteen ton on a load, and three miles per gallon of gas, they used their single axle truck, equipped with three spare tires. In half a year, they had their new $8000 truck and dump trailer paid off, working hard in several shifts.

When the Turnpike opened for business, a policeman came to Silver Hill School and talked to the children saying, "You had a lot of fun playing on the road, but now you must stay off! Those big trucks might not see you" he continued, "and you could get killed! You need to help keep your little brothers off the road also or they will be dead, and you don't want that."

The children mostly obeyed those orders and the parents backed the police officer's request. But boys were boys and enjoyed action. Fascinated schoolboys noticed in detail how the drainpipes beneath the roadbed, drained the center median. Skinny boys crawled in the outer end of the drainpipe and emerged in the center median, and still kept off the road. The boys knew the size of the square space beneath that grate in the median, where two boys could lift the heavy lid. It was worth all the bother, to surprise the drivers, when two boys poked up their head, like a gopher at his hole. They could always escape quickly, but never replaced the grate and left that for the maintenance crew. Those boys had kept the orders of staying off the road and not climbing over the fence.

The Black Creek was not always a clear trickling mountain stream. It drained a large area of rugged woodland and in a downpour; the creek became an angry raging current, flooding roads and low-lying areas. William Penn named it Muddy Creek. He considered Black Creek, the south branch of the Muddy Creek.

Back in 1938 when Dan Stauffers left Aaron and Amanda, they headed for home along the Black Creek Road, driving right beside the creek, after a downpour. The water got deeper and deeper until it came up to the belly of the horse. Mrs. Stauffer grabbed the diaper bag off the floor of the carriage to save it. They made it okay but they could have been swept downstream.

When the Turnpike crew built the arches beneath the roadway, a flash flood swept away the form- boards they had removed after cementing. Yellow- pine, tongue and groove boards floated in among the trees in Aaron's woods, and the boys used some of them.

A day or two before the new highway opened to traffic, Daniel and a few other boys rode their bikes all the way to Morgantown, starting at the end of Aarons Lane. What a great bike trip! The miles were level and easy and they almost made it back before two carloads of state troopers pulled up beside them. "You are violating the law," they said. "Bicycles are not allowed on the Turnpike!" the policeman were polite and professional, as they cruised the pike ready for their new job of patrolling the road, even so, the boys felt intimidated. Backwoods boys had never met with such authority. Daniel was ever so glad he was close to home, because if they had told him to get off at Morgantown, he would not have known the way home.

After the Turnpike opened for business, some teenage boys curiously wanted to see where it went and what the new road looked like. On a Sunday afternoon, they started driving west until it was time to turn around. In western Pennsylvania, one boy said, "If the world is this big out the other way, it's really a whopper!" Farm boys seldom ventured from home.

Aaron's section of the Turnpike was finished about half a year before the road opened for business. One nice thing about the Turnpike cutting through Laurel Hill was the smooth new black-topped township road that replaced the poorly maintained single lane dirt road. The thing that was not so nice was that the children's walk to school was much longer, as they walked west on the road, and then either cut under the Turnpike, stooping through a dark spooky tunnel, or walked farther and crossed the Turnpike over the new bridge.

The road connecting to the bridge soon had a problem as the roadbed sank, due to shoddy workmanship. The workers had quickly taken a shortcut, soon after the inspectors left the scene. They conveniently deposited some troublesome larger rocks as filler, thinking no one would ever know. They were called back to the scene for repair work.

Soon after the Turnpike opened, Sarah Ann, age 10 had a frightening experience. On the way, home from school Walter and Pete were in the house already, and Daniel was nearly at the bottom of the lane, when a man from the Turnpike walked towards Sarah Ann and asked, "where is your dad?" Sarah Ann said, "I think he is in the house." The man had a yellow car parked inside the Turnpike fence and said "come with me and you can earn a quarter. Follow me!" Therefore, with her mind on the quarter, the innocent nine-year-old turned to follow, without being the least bit scared. No one had ever warned children about strangers. When the man turned around to see if she was still following, Sarah Ann saw he started to undress. Suddenly she was terrified! She turned around and started to run faster than she ever did before. The man hollered at her, but Sarah Ann kept on running even faster, and by then Daniel was coming to see what was wrong.

After she was safely at home, she could not eat at the supper table, nor tell anyone what had happened. She was embarrassed and ashamed. Not until she was fully-grown did she realize, in how much danger she had been. Thank you God, for sending a guardian angel!

After November 20, 1950, a quiet neighborhood adjusted to the droning sound of roaring engines and spinning tires on pavement. It did not take long to get used to the traffic noise. When Uncle Ben's came from Indiana and slept at Aarons, Amanda asked, "Did you sleep good last night"? They said, "Well the bed was fine, but the traffic noise was bothersome," and Aarons no longer heard the noise.

The Turnpike became part of a map for small airplanes or helicopters flying east or west. Mrs. Charlie Weaver did not like to see any airplanes fly overhead because they could crash and fall on her. She said, "They do it on purpose because they know I don't like it!" Aaron saw an increased number of helicopters flying low, and he suspiciously wondered if they were looking for iron ore in the ground on his property, perhaps using strong magnetic instruments.

Aaron asked Marstella, the Turnpike superintendent, to build a new lane for him, due to the runoff from the Turnpike construction running down the lane. Aaron was not satisfied but eventually he gave up.

Earth moving equipment and rock blasting disturbed the natural habitat of wildlife in the hills, as they fled for safety. Snakes were much more common at Aarons that summer and they kept on the lookout for copperheads. One copperhead snake in particular, took up residence in the stripping room, living there quite awhile. It jumped out at one of the Kohl boys, nearly striking him, when they worked for Aaron at tobacco cutting time.

When Amanda came to the stripping room looking for something, she cautiously looked for snakes. She happened to see one coiled up under the table, on top of the stonewall foundation, sleeping beneath the windows. She immediately went to tell the men, who came and shot it.

⁓

Aaron's single sister Eva helped pick strawberries at Jesse Brubacher's and a snake bit her. This is her story:

I was 30 years old when a young copperhead snake bit me. Jesse Brubacher's baby Reuben was almost one week old and Martha Kilmer was the hired girl. Martha was a busy 17-year-old with much canning to do, so I helped her that weekend. I took eight-year-old Annie along with me to pick the last strawberries, just before dark on a Saturday night. We were barefooted among many thistles in the patch, so I did not bother to look what hurt me. I was tired and went to bed without concerns. On Sunday morning my parents took me to Elias's where I promised to help Nancy with Sunday Dinner Company. I helped what I could although I was not feeling well, with a fever and a headache, but I did not want to tell anyone. On the way home, I examined my swollen left leg and foot. Above the ankle were three flat marks 1/4 inch apart. Mother said it couldn't have been a spider, the marks were too big. When we arrived home, I soaked it in Epsom salts and bubbles moved under the skin of my arms and legs. The swelling went down overnight, so the next day I went to the factory at Terre Hill where I worked. By Monday evening, the swelling came out over my shoe again, and I still had a headache, so I promised mother I would see a doctor.

At noon the next day, I walked from the factory to Dr. Lauria, and he said, "it's snakebite!" Since I had a fever, he gave me sulfa drugs and so forth, and told me to drink a lot and to raise my leg. Poor mother, she went to the pump often, so that the water was cooler for me to drink. She was alone with a lot of canning and chores. Menno and Titus worked for Aarons, Jesse's, Elias's, and sometimes Reuben. They also helped Dad when he needed them.

Nothing changed much until the sixth day after it happened, when my heart took big jumps and breathing was difficult. Neither mother nor I slept that night. Mother milked the cow very early that morning, and walked up the hill to John Brown's telephone, to call Dr. Lauria, and she hurried right back. The doctor scolded mother for not calling earlier.

He said he expected this could happen, but did not tell mother when he made calls that week. Dr. Lauria sent for an ambulance to take me to the St. Joseph Hospital in Lancaster. There doctor Atlee gave me a dark green capsule to swallow. Then he stood in the doorway with about half a dozen nurses, and watched to see what would happen next. After a while, he came and asked, "How is the breathing by now?" I said I could breathe better now, and then they all left. I was in the hospital three days but recovering seemed an endless task. "

Eva ended up with nerve problems and a long recovery, while Titus helped with much housework that summer.

When Daniel and Jesse's Ivan worked in the field where the binder was cutting wheat, the boys grabbed bundles as they came off the binder while opening the outside round of a field. As Daniel came running up barefooted, to grab a bundle, he stepped on something rubbery, and to his horror he saw that he had stepped on a fat, angry copperhead snake! It was writhing and twisting on the ground, mad enough to strike, but it didn't. Daniel was puzzled! Why didn't the snake bite him? Upon closer investigation, he saw that the snake had a broken back from the binder wheel running over it.

Aaron wasn't the only one in the family in ill health that winter. His own mother was hospitalized in December because of breast cancer. Soon after Eva's snakebite, Annie's [Mommy Shirk] health began to fail. She tried to keep it all to herself, but one day she showed her daughter Lydia a lump under her left breast the size of a goose egg. The roots had spread to her lungs, making her feel uncomfortable. She had a cough for some years already. Sister Lydia said she must see a doctor about it, and after Dr. Wenger examined her, he made an appointment with Dr. Atlee. On December 15, 1948, she was admitted to the St. Joseph Hospital in Lancaster where it took four hours to remove her breast and tie many blood vessels. She stayed in the hospital two weeks and tried hard to recover, to no avail.

When Mommy Shirk turned fifty nine years old, Amanda sent Daniel age 11, to take a birthday cake to his grandmother. He took it on his bicycle and got it there without a mishap. His eyes sparkled as he gave her the cake with 59 corn candies on top. His grandmother said, "Thank you"! She noticed that Daniel might have liked a piece of the cake. His birthday arrived two days before hers.

Towards fall, Annie grew worse. She couldn't eat the last eight weeks of her life and food came right back up. The last two weeks she was short of breath due to lung problems, and relatives took turns staying overnight at their home, fanning her. She said," I can't live and I can't die." The doctor had doped her towards the end. She tried hard to talk but no one understood her parting words. On the last night, Jesse Brubacher was leaving when BW shirk told him it was all over.

Aaron's mother passed away on September 10, 1949 and the funeral was on the 13th. Eli H and Sam Horning preached to over seven hundred people at Weaverland Church. Two days later, B.W. Shirk had another grandson born to his daughter Annie and Reuben Weaver, baby Enos.

B W Shirk's children could not fully realize what a good mother they had until she was gone. She helped where there was sickness for miles around, even though sometimes there was sickness in her own family at the same time. She had so much to live for yet! How could this wonderful Annie, be taken so young at age 59, when her own blind mother Annie, with serious mental problems, needed help from her children until age 79? God made no mistakes and death was final!

People seldom heard of cancer years ago. There were other illnesses maybe, like typhoid fever from bad water, or "galloping tuberculosis", but seldom cancer.

Aaron struggled with health problems and money problems. He borrowed another five hundred dollars from his single sister Eva, who worked in the garment factory. Things looked so poorly that most people guessed Eva would never get her money back. Aaron and Amanda wanted to be an asset to their community and not a liability. It was an humbling experience to sink so deep, helplessly depending on others.

∽

Peter Brubacher's sister Barbara, [Bevvy], lived single with her parents, Jacob Burkhart Brubacher and Elizabeth Martin Brubacher (notion Jecky Brubachers). She occasionally enjoyed traveling to her brothers and sisters and other relatives, and she came to stay with Aaron and Amanda for two days and three nights in February, before moving on. The way it made at Aarons that entire winter, perhaps she felt fortunate to be single.

No matter how long and hard they worked, Aaron and Amanda could not make ends meet. When they were young and dreamed about marriage, no one could have told them how many troubles and trials they would meet. When Aaron was cutting wood at the end of the lane, he hurt his back seriously and crawled to the house in pain. The ambulance came and took him to the hospital again, where he stayed five days. Meanwhile Amanda had her hands full with ten young children and the oldest one was eleven years old.

Canadian travelers arrived when Ruth was sick. Lem Kiefer took Ruth to the doctor and Daniel got the flu. Dr. Lauria came out to the farm and called it an intestinal flu. Adin Kilmer came to do Daniel's chores and carried wood for Amanda, while Daniel was getting a little better, with Aaron still in the hospital.

Eli Huber's brought Aaron home from the St. Joseph Hospital, and Aaron could see how much Amanda needed help. Daniel was sick again and all three of them went to see Dr. Lauria. Aaron went to Noah Shirk to look for a hired girl to help in the house. Later, Aaron started improving and he could help do housework. He wrote in the diary "I laid around the house and Mandie planted the patch". Eight men volunteered to help Aaron clean the stables, haul manure, and pick more stones off the fields.

If Amanda had remained single, she could have perhaps traveled and spent her own money, as Barbara did. By the grace of God and his divine help, Aaron and Amanda were given strength to endure all the hardships even if they did not know where the next dollar might come from. Each morning God thrust a new day upon them and they kept on going. Amanda said,"We had no time for pity."

On some days Amanda was so far on behind with her housework, that if any modern-day official had stepped into their house on suspicions of child neglect, they would have found enough evidence to remove all of the children and put them into safe homes. Imagine the trauma and the loss! No one could have found a better home for the children. Dr. Lauria saw their poverty, but he also understood their love for each other and for every one of their slim, almost scrawny children. Some other children in the neighborhood also grew up among flies, dirt and poverty, without modern conveniences. The kind family doctor knew that the children never went to bed hungry.

Aaron and Amanda glued together old chairs, that were falling apart and they took Martha and Pete to the dentist in new Holland to pull some teeth, because one was abscessed. [None of them went to the dentist until it hurt].Just the week before, Walter and Pete were at the dentist, and they took baby Louisa to the doctor in Terrehill, after she fell off the couch and bruised her shoulder. Ruth had a turn to be sick with a bellyache and a fever in the evening. Aaron took a turn in the house one day, while Amanda went home to her folks for a much-needed break.

Aaron spent time mending and greasing harnesses for the horses. As the snow melted, the roads became impassable with mud, due to the turnpike construction. They all stayed home until the mud dried off. They found plenty of work around home, and Daniel helped Aaron dehorn four bulls, with their dehorner.

When a stranger arrived on Aaron's porch steps, he said, "I'm from United Way. We collect money for a good cause to help the poor people...".Before he could finish his request, Aaron welcomed the man inside, and exclaimed, "How wonderful to meet you! We have ten children and I just had back surgery...." after Aaron finished his lengthy row, the stranger could not get away fast enough.

When the grass turned green and birdsong filled the air, Aaron seeded clover all by himself. The hand- crank contraption, with a bag of seeds in a sling across his shoulder was too much for him and he ended up hurting his back again, in bed with pain. He had to learn his limits.

Neighbors came to help Aaron, and to cut firewood from the Turnpike. John Leinbach came for wood and burned some brush. Eberly hauled three truckload of saw logs on shares 50/50. When summer arrived, Aaron worked more and depended heavily on 14-year-old Victor Kohl, who mowed the grass and ridged the corn, etc. The reel mower worked best for mowing lawn when the grass was short. It did not work well for taller grass, and it stalled over every little twig or chicken bone scattered around. They only mowed a small area around the house.

Amanda had many trying days and not much time to get her basic work done. With Aaron laid up, Amanda could not invite dinner guests, nor go away to visit others. She could not see her way through when things seemed to keep going worse instead of better. She had little time to enjoy the birds and flowers or even spend time sewing necessities. Amanda had to remain strong for the sake of her family. What might their children grow up to see in this life?

All are born sinners and all needed the new birth to get to heaven. Aaron and Amanda felt the huge responsibility of teaching the important things in life, far beyond the schoolbooks. With so much evil on every side, how could they succeed?

If Christ returned soon, Amanda thought, their young children would be innocent and spared from the trials and temptations of the evil that prevailed. "Lord, come quickly ", was Amanda's wish and prayer. The heaviest thing in the world is a heavy heart, and Satan's most polished tool is discouragement! If he cannot get a person to break the Ten Commandments, he has an arsenal of other tools like pride, worries, and fears about the future, but the heavenly prize is for those that remain faithful until the end. Sincerely, many prayers ascended to heaven, and they received strength for the moment, the rest was out of their reach. They were sure of the promise,"God will never leave thee nor forsake thee."

Amanda copied just one Bible verse in the front of her diary, "Many are the afflictions of the righteous, but the Lord delivereth him out of them all." Psalm 34; 19.

They lived most of the summer with only twenty- five cents to their name. The quarter lay in the desk, and someone stole it, before the summer ended. Amanda suspected a certain worker that had come to help. Life went on without handling money and they did not go hungry.

Aaron and Amanda were in the summer time of their lives… comparable to a heavy-laden fruit tree in the relentless summer sun, with drooping branches threatening to break under the increasing weight. Their kind family doctor suggested family planning and they both agreed, and used the best to no avail. Daniel and Sarah Ann, out of school, where like two sturdy props under heavily loaded branches. They were indispensable except for short stretches of time. Amanda said, 'God would not give anyone more than what He is willing to help them bear. "

∽

Jesse and Aaron, next-door neighbors, and brother-in-law's, did not always agree. They did not think alike in many ways. Jesse was better at managing and making money. He took good care of his equipment and he might even work on a baler or a mower in the wintertime, getting it ready for summer.

When he loaned a manure spreader to Aaron for a day or two, it was in good shape, but too often Aaron returned the spreader with bale strings wrapped around the beaters. In a neighborly way, Aaron should have told his boys to remove those strings, but he did not notice.

In springtime, Jesse custom plowed with his D 4 Caterpillar tractor, and a big four-bottom plow. That plowed faster than a one -row-walking plow, but he constantly hit rocks in Aaron's field, and it was not a trip plow. With a breakaway hitch, the whole plow unhitched and he backed up, dislodged the rock, and hooked up the plow again. Aaron saw how much time Jesse spent backing up and he did not think it was fair to charge four dollars per hour for all the extra time. That was frustrating for both of them, and Jesse could have said, "Well then plow your own fields", but they reached an agreement.

Aaron had many ideas off-center or eccentric from the average person and he did not keep them to himself.

When Phares Shirk worked at Jesse's, he observed Aaron and Jesse clash and said, one man was as wrong as the other. No matter how much they disagreed, they needed each other and tried to overlook the many faults. No one could afford to be enemies. When it was time for thrashing or hay-making or butchering they needed each other. The whole community worked together very much. When Jesse was busy doing custom work in later years, or when Aaron had back problems, they depended on sending their nearly grown boys to help others. Aaron and Jesse's wives, Lydia and Amanda were best friend, closest neighbors and sister in laws, with never a clash.

Aaron's children walked to Jesse's nearly every day, to get the mail out of their shared mailbox. Why Jesse ever put up with it, remains a mystery. After the mailman went, Aarons children rummaged through Jesse's business mail, and took out what they thought was theirs. The children lingered to play as much as they dared, and stayed to swing on the porch swing. They knew Amanda might be putting the baby to bed for a nap right after dinner. Occasionally, a piece of Jesse's mail showed up at Aarons, but they faithfully returned it.

The schoolchildren trudged to school together every day, and sometimes they got into trouble together. One person hit the other one with his lunchbox on the way home, and had to explain to his mother why the glass liner in his thermos shattered.

Boys played bucking bronco with pigs on a warm summer day. Their fathers were upset when two pigs died from over exhaustion. The boys all knew better and would not have done it alone. Jesse and Aaron shared the loss 50/50.

Younger girls met at the stone fence at the property line, and lingered to play. A strong windstorm had flattened patches of wheat, giving them an idea to create houses for playing pretend. Destructively, they trampled more grain, to make more pretend rooms, and they had a lot of fun, not realizing the loss. They would never do that again!

When Lydi -Jes-sey needed eggs, she sent a daughter to borrow some from Amanda. The girls lingered again at the line fence, playing in the deep soft dust before parting. They wished to make mud pies and discovered that broken eggs mixed with dust, made super mud pie dough. When Jesse's Vera came home, she had a trip to the woodshed with her father, and learned another valuable lesson.

Fattening steers helped Aaron financially, but the tobacco crop meant survival. The labor-intensive crop provided work all year. Any person willing and able to help could pitch in, including women and children. Aaron owned a steamer for several years. He learned to steam tobacco beds and drive the steam engine. He worked at getting the steamer ready for fall steaming.

He bought his first coal-fired self-propelled steam engine at Kinzer's, on January 14, 1944 for $240. Aaron slowly drove home eighteen miles on the road, arriving three days later, for a late supper at 11 o'clock in the evening. The steamer crawled so slowly, that he averaged six miles per day! Steamers were a lot of seasonal hard work when everyone needed them about the same time, to sterilize the soil.

Aaron dug a path around his two long tobacco beds, which raised the beds and kept the soil in better condition. Nothing grew in the well-travelled, hard packed soil paths.

The huge black locomotive -type steam engine had a large boiler tank in the front part. Instead of using that steam to power the wheels, they channeled that steam beneath two pans placed on the ground much like overturned huge cake pans. The workmen sterilized the soil for 20 minutes, with scalding hot steam, hotter than boiling water. Then they moved the pans to the next spot. Sometimes a hose to the pan blew apart, and the pressure would whip the hose around spraying hot steam until someone shut the spigot. It was a two-man job to move the heavy pans, so when it was time for that, the operator pulled the shrill steam whistle to signal the farmer to come and help. The whistle gave signals in other ways and it let off some excess steam. A screen over the smokestack, kept the sparks from igniting a field.

Aaron bought bituminous soft coal for a fast hot fire and he piled the coal on the ground in easy reach. The two men that worked together timed the steamer pans and shoveled the coal to keep the fire hot. The steamer blew a flue occasionally and the men had to mind their business. The tank must never run out of water!

Aaron sold his Frick steamer, to Henry Garman for $500 and bought another coal-fired self-propelled steam engine, designed as a tractor. It had a drawbar for farming, and belt- power to run a sawmill, or a thresh machine.

The steamer made runs through the neighborhood working around the clock. Aaron charged so much per pan use... less than a dollar. After completing the job, the shrill whistle screamed three long toots, to signal the next neighbor to get ready. It took some time to get everything unhooked, loaded up and slowly moved.

while Daniel slept. Sometimes Menno was in charge. When Menno and Titus ran the steamer, they were gone all week, from Monday morning until Saturday evening. BW Shirk said. "If my boys can earn $10 a day, I will do my own spring plowing," and he did, even with a walking plow. Menno and Titus kept their eyes open for food along the way, glad to stop at any small country store, while moving from one farm to the next, with the steamer.

(Eventually steaming became obsolete and they gassed the modern tobacco beds.) Aaron farmed from six to eight acres of tobacco, according to the

As Aarons back had more trouble, he did less steaming. His brother Menno or Jesse Brubacher would do it. By and by, Aaron bought a third steamer, which he pulled with a tractor. Aaron got Jesse to pull it with his crawler, and that was not profitable for Aaron, so he sold it to Jesse.

When Daniel was through school, he helped Jesse with the steaming one spring. He operated the steamer for eight to ten hours, with the help of the farmer, while Jesse slept, then Jesse took over again

help available. With a cup full of tiny tobacco seeds, a farmer might earn $2000 in one year. Aaron raised many extra plants to sell as an added income.

In early spring, Aaron poured tiny brown seeds into a quart jar, with some water. If any of the seeds spilled, they rolled across the table, bounced on a chair and rolled on the floor, lost! Aaron watched for the first white sprouts several days after soaking the seeds in the jar, He carefully measured those sprouted seeds into a sprinkling can full of water and sprayed the fine tobacco seeds across the sterilized soil, as evenly as possible. Then he covered the tobacco bed with a mulch of cotton hulls or straw to preserve the moisture. Amanda and a few children helped Aaron spread a long white cloth over the seedbeds to speed the growing process. Just before covering the beds, Amanda sowed some radish seeds along one edge for early radishes. Some people sowed ground cherries.

Aaron pumped water from the springhouse, or the creek and he watered the beds every morning to keep the soil damp. He laid pipes to the source of the water, and connected the pipes to a gas powered pump for using the garden hose.

In order not to tramp on the tobacco beds, Aaron laid a four feet wide plank, designed like a low bench or bridge, to walk across or to lean on while pulling out the many young plants. Children loved to play on these planks, but Aaron sternly said, "Get off the board!" "Get out of the tobacco beds!" You may not damage the tobacco plants!" Their livelihood depended on tobacco.

Children often helped water the tobacco beds so that the plants grew rapidly. When it was time for transplanting those seedlings to the field, Aaron leaned across the plank bridge spanning the tobacco plants and gently pulled up the biggest plants. He stacked them neatly in boxes. The plants needed all of their roots and the ground must be soggy first, therefore a child stood holding the garden house, watering the plants just ahead of Aaron with copious amounts of water. The 500-foot garden hose did not have a nozzle on the end, because a nozzle made too much pressure and damaged the plants. It worked better with a person holding his thumb on the end, for a gentler stream of water. Daniel's thumb nearly froze while holding the hose long. The spring-water felt freezing cold, even after switching hands occasionally.

June was tobacco-planting time. Early in the morning, Aaron carefully removed tobacco plants from the wet soil and he stacked them neatly into wooden crates and covered them with a wet burlap sack. He set the boxes in the shade. Those crates fit on his one row tobacco planter, pulled by a two horse- team. Every farmer needed his own planter

because when the soil was fit for planting, he could not wait. Anyone available, helped to plant tobacco. Daniel could barely handle it at the age of eight, but he tried his best.

The tobacco planter consisted of two very low seats nearly touching the ground, followed by a water tank, with a driver sitting on top of the tank. When Pete and Dick were old enough to help, they had the boring job in the heat of the summer, monotonously poking in plants, with backs aching.

As the horses pulled, the planter made a furrow, released a shot of water, and immediately packed the soil together again between two rollers. Dick and Pete, each on a separate seat, alternately took turns inserting a tobacco plant into the same row at just the right time, to have it nicely watered and firmly planted. Any skipper in the row was a loss, and they had to keep a mind on what they were doing, with barely a chance to look around. Many times another child walked behind the planter, in case a plant needed more soil around the roots where a stone interfered. It was a monotonous job on a hot summer day.

Dick could hear the birds sing at the edge of the field, and out of the corner of his eye, he saw a rabbit run away, but he sat in a cramped position nonstop, until the end of the field. As Aaron turned off the water mechanism, the horses needed nearly a minute to turn around and start the next row. Those seconds were recess time, to straighten a boy's tired back, look around and stretch his arms.

Many a time, a bored worker snatched a weed or a flower- head beside him, to break the monotony. When Dick grabbed onto a milkweed plant at the end of the row, he underestimated the strength of the stalk, but he held on tight, thinking he could pull it loose. As the tobacco planter turned around for the next row, the tough milkweed plant swung Dick's arm behind him and beneath the wheel. He sat just a few inches above the ground, and the weed pulled his thumb beneath the steel wheel of the planter, right when the wheel went over a rock.

Ouch! Dick's thumb dangled in a bloody mess, nearly severed, as he cried out in pain. Tobacco planting paused, as he went to the hospital emergency room in Ephrata. Girls filled in when needed, in tobacco planting time. They wore straw bonnets with a long ruffle down across the neck, shielding them from sunburn. When the tobacco plants and the soil were just right, it was important to keep on planting. The doctor did not know if Dick would lose his thumb or not, but with the healing power of God, Dicks thumb healed nicely and even grew a new thumbnail.

Tobacco planting did not all happen in one-day. Aaron staggered the planting time because the plants were not all ready to plant at the same time, and neither could they harvest the entire crop at one time, due to the tedious work involved. After a good soaking rain, with mud pushing up between the toes, the boys got busy transplanting fresh new plants to fill any gaps in a row, or skippers in the field where a plant died.

After planting, came the job of keeping the field weed free, for a better profit with no competition among the plants. Daniel remembered hoeing tobacco by hand, many long days and years. As the tobacco plants grew taller, Aaron and the boys worked at topping tobacco, which meant removing the center of each plant, to prevent flowering. That caused new shoots or suckers to grow out the sides of the stalk, and then the children helped sucker the plants, by removing those sprouts. Aaron wanted bigger heavier leaves!

Tobacco worms, resembled tomato hornworms and both kinds had a voracious appetite, chewing big holes in the crop. The big green squishy worms with a horn at each end, held on tight to the plants, or to the fingers. Yuck! In a serious outbreak of those Carolina sphinx moths, Aaron sometimes sprayed the caterpillars, but mostly, the children helped to gather them by hand and dropped them into a can of kerosene. Boys simply ripped the worms apart.

Any fat green tobacco worms that reached maturity, dropped to the ground. They burrowed beneath the soil and stayed there in a cocoon, until summertime warmed the soil and they hatched into a moth. Those sphinx moths often hovered around Amanda's four- o clock flowers, because the four -o'clocks freshly opened at four o'clock

and the moths came out at dusk to lay more eggs. When Aaron plowed or tilled the soil, he helped to kill the cocoons in the ground, because they could not emerge when they did not face up.

When the tobacco plants matured, the hard work started. With long handled, sharp pruning shears, the men worked strenuously, cutting the full-grown tobacco plants close to the ground, saving every leaf. Aaron said, 'Get all the leaves...cut closer to the ground!"After they cut enough plants for that day, the farmers took a break for dinner. They knew the tobacco crop handled much nicer after it wilted in the field. Aaron also had less damaged or broken leaves with limply wilted tobacco, but he did not want sunburned leaves.

Lifting the hefty plants one by one, Aaron and his strong helpers speared the plants onto a lath with a dangerously sharp spear stuck onto one end. The men worked hard in the hot sun, spearing the thick tobacco plants. If a crisp stem accidentally split wide open, they turned the tobacco plant half a round and carefully speared the plant again, farther up on the stem, so that it remained on the lath when they lifted it up. Five heavy plants filled one tobacco lath, then Aaron removed the spear from the end of his lath, and lay those five impaled plants down on the ground again, strung up together on the four-foot long skinny board, called a lath.

He bent down to pick up the next empty lath, and the next tobacco plant, stooping and bending all day long. His weak back could not take much. Aaron often went to the house for a break, even while the others toiled in his fields.

While helping with Jesse's tobacco, Aaron had the misfortune of dropping a tobacco spear on his foot. That evening, he went to see Dr. Schnader to take care of the deep cut. Two days later on a Sunday evening, he went to Dr Schnader again, then again, a few days after that. The family Dr was almost like "family"

The smallest children capable, brought water to the field to quench the thirst of the hard-working men. Leddlin tseddlah [scatter laths] was a job for school children. They changed into everyday clothes after they came home and scattered tobacco laths throughout the row among the cut off plants.

Counting by fives, they estimated where to drop the next lath. Sometimes children hung around and handed a lath to a worker, or even lifted the end of a tobacco stalk to help an aching back.

It took a man or a strong boy to lift heavy, full tobacco laths onto a wagon, especially in a good year when the plants weighed more. Horses pulled the loaded wagon into the barn, where the workers handed one lath at a time to the next fellow, up higher. He hung each lath so that both ends of the tobacco lath rested on the rails in the barn, spaced the exact width. The stalks hung upside down to dry. It took a relay of maybe six people to fill the top tier of rails in the barn. The bottom row was easier.

Hanging tobacco was a hot sweaty job, grimy with sticky tar, in the heat of August. Sweat ran into the eyes and soaked their shirts, dripping down to the person below. Most of the rails were 4-inch square beams, but the ones at the top were round, like saplings with bark on them, secured in place with grapevines. Elias could walk like a squirrel on those round rails, even if they shifted a bit. The fellow on the wagon had to look up and always got dirt in his face, but the man way up top did not. He had the privilege of shoving dirt down or spitting.

Aaron hired help at tobacco cutting time, like Josie as usual, plus Henry, Andy, and Victor Kohl from neighboring Yellow Hill. Jesse Brubacher, and Aaron's brothers, Menno, Elias and Titus often worked together. When a group of men laid their tobacco spears down to go eat lunch, they all knew which spear was their own. Aaron had an old blue-tip, made that way from the factory, with a blue tip.

Josie eagerly helped, but he preferred to keep his feet on the ground because he was afraid of heights. He inappropriately wore a necktie while standing on the tobacco wagon, handing tobacco up to Jesse. His necktie wrapped in a tobacco stalk, and when Jesse pulled the lath up to the barn rails, he said, "Joe, negsht henksht dich noch!" ("Joe, next you'll hang yourself yet!") Aaron appreciated Josie's strong back when young boys could not lift the heavy laths high enough. Anyone that dropped a lath full of tobacco damaged the leaves.

With freshly cut tobacco in the barn, Aaron kept the barn doors open for air circulation. The cupolas at the roof were put there as ventilators for

Spearing tobacco onto laths

farming tobacco. The color of the plants gradually changed from green to brown, as the leaves shriveled. Tobacco sheds had ventilator boards along the sides, to open and close for better air circulation.

Then in winter, on any damp or foggy day, Aaron came in the house with an air of importance saying, "The tobacco is damp enough to move to the cellar and we need all the help available!" Even girls helped. The dried tobacco was no longer as heavy and taking it down was much easier than lifting it up. It took a brigade of six or seven people to pass the laths from the top-most part of the barn, down into the tobacco cellar, below the barn floor. Aaron opened the trap door in the floor. Working above others like that was the only time Amanda allowed her daughters to wear blue jeans, for the simple sake of modesty. They still wore dresses over the blue jeans, because jeans were men's clothes.

It took management to move tobacco while it was soft and pliable, so that the leaves would not crumble. Sometimes the men moved brittle tobacco, but that broke valuable leaves. The tobacco cellar was dark and damp with a ground floor, and Aaron occasionally misted water from a garden hose, onto the plants hanging there, to dampen them more until they were soft. They did not remove brittle leaves from the stalks, because that would crumble the leaves.

On a winter morning, Aaron started a fire in the stove when he went to milk the cow. After breakfast, he moved some softened tobacco from the dark damp cellar, into the warm sunny stripping room. The stripping room measured sixteen by twenty feet. Several people stood in front of the long sloped table along the sunny south windows, removing [or stripping], the softened tobacco leaves from the shriveled brown stalks. When Louise stretched a tobacco leaf wide open she thought it resembled the texture of bat wings, soft and velvety with ribbed veins.

Aaron and all the other tobacco farmers knew that the undamaged bigger leaves sold as wrappers, for wrapping up cigars. Broken and smaller leaves sold for much less money as fillers and might be cut up as chew tobacco or pipe tobacco. The leaves

did not sell at the same price, and Aaron sorted the leaves into "length boxes", separating longer leaves, from shorter, shorter and shortest ones. When he had enough of one size, he used a thin long leaf, wrapping it around the stem end of the bundle as he held that bunch of leaves in his left hand, and then he tucked in the tail end of the leaf in the center of the bunch to secure the finished bundle.

With young children underfoot, Aaron sometimes made pretend dolls, with a bunch of tobacco. He added some short leaves tucked crosswise in between the middle of the bundle for the doll hands, then another long leaf to wrap around the waistline. When the children went to the house, he used those leaves in the next bale.

On the floor, In the middle of the stripping room, set a bale box. Children that came out on a winter day to play in the stripping room, enjoyed watching Aaron make a bale. A big roll of heavyweight brown wrapping paper hung at the ceiling. Aaron lined the wooden bale box with a piece of that 'tobacco paper''. He neatly stacked many bunches of tobacco in the bale-box, and then he added the heavy lid, and pressed it down tightly, cinching it tighter by pumping the attached ratchet mechanism on the one end of the bale box.

With a special long needle and a piece of baler twine, Aaron securely knotted together the tobacco bale, wrapped in brown paper. Grooves in the wooden lid on top of the bale and grooves below the bale, made tunnels for the string, to go all around the bale. After knotting the string, Aaron dismantled the ends of the box, and the remaining sides folded out to expose a finished bale. Aaron lifted the bale into the wagon and had the children move it up to the barn floor, where the bales waited on a tobacco buyer.

Competitive buyers showed up from different companies like Bayouk, and General tobacco, buying what they needed. Without a telephone, Aaron did not know what price other neighbors got. He was disgusted when he sold to a buyer and then later he was offered a better price from a different company. Sometimes one neighbor received a cent or two a pound more than another neighbor making a noticeable difference in a paycheck. They never knew if the price might go higher or lower next week.

When the tobacco check arrived, Aaron sat down and wrote checks to pay many bills. All the doctors, grocers, dentists and feed companies rejoiced over good tobacco prices. The family doctor occasionally borrowed money to keep going until the tobacco sold. They were all in it together.

Stripping tobacco was a wintertime occupation among friends singing and talking. It was not all work and most farmers took a break, midmorning and mid afternoon. With tobacco pitch on their hands, they sat down to enjoy apples or pretzels as a snack. The stripping room was also a gathering place for neighborhood discussions of all kinds, trying to solve the world's problems. Any salesman or stranger that came to a tobacco farm, knew where to find the men, always on the sunny side of the lower barn.

When Josey moved to Aaron and Amanda, he brought along an old Victrola record player. It was nearly worn out, and needed continuous cranking to play a record. That Victrola did not last too long. When Daniel went with Amanda to an auction, he longingly wished for the Victrola for sale. The auctioneer came down to $.25 to get a bid, and Daniel bought it. The clumsy, hand crank, 4-foot tall record player was outdated and obsolete. Daniel did not mind that at all, and he found help to load it on the back of the spring wagon, records included. He did not ask Amanda first, as he knew things like that were *forbidden by the church. Aaron didn't mind, and found room for it in the stripping room. With a stack of* 78-rpm records, they stripped tobacco in style. The records collected dirt and the needle was generally dull, therefore the scratched records often stuck in a groove and needed a push. Children put some small object on the record player, and cranked all they could, to watch the thing fly off with centrifugal force. Aaron and Daniel both enjoyed music and songs.

Stripping tobacco lasted most of the winter and into spring. Woodcutting was also a time-consuming job. The stripping room did not stay warm without firewood and neither did the house. Aaron and Daniel worked at cutting down trees with a two-man handsaw, and trimmed the limbs with an ax. Two horses hitched to an open wooden-wheeled wagon chassis, hauled those poles to the woodshed. With a large circular saw powered by a tractor, they buzzed it into firewood lengths, and filled the lean-to woodshed. Daniel split a lot of firewood with an ax or a sledgehammer and wedges. Elm and beech trees split so hard he wished they had stayed in the woods. No wonder, the saying, "he who splits wood, warms himself twice.

Children carried wood to Amanda's kitchen, as long as children lived there. Keeping two woodstoves filled was an endless chore. The kitchen range took constant attention, with a smaller firebox. It was no wonder those women were "keepers at home", or the fire might go out. The second stove in the next room, held much bigger pieces that sometimes lasted all night. Firewood was plentiful and coal was expensive at $20 a ton. Aaron bought some coal to use in the coldest winter weather, or when they ran low in firewood.

Winter always ended and then it was spring! With children underfoot all winter, they raced out into the sunshine, returning refreshed, dirty and happy.

The modern-day farmer never heard the hushed sound of a plow going through the ground. Daniel learned to plow when he was barely big enough to handle a single bottom, walking plow, hitched to three horses. He held the plow handles with both his hands, and guided those big strong horses with the reins strung around his back. He learned to enjoy plowing with horses, and from then on, that was his job. He had more patience than Aaron did, to plow among the rocks.

After plowing, the horses pulled a two- section spring -tooth harrow across the fields, and then a wooden drag. Daniel enjoyed riding along on that drag until he got bigger. Then it was his job to pick stones, and that was an endless task. Sometimes they used the wagon to move stones, and at other times, they used the wooden drag to move the rocks to the stone fence at the end of the field. The piles kept growing!

When it came to planting corn, Aaron borrowed Jesse Brubacher's horse-drawn two-row planter. Aaron had only one farm wagon with large wooden wheels, until he bought a modern New Idea automatic steering wagon. It came with a hayrack or sides to attach for hauling hay and wheat bundles. For hauling tobacco, Aaron fastened tobacco ladders on the front and back end of the wagon, and for ear corn, a wagon box fit onto the wagon bed.

Daniel raked hay with a dump rake, and forked it with a three-pronged long handled fork. Aaron did not have a modern barn with a hay track, ropes and pulleys for unloading hay.

Weed control took a lot of effort with a hoe, and the shovel harrow and a two-horse, one row, McCormack riding cultivator. The cultivator was a one horse, one row, walk behind operation, but a two-man job. Daniel was barely big enough to reach the cultivator peddles, but Aaron desperately needed a driver. Daniel drove the horses while Aaron worked the hoeer, and later they switched. Aaron tried to be patient with Daniel and hide all the frustration when Daniel did just about everything wrong. Daniel was not fired, and he did not give up. Later in the season, he actually learned to control the thing and enjoyed cultivating.

Farmers did not use herbicides and the weeds kept growing. Aaron cultivated his corn several times and while cultivating the knee-high corn for the last time, he sometimes scattered many turnip seeds on the ground. He simply tossed them here and there from the cultivator -seat, and the seeds yielded many fine turnips that fall.

Without a silo, farmers cut corn stalks off near the ground with a sharp corn knife when the corn was half- green yet and tied the stalks in bunches. The half-green leaves did not crumble and break as easy and Aaron needed the fodder. Aaron wanted the ear-corn and the stalks to dry down in the field. To keep those shocks standing, Daniel made a 'buck' by tying together the tops of about six or eight stalks of corn still rooted to the ground.

Then he stacked the small shocks of corn evenly around the 'buck' that anchored them. After the corn dried down enough to store in the corn crib, farmers started husking the corn by hand and tearing apart the shocks. They removed every ear of corn and tossed it on a pile. They laid the corn stalks neatly on a small pile and then tied them into

a shock with a piece of twine. Daniel helped move those fodder shocks up to the side of the barn. Every morning and every evening he fed one bundle of dried corn fodder to each horse and one to each cow. The dry corn fodder made a substitute for hay and the stalks provided bedding.

Sarah Ann grew up among four brothers. Amanda needed her in the house as an indispensable helper; therefore, Sarah Ann seldom worked outdoors. She enjoyed the chance to help her brothers husk corn and she got good at it. "Wear these gloves and this corn husking hook," Daniel said. She was left-handed and so was Walter, but none of the rest.

Aaron laid down four dried corn shocks on the ground into a square shape and said, "Now toss the shucked ears in that spot to keep them together". All the workers had calloused hands from husking corn. The fresh air outdoors increased Sarah Ann's appetite, and when she returned to the house, food never tasted so good before. She enjoyed the luxury of sitting down to eat food that others prepared.

Aaron put the twelve-inch high sides on the wagon for hauling corn. They picked up those corn piles by hand, and tossed them onto the wagon with lots of help. Old Frank and Tony, the horses, walked along obediently stopping and starting as told. With a grain scoop, the big boys emptied the wagon in a short time, by scooping the corn into the window of the corncrib. Occasionally the children unloaded the entire wagon, by tossing one ear at a time into the open corncrib window.

Aaron brought in some fresh clean ears of field corn, and stacked them in the oven for roasting for making cornmeal mush. It took days to toast them, turn them and brown them just right, while a wonderful aroma filled the room. Amanda rotated them, so none blackened at the edges. After roasting to perfection, children happily shelled field corn in the kitchen, making a mess on the floor, for a broom and the dustpan. Amanda saved all the corncobs for starting fires.

She carefully winnowed the corn on a breezy day, by dumping it from one dishpan to the other, as the wind blew away the chaff. Aaron was fond of mush and he gladly took the corn to the mill for grinding into fine cornmeal. After everyone ate from a big kettle full of fresh cooked mush on the supper table, served with milk, the leftover mush filled bread pans for breakfast. Amanda sliced the stiffened cold mush in half-inch slabs and fried it in two frying pans.

Amanda preferred her fried mush with applesauce on top, and some of them liked it with canned pears. Aaron ate his mush with puddins [meat scraps from the cooked bones], eggs, or molasses on top. Amanda did not skimp on making enough mush, the cheapest food around. She pushed the leftover fried mush to the back end of the stove, where it stayed warm for the first person saying, "Mom I am hungry". The crunchy salty pieces compared to corn chips and were fit for a king.

Daniel worked hard, forking manure by hand when he was barely big enough. Aaron hitched a horse to the "misht-shlidda", or manure sled, brought it into the stable, filled it with manure, and then hauled it to the field spreading it with a fork. Most of the time, he used a wheelbarrow to pile it in the barnyard and forked it again later. Moving manure made for a lot of heavy work, needing plenty of sweat or elbow grease, and calloused hands, and blisters. Cleaning out a straw -bedded pen was not too bad, but cleaning out where long cornstalks tangled together, created a challenge. It was one tough tangled stringy mess and took management skills just to figure out how to tear- up one more forkful.

Jesse Brubacher owned a manure spreader and Aaron liked to borrow that. Aaron owned a de-horner and a pipe threader, which he swapped for tools he did not have. Aaron owned the butcher tools that the neighborhood used as one big family.

Most people butchered in winter so that the meat cooled properly, and the flies were dormant. Any time Aaron wanted to butcher, he started by cutting an abundance of firewood, because butchering required heat. Aaron fired up the butcher furnace, early in the morning, to heat the water for scalding the hogs. Titus shot the hogs or beef, because Aaron dreaded that job. He was not good with a gun, and one time when he shot a pig, it escaped, spraying blood all over Amanda's laundry

on the wash-line. Titus laughed so hard, he could hardly tell the story of the rodeo that followed. The ruckus resembled the fourth of July and a rodeo all in one, except Aaron and Amanda were both upset!

After killing and scalding several hogs, Aaron and Titus worked at scraping off the hair. They connected a "shill -shite" or singletree to the hogs back legs. Then with a rope and a pulley, they raised the hog to hang along the front edge of the fore bay of the barn. After removing the insides, and the head, the meat hung awhile to cool thoroughly.

Aaron's belt driven " Fairbanks Morse" flywheel engine powered the meat grinder. They stuffed baloney and sausages with a hand crank lard press. Daniel was too small to help, no matter how much he wanted to, and he heard Aaron say," Be careful with that knife, and don't cut your fingers...keep your hands out of the meat grinder, it could grind your hand... and don't get near the grinder belt... keep away from the hot lard...do not touch that gun... and keep your fingers out of the baloney meat. Ous vaag!Ga vek! (Get out of the way! Go away!")

Aaron had reasons for telling children to stay back. When Daniel was two years old, he already tried so hard to help. After rendering the pig fat, Aaron and Amanda put the hot lard into cans and set it aside to cool with the lids set loosely on top. Daniel wanted to put the lids on properly. He plunged his hand into the hot lard and burned it badly. Dr. Schnader came to the farm and bandaged the burned hand, making several follow-up calls, to dress the wound. Even so, butchering was one of the highlights of the year.

Meat never tasted any better than fresh from the butcher kettle, and the [greevah], warm cracklings left over from the lard press, made a delicious snack. Menno and Titus appreciated the saltshaker in the stripping room and nearly ate themselves sick with fresh meat. Sarah Ann remembered sewing long bags to fill with baloney, and she enjoyed watching the freshly ground squishy meat ooze into those baloney sacks. Her part of the busy day was to keep the toddlers out of the way. Liver was among the first parts of an animal eaten fresh on butchering day, and the"neeah-ly", or kidney, despite the fact of what it was and where and why. Aaron enjoyed eating the brains, fried in butter. Amanda served them just right, but most of the children "knew, before tasting them," that they couldn't be good!

Amanda worked to keep one step ahead in managing which meat gets ground up and which gets cubed. It was also Amanda's job to scrub all the greasy butcher tools and the grinder, before someone else in the neighborhood needed them. All the leftovers, the hide and scraps went to Sam Schaeffer, [duh shinnehonnis], the scavenger behind TerreHill. He paid for the scraps, or traded them for homemade soap. Amanda chose the soap, saving her a lot of extra work.

All the extreme amount of hard work that Amanda put into canning meat for her family, paid well at the other end. She had all her meat supply ready to heat and serve. Only chicken and fish were available raw during summertime. Fresh pork and beef was a rare treat!

Amanda knew the basics about home butchering, because her parents did the same thing and so did Aaron's parents. In Michigan Amanda helped clean the small intestines of the pig, so they could use those casings to make sausage. The intestines come in three layers. They saved the clean center layer and discarded the inner and outer layers. Aaron preferred to buy the ready cleaned casings.

Amanda's father in Michigan packed some fresh meat in the snow beneath a metal tub. He carefully placed a chunk of wood on top to keep it there. The weather stayed cold and the meat kept well that way quite a while. In Pennsylvania, the snow did not last long enough for Aaron and Amanda to try that.

Amanda remembered how her mother saved every last scrap and so did she. They cooked the bones to remove the last bits of meat and ground up the scrap meat to make puddins. She added salt and pepper and then poured the ground –up meat and broth into a crock and added a layer of melted lard. After the lard hardened and the broth jelled, her mother turned the crock upside down. The meat kept that way a long time in a cool place, without canning it.

Starting at a young age, Daniel worked long hours, days and years helping Aaron.

11

BW's Wedding

BW Shirk missed his wife more than words could tell. He had a family auction to dispose of his former wife's processions, so that his children could use their mother's belongings for happy memories. Sam Shirk, his son, and Jesse Brubacher, his son-in-law, auctioneered the best they could. The children bought their mothers house wares with memories to treasure. BW Shirk evenly distributed the proceeds from the sale among his nine children. Some of them did not buy many possessions, because they preferred more money. Aaron and Amanda bought many different lots. Quite a few of the things they bought cost ten cents or less. They paid three dollars for one of the high chairs that inventor Joe Shirk made for his twins. Aaron and Amanda used it hard for their five youngest children.

BW bought a Dawdy house, and his son Menno moved on to the home farm. Since he could not move into his new residence until springtime, BW Shirk lived with Jesse Brubachers and at Menno's that winter. Lydi-Jes-sey noticed that her father was homesick for his first wife. He chewed a lot of chewing gum. Anna Kilmer worked as a housekeeper for other people. When she helped at Jesse Brubacher's, Lydi-Jes-sey observed the beginning of a romance between her father and Anna. One time BW Shirk complained about Jesse girls having too much hair in the sink drain. When Lydi-Jes-sey told him, it was Anna's hair in the drain; her father did not have a problem with it.

When BW Shirk proposed to Anna, she thought that he is plenty old. He was nearly 60 years old and she was 42, only four and one half years older than his oldest son, Aaron Shirk was. BW wanted to marry before he turned 60 or next he is too old!

On June 10, 1950, Aaron's father, Benjamin Weaver Shirk married Anna Kilmer, daughter of Isaac and Katie Kilmer. She was the single sister of Martin and Christian Kilmer, and grew up in Michigan. On a Sunday morning, they married in the anteroom of Bowmansville church, before the regular church service started. Besides the bishop and ministers, only Benjamin's children and their spouses were present to witness the marriage. Benjamin's son Benjamin, from Indiana and his wife Grace served as attendants. Jesse Brubachers had the wedding dinner for her father, at their home, with quite a few guests present. The newlyweds took a short wedding trip to Virginia with Sam Horning as the driver. BW Shirk and his new bride moved into a small house, just up the road from the home farm.

BW Shirk's first wife Annie sat on the edge of her chair at the table, ready to jump up and serve! She moved quickly. When you want something done, you ask a busy person. Annie was a person like that. The busiest women anywhere were those that had children at home and cared for aging parents at the same time that they reached out to help their married children with challenging days. Annie had worked hard like that, and Anna noticed. She wanted B W Shirk to promise that if they marry, she is not required to fill in and help his married children as his first wife did. [She never knew how much she missed in life.]

The second wife, Anna, moved much slower, and seldom hurried. She had remained single over forty years, and when Dawdy wanted her to hurry, she panicked and froze in her tracks, and stared at him. They both made adjustments, and really did not need to hurry.

With Aaron's inheritance money, Aaron and Amanda went to ABC Groff's hardware store in New Holland and bought a new kerosene refrigerator, for $316, and a new white Colombian kitchen range for $145. Sarah Ann remembered that thrilling summer day when a truck unloaded a brand-new shiny white refrigerator. She was simply proud of it! Words could not express the marvelous thrill! Now they were really getting modern, and she graduated from carrying baby bottles to and from the springhouse.

Aaron and Amanda did not plan a spot in their new kitchen for a refrigerator. The huge new appliance did not fit in very well. Each wall had a door in the middle and three sides had windows. The big kitchen range hogged the north side, and they did not want to cover a door or a window with the grand new appliance. The refrigerator crowded the kitchen and Amanda had to stretch her extension table across the corner every time she opened it wide after that.

On August 27, 1950, another new daughter joined the family around midnight. This time Louisa at age one, picked a name out of a hat, and it was Irene. Amanda remembered a kind hearted, good-natured lady, named Irene that lived with Evanses in Brutus, Michigan, where she had worked.

Mary, age two, like all the rest, loved her new baby sister and could not let her hands off. When Amanda turned her back, Mary had baby Irene lying on the big bed, partly undressed and she gave her a baby oil treatment! Irene was not crying, and Amanda could not figure out how Mary had managed to get the baby out of the baby coach and onto the bed by herself. The Johnson's baby oil perfumed baby Irene, the bedroom and Mary.

Mary sat with Aaron on the men's half of the church-house. While he dozed off, the two-year old started undressing. First, she removed her shoes and stockings, and then she untied and removed her covering. Amanda's sister Betsy watched from the women's side of the room, wondering where Mary would stop. She could not reach little Mary near the center of the church, without a major distraction and a big show. Thankfully, that is all the further Mary went in undressing. She could not

open the buttons down the back of her dress and did not try to remove her underwear.

People came to visit Aarons after each new baby. Aaron enjoyed the social gathering of neighbors and friends. He welcomed the families heartily, and led the men into the parlor, for an afternoon of talking and smoking where he proudly handed out cigars, as many other new fathers did. Cigar smoke swirled in blue grey clouds, polluting the air, unaware of any harm in smoke.

Amanda entertained the women in the next room, beside the rocking chair. Ladies enjoyed the usual chatter of children, gardens and housekeeping in general. Most people brought a brown paper bag containing a baby gift. When Elias Shirks came in the lane, a brown paper bag set on top of the carriage roof, temporarily put there. It stayed for the two-mile drive, and they forgot about it, until Aaron commented on the bag. It was a gift for the new baby.

Many of the people gave Amanda a nice piece of useful flannel or print material, knowing she liked to sew. Every little gift meant a lot, like blankets, baby bibs, booties, stockings, nightgowns, straw bonnets, homemade felt shoes, washcloths, beads and baby rattles.

Martin Kilmers brought a pair of yellow rubber pants, [gum Huss, in Dutch]. The plain yellow rubber pants had three metal snaps down each side and Amanda opened them to change the diaper. The rubber pants had little yellow ribbons fastened at the front of each leg, and became the envy of sisters that squabbled for a turn to hold a baby dressed like that.

When Aaron and Amanda had twins, the baby gifts doubled. Dr. Schnader gave two baby books, when Amanda had very little time to write in them, but she did anyway. None of the other children had any baby books. Clayte Martins gave two homemade baby caps made with beautiful satin material, almost too fancy to wear. They saved them for Sunday best only, and the twins soon out grew them. Frank Martin made each twin a wooden rocking chair, which they used a lot and kept as keepsakes. Some people gave $.25 or even $.50. Aunt Eva gave a dollar for the twins. Aunt Lydia enjoyed making matching dresses for two little girls.

When company came for baby Louisa, Aaron had been in the hospital, and people gave more money that time, because they saw the great need. Baby number ten was the first one to wear rubber pants, and Amanda considered them uncomfortable, using them only for church.

When stockings wore thin, sometimes two worn-out stockings made a double layer for one leg, with a mismatched stocking on the other leg. This was a common way of totally wearing out stockings, but it was a stingy gift. Amanda said thank you just the same.

Amanda treasured baby gifts and stored them in a box under the crib, and showed them to the company, saying who gave what, until she memorized every item. "The material for that dress came from Jesse's and this piece came from Mennos," said Amanda. The gifts did not all go in the box under the crib, because they ate the food, and spent the money.

John Leinbachs brought a shoebox full of big soft fresh molasses cookies, and that was a thoughtful gift for a big family. The cookies did not last long, and Sarah Ann happily saved some for packing lunchboxes the next morning.

Mary wrote: "I still remember mom sitting in front of the kitchen range to bath a baby. She opened the oven door to set her washbasin there beside the clean baby clothes, warming everything from the heat of the oven. I know what that bar of Ivory baby soap looked and smelled like, also that Johnson's baby oil and the powder she used. The new baby wore a belly-band, or belly –binder tied on with the strings attached for that purpose, [or fastened with several little yellow safety pins]. Then a long- sleeved undershirt pinned to the diaper, to keep it from sliding up, and a kimono topped with a homemade flannel "sackly" [saque] on top, like a sweater. A baby cap prevented earache and a second diaper substituted for rubber pants. Mom warmed up a diaper and folded it up around the baby 's feet instead of wearing socks, and then wrapped the baby into blankets. A safety pin or two secured the blankets so a child could hold the bundle without unraveling everything.

Tending babies got stale, except for Sundays, when Amanda dressed the babies up and sisters nearly fought to hold them because they had to take turns.

Once a week on a Saturday evening, everyone took a bath, necessary or not! The galvanized wash- tub from the basement, sat beside the kitchen range, for warmth and because nobody wanted to carry the water far from the teakettle on the stove. The youngest children bathed first, and the water was grimy long before the oldest ones had a turn. However, they all used the same water, just adding a bit more hot water as needed. That same dirty towel was saturated, but the children all survived. Amanda worked hard getting ready for Sunday, like doing two days of work in one. After a busy day, she took her bath, scooped out the dirty water, and moved the tub to the basement. Amanda was ready for a good night's sleep.

∞

Preparing food for Sunday and having clothes ready for everyone, took a lot of management on her part. She did not rest when she served a big meal to invited guests, and yet it refreshed her spiritually. Aaron and Amanda both enjoyed hosting company and visiting others.

Aaron shaved once a week, every Sunday morning, using a straight razor honed on a leather strap. He had a cake of soap in a shaving mug, and added some water, brushing up lather, and then he used his soft shaving brush to apply the lather to his face. He was skilled with a straight razor, but it was common for him to nick his skin just a little bit, with a sharp blade.

Amanda packed a Sunday church bag on Saturday evening. Sarah Ann or the younger ones sometimes strung up Cheerios on a string and knotted the ends together, creating chewable beads. The Cheerios were quiet entertainment at church, and kept the baby from getting hungry.

On Sunday mornings, Amanda rose early and worked hard, even on a day of rest. Aaron did not want to be late for church, and the girls must be freshly combed. Someone needed to strain the milk, and clear the table. It all worked well, when children got up the first time Amanda called, but sometimes they stayed lying in bed too long.

The girls all wore coverings to church, beginning at the age of two. Amanda wore black covering strings, teenagers had white strings, and the youngest girls wore pastel colored covering strings or ribbons. The color-coded strings for the younger girls helped decide which covering belonged to which girl.

Occasionally girls wore short- sleeved dresses for summer at home, just for everyday, but Amanda considered it indecent to have elbows exposed at church. She never wore short sleeves on herself, nor made any short -sleeved dresses, not even for a baby, and she made many hundreds of dresses.

With all the work she did on a Sunday, getting her family ready for church, it was most practical to let some children at home, because the carriage did not hold them all.

To save time, Amanda occasionally combed some little girls the night before, and they wore old coverings to keep the hair nice overnight. On Sunday morning, it took less time braiding hair. As soon as breakfast was over and the young children were dressed for church, they gathered one by one in the carriage, tied at the maple tree. Amanda hoped the first ones stayed clean until the last ones were ready.

Someone in church asked Amanda, "How do you get around so early with getting all those little children ready?" Amanda said, "That's easy. We just go before we are ready!" It was true! Aaron wanted promptness and Amanda left home many times before she was 'ready'. When Aaron waited at the end of the walk with some children, he said, "See, Mom turned around again for something. When she comes out the walk for the third time, then she is ready."

Sarah Ann remembered Aaron and Amanda on the front seat of the carriage with younger children packed around them. The backseat was crowded also, and with only small "peephole" windows, one on each side of the carriage. Just one person could look out at a time. Sarah Ann sat in the back and when anything fascinating appeared beside the road, everyone wanted to see it at the same time, with squabbling and pushing, quick before the truck was out of sight.

When Aaron lit a cigar, while driving the carriage, no one could escape the smell of the smoke. The best spot in the carriage, was sitting or kneeling at Aaron and Amanda's feet, and looking out. The sights, sounds and smells were hard to beat. "Who lives there"? "What flowers do I smell, and why? A child could reach out and touch the horse's tail as it swished, and sometimes smelled the smell of fresh horse manure, as it plopped on the road.

Summertime in the carriage was much more pleasant when Aaron rolled up the back curtain, and everyone could see out better. Sarah Ann had to keep an eye on the little ones, that might lean over the backseat and fall out, but no one ever did.

In wintertime, some people drove with the storm- front window closed on the carriage, but Aaron did not like that. He just did not feel safe with the harness lines strung through the small holes of the storm front. Everyone needed to dress warmer, to keep from freezing. Scratchy wool army blankets, leftovers from World War II, were' buggy blankets', used by people and for covering horses at church, while the horses stood at the hitching posts several hours.

Aaron stopped the horse and carriage in front of the church to let off Amanda and the girls, before he tied old Frank at the hitching post. Men and boys walked around the church to the door where the men entered, while Amanda walked into the women's door. She gathered her girl's bonnets and stacked them on a neat pile on the shelf. She bundled all the younger children's sweaters and coats into her shawl, making them easier to find again after services.

Some of the children did not understand the services in German, but with enough Dutch mixed in they could grasp most of it. It was also hard to follow along in the German songbooks. Aaron and Amanda learned a lot of German, when they were young, but their children did not.

After the services, a stranger asked, "Who was that grouchy woman in church this morning?""Oh, that one! You mean Betsy Kilmer. Looks are deceiving, and she is the jolliest person around "was the reply. "It is just that the corners of her mouth turn down, and so does her sisters', Amanda's, and Mary's"

Aaron was in no hurry to leave when church was over, and Amanda was aware of that, as they both lingered talking with friends, unless they hurried home to get dinner on the table for company.

On the way home, Frank struggled with a load of passengers in the carriage, coming up Raymond Witwer's hill. With compassion for his horse, Aaron got out of the carriage and walked up the steep hill while holding the reins, and then he hopped in again for the last mile home. He did that for most steep hills.

In 1953, after Daniel was out of school; Aaron bought a single seat, two passenger, top-buggy from his brother Titus for $150. Daniel drove to church and took several children along, but some still had to stay at home with no room for them all, unless some of the older children biked.

Amanda sometimes enjoyed the luxury of a nap on a Sunday afternoon, unless they had other plans. She sometimes wrote a letter to a sister. Letters were the only form of communication she had with her sister in Indiana. At the end of each month, Amanda used the spent calendar page as stationary. Her tablet in the desk disappeared rapidly with many people wanting a piece of paper. She wrote in tiny writing and sometimes along the narrow margins when adding one more thought. She had no photos to share, no matter how much the sisters wished to see each other's children. Nearly every letter they sent, included several scraps of fabric, of whatever they sewed lately. Most women enjoyed the latest fabrics, or any fabric.

Aaron's younger sister Annie helped a lot at Aaron Shirks. Sometimes Christian Kilmer's Katie was there helping at the same time. Katie and Sarah Ann were younger and watched their chance to sneak out of work, by hiding in the outhouse, until Annie did the dishes. Annie jokingly called Sarah Ann and Katie, the "privy girls". Both of them did heaps of dishes while the rest went outdoors.

In October, Amanda helped chase cows along the edge of the stone fence. She broke out in poison ivy, so badly on her arms and face that she was

hardly fit to tend the baby. Dr. Lauria said, 'Do not slop in water more than necessary, and try to keep your hands dry."That was hard! He gave her salve to use, and she bandaged the worst part.

In Michigan Amanda did not get poison ivy. Then in Pennsylvania the first time she got it, was in cherry picking season. Aaron had spilled half a bucket of cherries on the line fence and Amanda tried to pick up most of the big dark cherries among the briars. She scratched her arms and perhaps that had something to do with it. She broke out in a serious case of poison ivy, enough to keep her awake at night. Later she became immune to poison ivy again.

Aaron's brother Menno married Martha Kilmer on December 7, 1950, daughter of Clayton Kilmer's from Michigan. She was born in Michigan, but she was only two years old, when her parents moved to Pennsylvania. Menno's newly married stepmother, married half a year earlier, was Martha's aunt. Eighty guests attended Menno's wedding including Aaron and Amanda, along with Daniel, Sarah Ann and baby Irene, in December 1950.

Baby Wesley arrived on November 4, 1951, the 12th child for Aaron and Amanda. He was named after Peter Brubacher's brother Wesley. After six girls in a row, Aaron and Amanda were pleased with another son. Menno and Martha kept one-year-old Irene awhile to help Amanda. They brought her back, before their own first-born baby David arrived.

> The best prevention for poison ivy is to eat a piece of a young green leaf in a sandwich or otherwise. One small piece, the size of a thumbnail can boost the immunity for a year or longer. If it does not work, try another leaf! For any person highly sensitive, it might be best to swallow the leaf in an empty capsule so the allergy does not swell the throat. This only works as a prevention and not a cure for a rash. Research is available on the internet. Try it at your own risk. The author and the printer are not responsible in case of problems.

Baby Wesley was just a few weeks old, when Aaron's youngest brother Titus, married Katie Leinbach, daughter of Clement Leinbach. Titus farmed the place on Pleasant Valley Road, which BW Shirk had bought for Reuben and Annie Weaver, and they did not want it. Therefore, Titus took it and lived there before he was married, and his single sister Eva, was a temporary housekeeper, until Titus and Katie's wedding on December 31, 1951.

When summer vacation arrived in 1952, Daniel said goodbye to school years. He was through eighth grade and quitting. Aaron needed him on the farm. For the first time in his life, Daniel went along to see the town of Ephrata, 14 miles away. On a warm summer evening, Aaron hired a driver to take him to Dr. Kaiser, a chiropractor, and Daniel went along. It was thrilling to see Ephrata, and even more exciting, to watch the train rumble through the town.

Daniel also got a chance to see Reading. Amanda and Sarah Ann wore glasses and regularly went to Dr. Rogers in Reading. This turned into a shopping trip, and searching the Reading mission for bargains. Daniel was thrilled to be eligible to go along on a coveted trip to Reading, until he discovered he was the "pack animal" for lugging parcels.

Ruth remembers: "from 1952 to 1960, I had to change lenses in my eyeglasses every six months for all eight school years. We would get up early and go to the square in Bowmansville to the center of town. There we would ask the old German grocer, Helmuth Spieler, who spoke German and some broken English, to park our carriage in the enclosed shed for the day, and we asked him to feed the horses the ear corn that we had packed in the carriage box. Then we stood beside the road at the square, waiting for a bus. Many times, it was just the three of us, my parents and me.

It was exciting to ride the bus, smell the exhaust and to hear the brakes. They took us to a depot, and from there we walked and walked all day. We went in big stores and bought many bargains, like gifts for Canadian travelers or gifts for Christmas gift exchange and glass dishes. At noon, we would get a nine-cent ice cream sandwich at Kresge's store. While we waited, they made the ice cream sandwich, by putting a thick slice of chocolate, vanilla, and strawberry ice cream between two flat wafers held in a big napkin.

The rescue mission was the highlight, looking for things like skates, coats etc. The man made our purchase on a pile on the floor, and estimated the bill, using us very well. Dad's back was usually over done on those days, as he carried our homemade cloth shopping bags heavily loaded. The last stretch to the bus was a drag, and we were careful not to miss the bus, or we had to wait for the next one. I remember Mom and Dad, all exhausted, sitting among lots of bags at the depot, ready to go home. Then we had to get it all into the buggy and head for home, where the rest were anxious to see what we got. Those who best fitted the nicest things, were overjoyed"

∾

Silver hill School was a big brown sandstone building and just behind the schoolhouse, a small creek flowed through a patch of woods. As the students arrived, they set drinks and glass jars of dessert into the clear creek to keep it cold until noon. Waist high, the children tied strings around the trees to mark off squares for their houses, and swept away the leaves to have a clean floor, and pretend housekeeping. They played baseball on a small diamond, with no room for a big one. A dandy hill sloped down behind the school for sledding in winter. The big coal stove warmed the school and turned out the best-baked potatoes you ever tasted. Initials on the potatoes proved who owned them, when it was time to eat. Salt and butter came along from home in the lunchboxes. Blanche Horning, the teacher, had a sandwich toaster to make cheese sandwiches, etc. She paid the older boys a penny a day to carry coal in from the coal shed, which they willingly did, because it meant going out during class sometimes.

Blanche Horning was an ideal teacher, but when Dick entered first grade, Mr. Coates taught school, and Dick did not learn much. The next year, when Ruth and Rhoda started in first grade Mr. Coates taught a second term, and he was not a dependable teacher. He hitchhiked to school from Pottstown, where he went for the weekends, often arriving late at school on Monday morning. He camped on the school grounds all week in a box from an old truck, setting at the edge of the woods, which he used as a camper. Mr. Coates told the big boys to cut small cedar trees and branches, to hide his camper from others, when it was school meeting time.

Mr. Coates did not teach the way he should have, and the students did not learn much. Occasionally, he put the upper grade girls in charge, while he went to the nearby neighbors, the Stamms, watching TV. Students found food missing from their lunch boxes, and once a student caught the teacher in the act of taking the food. Sometimes, when the Stamm s left their home, he ate out of their refrigerator. His socks did not always match, not even closely.

When Mr. Coates came late on a Monday morning, school started without him. Emma Huber and Anna Kulp, the eighth grade girls, were in charge until the teacher came. Emma skipped some grades because of her higher IQ, and she was smarter than the teacher was. Walter learned more from her than he did from the teacher, when Mr. Coates taught school.

Dick had Mr. Coates for first and second grades and he did not learn to read. People laughed at Dick for mixing Dutch and English words together and he did not like school. He had to stay in at recess one minute, for each mistake and he lost a lot of recess.

Mr. Coates enjoyed taking all the schoolchildren to the Stamms, where they sat down on the carpeted living room floor watching TV for President Eisenhower's inauguration. That was a new experience for most of the Mennonite children, watching television and hearing the Star-Spangled Banner.

When plans to consolidate all the little one-room schools into one big new school, met opposition, The public school officials purposely put poor teachers in the little one-room schools to help convince the parents that it's time to make changes.

At this point, people all over the neighborhood were encouraged to come and vote about consolidating the school system, and Aaron did. The next day Amanda wrote in her diary "we lost", and Silver Hill would be closing! Some of the plain people

Blanche Horning taught Silver Hill School

did not vote and insisted on separating church and state… don't get involved but sincerely pray about it. Mennonite women did not vote, and therefore the opposition had two votes against each big family with one vote. No matter who voted which way, small schools were closing all over America, and not just in Lancaster County, Pennsylvania.

Many young men went overseas during World War II, and those that remained in America did not wish for bigger families while supplies were rationed and horror stories abounded about what all was happening or could happen. Those that returned after the war had a desire for the better things in life such as family life, and children. That is when the baby boom started, and when those children were ready for school, there were not enough schools to go around.

Why not consolidate all the small schools and build a big new school system? Public education got a big push with the government helping build schools and furnishing big yellow school buses. It would be much better for children without the distraction of eight grades in one room, and just think how nice the teacher would have it, giving all her time to her one class all day, every day. The children would learn much more than those pushed back waiting on a turn for their class. (So they said!) The biggest obstacle of closing all the existing one-room schools was convincing the parents.

Silver Hill School was running smoothly, with Blanche Horning willing to go the second mile for her students. She even took time to make a call at each home over summertime, to better know her students and her school parents. Her fine Christian personality won full support from the whole neighborhood, so why would anyone want to close a school like that?

Aaron and Amanda's children had many fond memories of Silver Hill School. The annual Christmas gift exchange rated highly. Martha could hardly believe how Lena Shirk crammed so much into one small package. A pair of doll shoes and a ball just for her! Lena knew her cousins well and that is probably what she wanted for herself. Dick did not fare as well, and he returned home dejected. Bobby Kohl had his name and gave Dick a red,

six inch long, molded metal racing car. He had no use for such a toy and really wished for the nice color book and new Crayola crayons that he gave away. He would not get another wrapped package for a whole year and he had his hopes set high for this gift, a long time in advance. If any of Aaron and Amanda's children received jewelry, Amanda bought them a better gift.

Ruth remembers: "in my early childhood, I was not fond of being away from home. I cried in first grade, even if I shared a double seat with Rhoda and had four brothers and two sisters in the same room. I told mom my belly hurt, and blamed it on the applesauce in my lunch. We were taught to think of ourselves as less than others. In school when we played "20 questions" and my brother had his hand up, I didn't think I should pick his name, because our family should wait for last."

"At Christmas time, the bigger boys cut and dragged in a freshly cut evergreen tree from the woods just behind the schoolhouse. Students exchanged names and gave gift-wrapped packages for Christmas. One year at Easter, Silver Hill had a big egg hunt outside and that was fancy. The teacher allowed trading food in lunches, so therefore, jelly sandwiches made with crumbly dry homemade bread, were traded for bought bread with bought bologna. Every now and then, Aaron came to school in the carriage, during a heavy rainstorm, to get the children, at three o'clock, but mostly we walked. The teacher asked the big boys whose team of horses arrived, and then allowed each family to leave as the parents came to get them."

About once a month, John Smith came to Silver Hill School to teach Bible verses. Learning memory verses became a game, and the students enjoyed the break in routine. Pretty cutout shapes, like a lamb or flowers, had a memory verse printed on it. They set an easel up front with colorful flannel-graph pictures. Boys against girls tried to see who could learn the most verses, and the winners win a new baseball! Those boys tried hard enough, but the girls won. When John Smith returned to school, he said, "The girls usually win." I can see you boys are a pretty good bunch and I happen to have two balls along today so you may have one also. 'With grins of gratitude, two new baseballs in one day made Silver Hill the richest school of all! The Gideons came once a year and gave a New

Testament to each child in fifth grade.

Lem Kiefer put up with the whole neighborhood using his telephone as needed. His door was never locked and nobody else's was either. Someone painted "Wilkie" on Lem Kiefer's barn doors. He was. Sometimes picked on, and so was his nice daughter Shirley. Being influenced by local political opinions, Walter and Emma Huber threw stones at the word "Wilkie" and got caught in the act. When Lem Kiefer complained to the teacher at Silver Hill school, Blanche Horning got her two guilty students to write lines 100 times. "I won't throw stones anymore." The teacher only allowed recess time to write those lines. After several recesses, Emma was way ahead of Walter because he was left-handed and Emma could write much faster. She said, "You don't have to write nice, "Shripe shtarik" (write fast). Blanche had pity, and said, "You won't throw rocks any more will you? Walter and Emma said, "No I won't!" "Well then you are dismissed," said Blanche, "you better go out to play". Walter and Emma knew without a doubt, that Blanche was the greatest teacher anyone could wish for. She was kind and motherly and it was no wonder all her students adored her.

Sadly, Silver Hill School closed for always, and Brecknock opened in September 1954. The children had a lot of fun at the new school after some hard adjustments. They formed new friendships and had some good teachers. The changes were subtle, like skipping memory verses as unnecessary. The new teachers replaced the Christian hymns Blanche taught, with patriotic songs. The atmosphere was colder, more military style, than family-style. It used to be, that everyone knew who you were and where you lived.

On the first day of school, instead of walking two miles to the one-room school, a bus came to the end of the lane where Raymond Witwer picked up Aaron's children. The school was brand-new, so were the desks, the books, the friends and the big yellow bus. If best friends were not in the same grade, they barely saw each other.

Some of the schoolchildren talked about what they saw on TV, the latest invention! In small ways, TV influenced their mannerisms. Some of the new teachers wore V-neck blouses that exposed a "valley" in the bust line, anytime they leaned forward to help a child. That was shockingly indecent to children taught modesty, and it was so shameful that some children had a hard time keeping their mind on what the teacher said.

Not many plain people attended this new school, because they preferred their own parochial school. They wanted more Bible verses, less silly songs, and no TV influence from the other students. They also opposed the Pledge of Allegiance to the flag. They did not want to worship a flag or a country, when all their allegiance belonged to God. A group of Mennonite farmers worked hard to build a school, and find a teacher. It cost them more because they had to finance two schools, theirs and the big new elementary school. Money was not the important issue, but the children's futures were. The overall grade averages in the big new school did not improve in reading, writing and arithmetic. The older children no longer helped the younger ones.

Aaron and Amanda both had public-school educations, with Santa Claus and the Easter Bunny included. It was easy for them to overlook such childish traditions, and Amanda wanted her children to learn proper English. She did not know if a local teacher with an eighth, grade education could handle all that. Since Aarons lived further away from the parochial school than all the others did, Aaron agreed, "Let's wait and see how this new school turns out".

Laws stated that any child absent three consecutive days needed a doctor's signature on an excuse card explaining the reason why. In Amanda's childhood, school was a glorious privilege and Amanda seldom missed a day, but some parents kept children home to help work. That made it hard for the teacher, but compulsory schools win some, and lose some when school is 'the law' and not a coveted 'privilege.'

12

In the 1950s, Mary went along with Aaron and Amanda to an auction, where she met kind-hearted E K Fisher. He gave Mary a china knickknack shaped like a ladies face with a little pocket behind it, possibly a match holder to hang on the wall. On the backside, it said made in Japan, meaning it was not worth much. Mary marveled over the gift, and cherished it all her life, with memories of the kind man that gave it.

E K Fisher and his wife Alice attended many auctions and learned the value of antiques. They bought many items to resell at their antique store in Churchtown. They had no children of their own and perhaps the thought of fifteen children touched their hearts. . . or was it the innocent blue eyes that watched them at the auction? Amanda was a regular customer at E K Fisher, looking for bargains and for the joy of rummaging in leftover auction things. He also sold many practical necessities.

Mary was too young to understand who EK Fisher was, and she got him mixed up with Dewey Fisher the thief. In later years, she did not know why a thief had given her a nice keepsake. Dewees Fisher lived just north of BW Shirk. The Shirk's owned a good dog that barked when someone came and Dewey wanted to buy him. No, said BW Shirk, "that dog is not for sale!" "Then what can I trade for him? "the thief wanted to know.

Dewey had the reputation of being a professional thief, and one-time BW Shirk caught him red-handed. Dewey Fisher and his wife, Emma, came to their neighbors after dark, and while he came to the house to discuss business, his wife went to the chicken house and quickly grabbed some hens off the roost. Dewey Fisher tried to keep BW Shirk detained inside the house, but Ben stepped outside to show him something, and saw Emma putting hens in the trunk. Many people stole chickens back then for their monetary value. They were good for eating and readily sold for cash, or kept for eggs to sell. Almost every farm had some chickens and B W Shirk kept his farm dog, for good reasons.

BW was not in favor of using the law, and the thief simply put the chickens back where they belonged. He chose to forgive them. When Dewey Fisher went into a store, he soon noticed that the merchant worked alone. He asked"Do you still have some more of that twine for sale? " When the storekeeper went way out back, Dewey quickly filled his pockets up front with no one looking. He stole peaches off a porch and many other things. With a reputation like that, Aaron and others could blame Dewey Fisher for every misplaced tool in the neighborhood, even those that he found right where he used them last. Dewey Fisher had a marvelous voice for singing. People passing by could hear him sing melodious hymns with wonderful words, that he knew by heart.

❧

Chickens sold at Green Dragon farmers market and so did almost anything else. Every Friday rain or shine, crowds of people gathered at Green Dragon. Tweet !"Park over here ",directed Josie as he proudly blew his police whistle and waved his arms. Farmers converged there for the hay and straw auction in the afternoon, and the small animal auction. People bought tools, house wares, clothing, food, souvenirs, soft pretzels, fish sandwiches, produce and records among much more. Merchants of all types sold wares inside the buildings as well as outdoors, in fair weather.

Green Dragon was the best place around to buy produce in season. Peaches, corn, tomatoes and beans sold by the bushel or by the pound. Cotton candy was a specialty, and the aroma of handmade soft pretzels baking right there, tantalized nostrils. The soft pretzels cost $.25 each with an option of mustard on top.

Daniel enjoyed the record shack near the center of the market, and so did many others while the owner played any records they might wanted to hear.

Amanda helped Aaron catch some cats when they had too many. Most of the farm cats were wild, and Amanda had several nasty scratches and even a bite on her hand, determined to reduce the number of fighting cats. Aaron took three tomcats and several guinea pigs along to sell at Green Dragon. One cat paid for a 40-pound box of bananas, and Aaron and Amanda would not think of eating a cat! Selling two cats, paid for filling the gas tank on a car!

If Amanda overheard any plans of her children going to Green Dragon, she wanted them to look for cheap ripe bananas, her favorite. A 40-pound box of bananas disappeared rapidly among their big family.

∽

Sarah Ann and Annie Brubacher were first cousins the same age. They walked to school together and were as close as sisters were. Annie's hair was much thinner while Sarah Ann had enough hair for two people. When Sarah Ann opened her long dark braids, her hair was long enough to sit on it. Annie envied Sarah Ann's hair, but she did not know how much work it was just to shampoo it all, and how long it took to dry again.

Winters got long for mothers cooped up in a house with many children underfoot, instead of playing outdoors. Some flu or virus hit Aaron's family in the middle of January. Most of them had the sickness in the space of two weeks. Emma and Fannie Kilmer came to see Sarah Ann sick in bed. It was good that Amanda kept on going. She was really feeling bad if she complained, and that was very seldom.

After all the sickness, Amanda missed two Sundays of church and rejoiced to find a postcard in the mail inviting her to a quilting, at Martin Kilmer's. Amanda desperately wanted to go. She started planning ahead, to get the laundry done and food planned. Sarah Ann was well enough to babysit five lively preschool children with Wesley still half -sick. Five children went to school in a flurry, with packed lunches and braided hair. Aaron and Daniel went to an auction while Amanda went to the quilting.

"Look at that quilt pattern, now isn't that neat! The dark corners are on one side and the light ones on the other half. That's a great way to use up some small scraps of print fabric." Did you hear about the new baby? I planted my early garden when the soil was fit. Did you know that it works to plant tomato seeds in March. Just make sure you cover them in a cold snap. Titus came and got some cherry grafts from the better trees on the Weller Lot. March is a good time for grafting trees. Did you hear they had a party to strip tobacco at Harvey Zimmerman? He has cancer in his throat, and they need another gathering to help finish his tobacco. Discussing everyone's problems made their own problems seem smaller as they lifted spirits and helped women look on the bright side. A funeral, a miscarriage, and cancer…

Amanda could be content with her lot in life, with so many blessings to count. What would she do without Aaron and her children… her home… and her garden… and things taken for granted? No, she would not wish to trade with anyone else, and this is where she belonged. The horse didn't need any help in finding the way home, over the hills, to the woods and in the lane. Not only did a quilt get stitched with love but hearts were knit together with compassion for each other. Modern machines can quilt durable quilts, but it's the fellowship that ties the community together with understanding, and seeing the needs of others.

"Thank you God for everything, and thank you for a big girl like Sarah Ann," said Amanda. "So I could take a day off". More and more Sarah Ann was staying at home so Amanda could go way. Occasionally Amanda sent Sarah Ann to help someone else, and get out of the house for a change.

Aaron planted more sweet corn than necessarily, and gave surplus to his brother Titus. When Titus fetched a spring wagon full of corn, Amanda sent along Sarah Ann to help. She got paid one whole dollar to keep all for herself. That was fun!

Amos Ringlers needed help when baby Elmer arrived, as their seventh child. Harriet as the oldest was seven years old and in first grade. Aaron and Amanda had five preschool children, but these people had six, with no dependable help. On days when Amanda could manage, Sarah Ann biked about one mile west, to help them, and counted that a privilege. She didn't mind the work and commotion of little children, and went home at night. Sarah Ann helped them on butchering day, and when Amos 'went to a wedding. She learned that other people had many different ways.

Lem Kiefer apparently had a blood clot in his brain, and it seemed he had lost his mind. Someone had to watch him all the time, and his wife needed help. She watched him during the day and the neighbors took turns coming to help at night. Aaron took his turn like all the rest and slept at home in the daytime, after a tiring night. Kind neighbors volunteered what they could. After several months of this, Lem miraculously returned to normal.

Aaron and the boys spent time making a new fence through the woods. When it was finished, Aaron took Amanda for a walk showing her what they did among the beauty of the woodland. Walking in the woods brought back memories of her childhood and bringing water to her father and brother when they made fences in Michigan.

∞

Silver Hill got its name when people believed the area contained silver ore. Aaron studied the nickel mines area, and he dreamed about mining rights. In the spring of 1953, Aaron and Sam King went to Philadelphia several times and also to Lancaster about mining business.

When Aaron needed to go to Harrisburg to test some mineral samples, the trip was too far for a horse and buggy or a bicycle. Most people did not understand Aaron's ideas and often joked about his mining stories. They thought he must be half-crazy with such strange ideas, so different from their own. Instead of asking a driver to take him to Harrisburg, Aaron hitchhiked. All he had to do was walk to the turnpike, climb over the fence and put up his thumb. The soil samples fit in his pocket and so did a sandwich. Aaron got to Harrisburg and back in five hours time.

Not many people heard the details; so perhaps he could keep things secret after all. Aaron eagerly watched the mail for test results on those mineral samples. When the letter finally came, his dreams shattered into pieces. He had nothing worth mining and perhaps other people were right after all.

The whole thing went "greps gong", an old-time expression for things gone wrong, or fast reverse. A 'greps' is a crab or crayfish in Dutch and those little things are quick to disappear backwards, just when you think you have them.

After living with Aaron for fifteen years, Amanda tried her best to understand him, and his big ideas, even when she did not always agree. Just suppose he was right? They might even be rich some day! All she could do was listen intently and pray for him and let him have his own way. Aaron and Amanda had no desire for earthly riches but it certainly would be nice to have money to pay all the bills.

At Morgantown, about four miles east of Aaron's farm, Bethlehem Steel opened their new Grace mine. They announced an open house day, inviting the public to come see the above ground part of their new facility. That sparked Aaron's interest! He toured the building, with its huge steel I-beams and metal grated floors. Large magnetic rollers picked up powdered iron ore, and Aaron asked many questions. Bethlehem Steel owned hundreds of acres of land, digging for iron ore with high-manganese content. They found some gold...nearly enough to pay the payroll! Aaron still dreamed about finding iron ore on his own property. If Bethlehem Steel found gold...do you think... maybe...?   The main crop that keeps farmers alive is hope, because he is always going to be rich next year! Aaron dreamed on...

Amanda went all out to make Jell-O, for the last day of school picnic. The special treat sadly turned into a puddle of melted red liquid, on a sunny day. The boys thought it should be tossed out, but Sarah Ann knew that Amanda would not be pleased with wasted food. Surely, she could use it to flavor tapioca or mix it into something. When Amanda chilled that Jell-O mess, it turned out as good as new, to amaze and delight the schoolchildren.

Picnics and parties ended too soon, and not everyone rejoiced for summer vacation. Menno Shirks could hardly wait until school was over so Dick cold help with the farm work. He left home that day yet, to work there all summer. Menno and Martha, when they were single, helped Aaron and Amanda countless hours. Now with two diaper babies they needed some help, even if Dick was only nine. Spring work started and it was time to plant tobacco, make hay and work in the garden. Other children worked away also as the need arose. Dick rejoiced to come home every Saturday afternoon.

The entire neighborhood buzzed with activity. Aaron helped Martin Kilmer install a water ram for a running water system, while Amanda helped her sister Mary quilt. Sarah Ann was the busiest of all, stuck at home, tending children so Amanda could have a break. Daniel worked at Jesse's, while Pete was helping Titus. Daniel worked at Menno's; Walter worked for Jesse all day and then the next day to Titus. Daniel planted tobacco at Reuben Weaver's, and later cultivativated for Amos Ringler. No one sat idle!

There was no such thing as a combine. Jesse Brubacher cut the wheat with a three- horse team hitched to the binder, then they set up wheat in shocks to dry, and later they threshed with a thrashing machine.

Daniel and Walter helped work on the threshing crew all over the neighborhood in July. Aaron could not handle such heavy work. The thrashers started at John Leinbach and Aaron Leinbach, then on to Ike Kulps and Martin Kilmer's. Most fields were small and they worked fast, with a dozen men working together. It was hard work mixed with a time of excitement for everyone involved.

Sarah Ann remembered the thrilling event when the thrashers came, bringing extra teams of horses to help haul the wheat bundles to the barn hill. The noise and commotion of the thresh machine spooked some horses, as they pulled up alongside, to unload the wheat bundles. Nervous horses scared Sarah Ann as she helped Amanda prepare a big meal for the men. Lydi-Jes-sey came over to help also.

Some farmers hauled wheat shocks into the barn to keep them dry until the threshing crew arrived. Aaron and the boys brought in wheat with Amos Ringler and Manual Brubacher helping. They helped haul in the wheat at Titus and helped the threshing crew at Harvey Wengers.

The neighborhood worked together in synchronized unity, without using telephones. With Bicycles and horses, they delivered messages, as well as with children walking. The boys kept right on helping all over the neighborhood. Making hay, planting tobacco and harvesting wheat overlapped on busy summer days.

Farmers had to keep ahead of the weeds, without modern herbicides. Aaron had a two -horse McCormick riding cultivator, doing one row at a time, and the shovel harrow, which was a one-horse walk behind contraption. Children did a lot of hoeing by hand with the common garden hoe.

13

The New Pond

In January of 1953, Titus Musser came to Aaron Shirk to help plan a new farm pond. The marshy swamp in the meadow was a good location for a pond, but it was August before the action started. Boys eagerly started whacking brush a few days before the bulldozer arrived, and Pete chopped his foot with a hatchet. Amanda took him to the doctor for stitches. The bulldozer started working at noon on August six. Talk about excitement!

Children crowded as close as they dared and Aaron wished to supervise, while watching closely. He said, "Take off more dirt over this way and now over here." Any time Aaron paid hired help by the hour, his impatience showed more than usual. He liked to see things happen in' fast forward'. This worker spent much more time in reverse than forward because the dozer had low gear reverse. "You spend too much time backing, " said Aaron. Titus Musser was displeased with Aaron. He knew what he was doing and it just took time. When he had about all he could take, he kindly asked Aaron " Don't you have some other work to do?"

Children of all sizes watched the bulldozer in action and saw the colorful layers of sediment he uncovered. As soon as the dozer quit for the day, creative minds and busy hands made dishes for the playhouse. The fresh, silky smooth clay in assorted colors was as inviting as a mountain of play dough.

In one and a half days, the pond was finished... well almost. Titus Musser quit where the muck was too swampy for the bulldozer. He pushed dirt to channel the strong spring coming in from the side and therefore the pond had an island to the north side. The pond had a spillway on the west side and an overflow pipe at the deepest part.

The strong springs filled the new pond in four weeks time, without much rain. Many swimmers arrived before the pond filled with water. Aaron and the boys eagerly stocked some fish, they got at Paul Brubacher's near Morgantown.

The boys hastily put up a crude diving board, not meant for the job, and it soon broke. Before the next swimming season, Elias helped them install a better diving board. Work flew fast with the promise of swimming afterwards. Neighbors came constantly on the weekend as well as weekday evenings, swimming until dark. The boys claimed the diving board side of the pond and the girls had the east half. On the south side in the mud, the bloodsuckers latched on to anyone that stayed standing still long enough. Yeeeewwww, they were terrible, but not bad enough to keep people out of the pond. The children inspected each other's legs occaisonally and pulled off the ugly leeches while a trail of blood trickled down where they had been attached. Most of the time, the swimmers avoided that spot.

Aaron and Amanda had a clear view from the kitchen window, and could see what was going on at the water. Wesley walked in once as a toddler, but someone was right there to pull the spluttering child out again. The story goes that Wesley nearly turned green with algae from being in the water so long, and he could swim at the age of three. When he was four, he learned to dive.

The growing boys convinced Amanda that they did not need a weekly bath when they were not even dirty behind the ears. They quickly washed up with a wash cloth and tried to talk their way out of a bath in wintertime also.

Walter missed all the excitement when he worked away as a hired hand. Later on, he helped by burning the brush pile that remained. When the pile burned low, he wanted to add some kerosene to speed it up. Unknowingly he dumped a gallon of gasoline on the burning fire and caused a dangerous explosion. His hands blistered and his eyebrows disappeared. He was hurt, but thankful it wasn't worse. His coat saved his arms from the flames.

In October Aaron cut his foot accidentally with an axe and the doctor put a cast on it. He was handicapped a while and sat around the house helping Amanda can pears and get ready for company.

A party of men came to help Aaron cut firewood and butcher a cow because he could not work, so Aaron went to Peter Martin's store and bought cheese and pretzels for the party on the morrow. Only six men showed up, and they saw much more work. John and Benny Leinbach, Walter Martin, Ammon and Harry Hoover and Jesse came. Josie came to help cut firewood for Aaron, and perhaps others heard about how much work remained at the Aaron Shirk farm. The next day a group of fifty men showed up unannounced, husking corn and cutting firewood. Half of them went home for dinner, but Amanda cooked short notice, for twenty -five hungry men. Three days later the doctor removed the cast, and Aaron could work again. It took another ten days to finish husking corn.

∽

When Dick was in second grade, and eight years old, he had a lot of trouble with sore throat. He missed quite a bit of school but he did not mind, because he hated school so much that he would rather be sick. In the carriage, on the way home from the doctor, Aaron and Amanda discussed a tonsillectomy, when Aaron thought Dick was sleeping. Aaron said, "I'm afraid he will have to go to the hospital". Amanda promptly whispered, "Don't talk so loud or he will hear us."

Dick was on his knees in the carriage, and laid his head on Amanda's lap. His young ears heard more than his parents thought they did, and Dick feared for his life, but he was too scared to ask any questions.

When Clement Leinbach drove father and son to the Ephrata hospital for a tonsillectomy, Dick was tense and scared. People that love to talk are not always good at communicating and Dick had no idea what was going on or why? He never slept in a bed alone, and he held tightly to Aaron's hand. He was terrified when his father departed and left him at the hospital. Aaron slept a mile away at Eli Stauffer's overnight. The hospitals had no arrangements for a parent to stay with a child. When the attendants put an ether rag over his nose, Dick struggled and said, "I can't breathe!" They just held him down tighter and he seriously thought they were killing him. Dick survived, and it was the happiest day of his young life, when Joe Weaver brought Aaron to the hospital to take Dick home the next morning.

When baby Lydia arrived, she weighed 9 pounds and 12 ounces. Louise and Irene spent two weeks at Dawdy Shirks over that time. Wesley was a 13-month-old roughy- toughy, 28-pound boy, running all over the place, pounding and hammering things as though he might grow up to be a carpenter someday. Amanda said, "There is nothing feminine about him."He can even whistle already but I just hope he doesn't get hold of the new baby." The children all loved baby Lydia, including Wesley.

Dr. Lauria kindly donated a used playpen to Amanda. He often came out to the farm and kept an eye on those children. At Christmas time, he gave a generous amount of chewable multiple vitamins for the children, and each new baby received a small white dress as a baby gift. A" duktah frockly" or [doctor- dress] was a soft, thin, white,100% cotton baby dress, handmade in the Philippines, with detailed edges and embroidery.

Dr. Schnader, Aaron and Amanda's former Dr., also had the reputation of checking up on Amanda before leaving on vacation. Those family doctors had no way of calling people that did not have a telephone. On the margin of the filing card, Dr. Lauria listed a telephone number of some neighbors such as Clement Leinbach, Roy Hartranft, or Lem Kiefer. Those people did not want to run to Aaron and Amanda unnecessarily, and a Dr. seldom used such a number.

The kind-hearted doctors that came out at all hours saw all types of places. Some homes stayed neat as a pin and others had noise and disarray among the commotion of a large family. He smelled fresh bread baking and saw all types of action. Children often stared quietly as he opened his satchel of mysterious bottles and pills. He often gave sulfa drugs and he could amazingly open a medicine bottle with one hand! Aaron and Amanda trusted him totally. He encouraged baby shots and prevention and he gave all of the children their immunizations.

When the screen door slammed on baby Lydia's finger, infection gradually set in. At first, she lost the fingernail but it didn't want to heal, for several weeks. When one-year-old Lydia started with a fever, they took her to the doctor. After several visits, x-rays and different pills, there was no improvement. Amanda was concerned when she discovered a lump under her baby's arm. The doctor advised to hold hot washrags against it and try different pills, and that didn't help either. Surgery was the only sure way of knowing what was going on, in 1953, and Lydia was admitted to the hospital to drain the pus. It was infection in the lymph glands due to the injured fingernail. She stayed in the Ephrata Hospital all alone for five days. Amanda was pleased when Ammon Highs came on a Sunday and took them to Ephrata to visit baby Lydia. Eli Huber provided the transportation to bring her home again, and that was a day of rejoicing for them all. Dr. Lauria came out to the house for three more weeks to drain the surgery and to keep changing the dressings.

∽

Every morning Amanda started a fire in the heavy cast-iron kitchen range, to make breakfast. Kerosene was the fastest way she had to light the kindling when the chimney was cold, and she kept some close by. Amanda wore her black sweater with sleeves rolled up, to start working in the chilly house. She often wondered why the babies get up early in the cold mornings, while her able helpers like to sleep late.

From the bedroom above the kitchen, children could hear their mother through the open register. The baby jumper squeak -squeaked, with a bouncing baby. That was a happy noise and so was Amanda's singing, as the words drifted through the register." No never alone, no never alone, he promised never to leave me, never to leave me alone." The smell of frying mush was a sure warning it was time to get up, or soon Amanda would tap on the metal register with her broom handle as an alarm to "hurry up".

Sunday was a day of rest, unless company came. On a peaceful Sunday afternoon, Aaron biked over to Amos Ringler, while Amanda tried taking a nap, while four-month-old baby Lydia napped. Seventeen months -old Wesley found Amanda's tin can with kerosene in it, and he drank some. He coughed and spluttered until Amanda's nap was over before it started. "Give Wesley a drink of water" she called. "We did," they said. "It doesn't help and he smells like kerosene."

With Aaron not at home, Amanda did not know what to do. Someone went to Jesse's to ask for a home remedy or advice. Aaron's uncle and cousins visiting there, came to help and advised to give Wesley a raw egg or milk to get him to vomit. The vomit on the porch held enough kerosene to burn in a small flame when they lit it, so they were sure that was the problem. Maybe now the chemical was out of his system and he would improve on his own.

The advice to induce vomiting was fine for some things, but petroleum products could do more harm coming up, by forcing the kerosene into the lungs. Wesley was a sick boy! Dr. Lauria came the next morning but Wesley was not improving that day or the next. The doctor came out several more days before Wesley started improving. Thankfully, he survived!

∽

Aaron always had a touchy back and he still had backaches and pains in 1953. In March, neighbors gathered for a tobacco stripping party, to help him out. Neighborhood men and boys arrived on an evening, for fun and entertainment, while getting a lot of work done. Aaron enjoyed the party atmosphere and offered $.25 to whoever ate the most raw eggs. Leroy and Johnny Newswenger each ate two eggs. Pete ate five and Amos Ringler kept down four. Amos Kulp tried twice but the eggs came up. Aaron's brother Elias won the egg-eating contest by eating 20 raw eggs out of the shells, for $.25. Amanda and Sarah Ann served treat of cookies and drink.

Everyone had fun and one week later, many teenagers gathered for another party. Forty-five people didn't all fit into the stripping room, measuring 15'x18'. The tobacco-stripping table used up over three feet of that space along the entire south side and the wood stove demanded a large space. The youth accomplished a lot a work and they still had enough energy, for a rip roaring lively barn dance. A group of three local musicians showed up with a guitar, a fiddle, and a mandolin. They provided real live bluegrass music for the young folks. Daniel thought it was the most wonderful sound he ever heard, and from that day onward he was determined that he would someday learn how to play the fiddle.

Bart Horsts boys came with a pair of boxing gloves. Aaron's younger children peeped around the corners, and could not believe their eyes. It was the first time this neighborhood had seen boxing gloves in use, amid laughing and hitting, and seemingly no one getting hurt, while the boys said, "don't hit in the gut!"

Stories drifted to the parents about the entertainment at Aaron Shirk's that night and eventually someone brought complaints into church council about, "unsupervised tobacco stripping parties."

After Daniel was out of school, he often helped Amanda in the house. Many times, it was his job to do the washing. The Maytag, wringer wash machine had a troublesome two- cylinder gas engine. After sorting the laundry and heating the wash water, Amanda tired out stomping on that kick-start pedal. The gas tank was too small, and had a way of running out of gas just before the last load was finished. Restarting the engine was disgusting.

The engine made constant trouble and no one seemed to be able to fix it, not out back in that re-

mote location. A new washing machine was not an option, so Aaron removed the engine, and brought in his clumsy Fairbanks Morse engine with its two large flywheels.

Aaron needed to set the washer a foot off the floor on a platform so that the V. belt could reach the large engine beside the washer. That is when Aaron brought in the old"misht shlidda" [manure sled] for a platform. The whole thing was a rather awkward arrangement, but it worked and it was used that way for a long time. Daniel cranked that engine to start it, and actually did the washing from beginning to end. He helped hang the laundry on the line, but Amanda managed the art of sorting clothes.

Daniel used the poor little Maytag engine, to power a crude contraption of a go-kart. With his own imagination and limited resources available, Daniel brainstormed and constructed a wooden go-kart so badly underpowered, that only his little brothers Pete and Dick could actually drive it. He never even got one successful ride, but he had the wonderful opportunity of designing and dreaming about the gears and wheels.

Fastened to the wall behind the stove, Amanda had a drying rack for laundry. A dozen wooden arms fanned out from the wall when in use, and folded down out of the way otherwise. Wet mittens and socks dried beside damp baby clothes, in constant use.

The big old kitchen range was the heart of the home for warmth, and its many good smells of cooking, baking, drying and canning, plus the smell of wood smoke. Depending how the wind blew, a back draft pushed smoke down the chimney, seeping out of every crack the stove had. "Don't hold the lid open so long," was a common request when anyone put firewood in the stove. With utmost care, smoke still darkened the ceiling.

When spring arrived, Amanda's thoughts turned to housecleaning. She did not clean from top to bottom as many others did, but rather cleaned where it was so necessary that it could not wait. Every spring, the kitchen ceiling and walls needed a good scrubbing, due to the smoke from the stove. Amanda waited until the school children went out the door and then set to work. A few able–bodied helpers stood on chairs and scrubbed with warm soapy water dripping from their elbows to the floor. With aching arms and a stiff neck, they finished the job by mopping the floor.

When the school children burst in the door, they did a double take, saying…"oh, how clean, is that the color the paint was, or did you paint it yellow?"The walls and ceiling looked as bright as the sun coming out from behind the clouds. Everyone appreciated all the hard work, and it lifted the moods of those in the house.

Aaron and Amanda's kitchen was the most attractive room in the house, even with plain yellow walls, decorated with one calendar. The windows never knew curtains, because Amanda craved the sunshine. Each window had a green blind to pull down, just in case the sun came in a little too brightly. No one needed privacy in the kitchen, and neither did anyone wish to block out the great outdoors, and the activities of farm life.

14

Baby Rose Anna

When Peter Brubachers first bought their own place near Churchtown, it was not really what they wanted. Then, 10 years later, over public auction they bought the Frank Kiefer home for $2500, because it was more to their liking. They promptly sold their property at Churchtown for $3025, and moved to the Bowmansville area to be closer to their married children. That is what they wanted in the first place.

The turnpike loudly claimed all quietness in Dawdy Brubacher's back yard, on top of a steep bank, but they soon got used to the noise. A man needing help, climbed over the turnpike fence and down to Peter Brubacher's kitchen door. His vehicle on the turnpike needed water and when he met Mrs. Brubacher, he surprisingly recognized her. She had no idea who he was, but he introduced himself as John Brubacher, whose father William Brubacher from Indiana, was Bishop Daniel Brubacher's son from Michigan. Talking about Michigan and Daniel Brubacher, brought back many happy memories to Peter, who was bald, and his wife had white-hair.

While Amanda attended the auction of her parent's possessions in Churchtown, Aaron had a mishap working at home. He was helping the boys cut firewood, when an ax glanced and struck his leg. The axe severed blood veins and broke two bones. At the Ephrata hospital, they put his leg in a cast that stayed on for six long weeks.

In November, an early snowstorm hit and Amanda did not have enough boots for all their children. The boots she had for Dick were too small, since Pete and Dick needed the same size. She could not keep Dick home from school and she improvised by asking him to wear a smaller size four -buckle boots over a thick pair of wool stockings. Dick frowned and complained saying," The teacher has a rule against wearing boots inside the schoolroom!" Amanda fixed that, with a note of explanation for the teacher.

Martha in first grade did not have any boots either. Therefore, Amanda dressed her in long woolen stockings pulled overtop her shoes, then low rubbers over the woolen stockings to walk to school. As the snow drifted deeper, school dismissed early. Excited children hurried to dress and go home, all but Martha, sitting there with long wet stockings, slightly shrunken. Kind Mrs. Blanche Horning did not know how it all belonged together and Martha began to cry. With advice from her sisters, the teacher put the pieces together and they all trudged home in the snow.

By Saturday morning, the snow accumulated to eighteen inches and kept on snowing. Aaron and Amanda's excited boys shoveled the walk to the barn and did the chores. Then they brought out old Tony the horse, to ride him in the snow. When Tony came up to the kitchen door, he could not turn around on the deeply trenched, narrow path they shoveled through the drifts, so they brought the big horse up the steps on the cement porch to turn him around.

Snow came up to the horse's belly, as two of the boys rode horseback. They attended Bowmansville church preparatory services that Saturday for the excitement of getting out and going away. Only 36 members braved the deep snow. The roads were better the next day, and Aaron and Amanda both attended Sunday communion services.

The neighborhood teenagers often gathered at von Neidas dam, beside the old millrace, on the south side of Bowmansville. Daniel went skating there with teenage friends on Christmas day. The social life of skating was a highlight of the winter, even if he fell on the ice and sprained his wrist. He once broke into the ice up to his knees, close to the edge. He was not alarmed, but Amanda was greatly concerned.

Aaron started to work away from home for an income, because Daniel could manage the farm work, and they needed the money. Aaron worked at Terre Hill machine shop, assembling barn cleaners for Harvey Wenger. Occasionally Daniel went along to help. Aaron enjoyed welding, and on break time or after hours, he welded together strips of scrap metal, into a heavy-duty doormat, built to last a long time. The metal grate scraped piles of mud off the boots and shoes, before so many feet entered the house.

As a favor to Aaron and Amanda, Uncle Eli Stauffer and Aunt Lydia kept Mary, age 6, and baby Lydia just fourteen-month-old, when the next baby was due to arrive. At mealtime, Aunt Lydia tied baby Lydia's feet to the highchair, to keep her from standing up, or kicking her feet. This frustrated baby Lydia, and upset Mary, because she thought that looked cruel.

Eli and Lydia loved children and cared for them as their own, and desired to keep one for always. Aaron and Amanda refused to part with a child, no matter how many they had. Uncle Eli and Aunt Lydia took Mary and baby Lydia along to Ephrata for Eli's doctor appointment, and on the way home, Mary had the fright of her life, when the horse ran away! Eli hung on for dear life, and hollered "Whoa! Whoa!", but it didn't help. The next thing Mary knew, the carriage lay on its side, and the horse dragged the carriage along like that, until the terrified horse tore loose. No one was hurt except for bumps and bruises. Mary was shook and cried to go home. [Eli excelled in making and fixing carriages as a trade.]

Meanwhile Amanda was busy making more diapers, thick new ones for the toddler Lydia, while the thin, worn diapers were just right for another new baby arriving soon. She sewed two Sunday shirts for the growing boys, cleaned the parlor and made a couch mattress. Lydia Kilmer came to help all day and then Lydia Ann and Barbara Martin came to work all Saturday afternoon. Amanda had the day planned and they all worked together washing, ironing, cleaning, and baking.

Sarah Ann was just fourteen and still in school, so Florence Kilmer came to help when baby Rose-Anna arrived, on March 2, 1954, weighing 9 1/2 pounds. RoseAnna was four days old before she got a name because no one could agree on a name for another girl… not Hannah… or Harriet… and not Elva… so why not try something different, like RoseAnna? Yes! They all agreed!

Amanda sent a bunch of postcards in the mail as birth announcements. It was the best way she had to inform her sister Katie in Indiana and Aaron's brother Ben's family. The card addressed to her sister Mary and Martin Kilmer arrived the same day as she sent it, because they had the same mailman, and he just scribbled the stamp with an ink pen and dropped the card in Martin Kilmer's mail box that day.

Lydi-Jes-sey walked over in the evening to help, even when their own baby was due in a few months. Amanda stayed in bed seven days, and then she got up to go to the dinner table. New mothers had to stay in bed a week or up to 10 days, for fear they would ruin their health.

With baby number fourteen, Aaron and Amanda had nine girls, and five boys, but they loved each one dearly, and babies indeed were the greatest treasure on earth. Amanda rocked and cuddled and sang to another new baby, and so did all the rest. Amanda well remembered how her three young brothers were buried in Michigan, and how her sister Lydia longed for children all her life. So did Silas!

Aunt Lydia asked, 'Mary would you like to go home tomorrow and see your new baby sister named RoseAnna?" "Yes, yes! " Mary agreed excitedly, and she was ready to see her family again. "We received a postcard with the news just a few days ago," said Aunt Lydia, "but I didn't want to tell you for fear you would cry to go home right away," and Mary would have!

When RoseAnna had a sore mouth, Daniel took Amanda and baby Rose Anna to the doctor. Most of Aaron and Amanda's babies had thrush at one time or another. Amanda kept a small bottle of messy purple gentian violet in the (kallah holz) or cellar stairway shelf, like a dark hidden medicine cabinet for things little hands may not reach. That was the safest place to store drugs. Not only was it dark, dry and cool, but no child could set a chair on a stairway to climb into mischief.

When baby RoseAnna was only three weeks old, Martins needed Lydia Kilmer at home for their own new baby Anna Mary. The next maid for Amanda was Bart Horst's Sarah. She helped Amanda house clean the attic, and made homemade noodles, Aarons favorite! She worked fast at ironing, washing and cleaning, and then Daniel took her home on Friday evening. Amanda had schoolgirls to help her on Saturday, and to get ready for baby company on Sunday.

When RoseAnna was four weeks old, Amanda tried doing without a maid, but on Friday, she kept Sarah Ann out of school to plant the garden and help with the butchering, while Daniel got the garden ready for planting. It was springtime and warm enough that Amanda got out the straw bonnets for the girls to wear to school. When Amanda and RoseAnna went for a six-week check up, Mary went along for a smallpox vaccination, to start in first grade.

The new baby at Martin Kilmer's house, turned out to be a Down's syndrome child, but they loved and cherished her all the same. Peter and Sarah Ann Brubacher eventually had 49 grandchildren, and baby Anna Mary was the only one with a health defect.

As a frail child, she lived to be four years old, but didn't walk. She could sweetly sing *"Walking in sunlight, heavenly sunlight, flooding my soul with glory divine, hallelujah, I am rejoicing, singing his praises all the day long"*.

∞

Daniel was the right-hand man everywhere, even when he was younger. He worked hard at home and over the entire neighborhood, and even more so after eighth grade. He was out of school three years before Walter graduated. He worked long hours on the steamer, steaming tobacco beds, and helping with the threshing crew. Daniel worked dependable long hours at a slower pace than Aaron

did. He was natured like Amanda's side and Aaron said Daniel was born a day late. Daniel knew that was not his fault.

Daniel went to the store, after he took the scholars to school first, on a snowy day. He helped Amanda with the laundry on a regular basis and even got good at it, without complaining.

After Daniel was out of school, Uncle Jesse said to Aaron, "You should hire some of your boys out. With so many children at home, the boys will not amount to much if you don't. "Walter heard this conversation and it hurt him deeply. Worse yet, it was decided that since Daniel was the oldest, and already out of school, Walter would be the one to be hired out, because Aaron needed Daniel at home. Daniel and Sarah Ann couldn't be spared, but the next three boys could work away from home sometimes.

On May 31, 1954, Amanda packed clothes for a sad Walter leaving home. Some farmer needed a hired hand, with the spring work coming, and way over at Farmersville at that! Walter was twelve years old. Before the school term ended, Walter parted with his brothers and his friends at Silver Hill School. He finished the term at Farmersville public school and he had a hard time adjusting. Where four brothers slept in one bedroom at home, Walter now missed all the fun of being with them, day and night. He did not mind hard work and farming, but time got long and he was homesick! Were his brothers maybe swimming in the pond with the whole neighborhood gathering there without him? At a strange new school, he didn't know a single soul, but thankfully, the school term was almost over.

How Daniel envied Walter! He wished he could be the one to work away instead of being stuck at home. [The grass was always greener on the other side of the fence.] Aaron ordered brand-new bicycles for Daniel and Walter since Walter needed one to bike thirteen miles to work. Christ Sensenig's hardware store had only one bicycle in stock, so Walter got his first. It was a Raleigh bike with a Sturmy Archer three-speed shifter. The skinny tired, top-of-the-line bike, cost $62, but Walter wished with all his heart, that he could stay home, bike or no bike.

They ordered the second bike and Daniel went along with Uncle Titus in a hired truck a few weeks later to pick it up. Christ Sensenig said, "So you want a second bike before the first one is paid for?" Titus ended up paying for the two bicycles, but Aaron paid him back. Before the new bike arrived, Daniel had used a heavyweight Columbia bike.

In 1955, Walter attended Conestoga View private school in eighth grade. Even with the school privately owned and operated by Mennonites, the teacher was a public-school teacher, Mr. Rettew. One of Walter's duties as a hired hand, was to bike from school to the farm every lunch hour to give the chicken's water and to bring in the newspaper from the mailbox at the end of the lane. This automatically cut out all lunch recess and ballgames for him. He did not need a lunch box. He loved playing baseball and returned just in time to hear the details of the good game they had.

He also had a problem with some mischievous little boys where he worked. When Walter saw silage coming down the silage chute, he went to investigate, and found little boys hard at work being naughty. Hollering at them to stop, he started up the chute after them, amidst a shower of silage, and then a pitch-fork fell down towards him when he neared the top. Thankfully, the handle end came first! He scolded the little boys and spanked one of them right there, but the mother sided with her sons.

Not only did Walter have it rough, but so did Dick !He had to work for a neighbor, closer to home. He was only 10 and he had a serious battle with homesickness.

The first year that Walter worked as a hired hand, he earned a pair of new shoes. After a one year break from there, the farmer realized how much Walter was worth and he begged Aaron to have him back for $500 that next year. Aaron agreed and Walter had no say in the deal. He had to fulfill the agreement, and the worst part was when the farmer's wife heard the $500 figure, she insisted that Walter needed to help around the house sometimes at that price. Housework was not his thing!

Even when things went poorly, Walter was stuck there against his wishes. He overcame serious homesickness, and made new friends at school, but if given the chance, he would have pedaled for home as fast as possible to his parents and his brothers, where he belonged. He missed many things around home and occasionally people forgot to tell him things that they thought he already knew. When Jesse Brubacher's had another baby girl, she was in first grade before he knew he had another young girl cousin like that, living next-door. How could that be? He did not see them together and he thought they had only one younger girl instead of two.

Walter worked as a hired hand until he turned 16, then he could leave and get a better job. Meanwhile, Walter enjoyed skating and biking. He lived to skate! It was the brightest spot of the years that he lived away from home. When the ice froze over on the "arm" of the Conestoga Creek, Walter was there every chance he had. On ice skates, he could outdo anyone his size that he met.

Walter worked and lived, and even went to school at Conestoga, but he still felt inferior and he knew he was looked-down- on, as just a Bowmansviller. He felt as if Aaron Shirks children were the scum of the earth, and he would remain a nobody, because he was not from the Weaverland valley.

His good new bicycle had a mile gauge that recorded five thousand miles in one year. It was 13 miles to home and Walter biked that in 35 minutes, nearly as fast as the cars that drove slowly through all the small towns and stopped at the stop signs. He used his bicycle for more than just going home and back.

Walter, a scrawny teenager, ran many errands with his bike. He biked to Burkholder's stone quarry for 80-pound bags of cement one at a time, because it was faster than hitching up the horse. He made three trips in a hurry, while the men were busy concreting. If the bike had tipped over, Walter could in no way, have lifted up the bag of cement and started on his own again, but he made it.

Walter biked to Burkholder's stone quarry one time with a note for Dave Burkholder. "Give Walter four sticks of dynamite, two caps and fuse." The bicycle basket safely held the dynamite, but the caps were the dangerous part, and Walter put them into his shirt pocket. Loaded like a suicide bomber, Dave Burkholder said, "Be careful or this will kill you!" Walter knew all about using dynamite, and he was not afraid. He saw it used so many times that he respected the powerful tool and he drove carefully.

Walter enjoyed biking on Sunday afternoon, to wherever the action was. He met up with Davey and bought Winston cigarettes at Althouse in Hinkel town for $.23 a pack. In three hours time, Walter smoked the whole pack of cigarettes and got sicker than a dog, until he thought he might die, and then he wished he could die. It was the last pack of cigarettes for Walter, and the only pack he ever smoked in his life.

Walter froze his ears one time while riding bike, but he was too tough to get sick, and not used to being babied or pitied. He got tougher!

Growing boys worked hard harvesting tobacco all over the neighborhood. Lifting those heavy plants, was hard work in the hot sun, and the gummy dirt stuck like tar. A sense of humor lightened the load, and passed the time as they worked long hours without a break.

The smallest yellowed leaf at the bottom of each tobacco stalk was brownish, and gritty with dirt. It was called a sand leaf, and grew so close to the ground that the cutting shears missed many of them. Daniel knew that sand leaves contained nicotine. "Walter", he said, "let's see who can chew on one of those leaves the longest?"

Daniel and Walter each carefully brushed the loose dirt off a leaf and started chewing, but Daniel soon spit out his tobacco when Walter turned his back. Walter kept on chewing and got an overdose of nicotine. He went to bed sick, and missed the excitement that evening when Pete brought home a new dog, named Skip.

Sometimes the boys gathered those sand leaves and strung them on wire to dry. They also gathered any broken or loose leaves that fell from the tobacco laths onto the wagon, on the barn floor or out in the field. They could not spear them up with a tobacco spear to hang them on the rails, so they poked a wire through each leaf rib individually, and strung the long wire in an out-of-the-way place resembling a laundry line filled with tobacco leaves. They did not quite get rich, but Pete and Dick each got $6.75 one winter, when the tobacco check came.

Notion Jecky

Amanda knew many people in Canada. Her grandfather, Jacob B Brubacher, [Notion Jecky] was born and raised in Canada and married Elizabeth P Martin. Together they raised nine children. As newlyweds, these young people lived on part of Grandpa John W. Brubacher's farm in 1878, and then moved north into Wellington County two years later. They had two children there, Peter (Amanda's father) and a daughter named Catherine.

Jacob Brubacher's bought a farm of their own, at the sand hills, in Waterloo County, where they had five more children; Henry 1884, Mary 1886, Amos 1887, Christian 1891, Barbara 1895, but they did not stay living there. They moved west between Elmira and New Jerusalem school, and there they had a daughter Leah, but they did not stay in Canada, when the grass looked greener in May city Iowa. In 1901, A son Isaac was born, on a rented farm 1 mile west of May City, and later that same year, the family moved 2 miles north of Business Corner, Iowa, and rented a 200-acre farm there.

In 1905, they moved 2 miles east on a 120 acre farm they bought. They stayed there seven years, working hard, for a total of 11 years in Iowa, until the May City community fell apart. Then Jacobs relocated to Montcalm County Michigan, 6 miles north of Stanton. Jacob and Elizabeth's grown children scattered in many directions, while their parents farmed on the outskirts of Stanton Michigan, staying there for seven years.

After living at May City IA for five years, Peter and his brother Henry moved to Brutus, Michigan, starting out on their own, creating farms from scratch. Only Barbara remained single, moving with her parents from one place to the next. From Michigan, Jacob Brubachers moved to Lebanon County, Pennsylvania in 1926. They spent that winter visiting in Waterloo, Canada with many relatives, where Jacob and Elizabeth grew up. At the age of 70, no longer farming, they bought a home on a quarter acre of land in Farmersville, Lancaster County, Pennsylvania. Jacob's wife Elizabeth died there on January 5, 1930, and she was buried at the Pike church, at Hinkletown. Barbara could never understand why her father moved so many times, and yet did not return to Canada where his wife dearly wished to be. She was homesick for Canada so many times!

Barbara convinced Jacob, her father, to visit Waterloo, Canada for a few months in 1932. He liked it there, and sold out in March 1933, moving in with his daughter, Catherine and Eli Bauman, while Barbara worked for her brother Amos. After moving 12 times, Notion Jecky had come full circle back to his place of origin. At the age of 82, Jacob suddenly took ill, and died one week later, moving to eternity on May 25, 1937. Jacob was buried at Elmira Mennonite Cemetery beside his parents, a brother and his sister.

Any time when Amanda got a brainstorm, she would comment that she is one of Notion Jeckys granddaughters. She dearly loved visiting and traveling, much like her grandfather, but thankfully, Aaron and Amanda, stayed put without moving to other locations.

Amanda had several aunts and uncles, as well as many cousins in Canada. She also made many friends there, while traveling in 1937.

When Canadians came to the United States, some came to Aaron and Amanda for a call or a meal, or even overnight without an advance notice. Any time two carriages followed each other way out back, it was a dead giveaway, that someone was bringing travelers.

Amanda panicked, she might have five minutes or more to grab a clean apron, brush back her hair, wipe the table and move that slop bucket, while Aaron talked to the travellers and helped tie up their horses!

She greeted the guests at the door with a smile, "Koomet yoosht rie." (Come just in) We're glad to see you! After introductions and handshakes all around, the guests took chairs. "Do you have all your plans made, or do you need a place for dinner?" Amanda asked. Without telephones, it happened sometimes, that travelers came for a meal, or a night, without a warning. Amanda well remembered the hospitality shown to her in Canada, and she tried her best to return that appreciation, even if they were in the middle of canning peaches or butchering chickens.

Guests stepped into Aaron and Amanda's kitchen when Sarah Ann was sweeping the floor. She was pleased she had come thus far before company came, but Amanda looked at the huge pile of dirt, boots and miscellaneous that should never get so deep. She was embarrassed! Canadians lived, and dressed a bit more formal, using dessert plates and teacups with saucers. The Pennsylvania folks more likely saved a bread crust to wipe the plate, after the main course.

When the guests departed, they all gave the same hearty welcome. "Come see us in Canada!" Over the years, that looked inviting to Amanda, but not possible, but maybe... just maybe. ..when the children get older. An invitation to Aunt Barbara's wedding was the push they needed!

Years ago, at the age of 42, Barbara{Notion Jecky's single daughter], had married Enos Martin, a widower, with three children, on September 12, 1937, just two months before Aaron and Amanda's wedding. In less than 10 years, Enos Martin died, and Barbara was single again, with no children of her own. She was the one that tried to talk Amanda's sister Lydia out of marrying a widower. Now Barbara planned to marry a second time, to a widower, by the name of Noah Weber.

With Daniel and Sarah Ann both through school now, perhaps it was possible to leave on a trip. Amanda thought of her many friends and relatives there, and she set her heart on going to Canada. She began making plans.

Daniel could handle the farm work because they had planted most of the tobacco and made the hay. BW Shirks agreed to take six-year-old Mary and four-month old baby Roseanna. Aaron and Amanda could take along two children, and chose five year old Louise and Irene age three. Amanda started by sewing new garments they needed for the suitcases. Louise and Irene were fitted with new bonnets and new shoes, fit for traveling.

Martin Kilmer's Nancy came to help Sarah Ann with all the housework. Ruth and Rhoda were almost nine years old and could help work and so could Martha, at the age of seven, although they did not care about digging in to help unless they had to. Lydia was still in diapers. The laundry and cooking for nine people was almost more than Sarah Ann could handle, even with her cousin Nancy helping. Amanda kept sending home postcards for three long weeks, but there was no way to ask Mom how to do anything.

Eli Huber drove Aaron and Amanda to the train station at Allentown, and fetched them again three weeks later. Amanda's diary remained unwritten for two weeks or more, but mentioned the wedding they went for. On July 18 they attended Elmira church and then to Ammon Martins for the wedding dinner. Barbara married Noah M. Weber, a widower with seven grown children.

Amanda's Uncle Christian Brubacher's drove Aaron and Amanda around to different places in Canada, visiting friends and relatives with their horse and buggy. They greatly enjoyed the fellowship. They spent one night at the "new" Uncle Noah Weber's. Aaron and Amanda had dinner at Aunt Susanna and made many calls. It was cousin Wesley, that took them to see Niagara Falls and then to the train depot for the return trip, after Aaron and Amanda spent several weeks visiting in Canada.(the same cousin Wesley,

back in 1937, had taken Amanda, Lydia and Silas to Niagara Falls on Amanda's 22nd birthday.)

Irene well remembered the train ride, and walking up and down the aisle to get a drink at the water fountain. Louise dropped a fluffy bought cookie at the train station, and could not understand why Amanda did not allow her to brush off the black dirt and eat it. They ate lots of dirt at home and she could not believe Mom wasted a pink marshmallow cookie sprinkled with coconut.

When traveling in an open, two-seated buggy, Louise bit off the bottom of an ice cream cone on a hot summer day, and Amanda had only a hanky to clean up the dripping mess. Later when someone asked "What was the best part of the trip to Canada?" Louise said, "The thing you should not bite off the bottom first!" It was her first ice cream in a cone that she remembered.

At most places, the hosts gave gifts of appreciation to the travelers. Amanda politely said thank you for every tea towel and potholder and such. Irene and Louise came home with many souvenirs from Canada, such as a hanky, a glass knick-knack

or a jelly dish to put in the corner cupboard at home. Louise and Irene showed their souvenirs to the rest and then put them safely in the Ek-shonk, [corner cupboard] upstairs in a bedroom. The triangular cupboard in the corner had two glass-fronted doors that were supposed to stay shut. The things inside were fragile and just for pretty. When youngsters opened the doors, they could not reach the things inside easily. Occasionally a child hung on the doors to reach up higher and the narrow tall cabinet tipped forward with an awful mess and commotion and broken pieces. "Quick put the things back before Mom finds out!"Louise said. Amanda always found it out and fixed miscellaneous broken things with Duco cement.

Aaron enjoyed his first trip to Canada and especially the visiting. He enjoyed Niagara Falls on the way home and he didn't have any problems otherwise, except three weeks was a long time for him. Coming home was the best part of the trip, and they promptly fetched Mary and baby Roseanna at BW Shirks. Amanda was pleased that they could actually go on a trip, but she was just as happy to have her own baby again. Walter came home from where he worked, for such a happy family reunion.

After a good's night sleep in their own beds, Aaron went to work at Terre Hill machine shop where they manufactured gutter cleaners for dairy barns. Amanda took Nancy Kilmer home, then after she rested a bit, she got busy making supper for Canadian travelers! After Aaron was home about three days, he got lumbago. The next day was Sunday and Aaron had such serious pain in his back that Jesse Brubacher came over and rigged up a traction set, to help relieve the pain. The doctor came out the next day and Aaron was not supposed to sit up more than three hours a day, with orders of spending ten says in bed. Daniel helped on the threshing crew and the boys topped the tobacco without their fathers help.

Company dropped in regularly to "visit the sick", while Amanda worked as fast as she could, canning five bushel peaches and two bushel of plums. Her own mother and sister Mary came to help can sweet corn and a bushel of lima beans.

Aaron went to Blue Ball for x-rays on his back and starting on September 1, he went to Norristown for a series of shots for his back. After the first shot he was so much better, that he could walk out the door and also come to the table for the first time in a month. Everyone knew this was a stressful time for Aaron and Amanda.

Eli Huber took him for the second shot at Norristown and Aaron felt so much improved that he wished to go to church again. They knew the hard church benches were all wrong for his back, so Daniel took a rocking chair to Bowmansville church for his father to sit on.

Aaron and Amanda had missed nearly 3 months of church, being in Canada three weeks and then Aaron at home in pain. John Huber took Aaron for his third shot to Norristown, while Daniel was working like a man all over the neighborhood helping put tobacco away, as well as doing the chores at home.

Edward Martin took Aaron for the fourth shot at Norristown, but Aaron felt bad after that one. Neighbors came to help with tobacco, because that was heavy work. Aaron managed to go along to BW Shirks watermelon party on Sunday, and helped Amanda cut up a bushel of tomatoes for juice. A gang of men from the neighborhood hung Aaron's last tobacco in his barn. Uncle Joe Weaver took Aaron for the fifth shot while Daniel went to a big corn cutting party at Joe Horst's.

Aaron improved in October, and helped cut off corn fodder to make shocks. Alvin Sauder took Aaron for the sixth shot. All this time the family worked hard gathering and canning many pears and apples. They canned twelve gallons of tomato juice and lots of apple butter and butchered chickens to eat.

Aaron went back to work at Terre Hill, after a three-month leave. Rufus Nolt took Aaron for the last shot, while Daniel seeded wheat and cut corn to stack into shocks. Aaron and Amanda gathered twenty bushel of Baldwin apples from their own trees. The egg price increased to forty cents a dozen, but that did not go very far.

15

Travelers

After Aaron and Amanda returned from their trip to Canada, even more travelers came to see them. Amanda wrote in her diary "working like n------ [black people] getting ready for company. She had no racial slur intended, but much more had the opinion that such people worked hard without a break and accomplished much." She invited a house full of guests for a Thanksgiving dinner, and the day before that they spent the whole day driving Canadians from one place to the next. Amanda felt greatly honored to host those guests; Noah Weber married Peter Brubacher's sister... Amanda's Aunt Barbara... the wedding they attended the past summer. The guests came to Aaron and Amanda for dinner, then Martin Kilmer's and Aaron's, in two carriages, hauled them all afternoon making calls wherever they wished to go.

Meanwhile Daniel and Sarah Ann managed to butcher eight chickens for Thanksgiving dinner and with Amanda's help, prepared pies, cake, Jell-O and pudding for the next day, for company. With five preschool children underfoot, there was no way Amanda could have managed without Daniel and Sarah Ann's help. More Canadians came for a call! Ike Zimmerman's brought Elam Shantz's and Jesse Baumans in the morning on Thanksgiving Day.

On Thanksgiving, all the Shirks came for dinner and the boys enjoyed small game hunting. Daniel bagged two squirrels to please Amanda. Two days later, he brought in two more squirrels and a Ruffed Grouse (Pennsylvania state bird). The Grouse were plentiful and legal game, but hard to shoot in the woods.

Pulling a wagon across the field lanes, Lydi-Jessey brought her laundry to wash at Aarons, because her washer had problems. That's what neighbors are for... Sharing through thick and thin.

Daniel, Sarah Ann and Amanda went to Amos Ringlers apple snitzing in the evening, where a whole gang showed up for a good time, thriving on neighborly love. Walter had not been home for two months, and he enjoyed hunting with his brother Daniel again. The boys brought in "two bunnies" (worth recording in Amanda's diary). It wasn't just about the meat that she was proud of them, but the brotherly togetherness, enjoying the outdoors.

On November 16, 1954, Aaron brought Amanda a wedding anniversary package! Gift-wrapped! He knew how much Amanda meant to him, while he lay in bed... she cared for him, and managed all her other duties as well. It really did make poorly that summer and health was wealth... not fully realized until it was gone.

When Canadian travelers came to Aaron and Amanda's home for a visit, Aaron asked them "Where are you going next?" The Canadian replied, "We plan to go see Aaron Shirks. They say it goes so poorly with them." To this Aaron replied, "Yes, it sure does!", and he proceeded to tell his visitors just how poorly it really does make. He laid it on so thick, that the visitor soon tried to defend these poor Aaron Shirks, by saying, "Oh, it surely can't be that bad." As the travelers departed, their red-faced driver told his guests, "That was Aaron Shirk!" The humiliated Canadian had a hard time accepting his mistake.

Aaron didn't let it bother him one bit. On his next trip to Canada, there was one place he definitely wanted to visit. He wanted to meet those people again. When he arrived, the Canadian man told him, "I hoped I would never have to meet you again." Aaron said, "No, don't feel that way. I don't hold anything against you at all and I wanted to meet you again." From then on, those Canadians and Aarons visited with each other many times.

Anyway, things did go poorly at Aarons. It was a struggle to provide food and clothes for their growing family. Feed bills and grocery bills piled up, waiting on the tobacco check, while doctor and hospital bills stacked up. Yard sales did not exist, but occasionally people gave Aaron's family some out grown clothes, and Amanda did not waste anything. She skillfully mended and altered with a thankful heart. Several times a bundle arrived anonymously beside the mailbox, labeled " to Aaron Shirks". Aaron and Amanda could not see who stopped to drop it off, and if Jesses had a clue who gave it, they never said a word. Let not the left hand know what the right hand doeth. Most people gave in secret!

Daniel remembered as a schoolboy when he only had one pair of shoes. He wore them to do his barn chores, he wore them to school, and he wore them to church. He also remembered wearing Amanda's shoes that did not fit him. [Shoes were rationed in wartime.]He did not wear stockings and he got loose dirt inside those floppy low shoes while farming. They were not practical for walking in the field behind the horse-drawn harrow.

The children did not seem to mind, or even know it could be different. They never went to bed hungry, and their clothes were washed and mended. Sheltered in such a plain and simple home, surrounded by love, and not exposed to the world's wants and desires, they were a happy family.

Dick overheard his father talking to the feed man, saying, "It seems we can hardly make ends meet, and I wish we wouldn't be so poor." Eight-year-old Dick was greatly astonished and with big eyes, he went to the house and said, "Ich hop net gwist es me-ah orm sin! (I didn't know we are poor!) Aaron never forgot that statement.

∽

Martha walked to the mailbox to mail a post-card, and she played with her cousin, seven-year-old Mabel, until the mailman went. From a dis-

tance, they watched the men use dynamite to blast a hole for the foundation of a new stripping room cellar. Jesse Brubacher planned to put up a big new tobacco shed. At Eli Huber's sawmill, Aaron and Daniel helped cut the timber, and then they helped Jesse dig the foundation and lay concrete blocks. Clement Leinbach and his crew, were the carpenters that managed a raising.

On June 16, the neighborhood men gathered early to help put up the shed. Ladies stepped out of the buggies at the walk and went inside the house to quilt. Lydi-Jes-sey managed well, and prepared most of the food in advance. While the men hammered, the women sat at two quilts rapidly talking and stitching. Only at a raising, did the farm wives quilt in June, the busiest month of all.

Several sheets of plywood lay across some straw bales as a temporary table for a big noon meal. Ruth, Rhoda and Martha walked over the field lane to Jesse's, wearing freshly starched aprons and neatly combed hair. They were old enough to help Mary and Mabel carry food from the house and help serve the meal. They could fill water cups and do as they were told. The girls felt grown up and excitement filled the air, as they watched all the action. After the men ate their fill, the women got a turn to eat.

Aaron and Amanda's five youngest children had to stay at home, out of the way. It was even dangerous for those that had to help at a raising, because accidents happened and a hammer could fall down from someone working on the rafters.

Amanda and Sarah Ann each took a turn at Jesse's that day. Sarah Ann wanted to see the action and help Annie, her age. Amanda loved to quilt while catching up on the latest happenings. Did you hear about the new couple? ".Did your wash dry yesterday? Menno-sey spoke up and said, "I never washed yet that it did not dry... sometime anyway! Every quilting automatically turned into a recipe or pattern exchange. Perhaps it was just a simple cookie recipe of the treat they served, or another quilt idea, or as far out as CHOLERA BALM.

Cholera Balm.

Oil cinnamon,	½ oz.	Blackberry Brandy, 6 oz.
Oil Wintergreen,	½ oz	Guaranteed to cure all forms of
Oil Sassafras,	½ oz.	Cholera Infantum, Cholera
Laudanum,	1. oz.	Morbus and Summer.
Sulph. Ether,	½ oz.	Complaints generally.
Chloroform,	½ oz.	
Gum Camphor,	½ oz.	
Alcohol,	6 oz.	

Directions:

Adults one teaspoonful every hour until relief is obtained children, from 10 to 15; one-half teaspoonful every hour; infants from 3 to 10 drops every hour until regulated.

Cholera was a dreaded intestinal disease that sometimes spread rapidly. Many people died from it, with not much time to get help. Amanda knew such things happened far away in India, but thankfully, she never knew any one afflicted. She kept a copy of the recipe just in case.

A Christian's life is built on the solid foundation of Christ. Faith, hope and love form the walls, while thankfulness and praise, form the roof that keeps out discouragement and depression. In that case, going to a quilting and hearing about other people's challenges in life, helped patch any weak spots on a spiritual roof. It worked the same way for the men. Aaron loved to talk and heard many things, including the tobacco and steer prices. Aaron and Amanda had much to be thankful for, all of the time, and their problems looked smaller compared to other peoples' problems.

By noontime, a new building stood on the horizon, beside the lone walnut tree on the fence line, where Amanda often admired the sun going down in colorful splendor. A lot of work remained after the raising day and Aaron and Daniel continued helping what they could. They helped Jesse make hay and found time to help Clayton Kilmer who had a broken ankle. Pete started working for Joe Wenger and stayed there for the summer.

Aaron's father, BW Shirk was also building a new barn, and sometimes Aaron and Daniel took time out to help him. A team of four or five men worked on the roof with Menno in charge of the work. Half scared of the height, Daniel watched for a chance to get off the roof as soon as he could, but Menno kept him occupied until the end. Menno tried to get Daniel over his fear of heights.

Sarah Ann and Amanda seldom went to church on the same Sunday. They took turns staying home with nearly half of the younger children, because the carriage could not hold them all and sometimes there was a shortage of Sunday clothes. They shared what they had.

After the children cleared the table and washed the dishes, there was not much to do at home, because Sunday was a day of rest. Amanda considered sewing doll clothes as working on a Sunday. The children played church with their dolls on the stairway a while, and sang, but on a nice day, the outdoors called them to the pond, the woods or best of all, to the local dump.

Even their toughened feet needed footwear at the dump, due to broken glass, sharp metal, and some garbage. Louise grabbed a pair of boots that were much too small, but she needed them only at the dump." Look what I found. ..that is neat. ..maybe we could fix this...do you think Mom would use this? "Many hands started digging in the trash and someone disturbed a swarm of yellow jackets. Ouch! Oh, get back!. .. Children ran with flailing arms, shouting, "Yellow jackets… Run!" Louise could not run because her toes curled up inside the tight boots. She was the only one that was not stung that day, because the yellow jackets all went after the commotion. The treasures they collected at the dump were seldom worth bringing home, but they enjoyed it as much as a rummage sale. Some things could be fixed and some things went right back where they came from.

In Amanda's childhood, her parents had nothing to discard. Times changed and people soon had more empty tin cans than they could use. Food at the store came in packages and not just from bins and barrels. People that lived in towns, had no ditch where they could toss their trash. Before garbage trucks arrived, many people threw refuse at a dump on wooded brush land way out back. Plastic accelerated the trash heaps. At one time, the Terrehill Garment factory started a dump on Aaron's property so far out back. They paid Aaron to burn the pile every so often.

One day the boys came home from the dump with six dolls! That made quite an impression on their sisters.

Amanda had a doll with a ruined head, way back in her childhood in Michigan, and her mother bought a new tin head to replace it. With fond memories, Amanda was the best doll hospital around. Christian Kilmers had ten girls of all sizes, and when any of them met up with Aaron Shirks ten girls, they had an instant "buppa party", [doll party], while the brothers enjoyed action outdoors. The girls ages spanned so many years, that the children never all played doll together at the same time. Christian Kilmer's girls had the nicest dolls, but Aaron Shirks girls sewed the most doll dresses. Martin Kilmers had a real playhouse. ..a dream come true! Many girls played there and kept house with wild imaginations, as the dollies cried and needed attention. Their mothers encouraged doll playing as a form of training young girls to care for their own family some day.

Mary Dale

Like the older children, Ruth and Rhoda had many happy memories of Silver Hill School. The large brown sandstone building with no plumbing had electric lights. The twins shared a double seat with black cast-iron scrolled ends. Mr. Coates taught first grade and he had many shortcomings, but Ruth and Rhoda learned to read, even without a good teacher. Vivid memories remained of the bare wooden floors, the black cast-iron stove, the chalkboard and their friends.

The girls and boys learned to play jacks on the deep windowsills of those thick stonewalls. If the teacher caught anyone chewing gum in school, he had them promptly spit it into the coal bucket. They carried water from the neighbor's hydrant daily, and stored it in a five-gallon earthen jug, with a press- on spout at the bottom. A basin below it caught the dripping water.

When Martha started first grade, she knew very little English, but good old Blanche Horning returned for that term. She was a grandmotherly teacher, that understood Dutch, and she had a kind way with beginners. She also taught the next year when Mary started to school, with Dale Stamm and Norman Waltz in her grade. Mary and Dale were best friends but could not communicate well, because Mary knew very little English. When Dale asked her a question in English, Mary alternated her answers with "yes" and "no". If Dale asked, "Do you have a dog?" Mary might say "Yes". Then to "What's his name?" She might say "no", but Mary caught on fast and had a happy term.

Dale asked Mary to call her after school, and the next day Dale asked, "Why didn't you call me?" To this, Mary said, "I did, but you did not answer, I went upstairs on the top balcony and called, and called as loud as I could. "When Dale asked, "What number did you dial?" Mary realized, that Dale meant on a telephone. Mary did not know anything about a telephone or how the thing might work.

Children hurried to get to school on time and usually they took a shortcut beneath the turnpike, through the square tunnel, where the little stream tumbled. Elias's cows crossed through that tunnel and Mary was afraid. A cow in a barn or pasture did not look nearly as huge and alarming as a cow right beside her in a dimly shaded tunnel. She felt trapped in there with a cow so close-up. She wanted someone right with her and even that was scary!

On the way home from school one time, everyone started running and Mary was last. Coming through the woods, the other children wanted Mary to hurry, and jokingly said, "There are bears and wolves in the woods!" She panicked and ran until she had side stitches. All term, Mary could hardly keep up with the rest, and any time when she got too far on behind, while walking home, she sat down and cried until the rest waited on her. Sometimes she insisted they walk back to meet her, which really irked them.

Amanda tried her best to bundle up the children for a long cold walk to school, but there was no such thing as hood sweaters or tights. Heavy coats were not always warm coats. Children wore all in one long johns, or union suits, and woolen slips. Mary wore long woolen stockings overtop her four -buckles, to keep the snow from packing in around the top. The scarf around her head left only her eyes showing, and yet she was crying with cold when she came home. She would not cry

when she came near to the schoolhouse, because she was too big to cry, but a cousin saw her crying, and told the teacher. Mrs. Horning babied Mary as soon as Mary stepped inside the schoolroom. "Come closer to the stove and warm up," said the teacher as she rubbed Mary's hands to warm them, until Mary was ashamed of herself.

Mary and Dale remained best friends, and when they completed their work at school, the teacher occasionally allowed them to walk to Dale's house, just across the yard. Dale had a toy room with games and dolls of all sorts, and she even gave Mary one big baby- doll to keep. Mary proudly named the doll, "Mary Dale", and shared her among all her sisters.

When Mary turned seven, Amanda invited Dale Stamm to come for a birthday party. She heard so much about these school friends in Mary's grade, and here was a chance to meet them. Barry and Dale Stamm came, and so did Carol Weinhold. Ice-skating on the farm pond was the entertainment, and Amanda served cake and ice cream with bananas, candy and drink. Most birthdays came and went unnoticed.

Two weeks later, the Stamms returned the party invitation, for Dale's birthday. That was a rare occasion, with real balloons and party favors, and even party napkins at the table. The children sat in circles playing party games. Ruth, Rhoda, Martha and Mary needed a gift to give, so with feedbag material, Amanda quickly sewed an apron for Dale, as a gift from all of them. Printed on the fabric, were horse and buggies across a striped teal pattern.

When the twins turned nine, Ruth and Rhoda had a real birthday party in the chicken house. In their pretend playhouse, they decorated mud pies. Annie, Mary, and Mabel, (Jesse's girls) walked across the lane, all neatly combed and bringing a delicious cake. Amanda made a special treat of Jell-O and Kool-Aid, served on real dishes from the house, for a memorable day.

Those were the only birthday "parties" the children remember. A circle on the calendar number meant ", you are special!" Amanda did not decorate cakes, because most of them disappeared so rapidly, they did not need any frosting. Only the cakes for company needed icing, unless an inferior cake needed some disguising when it got stale, and then it soon disappeared.

Six girls in a row, had many happy times playing doll and pretending. When playing church, the many girls and dolls nearly filled the stairway. One person pretended to be the "preacher" and stood behind the tall wooden box that held Amanda's extra table boards, for her extension table. When it was time to sing in "church", the girls sang, "Yaysaw …yay -saw", (German for "Jesus"). At Bowmansville church, the congregation sang with German songbooks, but it was years later, when the girls understood whose name they were singing, because they did not understand all the words in real German.

Neither did they know what it meant, when the preacher said ", Duh drit ga-bittle" meaning chapter 3. "De blattah side, dry un fotzigh" meant page 43. German singing was very slow, and some songs were extra long. The children rejoiced when the song leader announced, "Un now nugh da letcht" (and now yet the last). That meant skipping some verses, and the song soon ended. The girls playing church copied all these details. Dollies fussed in church on their mothers lap and the biggest ones sat quietly beside them until they needed the out -house. They all knelt simultaneously for prayer in a hushed bish, bish, bish.

After "pretending church" dismissal, Amanda's daughters copied her way of inviting company for "dinner". Each one had a corner somewhere, claimed as "home". Amanda's house looked like a disaster, as her daughters practiced the art of homemaking. Amanda always did say, "the best housekeepers are not always the best homemakers."

The stairway had a hefty metal pipe as a banister, tough enough to endure the weight of several children sliding down at the same time. Hands created friction, but cushioned with a skirt, a child could glide or float down the banister smoothly, while hanging on with two hands and lifting up their feet. Aaron's banister was merely a sturdy handrail three inches close to the wall. Christian Kilmers had a deluxe open stairway, with a wide wooden banister, where a person could sit on and nearly fly down.

In the empty end of the chicken house, Walter made a wooden cupboard for the girl's playhouse area. Mary bubbled with delight, and felt it was fit for a king. When playing "pretend", the girls gathered "kase boppla" or mallow weeds to serve the little cheeses on their tea sets. Dandelion flowers and weeds, grandly decorated the mud cakes.

Children pretended to be the "buttla peddlah" (bottle peddler), with a basket full of jars, like the Raleigh man tried to sell. The jars contained colored water. Sometimes the children pretended to be the mailman, one of the most prominent people around! They had fun with a hand full of junk mail.

Every Sunday when the children had a chance, they gathered with Jesse's children for entertainment. The girls sat around the table coloring or playing paper dolls. The best games in the world were Chutes and Ladders, Sorry and Uncle Wiggly, besides playing "pretend playhouse" in their woodshed. Cracking black walnuts in the stripping room and horseback riding also rated near the top. Aaron and Amanda's land had no walnut trees other than the one on the line fence that divided their property. Jesses had a wonderful porch swing and Aarons did not.

When Sarah Ann attended eighth grade she went to Goods School along Route 625. Amanda bought her a brand-new red plaid book-bag with a shoulder strap, because Sarah Ann had to bike 2 miles and meet a small yellow school bus, nicknamed "The Yellow Jacket". This school had only grade eight, and Mr. Claude Beam was the teacher. He was an elderly man, old and wrinkled, but a very good teacher. Mr. Beam told the students to study for a test, and the four students from Silver Hill did not know how! They had learned very little in the past two years with Mr. Coates, an unconcerned teacher.

Mr. Beam divided his eighth grade students into group A, and group B. The poorer students caught up so fast to the smart ones, that Mr. Beam was proud of them.

By February 1954, work started on a brand-new elementary school. Aaron's older children biked over on a Sunday afternoon to see the new location and the construction work. In November, Brecknock Elementary School had open house.

Louise started in first grade, and she got seriously carsick. Very seldom in her life, had she ridden in a motor vehicle, and she might have been better off walking. The bus driver told the school-children to sit in the back, and fill up as they come, but Louise alone sat up front, for less bouncing and swaying. She did not like it, and neither did the bus driver, nor the school nurse that cleaned up her dress at school. The nurse commented on the pretty printed slip Amanda made from feed sacks. The sick feeling and the smell were bad enough, and worse yet, was the taunting name of "kutz koo" (vomit cow). There was no other way to get to school and no one knew about motion sickness drugs. She eventually outgrew it.

Aaron and Daniel, with the help of Elias and Titus made a bus shack, or shelter with two bench seats built into the sides, where children at the end of the lane could wait on the bus when it rained. Even then, Irene remembered crying from cold. The bus shanty served its purpose well and became a handy spot to shed bonnets, suspenders, or anything classmates did not wish to wear, among peer pressure, to such a fancy new school.

Mary remembered putting her straw bonnet under some big stones at the end of the lane to hide it, because other girls did not wear any. Rhoda quickly tucked her red flowered bonnet inside her lunchbox, when the bus came before she got to the end of the lane. She had intentions to remove it at school but forgot it until lunchtime. When she sat down to eat in the cafeteria and opened her lunchbox, she found her bonnet! Quickly she snatched it out and sat on it. A fancy classmate noticed and asked, "What was that?" Rhoda said,"Oh, a cherry pie!"

Half way out the lane on a snowy winter day, Ruth felt something move in her coat sleeve. She set down her lunchbox and grabbed with the other hand. It was alive! She yanked off her coat and gave it a hard shake, and a mouse scurried across the snow. She got her coat on again, before the bus came and was glad no one else saw it. The mouse was not as bad as," what would others think?"

Mice moved indoors every fall and Aaron's closet was a good hiding spot amid all the coats and boots of a big family. Amanda set traps and paid her children one penny for killing three mice. A rat earned five cents but they were scarce. Very seldom did one venture into the house.

Sometimes the bus was waiting while the first children came to the end of the lane, and the last ones were still exiting the kitchen door. In December, with the shorter days, the scholar's hardly got up early enough and missed the bus for the first time, and it was too far to walk to school, so they all stayed at home that day. A bus driver did not have to wait, if the children were not ready. It was a good lesson on tardiness, and the next time they were ready.

Silver Hill School did not celebrate Halloween, so it was something new for Aaron Shirk's children. That was one more reason to vote against Brecknock School.

When Walter did not work away, he went to school on the bus to Brecknock. He was not old enough to quit school, so he repeated eighth grade. Walter helped along with all the other students, to poke his fingers in the soft new caulking around the windows. Claude Beam was a good teacher, and he soon saw that Walter and Catherine Leinbach knew all their lessons. They were allowed to take time off and help work in the school cafeteria. Catherine Leinbach put milk on the school trays in an assembly line fashion.

Walter chose selling popsicles at five cents each to the students over the lunch hour, and as pay, he got one free popsicle every day. Orange dream sickles, ice cream sandwiches, ice cream cones and twin-sickles all sold for a nickel each. Amanda tried to see that her children each had five cents a week for ice cream in the school lunch boxes, for a real treat.

On each sticky paper wrapper, was a "Popsicle Pete" coupon worth saving for prizes, if any child gathered enough of them. Most of the prizes were flimsy things, but Dick one time earned a set of Indian beads, with fine wire to string them up into a bracelet. One little bump and the beads might scatter all across Amanda's kitchen floor, in the dirt. The Popsicle sticks were worth saving.

Mr. Beam saw Walter was wasting his time in school. He said, "Walter come up here a minute, you can help check arithmetic scores. "Mr. Beam was a kind but firm teacher that believed in spanking. He had a lot of order in his class, and he claimed that if he spanked one mischievous character at the beginning of the term, they all knew he meant business. Claude Beam always wore a brown suit, always, and brown shoes to match! He was a JP, [justice of the peace], and Aaron's children went there to get marriage license, when they were older.

At this time, the Mennonite families received the privilege of having their children work at home instead of going on to school beyond grade 8 or the foolishness of repeating 8th grade to fulfill the law. Fourteen-year-old children had legal permission to work at home all week and write a diary, and attend three hours of school every Friday afternoon, until age 15.

When Pete was in seventh grade at Brecknock, his classroom was right beside Walter's room. Pete lived and boarded with Joe Wengers family, where he worked and went to school from there. He just came home for the weekend, and enjoyed meeting Walter at school, even just for a few moments on the playground.

At Brecknock, schoolchildren had easy access to a new set of encyclopedias. Pete and Dick gained all sorts of knowledge in the books, and to their surprise, they discovered that gunpowder is made by mixing a few ingredients they had in their reach on the farm.

Pete and Dick spent many Saturday mornings in the stripping room helping Aaron with tobacco. At 11 o'clock, Aaron might say, "well, I have to go help Mandie make dinner," as he went into the house. After Aaron left, the real fun began for Pete and Dick. They brought down their supply of gunpowder material, which they stored on top of an open beam in the stripping room ceiling, where Aaron would never look.

After the gunpowder concoction was mixed, Pete poured a zigzag line of powder across the stripping room table. Then he lit one end of the line, and psssssstt! The flame raced around his track, licking up the powder in a flash. That was education!

Dick took empty bullet shells and packed them full of gunpowder. Then he tossed the packed shells into the stove and both boys quickly ran into the tobacco cellar and waited. Bang! The sound of the explosion thrilled their hearts!

The boys learned to make fire- crackers. With the availability of gunpowder as the main ingredient, along with an abundant supply of empty shotgun shells, and the readily available dynamite fuse, it was easy! First, the primer cap was removed from the empty shell. Next, the empty shell was filled with gunpowder. Then a piece of fuse was cut to a length of a few inches and the end of it was inserted into the empty primer hole. This was one of several models of homemade pyrotechnics manufactured in the tobacco stripping room.

This dangerous sport kept up quite a few weeks, and the boys became more daring, making their mixture a little more potent each time. The bang, in the stove got louder and more powerful! One day it cracked so fierce that the iron door of the stove blew off. When Pete and Dick saw this, they were greatly subdued. Maybe their hobby was getting out of hand, and they quit their dangerous game.

At the Reading mission, Amanda found a large collection of ready cut patches of print material. She was delighted! Someone else had done all the hard part of accurately cutting print patches, ready to sew. Ruth, Rhoda, Martha, and Mary all started piecing a quilt by hand. Dick was 13 already, but he helped also when he was home sick from school and home from working away.

When Aaron needed a new suit coat Amanda did not order a readymade one. She went to new Holland and bought material. She spent $120 while there. The fabric was rather expensive and so were the new tobacco muslins. Amanda also purchased a stack of colorful feedbags, washed and ready to use for all sorts of sewing, because she needed more than the feed-man brought.

Selling Tabacco

Aaron waited four years on his money from the turnpike, and some neighbors already had their money, but Aaron did not sign off when they did. He complained about the runoff problem of rain washing down the lane to his barn. With more fuss than necessary, he even hired a lawyer, which was greatly frowned upon by the church. [Why do ye not rather take wrong? 1 Corinthians6; 7] Aaron gave in later, when he saw the rain was going to wash down the hill, no matter what.

When the turnpike money finally arrived in the fall of 1953, the turnpike was in use for three years already. Aaron had charged bills at the feed mill, the blacksmith, the dentist, the doctor, and the grocer, and more. $2600 minus $400 for the lawyer fees was a lot of money, but he had it all spent, long before he got it, especially with paying part of that mortgage to his father.

Amanda could see they were not yet rich, and nothing really changed. The tobacco check for the current years' crop, might feel rich though, without all the bills stacked up waiting for the tobacco check. Maybe they could even get one-step ahead of all the bills for a change.

Jesse sold his tobacco crop for $.32 a pound, and that was a fantastic price, but Aaron wanted more money than that! What worked on the turnpike, by holding out for more money, did not work with selling tobacco. After a while, the tobacco buyers stopped coming and let him set, with his crop unsold.

Amanda tried to encourage him to sell like the other farmers, and to be content, but his mind was set and it was no use talking. In fact, he was not even listening! To her it made a lot more sense to sell the tobacco and put off a big new Sears order for boots and necessities. She had lived with Aaron long enough to understand, and to count her blessings, they were too many to count. Aaron's father, BW Shirk, was known to hold out for higher prices on steers and tobacco. Was it inherited or learned?

Amanda knew it was not in her place to sell tobacco, and this was her lot in life. She would not trade with others even if she could. Christian Kilmer's were moving again to another farm and Martin Kilmer's had a baby with Down's syndrome… and Lydia had a set of problems all her own. Amanda kept right on patching and darning, while singing praises to God. Money, after all was not the most important thing in life and godliness with contentment was her aim.

16

Sears Catalog

Look here! A new catalog came in the mail today! Everyone wanted to see the Sears catalog, and it was not a sharing thing, when Amanda wanted to browse the fabric section, and Daniel planned to study the tools. The children could hardly wait to look at all the pretty things they knew would never be theirs. The older out dated Sears catalog promptly went to good use in the privy. The thinnest pages made the best toilet paper, especially when they were crumpled and softened first.

Amanda sewed hundreds of dresses and she did not intend to order any ready-made ones. She allowed the girls to cut up any pages showing rows and rows of colorful dresses. Amanda had taught her daughters how to make paper dolls, to fit those many dresses. With cardboard and empty cereal boxes, the girls also designed detailed dollhouses and crude furniture to play pretend, with the paper dolls.

The Sears and Roebuck Company had a way of displaying the dresses in a row, but sadly, they overlapped the wide full skirts a bit and one corner of each skirt was damaged when cut apart. Worst of all, was the fact that the reverse side had more dresses to cut out, and they needed to make a choice of which side to save.

Amanda sent off many big orders to the Sears Company, but they always sent a check with their order and could not charge the bill. She bought Walter, Pete and Dick each a new thick brown corduroy coat, with a fake fur lining that looked like sheepskin. The durable "sheepie" coats lasted many years. Later Amanda copied the pattern from those worn out coats and made some home-made similar coats. Dick had a broken egg in his coat pocket one time and Amanda did not find it until the egg dried up.

The twins wore green homemade wool coats to first grade. Homemade coats were a little cheaper than the bought ones, unless a person counted time as money. The bought wool fabric and the sewing notions added up as Amanda saved everything but time. Sewing was a necessity but also a creative joy that helped preserve her sanity. She kept right on patching and skimping.

Shoes were not homemade, hence not so easy to come by. Some came from the Reading mission but Aaron and Amanda bought most of the shoes new. Amanda ordered many by mail from Sears and Roebuck and those, the children handed down until they were completely worn out. Amanda seldom went barefooted, but all the children did over summertime. Even Aaron went to church barefooted occasionally when the children were young.

When the geese headed south, the children appreciated the dignified, dressed up felling of comfortable shoes in the cool weather. Most everyone else their age, wore shoes to church. Aaron took several children to Bowmansville to the shoemaker. He didn't actually make shoes,but he repaired and sold many. Bells above the door jingled to summon the owner from the adjacent rooms where he lived. Amanda said to get black shoes and the styles did not matter much to Aaron, so he allowed the girls to choose black patent leather shoes with a swivel strap. That was the latest style, and some girls had shoes like that at Brecknock School. With the strap swiveled to the back, it looked like stylish slippers and made a nice flopping sound while showing off.

Louise could hardly wait until Aaron finished at the feed mill, so she could show off her new shoes. Amanda did not approve of the style and asked, "didn't they have anything better?"The shoes were soon worn out and forgotten.

Raymond Witwer was a prompt and dependable bus driver for many years. He lived just a mile or so, out the road and picked up Aarons children early. One morning before the bus got to school, the engine died and quit, and all the children cheered, "Yaaaayyyyy! Party time! No school and no classes... Whoopee! Raymond was concerned, and not in a party mood at all. He felt responsible to get the children to school on time, but they were late. Another bus fetched the children, and a mechanic worked on the bus. The next time he came, Raymond told the children that a fly stopped the school bus. How could a fly stop a big new yellow school bus? The fly was in the gas line!

The children respected Raymond Witwer as the boss, but he could never see what all happened on the back seats of his big long bus, even when he kept one eye on the rearview mirror. Louise and Lydia each had a turn being a school patrolman. The patrolman wore a big wide, white belt across the shoulder and diagonally down to the waist. The buckle at the waist opened and shut with a loud click and a touch of authority. The official-looking badge resembled a policeman's badge! They did not get out of the school bus and direct traffic like city patrols, but the bus driver needed them as tattletales, observing any misconduct or bullying, and reporting any mischief to the school principal.

The school children spent an excessive amount of time on the bus, and knew each other a little too well. They did not stay in their seats. Sometimes the children bounced around back there and scribbled names on steamed windows, teasing boy / girl nonsense. Louise outgrew some of her bashfulness and boldly reported some naughty boys, including her brother Wesley, when she thought it necessary. One time someone pushed Rhoda against the metal pipe along the top edge of the seat and broke her front tooth. For ten years, she had a corner missing and then she had it fixed very reasonably. Had she known, she certainly would have had the tooth repaired for her teen years and her wedding day.

Brotherly love multiplied among all the children in a big family, but privacy did not! A person could hardly find a spot anywhere for goofing off. "Mom, Martha is not helping," Mary tattled. "Did you know that Louise is finishing her library book?"

No one had any secrets... except in the outhouse... that unique toilet with two holes cut in the wooden bench -seat... used instead of a bathroom commode. The door locked securely with a hook and eye. Each hole had a tight fitting wooden lid, but nothing could eliminate the stench, especially in summertime! Outdated calendars decorated the walls more attractively than the latest wallpaper could. Occasional newspapers, and always the Sears catalog lay on the seat to use instead of toilet paper.

Their first outhouse had a hinged wooden flap on the back wall, where a man could fork the manure pile onto the wheelbarrow, and haul it to the field and spread it. Aaron changed that when they added an outhouse inside the woodshed. Beneath the hinged wooden bench seat, Aaron set two sturdy, metal five-gallon buckets on the concrete floor. Every so often, Amanda added a scoop of lime to reduce the smell and assist the composting. It was Aaron's chore to empty those buckets into the hayfield, close to the house, as sheet composting. No one played there. Everyone in the neighborhood, dumped sewage on the fields as the only option available.

Besides urgent necessity, the outhouse created seclusion, until the next person came knocking. Seclusion meant sneaking out of work, or sneaking a handful of raisins or candy and eating them without anyone watching. It also meant finishing the last chapter of a storybook from the school library, hoping Ruth washed all the dishes before anyone found out who was missing, or before anyone came pounding on the door demanding, "Hurry up!" Let me in NOW!"

The boys seldom used the outhouse, because they preferred a spot behind the chicken house. One time Dick used stinging nettles instead of toilet paper... but only one time! He learned the names of the plants in a hurry and never forgot the stinging hurt, burning like fire! The stinging nettle leaves closely resembled the soft velvety catnip leaves.

Outside the boy's bedroom window, the grass did not grow and the adjustable, sliding screens rusted out in a hurry! Amanda knew why, and so did the boys.

December 11, 1954

The new farm pond at Aaron Shirks attracted young people all year. The boys kept a close watch on the thickness of the ice and on Saturday, Dec.11, 1954 it was fit to go skating when the whole crew was home from school. Amanda said, "Yes, you may go skating when the work is done." The children all cheered for the first skating of the season.

With five girls in school, Amanda waited until Saturday for help in running the wringer washer, and the work of hanging wash on the line. Sarah Ann was busy filling kerosene lamps, and carefully washing the smoky glass lampshades, returning each lamp to its proper place in the house. Aaron chopped the heads off twenty chickens and busy hands helped pluck them rapidly.

"Girls, please wash and carry all those meat- jars to the cellar shelves," said Amanda, "dump the slop bucket to the pigs, burn the bonfire, fold the diapers that are dry, sweep the floor and mop it up. Irene and Lydia put those dolls and doll clothes away. Mary you may set the table as soon as the floor dries and Louise, see that the browning butter doesn't burn."

Everyone worked rapidly and dinner vanished in a hurry with the thought of gathering coats, mittens, boots, scarves, wool skirts, skates and sleds. It was frustrating when three children wore the same size skates, with not enough to go around, and not enough money to buy new ones. None of Aarons children felt deprived when they shared skates. With wobbly ill-fitting skates, nobody wanted to skate very long without a break! Amanda never owned a pair of skates, and neither did the rest of her brothers and sisters, growing up in Michigan. It looked like so much fun gliding across the ice, and she knew without a doubt, that she would have liked skating in her childhood.

This was the second winter for ice-skating at Aaron and Amanda's new pond, and Amanda gathered all the skates she could find at the Reading mission or at EK Fisher. Most of the skates were clamp- on and hard on the shoes, because shoe-soles were attached to the shoes with nails, and the skates pulled the nails loose. Any time the heel or soles needed reattaching, Aaron hammered them on his anvil. Misplaced nails made the shoes painfully unwearable.

Strap- on skates, with a leather belt all around the shoe, were wobbly and inferior. Shoe -skates were the latest and the best, but least available. It was style for the girls to wear white figure-skates, and boys wore black skates, but style had nothing to do with it. It all looked so easy until Louise tried to skate with ill-fitting, wobbly, dull skates.

The air was nevertheless, filled with festive excitement and the weather was fine. Children tried racing, twirling, swooping, skating backwards and figure eights, all mixed with showing off and falling on the ice. With or without skates, it was fun!

Amanda enjoyed some peace and quiet in the house, while ten-month-old baby RoseAnna took a nap. "Quietness" was scarce among a big family. She watched from the kitchen window and remembered the winter fun in her childhood … happy memories lingered. She enjoyed watching her lively children work so fast, and then play so hard.

Irene did not have skates, and did not like to be among the speed and action. She saw a circle of dark ice away from everyone else and thought it would make a nice "hut" for her. She wanted to sit on her sled, in this little house. The children had strict orders to stay away from that corner where the overflow pipe kept the water moving, and the ice was thin. Irene did not understand why no one may go there and she wanted a closer look.

With a sudden crack and a splash, she plunged into the frigid water, while others noticed and all the skating stopped. Irene desperately clung to the 6-inch wide overflow pipe, sticking straight up from the muddy bottom, while her sled sank eight feet to the bottom of the pond.

Daniel said, "Keep holding on Irene, I'll get you out!" Not far away, on the pond bank, lay a piece of the first crudely built, broken diving board. Daniel had recently seen a sketch about safely using a board on thin ice. He knew to distribute his weight evenly, as

he slithered across the ice to grab Irene's hand. The thin ice kept breaking away, until he got her to the stronger thicker ice.

Daniel worked like a man. He was big and strong for a 16-year-old, while Irene was small for her age weighing thirty some pounds at the age of four. He carried her to the house dripping and shivering.

Amanda's tranquil silence was shattered when a child burst into the house saying "Mam, mam! De Irene iss nie ga-bru-huh!" (Irene broke in) Amanda jolted to red alert and asked, "Iss see noch im vos-sah?" (Is she still in the water?) "Nay, duh Daniel hut see rouse grickt. See iss blotch noss un um shnotterah." (Daniel got her out; she is soaking wet and shivering)

Amanda glanced towards the pond and saw Daniel carrying Irene to the house. Piece by piece Amanda got the whole story as she dried off her frightened daughter. Irene was blue with cold and her teeth chattered! Amanda opened the oven door for more warmth, and sat closer as she cuddled Irene and loved her dearly. Irene felt the warmth of the fire, but the love she felt from her mother, warmed her more than a blanket could.

After Irene revived, she wore her high black Sunday shoes, because her other shoes were soaked. Amanda had a chance to explain to her children that they need to obey, even when they do not understand "why". (Swimmers retrieved the rusty sled the next summer)

Sometimes when one child tried to rescue another, they both went under and Daniel's calm thinking was appreciated many times. When the family sat down to supper that evening, and bowed their heads in prayer, there was an added pause of thankfulness to God for his mercies. Thank you for the Guardian Angels that hover around us.

Amanda worked long until the last laundry was put away and everything was ready for Sunday. Again, at bedtime, Aaron and Amanda had extra praise to God for their wonderful family and his promises to help them. "Thank you God for every one of our children, fourteen are not too many!

When the lamp was snuffed out and all was well under warm covers that night, every one of them was glad that they still had Irene. Aaron and Amanda were keenly reminded that raising the next generation was the most important job they had.

✎

Just before Christmas, Aaron bought a new gas lantern for $12.95. It used white gas instead of kerosene, and made a wonderful clear light, better than any his farm ever saw at night. The lantern was important for stripping tobacco after supper, but sometimes it hung on the sturdy ceiling hook where the baby jumper belonged, on the kitchen ceiling.

Amanda was not afraid of any people, animals, spiders or even snakes, but she had a fear of explosives such as gas and matches. While other people in the neighborhood used gas stoves for cooking and gas irons for their laundry, Amanda did not trust them. She did not want a pressure cooker either, due to many stories about pressure cookers exploding. Why take the chance? When canning, she cooked all her green beans, sweet corn, peas, and meat for three hours or so, sweating beside the wood stove, in the summer heat.

That was another problem. Many neighbors had a gas range for summertime cooking, but she did not want to mess with gas and matches, for some reason. She would rather sweat. As for the new gas lantern, even Amanda agreed to its cheerful presence. She was one that often worked late. She enjoyed the lantern light, and so did all the others, crowding around and saying, "Get out of my light"! Aaron used a lantern to do chores sometimes and the old kerosene lantern did not make nearly as much light as the new lantern. When the brightness gradually faded, someone had to pump it up again. Amanda missed the bright light when Aaron and the boys used it to strip tobacco after supper.

After Daniel turned 16, he got his first job away from home, other than helping uncles and neighbors. He started working at a tree farm in Angelica, close to Reading, where they cut down trees for making pulpwood. Rufus Nolt and his son Carl took Daniel along to work at Sherlund Forest. On a big tree farm, every third row of trees needed thinning. The trees, spaced five feet apart, were too crowded. Daniel helped cut down trees with chain-saws and hard work.

When the tree farm needed more help, Walter started working there occasionally, and so did Josie Latshaw and Amos Kilmer. A seasonal job only lasted one winter.

When Amanda had all the work she could handle and then some, she still enjoyed flowers. The gladiola bulbs she saved last fall were replanted again in spring, even with a two-month-old baby and much more important things to do. Saving bulbs from one year to the next did not cost money and the pleasure she got from giving flowers to sick people made it worthwhile. Amanda enjoyed the beauty of nature in all its forms, and especially the beauty in her reach, close to the house. Birds and blooms were a mental therapy and so were her hobbies of sewing and gardening. Any perennials Amanda collected from her sisters and friends held precious memories, as they emerged and unfolded every spring.

If Amanda's flowers were a hobby, sewing was an obsession due to necessity. Her mother taught her to sew at a young age, and she certainly wanted to teach her own girls. The first step in teaching a child to sew, was stringing up buttons. Amanda patiently showed her children how. She poured some colorful buttons in a pie pan, and gave a child a large needle with thread. When the child lost interest or forgot about the unfinished string of buttons, Amanda put them all back into the button jar, where she kept an assortment for her mending.

After mastering the needle and thread, came the challenge of hemming by hand, such as a hanky, a tea towel, a diaper or a scrap of cloth. Next came the grown up honor of piecing a quilt top by hand. Amanda carefully cut all the patches, and when a daughter sewed half the blocks together by hand, she allowed her to use the treadle sewing machine for the other half.

Amanda coaxed and ripped and encouraged patiently until every one of her girls learned to sew, even those that did not want to. It was part of "creating with your hands "and it was a must!

A virtuous woman needs to mend and darn, and sew for her family. Darning socks was one of those necessities. Nearly every laundry day brought more stockings with holes in them. The smaller holes were not hard to repair, but the larger holes were. Amanda slipped a smooth ceramic doorknob inside the worn sock, and with strong thread or yarn, she skillfully wove a new patch where the gaping hole had been. Stitching back and forth and then up-and-down weaving threads together, she mended as she sang. The doorknob was scarred from many years of stitching.

She saved denim patches from the backs of worn out pants, and appliquéd the scraps on the knees to cover the holes so commonly found on her boy's everyday pants. Even little children could sew buttons in place, at a young age. Sewing was not a hobby to enjoy after the other work was finished; sewing was the work, and a subject Amanda taught well.

When Amanda wrote in her diary at the end of a busy day, sewing was an accomplishment worth mentioning, because she felt she did something that day. Cutting out stacks of garments ready to sew was the hard part, and after that, she could sew without much concentration. She often sat sewing amid a cluttered house because sewing was more important than cleaning.

In a diary, Amanda wrote, 'Cleaning house while the children are growing, is like shoveling the walk before it stops snowing! "No matter how fast she worked, her time seemed wasted when nothing stayed clean. Old doctor Schnader often said ', Cleanliness is next to godliness'. Amanda tried, but she knew that saying was not from the Bible and God knows the thoughts of her heart.

When Amanda was not sewing, she spent her time with laundry and food. Canning was important enough to record in her diary many times, but on some days she had nothing much to say for herself. She wrote, "I just puttered all day", "I loafed all day with the daily work", "I just chored around all day", "I just bummed all day" and "puttered around making things to eat". On those days, Amanda worked hard. She got up early and worked hard, with a cheerful heart, meeting the needs of her family. She kept her mind and her hands busy, and did what she could.

She changed many diapers and washed them out in a bucket of water. Sarah Ann did more than her share of that also and carried the smelly bucket outside to empty it. Over summertime, they could not keep the flies away and they sometimes had maggots in the diaper bucket.

After working late, and all was quiet, everyone else went to bed. Amanda had time for herself, reading her German \English Bible and praying in secret, putting on her nightgown and her night covering, for a good night's sleep.

Amanda raised twice as many children as her mother did. It took twice the food, the management, laundry, and twice the sewing. It is true that she had twice the amount of help, but she had the job of training her helpers, and that was the tedious part. When a child was barely old enough for the job, that is when they enjoyed helping most, and wanted to learn, even if it was much easier for Amanda to do it alone. Amanda took time out to teach, not considering it a troublesome bother.

Her own mother had encouraged Amanda to sew, by making doll clothes with rags and salvaged thread, saved from ripping. Back then, in Michigan, Amanda remembered unraveling any scrap of yarn from a worn out garment, such as the cuff of a glove. They saved every scrap of yarn and string, wrapping it on a wooden spool, for hand sewing. Perhaps they used the unraveled yarn to darn stockings. With a six-inch piece, they could attach a button.

When Aunt Eva came home from the Terre-hill garment factory, with a pile of fabric and lace pieces from work, Amanda saved the best parts for quilts. Lace was fancy adornment that Amanda did not need, and anything was okay for the dolls. Amanda knew she could not wait until the work was done, to teach her girls how to sew. On a busy day in June, with the wash flapping on the line, she took a break to inspire her daughters and motivate them to use their imagination with sewing small projects.

Amanda showed the girls how to lay a doll on a piece of newspaper, and draw out around the doll, with plenty of room for seam allowances, creating a simple pattern. It took a lot of practice before anything fit on a doll, but it did not have to fit right. Many scraps ended up in the waste can, or salvaged for a smaller doll. It took a lot of encouragement, and patience to put up with tangled threads and lost needles. With several girls the same size, Amanda had triple the trouble, especially on the Singer treadle sewing machine.

Beginners started sewing by hand, but when they progressed to the sewing machine, Amanda had broken needles to replace, and she often heard, "the sewing machine doesn't work!" They all had to learn how to put in the bobbin and thread the sewing machine just right, and turn the wheel forward or it starts sewing backwards. Her efforts were well spent...

When Aaron's children brought dolls along to school one day, other little girls marveled at the talent of sewing. "Did you really make that doll dress by yourself," they asked. "Could you sew me a doll dress, with matching panties like that?" A few doll dresses sold at school, to classmates, and the honor was bigger pay than the coins in Ruth's hand.

Those other little girls at school could have learned to sew also, with a patient teacher like Amanda that took time out on a busy day, with encouragement to try again when they failed the first time. Even with a three-month-old baby in the house, and all the busy-ness of June, like strawberries, peas, haymaking, planting tobacco and pulling weeds, life is not all work… when sewing is play.

Rhoda learned to sew at a young age and in third grade, she wore a dress she had sewed by herself. Rhoda was a "ripsh" (worked fast) and she was soon finished, but not always to perfection, just good enough. She enjoyed action and did not consider sewing exciting enough, until ten years later, when she sewed her own clothes, as a must. Still Later, she became a whiz at sewing. She grasped the whole concept, and saw in her head how it should look, working without directions. She skillfully learned to adjust patterns, but did not like directions or recipes…. just do it!

An advertisement caught Mary's attention, "How to earn money!" Even without a need for coins in her pocket, Mary wanted to earn money-selling greeting cards. The advertisement made it look so easy, and without asking Amanda, she sent for literature. Several boxes of greeting cards arrived in the mail, and all she had to do was sell them for the card company, and then she could keep some of the profit.

The high-priced cards cost more than those did that Emma Good sold, and Mary did not think it would work to sell them at Jesse's, the only neighbors close by. She eagerly took them along to school trying to sell them to other students, who were not interested. Eventually she sold the cards to some kindhearted teachers that could not resist her sweet innocence. With Mary's long dark pigtails and big blue eyes, a teacher said, "My mother used to comb me like that."

Mary wanted to earn prizes way out of her reach, but she settled for a sweater clip she never used, and she knew she did not want to try selling any more greeting cards...ever!

The same gimmick grabbed Louise's attention, but she did not sell any cards. Amanda sent an explanation to the company, and Louise got out of the deal, and still kept the free salt and pepper -shaker set, shaped like cardinals. Amanda could have told her daughters that when things sound too good to be true, they usually are. It was supposed to be easy, so they did not ask in the first place.

The dentist's wife, Mrs. Halsey, taught music at Brecknock School. She enjoyed children, and often had action with her teaching, as "Here we go around the mulberry bush", while walking in a circle.

At Christmastime, Mrs. Halsey wanted a chorus of good singers. She took the students one at a time on the piano bench beside her, asking them to follow the piano notes as high and as low as they could sing. Aaron's children were not much of singers and might not be able to attend the school program on an evening anyway.

Amanda had the privilege one year, to go see the program and watched Rapunzel acted out. "They could have picked a better story, "she thought.

When Mrs. Halsey needed an angel, for a part in the Christmas story, she chose Mary Shirk, from among the hundred other girls in school. Any girl could dress in a white robe and wear a tinsel halo, but she wanted Mary's long hair for an impact. With her long nearly black braids unraveled, Mary's kinky dark hair rippled below her waistline and beyond.

As Mary stepped on the stage, the auditorium lights snapped off, and a strobe light shone on Mary, with her tinsel halo, dressed in a white gown, holding a foil star on a wand. She said her part clearly. "For lo, an Angel of the Lord came upon them, and the glory of the Lord shone round about them. (St. Luke chapter 2, verse nine.)" Mary slowly turned around and walked away quietly in stockinged feet, as her hair rippled and gleamed.

Many older teachers admired and fussed over long braids," like the hair I had as a child", but they had their haircut short. For 2000 years after Christ, most Christians agreed it was wrong for women to have cut hair, and then suddenly it was all explained away.

Mennonites insisted, Corinthians eleven in the Bible means, women should not have cut hair. Gradually, only the plain people remained with uncut hair on the women and girls, and eventually they were labeled as different or "plain people", because they did not change with the rest. Amanda insisted that long hair was a blessing, and not just for showing off in a program.

Amanda had long thick hair and she could sit on the ends of it, in younger years. The longest hair she measured was 45 inches long. Many of her descendents inherited that genetic trait, and a granddaughter measured a hair at 63 inches long, when she herself stood 67 inches tall.

Mrs. Rufus Nolt came to Aaron Shirks in 1955 asking if Sarah Ann could work for them, but Amanda had to say no. Dependable Sarah Ann was her only help while the rest of the girls were in school and they still had four preschool children.

Amanda had 50 people come for Sunday dinner, and 32 for supper: Manasseh Kulp's, Ike Kulp's, and Jesse's came for supper. After cleaning for company, she made it worthwhile. She always enjoyed preparing the food, more than doing the cleaning.

At the age of 15, Sarah Ann started her first quilt top by hand, a four patch. Walter came into the house and helped her make donuts, and popcorn. He shook the popcorn in big black cast-iron pan on top of the kitchen range. The pop corn did not last long and the fresh warm donuts vanished so fast that two days later the children tried making more doughnuts!

Martin Kilmer's oldest daughter Lydia married Enos Sauder in October 1955. That was a new chapter in Aaron and Amanda's life, that of being aunt and uncle at a wedding. On Tuesday, they went to help dress fifteen roosters for the wedding dinner on Thursday. Amanda finished her new dress so she could wear it for the wedding and she pressed the Sunday suits for Aaron and Daniel. She used gasoline as the best dry cleaning solvent available and then she hung the suit on the clothesline, until the smell vanished. Aaron and Amanda each needed a presentable apron to help as cooks at the wedding.

Amanda depended heavily on Sarah Ann at home with 11 children, so Aaron and Amanda could spend the day at the wedding where 130 guests ate dinner. Eli Huber's Anna Mary and Ira Martin married that same Thursday, in the same neighborhood, but not of the horse and buggy church.

Stone fences were an everyday part of life at Aaron Shirks, and there were so many. The property line between Aarons and Jesse was over ten feet wide, created with a ridge of rocks. Some years the freezing and thawing weather pattern heaved many more rocks from the fields. The rocks became a frustration, as Aaron piled more and more into the fencerows, around the edges.

A stone fence, sounded like something well built and beautiful, like those in the James Herriot books, but these were not walls, just heaps. The rounded rocks were worthless to a mason. They could not be split, or crushed or shaped, like the useful limestone slabs. The igneous diabase, rocks were granite or Ironstone, with enough iron in them to hold a magnet. They broke plowshares and caught at equipment. Aaron detoured some outcroppings, and farmed around them.

Many rocks were a bane to farmers, but a haven for wildlife. The boulders made crevices and crannies for a well-balanced natural habitat. Bears and coyotes did not live here, and deer were scarce but foxes and hawks dined on a healthy supply of small game of every kind. Dense bushes, briars,

vines and even small trees covered the rocky fencerows. As the trees grew taller, the roots zapped the crops along the edge, and so did the rabbits and the groundhogs. Yes, groundhogs, lots of them. They were another nuisance to every farmer. Horses could step into their large tunnels and break a leg. It was no wonder that small game hunters enjoyed such a habitat.

The swamp between Aarons' buildings and the clear Black Creek raised a generous supply of frogs, toads, snakes, fish, crawdads and mosquitoes. A person could not walk through the thick mucky swamp, and the cows detoured it most of the time. Song- birds hid nests where God directed them and a murder of crows circled raucously above the treetops. The heavenly song of the wood thrush thrilled a heart!

The varied habitat created a science class for anyone that noticed. It was living proof that God was real! It didn't just happen! The proof was in holding a new pink mouse, smell a perfect flower, study the clouds, find a mysterious egg or to see the beauties of nature all around. Where better, could a child grow up, than on a farm along the edge, with enough work to keep busy and yet time to create and explore?

Aaron was not a hunter and readily gave permission to other hunters. Some came every year and sometimes brought a few more from far away, like Philadelphia and Reading. With a hunter on each side of that fencerow, they might bag a limit of rabbits or pheasants in a short time.

It was more exciting than Christmas at Aaron Shirks, when colored cars parked on the barn hill, as many as seven or eight at a time. All the men wore new hunting outfits with a 4" x 6" tag displayed on their back, showing their hunting permit. They had an assortment of hunting dogs milling around them.

Several hunters brought with them coins and candy for the children, and sometimes a bottle of wine for Aaron. Mr. Lance usually gave toys, used puzzles and games. These were highly cherished and played with, for many years among many children. The "Lance puzzles" were carefully put back in the box, and dumped out again and again. The wobbly card table, with a puzzle on top, attracted many children, of all sizes. "Please don't push the table," they scolded. The puzzles were not interlocking, and one little push meant trouble. Every child scrambled to put the last fun pieces in place, even sometimes hiding a piece for last.

When Amanda cooked small game, her family enjoyed eating the squirrel, pheasants and rabbits, but not the groundhog. A neighbor, Melvin Reich enjoyed shooting groundhogs on Aaron's farm, and he talked Amanda into cooking one with plenty of onions. After she served the meat on a platter, it still smelled so bad that nobody wanted it. Perhaps it was an older woodchuck, and the young ones tasted better, especially if the hunter removed the glands promptly. Some hunter drove to Aaron's farm all the way from Philadelphia just to shoot groundhogs. Think of that! Aaron also gave permission for trappers to set traps for foxes and raccoons. Occasionly someone came to fish.

Whoever shot the game cleaned the game, unless he could successfully bribe someone else into cleaning it. In the stripping room, the boys hung a double hook from the ceiling to hold both legs of a squirrel or a rabbit upside down for skinning. After slitting the fur from one hind leg to the other, a person could skin a rabbit similar to pulling a tight fur garment off down across his head easily. The same plan worked for a squirrel, except for the fact that they were tough! Undressing fur animals looked easy until Louise tried it.

Fish were easier and Louise didn't mind cleaning some for her brothers. On the wooden porch floor, with a dull paring knife, she scaled the fish and removed the head, fins and insides. Everyone enjoyed the fish Amanda fried in butter, but when they met small bones in a mouthful of meat, they spit it all on their plate. Amanda carefully dismantled the soft, fried fish meat for the youngest children at the table before she gave any to them. She spent so much time removing fish bones at the table, that she hardly ate any fish. She did not want to see the fish wasted, with bones mixed in.

17

Baby Mandy

When Amanda turned forty, she had her last teeth pulled at the dentist, and got false teeth at the bottom. She had her upper dentures over twenty years earlier, before she married. Aaron and Sarah Ann got their teeth filled, and Aaron's family charged all the bills, waiting on the tobacco check. When Louise had toothache, she went to the dentist after school and Pete went with her. At 3:00, after school dismissed, Pete and Louise rode on a different school bus to get to Bowmansville, and to the dentist. Dr. Halsey fixed their teeth, and then Aaron picked them up with old Frank and the carriage.

Louise, in first grade, needed a second dentist appointment two weeks later. She bravely found the right bus after school, but she had the wrong day. The dentist was not looking for her and he had no way of notifying her parents. When the other children came home without Louise, they figured out what happened and Aaron fetched a rather scared first grader at the dentist all alone. The next day thirteen year old Pete, and Louise together kept their appointment, and Daniel brought them home again at four o'clock.

Aaron and Amanda's entire family had poor teeth. Did they eat too much candy, or lacked in brushing teeth? Aaron could not believe the dollar amounts when he came to pay his bill at the dentist, after the tobacco sold. He thought Mr. Halsey charged outrageously!

They had lots of fresh milk in their diet and they ate vegetables galore. They did not skimp on meat, Aaron made sure of that. He said he did not "eat" if he did not have meat on the table. Amanda loved fruit, desiring to serve it three times a day. They all had a sweet tooth, and Noah Groff sold candy by the case. The brittle clear-toy candy was almost too attractive to eat. Sometimes Amanda bought a whole case of black gumdrop candies shaped like little babies. The name of the candy is unprintable since people avoid racial incrimination. The same flavor candy is still available but in bear shapes, named anise bears.

Aaron's children sneaked candy between meals if they could find any. The younger children remembered begging for candy, and Amanda said,"If you can find it, you can have some." Amanda had many good hiding spots but sometimes the children found the candy. The family struggled through financial setbacks when they could not afford to buy candy, but fifty years later, quite a few of the fifteen grown children still enjoyed eating candy.

Anytime the children had chewing gum, they did not want to part with it. Sometimes one child tired of chewing a big wad of stale gum and passed it on to the next one for a turn. At nighttime, they carefully removed their gum before sleeping, and stuck the wad onto the bed frame. They all knew from experience, what happens when gum sticks in pigtails or onto a pillowcase. Gasoline was Amanda's best gum and tar remover. The next morning the gum went with them everywhere. At mealtime, the highly treasured gum rested in a drinking cup at the table. No one ever heard of sugar free chewing gum, but the old gum had long lost its flavor and sugar.

Wesley went to the hospital at the age of four, with a troublesome infection beneath his chin. Ever since he had swallowed kerosene as a toddler, he had a problem that did not clear up with penicillin. Finally, the doctor scheduled him for surgery. Wesley stayed at the hospital overnight all alone and he gave the nurses a hard time. Only one of them could speak his language.

Just a few weeks after that, Roseanna had her second birthday, and eleven days later, on March 13, 1956 she had a new baby sister. Baby Amanda Brubacher Shirk, had the nickname of Mandy, right from the start. She arrived at 11:45 PM, weighing 11 1/2 pounds. Sarah Ann was out of school, so Amanda did not need any outside help.

Amanda remembered so well, when baby Joshua arrived into their home and into their hearts, in Michigan. She remembered the warm soft baby, bundled in blankets, wiggling in her arms. His funny faces entertained her as he grimaced and yawned. Each new baby bonded the family more tightly. She did not want her children to miss out on the miracle sent from heaven. As a baby grabs onto a finger, it awakens a deep love in a person, to someday raise a family. Babies are precious, and grow up too fast.

Amanda approved of her children playing dolls and' pretending' to be homemakers, an important link in becoming keepers at home, but real babies worked better. Amanda kept her three oldest schoolgirls home from school, for one day each, even if the teacher marked that as an illegal absence. Ruth stayed home the first day on a Friday, and Rhoda got the next turn. Then Martha took one turn also, helping Sarah Ann. It was two whole years since a new baby arrived, and baby Mandy was a celebrity, at least most of the time.

Anyone that glimpsed into Aaron and Amanda's home, could see how much everyone loved another baby. Mandy was cuddled and rocked and sang to, more than any of the rest. She was used as a doll to play dolly and the only space alone, was sleeping in the crib. Babysitting got a little stale though, when everyone else went outside, except the one designated to watch the baby.

All the children in the family heard the request many times," Grick mich un vindle."[Bring me a diaper!]Amanda changed diapers on her lap for all fifteen of their children, even the bigger squirming toddlers. She never heard of wet ones or baby wipes. When she needed, a better clean up, she often asked," Please bring me some water in a cup." With a baby on her lap, she did not fetch the water by herself. She carefully poured water on the cleanest corner of the diaper for added scrubbing.

Within a two-mile radius of Aaron and Amanda, three other families raised fifteen or more children. (Elias Shirks, Harvey Zimmerman's, and Menno Shirks)

With a big family, Amanda had plenty of practice potty training toddlers. She thought she knew how until one of the last ones came along. Amanda said," It was good for me, so I could finally understand what the other mothers went through. I thought they just did not know how!"

A few days after baby Mandy arrived, a snowstorm started on a Friday, and by Sunday, the drifts deepened. Martin Kilmer's came through the drifted snow in a two-horse sleigh, to see the new baby. By Monday, the schools all closed and the Turnpike traffic jammed. The schoolboys dug tunnels in the deep drifts, and Jesse plowed open the lane after Aaron and theboys had shoveled half of it by hand. By the end of the week, the temperature reached 70° and the snow melted rapidly. It was springtime and the geese were flying, while the black birds sang,"oka..lee..., oka…leee!"

⁓

Amanda told her children many stories about her childhood in Michigan. "Our mailman came in a horse drawn wagon. John Brill, the mail carrier, took good care of his horses and each day he hitched them to the mail cart, which was a wooden box on a wagon frame. In early December as the snow deepened, he moved that box from the wheels, and put it onto sleigh runners until springtime. Everyone traveled with sleighs, and no one plowed the snow. The entire neighborhood all helped pack and maintain the roads for sleighs. Every place the snow melted we shovelled on more snow from the drifts. Mr. Brill heated the mail wagon with a small pot bellied stove and a chimney, to keep from freezing, because he had a lengthy mail route. One day the horses upset his mail wagon on the sleigh runners, and some of the mail started burning when the potbellied stove upset. John Brill quickly put out the fire with snow."

"You children just cannot imagine life in Michigan," Amanda continued." People put in long hard days and no one hurried as they do around here. Not many people had tractors or electric, but times were already changing there. Our neighbors were mostly Christians and people that trusted each other. Everyone dressed modestly and the ladies had uncut hair. There was not much difference between Mennonites and others, because nearly everyone farmed with horses. As modern trends and styles kept changing, the women cut and styled their hair. They tried to outdo each other with fancy Easter bonnets, pride and vanity. Mennonites did not want to follow that trend and encouraged their members to wear the plane bonnets like usual, and a black shawl as they always had. They studied the Bible and considered, "what would Jesus do?"Pride will not enter into Heaven and neither will immodesty.

Baby Mandy seemed to grow up faster than the rest did. When she climbed up on a chair for the first time Amanda recorded it into her diary. Perhaps she wanted to remember that grin of victory on her baldheaded daughter, her cute little namesake. Her mother-love included every one of her children, no matter how many!

Aaron and Amanda invited the Shirk family for Sunday dinner with baby Mandy only four weeks old. Dawdy Shirks, Sam's, Elias's and Rube Weavers came to see the new baby and to enjoy a Sunday dinner. Amanda certainly did the managing, but she had a lot of help. Aaron and Amanda took their new baby to church, even before she was quite six weeks old! They all had a very busy day on that Sunday when the Brubachers arrived for Sunday dinner. Amanda's parents, Silas's, and Christian Kilmer's came for a full course meal and other company arrived later in the afternoon, to see the new baby.

Aaron and Amanda always moved the bed downstairs into the commah,[temporary bedroom]for every new baby. When baby Mandy was six weeks old, they moved the bed upstairs again, because Amanda was allowed to go up the stairs after that. It was springtime and the baby stayed warm enough upstairs.

Aaron and Amanda never desired an elaborate trip of sightseeing, or traveling on a cruise ship to some faraway place. Wherever they traveled, they went to meet relatives. With fifteen children at home, they both understood that traveling was out of the question, and yet they wished to meet their cousins and many other relatives. They had no telephones! Post cards left many details missing between the lines.

With careful planning, Aaron and Amanda found time for a mini two-day vacation. With a horse and carriage, they took a few of the younger children along, and made reservations to sleep at Eli Stauffers. Amanda's sister Lydia gave them a warm welcome, and beds for the night. Eli put the horse in the barn and fed him well. By the next morning, the horse was ready to go and after a leisurely chat, Aaron and Amanda moved on. They had reservations for dinner at Aaron's cousin and a supper invitation, closer to home. They kept moving on, stopping at many different places for a short call and they arrived back home before bedtime on the second day. Only with Sarah Ann's help at home, could they enjoy leaving like that.

Small Game Season

In springtime, Amanda enjoyed gathering wild fruit, and spending time outdoors. In June, she wanted to check the cherry trees and look for wild strawberries on the sunny slope at the Weller lot. While Sarah Ann tended three-month-old baby Mandy, Amanda took some children with her and gathered one pint of wild strawberries, not enough to mess with, except for the satisfaction of knowing that her children didn't overlook huge quantities of ripe berries, going to waste. Amanda remembered picking up to 100 quarts in Michigan.

Two weeks later, Amanda returned to the Weller lot, with able helpers and a few ladders loaded on the horse-drawn spring wagon, to pick a bucket full of big red sweet cherries that she had noticed. Most of the nicest cherries hung at the top of the tree and stayed there for the birds. Amanda proudly canned seven quarts of their own cherries.

Amanda wanted to harness, and manage usefully, the abundant energy of her children. She worked long hours weeding and harvesting in the garden, but seldom alone. She possessed a talented way of saying, "children, come and help me!" rather than saying, "go do it!" Younger children picked some peas in the row ahead of her, as she carefully followed, gathering the ones that they missed.

Amanda knew the basics of seed saving, as her parents taught her out of necessity in Michigan. She seldom saved any seeds because of the abundance of quality seeds available right when she wanted them. The tall heirloom sugar peas growing on a fence in her garden were passed down from one generation to the next and those she saved. One section of the row remained unpicked all season, for plump top quality seeds, not just runts. Those pea pods stayed on the plant until they dried out. Then Amanda picked them and stored them carefully in a cool dry place where no insects or mice ruined them. If Amanda found mold on the seeds she saved, she knew her seeds lost their germination, and might not be worth planting. She then wrapped a dozen or so seeds in a wet cloth to see how many sprouted. Perhaps one of her sisters had a few to share, if she erred and ruined all of hers.

Amanda made sure all her children learned the gardening tips that her mother passed down to her, by hands on experience. Her parents showed her how to make a duster with a metal can or molasses bucket by attaching a stick attached straight up from the side. As she bumped it up and down, the lime or the wood ashes in the can, sprinkled on the dew-covered cabbage plants, like a big powder box.

Amanda sowed all the tiny seeds by herself, to make sure the children did not waste or spill any. She also did not want them planted too thick. She said, "All of you can help with the potato row. The potatoes should be planted about a foot apart, so space each one just right by putting your foot in between each potato in the row! "For the younger ones, Amanda gave each child a stick to measure the distance between the potatoes.

"The peas are planted like this. ..about one or 2inches apart...pick up all those spilled ones first! You should cover each seed with dirt, up to four times the thickness of the seed. "More was caught than taught as Amanda's children closely watched her every move. In springtime, Amanda planted tiny seeds of parsnips and salsify for fall. She dug the carrot -like tubers in late fall or early spring before they sprouted. Freezing did not hurt them.

Amanda had no desire to plant any round jack o lantern type pumpkins, because the squash type neck pumpkins made better pies. Aaron liked the long curved neck pumpkins sliced in thin slabs, fried in butter, and seasoned with salt. Many fruits and vegetables were highly perishable, but not the potatoes and the pumpkins. When Amanda wanted to make pumpkin pie, she used the ones stored upstairs beneath the children's bed, where they seldom froze. Those nice big pumpkin seeds were among the easiest seeds to save for spring planting.

Children could not peel the hard rind on a pumpkin, but Amanda gave them the chore of chopping pieces of the pumpkin she peeled, as a good way to first use a paring knife at a young age. Every child needed a chance to cut a finger or two, while she worked nearby. Amanda did not have band-aids and most of those nicks did not need any. After a child learned to use a paring knife, Amanda wanted each one of them to master the art of peeling apples and potatoes thinly. For the rest of their lives they needed the basic talent of making less waste.

When Dick ran out of work, he pestered Amanda and bombarded her with incessant chatter. Eventually Amanda said,"Gay boddah de kotz!" [Go bother the cat.]After several minutes of peace and quiet, Amanda heard the unmistakable sound of a cat in distress. Dick followed the assignment his mother had given him, even when she did not mean it...

Amanda asked Aaron to stop and buy her some sweet potato plants, and he did. He came home with 350 plants, a lot more than she wanted, but they planted them all.

In two meals, Aaron's family ate one and a half bushels of sweet corn as roasting ears. It took a lot of food of every kind, and they served what was in season. Amanda pickled pickles, made cookies, butter, and a large amount of fresh apple dumplings. It made her day when Daniel Brubacher stopped by for a call, on the way to Jesse's for supper. He was the bishop that married them, nearly 20 years earlier.

Aaron and the boys worked in groups all over the neighborhood, topping tobacco at home, and then helping Jesse put away his tobacco, and attending a tobacco party in the evening. Amanda and her helpers, canned 96 quart peaches, costing one dollar a basket from Dan Esh, and the next week Noah Groff brought peaches, grapes, and tomatoes to can.

When a group of men arrived to help Aaron with tobacco, Amanda cooked for the workers. Jesse and his son Ivan came to help and also Ivan Oberholtzer. Aaron needed Josie. Every one worked extra hard, because of frost predictions. The temperature dropped and froze three acres of Aaron's tobacco. Tobacco is as frost sensitive as tomato plants. The shriveled leaves, turned brown and it was not a good year for Aaron's cash crop. Three acres amounted to half the crop, and the profit would be much less for the same amount of hard work.

To start with, in early spring, Aaron lost many young plants to hailstones as big as egg yolks. The loss was so great that he reseeded some tobacco beds for a late start, and then a killing frost nipped some of those young plants on May 17.

To make matters worse, the next year in September another killer frost hit the area early. All the farmers and merchants knew their community would suffer together.

Frost in the light of the moon only nipped the edges and did not usually kill the plants. After full moon, when the moon gets darker, is the 'dark of the moon' for two weeks, until the moon starts getting lighter again.In the dark of the moon, is when a frost is killing.[When the moon gets darker, the plants get darker!] Aarons great grand -father, inventor Joseph Shirk wisely studied astronomy and all those things. Somewhere along the line, people confused all moon signs as evils of astrology and fortunetelling. They wanted to err on the side of caution and tossed out many wonderful facts. Aaron and Amanda did not go by any moon-signs.

Aaron's brother Titus and his cousin Phares Shirk were helping Aaron strip tobacco when General tobacco buyers arrived offering 39-1/2 cents a pound for Aaron's tobacco crop. That was the best price they ever heard of, but Aaron wanted $.40. Titus and Phares could not believe Aaron wasn't going to sell, and urged him several times to sell, but Aaron didn't. Aaron packed that baled crop of tobacco in the top floor of the barn, and held on to the two next year's crops as well. It was all a game to him and he was not forced to sell.

Wesley returned to the hospital for a second cyst operation beneath his chin. After returning home, Dr. Lauria came out and gave Wesley a shot, and came again to change a bandage. Wesley missed sixty days of school in first grade and did not want to go back to school. Somehow, he learned enough to pass to second grade.

When Aaron and Amanda took Wesley to Dr. Riffert for a checkup, he gave Aaron an appointment to remove the lump at Aaron's ear, and one on his back. Dr. Riffert removed it and was concerned that it could have caused cancer some time. As the twins were swinging RoseAnna, they possibly cracked her arm, so the doctor also checked RoseAnna. Dr. Lauria often prescribed sulfa drugs for all sorts of problems.

Corn husking kept everyone busy and even Josie helped in October. Daniel went to a husking party at Dan Risslers, and to one at Allen Brubaker's, as well as husking corn at home. Teenagers wanted an excuse to gather somewhere and husking corn in the moonlight or with lanterns made a fun evening. Husking corn hardly seemed like work among a crowd and they enjoyed a treat afterwards.

When hunting season opened again, ten cars arrived for small game season in 1956. Aaron went along out as a hunting guide, for several doctors, and they got six pheasant roosters. Those doctors from Lancaster paid eight dollars just for the privilege to come and hunt, and the people from Chester County gave three dollars and candy. It was hard to tell who was most pleased, Aaron or the doctors! Daniel brought in two rabbits and one ring neck pheasant. Amanda stewed them until they were soft and the wild game disappeared in one meal, even if a few people bit on splintered bone or ammunition. Amanda made sure the boys understood that it was a crime to discard any shot -up game, which they did not feel like dressing. The Bible says in Proverbs 12; 27, The slothful man roasteth not that which he took in hunting.

Aaron and Amanda did not see many deer, but occasionally someone managed to get one in hunting season, especially in the state game lands, just across the Turnpike. Aaron's brother Titus enjoyed hunting much more than Aaron did. He bought a hunting permit and pinned it on his back. The license started with the letter H and he told Aaron's boys that H is for hosh [deer], and sure enough, Titus shot a small deer over there, and the easiest way home, was walking along the Turnpike. He draped the 50-pound deer across his shoulders and walked along the edge of the road, towards home. Carrying the deer half a mile, made it feel much heavier than it was. Any deer was nevertheless a wonderful bragging right, even if it did not have much meat for the table.

Canning Peaches

In August, as the peaches ripened, peddlers came driving through the neighborhood selling peaches with no schedule or warning, and sometimes the tree -ripened peaches needed prompt attention. All the other work stopped around the house, and Amanda ran an assembly line of workers, preserving fruit for winter.

"Go fetch empty jars and wash them clean," said Amanda." See if you can pull the skins off and stuff the peaches in the jars faster than I can blanch them?" Amanda put peaches in a pillowcase and scalded them in the boiling water, by dipping them up and down, because that saved time in removing the skins and made much less waste. With dishpans full of peaches, children of all sizes dug in to help and even Aaron, when necessary. Ruth cut each peach in half and Martha removed the pits, while several girls slid the skins off the fruit, and the smaller children

stuffed them into jars, because their hands easily fit inside the canning jars.

Steam from the canner and from the scalding water, mingled with sweat and dripping hands. "Now dump one cup sugar into each two- quart jar, and fill it with water," Amanda said, as she carefully screwed the lids on just right. She did not trust the children with zinc tops and rubber rings, as she carefully sealed each jar with the heel of her table knife, slightly bending the zinc against the rubber."No fooling around girls, because the next canner will soon be ready to fill. I need more peaches ready as soon as I lift those jars out," she said. Two big oblong wash boilers kept boiling the half-gallon jars as Amanda timed them, and lifted them out. In the sweltering heat of summer, amid the heat radiating from the wood stove, Amanda worked hard.

Canning peaches was a major task every summer, because they ate four hundred quarts, over winter. Amanda did the hard part of standing at the woodstove, managing well. With no fan anywhere, she wiped a lot of sweat. To save time, and do more peaches, she sometimes boiled the peach halves in a huge kettle and dumped them into jars, using her funnel and a big ladle. The open kettle method worked well and she understood the danger of scalding hot liquid, among children everywhere. She did not serve those inferior looking, everyday peaches to company.

At bedtime, Amanda liked when the children went to bed, so she could work late. Many of the children would rather do things at bedtime, and sleep in the morning. Amanda looked tired and worn out. Sarah Ann could hardly go to bed, knowing her mother worked late, but Amanda insisted, "After the house is quiet, I can keep on going."

The cold- packed peaches stacked in the jars neatly, looked nicer, but quantity counted more than quality. Amanda saw that every sticky jar was washed. Only the older children carried more than one jar at a time, down those cellar steps. One little oops made a ferocious mess of splintered glass and wasted food to clean up! Ach, My!

One time when Aaron came home with a whole spring -wagonload of peaches, picked up at the orchard, they needed prompt attention, and that is when Canadian travelers arrived for a visit, among the sticky mess.

Canning sweet corn involved yet more work, because corn had to cook much longer in the jars. The men helped to bring in the sweet corn and remove the husks. After cutting the corn from the cob, children helped Amanda fill the two -quart jars, then she shook them down, not packing them tight full. She added salt and water, and sealed them carefully with rubber rings and zinc tops, cooking them fully three hours.

The family canned eighty-nine quarts of sweet corn in one day without outside help. Aaron and the boys picked the corn on the evening before, and helped husk it the next day. After dragging the corn around too long on a hot day, the sugar turned to starch and all the corn spoiled after they canned three or four hours. The neatly washed jars of corn, hoarded in the cellar for wintertime, spoiled. That was a smelly, disgusting mess! The children thought they had the worst part, by emptying those stinking jars. Little did they know how hard it was to raise that corn… planting…thinning…hoeing … weeding… picking… husking… cutting… and canning. Beyond all the hard work and wasted time, Amanda had a hard time seeing so much food wasted like that, but she had tried her best. That was all she could do!

Many other peddlers came besides just peach peddlers. Sparky Weaver made homemade knives and came around the neighborhood selling them. He was lame, and stuttered while speaking Dutch. He had knives of all sizes, from paring knives to butcher knives. He made them in winter and peddled them in spring and summer, to make a living. Amanda liked his good knives, and she wanted to help him out. The small sharp paring knives were worth their weight in gold, as Amanda used her favorite knife every day… serving fruits and vegetables in season.

One knife lasted her a long time. She kept it sharp and in use. With so many inexperienced helpers, she had a hard time keeping the girls from losing a good knife. One time Amanda went to the barn and searched beside the pig trough where she triumphantly found her knife. She scrubbed it clean

and learned to run her hand through every dishpan full of peelings ready for the slop bucket.

Amanda welcomed Emma Good's portable store in a large van. Emma arrived on schedule, after sending a postcard announcing when she might be coming. Emma sold all sorts of pretty things that little children should not touch, but did anyway, such as hankies, Golden books, stockings and pretty fabrics. Amanda usually bought some prints, and wanted to patronize Emma Good, because Emma worked hard for her living. The children did not understand that part, but they knew Amanda would buy something, and that added excitement.

When the store arrived all the children wanted to look inside, and there was not room for that many, so they took turns, and wished to" help" pick something out. Amanda bought pretty hankies to keep on hand for souvenirs, as gifts to travelers who brought some children along. The girls liked the latest bob-retts when they put up their hair. Some of them kept the same slim pair of barrettes over many years, and wished for more when the company quit making them. One pair is still in use every day 50 years later.

Horace Eshleman, a salesman who spoke Dutch, sold Raleigh products. He came with a basket full of colorful bottles with things like liniment, vanilla, shampoo, golden oil and so forth. He showed his wares and talked about "de hooshta druppa" (cough syrup), and "duh vise vanilla" (the white vanilla). Then he gave each girl a tiny bottle of perfume, labeled "toilet water". Mary saved hers all her life, unused.

Noah Groff, a regular peddler, also made his rounds through the neighborhood. He was a heavy man with one front tooth missing, and he talked Dutch in a slow drawl. He came regularly with an assortment of salvage food, and he preferred to barter. His prices were not firm, and he enjoyed dickering with Aaron. Many times, he would ask, "What would you give me for this box full?" Or, "if you take this box, you can have the next one for one dollar." When he opened the side of his van, you never knew what he might have, as he proudly showed his wares and begged for a sale.

Aaron and Amanda treated him kindly and tried to help him out, even when money was scarce.

Sometimes, they bought a case of raisins, Amanda's favorite. Many times, he sold candy by the case, and the whole neighborhood had the same kind in their lunches. He also sold oranges, watermelons, ripe bananas, broken cookies and pretzels by the case. Sometimes Noah Groff brought along his retarded daughter, Gloria. She wanted to get out of the truck and play among the children at Aarons, but she was afraid of any dog.

Trusty, another salesman arrived, peddling bakery surplus and stale bread. When he left, Amanda usually came in the house holding the bottom corners of her long apron as a bushel basket, filled nearly full. Trusty did not have enough empty boxes and no one ever saw a plastic bag! Amanda certainly could have used some.

"Mam, duh Bucky iss doe!" [Mom, Bucky arrived!], one of the children said, as the grocery man brought their order. He was a local merchant that started a delivery service. Bucky dressed neatly and he wore a well-trimmed beard. He helped check off everything on Amanda's grocery list to make sure it was satisfactory, then he politely said," thank you "and he left, jangling his keys. Little eyes followed his every move, all the way. The moment he left, they eagerly looked over the pile of food he brought. Was anything attractive on the back of the cornflakes box?

Aaron and Amanda depended on Buckwalter's grocery store in Churchtown, and he came to their house every week. (Later the business name changed to "B and E Market "for Buckwalter and Esh.]The grocery store ran a business, catering to Amish and Mennonites, or anyone else wanting to order groceries brought to their door. Without going shopping, Amanda sent a postcard stating her grocery list. If she put it in the mail on Tuesday or Wednesday, the groceries arrived on Friday, and she charged the entire bill until the tobacco sold. The grocery man quickly learned to know his customers. When Amanda wrote down two boxes of strawberry Jell-O, he knew she meant the larger size boxes.

One other peddler was quite a storyteller, and he might visit with Aaron for an hour. When he brought along a wooden box, he convinced the children it contained his pet mongoose, and he asked,

"Did you ever see any mongoose?" The children crowded around, shaking heads, "no", and tensely stared into the screen covered box. Suddenly a trap snapped, and they all jumped! The only thing in the box was a bushy tail like that of a raccoon. He laughed and enjoyed tricking people.

Another time a salesman arrived and Aaron's dog just kept barking at him. Amanda said "Hoont,sie rooich!" ("Dog, be quiet.") The salesman reached down and patted the dog saying, "Aaaahh, Hoont." He thought that was the dog's name.

Many people did not know his last name, but everyone in the neighborhood knew,' Horry Flooha'. [Harry the swearer].He came to buy rags, bags and scrap iron, to resell at a profit. The cotton, linen and wool fabric had many recycle uses but Amanda recycled most of her own. Sometimes Aaron had scrap metal saved for him. As the men agreed on a price, Aaron's boys listened, in wide –eyed amazement at Harry's many by-words. When he left again, Dick asked, 'Mom why does Harry use so many swear words?"She said,"People just use words they hear others use and he picked up a bad habit. Just do not ever repeat the swear words you heard him say! Spreading those words is like spreading troublesome weed seeds. Let all your words be clean. In Matthew 12, verse 36, the Bible says we must give an account for every idle word we say."

It was not easy for Aaron and Amanda to pack up and go shopping in those days, and they welcomed peddlers at the door. What they could not buy from the peddlers or the local store they mail ordered from the Sears and Roebuck Co.

The Sears order came in a large corrugated cardboard box, unless it was too big and someone picked it up at the post office, with an order such as a stepladder. Any big box with their name on, beside the mailbox created excitement. "My! What could be inside?" They hurried home for the wagon saying, "The Sears order came!"

Inside the package, they might find things like new shoes and such. One-time three packages came from Sears, and Walter picked up a good-sized package ripping into it excitedly. Amanda knew what was inside the lightweight package and she watched, with a sly smile on her face, as Walter kept on ripping and digging eagerly. When he found the contents, it was nothing but a chamber bucket for using at night, instead of making a trip to the outhouse. The look on young Walter's face showed disappointment. If that is all he had, he was going to be the first one to use it. Right then and there, There was never a dull moment!

∽

Young girls learned to braid hair at a young age. They braided the hair on their dolls, braided baler twine into jump ropes and even braided the horse's tails sometimes. Each daughter wore pigtails for approximately twelve years, and they each had two pigtails, or more. Take that, times ten girls, equal 120 years of pigtails.

The smallest children had six pigtails to keep all the fine little hairs tucked in tighter. Sometimes Amanda twined a piece of string among the braided hair to keep the shorter finer hair from unraveling, and to make that little short pigtail at the front, reach to the next one, and again to the third one.

As the hair grew longer and thicker, four pigtails worked better. Before school age, the girls did not all get combed every day. Rhoda learned to comb her own pigtails at the age of seven, even starting the braids behind her head where she could not see. We can be sure those first braids behind her head, did not quite pass Amanda's inspection, but she needed all the help available.

At the age of 14, the young girls stopped wearing braided hair and wrapped it up in a bon, as their mothers did. That is where Sarah Ann had a big problem, with too much hair to fit decently underneath a covering. Amanda helped her daughter, but she had her hands full with too much hair. Where do you go with it all? A woman's long hair was a blessing to her and should not be cut. Sarah Ann looked rather odd with her slim figure and so much hair beneath a big covering. Mrs. Hettie Horst made a new bonnet for Sarah Ann and a one for Amanda also.

Amanda combed many small braids all the way to the end of the hair.

18

Martin Kilmer Quilting

In 1955, Martin Kilmer's had a barn raising and Amanda set her heart on helping her sister serve a big meal for the workers. Since Sarah Ann was out of school, she could babysit Louise, Irene, Wesley and Lydia, while the others were in school, and baby RoseAnna went along.

Sarah Ann constantly stayed at home babysitting so much, that for something different, Amanda took her and the younger children to Elias Shirks. There Sarah Ann helped babysit Elias 'children as well, so Nancy could also attend the raising with Elias. The children kept Sarah Ann busy, but she excelled at understanding little ones, giving Nancy a much-needed break. Eighty -five workers ate a big meal at the barn raising in May.

The women enjoyed the day, and especially the quilting. The usual quilting chatter rambled on while nimble fingers stitched many tiny stitches. It sounded as though everyone talked at the same time and no one listened." Did the Raleigh man, come out your way also? I heard Ike Hurst's funeral was a big one. He was only 64 years old. Oh yes, and Dawdy Jesse Brubacher was buried nine days ago. [Jesse Senior]. Did the Canadian couples stop by your way for a call... they were Dillman Brubacher's, Ezra Martins and Israel Baumans.? Daniel kept busy steaming tobacco beds into April when it was already time to seed them. He came home at 3 AM, all tired out! Our boys went fishing in the creek and got two suckers. Is it true that vinegar helps de-tangle long thick hair? The girls wore straw bonnets to school…. and that is a sign of spring. It was fit to go barefoot early this year! Daniel helped put in a water- ram at Titus and it saved them from pumping all the water by hand. Oh, did you see Titus's new house already? They moved in and everything is fantastic. How do you fix asparagus so that your children like it?" How is it going at the new Goods private school by now? Some of those stories might not be true...Es coomt ivver dem un hoont mit un lengrah shwonz! [There soon comes a dog with a longer 'tale'.] All too soon, it was time to go home.

The men worked as fast as the women talked, and accomplished a major improvement. The new roof already covered the barn. Aaron enjoyed the fellowship among the men as much as Amanda enjoyed the quilting, but much work awaited them at home. Sometimes Aaron would say, "Before you go to another quilting, would you sew a button on this shirt? What he really meant was "Please do it right now!"

When Amanda asked Aaron for five minutes to fix something, he would say, "I'm very busy right now, surely we will get a rainy week one of these time, so that I can catch up around here." He was also fond of requesting things on paper. "Get it on paper, and I'll do it later."

When he turned his back, Amanda tried to improvise and make do, the best she could. Many times, she patched, glued, wired, taped, screwed, hammered and fixed all sorts of things others considered unfixable. She killed snakes, bat's, mice and spiders quickly out of necessity and no screaming ever! Never! Unless a life was in danger.

When the tent caterpillars spun cobwebs over the apple tree branches, Amanda complained, "tz-soo feel rou-vah!"[Too many tent worms]. "Gay grick mich un misht govvel."[Go get me a pitch-fork].She carefully dipped corncobs into kerosene and speared them on the tines of a pitchfork, and with the help of her boys, Amanda lit them like a torch, to burn down the worms, before they defoliated the apple tree. Amanda was a teacher all day long, multitasking, with one eye on the clock, knowing what goes on around her back, while teaching, scolding, rocking and encouraging. Aaron and Amanda gathered their children around the table 3 times a day, just like their parents did, before them.

Aaron and Amanda felt that Bible teachings were given by inspiration, and shall be taken by inspiration! They opposed Bible School and Sunday school, because people should not be graded on their understanding of the Bible, like just another school test. Bibles were highly treasured and not for show. They should never be on the floor or covered beneath clutter. Everyone needed to use the talents given to them and not compare themselves among themselves, but on their individual understanding.

Amanda had a German/English Bible that she used a lot, but her children did not see her read it. She walked the walk in sincere faith, by letting her light shine. Aaron also read the Bible, but none of them read to their children. They taught by example and did not tolerate wrongdoings.

Everyone had different talents! When Bowmansville church needed more hitching posts, they preferred a certain size and kind of wood. They knew where to find the seasoned locust posts they wanted, but getting permission from the owner took a skill in public relations. The trustees knew that the owner was negative toward the project. They knew that Aaron Shirk had a way of talking and convincing, that just might work. They sent him to get permission to buy the locust posts, and he did. It was not so much about what Aaron said, but how he said it.

The freezing and thawing of wintertime heaved yet more stones from the ground. Aaron knew those rocks made troublesome farming. It was hard monotonous work to load rocks onto the wooden drag pulled by horses. Every spring Aaron threatened to sell the farm and move, due to the many stones, but he never did. Younger children went along for a ride on the drag, and could help gather smaller stones to unload at the piles called stone fences. Aaron said; Don't pick up any rocks smaller than my fist. _No cattle crossed over the rocky fencerows, but the rocky heaps were a bother, needing pruning or burning -off regularly.

With so many rocks to pick, Aaron asked Josey Latshaw to come and help, first thing in the morning. Pete and Dick started the detested job of picking rocks that morning, with the consolation that Josey was coming to help them. They labored long and hard until about 11 o'clock when Josie finally came walking in the lane pulling his wagon and shouting, "Let's go!" Josie was the only one around that did not balk about picking rocks, but he was not prompt and Pete and Dick were tired out before he came.

Saturday Singing

Nearly every Sabbath day, Aaron and Amanda enjoyed having company for Sunday dinner, just as much as they enjoyed dinner invitations to others. These social invitations were important, and more so at Christmas time. BW Shirks invited the entire family for Christmas, including all their children and grandchildren.

Seventy-four people arrived, on Monday; the day after Christmas, to be able to include Ben Shirks from Indiana, who came on a business trip. Benjamin Shirk enjoyed meeting his son Benjamin Shirk and his son Benjamin Shirk, as well as four other grandsons named Benjamin. They seldom got together in a group, on the same day. Grandpa BW Shirk enjoyed visiting with his descendents, of all ages. He gave each of his 55 grandchildren a quarter for Christmas in 1955, but he did not keep it up every year. Some of his grandchildren remembered how he handed out Black-Jack chewing gum after a Sunday dinner. Each child claimed one stick of gum and chewed it a long time. ..even the next day or week.

It was always exciting to have out-of-state guests, but even more so when Ben's family stayed five nights. Ben and Grace with their seven children came from Indiana for Christmas and about business at Kinzer's. Amanda and the girls cleaned rapidly, when they heard Aaron's brother Ben and family were coming for the week. Ben and Grace slept in one bedroom, while their three oldest children, Bertha, Anna Mary and Benny, slept with Aaron's children, and the remaining four children slept at Jesse's. The cousins had a lot of fun together, making up for lost time by living so far apart.

After the Christmas reunion, and company overnight all week, Aaron and Amanda hosted a singing for the youth group on Saturday night. Daniel was already 17! The whole family pitched in working hard, but the guests arrived in the dark, and maybe did not notice all their efforts.

After 7 PM, teenagers started arriving in buggies and on bicycles, with the boys going out to the stripping room, and big girls giggling upstairs. After a while, they assembled in the big kitchen, packed full of people with standing room only. Boys and girls mingled their voices together singing lovely hymns, with familiar songs and some that Aaron's children had never heard. Young children peeked around the corners, and marveled at the four-part singing.

After the parting hymn, several young people pushed the kitchen table, minus all its table-boards, into the corner and the games started. Eight couples swayed gracefully, as Maynard Kilmer chanted square dance calls.

Joe Wenger couples did not have a date on Saturday night; therefore, no one was in a hurry to leave. Raymond Nolt and Florence Kilmer, as a couple, stood together in the cluttered and dark summerhouse, simply wanting a chance to talk.

After the singing was over, Christian Kilmer's four children stayed overnight with permission. Katie, Naomi, Florence and Maynard, had far to drive home. Aaron and Amanda had room for one more as the teenagers crowded in with their cousins overnight, and went to church from there in the morning.

∽

Four long cupalos topped Aaron's barn roof, for better ventilation, and they attracted pigeons. The ledge up there created an ideal place for pigeon nests. After the tobacco was out-of-the-way in the barn, it was easier to catch pigeons, and sell them for pocket money. With Daniel way up at the peak of the barn, close to the cupolas, Pete shown the flashlight right at the pigeon and wobbled the

light back and forth confusing the bird. One boy could not easily do it alone, because he needed one hand to hang on the rails up there, and grab the pigeon with the other hand. After capturing a bird, Daniel carefully interlocked the feathers of both wings, behind the birds back, and tossed it to the barn floor where Pete used the flashlight to find it and fill the chicken coop. The pigeons naturally landed on their feet, but if they did not, that might unlock the wings and let them escape unharmed. This was entertainment and excitement, with a little profit. As long as the tobacco hung in the way, it was inconvenient to get the birds down to the coop. One time when the boys were fumbling for pigeons in the dark, someone reached into a bird-nest and touched a big blacksnake that had beaten them to the job. February was an ideal time of the year for catching pigeons, before they nested, and so was late summer before the barn filled up with tobacco.

Pigeons multiplied rapidly, and every barn in the neighborhood had pigeons to spare. The boys brought some home from Joe Wengers barn in a burlap sack on a Thursday night. After carefully counting them and packing them into orange crates or cardboard boxes, Harvey Zimmerman drove them to Green Dragon the next day. He was a kindhearted friend that often helped his horse and buggy neighbors, in need of transportation.

∽

Aaron did a lot of talking on Sunday, as well as at every social gathering around, but he still took time off to go visiting during the week. On a lovely day in May, with plenty of work at home, Aaron and Amanda went visiting with eight week old Mandy and two-year-old RoseAnna along in the carriage, while Sarah Ann kept three pre-scholars at home. They stopped at Ezra Zimmerman, Davey Eberly's, Elam Sensenigs and Mose Berkeys with a dinner invitation at Eli Stauffer's, Amanda's sister Lydia. It was a long way to Murrell, so they made it worthwhile. Leisurely driving was also a time of discussions between Aaron and Amanda, without children listening in.

With a horse and carriage, it was a day's journey to travel 15 miles, and back, resting the horse in between. Eli Stauffers invited Aaron and Amanda, and the whole family for Sunday dinner, on Wesley's fifth birthday. Not all of the children fit into the carriage, so Aaron hired a neighbor, Charles Stamm to take the family there in his station wagon. It was a day to remember as the family traveled there and back without being on the road for long.

Daniel and Walter made their own teenage plans. Aaron and Amanda, Sarah Ann, Ruth, Rhoda, Martha, Mary, Louise, Irene, Wesley, Lydia, Rose-Anna and seven-month-old baby Mandy crowded into that station wagon, and still made room for Dale Stamm, the daughter of the driver and Mary's best friend at school.

Eli Stauffer's house was crowded with the Christian Kilmer family being there, as well as Horace Stauffer's, Norman Stauffer's and Katie. The men and boys always ate first, while the schoolgirls hungrily waited on their turn, after resetting the table. Fascinated children watched food disappearing downstairs on Lydia's dumbwaiter, like an elevator shaft going up and down to the cool basement and back up again. The day ended with many happy memories for years to come.

PP & L

Aaron kept on buying woodland, whenever he could. The land on the other side of the turnpike belonged to the Pennsylvania state game commission. In no way, could Aaron buy that land. The well-kept farms to the west of him were not for sale, such as Jesses, Joe Wenger, and Titus and beyond. To the south and east of Aaron lay a patchwork of odd parcels of land, all among rocks and hills, certainly not tillable. That was the land Aaron had his eyes upon; and he mostly wanted the mineral rights. Who cared what lay on top?

When Henry Burkholder owned woodland next to Aaron's farm, he put up a new sheep shed about 100 feet from Aaron's barn, between the barn and the woods. Aaron's children traipsed out to watch the workmen. At the age of two, Walter went along out to watch, wearing pajamas, and carrying his baby bottle. The workers

teased him about that. That was the last time he needed a bottle!

Henry was ordained as a deacon in the church, and lost all interest in the sheep ranch. He never had even one sheep in his new building, and he remarked, "I didn't know that I would have sheep in the church to take care of." The ordination changed his priorities.

Aaron eyed that chunk of land and watched his chance to buy it. When he came to the Blue Ball Bank, asking for money to buy land, Raymond Baxter frowned. He said, "Aaron, you will never see a return on such an investment. While other farmers wisely spend money on farm improvements, you waste too much money on trash land, but I can give you the money." The banker gave $2500 to Aaron and he purchased the 124-acre sheep ranch. He received the original old deed printed on pigskin, on the real hide from a pig! The hide looked like heavy parchment paper but where the official seal was punched, a person saw it was not paper.

Not much later, The Pennsylvania Power and Light Company contacted Aaron about purchasing a right-of-way across his property. They planned a big new power line just south of his farm, paying one dollar per foot and Aaron could keep his mineral rights. He could use the land as pasture and in many other ways, as long as he did not plant trees or anything that obstructed the clearing. On December 20, 1955, Aaron signed off the power line, all 3400 feet of it, for $3400. The power line ran full length across his newly purchased rugged woodland and sheep ranch.

When Aaron received his share of the money from P P and L, he eagerly took the check to the Blue Ball bank and made sure he talked with Raymond Baxter. He proudly said, "Here is the money I borrowed, what do you want me to do with what's left over?"

In March, the men came out to survey the land. Aaron and the neighborhood had the privilege of removing any lumber or firewood they wanted to save. Aaron collected $100 from selling better lumber trees to Elias and to John Sauder.

Aaron kept right on purchasing other small tracts of woodland: From Wayne Steffy, he bought the Steffy (hecka) or brush land costing $200, for 12 acres with no trees worth taking to a sawmill. Rufus Nolt took Aaron to check into buying the Witwer woodland. Aaron paid $301 to Sam Nolt for a woodlot. Aaron purchased four acres from Sally Yohn for $55, and he spent $150 for five acres from John Hoover in 1956. In 1957, he bought woodland from Ammon B for $276.

Aaron wanted to borrow money to buy a triangle of land close to the end of his lane. He mentioned the road frontage along his property, and the banker mockingly said, "What is frontage way out back on Laurel Hill?" Amanda did not always understand his way of thinking either, and Aaron often said, "I cannot make money without borrowing money!"

⁂

In October, Aaron bought his first tractor at Eli Goods sale for $250. It was a V. A.C. Case with a one-bottom hydraulic lift plow. After farming with horses for 18 years, the tractor was a joy to use. Daniel and Walter could hardly get enough of it, and even Sarah Ann learned to drive the tractor, as she helped Daniel pick corn. The tractor was a major improvement in modernization, but there was a problem. Rubber tires were a test of membership in the Joe Wenger church and no members took communion while owning rubber tired equipment.

Before spring communion time, Aaron had the rubber removed from the tractor wheels and sent the tires to the Morgantown relief sale. Some tractors worked better on metal cleats than others did. The tractor wheels that had good traction on rubber, slipped and spun over embedded rocks in the field, with an ugly grating noise. Some cleats broke off, for even more problems, and less traction. Jesse's Caterpillar tractor worked fine on cleats, but Aaron's tractor did not. The wonderful new tractor was a cripple, as it jerked and grated against the rocks. The teenage boys could not understand! The whole thing seemed ridiculous to them, with their first-hand experience of before and after rubber tires.

With horses, the farmers used a one- row tobacco planter because the horses did not walk slow enough for a two row planter. After Aaron had a tractor, he bought a brand new two-row tobacco planter from Jared Stauffer. That one still needed one driver and two people planting but they preferred doing two rows at a time. They each planted an entire row alone, rather than alternately, and the driver on the tank, sat in front of the planters. At the age of six, Wesley learned to drive the tractor and planter, when he was still too young to plant tobacco.

19

Jesses Ivan

"Help!", "Help!" There it was again! Sarah Ann distinctly heard a desperate call for help and it came from the woods! Greatly alarmed, Sarah Ann hurried back into the house and told her parents. None of Aaron's family was missing!"

Aaron and Amanda stepped out in the cold and heard a wailing call for "Heeeelllllpp!" Whom could it be they wondered? Greatly concerned, Aaron wasted no time and hurried to the woods, where he found Jesse's 16-year-old Ivan, lying on the frozen ground with a badly broken leg. He was trying to haul in some poles, from the power line right of way. When the horses pulled the load of logs across a dip, the tail end of the long load bumped on the frozen ground and shifted the logs, smashing Ivan's leg.

Jesse was not at home at the time, so Aaron called the ambulance and went along to admit Ivan into the Ephrata Hospital on November 27, 1956. First, the doctors tried a pin and later a body cast, but it was a long ten months recovery. Amanda wrote details in her diary as though Ivan was her own son. He grew up so close with Daniel and Sarah Ann, that he was more than "just a nephew".

Aaron, Daniel, Jesse and Amos Ringler donated blood for Ivan who spent time in a wheelchair and on crutches a long time. Sarah Ann was deeply touched! This cousin was her age, and they walked to school together for seven years, sharing much in their lives.

The day after the accident, Sarah Ann again thought she heard calls for help. When Amanda came to listen she realized it would be quite a while before Sarah Ann stopped recalling those vivid memories, and calls for "help!"

For $1.60, Sarah Ann bought an 18-inch glass fishbowl at E K Fisher. She added three small bass from the farm pond to amuse Ivan and baked a cake to take along when they went to visit. Many prayers were sent heavenward for Ivan's recovery.

Daniel, Sarah Ann, Walter, Pete, Dick, Ruth, Rhoda and Martha walked over to visit Ivan on Christmas Eve. Ivan was not much into entertaining that evening, but he could tell his cousins how he had just come home in the ambulance, and this time the sirens were not screaming. Daniel, Walter, Pete and Dick appreciated Ivan and Jesse Junior about their size, and Annie was close to Sarah Ann. The twins and Martha were the same size as Mary and Mabel, and it was no wonder they watched every chance they had to get together. The younger set also had close cousins their age. Reuben and Benny had Wesley, while Eva, Naomi and Vera, played with Irene Lydia RoseAnna and Mandy.

Jesse Brubacher had the best hill for sledding, right past their house, on the public road. Aaron's children bundled up and walked over to Jesse's, pulling sleds and carrying a kerosene lantern. With not enough sleds to go around, two people shared each sled. They set the lantern at the top of the hill where one person remained as a "lookout" for traffic, while awaiting their turn. Very few cars came this way but if one did, everyone hollered, "machine!" (Car!) Quickly, the sleds steered into the ditch, dumping passengers into the snow banks!

Fresh snow piled up several inches while the children were in school. Amanda knew they did not wear any boots that morning, so at three o'clock Daniel waited with a box full of boots at the end of the lane, at the bus stop. All eight children found boots to wear except Irene, in first grade. The remaining pair of rubbers was not tall enough for the deep snow, so Daniel lifted Irene onto his broad shoulders and gave her a memorable piggyback ride down to the house.

Amanda's cozy kitchen cooled off rapidly, after eight schoolchildren returned with cold air and snowy boots. "Close the door!" she repeated. When the north kitchen door to the cold summer house stood open a crack Amanda said,""Moch de ice —box tzoo! [Make the ice-box shut]

Hungry children coming home from school after three o'clock sometimes met Aaron in the kitchen stirring up a snack for himself. He offered some of it to the children. His favorite snack consisted of a raw egg in a coffee cup, stirred together, with broken pieces of buttered bread and salt. The children that tasted it actually liked it especially at that time of the day and he helped them fix their own, to Amanda's disapproval. "Agh Aaron!" she would say. Aaron said, "See, they like it!" As the children got older, they refused to eat eggs in such a slimy way, even if it did not taste much different than an egg for breakfast, slightly rare, served on buttered bread instead of toast.

Anytime Amanda had fresh churned butter in the house, Aaron enjoyed butter as a dip for his pretzels. He also had a craving for salt, and poured a small pile of salt on the table sometimes, as a dip for celery or carrots, or even raw potato slices.

Amanda grew up without pretzels in Michigan, but Aaron liked pretzels in any form, at almost any time. When some pretzels turned stale, Amanda toasted them in the oven to renew the flavor and their crunchy texture. Pretzels always came in a big metal tin can with a tight fitting lid. Amanda sometimes stewed the big fat stick pretzels into pretzel soup, by scalding them in hot water, then stewing them in milk. She added browned butter on top. Aaron seldom ran out of pretzels. Amanda learned to like them and found pretzels convenient to drop in the many lunch boxes.

After the Shirks gathered for last Christmas, Amanda's side gathered for a family reunion, on the next Christmas. Uncle Dan Martins came from Indiana for Christmas dinner at Martin Kilmers. A postcard in the mail from Nappanee, route three, cheered Amanda, as her sister and family announced their plans.

Dan and Katie joined the Wissler group in Indiana, and owned a car. Aaron's children looked up to them as being of a higher class, maybe because Amanda treated them as royalty, when she was so glad for their arrival. A dear sister and her family deserved the best Sunday china on the table, and the Sunday tablecloth for breakfast. Perhaps it was also the idea that Amanda encouraged her children to clean better for company coming, telling them," Not everyone lives in so much disarray. Get busy and help clean up for these special guests!"

Amanda needed help to clean the mess on the girl's bedroom floor. Some garments belonged to "nobody" and many things were shared by two girls. Boxes under the beds collected childhood treasures among bed woollies. Amanda utilized every bit of space in such a crowd of people. She helped organize to make room for the cousins to sleep there as special guests. If everyone cooperated, they could move mountains.

When the greatly honored company arrived, the children did not lose any time in finding things to do. Ida, Betsey, Barbara, and Lavina mingled with Aaron's girls and Joe, Manasseh, Ephrim and Emerson found boys their size. They had a good time going away for dinner and sleeping with their cousins.

A lively game of 'Bloomp Sock' in the barn created action for anyone brave enough to help. "Here is the knotted sack we used last time...who is IT?" Children hurriedly ducked behind a barn-wall or the farm wagon, before the' itter' tossed the sack and nipped him with it. The game got wild sometimes as the cats ran to hide and the pigeons flew out of the cupolas. When the younger ones tattled or cried to Mom, she told them to stay out of the way and go play something else. She was once a tomboy of sorts and knew the game well. It compared to a rough snowball battle, all in fun.

Aaron knew Dan's did not farm, nor use tobacco and he embarrassingly rubbed in the fact that tobacco was their way of life. He asked", Daniel, do you have a chew?" None of them chewed tobacco regularly, but Aaron chewed some halfheartedly in front of Dan, his brother in law, and he might even offer him some tobacco when he knew Dan despised it.

When it was time for them to leave for home, the children seldom left without a game of "got you last", as everyone tried to get the last touch or tag, before the car door slammed shut for the last time.

Fifty years later, when those cousins reminisced, Ida said, "Did you think you were sloppy?" Now that was a real compliment! Actually, Amanda was precise and neat in what she did, but the rest was not done until 'urgently necessary'. She did not reach around. Housekeeping and homemaking are not the same! Dr, Schnader occasionally reminded Amanda that cleanliness is next to godliness. That verse was not in the bible and Dr.Schnader had no children, not even one.

Amanda's father liked perfection and neatness. If he found a hair on his clothes, he would not drop it onto the floor, but he carefully put it in the trash. Amanda also liked neatness, but she could not always afford it.

Aaron's mother, at a young age, saw a need to cut corners, when her own mother had mental health problems. It was better to get sloppy than to go crazy! She was always ready to jump up and serve others. As saintly as she was, Amanda thought Aaron's mother was sloppier in washing and in cooking, than Amanda was. One person cannot have it all.

When washing dishes, Amanda taught perfection!"Wash all the clear glass cups or tumblers first when the water is clean. Next, wash the silverware, and do not soak those wooden handled knives and forks. Wash them thoroughly without putting them under water, or the wood might swell and the handles will come apart."The kettles always came last and then the water was dirty and nearly cold, with no suds left. It was tempting for her daughters to put those dried-up kettles in soak for the next meal, and the next girl's turn to wash dishes. Sometimes that worked, and at other times, they got more clean water and started over, washing every piece.

Learning by doing was by far the best way to teach anything. Observantly watching might be a good start, but Louise had to know just how hot to make that pan, learning by trial and error. "You must wait until the pan is hot before making pancakes, "said Amanda, "or see now how seriously they stick to the pan."

Amanda was never quite sure which girl made pies the last time, and which one had not tried it yet. "Take that dishpan and make it half full of flour, "she said. 'now use almost one third that much shortening...rendered chicken fat makes the nicest golden piecrust, but we don't have any... here is the lard...add some salt... then go in with both your hands.. .Did you wash your hands first? Better wash them again! Now put both hands in there and rub the lard until no big pieces are left.. .Oh, don't make it come out over the edge of your dish like that!...keep on rubbing the flour and the shortening together...that's not good enough yet...you want it as fine as possible... Now, that looks better.. .Pour just enough water in to hold it together like dough... You don't want much... you can always add more... no, don't work the dough very much or it will really get tough... don't squeeze the dough. ..gently make the dough balls just big enough to fill one pie pan like this... now you're ready to roll them flat...see if you can make a round shape without trimming much waste around the edges.... take the rolling pin this way across...and then the other way...see. ..you can shape it round...fold it and lift it gently so it won't tear... you must keep more flour sprinkled beneath the dough. ..or it will stick to the table if you don't. .. it takes more than that...now gently lift the dough into the plate and I will fill it with these apples....trim the edges...add about so much sugar and cinnamon...and some tapioca...now use those leftover trimmings mixed in the next ball of dough... make another crust. ..add some vent holes in the lid to let the steam out...You might want an 'A' on top so we know which ones are the apple pies... now crimp it like this. ..and bake it... You may make a little pie with those scraps. ...or roll them and sprinkle them with salt, baked for a snack later...and before you run off to play... put the rolling pin back where you got it. ...but don't wash it,.... just wipe it clean... it works better when it is oily"

Pie making always looked easier than it really was to a beginner, and Amanda could do it ten times faster by herself. Peter Brubacher's family ate many pies in Michigan, because pies were cheaper than baking cakes, when they had an abundance of fruit, and a shortage of eggs. Amanda had no recipe and neither did her mother.

Sometimes Sarah Ann baked twenty-five pies or more, in one day, just for their own use. Warm fresh pies served with milk disappeared rapidly and that might be half the meal.

Amanda learned cooking and baking without recipes when she grew up, and they used what they had without buying things at the store first. Eventually she had a cookbook, but she still preferred to cook with what was available and in season. Buying things in the store and stirring them together was not called cooking.

After butchering day, Amanda saved scraps of suet, for making suet pudding, where the ground-up tallow replaced the shortening in a spice cake, with glaze on top. It remained moist and tender when she baked it. She did not want it dried out around the edges, and placed the suet pudding pan in another pan of water like a double boiler, while baking it in the oven. Squishy plumped raisins also kept the cake soft inside.

Sinkers

Against his wishes, Dick worked on a farm west of Aaron and Amanda. When he was in the sixth grade, at the age of 12, he was paid one dollar per day as a farm hand, and Dick received 10% of that.

Joe had one cow, three horses and some steers to feed, besides farming tobacco. Dick helped him with chores and stripping tobacco. He slept there and went to school on the bus from that location. Joe was a very kind man to work for, but Dick seriously missed his brothers and sisters. It was not far to walk home, but he could not leave there before Saturday noon and then he just stayed home for one short day.

Joe's wife baked the best homemade bread Dick ever ate and he could hardly control himself at the bread plate, but he missed his brothers more every day and he got severely homesick. After school let out, Amanda sent Ruth over to help at Joe's but that did not make matters any better. Ruth and Dick both ended up so seriously homesick that they could not eat anymore, not even the

best bread. They just could not handle living away from home. So they both spent most of that summer at home, but by September first, Amanda was packing Dick's clothes for another stay at the same place, working there before and after school. On a sad Monday, Joe fetched Dick for the entire winter, but one week later, Dick returned home, seriously home sick!

Not all was "work" for the boys in summertime, and they rejoiced to go fishing in Titus's farm pond. Occasionally the boys killed sparrows with a BB gun, dressed them like chickens, cooked them and tasted them. The good dark meat was only a sample and not because they were hungry. The same went for eating frog legs over an open fire for entertainment. The boys swiftly caught a frog and whacked it against a rock while holding it by the back legs. They made sure the frog was dead. When Aaron was a boy, him and his brothers caught frogs to eat and removed the hind legs. They tossed the rest aside. The next day they met a frog in the springhouse sitting there alive, minus two big legs the boys had eaten. They never forgot that cruelty and Aaron told his sons to kill the frogs first.

Making sinkers was a big thing! The boys gathered lead at the dump from old car batteries, and melted it in an old hand cranked forge, or at the stripping room stove. They owned a two-piece, clamped together mold to make fish line sinkers, but they had a lot to learn the hard way. They used Amanda's good long handled ladle from the butchering tools as a melting pot, and sadly melted a hole in the middle of it, spilling their precious melted lead into the fire.

When the sinker mold was too cold, the melted lead hardened before it filled the air space in the bottom. The boys kept on practicing until they were good at it and most everyone in the neighborhood had some of their fish-line sinkers. If Amanda had any worn out zinc jar tops, from her canning supplies, they eagerly melted the zinc for their mold. In later years, they discovered wheel weights were easy to get from Dicks Sunoco service station. Another improvement was a bigger nicer, hinged mold, with a row of sinker forms of assorted sizes.

When Aaron bought a new black, high- spir-ited horse, he gave his boys strict orders "Do not ride him!" That was a mistake! Aaron knew the horse was not safe and hard to hold back, but when Aaron left home, the boys wanted to try the horse. "What would it be like to have a fast ride?" Pete and Dick carefully saddled the horse and led him out of the barn. Dick turned "chicken", so Pete swung into the saddle. In an instant, the horse shot straight ahead, across the open field, going wide-open, heading east towards the dump at the woods! The next thing Pete knew, he had fallen off, land-ing on his back beneath the horse.

Thankfully, the horse did not step on Pete, and soon stopped running. Pete got off the ground, reached for the bridal, and led the horse back into the pasture behind the barn where Aaron had made a new gate out of pipes. Four pipes, each 21 feet long and two inches in diameter, slid into a wood-en frame on each side of the gate. Anyone pass-ing through, opened the gate by lowering one end of each long pipe. Pete removed three pipes, and thought the top one did not matter, and he led the horse beneath that top pipe. Half way through the gate, the saddle horn caught on the only remain-ing pipe, and scared the horse. He frantically shot straight ahead and bent the pipe into a U shape, as the pipe popped out of place, sailing high over Pete's head.

When the horse calmed down, the boys re-moved the saddle. They returned the pipes at the gate including one badly bent one. Pete sent Dick into the house to get him another shirt, while he stuffed his torn shirt between loose rocks in the barn foundation. The scabs on Pete's back took a long time to heal, but his parents did not know it. Aaron noticed the gate a while later, and never fig-ured out how a pipe might bend like that. His boys never bothered telling him because they thought he might be happier not knowing.

Those pipes behind the barn made dandy gym bars for daring acrobatic children, at a spot Aman-da could not see from the kitchen. She might have scolded many a time about young girls hanging up-side down. Had she seen, she certainly would have put them to work!

As for their father not understanding...Pete and Dick might have been surprised. When Aaron and Sam lived at home, their father wanted to trust his oldest sons at home alone for a short time. Just be-fore leaving, he said, "Don't open the desk and do not mess with the clock! With those words ringing in their ears, their parents were barely out of sight, before the boys did exactly that. Those temptations are part of human nature, way back to Adam and Eve, in the Garden of Eden.

Dynamite

Kaboom!" What was that?"Amanda quickly viewed the sky for an approaching storm, always on guard to save the laundry from a sudden show-er. Many times, all available help scurried to snatch the wash off the line. Drenched laundry multiplied her chores, and she knew it wasn't good for the wash. Aaron studied the sky, and they both knew it was not an approaching storm. Maybe someone in the neighborhood discharged some dynamite.

Titus worked countless hours and years for Aaron and now Aaron's boys could work for Ti-tus. Pete enjoyed helping his youngest uncle, as they worked and played together. Titus ambitiously started a good-sized orchard. They did not work hard digging those many holes for the new fruit trees, but instead, they played with dynamite! Ev-erywhere they wanted another hole; Titus planted another stick of dynamite and lit it, before taking cover. In childish glee, they set another cherry tree in the hole as grand entertainment. Pete did not mind working like that, and he certainly did not get homesick working at Titus.

Children in the neighborhood had easy access to dynamite, somewhat like fireworks. Grandfather kept some in his desk where the children had no business, but they still tried some out. The boys put a metal bucket upside down in the grass, and laid a board across the top. After lighting the fuse on a piece of dynamite, the boys quickly placed it beneath the bucket and stood on top to see how high it could lift them.

Those children also had easy access to the 'strike anywhere' wooden matches that hung on

Amanda's kitchen wall. Aaron used them to light his cigars and Amanda needed them every time she started the fire in her kitchen range. Occasionally a child sneaked a few matches from the metal dispenser on the wall. Most of the time, Amanda had eyes on the back of her head and asked, 'Where are you going with those matches?" The children had permission to use them as necessary, but Amanda knew the danger involved and she did not want her children to wastefully, strike two matches together to watch them ignite.

Daniel, Walter and Pete helped assemble Titus's brand-new sawmill. BW Shirk was there to help and so was Aaron's brother Elias. Elias and Titus planned to work together sawing local trees into lumber. BW Shirk did not have much confidence in his two sons as he said, "I never saw a rich, lazy saw- miller!" He was hinting that his sons would be too lazy to work at such a strenuous job.

Titus worked hard at the huge circular saw, as he moved the logs and sliced them into rough lumber. The sawmill was a vital part of a growing community, because everyone used native lumber, grown locally. Titus had a tobacco shed raising in 1957, where the entire neighborhood congregated for a day of work.

John Leinbach moved to the Bowmansville area, from Brutus Michigan, back in 1935. He married and raised a family. When his son Harvey needed lumber for a tobacco shed, they came to Aaron Shirk for trees. John brought along his son Levi, but first they went to get Peter Brubacher. He lived back close to the turnpike. They brought seventy -eight year old, white haired Peter [Amanda's father]and his sharpened two-man saw, to Aarons woodland, back where the turnpike crew pushed those huge boulders into the creek.

Peter excelled in cutting trees! He spent many happy hours felling trees in Michigan and he enjoyed that work much more than farming tobacco. Peter manned one end of his long two-man saw and seventeen-year-old Levi had the other. The teenager soon saw that he was no match for Peter, even if he was much younger and stronger. Peter really knew how! Those lumberjacks did not push the big long saw, but each man pulled it his way,

after the other man stopped pulling.

After felling trees, they removed the branches and used their horses to snake the logs to the road-side. After a substantial snow, they used their sturdy log-sled to move the logs to Titus Shirk's saw mill. In March of 1960, Titus had a mishap and cut his knee-cap in half while sawing lumber. He spent thirteen days in the hospital, and the doctors fixed his knee the best they could. They did not know if they could save his leg due to the critical loss of fluid in the kneecap. Titus could not work for quite a while and depended on outside help, but his leg healed, even though he limped for the rest of his life.

Titus often told other people, "quick worry while you can, because it will soon be too late! "In most cases, he was right! Even where the fear did not soon subside, it certainly did not help to worry.

Titus remained spry and active for another 35 years or more. He had a strong heart and lungs from biking many miles. The entire horse and buggy neighborhood used bicycles extensively. Menno Shirks son, Alvin had a girlfriend in Penn Valley, near Fleetwood, and he biked thirty miles one way, to see her every Sunday. While biking through Reading in the dark, a cop stopped him and asked, "Where do you think you are going at this time of the night?"He said, "I am on my way home from my girlfriend's place." As the officer dismissed Alvin, he said, "She must be one beautiful girl!"

When Aaron Shirk heard that story, he repeated it several times and Allen Musser at Bowmansville put the amusing bit of 'news' on the radio.

Pete and Dick helped Uncle Menno plant tobacco and took their fishing rods along. At the first chance they had, they slipped away for a break in the day. Mary happened to be working for Aunt Martha as a "kindts maude" or babysitter right then, and she wanted to join her brothers in their excitement. She trailed after them through the meadow of Mary Bauman and Lydia Zimmerman where the goats browsed. The biggest billy- goat with long curved horns charged and came right towards Mary, while her brothers were nearly at the fence. She screamed all she could and ran faster, but the goat easily outran her, at the age of seven. Pete called loudly and said,"Lay down! Mary, lay down so he won't get you!" Mary panicked and continued to scream and run! Pete had no words in his vocabulary that could convince his sister to give up and surrender in front of such a beast. With all that commotion, the goat owners came to the scene quickly and Mary lived to tell the tale. The goats did not hurt her, but if looks could kill, she might not have survived, because she had never seen Pete so upset in all her life. He said, "Next time we will not take you along!" That was ok with Mary because she had quite enough and declared, "I don't ever want to go along!"

Miss Fox

Miss Fox said, "Ruth, I want you to stay in at recess!" Ruth cringed because that was mostly for people needing a punishment or someone not finished with her schoolwork. Ruth's mind kept racing and wondering " now what?" She was a teacher's pet in sixth grade, and had nothing to fear.

Miss Fox smiled and talked sweetly, "Ruth, you should go on to a higher education. You are talented and need to use your life for something worthwhile. What would you want to become in your future? " She went on talking and said," Think about it, and if I could help you, let me know!"

Ruth was flattered about the comment about her IQ, but Miss Fox talked on deaf ears. Ruth, Rhoda and Martha grew up like triplets and shared everything. Why would Ruth want to go to high school, when Rhoda and Martha could stay at home with Mom? Ruth knew what homesickness felt like, while working away for other people and she was a homebody. What would she want to become anyway? Aaron and Amanda already had done a thorough job of programming Ruth to become a" keeper at home."

As a child, Amanda stayed home from school to work for her parents whenever they needed her, and school was a glorious privilege, with no problem in catching up with her lessons. She had many friends and good teachers, and she cried when she had to quit after eighth grade. Higher education for her in 1930 was out of the question, and she never wished for more book learning all her life. It was the friends that she missed most... recess

....art classes… spelling bees...and the fellowship! She learned proper English and enjoyed spelling all her life, almost like a walking dictionary. Amanda learned easily in school -work, and so did most of her children.

Amanda had wished to continue school in Michigan beyond eighth grade, mostly for entertainment, and because school was fun. Meanwhile she saw another side to this thing called life. If Ruth made it to the top, and became a skilled nurse... or whatever... what then? If she spent her life without a family and children, would she be deeply satisfied as Amanda now was, with 15 children? What was more important in the Christian life? Being a mother and homemaker, was the most needed job...nothing rated higher!

While peeling potatoes for supper that night, Ruth and Amanda discussed education and, Ruth asked, "Why don't more plain people go to college?" Amanda tried to explain that many decent hard-working people learned a tremendous amount to help others, such as their remarkable family doctor. On the other hand, book learning makes knowledge and wisdom is from God. The fear of the Lord is the beginning of wisdom.

"Think of that paring knife in your hand, it is a wonderful tool if you use it the right way. Without putting God first, a knife could be used to kill somebody. The fire in our wood stove is a tremendous help when it is controlled and used for our good, but think of a fire burning down a house or a barn. Bigger is not always better, and neither is it in education. In second Timothy, chapter three, verse seven, the Bible warns against" ever learning and never able to come to the knowledge of the truth", comparable to going through college and not believing the Bible. Among the happiest people, are those that are satisfied with less.. Contentment with godliness is great gain, whether single or married.

You will need your reading, writing and arithmetic all your life, but we prefer working with the soil close to nature and helping others.

Ruth went for a bike ride and thought about all that. Maybe someday she might understand it. For now, she was happy where she was. Her brothers taught her how to ride bike and none of them used training wheels to learn. Ruth had Pete on one side and Dick on the other side of the big clumsy bike. They helped her get on, and gave her a shove and said, 'Remember to leap off the bike, just before it falls over!" She had bruises and bumps, but every time they praised her, she tried to go a little farther the next time. All fifteen children learned to ride bike by coasting down the slope in the grassy meadow, because they wanted to and did not give up.

Amanda worked hard in teaching, managing and cleaning up messes. There came a day when Amanda looked around and said in amazement, 'The work is all getting done and I'm sitting down!" It took many years to get to that point. Most of the time, it was easier to do the work by herself, than to encourage and teach beginners. Teaching children dependability took time and needed all the patience she had, but in the end, it paid off.

20

Josie

"Run! Quick, where could we hide? Josey is coming in the walk!" said Martha in a scared half-whisper. Mary and Martha stampeded up the stairway to escape. With flashing eyes and pounding hearts, they panicked and wondered," why didn't we run out the back door, and over to Jesse's, because now we are cornered! Who wants to feed the dirty old tramp?"

Josey entered the kitchen calling loudly, "Anybody home? Hey! Anybody home? Voo sin deah? [Where are you?"]He heard the girls run pell-mell up the stairs, and he called up the steps. "Hey! Hey! Anybody home?" Mary and Martha scurried up to the attic, scared more than ever in their life. "What would Josey do if he found them...he never hurt them, but what might he do when he was mad? They tiptoed to hide beneath a row of winter coats hanging on a pipe, out of season. Only their feet showed beneath the row of coats hanging down to the floor, and both girls froze in great alarm.

Aaron and Amanda were not at home. Martha age 13 and Mary age12 did not want to meet up with grisly old Josey. They stood still and sweated among the coats for a long time. Then slowly they emerged from their hiding spots and looked out the small attic window to the west. With great relief, they saw Josey leaving towards Jesses, and just like that, he turned around and looked back. Would he come back, did he see them? Both girls froze again in fear! Thankfully, Josey gave up and kept right on going, but he knew someone did not want to meet him. The girls knew that Amanda would have fed him kindly...was Josie hungry? Surely, with her kind generosity, Lydi-Jes-sey would feed the hungry tramp, but Josey felt a great loss anytime he missed finding Aaron and Amanda at home. He walked over three miles for nearly nothing!

All these years, Josie Latshaw made his regular rounds through the neighborhood, pulling his little red wagon. People usually heard him coming, long before they saw him because the wagon wheels screeched, in need of oil, and the tin molasses buckets rattled...but not always!

Walking in big strides, Josie came to Aaron and Amanda every week for food and a shave. Most often, Children heard him coming at a distance, and announced, "duh Josie iss um kooma!" (Josie is coming!) Young children were afraid of the unsightly, unshaven man with slurred speech, and they hid behind Amanda's skirts, or even in the next room. Skip, the dog sniffed the contents of the rattly wagon, which did not suit Josie at all, and he used his cane to chase away any dog. There was a time when Josie brought along his dog-named Rosie. He was not afraid of Aaron's dogs, but Josie became overly possessive about his wagon and it even upset him when a toddler sat on it.

Josie stopped at the stripping room, where he used an excessive amount of oil on his wagon wheels, leaving a puddle beneath each one. At the corncrib, he helped himself to ear-corn for his chickens and filled a bag to take along home. Then he carried his tin molasses bucket into the kitchen and set it on a chair, as Amanda asked, "Husht ennich eppus cot fu essuh hite nuch?"[Did you have anything to eat today yet?] The answer was always the same as he said, "Naaaaaaaaaaay" in a lazy drawl, even if he had just eaten at Jesses.

"Would you like some oatmeal if I fry it?" asked Amanda. "Yaaaaw," said Josie. "How about coffee?" Amanda knew before he answered that coffee was a favorite, and he usually ate everything she set before him. Josie preferred an abundance of sugar in his instant coffee, with half an inch of sugar crystals remaining at the bottom when he left. While Amanda warmed up leftovers on a slow wood stove, Josey sat rubbing his thighs, saying "Aaaaaaaaaaaaaaaahhhh……Aaaaaaaaaaaaahhh……….."in a relaxing way.

Besides a large cup of coffee and two pieces of buttered bread, Amanda served whatever else she happened to find, even leftovers others did not want to eat anymore. Watching from a safe distance, a child stared as Josie sopped his bread into his coffee, sloppily drooling coffee off his chin and onto his plate.

If Amanda asked, "Now, what do you need?" Josey replied, "Oh, mit nem soch." (Take along things). Amanda removed the lid from the smelly tin bucket and washed it out, before filling it with fresh milk. The repulsive stench that met her nose proved that Josie did not wash the tin pail, after using the milk.

After his meal, Aaron gave Josie a shave, every time he needed one. After practicing many years on Josie, Aaron enjoyed shaving anyone sick in bed, or otherwise. Sometimes Josie needed a haircut and Aaron gladly cut his hair, but when Josie asked for a flattop hairstyle one time, he was out of luck. After Josie left, he stopped in at Jesse Brubacher's and said,"Ich hop nix cot hite nugh." [I had nothing today yet.]Nobody had any idea how many days he lived without food, and then filled up big time.

Cleaning up after Josey, Amanda's girls did not care to touch his dishes or the towel he used. Amanda thoroughly washed the dishes and the table, and somebody else quickly changed the towel, gingerly holding it by one corner.

When Josie dumped his dirty laundry pile on Amanda's kitchen floor, the [shroat caffah] grain-bugs crawled out. Lydia RoseAnna and Mandy remembered moving Josie's dirty wash -heaps with the pliers, to keep from touching things.

On a nice laundry day, Amanda washed twice. First, she washed for her own family and then she drained the washer and started all over to do the heap of dirty clothes that Josie had trampled in the dirt. Sometimes Amanda washed a third time, because she had no water shortage and she washed the many Sunday clothes and good dresses in clean water that did not contain all the cotton lint from her regular laundry.

RoseAnna did not mind her nickname of Rosie, except that was the name of Josie's dog. If anyone called her Rosie, she tattled to Amanda who simply said, "Don't worry about that!"

Lydi-Jes-sey gave Josie a clean gallon bucket for his milk, and then later she discovered that the milk he hauled home, all went to his dogs.

Due to his simple mentality, Josie became a common target for teasing. It made matters worse that he scared easily and became rattled. Boys of all ages loved to torment him, even if they knew it was wrong. If any driver swerved at Josie and blew the horn, he panicked, and jump into the ditch, wagon and all. One-time Josie cleared a meadow fence and landed on a cow. Another time some boys caused a vehicle to backfire outside his house. That scared him so bad that he fell out of the bed and complained to Aaron about it the next day. Josie said he could only lift his arm up half way now. Then Aaron asked him, "How far could you lift it before this happened?" "Why, like this," Josie answered, painlessly holding his arm straight up.

Josie helped himself to a bicycle at Paul Risslers, to try his hand at biking. He pushed the bike to his shack and tried to ride it, but it did not work. He was completely exhausted and dripping with sweat when he returned the bicycle on the same day. He would rather walk!

For some reason, Josie was afraid of policemen, and yet he liked to dress up like one. With his police badge and a cap, he loved directing traffic like a real policeman. Anyone having an auction gladly gave him permission to direct the traffic and paid him a few dollars for the job. He was good at that! This presented a good opportunity for boys to watch him jump, especially a group of boys hanging out at an auction.

On one occasion, local people took Canadians along to a sale, where they met Josie dressed like a policeman. The unkind Pennsylvania man said "Joe, ga veck, oddah ich schlaagt dich um!" ("Get away or I'll knock you over!") Josey ran up over the bank on a fencerow, terrified! There he stood with big eyes, not saying a word. The astonished Canadian man said, "sell dot date net schoffe in Canada fa so shwetza tsu un policeman." ("That would not work in Canada to talk like that to a policeman.")

At Paul Oberholtzer's auction, Josie had the job of carrying the sale papers in to the clerk. For pay, Benny Weaver, the auctioneer promised Josie all the hot dogs he could eat that day. Half way through the sale, the hot dogs got all. Josie rushed up to the auctioneer in a panic, and brought the sale to a halt saying, "Halt a moll! Halt a moll! De doggies sin all!" ("Hold it! Hold it! The hot dogs are all!") After the auctioneer promised Josey plenty of other food, the sale continued.

At that same auction, Wesley observed some young boys tormenting Josie. Their fathers found out about it and straightened them out. They knew they might not behave like that. After they left him alone, Josie he came looking for them. He often asked for attention, and he did not want to be ignored.

Other neighboring farmers sometimes hired Josie, paying from $1-$3 a day for his work. He was strong with all that fresh air and walking many miles. With a long stride, he sometimes traveled 15 miles to Green Dragon on a Friday. Josie understood the value of the different coins, but dollar bills confused him. He did not like pennies because they were not shiny. He was shrewd in some ways, and when someone asked, "Josey, how much money do you have?" he might open a snapping purse with a few pennies in it. In a separate pocket, he had a billfold with greenbacks, which he really did not need.

Josie seldom stole anything, but sometimes he borrowed things without asking and did not bother to return them. The neighbors knew where to look for missing tools.

Josie fell asleep on a Thursday afternoon and awoke at dusk, thinking it was Friday morning. He pulled his wagon and started for Green Dragon, when a neighbor stopped him and asked, "Where are you going?" It was hard to convince Josie and that it was evening and not morning.

In earlier years, Josie walked to Bowmansville and attended the Joe Wenger church where Aaron and Amanda went. He preferred to sit with the smaller boys that were not quite as smart as the teenagers were. While his mother lived, Josie would take the bus on a Sunday morning about once every six weeks and travel to Lancaster to see his mother at the county home. He dearly loved his blind mother!

The shack where Josie lived was in a sorry condition, living with Mattie, a woman that he did not get along with. The neighbors constantly heard them fighting, hollering, banging things and throwing bricks and kettles. Henry Highs, who lived about a half-mile away, could plainly hear them on a clear summer night and it scared their girls. When Josie came home to his shack, many a time the door was locked, and he forced his way inside loudly. After a while, the boarded broken windows and the broken door remained beyond repair.

The place had a terrible stench among rats everywhere. Aaron wondered what Josie did with all the corn he took along from his corncrib, for so few chickens. Upon investigating, he saw the corn stored in the outhouse where the rats ate it. Josie wanted cats and dogs, but when an animal died, he put the remains in a box in his attic.

For a while, Josie's mother owned the place where he lived, and his brother Clarence paid the taxes. Eventually the land was sold at a tax sale at the Lancaster courthouse. Adin Leinbach bought the land for $500. The neighborhood planned a new house for Josie, just across the road. Aaron was in charge of the building project.

At this time, Josie attended the Bethany Mennonite Church and they considered him a member there. Wilmer Lehman was the deacon and he made sure Josie had a bath and clean clothes every Saturday to get rid of the smell. Josie carried a Bible to church, but he did not know the difference when he held it upside down...or not.

The Bethany Mennonite Church collected the needed money for Josie's new house, a little over four hundred dollars and gave it to Aaron. At Wickes Lumber Company, Aaron purchased roofing, siding, flooring, rock lath and nails. Local volunteers cut the rough lumber from trees in the neighborhood. Volunteers also supplied the sawing, trucking, and carpenter work.

In April of 1964, Josie's new house stood completed and the time had come to burn down the old one. Aaron was in charge of thoroughly inspecting the old house before burning such things, as old Bibles, the American flag, deeds, insurance papers, or birth certificates.

Ira Martin helped Aaron search through the filth. After looking inside a box, Aaron handed it to the men outside. "Be careful", said Aaron. "Don't spill this box." They set the box neatly on the lawn, and opened the lid. Inside were the remains of "Cookie", Josie's big dog laid to rest with only the bones, hair and smell remaining.

Volunteers notified the local fire companies before they lit the house. Among the blazing flames, numerous rats screamed out. Racing around with their hair burned off, the rats quickly perished among the various spectators. That night the wind blew in the direction of Bart Horsts, and their house filled with the odd smells of the fire, on a warm night.

Mattie moved elsewhere, and Josie lived alone in his new house. He now had electric lights, a refrigerator and even a few receptacles along the wall. "What would you do if the electric went off Josie?" Someone asked. Josie said, "I would plug things into a different outlet."

When Amanda wanted to give Josie some fresh milk, he said he had a problem that it just turns sour. "But why, wondered Amanda?"You have a refrigerator now!" Josey shook his head and said, "There is no room in there." Aaron found the refrigerator filled with ear corn, cereal and things that needed no refrigeration, while the milk set on the table. Josie had tin cans and a can opener but he could not read the labels, and he occasionally opened cans, just looking what was inside, and he allowed the food to spoil.

Mrs. Weaver from TerreHill had washed Josie's laundry for many years but she was aging and couldn't do it anymore. Therefore, every week Josie brought a sack full of dirty clothes for Amanda to wash. Amanda did not require that her girls helped with Josie's wash, but sometimes they carried it to the basement for her, where she washed it. She also did the mending and altering. When Josie complained, "My pants are too tight around the waist." Amanda looked and said, "Here in the back I see where I can make them wider." Josie said, "No, it's not in the back that they are too tight, it's in the front."

Amanda and Mrs. Aaron Leinbach went every two weeks to clean Josie's house when he was not at home. Years later, Aaron wrote these words: "Josie was the most trying person to deal with. We never had a right to mistreat him, and yet he had the dumbest ways of any person we have experienced so far. It just seems to me it was God's plan to have Josie in this world, for a test on the people around him, to see if we use our talents to the best the Lord gave us, and to see if we are willing to shed light and mercies to the less fortunate one. This is always part of our daily walk of life, to have love, mercies, and patience with others around us. The Lord has a way to teach such lessons if we are just willing to let ourselves be used. There is still work for us to do. Aaron and Amanda could not go overseas in missionary work, but they helped people closer to home.

Anonymous poetry in memory of Joe Latshaw, a lifetime resident of the Bowmansville, PA area: Departed this life eight years ago:

J	Joseph Latshaw, we are glad to say,
O	opened some hearts a special way.
S	survival a struggle, problems many
E	education, (hardly any),
P	pitied by neighbors, along Spook Lane
H	his cabin they built, clothed him the same.
E	essentials scant, privileges few.
L	lived perhaps the best he knew.
A	as most were kind, some acts were bad,
T	teasing insults often t'was sad.
S	seventy four years, his cares did end.
H	he lies beside mother, his only close friend.
A	A challenge for us to amend our ways
W	we should have cared more to brighten his days.

-Contrite   Printed in 1994

Thrashing

When the heat of summer ripened grain in the fields, the farmers cut their oats and wheat with a horse-drawn binder. They hand tied the bundles into sheaves, and then stacked them into shocks to dry in the fields. To all the farm wives, those golden wheat shocks signaled a time to get busy planning a feast for hungry work men. By harvest time, most of them depended on chicken as a summer meat supply, and they dressed some chickens for the threshing crew. It was exciting to hear, "The thrashers are coming tomorrow!"

An assortment of strange horses and wagons arrived, among much noise and commotion. Jesse Brubacher owned the thrash machine, and he was responsible for all the repairs when things went wrong. He was in charge of a big area around Bowmansville and Churchtown. The "service truck" consisted of a horse-drawn greasy wagon (shpring vugha), complete with wrench sets and all. The well-stocked wagon had bearings and the most needed parts like belts and pulleys, because they could not afford to run for parts unnecessarily, while a whole crew of men waited.

Eugene Weaver was a regular on the crew, arriving among Titus and Menno and a group of others. Daniel worked hard on the crew for several years, and Walter was just a little fritz, when he went along threshing. It was his job hooking empty sacks on the grain chute, as fast as they filled. He even got pretty good at the job, but occasionally a bag ripped before Jesse grabbed the full one away. (2 bushels per bag). Walter could not move a 120-pound sack of wheat, and the grain kept on coming. He tensely tried to keep ahead, while Jesse tied the bags and moved the full ones.

At noon, the threshing machine shut down and all the workmen headed to the house for a big meal. Amanda set up rinse tubs in the shade of the apple tree, where the men cleaned up before eating. Working in the dust and sweat, they no longer looked like white men, because only their eyes and teeth looked white. The water they used for washing soon looked muddy and they needed the second tub for rinsing. The workers were laughing and talking and joking as the towels turned dark. Someone wondered if skinny little Walter worked enough to earn his meal, and Walter wasn't sure, but Aaron's brother Menno kindly stuck up for him. He was needed!

Sarah Ann worked just as hard helping Amanda prepare and serve the meal while tending children and washing many dishes. Threshing always made an exciting day, seeing an occasional horse rearing up on his hind legs, and sometimes even a runaway among the noise. It was comforting to see the grain harvested and stored for winter use before the next rain arrived. Walter showed Louise how to chew a hand full of wheat kernels, and to keep on chewing until the wad resembled chewing gum. The flavor did not match that of bought gum, but the bragging did. "Who gave you chewing gum?"

The farmers vied for the best time of the season, because the grain ripened at the same time and they had to share the thrashing rig among the entire community. When Aaron and the boys had the sheaves properly stacked into shocks, they repelled rain, but a week of rain sometimes sprouted the wheat before it was thrashed. With extra work, the farmers occasionally forked the dried wheat shocks onto wagons and stacked them in the barn, awaiting their turn. That way the other fields were more urgent and such a farmer had to wait until last. Aaron had about 5 acres or even less, and the straw was more important than the wheat. Farmers seldom discussed how many bushels per acre they raised, but "How much straw did you get?"

All the thrashing must be out of the way before tobacco cutting started. The crew traveled all over the neighborhood, and stuffed themselves with good food, but none of them gained weight, as they worked hard. One fussy hostess drew attention to herself and said "Es hut feel mooka room!"(It has many flies around), the flies were scarce and Titus piped up, "Yah ich hop gnoticed." (Yes, I noticed), to embarrass the hostess who was seeking reassurance that not many flies remained.

Fresh straw in the haymow, made a perfect playground among children bouncing with energy to spare. Even bigger boys enjoyed the rope swing and dropped down into the soft pile of slippery loose straw. Aaron and Amanda did the same thing when they were children.

In Michigan, Amanda's mother came out to help her daughters level the loose hay in the barn, before the men came in with the next load. The girls also helped rake the hay and drive the teams of horses. Amanda had fond memories of swinging so high above the hay, that her skirt touched the beams as high as the top of the swing. She also tried climbing all the way around the inside of the barn on the frame, without getting down. Time brought many changes and Amanda happily stayed in the house and relived those memories through her own children.

Children came out in the barn to choose the biggest cleanest sections of fresh straw. They cut away the joints, and used the straws as soda straws. Only the rich people bought paper straws for drinking drinks, but nothing tasted better than root beer through a wheat straw. They were in style!

When D. Walter Martin purchased a Massy self-propelled combine with a five-foot head, local farmers couldn't imagine the combine ever out- doing a binder with a ten-foot swath. It was not about the width; it was more about one man replacing twelve men, plus many horses and wagons. When thrashing went out of style, some people said "good riddance," while others felt a loss, due to the lack of community togetherness, and helping each other.

Haymaking soon followed, with the arrival of the baler, and no more farmers forked loose hay onto the wagons. Bales saved a tremendous amount of space and labor, replacing the need of outside help. Several years later, farmers quit butchering at home and put their meat in the freezer, ready frozen from the locker. And, believe it or not, people began putting up buildings without a barn raising, because they could order them raised professionally and labor became a valuable commodity, as more people sought an off the farm income. Times changed rapidly, but not all for the better.

Sunday Dinner

All her life, Amanda liked working with food and inviting guests. The fellowship of friends made it worthwhile. Both Aaron and Amanda never quite got their fill of inviting company of all kinds.

Sometimes Amanda planned ahead and sent postcards in the mail inviting their guests, but many times, she opened her heart and home without getting ready in advance. One time a family came to Aarons on a Sunday dinner when no one was looking for them. Someone had the date wrong and Sarah Ann was embarrassed! They were not at all ready for company. It took a while, but the company stayed and Amanda got a meal together. The many jars of canned food in the cellar were as convenient as opening tin cans.

To do it right, a lot of work went into inviting company. Amanda worked ahead all she could, because she did not approve of working on a Sunday. The cast-iron kitchen range was a mess to clean, with bits of food spilled and the black dirty corners needed regular cleaning. Amanda often used a wad of any waxed paper, like the layer inside of the cereal boxes, to clean the range top. She crumbled the waxed paper in a wad and swiped it over the warm stovetop, rearranging the paper until all the wax melted off as a polish for her stove, and then she tossed the paper into the fire.

As time went on Amanda had more helpers to prepare food and to help clean for company. It did not matter if the people were young or old, rich or poor, neighbors or travelers; Aarons invited many guests.

Amanda and her helpers stretched the 14-foot extension table wide open, and covered it with the best white Sunday tablecloth. Amanda used her Sunday china, and she did not skimp, down to the last saltshakers and toothpick holders. As the dinner guests entered the house, the men hung their hats in the living room, on a row of hooks, and the women put their wraps upstairs on a bed. They took seats, or stood around waiting. It was polite to offer to help the hostess, but sometimes it was best to keep out of the way when the potatoes were not ready yet.

Butter browning in a pan smelled tantalizing! Amanda drizzled it over the filled noodle and potato dishes, about the time she told Aaron, "Everything is ready now!" Aaron sat at the head of the table, and any minister or guest of honor sat at the other end. The men always sat down first and next came the boys. Children watched in eager anticipation to see if they could get to the first setting because they were hungry. It was already past their usual mealtime.

With the table filled to capacity, everyone bowed their heads in reverence for a silent prayer. Amanda removed the tea towel that covered the bread plate and passed the bread first. No one passed the butter and jelly, as everyone reached in to help himself.

The most convenient Sunday meat was beef, canned in wide- mouth two-quart jars, ready to heat and serve. Amanda cooked homemade noodles with a pinch of saffron. Mashed potatoes took much longer, and many a time the meal waited on the potatoes, because the canned vegetables were ready quickly, and so was the fruit.

The meals were not perfect, but Aaron and Amanda enjoyed the company, and the joy of using Sunday dishes filled with good food. Amanda reserved the pink Depression glass dishes for fruit salad. The gold glass dishes generally contained pudding, and she used the green glass dishes for salads. Amanda often made Jell-O on a Saturday evening for a special treat for her own family on Sunday, or just in case company arrived. She put the jello in her clear dishes. Many times she had no idea how many people she might be serving, if any, but she knew extra food was no problem as she made two cakes, or many pies.

Instant pudding was a wonderful invention that simplified a Sunday dinner. With an abundance of fresh milk, a child could make the pudding after the guests arrived, as the potatoes softened. Sunday dinner guests were not in a hurry, and it is good they were not, because sometimes the meal took a while.

Preschool-age children, unable to wait so long to eat, filled a soup bowl and sat on the wood chest or out in the summerhouse while big girls and mothers waited for the second setting. Any time a huge crowd of guests gathered, those hungry pre-teen girls nearly faded away with hunger and self-pity, when they had to wait half the afternoon on a second or occasionly

even a third setting of dinner guests. No one had ever heard of eating from trays.

After Amanda passed all the food a second time and last of all the toothpicks, the men left the table and retreated to the parlor, where they often smoked cigars, while talking. Any boys exited the closest door to the outdoors.

With a flurry of activity, all the available girls and women helped to wash the Sunday dishes and then quickly reset the table. Amanda retrieved the half-warm leftovers from the oven, and the women ate their fill, in a relaxed mood. After the meal, the girls quickly helped to clear the table one last time. Sometimes they caught up with the boys playing 'bloomp sock' in the barn[a type of playing tag, by tossing a tied up gunny sack at the next 'itter'. They played croquet in the yard. Depending on who the company was, the girls did not want to meet the boys, but cousins could be fun.

After the last guests ate, the women spent time leisurely washing and drying all the Sunday dishes as they talked about the flower slips at the window and the latest quilt inspirations.

Amanda carefully put most of the Sunday dishes away, but some remained until the next day. Each bowl and each platter fit in its exact place in the china cupboard, and only she could pack it precisely as it had been. Inviting company took a lot of food and hard work, but none of them considered being host as working on a Sunday.

Sometimes when the guests were ready to leave, no one knew where to look for the children. Amanda did not like when the children boldly went too far, but neither did she like when they hung around saying, "what can we do?" "Go Play dolls, or get the color books and colors" she suggested, (unless they were all filled already.)"Let's go feed the fish in the barn yard, said Louise" That meant catching shroat caffah, or mealworm beetles, to drop them into the water trough, watching the fish slurp them in a big gulp.

[Scientifically known as Tenebrio], the mealworms multiplied beneath the feedbags, and as spring turned into summer, black beetles emerged. Aaron wanted to get rid of the destructive pests, and feeding the fish was fine, but the children must be careful when moving feedbags or they might damage the bagged feed among their innocent fun.

When it was not raining, the boys headed for the pond or the woods, and occasionally enjoyed the primitive entertainment of roasted frog legs on sticks, over an open fire. The boys ate them all, even without salt. It never failed that the children were having most fun when it was time to go home.

❧

Aaron and Amanda did not own a coffee pot. Besides Josey, Aaron was the only one that enjoyed coffee. When he came in for a break between meals, he helped himself to instant coffee. He preferred the Nescafe brand name. Aaron needed a saucer or a plate, because after stirring a spoonful of instant coffee into a cup of hot water, he added an abundance of heavy cream, deliberately causing the coffee-cup to overflow onto the saucer. Sometimes he used a second cup and poured the coffee back and forth, playfully cooling it. He appreciated cookies with his coffee.

After drinking the coffee, and speaking what was on his mind, Aaron reached for his tattered straw hat and headed outdoors again. Many times, he could not find his hat, because he had no idea where he last put his hat and his coat. When he wished for help in finding anything, he said, "Somebody stole it!"He enjoyed being served like royalty, and he appreciated when Amanda helped him find his things, even when he knew he had them last.

At one time Aaron had a bad habit of tossing his hat and coat in a corner on the floor. To help him break the habit, Amanda threatened to set a tub of water at that spot...but she didn't!

Amanda preferred hot chocolate milk over coffee and served it any time she had surplus milk. She stirred together equal parts of cocoa and sugar and simmered it in a bit of water, with a pinch of salt, to make chocolate syrup. She brewed tea from the patch behind the house. Fresh tea often filled the baby bottles, and she served it cold by the gallon, on a summer day. When the family first tasted tea like Nestea, not one of them would drink it, they preferred homegrown meadow tea, wooly tea, and mint or spearmint tea.

Amanda spent a lot of effort in teaching ten daughters how to cook. When a cake burned at the edges or flopped in the middle, she served it anyway. Sometimes the potatoes turned black on the bottom of the kettle, and sometimes the pudding scorched, especially due to her lightweight cookware.

When everyone sat down to eat at suppertime, the children occasionally frowned and said, "It's not good!" Amanda said, "If all of you take just one serving, the dish will be empty!"She did not want to waste any food, and the teenage boys called those inferior dishes" muss-fress", translated as 'must eat'.

When Amanda served some exceptionally good dessert, they also shared, by not taking more than their share. Amanda cooked a lot of pudding and made tapioca, trying to use up the fresh milk. The children often said, "Jell-O, junket and ice cream, are the three best things in the world!" Junket was fun to eat, as the sweetened milk thickened smoothly, in individual custard cups. When Amanda couldn't decide what to make as a quick meal, she made cold milk soup. She tore up some bread and added milk sweetened with sugar, and flavored with vanilla. She served it with fresh fruit and set the large aluminum bowl on the table for a simple meal in summer. Ice cream was best of all, and they seldom had their fill.

For a short time the ice cream truck came out back to Aarons, and he tried to sell expensive ice cream. They seldom could afford even one box of the bought luxury, and the truck quit coming.

Sometimes Aaron and Amanda served one box of ice cream among a family of 17 people. Amanda waited until everyone had cleared his plate of meat and potatoes, before she reached for the box of ice cream in the refrigerator. With all eyes watching, she carefully opened the box and flattened it. Then with a sharp knife, she cut the ice cream in half and in half again. Without using a ruler, she cut each piece in half and in half again. She cut all 16 pieces as equally as possible, and she placed one piece on each plate around the table, with no one having a chance at even a teaspoon –full more. Each person got a ½-cup serving, and they all wished for more of the velvety smooth ice cream! The children savored every delicious spoonful and ate it slowly. The only thing that could have made it taste any better, was seeing their mother eat some also. She scraped the box with her knife, and barely had a sample of the sweetness.

Aaron and Amanda seldom bought ice, because the iceman did not travel to their area. When the farm pond froze a foot thick, Titus came over and cut chunks of ice with his oversized saw. It was heavy work! He hauled the ice home and kept it insulated among sawdust, keeping it a long time that way. Aaron also stored some in his haymow, wrapped in canvas.

Naturally, ice cream tasted better in the heat of the summer, and on a rare occasion, the children eagerly gathered enough hailstones, to make a batch of ice cream in a hurry. Jesse's and Aarons could not both make ice cream on the same day be-

cause they shared the same freezer. When Amanda tried basic flavors, everyone dug in for huge servings, and seconds, but one time she tried coffee flavor and disappointed everyone, even herself. No one remembered what happened with that ice cream, but surely, she did not waste it!

Children gleefully chanted, "Were making ice cream, we're making ice cream!" Amanda did not use a recipe, but knew from her memory, how much junket and how many eggs worked best in the 8-quart freezer. She never skimped on cream, because she had plenty from the family cow. Sometimes Amanda over-filled the freezer with more than just up to the "full" line.

The brittle ice chipped easily with a sharp ice pick. When the big boys helped, they worked faster and put a chunk of ice in a burlap bag, lifted it up and slammed it down on the concrete walk several times. To crush the ice finer, they used Aaron's

Eating ice cream. Sarah Ann got up to take the picture. Aaron and Amanda sat at the head of the table and beside them was the high chair. Dessert dishes made the treat even more special. Notice the eight quart ice cream shtennah [canister].Louise turned her dirty plate upside down and put her dessert dish on top.

heavy splitting maul, pounding the ice in the bag until the bag had holes in it.

After carefully packing layers of coarse salt among layers of finely crushed ice, Amanda covered the White Mountain freezer with a burlap bag or a rug, and a smaller child sat on top, while others took turns cranking. As the salt melted the ice, water flowed out of the small round overflow hole on the side.

After cranking a while, Amanda said " Scoop out some of the soft ice cream, so that the rest can harden, and please keep the salty water out of the ice cream". Girls that cranked the ice cream rapidly, slowed down when it turned harder, and asked Pete or Dick to take a turn. Dick asked, "Whose ice cream freezer is this, Jesse's or ours?" Pete said, "It doesn't really matter, keep on cranking." The wooden White Mountain ice cream freezer traveled back and forth on the wagon, between Aarons and Jesses, so many times, that no one cared who owned it. It would not make any difference as long as it worked. Sometimes they wanted it at the same time, but they shared and someone changed plans.

Amanda planned a simple supper, making sure they had room for ice cream. When Aaron lifted out the paddles, eager hands reached out to scrape them clean, because the paddles came first. Every one kept on eating until the ice cream was gone, because they had no way to save the leftovers. Generally, that was no problem but sometimes Amanda coaxed children to help eat the last serving, even when they had their fill.

Homemade ice cream was a highlight brightening any day. It was Aaron's favorite, and he recorded the event in his diary. The anticipation of the finished product was greater than the ice cream itself. In fact, sometimes it was imperfect but in their minds, it really was a wonderful dessert.

The dirty salt water that remained in the ice cream freezer, worked as a weed killer along the edge of the walk.

In springtime, when the grass turned green, Aaron turned the cows out to pasture, and the cows found the wild garlic that grew abundantly. The cows loved it! Before Aaron brought in the warm fresh milk, he dumped some of the bad-smelling milk to the pigs first. Pee Yew! Nobody liked the garlic flavor or the smell in the milk, and even Amanda considered it spoiled. Some of the children held their noses shut while swallowing. If they had nothing better than that, they would rather put water on their breakfast cereal, because they could not disguise the garlic flavor. Sugar could not hide it, and neither could ice cream, not even with a lot of vanilla or strawberries added. Amanda did not even make the cream into butter.

21

Salesman

A salesman arrived on a winter day when the stripping room was cold. Since Aaron wanted to warm up beside the kitchen range, he invited the man into the house. Aaron loved to talk, even to a salesman, and each man pulled a chair up to the cook stove, sipping coffee. The stranger marveled at the action all around him, for he had never seen anything quite like it. Children put away the freshly folded laundry piles and set the table, while Amanda was busy making supper. People swarmed all over that room, each doing their own thing. "How can so many people work together without knocking saucers out of each other's hands?" He asked.

He left before everyone washed up and found their usual seat at the table, where a six-foot bench crowded each side. Eight-inch aluminum pie plates served as soup plates or flat plates, no matter what the menu and they did not break. When Amanda bought the new pie plates, the eager children scratched a name on the bottom of each plate. Amanda did not appreciate when the girls spent extra time deciding who gets which plate, when they were all identical. Everyone had a plate and a spoon at the table, but they often shared forks, knives, and water glasses, without complaining, due to a shortage.

The kitchen, built in 1945 was big by the standards back then. Aaron and Amanda thought they planned plenty of room in the 16' x20' kitchen but they had no way of knowing their family would double in size. Hunger and respect drove the family together three times a day, no matter what they were doing and no matter what the food was. Aaron and Amanda, with their table full of children, silently bowed their heads in prayer, thanking God for food and for each other. Amanda cooked large amounts and baked many pies, just as her parents taught her. Pete cut a pie in half and asked, "Dick, which piece do you want?" Each of those growing boys ate half a pie, because they saw all the remaining warm pies, fresh out of the oven.

When the meal ended, people scattered! Some went to the barn, upstairs, or outside. Mary said, 'let's run to the scales and see who weighs the most!' As Amanda looked around, she said, "Where are all the people who ate here?" The girls soon came back to help with the dishes, sometimes reluctantly. Gaining weight was something to brag about among such a skinny bunch. Mary was proud when she weighed more than her sisters did! Aaron's platform scales weighed things accurately, whether it weighed people or tobacco bales.

Boys often helped with the laundry, but they seldom got involved with doing dishes at Aarons, when all five boys, each had ten sisters.

Bantam hens multiplied naturally and hid their nests in surprising places. Sometimes the biddy hen remained unnoticed until she had soft adorable chicks chirping loudly, trying to find their way down from the hayloft. Louise loved to scoop baby chicks into her skirt to show them off to anyone interested, especially to Amanda, but she knew she had to release them again.

Many times, the children playing in the barn, found a large nest of hidden banty -eggs. Each egg came with a built-in freshness tester. Amanda put the eggs in a dishpan of cold water and if any floated, she gave them to the pigs, because they were rotten. Those that sank to the bottom were fresh enough to eat for breakfast, unless they were nearly hatched. The eggs that half way rose to the top, or stood on one end, were stale but still fit to eat after a careful inspection. Eggs like that made good homemade noodles. Amanda carefully opened and checked all questionable eggs before using any of them. She did not want to waste food, but neither did she want anyone to get sick from her cooking. None of them ate pasteurized food of any kind, because it was not available to them. Perhaps the honey crystallized but Amanda set it on the reservoir end of the range and it softened slowly. The apple cider sometimes turned to hard cider or vinegar and they used it that way.

The United States Department of Agriculture did not recommend canning low acid vegetables without using a pressure canner, but Amanda did it all her life, without any health problems. Pickles with all that vinegar seldom spoiled. She knew that fruit, fermented like wine, could still be safe, and so was fermented sauerkraut, after skimming mold off the top.

She served many things others might not, as she trimmed mold from cheese and skimmed mold from sour cream, because her mother taught her that moldy cream, with the mold removed, made butter all the same. Amanda skimmed mold from homemade jams and trimmed mold from cakes and bread if it was not too bad. Pioneers without refrigeration learned that moldy bacon was not harmful.

Amanda fetched a home cured ham from the attic, with plans for a big ham supper. Aaron had helped her soak it in brine and rub the ham with sugar cure. Then they applied liquid smoke and hung it to dry in the attic. Upon close inspection, she discovered that the huge chunk of meat they had tried to cure, had maggots crawling near the bone at the one end. She could not toss out all that meat! Disgustedly, she fetched the meat saw and started trimming. She threw away all that looked bad and even a tad more. She never served worms or bugs to anyone! After thoroughly cooking the ham, she knew it was safe to eat. Amanda did not want to waste any food that God trusted to her.

She knew about botulism and those deadly poisons. "If in doubt... throw it out!" That is just what she did with spoiled tomato juice, and any suspicious looking canned vegetables such as corn. When she found a chunk of baloney in the refrigerator, all covered with a fine layer of white mold or a sticky surface, she washed it with vinegar and

carefully trimmed off the first slice, and then she served the rest without any problems.

In later years, Amanda found bugs in cereal and bugs in flour. If it was just one bug that fell in, she removed it and went on. When she saw spider webs in the corner of a cereal box, she gave the contents to the cats or to the chickens, with visible regrets. As fast as their family devoured food, they seldom had a problem.

Food was a sacred gift and she did not like to discard any, and none of her cooking ever sickened any of her family or guests that she knew. Spilled popcorn never went into a waste can to burn, and neither did any other food, because she could not destroy food! Surely, the birds or the chickens would eat the crumbs she threw out the door. She tried her best to teach her fifteen children, to never burn or destroy food. God was watching!

In Michigan Amanda seldom had sweet drinks. Mommy Brubacher occasionally made a thirst quenching vinegar punch by stirring together one half cup sugar, one half cup vinegar, and a little nutmeg in a gallon of water.

They spread lard on a slice of bread, because the homemade butter went to the store. The eggs also were too valuable to eat, but they never went hungry. They did not have any trash. They saved every scrap of paper with a blank spot remaining on it, to figure or to write on it. Snavely flour came in pretty paper bags with a blue liner inside, and they used them to wallpaper the outhouse. If they had an unusable piece of paper, they used it wisely to start a fire in the stove. None of them had any tin can trash, because they used every empty tin can as a flowerpot on the windowsill, a pencil holder, or for sorting nails in the shop. Broken dishes went out to play pretend in their crude playhouse at the lean-too. They lived before plastic, and they did not need a dumpster or a landfill area because they kept everything they had. For the rest of her life, Amanda automatically remained a packrat.

First of May is Barefoot Day

First of May is barefoot Day! The holiday Aarons children counted down to most, was" barefoot day, "no matter which day it first arrived. It meant going without shoes and connecting with oozing mud, soft grass, plowed fields, prickly stubble and the real feel of nature itself. Naturally, there were also things like thistles and splinters and stepping on a bee. The soles of the feet soon toughened to the feel of tanned leather. Amanda asked that her children gather every sharp object first, such as a shard of glass, a piece of metal, wire, or anything that cuts. After several trips, of searching around the house and the shed, children abandoned shoes in a gleeful celebration of running and tumbling with energy to spare.

Bare feet resulted in the extra chore of washing feet before bedtime. A basin of water on the porch steps, was sufficient for the whole bunch, and saved washing more sheets. After dark, it was nice out on the steps to watch the bats flying out of the attic and to hear the first distant whippoorwill calls. Then came the lightning bugs, flashing with their "catch me if you can" attitude.

Amanda tried her best to keep all the bats out of her attic. She looked carefully to see where the morning light shone in the cracks on that east gable end of the house. She stuffed all possible cracks with rags or wooden wedges, but the bats always won.

Lying on a blanket in the grass, children counted a steady stream of bats exiting the attic eaves, 93, 94, 95, 96,. .. 97.... Occasionally a stray bat came down the attic stairs and into the girl's bedroom, in the middle of the night, creating lifetime memories.

Mary was scared of bats and she hid under the covers ! Most of the girls grabbed a shoe or something, and created quite a ruckus, amid squeals of laughter and ripples of panic. Half a dozen girls chased one scared bat. Amanda came over in her nightgown and housecoat to help with the battle, and to quiet things down so the rest of the family could get some sleep. Someone dropped the dead bat into the chamber bucket or else tossed it onto the balcony until daylight. The poor little bat would have escaped in a hurry if anyone had opened the balcony door or a window, where the bat could feel fresh air and a way of escape to the outside. Any bat wanting to tangle into long hair, missed many

an opportunity. All the girls understood that 'bats getting into hair', was an old wives fable.

Bats were a sign of spring and so were the whippoorwills calling from the woods. They returned several weeks after the last frost and set up their nighttime serenade, calling to claim their territory. Even with a late spring snow, the whippoorwill's returned on time, around the middle of April. Amanda recorded such an important fact in her diary because the birds were a joy to her and a promise of spring. When the whippoorwill called, it meant the ground warmed up enough for planting corn, and the rest of the garden.

While lying on the grass and looking at the bats, no one could miss the display of stars overhead on a clear night. "Look at those stars! They are so far away that they just look tiny... the books say each speck of light we see, is as big as our sun... how can that be? There is the Big Dipper... and I see the North Star... See the Milky Way over there... That constellation is one gigantic group of stars rotating like a pinwheel with different arms reaching out... our sun is part of the Milky Way.. .If each speck of light in the Milky Way is a sun... those could all have planets rotating around them as our sun does.. ."God telleth the number of the stars and He calleth them all by their names. Psalms 147; 4". Man is really, really tiny! What is man that thou art mindful of him? In Psalms, The Bible says man is just a little lower than the angels are, and he has dominion over all the animals. Thank you God for the works of your hands... thank you for making the whole world and for all of our family."

After a while, the mosquitoes drive the children indoors. Amanda set the kerosene lamp on the table, and children lingered, not quite ready for bed. Amanda simmered cocoa with sugar, water and a bit of salt to make chocolate syrup. A gallon of chocolate milk disappeared as a bedtime snack, around the flickering lamp. Many a time, someone pulled out a longhair from a pigtail, and held it above the glass lampshade, watching it curl up in the heat. It sizzled and curled in a neat pattern, followed by the smell of burning hair. Amanda tolerated some of that, but nobody liked the strong smoky smell of burnt hair. Two by two, the girls went out to the outhouse and used the 'double seater', one last time before heading upstairs. It was scary going alone, even with a flashlight.

Most of the family had a long busy day and fell asleep instantly, but anyone not totally worn out could lie awake and count the whippoorwill calls. It worked like sleeping pills. Aaron's family did not count sheep…. Birdcalls and croaking frogs pleasantly sang them to sleep… Thank you God!

School Sewing

Farmers generally had a slight break after threshing, planting tobacco and making hay. Even the garden had a break in the heat of the summer, and that is when Amanda liked to start sewing for back-to-school. Keeping their 10 girls in dresses required management, and she knew she could not buy dresses ready-made because she wanted simplicity and modesty, without lace and trim in the latest styles.

Amanda kept her Singer treadle sewing machine inside the north window. It stayed there always! She needed the window as the source of light for her sewing. She did not want the glare of the bright south side, and she considered any harsh sunlight too hard on the sewing machine. Some things she could sew in a dim light, and she even enjoyed working in semi-darkness for her usual chores. As the sun went down, Amanda's eyes adjusted to the softness of the dim lighting and she did not mind. Seldom did they light the lamps, until it was truly necessary. When Amanda had things to sew by hand, she did it in the daytime for a better light. Any time she sewed a black dress or a black suit, she needed the bright sunlight.

The school girls could barely wait until the feed man unloaded Aaron's order. 'Let's race to the barn and see what feedbags he brought, 'said Rhoda. "I want this one," said Mary. "This one is mine," claimed Martha. "You have to have two matching bags, or mom can't make you a dress," said Ruth. Amanda always got the final say, deciding who gets what, and which bags she might return to the feed company for a $.25 refund. The colorful printed feedbags came as part of the animal feed purchase, but occasionally Amanda returned some bags if she did not think they were suitable colors or patterns. Mostly, she used them up, because she could use feedbags for anything from quilt backs to tea towels, aprons, bloomers, bonnets, slips, dresses, shirts and table- cloths etc.

If the mice chewed a hole in the corner of a feedbag, they could not return that one. After Aaron used the feed, Amanda turned each bag inside out, opened the seam, and washed it. At Harry Goods store, Amanda bought sheets of woven straw, by the yard. She cut and sewed that for the front half of a straw bonnet, and the back half, she made with gathered printed fabric, with a ruffled edge along the front, covering the edge of the cut straw. Sometimes the new school dresses matched the straw bonnets. For winter wear, Amanda made velvet caps with heavy lining.

She collected material of all kinds, wherever she could find it. Some came from the Reading mission in the form of lady dresses to alter. Many pieces came out of her "gift" collection beneath her big china cupboard, given as baby gifts. By now, she had used up all the sugar sacks from the bootleggers. She enjoyed any fabric sale at Rubinsons in New Holland, and fabric of all kinds attracted her.

Amanda did not want to cut into her tablecloth, so sometimes she folded back the oilcloth on the table and cut fabric on the bare wooden table boards. With just a few crude newspaper patterns, Amanda called each girl individually to measure her, making sure the dress was big enough. It was hard for Louise to stand still long enough for Amanda to fit, one piece at a time. "Now bend your arm so I can measure from your shoulder to your hand," Amanda said.

She cut the bodice front piece last, especially if it looked like the fabric might not reach. Due to necessity, Amanda pieced the front in three sections. She split the dress front down the middle, and in the center, she created a ladder of tucks running horizontally, from the waist up to the neckline. Sometimes she even pieced that narrow center strip, from barely a handful of scraps left over. Other girls marveled at such decoration, but it was not for vanity.

Amanda sewed many straw bonnets like these. Notice the tucks Amanda pieced in the front of a dress due to necessity.

Two-toned dresses were fancy and Amanda could not buy more fabric to match. Feedbags had only so much material, measuring 36" x 46" and Amanda knew exactly which apron or dress pattern fitted on that size. Jesse Brubacher's girls sometimes wore two-tone aprons for every day when the print was almost the same. Sometimes women could trade feedbags or share the scraps if there were any. Every small left over print scrap went into a collection for making quilts.

Amanda concentrated on cutting the right size without making a mistake, because then the fabric only made a smaller dres. Lydi-Jes-sey walked into Aaron's house one time while Amanda was busy cutting fabric. She saw Amanda cutting out a garment on her lap because no one had cleared the table. Beneath the table sat a small child crying, and Amanda desperately wanted to finish what she had started. Every now and then, she peeked

beneath the table saying, "peek-a-boo!" to distract and amuse the child. Lydi-Jes-sey knew she could not make things holdout, without a better pattern, and while listening to the distraction of a child crying, as Amanda did.

Amanda was hard on her dresses, as a child growing up in Michigan. Her mother made her and Betsy some heavy blue denim everyday dresses. Amanda cut a hole in the front of the dress with a knife when she whittled a stick. When Louise came along ripping holes in dresses, Amanda tried that idea on her daughter. She sewed two identical everyday dresses out of heavy-duty material, and the next week Louise tore a triangle in her skirt while climbing down from the hay-loft. "Husht due un dri-eck in die frock grissah?"[Did you rip a triangle into your dress?]Amanda asked, and she patched it!

Amanda used her sewing machine regularly for sewing of all kinds. On laundry day, any mending that she did not fix right away, accumulated on top of the Singer treadle sewing machine. When Amanda came to sew, she tried to do the mending first, and that was almost endless. Amanda had a second "poor" treadle sewing machine in the bedroom, just for the girls but any time Amanda was not sewing or mending, the many girls used her good sewing machine, impatiently waiting for their turn. Their dolls had a "need" for many dresses.

When Ruth sewed right through her finger, she loudly called "ma-am!" Amanda was there in an instant, turning the wheel, and removing the needle from Ruth's finger. She could tell by the urgent call what took place. Sewing a finger was an important part of learning to sew.

"Use duh selvin," Amanda said. [Do not waste the selvage edge]. That is the strongest part of the fabric! Amanda knew that what her children learned by experience was as important to them as money in a bank account. She bought bias tape for some sewing projects, such as slips and aprons, and each package of Wrights trim had a coupon or wrapper to save. For $.10 postage and three coupons, the Wrights Company sent a scrap bag of lace and trim ends for crafts or sewing. The girls dreamed what all might arrive for ten cents, and the dreaming was even more fun than opening the package. When

Amanda parted with a dime, she knew the money was well -spent, because it taught a child how to send for things in the mail. A personalized envelope "just for me" put a sparkle in the day it arrived. It helped teach children not to open another person's mail, no matter what it was, even if they knew what was inside, and it was for everybody. The bits of metallic rickrack or gold braided trim were as important as holding real gold, to fire the imagination. Their dolls wore the latest, with lace and ruffles and nothing was too fancy for them.

The ragman bought some rags to recycle, but most of the rags disappeared as cleaning rags and rug rags. Amanda had a ragbag in the summerhouse, but after the growing girls salvaged scraps for doll garments, not much was left. Amanda saved a barrel full of old clothing, for making rugs, especially wool. She gathered her daughters together in a circle in the kitchen, ripping out pockets and removing collars. "Save those buttons and snaps for the button jar," she said. Amanda supervised the messy job, with dust and fuzzies getting into noses. She showed them how to cut thin long pieces and sew all the strips together, wrapping them into balls for crocheting. Her daughters learned to crochet rugs, because Amanda did not want them to discard anything usable.

Amanda came home from an auction one day, with a box full of material strips; ready rolled into balls for crocheting. She was delighted with the bargain, all ready for making rugs! Upon closer inspection, she discovered brand-new fabric in pretty colors, suitable for making a nice log cabin quilt. She unraveled some balls and cut out sections to her liking, because it was good strong fabric. After she salvaged the best, she had enough good printed material for two log cabin quilts. She cut one quilt for Louise, and sewed the other one for herself. She added some of Louise's own dress scraps, to add more meaning. When the quilt needed binding, Amanda asked Louise to hem it by hand. That was asking too much, because there in the living room sat Amanda's new Necchi sewing machine, recently purchased. It had a zigzag stitch that she wanted to try out, much faster than hand sewing!

When Amanda was getting ready to go to a quilting, she could not find her good covering. It was a mystery to her, how it could totally disappear. Where had it gone? She did not want to leave wearing her every day covering, so she quickly made herself a new one!

Months later when the leaves dropped from the trees, Amanda noticed something in the big apple tree outside their bedroom window. She could not imagine what it might be, until suddenly she realized it was her missing covering! Apparently, a strong breeze had floated the covering out through the screen -less window.

Eastern bluebirds lived in a birdhouse on the wash line post, amid many children, cats and noise. They came back every year, fascinating anyone hanging laundry on the line, or swinging on the baler- twine swing beneath the birdhouse. As Sarah Ann hung up one basketful of wash after the next, she noticed how hard the mother bluebird worked to feed her babies. She pitied that mother bird and searched until she found a fish worm. Now what? After thinking it over Sarah Ann draped the worm on the peg at the entrance of the birdhouse. She was horrified as she watched the young birds panic and bail out of the nest, creating a major problem among the cats. Never again would she offer to help feed fledglings!

Louise also enjoyed the birds and especially listening to the pigeons coo in the upper barn. When Daniel had a small workshop in the loft above the pigsty, Louise enjoyed that secluded spot among his tools. He had a cheap vice from E K Fisher, a hammer, screwdrivers and such among boards and nails for making birdhouses. Some of the boards were empty crates. Louise enjoyed the entertainment, of climbing up the ladder, and quietly watching the pigs, but best of all she watched the barn swallows, just a few feet away. She amused herself a long time watching the mother bird feed her young, as she wondered which baby bird might get the food next.

Daniel's first bike came from EK Fisher and so did his first gun. With influence from Titus, he bought a 410-gauge shotgun for $30.Daniel worked hard for little pay and that was a major investment for him. Later he preferred the 16 gauge with more power. Others sometimes called Louise a tomboy because she enjoyed the outdoors. When her brothers were sighting in their gun, they wanted to demonstrate how much kick a gun had, so they talked Louise into shooting target. When she squatted down and pulled the trigger, the gun kicked so hard that she fell backwards, while her brothers laughed! Most of the boy's things were more fun than doing dishes. Louise squirmed and protested when Pete or Dick put a fish worm down in the back of her dress, but she knew better than to run to the house and tattle. Amanda had plenty of housework waiting.

When Skip chased a groundhog up a small tree, Louise shook it down to watch the fight. As the dog violently slung the groundhog back and forth, he tossed it her way. The groundhog bit her in the ankle and left a scar, but not seriously. She also messed with a bat spread out on the bark of the apple tree, and it bit her when she stretched out the wings and admired the downy softness. Rabies was just an uncommon word in the dictionary.

Most scratches and bruises healed by themselves without a fuss, but Amanda's medicine cabinet included the basics of rubbing alcohol, peroxide, witch hazel, Soothie, toothpaste, Mercurochrome, and Merthiolate. It burned like everything!

She could not afford Band-Aids but she usually had a roll of white adhesive tape and some soft worn -out cotton scraps she used as gauze when necessary. She seldom ran out of Vicks Vapor Rub, and anyone with a sore throat had the stuff rubbed on generously, like it or not. Amanda carefully warmed up a woolen rag, or a stocking, to wrap around the neck, steaming the Vicks medication down in deeper.

Mercurochrome and Merthiolate both contained a warning on the label. "Do not use a large amount on a large wound because this product contains mercury.' 'Eventually it was outlawed. Amanda saw no harm in mercury. She used a glass fever thermometer with the silver metal inside, and when it broke, she gathered the liquid mercury in a small dish to entertain her children. The funny stuff split into many tiny balls and snapped together again in a strange way.

Inside the wooden cabinet door hung two rows of hooks to hold enough toothbrushes for everyone in the family to have their own, at least in later years. Each toothbrush belonged on its own personal hook and the shorter children had the bottom row. Aaron and Amanda did not require their children to brush their teeth, but it was a great way to stall for time, before going to bed.

None of Aaron's children needed braces in a major way. Some of them had crowded teeth but they inherited wide jawbones. Lydia had a noticeable problem with her front teeth, because the one permanent, front, top tooth never grew. The x-rays showed one tooth never developed. The remaining front tooth drifted to the center in a deformed way. For many years, she hid her teeth with a shy smile. Only one time, did the school photographer manage to show her teeth. When she turned fifteen years old, Amanda knew Lydia should be able to smile, without hiding her teeth. They took her to a dentist and had all her top teeth pulled, and he made false teeth for her, before she turned sixteen. Dr. Wenger did such a good job that two years later, Rose Anna got upper dentures at the age of sixteen. She had her front teeth knocked loose in a snow -mobile accident. She had a lot of pain and not many options available. Dr. Wenger pulled eight teeth in one sitting, and Yes, she had a sore mouth!

Homemade root beer was a delight

Homemade root beer delighted everyone! Amanda 's big canner barely held a full batch of the Hires root beer recipe, and the canner filled to the brim, with 4 1/2 gallons of water, the jar of bought root beer extract, some yeast and lots of sugar. The eager children wanted to be involved, and rejoiced to even smell and see it, and especially to taste it. Amanda managed to provide clean glass containers and she supervised the entire project, as several children funneled the drink into the glass gallon jugs, using a dipper.

It also took a mother's special touch to help clean up the sticky mess where a little sugar spilled and some root beer puddled on the chair and to the floor. Houseflies loved it!

The wonderful drink- to- be, needed three days to ferment. Yeast is a plant and too much heat in direct sunlight could kill those plants, or even explode the glass jars. The drink might even turn out bland without any fizz, but if all went well , root beer was the best drink anyone ever tasted !It was the only soda pop that Aaron's children knew. They checked off the numbers on the calendar with high expectations, and gladly transported the finished root beer to the springhouse! Root beer was a rare summertime treat that Aaron and Amanda also enjoyed.

Summer always meant hordes of flies around the house. When Aarons built the new kitchen, they added a generous porch and upstairs balcony on the southeast side of the house. The porch was in constant use, with a small laundry line strung across the porch posts, sheltered from the rain. Tomatoes and peaches by the bushel ripened there until ready for canning. Children played on the porch.

Aaron said, "Us shtate un gviddah ra-ah in de west,[a thunder rain stands in the west,"] When a storm arrived, Aaron reverently sat on the south porch watching, as the lightning flashed and the thunder roared, displaying the power of an Almighty God. As the raindrops fell, Aaron considered each one a miracle. He knew that all the water from the run-off, trickled into streams and into the ocean, condensed and fell again, purified like new. Perhaps these same raindrops, once long ago, fell on Noah's ark or traveled through the insides of an animal. Any way you looked at rain, it was awesome! The children were not afraid of storms, because Aaron and Amanda showed no fear on their faces. The main concern was "Quick get the wash off the line!"As every person available ran for an armful as the first drops began falling. Amanda did not want any muddy clothes, but after a warm rain, the children occasionally slopped and waded with permission.

Sometimes a steamy mist rose from the woods after a rain, and Aaron said, "De fox's sin um soup kucha," (the foxes are cooking soup) an old-time saying that predicts it will rain again soon, and sometimes it did. "Mar-yuts gviddah...o-vuts viddah! " [Translated as thunder in the morning, thunder again in the evening]. Occasionally an early morning shower soon cleared off, prompting the saying of, "Rain before seven, clear before eleven," and that saying often held out. Aaron could also predict showers by watching the chickens in the rain. "see those chickens scurry for shelter," Aaron said... "That means the sudden shower will soon be over, and the chickens come out to eat again." If the chickens do not run for cover, Aaron knew quite certainly that the rain came to stay awhile before clearing off, and somehow the chickens knew they would go hungry, unless they kept on eating during the rain. Rain on a Monday, meant rain again that week. Aaron and Amanda studied the skies for their weather predictions and so did all the other's. Sometimes Aaron felt arthritis aching in his bones before a storm approached.

Aaron always marveled over the rainbows, and heralded them in reverence, removing his hat and saying, "Did I ever tell you about the lovely rainbow in 1937. Your mom worked at Dan Goods when I came to see her, on a lovely evening in April, when the rainbow was brighter than this one. That was one of the happiest days in my life!"

The screen door slammed constantly among many children. Amanda patched and darned any holes accidentally punched in the old screen. The porch on the southeast corner darkened with flies seeking shelter. Every time the door opened, more flies came into the house. The sticky table and chairs, and the slop bucket beside the kitchen range attracted more flies.

Aaron did not like the flies and he said, "They all use my bald head for a landing strip." Uncle Titus commented on the excess amount of flies, but he worked up an appetite, helping his brother work and said," Despite the flies, Amanda was a very, very good cook. "

All those flies bothered Amanda, and she didn't like them anymore than others did. Occasionally, she asked some children to help her chase them out the door. She darkened the room, by pulling the dark green blinds, as everyone used a towel, an apron or something, waving wildly, herding flies towards the open door.

That always reduced the number, but it didn't keep them outside. Amanda liked to see them dead, and offered her children one penny for swatting 100 flies. They had little use for the pennies, but the contest was fun, as they kept swatting and counting. Rhoda found an empty metal band-aid box, wherein she collected and saved all the dead flies she could gather. As she proudly counted and recounted the flies, Amanda said, "Please throw out those filthy flies, and I will believe your numbers."

Sometimes Amanda bought sticky fly ribbons, to hang on the south porch and in the kitchen, dangling from the ceiling. When her tacky "mooka bop-ah "[fly ribbon] filled, she carefully rolled it up and tossed the messy thing in the wood stove, knowing those flies would never return.

She also used a flytrap over a large container to trap many gallons of flies. Inside the large clear glass flytrap, Amanda put any garbage that might attract flies, even the contents from a messy diaper, if that was what worked. She saw that those dead flies could not spread any more germs. Most of the time flies were just a part of life, but every now and then, Amanda sprayed the flies. Aaron brought in a sprayer from the barn; a metal can with a long pump handle, filled with fly spray.

It took a lot of effort to ready the house for spraying, because Amanda did not like poison on anything and she carefully covered all the food items inside a cabinet or inside the refrigerator. After spraying flies, everyone needed to stay outside and that was the hardest part. Occasionally Amanda sprayed flies just before everyone left for church. If they invited guests that Sunday after church, it so happened that the guests might help sweep up flies and wipe the table before Amanda served dinner.

Every Sunday was a holiday, a day of rest! Hosting Sunday dinner guests happened regularly, and when the guests went home, Aaron and Amanda decided where they could go for the evening. Isaac Weinhold's lived just a mile out the road, and the children always cheered when Aaron suggested,

"Let's go see Weinholds." They had children of course, but more importantly, they owned a TV! Youngsters that never watched TV in their lifetime sat and stared in disbelief as Lassie entered the screen, and barked. They were mesmerized and needed no other entertainment. How did it work?

Linda Weinhold wore pretty blond curls and she had a record player! She played the latest hit of "Itsy bitsy teeny weenie yellow polka dot bikini. She swayed to the music and those memories made long lasting impressions.

Isaac Weinholds owned a hand crank telephone on the wall, and they had unlocked doors for any neighbor that needed a telephone. Everyone liked Lily Weinhold, a kind and giving neighbor. Lily gave generously, and sometimes she even gave such coveted things as a color book and colors. Their son was opposed to conscientious objectors and C.O. status during World War II. One time he planted a patriotic flag close to Titus's house, to show his opinion. Every winter, the Weinhold family decked a large evergreen tree in their yard with Christmas lights and a star on top. None of the Mennonites in the neighborhood decorated Christmas trees, due to the verses in the Bible, in Jeremiah, chapter ten.

All the neighbors needed each other. In Feb. 1965, Isaac Weinhold's house burned when their radio exploded. The firefighters doused the flames but the house needed a tremendous amount of help cleaning up smoke and water damage. The next day the neighborhood gathered to help, with Aaron and Wesley among the group. It was payback time for kindhearted neighbors.

Valentines

Amanda had happy childhood memories of Valentine's Day in Michigan. It created a bright spot in the dull days of February, and she loved artwork and the joy of giving. She was good at art and drawing. Other children sometimes asked for her help in sketching and drawing things when she went to school. In her spare time, she doodled on paper and excelled in drawing horses. Her parents frowned upon creating an image of things.

In a one-room school, Aaron and Amanda's children did not need many valentines to reach around, but in the elementary school with eight children in seven different rooms, giving to several dozen friends each, they needed many more valentines.

Soon after Christmas, stores like Rubinson's displayed Valentines and Amanda liked to get some before they were picked out. Cardboard punch-out books contained enough to make 50 valentines each, so she bought several. Amanda enjoyed the Valentine making nearly as much as her children did. With eager anticipation, many hands punched adorable puppies and kitties among fuzzy flocked red valentines, roses and Victorian lace. Scattered throughout the book remained many small optional cutouts to glue on with paste. Their only paste was homemade "male paste "or (flour paste). It did not take long to stir up a tablespoon of flour with just enough water to dampen it to the right consistency. After drying, the slimy goo stayed put on any paper.

Some of the homemade valentines had real lace scraps sewed on them. Amanda saved every scrap of paper in the house that still had one side unused and she tucked it beneath the tablecloth where she sat at the table. This was sometimes used as stationary, or as her only notepad. Some scraps of this paper might make homemade valentines. After the paste dried it, came the thrill of choosing valentines. Girls cleared the long extension table and spread out the entire assortment of finished valentines. No matter who assembled them, the scholars enjoyed choosing the nicest valentines, in an orderly fashion; all in a row while walking circles around the table and choosing one card each time around. Then came the hard part, of deciding who gets which one, as they signed the valentines.

The teachers at school made a big to- do over Valentine's Day, with fancy decorated boxes to collect the valentines, quite awhile before the day arrived. The children cherished all the pretty valentines, long after the excitement ended and they did not discard any, as they stored them under their beds with their other treasures. Sometimes it happened that mice nibbled on the flour paste, and then Amanda trashed some.

Amanda cherished every clean sheet of paper, and not just for scribbling. Next best for doodling, were the steamed kitchen windows. All the children practiced making pictures and words on the windows. Later, Aaron and Amanda bought the one- foot by four -foot slate blackboard at Peter Brubacher's auction. They had it in Michigan. Several children crowded together with each one claiming a square foot of slate marked off for their own spot of creativity. Games such as tic tack toe and hang man did not need paper.

Mommy Brubacher also had three dolls at that auction, with cast iron heads. The heads were about the size of a chicken egg and the paint scratched off so badly that the thin twelve-inch long dolls resembled Aunt Jemima. The hands and feet were cast iron, attached to cloth bodies. Mommy did not want young children constantly undressing the dolls; therefore, she sewed the floor-length dresses onto the dolls.

Amanda encouraged friendships among school–children. Louise, in second grade, had an invitation to Amos Goods overnight, when Amos was sick in bed with cancer. The Goods lived just across the road from Tom's Pies and Aaron knew them well. Aaron and Amanda visited there, and Amos appreciated when people came to sing for him. His wife occasionally invited a daughter's classmate to stay overnight, for something to do, when 'daddy lay dying'. Lorraine Good and Louise Shirk shared the same birthday, and were in the same classroom at Brecknock School. Therefore, with her parents' permission, Louise had the privilege of getting on a different school bus with Lorraine, and return to school on that bus the next day. It worked so well that it happened several times. The 'twin 'girls had a great time pretending.

At home again, Louise thankfully appreciated they did not live along the blacktop, with close neighbors on every side. Likewise, Lorraine had fun at Aaron Shirks a time or two, and she returned to her home thankful for electric, telephone and a bathroom.

Irene came home from school with an invitation to spend the night with Martha Musser. Aaron and Amanda allowed her to sleep there one night, even if they did not know the parents, and had no telephone connections.

Half a century later, Irene chuckled with fond memories, how two innocent six-year-old girls discussed toilet paper! The Musser family taught their children to save, and Martha was pleased to announce, "I may use four sheets of toilet paper. How many may you use?" Irene quickly calculated that two squares of soft tissue might equal to one sheet of paper in the Sears catalog in their outhouse, and she said, "I use two!"

Amanda's five-year diary had very little room for details but she recorded that Irene went home with Martha Musser. Was it a prayer for the well-being of a child missing in their home at bedtime?

Amanda tried her best to teach her daughters modesty, and a sense of shame. If any daughter had her knees showing, Amanda demanded,"Put your dress down! "Seeing underwear was dreadful! Amanda occasionally went all out to spritz water with a wet hand to make a lasting impression, when a daughter sat indecently. She also had an empty threat of making black underwear for any girl that had panties showing; surely, she would keep her dress down then, such as a threat of adding lace on a boy's shirttail to keep it tucked in just right. Eventually the threat of shameful black panties became a reality as Amanda made some for a daughter. Not many years later, black underwear sold as the latest style in the catalog! How awful?

∽

Among all the 15 children, only Lydia had a problem with sucking her thumb. Perhaps she had a problem with loneliness when she spent so much time away from the rest and lived with Aunt Lydia. At the age of five, she still had a problem and Amanda wanted her to stop before she starts in first grade. "If you stop sucking your thumb, you may have a brand-new color book all for yourself," said Amanda. A coloring book for her alone, among so many sisters sounded like a small fortune. Lydia desperately tried her best and won the prize!

22

Aaron did not have anti-freeze so he drained the water from his Case tractor. On a cold day, he needed to haul manure on a frozen field and said," Walter, go put water in the tractor awhile, so we can use it today." As Walter poured hot water on cold cast-iron, he split the block wide open. Walter innocently did not know that hot water poured on frozen rocks is a poor man's dynamite. He just wanted to warm the tractor quickly, but regrettably, they could not haul manure that Saturday. Aaron went to Morgantown and bought a Farmall Super C tractor for $1200 because the old tractor was not worth fixing. On Monday, he asked the banker for a few hundred more dollars.

Aaron spent $90 for a brand-new harrow for his two-point hitch super C tractor. It was a failure from the start, because the front end of the tractor hardly stayed on the ground when he pulled it. Experience was the best teacher in many ways! After Aaron and the boys husked all the corn by hand and stored it in the corn crib for winter, they discovered the moisture content was too high and the huge pile started molding. They needed the corn to feed the animals and started shoveling and rotating and putting some on the wagon and on other piles to dry it out save it. Farmers worked hard, even with the best of management!

A steer kicked Aaron above his eye and he needed five stitches!

Aaron's children spent many hours watching cows grazing in the fields due to a shortage of fences. With plenty of helpful children, their two cows were not hard to watch as they browsed on Aaron's small fields of rotated crops, after harvest. Sometimes though, the children goofed off, forgetting the cows until they got into the cornfield...

When Aaron's girls watched cows so close to Jesse's, with cousins their age, they planned on the sly, to meet there with their dolls. They had a grand time until Jesse fetched his daughter, saying sternly, "There is work to do at home!"

When Amanda grew up in Michigan, her father needed his children to watch eight milking cows and about six head of younger cows. When the pasture got short, they grazed their cows along the raod banks. With fences along each side of the road, one or two girls watched each end of the allotted stretch of the road. One section had a fence only on one side and the cows wanted to wander in the woods.

Huge stumps remained among Peter Brubacher's recently cleared pastureland. Amanda and Lydia sat upon those stumps, pleasantly enjoying the outdoors, while watching the cows. Their mother taught them to keep their hands busy even out there, by hemming feedbags among the slowly grazing cows. Aprons back then sometimes had reversible seams neatly stitched by hand. They soiled both sides before the apron needed laundry.

When Amanda's parents bought eighty acres of more land, Silas and Joshua worked hard at helping Peter put up a barbed wire fence. The cows had such a big area to roam, that the children met a challenge rounding up all of them, at milking time, especially if they were down at the swampy end. Some of the cows wore bells, but they did not all stay together. The quarter mile long stump -fence, kept diminishing because Peter and Sarah Ann sawed off the protruding pieces of dried wood, to use as kindling and firewood.

Out in those woods the children helped gather wild strawberries, raspberries, blackberries and huckleberries in season. Amanda learned the names of many of the flowers and watched the birds, but they seldom had time to play out there. The girls watched their chance to pick a bouquet of flowers and in springtime, they enjoyed a taste of morel mushrooms. The birds and flowers in Michigan were much the same as in PA, but Amanda remembered trilliums and the bank swallows that she did not find in Pennsylvania.

Drinking water was a problem for the children watching cows for three or four hours. The girls took turns one at a time to go home for a drink, but they often got extremely thirsty. After Betsy and Amanda returned the cows to the barnyard, the girls were extra hot and thirsty. Their mother had just brought a fresh bucket of cold water from the pump and Betsy drank like a camel, all she could hold. She collapsed on the kitchen floor and mother took her out in the shade and put a wet washcloth on her fore head. It seemed like a long time until Betsy came to again, maybe an hour. Mother called it sunstroke!

∞

"Sis tzite fuh groom-bear-uh kima!" none of Aaron and Amanda's children liked that announcement, because that meant, "it is time to sprout the potatoes." Every one of the younger children followed Amanda down to the dark spooky basement, [or rather the cellar part]. Every fall, Aaron enjoyed filling that potato bin with hundreds of pounds of potatoes for winter.

Amanda cooked potatoes nearly every day, in a variety of different ways. A huge kettle full of cooked potatoes one meal, meant fried potatoes for the next meal. Aaron preferred the potatoes fried in butter, but no one complained about potatoes any way they served them, providing they did not scorch against the bottom of the kettle.

Potatoes kept well beneath the old part of the house, in a bin on the hard packed, dirt floor. It was cool down there and only dim rays of sunshine squeezed through the metal grate of the one small window. The grate had a child's face molded in the center of the heavy cast iron. God somehow gave those potatoes a signal late in winter, to start growing roots and sprouts. "Come, "said Aman-

da, "if we all go at it, it will not take long!". The job was easy enough for a three-year-old, but no one enjoyed the dreaded chore of removing those white sprouts growing from every wrinkled potato. Amanda did not like to peel wrinkled potatoes. Everyone dug in to help.

They were soon finished and Amanda went upstairs. After the children's eyes had adjusted to the dim lighting, they wanted to play in the cellar. Amanda had the canning shelves well -filled with colorful food of every kind. When the shelves could hold no more, Amanda set the remaining jars on a wooden platform in the corner. The girls got busy rearranging jars of canned food, making paths and small 'rooms' to play in. Imagine their mother's disapproval when she saw what her daughters had done. Amanda had ever so carefully arranged the jars so that they would use the oldest ones first.

Children innocently made many mistakes! Rose Anna promised to stay out of the way if she may just watch Ruth and Rhoda paint the kitchen. The color transformed from yellow to pale blue and she did not touch. She kept her fingers off the wet paint, but the next thing she knew, she had backed against the other wall and her hair had a patch of blue paint all dried on before she noticed. In the middle of a busy day, Amanda spent time cleaning Rose Anna's hair with gasoline. Some of the paint in her hair stayed awhile and faded on its own.

Changing Churches

As the oldest in the family, Daniel had more spankings as a child, and he walked the line as the rest followed without spankings. When he was a teenager, his parents watched him closely and guarded every move he made, more than any of the rest. On a Sunday afternoon Bart Horst's had a half -crowd, a teenage gathering where he attended with permission. When it was time to head for home, one of Bart's boys wanted to talk yet and invited him to linger at the strawberry patch, eating ripe berries. It got a little later than Aaron and Amanda thought it should, and Aaron came looking for Daniel. He was biking home along the

Black Creek Road, when he met his father coming towards him, and not very happy. Being the oldest in the family was not easy and Daniel had many decisions to make.

Katie Kilmer, the oldest of Christian Kilmer's girls had it tough also. She currently worked at Menno Shirks; therefore Daniel occasionally picked up Katie and took her along to singing school. That worked fine for both of them, as neither of them wanted to go alone. Katie gave Daniel a thank you gift! She spent a lot of time decorating a buggy blanket for him, with colorful yarn and a punch hook. She punched a picture of a large horseshoe, with a horse head in the middle, surrounded by brightly colored flowers, flocked on a navy blue wool blanket. It was almost too pretty to use!

Daniel had a horse, and his buggy was no problem. Walter helped Daniel stripe the buggy wheels in detail. They jacked up the buggy so a wheel turned freely, and while Walter turned the wheel, Daniel painted gold stripes and intricate designs, with a striper made for this; a container held the paint and it had a roller wheel on top.

Daniel felt inferior, coming from a poor family, and a remote area out back in the sticks. He had many friends for the most part, and good fellowship among the young folks. He bought a Whizzer motorbike, which was nothing but a bicycle with a small motor attached. That one was okay, but Aaron said he would want to disown any son of his, that owned a motorcycle or a revolver.

From one of his friends, Daniel purchased a cheap camera and hid it under his buggy seat. Cameras were forbidden in the Joe Wenger church. For some unknown reason, Aaron looked under the buggy seat and discovered the hidden camera. Daniel could not believe the fuss his father made over finding the camera. Aaron told everyone he met! He barely mentioned it to Daniel and didn't actually oppose the fact that his son owned one. Daniel would have preferred a punishment rather than the humiliation.

He learned how to use a camera but he rarely got to Althouse in Hinkletown to drop off his film for developing and then he waited another three weeks to get the pictures. He did not know much about the outside world and neither did he have much money. Amanda was no longer slim and Aaron lost his hair. Nobody had a camera to take pictures of Aaron and Amanda's rapidly growing family, before Daniel was grown.

On Amanda's 36th birthday, in 1951, a cloud hung over her head, as Aaron went to Bishop Aaron Sensenig to give reasons why he was leaving the Joe Wenger church. After sincere discussions, Aaron changed his mind and patched things up. That was a big gift to Amanda… a major relief because she preferred things as they were. She was concerned about their large family, with so many girls eventually wanting partners. Amanda thought it might be easier on the children if they did not need to switch over to another church, stressfully making new friends. She did not forget Joshua and how he sought acceptance.

For the next six years, Aaron still kept looking at other churches. He attended nearly every church around, just looking, and comparing. It was no secret that he was not quite satisfied with the horse and buggy way of life, but he could not find a perfect church because there was none. Many times, he hired a driver for transportation to go a distance and riding in a car was not wrong. He preferred rubber tires on tractors and farm equipment, among other reasons for change.

Daniel noticed all these discontents and more. He didn't see any reason for removing rubber tires from their tractor. (The reasoning was that steel wheels would stay on the farm, and not tempt a person to use them to seek entertainment). When the boys Daniel's age, started joining church he held back because he wanted a car. It was not an easy decision, to leave his friends and start a new social circle.

He heard about good pay rates at the hat factory and he got a job there, as an equipment maintenance worker. He biked to the 625 and went along to work with Bobby Hammond. Before this, Aaron thought he could not spare Daniel and he kept him at home, but a taste of those paychecks changed the story. All of a sudden, Aaron realized how much the other boys had grown, and they could spare Daniel, for a much-needed paycheck.

The environment in the Bollman hat factory was none too good. When a girl made up to Daniel, he winked at her and did not see anything wrong with it, until another worker kindly informed him that she was a divorced woman.

Daniel carefully saved his part of the paycheck, which was 10%. He pooled that money with all he made from selling pigeons at Green Dragon and came up with $130. With that money in his pocket, he got Bobby Hammond to take him to E.T.Line in Denver, and made a deal on a 1949 dark blue Pontiac for $235, on May 25, 1957.

Daniel was 18, and never drove a car on a road before, but the Kohl boys, that sometimes helped put tobacco away at Aarons, allowed him to drive their hot rod in the field lane. Daniel bravely drove his own car home without license or insurance and no drivers license. The next week, Aaron went with Daniel to purchase Brotherly Aid vehicle insurance. He said, "Mom and I didn't sleep good last night." Aaron also said, "You should have a better car than that, Daniel."

Bobby Hammond kindly took Daniel for a driver's exam and he did not pass the test on the first try. Two days later, they tried again and he had a driver's license, on that summery Friday, June 7. That day yet, Aaron and Amanda hired Daniel to drive them to Terre Hill to Dr. Lauria, because three-year-old RoseAnna had tonsillitis. Aaron was pleased, and to impress Amanda, they made a call at her uncle Joe Brenneman. Aaron celebrated with buying a whole gallon of ice cream for supper. It was getting soft and really smooth, and each person had a whole cup full.

Siblings stared in wide-eyed wonder at a car parked on the barn hill…. cars were forbidden…. now what? Daniel had it all planned out. He made application that month, to join the Weaver land Conference Church where they allowed cars. If it was ok to go to work in a car every day, he saw nothing wrong with owning one. Daniel soon had his car painted black, and that fall he was baptized at Weaverland Church. Later, Daniel got a better car, a 1954 Ford for $1000.

Aaron did not scold his son, but instead, he was impressed! "Was it really that easy to get a car

and learn how to drive it?" he pondered. "Maybe he could do it too!" Walter and Pete understood what was going on and seriously hoped their parents might get a car. Amanda plainly understood Aaron's longings and discontent. She said, "if the steel wheels are as cumbersome as you make it sound, surely the church would soon allow rubber tires and cars. Try more patience and wait and see" she encouraged, but that was asking too much.

Six weeks later, Aaron purchased his own car. It was a green and white 1956 Ford station wagon costing $2000. Walter, Pete and Dick, ages 12 to 15, celebrated by sleeping in the car without covers, and they got cold that night. The station wagon was green and white only two days before it went to Lichtey Brothers and came back black.

Amanda was keenly disappointed in changing churches. How could she forsake what her parents taught her? Those decisions were far-reaching. She could keep her membership where it was, but then what would their children do? She knew all fifteen would follow Aaron, and how would she alone get to church? …..always in a car, to a horse and buggy church? She did not want that, nor did she want to drive the horse by herself. How would such a change affect all their young children. Would all that row of girls remain single?

The deacon and bishop strongly discouraged parents from attending separate churches. They said, "Parents need a united front for the sake of their children!". Amanda was troubled and studied the Bible. This was not about styles and memberships, but about getting to heaven and meeting her family there. Which way was she to go?

Silas bought a car and changed churches when he saw that he would not find a wife among the horse and buggy group. Katie and Dan Martin also switched churches, but far away in Indiana. Amanda knew her parents would be disappointed, because Peter and Sarah Ann left Michigan for a plain church. Perhaps they could all have stayed in Michigan, if their children wanted to forsake the horse and buggy church anyway. Her parents still missed Michigan at times.

Amanda had joined church at the age of seventeen, in Michigan. The vows she made on bended knees, before God and many witnesses were sincere and not taken lightly. She promised to follow the teachings of Jesus Christ faithfully and obediently onto death. Heaven is all that really mattered!

On their wedding day, she promised to stand by Aaron in sickness and sorrow, and to live with him peaceably, in a Christian like way, and not to forsake him as long as God grants her life.

The Bible says to honor thy father and thy mother. Peter and Sarah Ann lived close by, and she did not want to hurt them by rejecting their teachings. There is not just one right church, and all of them seem to have some faults. She wanted a plain, spirit-filled church, for her children, with no fancy clothes and less pride in its many forms. A fancier church seriously bothered her.

Amanda was seldom discouraged. She excelled at overlooking the faults of others, knowing that no one was perfect. She was not easily offended and tried her best to ignore insults, while dwelling on her many blessings with a thankful heart, but this was too much. What was life all about?

Make sure that none fall by the wayside! Meekness and humility were the way to heaven and she did not want to miss that happy end. With lots of prayer and deep thoughts, it was the hardest thing she ever did, but she left the church of her choice and stood by Aaron. He was the head of the home.

Aaron convincingly said ", We know it is wrong to steal ducks, so why do we want others to steal them for us? Compare that to driving in a car... if it is wrong to own a car, then it is also wrong to drive in a car. "Amanda gave up... the "stolen ducks", were the last straw between right and wrong.

Years later, Amanda wrote in a letter, "Really, it was the hardest thing I ever did in my life. For a while, I did not think I could ever sing or be happy again. The fancy dresses bothered me about the most. I was never in church without wearing long sleeves and an apron. We dressed more like the Pike Church when I grew up. Little girls' dresses buttoned-down the back, then at teen age, the girls dressed just like their mothers. They opened those dresses with buttons down the front and wore a cape over the dress. Collars on dresses were much too fancy! Some girls in the Horning church still dressed plain and I felt sorry or guilty for letting you girls try all kinds of patterns and styles and capes that opened in the back. Aaron insisted that you may dress like the average of the Horning girls, and that hurt!"

In June, Aaron went for a driver's test. First, he needed to pass the questions and he was not good at that. He gave vague answers. The policeman asked, "When you are following someone, how many feet should you allow between the two vehicles?" Aaron said, "I'd stay way back and leave plenty of room!" To another question Aaron replied "Sir, that question was not in the book that I studied." The policeman said, "Well, it was in there." "No sir, that question was not in the book!" Aaron insisted. Finally, the policeman got the book and showed Aaron the question, and right there he saw the answer. The question was worded a little differently, nevertheless Aaron got the answer he wanted and passed his questions.

Aaron surprised everyone, including himself, when he passed his driver's test on the first try. His sons jokingly agreed that the cop probably did not want to see Aaron come back again. At first, Aaron used the turning signals around every bend in the road. He had to learn all about dimming lights to oncoming traffic and much more. It was easier in teenage then at the age of forty -three. He wished he could see the wheels the way he could see the buggy wheels, because he had a hard time to tell where the tires went.

On September 1, 1957, Aaron and Amanda joined the Weaverland Conference Church, at Bowmansville Mennonite Church. The entire family was present from Daniel age 19 all the way down to 17-month-old baby Mandy.

On the next Sunday, Aaron's family went to the same church house, wearing the same clothes, but met a different congregation of people. On alternate Sundays, both groups shared the same church house. On one Sunday, cars filled the churchyard, and on the next Sunday, the men tied their horses to the hitching posts. The church split thirty years earlier, about owning cars and having rubber tires on equipment.

Bishop Joe Wenger was the leader of the horse and buggy group while Moses Horning was the Bishop of the group that allowed cars. They did not want pride in showy vehicles, so they asked their members to humbly paint their vehicles black, like the buggies were. Not long later, car models sported wide shiny chrome bumpers, so the church leaders asked members to paint the chrome black for less show and for avoiding the latest style. The theory was that conservative vehicles would not be seen among entertainment like sporting events, fairs, movies, taverns, or forbidden places. Using cars for luxury and entertainment was the number one reason why cars might be wrong in the first place.

Any time horse and buggy people switched over and got a car, others might say things like "they used to be decent." While hanging out the back of an open carriage window, a neighboring child saw Aaron driving his station wagon and thought, "Oh, it's Aaron, he's a nice enough man, but too bad he is going to end up in hell, because he owns a car now."

Amanda's problems persisted. She told Deacon Walter Martin that she is not interested in fancy clothes and intends to wear the same simple styles, as she always did. "Yes, that is good," said Walter Martin "but those girls will want lace on their dresses soon enough", and he was right. Teenage girls were quick to catch on what others wore. The first change the girls made was to braid pigtails just a little over half way and let the rest of the hair hanging open. That was fancy but it also saved time because nine of the girls wore pigtails. Sarah Ann was old enough to put her hair up.

At the age of 14, all the young girls suddenly stopped wearing pigtails and put up their long hair into a bon or bob beneath a covering, even if they did not join the church yet. At the same time, they added a cape, as part of the dress pattern. They wore the separate cape with an attached belt, overtop their dress to help conceal a showy figure...very grown up!

In church, these teenagers sat beside their friends on the back row of benches and sometimes they whispered disrespectfully. They had

much room for improvement! Other parents once brought their girls to Aaron Shirks on a Sunday afternoon so the girls could talk until they had nothing left to talk about. Bowmansville church had very few teenagers back then.

When the twins were through school and put up their hair, Amanda was sorely displeased with the smaller sheer coverings and the shorter dresses on her growing girls. The boys quit wearing suspenders, but their styles did not change otherwise.

When Aaron and Amanda ate Sunday dinner at Dawdy Brubacher's place, they could feel their hurt. After the meal, when he children ran out to play, church issues became the talk amid heartfelt tears. What had their daughter done? Not since Joshua died was anything so sad. Would they get to meet again in heaven? Amanda sobbed hard with her dear brokenhearted parents and wished she could somehow comfort them, but she did not know how.

The best part of having cars was that now the whole family could attend church together. A dozen people could pile into the station wagon while the carriage held much less and some children had to stay at home. Walter, Pete and Dick happily drove to church with Daniel in his car. Unloading Aaron's station wagon at church was quite a sight with so many people exiting one vehicle. Four children sat squaw -style in the back part of the station wagon and Aaron called that "de hummley pen". (Calf pen). It was grand and no one dared complain about sitting too tight. Amanda said many times, "Es gain feel ga-dolt-igh-y shoaf in ay shtoll" (many content sheep fit into one stall).

It happened very gradually, but Amanda began to sing and smile again. She eventually had many prayers answered when her daughters grew up and put away their childish styles.

Two months after purchasing the station wagon, Aaron suggested taking the entire family to the Philadelphia zoo, in two vehicles. Amanda opposed entertainment as the main problem with owning cars, but she gave in. They could see how fast their family grew, and this might be their only chance doing something special all together. When looking back Aaron could see it was only 16 years ago, that Daniel was a diaper baby, and 16 years in the future, baby Mandy might have a driver's license.

Neither Aaron nor Amanda had ever been to a zoo in their lifetime, and wondered about seeing exotic animals that God created. On a Saturday morning in September, fifteen excited children helped get an early start and eagerly packed lunches for the day. Aaron and Daniel planned to follow each other through Philadelphia, but the traffic separated them, creating stressful driving conditions. They all arrived just fine and spent the unusual day together. For $.50 they rented a stroller for baby Mandy, and Lydia age four wished she could ride in one also.

Among favorable weather and sunshine, Aaron obtained permission to bring their packed lunch to a picnic table. Hot dogs at the zoo cost $.35 each, and that was too much, so Aaron and Amanda brought along half a case of hot dogs, for a special treat among their group of 17 people. They had an enjoyable day, with vivid memories for a lifetime. Occasionally it appeared that Aaron's group of children got as much attention as the animals.

With their own transportation, Aaron and Amanda planned another trip to Canada and this time it involved some business. The over-loaded station wagon with the tailgate open dragged low with heavy barn cleaners headed for Canada. Thankfully, the tires held up, because trying to find a spare tire beneath that extreme load, could have been a major problem.

Irene and Louise went along last time, so now it was Lydia and Wesley's turn. They were ages four and five and not yet in school. It was three years since Aaron's last trip, when they went on the train. They had no problem with the driving, but Aaron and Amanda did not have the necessary paper work to cross the border, and they were delayed quite a while, with their unusual load from Terramatic, where Daniel and Aaron worked.

After unloading the barn cleaners as planned, Aaron and Amanda did a lot of visiting for two weeks. Lydia and Wesley received gifts such as handkerchiefs, and even a whole pack of chewing gum to themselves. The Canadians driving them around had a boy and girl along about their ages. Amanda asked Lydia and Wesley to share their chewing gum with the children that did not have any, but Wesley already had his entire pack of five pieces in his mouth at one time, therefore Lydia had to share with the boy and the girl. She never forgot that! She also remembered the extraordinary gift of two yellow china birds bestowed as a keepsake just for her. She felt rich! One evening, Amanda's cousin Wesley and Olive Brubacher, showed slides with bear pictures, and Amanda thought their children might have nightmares about bears, but they didn't.

Sarah Ann and the rest were stuck at home running the household to make that trip possible. Aaron first went to the bank and bought a roll of quarters for buying lunches at school, and that saved all the hassle of packing lunches. Pete managed to wash and hang the laundry for Sarah Ann and he helped butcher chickens several times. With Sarah Ann in charge, they made 18 quarts applesauce, mended, ironed and made cookies. They sold a dozen eggs to a hunter in small game season, and cared for two diaper babies. One day everything seemed to go wrong. Mandy hurt her toe, and the baby bottle broke. The butter churn full of cream upset creating a terrible mess, with no mom to clean it up.

Worst of all, the running water quit coming, because the water ram had problems for the first time in many years. Children couldn't fix it, and they carried water uphill from the springhouse, even for washing. Every few days, a postcard or a letter came in the mail from Aaron and Amanda in Canada, but sadly, Sarah Ann could not contact them. One postcard stated that Aaron's business would keep them four days longer than they planned.

On October 16, Aaron and Amanda left Canada at 4 AM and returned home at 8:20 that evening. They all rejoiced to see each other. In 1958, everyone travelled slower and drove through small towns.

At Christmas time, Aaron and Daniel each got a dressed turkey given to them from Terre Hill machine shop, and each of the 17 children received a basket of nuts and candy, plus an orange. Perhaps that was a bonus for taking the barn-cleaners to Canada.

At the age of 78 years old, someone gave Peter Brubacher his first grapefruits and he was not sure how to eat them. He thought that maybe Amanda should cook them first. The grapefruits Amanda purchased at the local store were not the sweet pink kind. They were sour! She cut them in half and put one on each plate at breakfast, after she carefully cut around the edges first. Aaron put a heap of sugar on top of his grapefruit half, and the children followed his example, but they just couldn't eat them. When Amanda cleared the table, the expensive uneaten fruit disappointed her. She enjoyed her grapefruit without sugar, and would have eaten them all, but not with sugar. Perhaps she salvaged the leftovers and made them like orange juice, because there was no way she considered discarding them.

On Christmas Day, Aaron and Amanda had the entire Brubacher family for a turkey dinner, serving the two plump turkeys given from Terramatic. Uncle Dan's could not come from Indiana but the rest showed up. Uncle Silas and Aunt Sarah came without hurrying. Like usual, it took him a while to get his car parked just right, the way he wanted it.

When Silas arrived, he wanted to talk with every child in the extended family, but the children did not like to talk to him. He did not talk plain and even with a hearing aid he was hard of hearing. With a shaky hand, Silas reached out to greet little children, and some were scared of him. They cringed as he said; "Do bid aw wite" (you are all right). He enjoyed finding and holding a smaller child that was not scared of him, because he dearly loved children all his life, and never had his own.

Silas's wife Sarah brought her delicious double fudge at Christmas. The bottom layer consisted of peanut butter fudge, topped with a layer of soft smooth chocolate fudge. The confection was sickeningly sweet, but the pan always returned empty and furthered Sarah's reputation.

Christmas dinner was a special occasion, even without a Christmas tree and special gifts. Amanda

enjoyed giving, and in 1957, she wrapped a gift for each of her children, for the first time. Up until then, the gifts they received in school at a gift exchange were their only wrapped gifts they received all year. She gathered together gifts for several months and added some homemade things. Most likely, she enjoyed the idea more than the rest of the family.

∽

On Friday, Aaron started with a boil on his back, close to his shoulder blade, and it irritated him when he moved his arm. Boils were nothing new, and Aaron's family often had painfully sore boils, but this one became extremely bothersome. Aaron helped drive two loads of relatives to the Lancaster train station when Martin Kilmer's William planned to marry Lena Kulp in Indiana. Aaron and Amanda did not attend the wedding of a nephew so far away and Martin Kilmer's could not attend their own sons wedding. On the same day their oldest son got married, they welcomed another newborn son at home, named Rufus.

On Saturday as the snow swirled, Aaron went to Dr. Lauria about the boil on his back, and he took Ruth to Dawdy Brubacher's for her usual Saturday cleaning job. By the time Aaron brought Ruth back home; wet snow came faster and piled six inches deep. It thundered in the night, while the snow kept blowing and drifting. On Sunday morning, no one went to church, due to the snow. After sitting around the house a while, Aaron rode horseback over to Jesse's, just checking on neighbors. He learned how helpless a car was in the deep snow or ice. That morning before the snow deepened, Daniel walked over for a chat with his cousin Ivan. In the evening, Jesse's five oldest children came over to Aarons in excitement, just to see if they could brave the storm. The snow still came thick.

On Monday morning, all the roads were closed, even for horses! Daniel, Walter, Pete, and Dick spent their time stripping tobacco, while Aaron spent some time around the house nursing a sore boil. Amanda saw all the lively ambition around her and framed a comfort for knotting. Many hands finished it rapidly, and she promptly put a quilt in the same frame next.

The younger children said," Let's go play doll...I want the Mary Dale doll this time...no it's my turn, she is not just yours... mom said we must take turns...I'm going to be the preacher. .. who is going to invite us for dinner?" Off they ran up-stairs...at least for a while.

When Aaron had a boil, everyone heard about it, because he could think about nothing else. He could not go to the doctor and the sore got worse, as a massive cluster of boils. Aaron needed Amanda's sympathy and a hot compress of warm water to soften the spot he couldn't reach.

The treadle sewing machine ran all day, with a waiting line of girls wishing to sew. With a two-year-old baby in the house among all 17 people, Amanda kept order."Mam ich vill un pinny." (Mom I want a safety pin,] said a daughter among the doll-playing group. Amanda reached beneath the cape of her dress, and handed over a small yellow safety pin, worth less to her than the bigger ones. She nearly always carried an extra safety pin beneath her cape. When she could find no more safety pins for her own needs, she raided the doll clothes box, upstairs beneath a bed. Safety pins seldom reached around.

Amanda planned and organized the best she could. The entire day ticked as fast as other days but no one watched the clock. Aaron and Amanda thanked God that all their family were safely snowed in at home. The day had a festive touch and excitement. No school and no factory meant one big recess all day long.

The boys found a spot to set up a game of checkers. The lively tournament rang out with,"I'll play the winner!" Some of the children set up a card table for a game of Monopoly..." Rent!... I own the Boardwalk and Park Place!. ..Go to jail... Mom, Wesley kicked the card table leg on purpose, because he saw he was losing, and all our pieces slid to the floor! "It was not hard to see, that a mothers boundless love kept all the gears in motion, sooth-ing any squabbles. The only quiet moment all day, happened at mealtime as they bowed their heads in silent prayer. They were richly blest!

The heavy wet snow piled on roofs danger-ously. The roof of Silver Hill School, no longer in use, had the roof cave in, and so did many other buildings. Aaron and Amanda's family, snowed in, did not know how it affected others. They had some inconvenience getting to the barn and back, but they shoveled a path to do the chores. The wet snow scooped in neat square chunks, making clear-cut trails. The animals and the people on the farm had all the food, water and warmth they wanted.

Girls dug out embroidery, among quilting and knotting comforts and such, while the boys went outside. A beautiful white world awaited them, with snow four feet deep! An unusual calm hushed the countryside, because even the Turnpike was quiet. Children delighted in sliding on the drifts piled as high as the corncrib roof, after the storm abated. Behind the house, Amanda had a mock orange bush bowing to the ground beneath the heavy wet snow. "Look! Beneath that load of heavy snow, the bush formed a cave. ..a beautiful hut to play in!"

When they were not stripping tobacco, Walter and Pete, in their mid-teens said, "Let's go up to the Turnpike!" That was hard, because they could not walk without pushing and pulling each other through the deep drifts. Only an inch or two of the Turnpike fence, extended above the snow. Af-ter pausing to catch their breath, Walter and Pete realized their strenuous efforts left them exhausted and dehydrated. On the Turnpike, they saw cars stranded under huge mounds of snow, hoping the people were no longer in them. The Turnpike maintenance crew had tried hard to keep one lane open as long as possible, but eventually the traffic stalled, and all was silent.

Suddenly, a rescue helicopter came into view, passing over the boys. As they stood watching, it suddenly made a U-turn and came back towards them. "Oh, no!" said Pete. "He saw us, and he's coming back to get us!" "Let's hide!" said Walter. "Quick, let's get beneath that truck!" They couldn't move very fast, but as quickly as possible the boys dug underneath a stranded tractor-trailer truck and waited there, as nervously as rabbits hiding in a clump of grass in an open field, when a hawk glides about. After all, they were on the other side of the Turnpike fence, a place where they had no business! They watched as the helicopter made two more circles above them, and then to their great relief, the helicopter disappeared! It never occurred to them that maybe they could have had a helicopter ride down to the house. They worked hard to get there!

The storm was a major disaster to many people without electric and telephone. Many had no heat and some ran out of food and water. The Aaron Shirk family felt no hardship, beyond the usual, because they never knew the convenience of electricity, telephones and radios. The wood stove kept them warm and cooked their meals like usual. The woodshed contained wood, the cellar had an abundance of food, and the spring never went dry. Other people faced serious problems!

Bart Horsts had a wedding and not so many people showed up. Sam Sauder shoveled snow from his roof and he fell on a fence post and died. Many roofs caved in and schools closed for quite a while. After the storm, Daniel went to Bowmansville on horseback, and came home with boxes of half melted ice cream, which disappeared rapidly as a special treat. The storekeeper had no electricity.

The February blizzard hit the area hard. After three snowbound days in a row, Aaron and Amanda both thanked God heartily for the bright sunshine and the open roads on Wednesday. Aaron promptly went to Dr. Lauria, who gave him all the sympathy and attention he craved. With a razor-sharp tool, he opened the massive boil and called it a carbuncle. He asked Aaron to return each day for the next three days, so he could change the dressing and make sure there would be no infection in the wound. Aaron did, with much faith in his family doctor.

When Raymond Witwer came through with his big yellow school bus, children chattered excitedly about what all happened on their "unplanned vacation". The children from town said, "We were out of electric and went to our grandparents place to keep warm." One of Mary's friends, Bonnie Youndt, asked, "Did you have electricity?" Mary, age ten, proudly answered, "No, but we are going to get some soon!" Electric arrived later that year.

Aaron's children remembered the happy warmth of love and togetherness, every time they reminisced about that snowstorm.

∽

When Mary went to bed at night, the bedroom was pitch black, after the last girl blew out the lamp. Maybe she dreamed about cats, because she sat up and called,"MOM!" When Amanda came over to the girls room, Mary said, 'There is a cat in my bed!"Amanda said, 'That is just Louise's head, feel the hair."

Aaron and Amanda lived far away from streetlights, and the nights were dark indeed. They had no monthly bills, no TV or movies, no radio, no electric and no telephone, no garbage man, no sewer system, no library and very few books, no sports schedules nor dancing lessons and nothing like music lessons, no water bills to pay, no life insurance, no airplane rides, no money or time spent at a fair, nor any other entertainment, no fur coats, jewelry, or makeup, they needed no barber, firemen or policemen, they had very low taxes and did without showers, and had no bought drinks of any kind. Kleenex, paper towels, toilet paper, or even plastic bags were not found in their house. They lived without government assistance, and didn't need an auto mechanic. Locks and keys were for city people. Without electronics, telephones and entertainment they did not feel deprived.

Sarah Ann was shy, even as a child. When Amanda coaxed her to sit on the church bench with the schoolgirls her age, she preferred to sit beside her mother. She stayed at home more than the sisters that were hired out because Aaron and Amanda needed her at home. Changing churches stressed her!

In teenage years, Sarah Ann was more bashful than ever. She worked at home, with not much social life, until she turned eighteen. She did not seem to belong anywhere and she was self-conscious about her clothes. After Daniel had a car, he dropped Sarah Ann off at the horse and buggy singing school. When he picked her up again, some boys threw stones at Daniel's 49 Pontiac, because a car was a sinful thing they looked down on. Sarah Ann did not want to go there again. Amanda encouraged her to attend social events and Sarah Ann preferred hiding behind the door while she was there. She was slender with a huge amount of hair beneath a big covering and her common dresses were made like her mother's. She felt awkward!

Amanda made sure that Sarah Ann's parlor was freshly papered and painted with new linoleum, a rocking chair and a nice couch. Other girls had nicer electric lamps, not a kerosene one and they had carpeted floors. Without a telephone, Sarah Ann missed many short notice plans. The Horning girls had no way of reaching her, way out back and they went to Washington DC, to see the cherry blossoms without her. Youth gatherings stressed her until Maggie Burkholder included Sarah Ann and helped her make many friends. Maggie was full of fun and ideas, with no room for self-pity.

Some of Sarah Ann's friends came to see her on a Sunday afternoon, ready for some action. When they met Pete and Dick driving a horse and buggy, they asked for a ride! In their early teens, Pete and Dick wanted nothing to do with big girls. They got out of the buggy and handed over the reins to the strangers and fled! The girls did not usually drive a horse and buggy, but the tame horse cooperated and they had a grand time, making life-

time memories. The ironic part was that one of the girls turned out to be Daniels wife. He did not know her yet.

Working in the Walter W Moyer factory, among other girls her age, helped Sarah Ann make new friends and plan her social life and weekends. Sarah Ann cleaned her parlor when Aaron wasn't around, because she didn't want to be teased about why she is cleaning the parlor. This was a new chapter and the younger sisters were not teased. In Aaron and Amanda's youth, boys outnumbered the girls, but now that trend reversed, with more girls than boys, and Aarons had ten of them. Aaron and Amanda each had a single sister and agreed it would be nice to have a daughter "left over".

Walter also minded the adjustment of changing churches in teenage years, and he did not fit in anywhere. Daniel was ' Shirkey ',because there were no other Shirks among the youth group, and when Walter came along, rather small for his age, he was called "da glay Shirkey" (the small Shirkey). Walter joined church at seventeen and found two good friends to cling to, Ally and Phares Martin. They helped him a lot when he met so many strangers from Lebanon County. Walter was gun -shy around the girls and self-conscious about fitting in at singings for quite a while.

When Daniel bought his car, Amanda wanted Aaron to give each of the boys a chance at Daniel's buggy, in hopes that one of them wanted to drive it. Walter said "No." Dick said right away "If Walter doesn't want it, I don't want it either!" Neither did Pete. Aaron sold his carriage to Joe Shirk for $275. He worked with horses all his life and did not want to part with all of them. He kept the children's favorite, tame old Tony who safely tolerated many children on his back, and good old Frank. Aaron had paid ten dollars for Frank because he was blind in one eye. That horse served Aaron well for many years. Anytime a person brought a nearly dead horse to the slaughterhouse, they could trade for any horse there, of equal size.

Aaron understood all about horse harnesses, but he was not much of a mechanic. He could see how gears and pulleys worked, but looking under the hood of a car overwhelmed him. He checked the dipstick and he added oil because that much he understood and gas, a car would not run without gas. When it came to changing oil or troubleshooting, he took the car to Dicks Sunoco at Bowmansville. Aaron didn't have any interest in learning auto mechanics at the age of 44.

The boys were better at it. Pete even studied towards getting a college degree, with a home study course to become an auto mechanic. He worked at Dicks Sunoco awhile and then at Carlos Leffler at Richland, for higher pay, after he passed the test. He started at the bottom by fixing flat tires. He had dreams of working his way up, but he remained stuck at the bottom too long and he quit that job to work at Wickes Lumber Company.

Teenagers all had to learn to drive, and so did Aaron. He bought a 49 Dodge car for $50, to drive to work. He wanted the car painted black, but it was not worth the price of a paint job, therefore Daniel and Walter painted the car with a paintbrush. Aaron backed that Dodge sedan into a parked lime spreader truck at Jared Stauffer's Case dealer parking lot, in Martindale. It was hard on Aaron's pride, but according to his explanation, he said, "it was a totally unavoidable accident!". The boys grinned inside, but they all knew better than commenting. Years later, the phrase "unavoidable accident" brought back memories. Aaron also hit an impossible to see, tall white fencepost, scraping the new paint job.

Aaron delighted in going places with his own car and he certainly made use of his driver's license. He said," I miss the horse and carriage most in springtime. We no longer linger long enough to smell the honeysuckle along the road-banks and I barely get one whiff of the new-mown hay in the fields we pass."

Children on the farm usually found their own creative toys, or made up their own games. They often played 'Mother May I?' When the hollyhocks bloomed beside the south porch, bumblebees and honeybees came to visit the blossoms. Children found time to harass the bees. They sneaked up slowly and then trapped a bee inside a blossom by suddenly bringing together the ruffled edges of the flower! What an adrenaline surge! They securely held a trapped bee inside a blossom, as the angry bee buzzed and vibrated ferociously. The bee could not sting through the flower petals that a person held by the tips.

Amanda's perennial Hollyhock flowers in pastel colors, made attractive doll families. One open blossom facedown made a lovely ruffled skirt, and a rounded flower bud, fastened with a stick, made a head. The dolls paraded up and down the steps and made a pretend family.

Any spent dandelion blossom on a tall stem, made a small bicycle, by splitting the long stem lengthwise, and curling up each side of the stem into a tight wheel. In a bucket of water, split dandelion stems curled up tightly and neatly, in a mysterious way. The girls sometimes gathered lilacs and inserted one tiny blossom end into next one, trying to connect them into a chain long enough to make a fancy necklace.

Louise worked at a place where the mother called every insect a "bise-ah!" [biter] and the children there learned the same. Louise knew all the insects had names. Amanda had no reference books but maybe her parents and their parents passed the information to those children that wanted to know. Amanda taught the difference between honeybees, bumblebees, yellow jackets, hornets, mud wasps and paper wasps. She understood that only one insect out of ten might be harmful, and the rest are here for our good, even if she did not like bugs and declared war on all the flies, potato bugs and cabbageworms, etc.

Aaron's children met up with wood ticks and chicken lice, plus many tiny annoying harvest mites in harvest season. Thankfully, they did not meet the nasty ones such as head lice, bed bugs and body lice. Grand- daddy-long -legs are spiders and [sh-longa duck-tahs] snake doctors, are dragonflies. Is it true that dragonflies cannot walk, and what makes the lightening bugs flash? God planned a tremendous amount of detail when he planned every tiny bug! How can an armadillo bug be called a cal-ah ase-el? [cellar donkey] some things remained a mystery.

"Mom, look what I found!" said Wesley excitedly digging in his pants pockets. He pulled out his hand holding a pretzel and laid it on the table. That was not what he wanted, and the next handful only produced more pretzels. Next, from the same pocket, he eagerly brought out a nest full of pink baby mice, in his hand! "Oh, Wesley! Get them out of here," exclaimed Amanda. Quickly Wesley snatched up the pretzels and ate them, making sure Amanda did not deprive him of his pretzels.

For many years, Aaron and Amanda asked other people to take them where they needed to go. Suddenly the tables turned, and Aaron had many requests for taking people to the hospital or just a doctor appointment. Most of the time they did not mind, but sometimes people tried Aaron's patience too far. Many a time, Aaron gathered together volunteers for a barn raising, storm cleanup, a blood drive, and who knows what. One time when he came to Elias Shirks to pick up Benjie, Benjie was slowly milking the cow. Aaron wanted him to hurry, and he said, "Let me show you how to do that!" The lad stepped aside and gave his Uncle Aaron the privilege. Aaron sat on the milking stool, moving his hands rapidly, as he milked extra fast! Benjie understood the nature of the cow, and...BAM... he was not surprised to see the cow kick violently. The pieces flying in all directions resembled an explosion. As Aaron struggled to his feet, he said, "would someone go and get the milk bucket, and fetch my hat at the Turnnnpike?"

23

When the schools consolidated, not everyone agreed to the big new elementary school. A brand-new one-room school was built on Dan Hoover's land, along 625, with the management of John Leinbach, Dan Hoover and D Walter Martin. The original Goods school sold over auction to a private buyer and this new school took on the same name of "Goods school." Lydia Hoover, a 35er, was the first teacher there, when Aaron's children got on the big yellow school bus for their bigger brand-new school.

Brecknock elementary school had all eight grades for only three years until the rules changed. All seventh and eighth grade students must attend high school! Only first grade through sixth grade would remain at the elementary school. Dick was already through seventh grade, and he went to Garden Spot High School for eighth grade. He had poor reading comprehension, and he did not like school, much less the thought of high school. He attended against his wishes and did not understand the system, of moving classes to different rooms for different subjects.

Ruth and Rhoda lucked out with staying in Brecknock that term, where two grades shared one classroom, combining sixth and seventh grades for that year.

Dick wore suspenders to high school and they labeled him as "different". He had no brother, cousin, or neighbor to lean on for support and his confidence was sadly lacking. Everyone else seemed to know where to go next, and how to find the right classrooms, except Dick. Teachers carefully explained the details to the beginners the preceding year and the eighth graders were supposed to know what they were doing. The whole term was a disgusting ordeal for him, as classmates snapped his suspenders. He slumped his shoulders and wished to hide.

The teachers put pressure on all the students to finish high school and not drop out. Teachers all insisted,"Dick, if you quit school, you'll never be able to get a job!" He worried about that! He also had a hard time with the public shower idea after gym class and refused to take a shower while others watched. "You didn't shower," the teacher, questioned, "You'll stink!" but Dick did not care about that. Even the teachers had a difficult time liking the gangly farm boy with big ears and huge feet. He was an outcast, a Mennonite from a large poor family, and not very smart to their way of thinking. To complicate matters, Dick was saddled with homework, and his teachers urged him to catch up. That was misery in itself, when he would rather do manual work. Eventually the term ended, but not too soon for Dick. He never wanted much to do with books for the rest of his life, but he was ready to dig in and work helping others every chance he had.

After Dick had been teased and mocked to tears, Aaron and Amanda tried the Goods one-room parochial school for the next term. Ruth, Rhoda and Martha attended there two years and Mary went one year. They lived 3 miles from school. They thanked Daniel for giving them an early morning ride to the 625. Daniel stopped at the stop sign, where he turned north towards Reading and they hopped out for a short walk south to school.

They arrived before anyone else did and sat on the porch watching traffic. Certain cars passed at the same time every morning and Mary found nicknames for the most familiar ones.

Selestia Weaver taught all eight grades with 40 students, including some slow learners and blind Mabel Hoover. Selestia was a talented teacher and fair to all. She had no children of her own, and stayed single all her life, putting her all into helping raise the neighborhood, as she taught right from wrong.

Selestia ate her lunch inside school, while tutoring the slow learners, and she kept looking out the windows to patrol the playground. She stood close to the coal stove overwinter with her black sweater draped across her shoulders. She was talented in singing and the song still rings clearly,"Elijah's God still lives today, oh blessed be his name. When his children to him pray, he answers still the same."

In a baseball game at recess, Rhoda had a collision at first base, which broke her arm and knocked her unconscious. When she came to, her right arm hurt so badly that the teacher sent two students on bicycles to tell Aaron and Amanda to come and fetch Rhoda. It was not long until Aaron arrived in the station wagon, with the four -ways flashing and the horn blowing. He considered it an emergency! On the way to Ephrata, to put her arm in a cast, Rhoda did not know which was worse, the pain in her arm, or the embarrassment of a father like that, with some classmates grinning. She wore a cast six weeks.

Ruth already knew most of her lessons and enjoyed helping blind Mabel Hoover. Together they shared one desk as Ruth quietly whispered the lessons to Mabel, very close to her ear. Mabel propped her chin on her fist, while her blind eyes stared into space. Ruth marked the answers Mabel told her.

Mabel always dressed clean and neat, with extra shiny black hair. Ruth marveled how Mabel groped along the wall to find her own straw bonnet, on the first hook in the row, and how her face lit up in a smile when she found it. Mabel often picked the song, "no tears in heaven". They became good friends and at Christmas time, Ruth was surprised and honored to find a small gift, wrapped and labeled, "to Ruth Shirk". Inside she found a wind chime as a thank you gift from Mabel and her parents, Dan Hoovers. Ruth felt unworthy, and the gift was a real surprise. It never occurred to her that she did a good deed for someone.

Aaron and Amanda's three teenage girls made new friends and their grades were no problem. They had many good times with sliding and sledding on frozen slopes. Ruth brought along crocheting, and at recess, she showed left-handed Rosene Martin how to crochet. Ekka Bolla or corner ball included everyone in a fun game, but stories circulated about misconduct at recess when children went off school property into the woods and tardy in returning. After two years in this school, Aaron and Amanda sent the remaining children to Garden Spot High School. Mary had it tough switching over, after missing seventh grade at Garden Spot, as Dick had.

Mary did not understand the system because she was in the one-room school for seventh grade. When the bell rang, everyone else scurried to the next classroom. Mary tried to follow a classmate, and found herself in the wrong room, with the wrong class. She turned around and went back to Mr. Cully, her homeroom teacher, and he kindly told her where to go. When she arrived to the proper destination, class had started without her. It was like a nightmare to her and she occasionally dreamed about that for the rest of her life, being lost in a big school, not knowing where to go.

After Dick finished eighth grade he worked at home full time with his parents for one year. He thoroughly enjoyed himself learning many interesting things, about farming and helping Amanda in the garden, picking anything from strawberries to pickles. Dick did most of the laundry that winter with the Maytag wringer washer run by a loud gas engine, that gave off a blue smoke from the exhaust pipe that probably leaked fumes into the basement. In the fall, he helped cut firewood from the woods, and he loved this type of work helping his parents.

Dick's suspenders

Ruth, Rhoda, and Martha had the privilege of going on a school trip to see the Lancaster planetarium. Amanda gave each of them $.25 to spend as she please on the trip. Other children had more money along then that. Rhoda bought cheese curls and they sure looked good, even if Martha never tasted any, but she wanted root beer. After waiting in line awhile, she heard all the fancy girls in front of her asking for Coke. If Coke was better than root beer thought Martha, "This must really be great!", and she ordered Coke. To her surprise, it tasted much like medicine, and how she wished for that root beer! Her drink tasted so bad she could not drink it all. When everyone was snacking but her, she miserably hoped nobody would notice, and the group might soon move on.

Irene, in second grade, tried hard to be like the fancy little girls in school, who had cut hair and wore short dresses. She could keep up with their grades, and she did not want cut hair, but she wished for a shorter dress. When Irene, Lydia and Roseanna, were playing in the corncrib, they heard a car driving in the lane. They did not know who might be coming, but they quickly smoothed down their hair and tried to make the dresses shorter by tucking them up at the waist, to look fancy. Oh, the driver of the car was just Daniel!

After Aaron and Amanda owned a car they attended an occasional school meeting. When Aaron attended a teachers meeting, he talked to Mrs. Zimmerman and said,"We bought our first car now." He continued talking to Mary's third grade teacher about details that embarrassed Mary seriously, while she stood listening. Getting parents to school did not happen often.

Aaron Shirks children attended a spelling bee at school one evening. When Irene was up on the stage, waiting her turn to spell, she again desired to look like the" fancy" girls. She folded her dress up at the waist and crossed her arms over the fold. Now her dress appeared shorter in the front all right, but still hung down long in the back! She spelled the word "running" with only one 'n' and took her seat. Her older sisters were ever so glad!

Most of Aaron and Amanda's children excelled in spelling and they liked spelling bees. After drilling each other at home for the coming big event at school, Pete and Dick went up in the rapid calculation class. They were sharp with numbers any time, and with all that practice, they won! The last three people in the rapid calculation class, were Pete,

Dick and Allen G. Musser, one of Bowmansville's most successful businessmen. Pete ended up as the winner! Several days later, Allen Musser remarked to Aaron, "I thought I was pretty good at numbers, but your son beat me!"

Dick's third-prize was a hard- cover storybook titled "Old Yeller", by Fred Gipson. The new book, fresh off the press in 1956, told a story about a young boy in pioneer days and his old yellow dog. The story was appropriate at Dick's level, but he was disappointed because he had not mastered words as well as numbers and reading was "not his thing". He kept the well-worn book as a trophy, and passed it around to others. Inside the front cover, over 30 people signed their names after reading it, but his name did not make the list

When Louise went to school, her teacher suggested her name sounded better with an 'e' at the end. Louise did not care, because most commonly she was,"La Veese", a dutchfied variation. For the next fifty years, she spelled her name as Louise. In later years, she changed her name back to the original spelling of Louisa, for legal purposes.

Most of Aaron and Amanda's children met language barriers of some kind, due to speaking Dutch at home. Louise and Virginia Redcay had a minor spat at school over some trivial thing. Virginia told her mother about it, and her mother asked her to apologize. The next day she asked, "Louise, would you please forgive me?" Louise did not understand 'forgive' and said, "No! What must I give you?"She was not going to promise to give Virginia anything, afraid of what she had to give. Only in a higher grade did Louise catch on to the meaning of forgive. She would still like to tell Virginia, that she had been forgiven right from the start!"

Irene came home from school with a serious problem, and tried to make a paper plate, because she knew they had none in the house. Amanda asked, "What are you making?"Irene said, "My teacher said I should bring a paper plate to school, for a special treat tomorrow!" As Amanda watched her daughter trace a dinner plate onto a corrugated box, and then cut it out, she kindly said, "You may take a Sunday best plate instead. Surely not everyone else will have a paper plate either."Irene was not the only one at school without a paper plate, and most of all, she could hardly believe that it did not even matter!

Books were treasures, because Aaron and Amanda did not have many books. The hunters gave a book about Little Black Sambo, where the tiger ran around the tree until he melted into butter. Amanda knew most of the nursery rhymes and the silly songs she learned at her school. Aaron's children knew about fairy tales and Santa Clause. He was as far out as putting Humpty Dumpty together again.

Every so often, a bookmobile came to Brecknock School. The portable library had rows and rows of books in a panel truck. A few students from each of the many classrooms chose a dozen books for their room to share. Several times Louise had the privilege of choosing books for her room. Maybe the teacher saw she had her lessons finished or else she trusted her choice of books. When children brought library books home from school, they knew they must do their work first. Reading was a special privilege and those restrictions encouraged them to read more. Dick, Rhoda and Martha did not read as much as the rest.

Hackman's

Aaron offended some people with his much speaking, while others did not seem to mind. Warren Hackman was among the people that enjoyed lively discussions with Aaron Shirk, especially on church issues. On a Sunday morning in December, the Hackman family drove over thirty miles to Bowmansville church, with hopes of going to Aaron Shirks for dinner.

Amanda was home tending sick children, six of them had the measles, and it was not necessary that Aaron stayed home also, so he went to church with several of the boys. After church services ended, Warren hinted to Aaron that they want to come for dinner. Aaron knew what the house looked like when he left home and he did not know what to say. "Amanda is home with sick children", he hesitated, "Did you all have the measles?" All six of them had the mea-

sles, so they came along for dinner; or rather, they followed Aaron in their own car. Without a telephone, they had no chance to call ahead that morning, announcing their intentions.

Mrs. Hackman wanted to back out, and not go to a place where the mother was tending sick children, totally unprepared for company, but her opinion did not count. While driving in the lane, Katie Hackman said, "I bet Amanda's hair is standing on end, when she sees company coming!" And it was nearly so.

In the middle of the kitchen floor, was a bushel of miscellaneous items swept together to sort later. Amanda was in the process of sweeping the floor, and there was no place fit for a guest to sit down. Aaron apologized to Amanda, and slipping out of his Sunday suit coat, he said "Mom, now what can I help you with?" He didn't help much as the men sat down to talk.

Amanda somehow got a meal together and made the best of the situation. Mrs. Hackman felt sorry about the poor timing, and Amanda felt humiliated that anyone would step into her house in such a mess. Special guests at that! What might they think about her housekeeping? Mrs. Hackman dug in to help the best she could, setting the table and helping get the meal ready.

In the next room lay sick children, not caring to eat, while the lowered green blinds shaded the bright light from their eyes. Four-year-old Rose-Anna, laid across two rocking chairs for her bed, like a "crib." She pretended to be sleeping when visitors came fussing over her when she felt sick. Martha, Louise, Irene, Wesley, Lydia, and Mandy were so sick that Amanda wondered if they would all survive, but they did.

Aaron's older children had the measles earlier. Ruth and Rhoda showed the Hackman girls the new dress material Amanda had laid out to sew, with bought matching buttons for them. The guests looked on enviously. [Amanda did not attach contrasting or showy buttons.]

The mothers had compassion for each other and the visit gave them each a lift. The men enjoyed the visit also, and when the Hackmans left, Amanda's house was much improved, and her thoughts turned to other things, beyond herself. Other people also have problems!

Uninvited guests for Sunday dinner were nothing new to Amanda. Back in Michigan, it was so common that people sometimes even invited themselves for Sunday dinner when the owners were not at home. The company helped themselves to whatever food they found, and any simple fare sufficed. They just stopped in for a bite to eat, when they were moving on to visit elsewhere. It was too far to return home for lunch if they came from a distance, with a horse and carriage. They expected to return the same hospitality to others.

Six sick children at one time were almost more than Amanda could handle. The mumps also made their rounds and quite a few children could not attend the Christmas program and gift exchange at school. Amanda sent gift-wrapped gifts along to school, with those that were not sick. The students exchanged the gifts at school. Those at home sick, wondered what they might get. They knew they just missed the most exciting day of the school term. Mary was not pleased with a red wallet, which she had no use for and Louise never used her pen and pencil set, studded with rhinestones. Perhaps the gift was grand to look at, but they did not work well. Martha also frowned at what she got. How could people be so dense and not know how much she longed for a color book? She did not appreciate a dustpan and brush, not even a pretend one. Bobby gave Dick a useless metal car and Dick gave away a nice color book and colors, the best gift of all.

A pleasure is greatest in its anticipation and the children looked forward to such a grand moment all year. Only once a year did they get a gift-wrapped package. In Amanda's childhood children were easier to please. They gave simple homemade gifts or a piece of candy.

Benny Weaver fixed that problem when his teacher simplified the exchange system and asked each boy to bring a boy gift and each girl to bring a gift for a girl. His mother bought a mouth organ for him to give away, exactly as he coveted. He wrapped the small package crudely in newspaper and it was still there when he chose a gift from the pile. He chose his own gift, and went home happier than all the rest!

When Warren Hackman's invited Aaron Shirks to Lebanon County for Sunday dinner in return, Aaron felt greatly honored, but how could he find the place? D. Walter Martins were invited also, and therefore they followed each other. Traveling to Lebanon County was an exciting venture, but stressful, as Aaron tried his best to follow another vehicle, not knowing the road, and with thinking of getting lost. Aaron did not want to be late so they allowed plenty of time to travel about 33 miles to Mount Zion church. Amanda started combing girls the night before. It took a while, but French braids stayed good enough until Sunday morning when a daughter wore Amanda's old covering all night. They all arrived at church on time and enjoyed the day.

Aaron's cousin Lem Martin generally enjoyed Aaron's discussions, arguments and fellowship. Sometimes when those two men started talking, Amanda embarrassingly said, "Ach Aaron you don't have to say everything!"

If someone asked, "Aaron, how much land do you own?" Aaron might say, "oh hundreds and hundreds of acres!" And that was true, if people translated it properly, as 100+100+19 acres. Aaron didn't mind boldly differing viewpoints. After nearly a quarter-century without success in mining, he was used to opposition. Even the big new Grace Mines closed, to his dismay.

Others joked, and Aaron just smiled about the stories of his much talking. One story said that Aaron and Christ Shirk traveled to Virginia together and they were tired, but they had so much to talk about, that while one slept, the other one talked and then they switched off.

Aaron was accused of sitting too close to the cellar stairway, leaning back on his chair. When the chair tipped over too far, it fell against the un-latched cellar door, tumbling Aaron and his chair backwards down the stairs, and he never stopped talking all the way down!

Other people sometimes made fun of A M Shirk. They misunderstood him and even misused him at times, but he was a generous person when you got to his heart. When relatives came for a call, Titus watched Aaron and Amanda load some of their hard- earned canned food into the poor people's carriage, before they left. Sometimes Aarons sent a Sears order anonymously, to those in need.

Many Shirks had a reputation for talking too much, and talking their way out again. Aaron remembered how his father, BW Shirk, worked out in the field cultivating close to the end of the lane, when old jockey Groff stopped and asked, "How much would you take for that Guernsey cow over in the meadow?" BW Shirk thought awhile and made a price so high that no one would buy her, because his gentle family cow was not for sale. Mr. Groff said, "I'll take her!" After chatting a while, BW Shirk asked Mr. Groff, "Would you take a one dollar profit on that cow?""Yes," said the jockey, "I believe I will." BW Shirk handed a one-dollar bill to the jockey and bought back his own cow.

The Shirks could exaggerate and lay it on thick. Aaron had a way of getting his point across, and his children saw how he did it. People did not need to guess what he meant in his convincing way, hence the saying, Give them an A M row.

Sarah Ann

Ruth

Rhohda

Martha

Mary

Louise

Irene

Rose Anna

Mandy

Left to right: Wesley, Dick, Walter, Daniel, Pete
Sarah Ann, Ruth, Martha, Mary, Louise
Rhoda, Irene, Lydia, Rose Anna, Mandy, Amanda

15 children and their partners standing in three rows.
Front row of couples: Marlins, Wesleys, Carl Hoovers, Lewis, Henrys
Center row: Mervin B's, Carl W's, Mervin H's, Rolands, Ivans,
Back row: Petes, Dicks, Daniels, Walters, Mahlons
(Ruth wore a wig after chemo)

Front: Irene, Wesley, Lydia, Rose Anna, Mandy
Center: Ruth, Rhoda, Martha, Mary, Louise
Back Row: Daniel, Sarah Ann, Walter, Pete, Dick

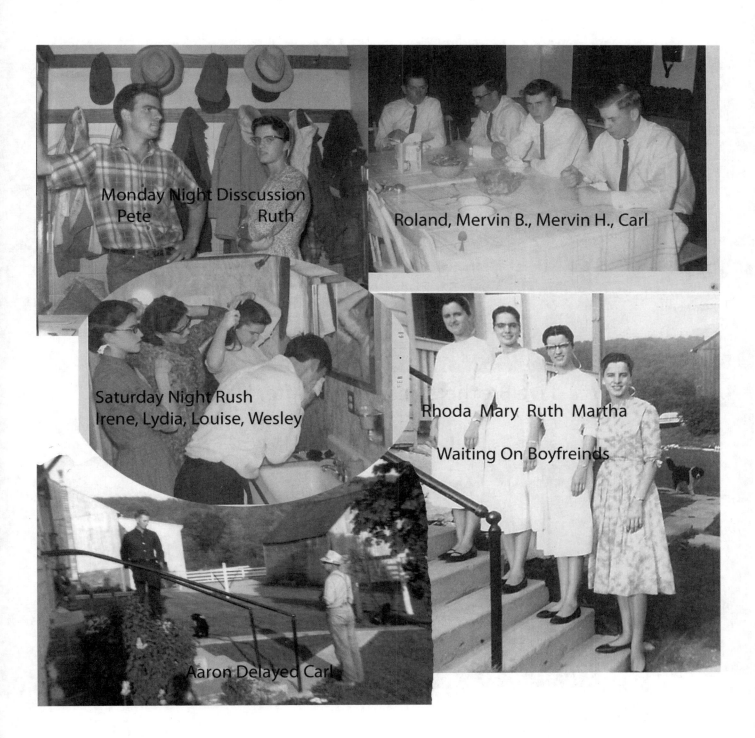

Monday Night Disscussion
Pete   Ruth

Roland, Mervin B., Mervin H., Carl

Saturday Night Rush
Irene, Lydia, Louise, Wesley

Rhoda Mary Ruth Martha

Waiting On Boyfreinds

Aaron Delayed Carl

Five Brothers Before And After Hair

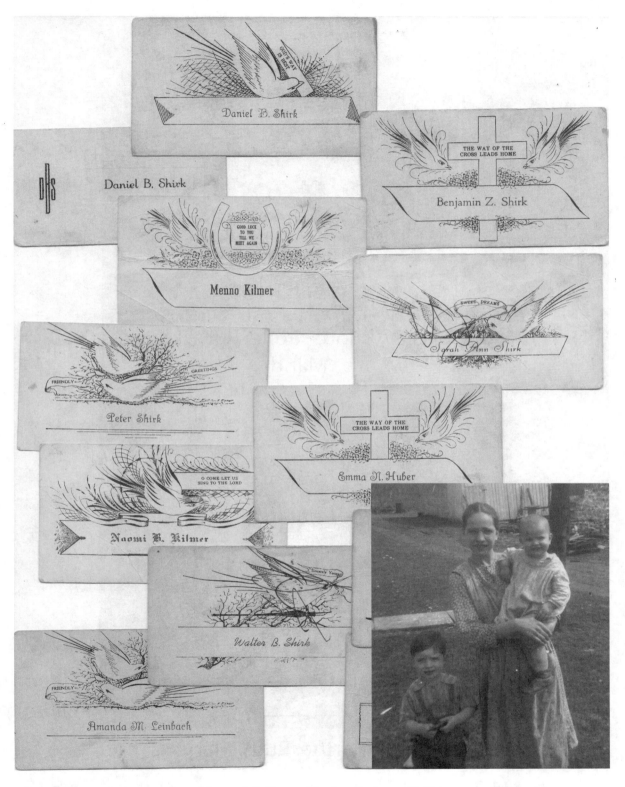

Sarah Ann spent most of her childhood babysitting. Children scribbled her namecards everyone traded.   (Wesley, Roseanna)

Lydia, Wesley, Rhoda, Irene, Ruth, Louise
Mandy

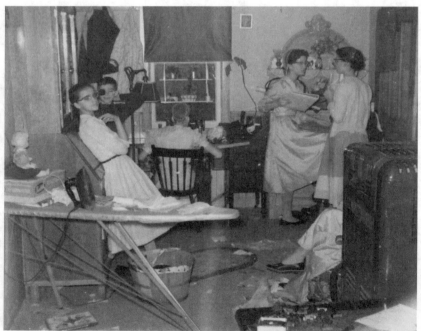

Irene, Wesley, Martha, Ruth, Mary

Dick   (Skip)   Pete   Daniel

Peanut   Daniel   Chester

Top photo taken in April 1956. The tallest section is the same house Aaron and Amanda bought in 1937 .The chimney needed replacing back then already .The house is old but solidly built. The apple tree to the right is where Amanda found her covering caught in the branches after the leaves fell from the tree. Aaron and Amanda added a bedroom, balconies, and a large kitchen with a basement in 1945 when they had twins. The new part connected the old house with the summer -house on the right, which was there before they arrived. The summer -house disappeared to make room for a big garage in 1975, before another wedding. At the corner of the barn, notice the stack of wood used for butchering out there, or for stripping tobacco .The stripping room door starts about where the photo stops. The single strand laundry line on three posts sagged overloaded with laundry every week, until Aaron put up three long parallel lines. Amanda planted flowers in the black tire, every spring, right there beside the Rose of Sharon bush.

Bottom photo: To the far right is Amanda's new retirement home, making room for others to live and work on the farm. Walters saw a need for replacing those two rooms Aaron and Amanda had added. In 1992 they razed the east end and added this new addition.

Center: Aaron & Amanda   Children; 1: Daniel, 2: Walter, 3: Pete,
4: Dick, 5: Ruth, 6: Sarah Ann, 7: Rhoda, 8: Martha, 9: Mary,
10: Mandy, 11: Louise, 12: Irene, 13: Lydia, 14: Roseanna, 15: Wesley

24

10 Girls

Most people in the area knew about the family with ten girls, and with that many, surely, they could spare one as a hired girl. Christian Kilmer's had ten girls and many of them worked away from home also, and so did others. Hiring out children was a common practice, somewhat like an apprenticeship, but more importantly a form of helping others. Just before school let out in springtime, postcards arrived in the mail from people needing hired help for the summer and that was trouble! No one volunteered! No one wanted to leave home! "Oh, that dreadful feeling!" Amanda well remembered the days when she needed help and she encouraged her daughters to work for others, and learn their way of doing things."

Sarah Ann rarely worked for others because Amanda depended heavily on her, until she was old enough to work n the factory. Sarah Ann considered it a privilege to work at Aaron's brother Menno when they had a baby Menno Junior. Working for others looked more glamorous than the drudgery around home with an endless amount of routine housework. For the rest of the girls, Amanda had helpers to spare, against the girls wishes. Sometimes when she said, "Irene, go fetch some peaches from the cellar, "she might get a reply like, "I'm busy, Louise isn't doing anything," or "it's not my turn, I did yesterday." Separating the girls and getting them to work for others was the best way to break that habit, she thought, and she was determined to help needy people by sending help.

Ruth enjoyed helping at grandmother Brubacher all day Saturday every week. It was fun because Ruth came home every night. Ruth rolled out the pie dough and shook off the rugs; she filled the wood box, and did the dusting.

Mommy Brubacher, like the grandmother before her, scrubbed with a passion, and kept everything neat and orderly; she even scrubbed the wooden walk to the outhouse, as well as the outhouse itself. Everything smelled like pine oil! Her maiden name was Brenneman and those people had a lot of ambition and 'get-up-and- go!'Grandmother saved all her eggshells, dried them, and crushed them to use as fertilizer in the garden. She had the prettiest garden of raised beds, and regularly swept the garden paths with her broom.

Every time grandchildren came to her house, she wanted them to remember her. She treated with round pink lozenges called wintergreen candies, or "mommy Brubacher" candy. No one ever dared ask for a second piece. She sent some of the pink mint lozenges in the mail to her grandchildren in Indiana. Pleasantly and cheerfully, grandmother chuckled and laughed a bit as she told Ruth "Where so many girls are together, it is good to help and learn from others. "

Ruth got homesick working away from home overnight, especially at a place where the mother had depression problems. She did not mind driving a team of horses so the men could plant tobacco. The housework was not hard and she enjoyed the little children, but when the lights went out at night, Ruth cried. She cried herself to sleep and had a hard time eating in the daytime. She struggled with pain, fever and bellyache, until they took her home. After that, every time when someone asked for a maid, Ruth cringed and stubbornly refused to leave home.

When David Zimmermans, asked for a helper Amanda planned to send Ruth. He came to pick her up, and Amanda thought surely Ruth could try just one week, but she refused to go along. Standing in the old kitchen, with her head down on the sideboard cupboard, she cried into her arms, sobbing hard. She remembered her last job and flatly refused to go!

Amanda was disappointed and didn't know what to do. She could not send Ruth like that. Some of the other girls already had jobs, so she took nine-year-old Louise, and kindly said she must go and work for the strangers she had never met. Amanda quickly gathered some clean clothes and put them in a bag for Louise, while she tied on her sunbonnet, rather alarmed! The strange man stood patiently waiting. Amanda talked kindly and said, "Many people have helped us and we must help others."Louise did not have a clue what her mother meant, because she did not understand that anybody ever helped them. Amanda went on to say, "Each day I'll do a golden deed, by helping those who are in need." No matter what Amanda said, Louise truly did not understand, but she had no choice.

She was numb with astonishment as she sat directly behind the driver not saying a word, while her mind raced in all directions…why me...where was he taking me? She had no idea! The five miles to Churchtown, were not much different from five hundred miles, because after they drove beyond Laurel Hill and the dump, Louise did not know the way home.

David's two small boys, Ricky and Johnny, were not much work for Louise, but then again, she didn't notice work of any kind unless someone told her what to do. Nighttime was the hard part, when she knew her sisters went to bed at home without her. Were they laughing and having a ball, while she was in a room all alone? Was that what a new puppy felt like when it whimpered all night with no one to touch? She knew the slaves in the storybooks suffered much more, and yet there was a strange likeness because she had no say whatsoever. Yesterday she was free and now she felt trapped! Doesn't anyone care, and why would Mom do this? She cried herself to sleep, dearly clinging to the promise of going home on Saturday, but that was a very long way off.

The people were kind to her, and when the longest week of her life ended, David took her home.

Amanda knew a nine year old was not worth more than room and board so David paid fifty cents a week, of which Louise kept 10%. All her hardship and tears, for three months of her young life, sold for 65 cents. She cried into her pillow at night, and got over her homesickness, therefore she was doomed for seven summers in a row.

On Saturday, after the weekly cleaning was done and the children had their naps, Louise returned home. Going home again was wonderful and yet sad. It seemed like they did all the fun things while she was gone. She missed so much in life. The girls were just drying their hair after their noontime swim, and no one cared to go to the pond again. Monday morning came much too soon, and she sadly returned.

One time Louise received a pair of barrettes, the envy of her sisters, and even a nice new color book. Those gifts meant much more to her than any money, which she had no need for, because she didn't go to any store. All the pretty things in the Sears wish book were as far out of her reach as the stars in the sky, but one time she even came home from David Zimmerman's with a doll just for her.

 Eventually summer disappeared. On a cool crisp morning, Louise heard the first geese flying south. It was back-to-school time and that meant nine wonderful months at home again, among the love of a big family. She could hardly wait, no matter how humble the setting.

At age seven, Irene worked at Martin Wengers as "kindts maude" (nursemaid). They had two small children and Irene missed home, but she did not stay full-time for the entire summer. She remembered how the Wengers served goat milk, and she stayed there one weekend without going to church. She was "paid" with a piece of dress fabric.

All the hired girls learned how to work, to the full meaning of the word! Sometimes at home, one of them might ask "But what must Lydia do?"When working away, young girls listened more carefully to detailed instructions, and when told to do something, they obediently went!

Mary remembers swinging and singing to young children and kindly reading to them. All of Aaron's girls enjoyed little children, and playing with them, but sometimes those same young helpers had room for improvement, when they really did not want to be there at all. Life wasn't fair!

Rhoda worked at many different places. At age 11, she worked at Uncle Menno Shirks, coming home every other weekend. At a very young age, she helped work at Uncle Silas Brubacher's and while there, she was required to rub aunt Sarah's back with ointment. She worked at David Zimmerman's, Ivan Zimmerman's and Isaac Horsts, among others.

For a while, she also worked at D. Walter Martins. Daniel dropped her off on his way to work, and then picked her up again on his way home in the evening. While there, she made many French braids on the little girl's hair, and Rhoda got her first taste of marshmallow cream. Yum!

Mary worked for Martin Wengers, Joe Wengers and for Iky Horsts. The next summer Martha and Mary worked for Mose Hornings. Laverne Zwalleys fetched Martha as needed. Seven-year-old Irene went along with Ruth to Martin Wengers, to see if that makes things better for Ruth. She still could not handle that, and came back homesick, so Irene went home also.

Irene worked for strangers, and bravely walked into the strange house by herself, staying all week, when she was ten. At the dinner table, the husband and wife had a disagreement, which Irene did not understand. The husband slammed his fist on the table so hard that the dishes jumped! His wife fled to the bedroom, and Irene looked scared. He asked her, "Don't your parents argue?" Irene said, "Not like that!"

Some people did much more ironing to perfection, and that was usually a job for the maid. The majority of the laundry was 100% cotton and on a wind-still day, it wrinkled more. One time Mary and Louise worked away and hung up heavy laundry. The wash line ripped down accidently. They deserved their scolding, for not coming to tell what happened, as the laundry lay in the dirt.

Mary worked where the little children did not empty their cereal plates each morning. On the Kellogg's corn flakes box, in bold letters it said, "The best to you each morning!" As Mary cleared the table she said, "The best to the cats each morning". Amanda did not allow such waste.

At one place, Ruth accidently dropped a glass dish and it broke! The mother cried and said, 'That was my nicest one!"Such a comment caused a flood of tears, since Ruth already battled homesickness.

With a lot of coaxing, Ruth tried again, but Daniel soon came and fetched her. When she turned 15, she worked for uncle Silas and Aunt Sarah Brubacher. Sarah was sick and needed help, so Ruth helped give her a sponge bath, and worked there as needed. They lived in a house in town, with deathly silence. After several days of crying, they again took Ruth home.

Amanda said," Ruth, we plan to take a trip to Indiana and Brutus, Michigan, to see the home place where I grew up, and we want to take you and Rhoda along, if you try again to work as a hired girl." Ruth ignored all the bribery, and flatly said, "Just take Martha along, I don't want to go!"

As the time neared, Aaron and Amanda planned their trip, taking Dick, Ruth, Rhoda, Rose-Anna and Mandy along. Ruth did not ask to go along, and promised to work any place where she could come home to sleep at night. She learned to help at a large Amish family by the name of Isaac Zook, close enough to come home again at the day's end. She did not work there every day, and did not cry. She understood all about washing with a gas engine wash machine, and she enjoyed using the long pulley line, reeling the laundry high up into the breeze.

Irene worked at Ivan Zimmerman's; taking an occasional turn with Louise, and remembered tending baby Elmer. She was young and immature enough to enjoy driving the children's tricycles! The mother always cheerfully worked with her, rather than sending Irene alone to do something. Working there later, Irene learned to hang cleaning rags in a hidden spot on the laundry line, so that nobody notices the rags. That was a new thought to her, because it did not matter at home. She thoroughly enjoyed combing the curls on baby Grace.

At one place, Rhoda did not enjoy her job. She was half-scared to iron the laundry, because they had a gas iron and the flames shot out the back...

alarmingly! Rhoda got so badly homesick, that she couldn't bear it anymore. She packed her bags and said, "I'm leaving!" She walked up the road to the Union Grove crossroads where she knew Sarah Ann came by on her way home from the factory. As Sarah Ann stopped at the stop sign, Rhoda opened the car door and hopped in the crowded car. When she arrived home, she marched right past her mother and went upstairs to her own bedroom. That was the start of something new. Since Sarah Ann drove that road daily, Rhoda only worked for those people two days a week, and spent more time at home.

Then there was Aunt Lydia, Amanda's childless sister that enjoyed claiming a girl whenever she could. Lydia's house was always clean, and she sometimes did invisible weaving for the dry cleaners in Ephrata. Irene remembered working at Eli Stauffer's and fetching milk next door at Amos Stauffer's where the girls walked on stilts and climbed the tobacco rails, with pep to spare!

Sometimes working for others really was not so bad, but at other times, it seemed like Mom did not understand. "Why do girls have to work away from home?" Back in Michigan, when Amanda was 12 years old, she worked four summers in a row for others, and she understood much more than her daughters realized. She stayed at Manasseh Kulps, and her parents decided that Amanda could keep on working there, living with them, even going to school from there. Manasseh Kulps lived in the Ayr school district, too far away for Amanda to attend her home school of Woodland. She had no familiar classmates, and no brothers or sisters at the strange school. After about a month, Amanda suffered from homesickness so badly, she could hardly cope, and she returned "overjoyed "to her home and her family.

If Amanda knew all about the hardships away from home, her young daughters wondered, "Why did it need to be that way?" Amanda could see the other side, after Aaron and Amanda had many years with more work than they could handle. Now they had the glorious opportunity of doing unto others, as others had kindly given them. They could not help the same people perhaps, but they saw much

good in sending help to the needy. Amanda had a hard time turning down any requests for help.

Some of the girls enjoyed walking through the woods, like on a Saturday afternoon at home. Irene was afraid of snakes, so she did not go hiking unless Louise went along. Just behind the barn, the girls climbed through the pipe gate,"fol-doah" [fall-door], and passed the row of persimmon trees, past the "shoaf shtall", or (sheep shed). As they crossed the creek, they lingered at the 6 inches of clear water, wading and overturning several rocks, looking for crayfish, before heading up the wooded hill, to the Weller Lot. Only a stonewall and foundation remained of the former homestead of Sal Weller and her witchcraft..

The girls reached their goal when they came to the big lone hemlock tree, where owls roosted and regurgitated owl pellets, dropping them beneath the tree. The furry pellets invariably held a skull or two from mice the owls had eaten. Beneath the tree stood a crude homemade chair, as royal as a king's throne, made by one of the boys who found time to spare. The stately [tsattruh baum] Hemlock "and state tree of PA" was the only evergreen tree in the area. Beyond that point, young children could become disoriented and lost without a trail, but only if they crossed the road or the power line. Downhill always led to the creek, and that went home. Children played there a long time, raking leaves, carving initials, slopping in the creek and even going to the arch beneath the Turnpike sometimes. The entire hillside was a natural playground for climbing trees and digging clay at the "clay hole", merely a puddle with soft smooth clay, ready for pottery. In some of the older trees, they found initials of big brothers and perhaps even an uncle. When heading for the house, the children first picked Mountain Laurel for Mom or wintergreen leaves to chew. If nothing else, they gathered a bouquet of abundant buttercups in the open pasture. The buttercups in a vase on the table soon "cried" with homesickness and dropped all the petals they had. The woods became a healing balm after working away all week.

Lydia stayed with Aunt Lydia and Uncle Eli Stauffer every summer from age five to twelve.

Since Aunt Lydia had no children, she still wished to keep her little namesake. She knew that Amanda had so many children, that she did not need them all. On Monday morning, Sarah Ann took Lydia along to Ephrata and dropped her off at Eli Stauffer's, but Aunt Lydia did not keep little Lydia, and they brought her home again on Friday evenings. Only once, did Lydia cry for homesick and bellyaches.

Lydia Shirk

At Aunt Lydia's clean and quiet house, five-year-old Lydia was somewhat pampered. She got a penny for washing dishes and often had candy. Lydia felt rich one day when Aunt Lydia gave her a shiny nickel for cleaning away the row of dead irises. She helped tend the garden and the fruit trees, and watered the blueberries. She enjoyed the lively children just across the pasture at Amos Stauffers.

Coming home to a big family was quite a culture shock, with all the dirt, noise, flies and the commotion. Lydia felt that no one cared about her, even when all of them did care!

Amanda spent many stressful days at the bedside of her mother in the winter of 1959 and 1960. Mommy Brubacher had weak lungs, for many years; perhaps the problem resulted from damage in 1918 when she nearly died in the flu epidemic. Her children thanked God many times; that he spared their mother another 40 years. She was frail now and coughed a lot. Just two years ago, Mommy Brubacher had pneumonia with pleurisy, and she was flat in bed near death. One week later, she could sit up some, and came to the table. Slowly she recovered.

Peter and Sarah Ann shared the kitchen table, the busiest spot in their small house. He needed the table to clean the eggs to sell, and mommy watched her chance to cut out pants to sew for Peter, or work on her large braided rug, when she was well. Katie was far away in Indiana, but Mary, Betsy and Amanda helped all they could, while still caring for their own big family. They took turns bringing girls to help clean their parent's house."

Mommy Brubacher wrote a letter to her daughter, Lydia, saying, "I guess your windows are almost getting holes, where you look so much for a letter from us. It is not so good with me. When the doctor came out, he gave me heart pills and dropsy pills. Getting meals together is all I can do. I cannot sleep more than two hours at night before waking. The last three nights, I just could not lie down."

The kind parents that raised Amanda now depended much on their children's help. Thankfully, they lived close by. Aaron and Amanda came to visit Dawdy Brubachers one evening and told the children to keep the noise down, when the children thought the place was boring enough already. Rose Anna and Mandy went to the kitchen, and Mandy found a paring knife. Rose Anna, nearly four years old, panicked to see her twenty months old sister get a sharp knife, holding it by the blade. With a quick yank, Rose Anna jerked the knife out of Mandy's hand, while Mandy knew she has it first and defiantly held the knife tighter. A deep gash in the palm of her hand needed stitches that night yet. Amanda thought it could not be!

Peter tended the chickens, and cared for his horse. Martin Kilmers lived the closest and sent their children to do the dishes each day. The egg prices kept dropping and when they thought the price could not go lower, it still did. They had many doctor bills, and life became a struggle.

Amanda and her sisters took turns staying with their parents every night, even with heaps of work among their own big families. They automatically taught their children how to care for the elderly. Mommy Brubacher was deathly ill with pleural effusion pneumonia, and they made meals for her and combed her hair. Amanda mended a dozen pairs of stockings for her parents while she sat at her mother's bedside. After Amanda came home again, she saw how much her own work had been neglected, and she kept Sarah Ann home from the factory due to a desperate need for help.

Christian Kilmers showed their first grandchild to Mommy as she lay on her deathbed, when baby Marvin Nolt was about six weeks old. Martin Kilmers had three grandchildren and the others had none. Daniel had started dating Edna. On March 10, 1960, Sarah Ann Brenneman Brubacher, died at the age of 73 before meeting any more of her descendants. Christian Kilmer's Ada was at her grandmother's bedside, when Mommy Brubacher moved on to eternity. At the end, Mommy sat up in bed and pushed away her covers. While looking upwards, she said, "Glie mole binnich ous deah kosh-tuh, un mit duh Yuss-vah."(Soon I will be out of this dwelling and with Joshua). By the look on her face, it appeared she was seeing Joshua, and heaven.

The funeral was not a surprise, but it kept Amanda extremely busy! After her mother died, Aaron and Amanda spent the first night with Peter Brubacher. It was eight years since there was a funeral in the family and some of Aaron and Amanda's children did not understand what a funeral really was. The children did not regularly go along to funerals unless it was a close relative. The girls all needed dark dresses, showing respect for their grandmother, and Amanda quickly sewed four more dresses for the twins, Mary and Louise. When she sewed the navy blue dress for Louise,

she used the buttons from her own wedding dress, knowing she would never wear it again. Amanda had designed her original wedding dress with tucks for enlarging the dress as necessary. Since Amanda nearly doubled her weight, she could no longer alter her dress any larger.

It wasn't just sewing four dresses, that kept Amanda busy, she worked fast to get ready for Uncle Dan's, traveling from Indiana, and coming for the night. Three hundred and fifty people attended the funeral at Bowmansville Mennonite Church and over a hundred ate dinner at Martin Kilmers. After the travelers left again, everyone returned to their routine except Peter Brubacher. He was all alone, with the cold hard facts of life. He was sick and Amanda spent another night, staying there with him. Peter slowly recovered.

Soon after that, Aaron went to the hospital with a hemorrhoid problem. He stayed in the hospital for five days and during that time, Amanda helped her sisters divide their mother's clothes among them.

Amanda could not be everywhere! Travelers came overnight and her father needed her and so did her husband in the hospital. When Dan Martins came for the funeral, they stayed in PA for ten days. They took Amanda to see Aaron in the hospital and so did Uncle Joe Brenneman. Dan's boys Joe, Manass and Ephraim helped Dick strip tobacco and then they went together to the New Holland Sale Barn, just looking. When Martin Reed brought Aaron home from the hospital, Aaron wanted all of Amanda's attention. She stayed in his bedroom and did a little cleaning, as she' waited 'on him hand and foot!

After the Indiana travelers left again, Amanda hosted many visitors who came to see Aaron, sick in bed. A steer bloated, and they sent it to market quickly. Aaron recovered and so did Peter Brubacher.

In January, Aaron and Menno had ordered new kitchen cabinets at Wickes lumber company for Amanda's kitchen. She did not go along to order the cabinets, and they chose the most practical style available. The new sink and formica top arrived one week before mommy Brubacher's fu-

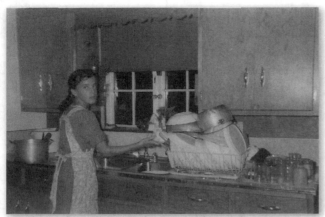

Martha washing dishes at the new kitchen sink.

the dirty dishwater out beside the front door where nothing grew. The spacious cabinets had more room for organizing, and it had one row of drawers. The new kitchen was simply grand, even if it was less than eight long, due to limited space. Washing dishes for a big family, three times a day, was still the same old drag. Dirty dishes came around much too often, and arguing about turns was a lot more fun than doing dishes. Taking turns among so many girls became so complicated, that they solved the problem by taping a piece of paper inside the new cabinet door where everyone signed their name for credit after washing and drying the dishes.

Among themselves, the girls made a law that whoever washes dishes and catches up may quit. Whoever cleared the table and did not bring the dishes to the sink fast enough had to finish washing the rest of the dirty dishes. Perhaps next time she would not be so pokey. That did not happen very often but made the dishes disappear much faster while racing. With enough dried up kettles and pans, they had no chance to catch up, but the chant often rang,"Voss evers deah net rivvoh bring-ut missuh deah sellvot vesh-uh! [What ever you don't bring over you have to wash by yourself!]

After baking pies and cakes and making pudding with surplus milk, the dishes piled up into a mountain. That was when Amanda brought out her big metal tray and set it on the kitchen table. With a dishpan of warm soapy water, two girls washed dishes at two different places and several girls dried dishes, hoping to finish faster.

1960 proved to be a busy year all around. Sarah Ann went to Rutts furniture for a new couch and chair for her parlor. She spent two weeks traveling to Canada in June and two months later Walter and Pete went for a one-week stay. Later the boys went clamming to Delaware Bay, and waterskiing at Perryville. Amanda appreciated when they brought home some fish to eat. Pete made"au-shpruch" [application to join church] and for every one of their children, that was a bright spot to Aaron and Amanda, worth recording in their diary.

Aaron came home with 500 tomato plants and he helped set them with the tobacco planter. He enjoyed tomatoes! He also came home with 600 celery plants, and helped to plant them. He excelled in buying and planting, but when it came to weeding, harvesting and preserving, he had no idea how much hard work and management it took. As the celery grew, Dick helped Amanda mulch and blanch it. They shared some with others. And tomatoes...they had more than they could eat and canned many gallons for winter. Aaron liked chunky pieces of tomato in his tomato soup. The old-fashioned kinds of tomatoes did not yield as many bushels as the modern varieties. With fifty heads of cabbage, Amanda canned sixty quarts of sour- kraut. Preserving food was a way of life she learned from her parents, a common necessity.

She had her sons bring in some saplings from the woods that she used as beanpoles in the garden. Amanda's garden simply was not complete without string beans climbing up the poles.

Amanda seeded marigolds, zinnias and calendula seeds in her early garden and transplanted them into her flowerbeds in late springtime. She took time out to plant the dahlia flower roots that she had saved over winter. They stored just fine in the cellar, and she had a joy in watching the flowers unfold perfectly, as a remembrance from her sister, and a miracle sent from heaven. She took a bouquet of cut flowers along to visit the sick and injured, every chance she had.

Anytime Amanda smelled a whiff of marigolds years ago, while working in the house, she knew Louise was at them again. As a young child, Louise delighted in dissecting the pretty flowers and playing with the petals.

When Aaron and Amanda needed time to themselves, they found the perfect spot while slowly driving in the horse and carriage. On a Sunday evening, they took Louise to work for Frank Hoover's, Irene to Aden Oberholtzer's, and Lydia to Aunt Lydia. Sometimes they made that run on a Monday morning, and on the way home, they could discuss any topic little ears should not hear.

Peter Brubacher had no desire to do his own housekeeping, and at the age of 80, he did not try to find another wife. He was ready to quit also and move on to heaven… to his wife and his sons. "This world is not my home, I'm just passing through". However, his passport was not yet sealed and he had to wait.

After much thought and prayer, he sold his small farm and most of his belongings, and lived with his children, taking turns at each place six weeks at a time. He had eight years to wait yet on earth, eighteen years beyond man's allotted time of three score years and ten, and he had much time to think. Why was he here? Why did life turn out like this? Hindsight was 20-20 and everyone only had one chance in life. Once to live and once to die!

When Peter came to stay at Aarons for six weeks at a time, Amanda tried to keep things orderly and a bit quieter. Peter talked very little, except to Amanda, and the children did not bother asking him any questions. They were not interested in discussing distant relatives from Michigan or Canada. Peter remained a Canadian citizen, even if he spent less than one fourth of his life there. He was an alien resident, and that did not matter.

All his life, after a hard days' work of farming in Michigan, Peter liked best of all, to sit on a rocking chair and smoke his pipe. That remained as his favorite hobby! No one knew smoking to be a bad habit. After carefully tamping tobacco in his pipe, he lifted his left foot and struck a match across the bottom of his shoe, to light the match. Slowly he lit the pipe and puffed away, while tapping his foot on the floor, with nothing more to do, as the clock kept ticking and his grandchildren played around him.

Over the years, he tried his best and lived a good life, but deep thinking appeared sobering.

Things could have been different in May City Iowa. That was where he should have settled and stayed. Seeing the Michigan church dissolve with all his roots still there, was a shock from which he never quite recovered. He had tried so hard to stay there …. And Joshua…? Oh, Joshua… it hurt too much to think!

Yet, in thinking back, Peter did what was best for his family. The Funk church group in Michigan where he might have joined, had lost all the conservative standards that Peter wished to keep, they even allowed such things as divorce and remarriage, with cut hair and slacks and TV and all…Peter contentedly knew he tried his best! Why does every church that loses the prayer veil always lose the plainly taught message of God first… then Christ… man…woman…in that order, and no divorce?

Aaron's children in their childish ways had no idea what all might be going through Peter's mind… thoughts of reminiscing. They were too young to appreciate history. Peter was not a talkative person like Aaron, and the children ignored him, doing what children do with bumping noises and bouncing with ambition. Amanda requested, "Please respect Grandpa with decently combed hair, and not so much noise."

Aaron and Dawdy Brubacher were opposites in temperament, and Peter had the habit of being seated last at the table. Therefore, any time when Aaron came in to eat, in a hurry to go somewhere, Peter tried his patience, of which he did not have enough. Dawdy Brubacher waited until last to sit down at the table and then he jerked his chair forward three times rather slowly, edging closer to the table, before anyone said their prayers.

Amanda made mental notes and verbal comments, that when she is no longer able to work she would not want to keep people waiting. Always being last even irritated her. But Amanda saw a different man than what her children did. Peter was her kind father who worked hard in Michigan, only to give up all those efforts and dreams, after starting from scratch. He lost three infant sons in MI and one son in wartime and maybe he saw some things that should have been done differently. Peter was poor all his life, and now penniless also. He never really got ahead in life, but when it came to things like faith, love, peace, patience, meekness and temperance, he was richly blessed. Especially temperance and the temperance he taught to Amanda, helped Aaron and his 15 children. Amanda often stressed temperance in all things!

The Brubacher name was among those steadfast Christians that endured Anabaptist suffering, and it was not just something to be ashamed of when Aaron and Amanda's children wrote out their middle name as Brubacher. Classmates wrote short feminine names, not Brubacher!

Aaron and Amanda's children could have asked Peter many things about his past, even if he mumbled and talked softly. They bought furniture and planned weddings, while younger ones played rough and practiced broad jumps in -doors. Amanda was very busy in many ways. She loved her father and did all she could to accommodate him. The children did not understand much about their 86-year-old grandfather and mostly just treated him like a guest or a stranger. Mail arrived in the mailbox for AM Shirk and PM Brubacher. (Morning-evening)

Amanda regularly cooked for eighteen people without complaining. The long and full table had seven people crowded on each side, with the benches, and chairs packed as tight as possible.

When no more chairs fit into the row, three people shared two chairs, by one person straddling across the gap between the chairs, at suppertime when everyone came home. They couldn't all have room to eat with two hands and kept the left hand down. Irene remembered eating with her left hand to irritate Louise, but no one was allowed to squabble.

Daniel had a special friend, and dated Edna Horst of Lebanon County, the only child of Michael and Mary Horst. Daniels sisters and brothers could hardly comprehend the life of an only child. No sisters to confide with and no brothers to fix things, how lonely that might be? Perhaps the table would be quieter, with plenty of room and no limit on how much ice cream a person may have, but my, what all else would be missing?

Daniel brought Edna along to Aaron's, for a family picnic in the woods, roasting hot dogs over a fire. They enjoyed ground cherry pie for dessert. Edna enjoyed such a huge family picnic, and it was nice to see all of Daniel's brothers and sisters together.

25

Packing Lunches

Amanda was the last one to bed at night, and the first one up in the morning. With kindling and kerosene, she tried to coax some heat out of the cast-iron kitchen range that went out at night. Aaron headed to the barn for the morning chores of watering horses, feeding steers and milking the cow. When he returned with a bucket of warm milk, he wanted breakfast ready, but many times, he had to wait on the stove, especially when the air hung heavy and the chimney was cold. With a lack of patience, he recommended Amanda should lift the stove-lid off the stovetop and set the black pen directly on the flames, but Amanda preferred to keep all that soot out of her dishwater when cleaning the pan. It simply took patience to fry eggs!

Packing ten lunches in the morning, took a lot more management than cooking for ten people at the table. Amanda worked to manage enough ready to eat food, ready to drop into lunches. A row of girls packed lunches in an assembly line fashion. While one did all the sandwiches, another one wrapped up cake in wax paper or empty bread wrappers, and another girl, filled the jars with canned peaches. While looking around and deciding what to put in next, the girls chanted, "Sandwich, jar, cake/bun, apple and pretzels."

Before plastic bags, Amanda bought Cut-Rite wax paper. Punched in the waxed paper at the end of each roll, it said 'Time to reorder Cut Rite', and she reordered often. She carefully saved all the clear bread wrappers and reused them. The bakery had a way of printing words on a removable band inside each wrapped loaf. Where the cellophane ends met, tacky yellow 'glue' secured each wrapper. Dick did not like mustard and he threw away every wrapper that had a spot of yellow on the edge, un-til Amanda wondered why he is wasting so many wrappers. She wanted him to return each one for wiping and reusing.

The big boys carried lunches to work and so did the girls in the factory. A gallon of fruit a day barely reached. Amanda and her helpers baked a tremendous amount of cakes, pies and cookies. They had no recipes for bars and seldom made brownies. Flop cakes, soggy in the middle, disappeared as fast as the perfect ones, and after every family member ate one piece, the cake vanished. When Aaron came home from Bowmansville with day -old bakery items, they saved the best for lunches.

Amanda had her hands full trying to get everyone out the door promptly on schedule. The factory workers left first, and then the children headed to school in a flurry. The bus driver would not wait, and the factory workers must be prompt, to punch in their time cards. One morning the big girls soon returned, because Irene forgot her covering. They drove one-mile before anyone noticed!

The schoolgirls did not go to school without opening long pigtails, and braiding hair, so occasionally one girl combed the next girl, while that one combed the next girl. It was hard starting their own pigtails on the back of the head where they could not see. Many times Amanda heard, "Mom, I can't find my….mittens… book…. boots… ."Then, Ah…, peacefully, she relaxed again!

Amanda learned to peel potatoes ahead of time, because she had no burners to turn on high. She cooked on the kitchen range that supplied the heat for the house, and the heat to warm the irons for ironing and the water in the teakettle.

Sometimes the potatoes were not quite soft enough for mashed potatoes, a special treat. To mash the potatoes, Amanda squashed them with a handheld masher, than added milk and butter, and pounded some more with the wooden handled masher. It took longer to make potatoes, than it did to make the meat, because the meat was canned and ready cooked. When Aaron and Amanda spent long hours and many days with butchering and meat canning, they worked ahead, because all that canned meat was ready to heat and serve. Fresh meat on butchering day was the best meat available and second best, was the home canned meat. Other then smoked bologna and cured ham and bacon that was all they had. In summer time, they ate more vegetables in season and ate fresh fish sometimes and lots of homegrown chickens.

When the schoolchildren returned, everyone changed into everyday clothes. "Someone better bring in the wash soon, and please fill the wood box, I need some now," said Amanda. She had folded diapers as soon as they dried, because she needed the wash line space, and the diapers should not wrinkle into a pile. "Please don't wrinkle the Sunday shirts into that laundry pile, and hang up the dresses right away. The last wash must come in before the sun goes down, or the laundry will get damp," said Amanda. "Won't one of you girls bake a cake because the oven is the right temperature now?"

Everyone living at home gathered around the table for supper. After the last person sat down, Aaron bowed his head and all the others followed. They said a silent prayer with thankful hearts. Little children turned their eyeballs to the corner of their eyes, looking for a signal when the prayer was finished. A deep breath from Aaron signaled, Amen! Everyone dug in and helped themselves, passing dishes to the left. No one was greedy, making sure there was enough to go around, before taking seconds. Amanda often waited for last when anything looked like it might not reach.

She did not have a 'favorite' piece of chicken, but most often, Amanda chose the back or the neckpiece because all the others might overlook some scraps of meat that remained hidden in the crevices. She used her thumbnail to neatly round out the meat in the curved bones. She ate the kidneys, and enjoyed every chewable piece, even the cartilage of young soft bones. If anyone else had

the chicken back on their plate, she scoured the bones for tid- bits of meat, before tossing the bones out to the cats.

Perhaps her parents taught all of their children such necessities during the Great Depression when they had growing children to feed. Amanda tried her best to pass on the art of skimping on self, and giving to others. She did not consider taking a drumstick or a thigh off the chicken platter until everyone had seconds. Amanda most often chose white meat because she saw it was everyone else's least favorite choice.

Supper was a lively time, with many discussions, and happy memories. Every now and then, when children squabbled or got out of hand, Aaron scolded, "sell lunked!" (Meaning, that is enough!), and that settled things down.

Cleaning up after every meal was quite a chore. Amid some complaining, and squabbling about turns, someone asked, "Mom did you have to wash this many dishes when you were young?""No." Amanda said, "no one in Michigan owned this many dishes. We washed the pudding kettle before we could cook the potatoes. Our kitchen was small, and so were the sink and the table. Our entire family numbered half as much as this one. We certainly do have a lot to be thankful for. I remember the three little brothers buried in Michigan. My grandmother always said," Lee-vuh full vee la-ah!"[Rather full then empty!] She saw times when the shelves and cupboards were too empty. What would that be like?"

The girls kept on scrubbing dishes, even some left over from noontime, plus the dried-up canning jars.

Amanda met many challenging days when things went wrong. Children spilled things, wasted things and broke things. Fifteen children ruined many things while trying out scissors. Four-year-old girls cut hair and one cut-off a pigtail from a younger sister. Winters indoors could be long! Amanda had good nerves and much patience, but sometimes even that was taxed to the limit. When the noise and commotion became almost unbearable, Amanda said in an empty threat, "I guess I'll run away!" Sometimes that quieted things down, but Lydia was worried. At her young age, she knew the family could not go on without a mother! What was a mother worth? No one knew, and neither did she want to find out! They all took her for granted! She was there for all the important things, as well as all the little hurts, and for cleaning up messes.

Upstairs in the girl's bedroom set a chamber bucket for nighttime use, because the outhouse was far away in the dark. No one was supposed to use the pot regularly, and who ever used it, was supposed to empty it. Like many other things in life, "Miss Nobody" used it, until the pot smelled strongly like ammonia. Sometimes the girls said, "Last one down must bring the pot", as everyone scrambled to avoid being last. On one such occasion, a child accidentally dropped the agate bucket and it tumbled down the stairs splattering its messy contents all the way.

Amanda showed keen disappointment, as the brittle white agate chipped and popped, causing a small hole in the bucket. Guess who cleaned up the mess?

Amanda didn't run away, no matter what! Before using the pot again, she mended the holes with tiny bolts and nuts with washers, called "mend-its", made for such agate-mending purposes. The canner bottom had an assortment of such little mended spots, and it didn't matter so much if a few drips leaked out onto the stove, but for the chamber bucket, any leak did matter, and even a few drips were too much. She would order a new one soon. Most of the time, mended spots on agate, added several more years of wear without a problem. Amanda usually had a washable rug beneath the chamber bucket

Amid extra noise and people everywhere, Lydia complained, "Why do we have so many children?"Amanda promptly replied, "Which one don't we want?" Lydia did some deep thinking... she wanted everyone of her sisters. ..without a doubt. .. and her brothers. ..no matter how much Wesley teased. ..she did not want to part with any of them!

With seventeen people in one house, Amanda needed more drawers, but the crowded rooms had no more space for dressers. She used her ingenuity and the help of Walter's woodworking ability. She

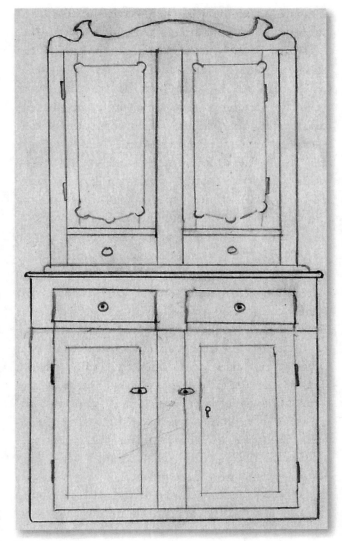

Upside-down cupboard

planned one "jelly cupboard" upside down on top of the other one. Walter questioned,""What about those upside-down drawers? "The top dresser originally had two small drawers along the top edge, and those drawers were now along the bottom." They will work just fine if we turn the drawers upside down from their original intention", said Amanda.

She saved the trim board along the back of one dresser and Walter placed that board along the front edge of the top dresser where he sawed off the legs sticking straight up. She refinished the entire project until it all looked as though it belonged that way. The upper section then consisted of two cabinet doors where she stashed her colorful assortment of prints and backs for making quilts.

Amanda used the [unnahsht savvasht shonk] or upside-down cupboard combination for another 50 years. Then the next generation bought the sturdy cupboard over auction.

Sometimes Aaron minded the extra noise with nobody listening to him. When he came into the house with something on his mind, he occasionally said, "News flashes, news flashes!" That was a sure way to get the attention he wanted, even if it had nothing to do with news. His demanding ways were embarrassing at times, especially among some that did not know him. Others understood his ways.

Aaron's big family got into the station wagon to go to Uncle Christian Kilmer's for supper. Dick, the oldest one along, complained, "It's too full in here. How many are there anyway?" After taking a headcount, one turned up missing! Irene was not along!

Instead of turning around, the family went on to Christians and unloaded the station wagon. Then Dick and a few sisters turned around and went home to look for Irene. They found her upstairs sleeping in her own bed with a slight headache, trying to get some rest, but she went along. Instead of twelve people in the station wagon, on the way home there were thirteen.

Before Rose Anna started to first grade, her future teacher drove in the lane unannounced. Miss Kutz surprised them on a summer day and Rose Anna was not combed, so she ran to hide, not knowing whom the stranger might be. Mary soon found Rose Anna and brushed back her hair. Miss Kutz gave Rose Anna a Golden book to keep, and sat beside Rose Anna on the couch to get acquainted. She certainly made a lasting impression and Rose Anna cherished her book. Fifty years later, she still had the Golden book and the vivid memories.

Mandy had no problem with younger children messing up her things, and getting in her way, because she was last. She could never change that fact. She had to wait two whole years to start school after RoseAnna did, and that was long! She said, "Mom why didn't you get me first?" Amanda said, "Someone had to be last!" Everyone took turns being last in a game, but none of her brothers and sisters could take turns with Mandy, being

last in the family. She wished for a younger sister or brother many times, and it seemed like her parents never had a baby in the house.

∽

After one half year at the hat factory, Daniel got a job at Terramatic in Terrehill and earned $1.30 an hour. Then he got a better job at a machine shop in Reamstown, known as Craftwell, owned by Victor Kingswell, who came from Reading, England. While earning $2.00 an hour, Daniel eagerly learned a mechanical trade. He greatly enjoyed this type of metalwork for 2 ½ years.

Sarah Ann joined many other Mennonite girls working at the Walter W. Moyer Company. With a one-hour lunch break, the girls found all sorts of entertainment. Sometimes they played baseball on a crude diamond on the other side of the Cocalico-Creek, next to the factory. Often they walked to the center of Ephrata, shopping in many different stores. The factory had no air conditioning, so it got exceedingly warm with many sewing machines running close to the low hanging electric lights above their heads. Eight-hour days in the factory were tiring.

While working there, Sarah Ann tasted a new food…called pizza! Someone treated with pizza for a birthday at Moyers, and Sarah Ann was impressed. After thinking it over, she wanted to try the new food on her brothers and sisters at home. She bought a box of Chef Boyardee pizza mix, and carefully followed the directions. It smelled strange, and not one of them liked it at the supper table. Someone said, "It looks like vomit", and it took years before anyone wanted more pizza. They did not eat at restaurant and neither did most other people. None of them barbecued meat over open flames and considered slightly rare meat unfit to eat. They refused to eat fat. Yuck.

Aaron had a box of colorful leg bands for labeling chickens because they all looked alike. He color-coded the younger ones from the older hens. The boys sneaked some of those rings and put them on the bicycle spokes for style. The girls played with them also and connected the rings as beads.

Amanda put a string of them in her Sunday diaper bag to entertain a baby. Aaron and Amanda could still use the durable plastic bands on the hens later, as needed.

Any one that sold eggs to a hatchery did not wash the eggs first. If any dirt clung to the egg, they removed it with fine sand paper. Clean bedding in the nesting boxes eliminated most of the scrubbing.

All the farmers in the neighborhood knew about DDT and they commonly used it as the recommended way to eradicate disease. It worked, but it caused environmental problems and the government outlawed it in later years. More things changed and prices kept dropping until even those farmers with good management could no longer turn a profit. They quit selling eggs and just kept some hens for their own use.

One Saturday at noon, Aaron's family was waiting for the big boys to come home from work. The younger children were impatient and hungry, as they watched out the lane for the boys to come home. Rose Anna said, "Dad, I see smoke up in the woods on the other side of the turnpike!"

"Smoke?" Said Aaron in a great concern, "I better see what's going on!" With that, he grabbed his coat and headed towards the Turnpike. Aaron owned a small acreage of woodland over there, and it was burning. On their way home from work, his boys had seen the smoke first and went to fight the fire. Using their jackets, Walter, Pete and Dick beat out the flames!

They had no time to go for help, as they desperately worked with all they had. They were exhausted, hot and tired, but they won the battle as the flames died down. No one ever figured out what started the fire, but the boys arrived just in time, saving a large area of deep woods without roads for fire trucks. Dinner was nearly forgotten, and everyone was thankful for the black, smoky faced boys, cleaning up at the sink. Their teeth and the whites of their eyes shone extra bright, almost like Negroes.

Aaron and Amanda never called the fire engines to their farm, but one morning it was close enough. When Lydia awoke, she went downstairs earlier than usual, and she was astonished to see the stovepipe red-hot with her parents both working around the stove. Amanda dipped rags into a bucket of water and they held them against the stovepipe. The heat from fire roaring up the chimney created steaming rags and Lydia was scared! "Stay back, Lydia!" Amanda said. When the fire calmed down, Aaron said to Lydia, "that was a chimney fire."

One other time, they nearly needed a fire engine, when some bedding started smoking against the bare stovepipe upstairs. The exposed stovepipe helped warm up the upstairs. When Mandy opened the stairway door she smelled smoke. Amanda took one glance at the thick smoke and said,"Quick run out to the stripping room and tell Dad to come!"Amanda tossed some covers out the window and Dick helped Aaron carry a smoking mattress down the stairs and out the door. No one was hurt! The guardian angels had many a busy day around that farm.

Helicopters

"Whoomp —whoomp-whoomp the sound of low flying helicopters were nothing new, but these three flew rather low and the army was coming! "Let's shoot at them," Reuben and Benny agreed. With that, the brothers raised their weapons and shouted, "Boom! Boom! Boom!" To their great surprise, two helicopters promptly descended! The boys were innocently walking home from Uncle

Elias's and each of them held a cornstalk as a pretend gun, but sudden fear and terror gripped their young hearts as they worried 'Did the pilot think we had real guns? Are they coming to arrest us?" With pounding hearts, both boys raced home as fast as they could. They panicked and hid, afraid of what might happen next. They were dumbfounded and shaking with fright! On the side of each helicopter, it plainly said U S Army.

Aaron and Amanda were at Martin Kilmer's for Sunday dinner, and Daniel was at home taking a nap on a quiet Sunday afternoon. On their way home, Aaron and Amanda noticed the low flying helicopters. When they got closer to home, they saw that two of them landed in Jesse's field! How exciting! Why ever did the helicopters land there? In no time, they joined the growing crowd of neighbors gathered around both helicopters.

The extra loud noise of the choppers awoke Daniel from his nap, and when he looked out the window, he was astonished at what he saw at Jesse. "I wonder if they are the same ones we saw the other day, "he thought. On Friday, Daniel and Pete noticed three orange army helicopters flying west, but what might the army want at Jesse?

It did not take long to learn what happened, as the pilot explained, 'I made a forced landing because my warning lights indicated mechanical problems. Yes, these are the same helicopters that flew over on Friday, headed west from Willow Grove near Philadelphia, to Middletown, close to Harrisburg."

The neighborhood children gathered excitedly. Most of the older ones had a chance to crawl inside and sit in the pilot's seat. Lydia would have liked to see the inside also, but she was classed as being "too little". The second helicopter soon left, after checking out the problem.

Two young boys still scared and hiding missed all the excitement on their own farm, as neighbors gathered in their hayfield, staring in amazement! "The boys remained hidden in the barn where no one found them. Many thoughts tumbled through their young minds."What does a jail look like and how long could they keep us? Would people come, visit us, and give us food? What would our friends say? Our parents told us to never point a gun at anybody! I am hungry; do you think the rest are eating without us? They know we did not have guns, but what about those army people? " It took long hours before Reuben and Benny realized that no one tried to find them and they were free!

A newspaper reporter picked up their story and wrote," Two boys headed for parts unknown". The New Holland Clarion, later picked up the story and put it in the Old Oaken Bucket column, somewhat like a comic strip.

A tractor-trailer truck came to load the stranded helicopter. Jesse offered to help with his caterpillar tractor, but they preferred manpower, pulling on the ropes to prevent scratching the paint job, or denting the metal. Many men and boys volunteered to pull. The army crew spent time removing the propeller, so the loaded helicopter would fit underneath the bridges.

In the meantime, Aaron invited the pilot to his house to stay, but he could not leave his craft. Therefore, Aaron brought food and provisions out to him. After loading the helicopter, all the excitement died down, and Aaron took the pilot to Harrisburg, which the pilot greatly appreciated. Several years later the pilot and his wife came back to visit Aaron and Amanda.

Electricity

After changing churches, Aaron and Amanda agreed they both wanted electricity on the farm. No close neighbors had electric. The utility company required Aaron to pay for one whole mile of electric poles and wires. Construction and wiring the house, took a while, but it was a big event when it finally happened. The flip of a switch on the wall, lit the entire room… like a miracle! The light was almost as bright as daylight and they no longer needed the smoky kerosene lamps.

A shiny new electric iron replaced the old heavy sad- irons, known for scorching clothes, especially among beginners. Aarons family marveled at the texture and flavor of what real toast tasted like, besides the occasional bread toasted over open flames, or the slices of bread that Amanda laid flat on top of the cast-iron range. Making toast was quick and easy!

A new electric refrigerator replaced the kerosene one, and Amanda no longer had dark corners inside the refrigerator, because even the refrigerator had a light inside. A second hand electric range accompanied the big iron kitchen range. No longer did they heat the entire house when canning over summertime and the dependable oven temperature was always just right for baking. Come wintertime, Amanda still preferred the heavy kitchen range, but over summertime, they removed the stovepipe and shoved the stove against the wall for two feet of more living space towards the center of the room. Amanda cut a piece of linoleum to fit the stove top and then she used that stove as counter space until the geese started flying south and the children returned to school. A cozy wood fire warmed the house and turned it into a home with all the slow-cooking and baking smells.

Among the major changes was the luxury of a hot water heater! The water pipes in the old kitchen range had a way of plugging up with mineral deposits, and one teakettle heated water for the big family. They moved the galvanized washtub down in the basement to stay there. They had more privacy among growing children that way; and they could have all the hot water they wanted with the new water heater. They simply tipped the big oval tub on its side and the dirty water swirled down the drain. Wasting warm water seemed extravagant and several children still used the same water until it looked dirty.

A whole year went by, and Amanda still did not own an electric mixer, so Sarah Ann bought one with her own money and gave it to Amanda. She wanted to try a mixer such as her friends used. Amanda was not in a hurry to get rid of her old ways. "What if the electric goes off?" she said. They moved the old kitchen range to the summerhouse, and Amanda kept some kerosene lamps and old irons just in case.

The electric freezer rated higher than all the smaller gadgets. The freezer saved a tremendous amount of canning in the heat of summer. Peas and corn were nearly as good as fresh ones and none of them spoiled. Frozen strawberries stayed red and gone were the rubbery brown canned ones. Yes, the freezer was just all right! On butchering day, Amanda finished quickly by freezing the meat. She still preferred to can some beef for short notice meals and for any travelers that arrived unexpectedly. The school children put the nicest biggest apple in the freezer overnight to make a nice crisp gift for their teacher the next day. Oh! What a surprise on them.

The biggest improvement of electricity was the wonderful electric Maytag wringer washer. One bare light bulb lit the entire damp dark cellar by one simple jerk on a string. That alone was a huge improvement in the dark basement, but gone now was the polluting smoke and the noise of the gas engine. The electric motor on the washer ran so quietly that two people could hear each other talk while washing, and it never ran out of gas before completing the last load. Best of all, Amanda could promptly start the washer without a man's help. All she did was plug it in!

Amanda used her Singer treadle sewing machine two more years without feeling deprived. Then she came home from an auction with a Necchi electric sewing machine, with a new-fangled zigzag stitch, which she appreciated. She used it for mending and reinforcing seams. The zigzag stitch even kept seams from fraying! She still used the treadle sewing machine regularly for straight sewing.

Without a shortage of ice in the freezer, the children could make ice cream anytime of the year when they felt like it. Aaron put pans of water in the freezer to share with several neighbors. Titus came and fetched some in summertime.

The downside to the freezer was the fact that they could now buy ice cream on sale at the store, and it was not long until they preferred the smoothness of bought ice cream. A big new store opened in Shillington, called Two Guys, and sometimes they had ice cream on advertised special for $.29 a half gallon. On the way home from Reading, they stopped there and bought a pile of it. IGA opened in Terre Hill and they ran specials on ice cream. It was smoother, creamier and always ready to serve. After a while, Aarons seldom used that hand cranked White Mountain ice cream freezer.

Why bother? It was hard to explain, but something special was lost in the anticipation of how good that ice cream was going to be, no matter what.

In the summer of 1959, Amanda needed surgery to repair a cystocele and a rectocele. At the same time, Sarah Ann had planned a trip out west with some girls, including Maggie Burkholder and some other friends. Sarah Ann considered canceling her trip, but her mother encouraged her to go. Amanda said, "after all the hard work you did at home, tied down over the years, you deserve to go traveling with your friends. "Amanda planned to be in and out of the hospital in a short time, and Sarah Ann went!

Nearly 14 years old, Ruth took charge of the home, while Rhoda worked as a hired girl. Martha age 12 helped Ruth manage, while Mary and Louise worked away. Lydia spent the summer with Aunt Lydia, leaving Irene, Wesley, RoseAnna and Mandy at home. Baby Mandy was three years old and no longer in diapers.

Ruth and Martha learned in a hurry, about all the detailed things a mother does. They were in charge of gathering the wash, sorting, washing and drying it. (Thankfully, they used an electric washing machine). At the table, they set 7 plates for dinner, and 10 for supper when three big boys came home from work. Packing lunches looked easy when Amanda told them what to put in, but not when they had to manage preparing things, ready to eat.

One week turned into two, and then lengthened into three long weeks because Amanda had complications. She stayed in the hospital longer than expected. She had a hysterectomy, and she struggled emotionally to sign for such a surgery. Amanda later admitted that it took her several years to recover from the fact that she would never hold another new baby of her own. She loved them all!

Ruth and Martha tried putting asparagus int he freezer raw and that did not work. It turned dark and they threw it out. The girls learned about blanching and freezing vegetables for their big new freezer, but they worried about their mother. Aaron's concern showed very much! He said, "Mom is seriously sick and we just don't know if she can get well!" She has problems with getting off a catheter.

Aaron often went to the hospital to see Amanda,. The girls at home thought things were tough, but Amanda had it worse. She missed her fifteen children and knew they needed her. Their seven children under the age of twelve were not allowed in a hospital beyond the waiting room. Amanda begged to see them and Aaron got permission to bring some along. Amanda walked to the second floor balcony and waved at the children but they could not talk across such a distance. Their mother looked sick in her robe and strangely wore pigtails for comfort, without hairpins poking her. She tried to tell them to obey their sisters until she returns. *Sint shay!* (Be nice!)

One time Aaron took along twelve year old Martha. Her pale mother discussed details about housekeeping and wished to go home. Before leaving, Carmi Stauffer, the custodian, gave Aaron a tour of the Ephrata Hospital. "This room is the laundry," he said. They saw huge rollers that pressed the linens and bedding. Then he led them to a dark basement room and snapped on the light. Martha did not like what she saw. Hanging from the ceiling were rows of long glass tubes about four inches thick, filled with blood in assorted shades of dark red. It nearly grossed her out! "This is the blood bank," said Carmi.

Aaron was in the hospital many times, but this was a first for Amanda. She survived the flu epidemic in 1918, when her mother nearly died. She did not get scarlet fever when she was quarantined and helping the sick. She had varicose veins and suffered many pains over the years, but she suffered in silence. She had a good immune system and everyone took her for granted!

The girls could fill in as temporary help, but what would ever happen without a mother? It was hard to comprehend what she all worked without complaining. They prayed silently, "Dear God, please heal our mother, we need her very much."Amanda gradually recovered, and everyone rejoiced when she came home from the hospital. A mother would be hard to replace!

In December of 1960, Amanda had a gall bladder problem. She invited the Brubacher's for Christmas dinner and Aaron fetched Doddy Brubacher and Eli Stauffers because the distance was too great for a horse. After the company all went home, Amanda went to bed, but she did not sleep all night long due to pain. Dr, Bender came out in the morning and put Amanda on a liquid diet and bed-rest. The next day Aaron took her for X-rays and Amanda cut out a robe for herself, just in case she needed surgery. She completed the robe and that night she had a gall spell and went to the hospital in the middle of the night. The doctor removed her gall bladder and she stayed in the hospital a full week and then spent time recovering at home. Lydi-Jess-sey understood and came to help catch up on necessary mending. None of the children realized how much a mother does in a day until they did the regular housework, packed a long row of lunch boxes and helped butcher a pig. Amanda rested at home, but she still supervised all she could.

Pete's Deer

Aaron's children never saw their father shoot a gun. His brothers enjoyed hunting and shot small game on his farm, which Amanda gladly served. Aaron's children learned about hunting from their uncles. The only time Aaron had a need for a gun, was on butchering day, and even then, he asked his brothers to do the shooting.

Whenever the boys brought in a gun to put it away, Aaron asked, "Is a shell in that gun?"Please be careful!" Aaron repeated many times that, "the two most dangerous things on the farm, are the "empty" gun and the "tame" bull". He liked neither!

In younger years, Dick asked, "Mom, why is Dad leading our cow over to Jesse's?"Amanda had a ready reply and brushed it off with, "Don't you think a cow likes to meet other cows sometimes?"Aaron did not want a bull on the farm.

At the age of 17, Pete was the first one in Aaron's family to shoot a deer. He traveled 50 miles north to the Blue Mountains, and he made exciting headlines at home! He posed for pictures with the 130 pound, six-point buck, tied across his car fender. The younger children all around him marveled at the nearly exotic animal that he brought home for them to eat. Deer were scarce in Lancaster County! His brothers helped him hang the

deer and three days later, they skinned and butchered it. Three weeks later, Titus came to help Pete mount the deer head. Uncle Titus was a self-taught taxidermist, with a den of mounted animals in his living room, beside their impressive cuckoo clock. Children stared in amazement!

Every now and then people saw deer locally, especially at night. Aaron's boys set up a prank at the end of Jesse's road at the stop sign. At that spot, any headlights shone across the Turnpike into the brush of an old fence line. Walter and Pete went out around and through the brush, about a mile and arranged reflector tape to look like deer eyes, exactly where the headlights shown at night. It appeared like three deer came out each night, and motorists took notice of these "deer". More and more, people spotlighted them, but they never moved. Any person that went out around the Turnpike to this secluded spot could not find any deer.

Walter and Pete enjoyed the mounting excitement of listening to other's opinions and stories, about the three deer that came out every night. Eventually, the truth leaked out.

26

Walter and Pete both quit working at Victor Weaver when they had the opportunity to help their friends; Ivan High and David Hurst unload lumber at Wickes Lumber Company. When they needed more help, the boss asked "Don't you have any younger brothers that could work?" That is how Ed High and Dick joined the crew. Dick started working before he turned 16, and he could stop worrying that he would never get a job without a high school education. Dick liked to work.

The boys worked for Walter D Wolfe, who was a subcontractor in charge of unloading train cars at Wickes. He also owned a business of Wolf Moving and Storage. When he needed help in moving furniture and such, he had those strong able farm boys to load and unload his moving vans.

At home at the supper table, Aaron's boys discussed how they helped move a huge piano from one end of town to the other. The piano came into the house through the upstairs window and that was the only way out. Dick helped lay a long heavy plank on the flat house-roof. One end extended about 30"beyond the roof edge and they weighted down the other end with heavy sandbags. They removed window sashes from the windows. After wrapping the piano in padding and a harness of strong ropes, they used a pulley chained 4" near the end of the plank. Dick carefully fed rope to the pulley after all the others managed to shove the piano out the window. The rope looped through a hook on the truck bumper and Dick hung on the rope rather nervously as he watched the plank bend with the weight of the piano. The whole thing could splat onto the ground from that third story window. But it worked!

At another moving place, the workers needed to hurry. "Get all these things moved out of here before my husband comes home, because I am leaving him" she said. That day Aarons boys came home with a detailed Lionel train set that had to go. It was a little boy's dream come true. Aaron's house was full, with no room to set up so many intricate pieces out of the reach of little hands. The boys' busy minds schemed a plan, and made a flat canopy of plywood above the boy's bed. Wickes sold 5X9 sheets of plywood for table tennis games, around Christmas time. The boys set to work trying out all the many pieces as the train looped around the tracks, over the trestle, and under the tunnels while puffing real clouds of smoke, past the trees and houses to the depot. Keeping it in working order became a challenge among company children and the hands of preschool children. The man that lost his train set never knew how many children stared in awe. The train set stayed there for eight years.

Walter Wolf was not a church going type, but more involved with wine and women. "Would some of you apostles go on this next job? "he asked. He saw these plain people had higher standards and he was pleased with their work. Eventually Walter Wolfe lost that job to Henry Brubaker.

Workers worked in teams to unload lumber. Dick enjoyed working with Ed High and appreciated how Ed offered to take the most undesirable job. Taking those first pieces of lumber out of a fully stacked train car meant crawling into tight spaces. In winter, that was a cold job and in the heat of the summer, they nearly fried under that dark tin. Half the time it was easier to work inside the train car and half the time, it was easier outside on the pile. Ed was a fine person to work with.

Occasionally the boys put in overtime-unloading train cars, and it happened several times that they spent the night there, after working late, grabbing some sleep, and then starting early the next morning again.

Aaron and Amanda considered Ascension Day a holiday, but Pete worked all that day at Wickes lumber company while Dick went fishing to Maryland, with a group of friends. Walter went to Walker Gordon dairies, and lost his wallet, including the whole week's pay of $80 cash, and his driver's license.

At Wickes, an announcement over the loud-speaker said, " Would one of the Shirk boys please answer the telephone?" After the second or third announcement, Ed High said,"Dick that means you, because Walter and Pete are not here right now."Dick panicked in a major way and said,"I can't, I never talked on a telephone!" Ed High encouraged Dick to try and told him. "You can do it !". Dick started off with his mind in a whirl, wondering to himself "what could be so important anyway?" As he got closer to the office, his heart beat faster and he sweated profusely! He nervously admitted, "I do not know how to answer a phone!"The secretary pressed the right button and gave him the receiver but Dick could not hear. She noticed he had the wrong end to his ear while saying "Hello. Hello" so she showed him how to turn the receiver end for end. He could hardly hear among the noise, and he did not know to hold one ear shut to hear more clearly. "What? What did you say?" After awhile Dick got the message. Adin Kilmer wanted the boys to bring some building materials along home from work. Dick survived the ordeal, but he was wet sweated from all the stress and ashamed that he was so dumb. He was almost 16 years old!

On a different occasion, Amanda answered the phone at home and a stranger asked to speak to Paul or Richard. 'I am sorry, "Amanda said, " You must have the wrong number." Before hanging up, she caught on that it was a business call about the boy's jobs at the lumber company, and they wanted Pete or Dick.

A bonus from working at Wickes Lumber Company was free scrap lumber. The car trunk could not haul the big pieces, so the boys cut those choice pieces in half with a handsaw until everything fit into the trunk. The generous yard foreman appreciated when the boys took along the scraps; otherwise, they returned it to the sender. Before Walter got married, he bought a 56 Dodge pickup. That is when they could haul nicer lumber home.

Elias and Titus filled in as needed at Wickes, and Jesse's boys helped for a short time. They had some good times out in their break room and even moved in a refrigerator. They wrote Names and dates inside boxcars to see how long it went until the cars come back. That took long. To move empty train cars the workers climbed on top of them to release the brake and then used a hand jack like a pry bar to move the wheels a few inches at a time.

Walter and Pete learned where everything belonged in the lumberyard, and after a while, they quit working for Wolfe, and started as sales clerks for Wickes Lumber Company.

After bringing home a generous pile of scrap lumber, Walter designed his first house. It stood about eight foot tall, as a playhouse for his younger sisters, out under the apple tree. He asked Amanda for an old window, unused in the attic for nearly 20 years. Aaron removed that window when he added the new kitchen in 1945. Walter used that old window sideways. He purchased another window and the yellow pine flooring for a total of eight dollars and some cents. The barn siding needed some extra seams where the boards were not long enough. Some of the siding boards were too short because he cut them in half to fit in the car trunk.

Aaron and Amanda did not divide their love among fifteen children. Love kept right on multiplying!. The little girls admired Walter's every move as he hammered and sawed. Amanda was pleased with Walter's creative talent and ambition to complete a playhouse. She knew she and her sisters certainly would have enjoyed such a luxury thirty years ago in Michigan. Aaron and Amanda's children used the playhouse so regularly that Amanda did not want Walter to take it along when he married and left home.

Children pretended to cook and keep house while keeping order with crying dollies. Irene, Lydia, RoseAnna and Mandy spent a lot of time in the playhouse. Glass liners from zinc jar lids became plates for dolls, and some things were treasures

Wesley's pony cart and notice the playhouse!

from the dump. Children collected seed heads from the kase bopplah also known as common mallow weeds. They ate the wedge shaped 'cheeses" for a snack and put some in jars for pretend canning. Not so long ago, came the train set, and now a mansion for the dolls. Amanda paid a little something to Walter, and the playhouse became a useful addition to the farm. Thank you Walter!

Daniel, Walter, Pete, and Dick all enjoyed working with wood. Dick cut and assembled a well-made bookshelf as a gift for his girlfriend, Ruth Zimmerman. Not many years later, Pete started building real houses, for real people.

By now, Ruth and Rhoda worked at the Walter W. Moyer Company and earned big pay. A $104 check, meant they earned $52 in one week, at the age of 17. Since they kept 10% of each paycheck, Aaron and Amanda were raking in nearly $100 a week from the twins.

Aaron and Amanda gave ninety percent of their money home to their parents until they were 20 years old, so that is how they did it for their own children. After the children reached 20 years of age, they paid rent, for staying at home. Twenty dollars a week covered all their room and board, including telephone, food and laundry.

Aaron and Amanda carefully tried to keep things fair from the oldest to the youngest. When

Wesley came along he thought that was rough, and so did his brothers. "How can a person make car payments and still have money for gas on the weekend", he questioned. As the boys grew up, they noticed they had better practice budgeting their money than the boys that were given a car from their parents, and spent money unnecessarily..

Amanda had her mind on several things, when one of the boys handed her some 'rent' money. When she opened the big brown wood stove to toss in a handful of paper trash, she astonishingly discovered she still held the trash and had tossed the money in the fire. She had a hard time accepting her mistake, and just couldn't believe it! Some melted coins ended up in the ash pan, as proof of what happened.

Aaron called this heftier brown coal/wood-stove combination a "glutz uffa" or (chunk stove) because it held large pieces of wood to bank the fire overnight. In the coldest part of winter, they made sure no pipes froze, by banking the stove with coal.

Louise hid behind that stove with a broken crayon and scribbled on the warm stovepipe. The crayon melted smoothly and puddled like paint, but the smell of the smoking stovepipe tattled on her and spoiled the fun. She had to stop!

On a cold winter's night, RoseAnna and Mandy sat on top of the big brown stove until they warmed up thoroughly and then they made a wild dash up the stairs to a very cold bed.

Irene remembered sitting against that same big brown stove in the nighttime when the warmth felt good to her aching ear. Earache was not a common thing at Aaron Shirk's, but most children knew what it was, and had earache at one time or another. The only instant relief available to Amanda was having Aaron blow smoke in the child's ear. It looked truly alarming to the siblings, as Aaron lit a cigar. While Amanda restrained the baby, it screamed loudly, Aaron put the lit end of that burning cigar in his mouth and very gently blew tobacco smoke in the crying child's ear. Amanda promptly put a warm cotton cap on the baby and cuddled it against her, rocking and soothing, and singing as peace returned to the farmhouse.

Late one evening, Aaron stopped at the end of the walk and the sleepy children got out of the station wagon and went to bed. Amanda carried in the sleeping baby Mandy. After Aaron parked the car, he carried in sleeping Roseanna and put her to bed.

The next morning, while getting ready for school and combing many pigtails, someone looked for a certain pair of barrettes. They remembered that Lydia wore those barrettes the day before. Amanda said, "You may go upstairs and take the barrettes out of Lydia's hair while she is still sleeping." When the girls got to Lydia's bed, they discovered she was not there!

Where was Lydia? She couldn't just disappear," do you suppose she was still sleeping in the car from last night?" they wondered. Sure enough, there was Lydia, still sound asleep in the back of the station wagon! She slept soundly all night, not realizing that her family actually had forgotten her. They missed her barrettes more than they had missed her.

Churning Butter

Churning butter was the easiest job in the house, but among the most detested. It compared with washing dishes, because it happened so often. When Amanda said, "I need someone to churn the butter," she seldom had any volunteers. It was not fair that one person could go outside and play, while the other one sat on a chair, cranking that handle.

Anyone sitting around the house with absolutely nothing to do, could instantly think of all sorts of fun things they would rather do, the moment their hand turned that crank. The flies buzzed, and time seemed to stand still, while Louise dreamily looked out the windows.

With two Guernsey cows, Amanda skimmed a lot of heavy cream off the milk. She sometimes traded butter for groceries in Bowmansville. She used bought parchment paper to wrap each pound individually, after molding it in a simple wooden butter mold. Sometimes when the cream was too old before making butter, she used it anyway. She did not discard cream and after awhile, her butter did not sell very well, because a strong butter flavor cannot remain hidden. Jesse's girls leaked out the truth that Aaron's butter did not sell as well as theirs did at the store. Eventually Amanda gave up and used all the butter for her own family.

The butter churn had wooden staves, held together with metal bands. It looked like a small short barrel lying on its side, with a tight fitting lid covering the rectangle funnel -type opening on the top. Any time a gallon or more of heavy cream accumulated in the refrigerator, it was time to make butter. Amanda carefully scraped the cream into the butter churn and asked for help. "It's not my turn, I did it last," Therefore, two girls ended up taking turns! Slap, slap, slap," let's get done really fast," they agreed, but that was not allowed! Amanda said, "Mother taught us that turning fast will not help, so just turn slow and steady or you will chase the butter away, ".

After peeping in the top every now and then, the girls finally discovered butter lumps, and Amanda dismissed them. She carefully finished the butter by washing and rinsing it, until the water ran clear. With a wooden spoon, she pressed out the last of the water and added some salt. She saved some buttermilk for baking and the rest went out to the pigs and the chickens, unless Uncle Titus happened to be there, and he would drink the buttermilk.

Amanda poured some hot water into the churn and cleaned it carefully, before returning it to the damp cellar. Anytime the wooden staves dried out, the churn might leak. That meant re-soaking and swelling the wood before using it again.

With the arrival of electricity, the wooden churn stayed in the basement. Amanda found a wonderful electric churn, with a glass see-through container. It was much easier to clean, and removed all the mystery of when the cream turned into butter. The Dazy churn plugged into an outlet on the counter, with no more children arguing about turns!

Amanda had no problem parting with the old wooden churn, when a total stranger knocked on her kitchen door, asking for antiques. Amanda welcomed her into the house, as she would a beggar. The stranger was hard up for a wooden clock or maybe a wooden butter churn. Amanda had no clock, but she sent Louise to the cellar for the butter churn. The beggar wanted it really cheap and paid $2.50 not realizing she could have had it for nothing, because in the Sermon on the Mount, the Bible says, "Give to him that asketh thee."

Amanda treated all beggars as angels unaware. This person did not dress like a beggar or an angel! She drove a decent looking car. Was she perhaps in dire need, or maybe so really poor that she had never learned the joy of giving? Perhaps her mother did not teach her the golden rule, of doing unto others, as you would have them do onto you.

Amanda knew that EK Fisher sold fine old antiques for outrageous prices lately. As she glanced at the coins in her hand, and then at the stranger going out the walk, she wore a puzzled expression. She did not like the feeling of being ripped- off, but neither was she going to use that churn again. It was leaking a bit, and even showed a few wormwood holes lately. Years ago, Aaron and Amanda had purchased the churn for one dollar at an auction, and they had used it hard.

Amanda parted with it, "As though the Lord had need of it!" To her, this was merely an earthly possession they no longer used and she much more desired the joy of giving, and the thought of having her treasures in heaven.

In later years, her grown daughters would have enjoyed turning the crank of that old wooden churn for sentimental reasons. Might it bring back vivid memories of how time stood still, while the flies buzzed and mother worked in the kitchen? Just maybe though, the churn would have disintegrated, unused in a damp dark corner, long before that.

∽

Aaron and Amanda learned to enjoy the benefits of electricity, about the same time that Daniel O'Hagan and his wife desired to get off the grid. Several miles away, in a secluded spot, the O'Hagans built a homestead from scratch, working with their own strength and imagination. They enjoyed showing neighbors and visitors how they lived, with back to basics. Both man and wife appeared highly educated and enjoyed nature. He had worked as a government employee and had his fill of city life in New York City and Washington D.C.

On a Sunday afternoon, Aarons girls walked there with Walter Martin's girls, and Daniel O'Hagan told them about poison ivy... leaves of three... let them be! He concluded by explaining how the urushiol oil in the leaves should be washed away with soap and water, after touching poison ivy. A house wren built a nest in the bicycle carrier attached to Mrs. O'Hagans bike, and she parked her bicycle until the wrens could fly. The O'Hagan's had an attractive place and enjoyed nature but Aaron's girls could not imagine why they didn't want electricity when they could have it.[In later years, the O'Hagens seperated and went back to modern living.]

As the girls hiked a little farther, they scrambled over a heap of boulders called 'Devil's Den', an unbelievable heap of huge rocks, locally called "icy shtay" [iron stones].The rocks contained enough iron to interfere with the needle of a compass.

∽

In 1960, John F Kennedy and Richard Nixon ran for president. Young children heard political discussions that they did not understand. On the school bus, someone asked a first grade farm boy, "Do you want Kennedy or Nixon?" He barely understood English and did not know what they were talking about, and said, "Ich het leevah un penny us nix!" (I would rather have a penny, then nothing.)

Louise overheard Aaron and his brother Titus discussing the upcoming election. The whole thing sounded rather alarming, when Titus said, "The world will come to an end sooner if Kennedy wins!" Aaron certainly did not vote for young Kennedy as president, but he was not as pessimistic as some of his brothers were, and the world did not end in their lifetime.

Three years later, Aarons children heard about Kennedy's assassination in an announcement over the speaker system at school, as lessons paused for a moment. Flags flew at half-staff, and the newspapers had many headlines about the details. Classmates discussed what they saw on television, and wondered what happens without a president. On the day of the funeral, the factory and the schools closed at noon. Jackie Kennedy, the new widow, had two young children to raise, and everyone felt sorry for them.

Amanda thought the school system should teach children to memorize all the Presidents of the United States, as she did in Michigan. Some teachers tried, but the list kept increasing.

∽

School laws required that children attended school until they turned 15 years old, and Aaron and Amanda respected those laws. After the one-room schools closed, the younger half of their children finished their schooling at Garden Spot High School for seventh and eighth grades. [The fertile Weaverland Valley was nicknamed the garden spot of the world].

Fashions in the sixties changed dramatically. Some classmates had teased hair piled high on the head in a tangled mess. Others wore plunge necklines or mini-skirts. Some wore heavy make-up. Some girls wore knee-high stockings perfectly matched to the outfit, with the knees exposed, and some wore boots. The skirts got shorter and shorter and some girls had a hard time sitting modestly.

Backwoods farm children did not understand modern music and did not actually care if that record played Beethoven, or Peter and the Wolf. It was rather foreign to people that sang for the words and not the music.

For the regional spelling bee, a teacher announced twenty unusual spelling words over the speaker system, and after grading the papers, Louise had 100%, spelling correctly a word like communiqué, that she never heard before. Several of the top spellers went on to the next school, and Louise found herself on that bus, as the only Mennonite among strangers. She nervously chewed her fingernails! Spelling on paper was one thing and facing a crowd was a completely different story. She went down on her very first easy word of 'bungalow' and she rejoiced to get off the stage, even if her teacher had reasons to be disappointed.

One team won a greatly honored basketball award at Garden Spot. The high school coach found his way out back to Aaron's farm, wanting permission for their daughter to play against other schools. Amanda met him on the porch, when Aaron was not around. The coach politely stated his request, but he had no idea how strongly Amanda opposed all organized sports.

Amanda believed the Bible and knew about the twenty-fifth chapter of Saint Matthew, where Christ taught the parable of the talents. She believed that time and money were the talents of which every individual must give an account at the end of their life. If all the spectators and all the players put their time and money into something worthwhile, they could move mountains of work for a good cause. Amanda knew that two hundred men could erect a barn in one day. How many thousands of people might fit into one crowded stadium? She could not fathom how much money the total of them spent getting there and paying admission. Are they putting God first?

She certainly enjoyed recess at school in her childhood, and organized sports at that level were fine. She wanted her children to practice the verse in first Corinthians, chapter thirteen, verse eleven, where it says, "When I became a man I put away childish things." Amanda did not say everything she thought, but the coach got the message. Amanda said, "Ach go on! "...and he did...even if he just lost a valuable player on his team.

The school coach did not see Amanda's point of view. He saw a talented daughter with parents that hindered her from becoming all that she could be. Aaron and Amanda plainly saw a different side, and wanted their children to grow up helping others. Organized sports were a waste of time in their opinion. Aaron and Amanda did not want their children to compete for a blue ribbon at a fair or a trophy of honor for any reason. They should always try their very best, but all honor and praise belonged to God! He gave the talents.

During Lyndon Baines Johnson's presidential election, a history teacher plainly stated that all his students must know which President and which Vice President are running for election. Republican or Democrat? He would mark an automatic F (failure) on any history test paper, not having that information correct. Louise knew Lyndon Johnson was on the one ticket and Barry Goldwater on the other, but where did Hubert Humphrey come in, and what was the difference between Democrat and Republican? She had something wrong and got an automatic F on her history test. Sorry, Mr. Huber! She tried her best. Others heard those political names discussed freely on radio and television and Aarons did not have any. Perhaps she should have studied more.

Delightfully, home economics class included sewing machines. That was something Aaron and Amanda's girls excelled in, with their mother being an expert seamstress. The high school teacher commented that Louise already knew how to sew, and she gave her an A, on the half apron she sewed in class. She said, "You could have had an A+, if it were not for the ironing." (Sorry teacher, ironing was Mary's job.)

RoseAnna went on to earn an A+ on a dress she sewed at school. In another school term, Rose Anna sewed a skirt, but that was 'fancy' and Aaron's girls were not allowed to wear separate skirts and blouses. Aaron and Amanda faced many decisions about school things. Rose Anna did not wear her finished school project until she converted it into a complete dress with less fashion and style.

Friends at school chose careers in higher education while Aaron's girls preferred to become "keepers at home". The teachers tried their best to convince all the students that a person is much better off with higher learning. Half a century later, people could see where that took them. America was in desperate need of more mothers teaching children right from wrong, and putting others ahead of self and careers. Amanda taught much more about giving and not just about getting. An ounce of mothering is worth a ton of schooling.

"Be somebody important, "the teachers advised. Higher education did not consider the value of motherhood, and the important part of teaching at home. One teacher said, "All of you girls must have a career planned, just in case of singlehood or widowhood!" She did not consider what the Bible taught about others supporting the widows. Any time a wife saw she could earn a living without a husband, divorce became more tempting.

Evolution theories appeared in the newest schoolbooks, and how could anyone prove that the Bible is not just a myth?" If Aaron and Amanda could have seen everything their children endured, they might have sent them elsewhere. Someone stole two dollars out of Rose Anna's purse and when she complained to her teacher, Rose Anna found no sympathy. She received a scolding for not having her purse locked up.

RoseAnna combed her hair into a long braid hanging down her back. Long hair, like suspenders

were a temptation for tweaking by mischievous students. Seated right behind RoseAnna, sat a boy inclined to mischief. He often pulled her hair and irritated her. She felt looked down on, in many ways at school. When she complained at home, Amanda said, "Just ignore him and after a while he will stop", but that did not work. No matter how much RoseAnna ignored him, he pulled her hair until it hurt. When her head jerked back often enough and hard enough, the teacher took control and English class came to a halt. Mrs. Campbell spoke up. "Rose, why don't you stand up and kick Ricky in the shins?"

RoseAnna was startled... how could she...? That was not what her parents taught her to do. A hush fell over the room as all eyes turned on RoseAnna. She hesitated in astonishment, as the classroom suddenly broke into a chorus of requests for action. "Do it, Rose, do!" "Yes, Rose, do it!"

Among all that prodding, RoseAnna did just that. She stood up and kicked Ricky in the shins as the entire classroom erupted in cheers!"Do it again!"Rose Anna did not do it again, because deep down in her heart, she didn't think it was right, even if that ended the problem. She was taught to obey her teachers but the Bible says to 'turn the other cheek also'. When a tragic traffic accident killed Ricky several years later, RoseAnna truly felt sorry.

Teachers hesitated to spank a child, and discovered such a punishment worked even better. Mandy's teacher tried the same thing when a boy in the seat behind her could not resist tormenting her. The teacher politely asked him to stop jiggling his feet beneath Mandy's seat. He did not stop and seemed to enjoy the attention he had from his classmates. The teacher reinforced her authority, by saying,"Mandy, Why don't you hit him on the head with that arithmetic book?"She did!

One boy asked Louise for a date, for so and so. He appeared to be setting up a blind date for someone else, and her half-scared no, was short and firm.

One boy insisted, "You are my Amish girlfriend!" But RoseAnna said "No." "Yes you are," he insisted, not wanting to give up.

For the first girls, Amanda did not consider it necessary to spend so much money on bought gym suits, so she made homemade ones, just a bit longer than what the other students wore. The gym teachers suggested the proper length of a gym suit, was at the level of the girls bent —over fingertips when their arms hung down at the sides. Amanda knew her daughters learned to keep their skirts down in modesty, but she had no clue they dangled upside down on rings and bars.

When choosing teams, one of Aaron's girls was last every time. The message came loud and clear, even without words. "We don't want you on our team, but today we are stuck with you!"

Aaron's girls often jumped rope, whether on a Sunday afternoon or among just a few girls at home. They jumped for a wonderful pastime with a homemade baler-twine rope. Some of them excelled at playing 'high waters'...leaping higher and higher. When Rose Anna nimbly cleared the rails over four feet high, in the high- jump at school, she impressed her teacher. "Perhaps with a little practice you could even do better than that", the teacher suggested. The gym teacher kept Rose Anna after school for athletic training, but Rose Anna tensely could not even jump that high. She also had no interest in practicing or competing in jumping. Rose Anna most certainly preferred to go home with her sister after 3:00.

Lydia and Mandy had the privilege of joining the National Honor Society and attend a candlelit ceremony on the high school stage one evening.

Irene was picked last in a boy-girl square dance at school in gym class, because she was different and could not dance. No matter how they combed their long hair, hair was always a temptation for pulling and yanking, in a mocking way. The girls never thought to complain to their parents, or to the teachers because in the "pecking order of life", they did not know they had any rights.

RoseAnna grew up feeling unworthy, and had to work hard to get good grades. She was sure the Shirk's were looked down upon; why else did they not have a mailbox at the end of their lane? To make matters worse, in sixth grade Mr. Hess started calling her Rose. Everyone turned their eyes and started snickering. It was impossible to convince Mr. Hess that her name was Rose Anna. He said,"Your name is spelled in two words and so your name is Rose in our class. Rose Anna had no say and the matter was settled.

RoseAnna and Mandy did not carry lunches to school because Amanda saw the convenience of buying hot lunches, and for their last children they could afford to pay for lunches. The younger children also wore bought gym suits.

Wesley didn't have it any better than his sisters. He was a misfit, even without wearing suspenders. He wore a bought gym suit and he dressed much like the other boys at school, but he was a Mennonite. They teased him...and called him "Yohnie"... like the newly printed story about an Amish boy. He did not belong at GSHS!

Wesley was small for his age, but tough and wiry. Picking up rocks in his father's fields, swimming skating, climbing and hanging tobacco in the rafters, strengthened every muscle he had. All gymnastic stunts or sports came naturally for him and climbing a rope to the ceiling was easy. Wesley and a friend, once climbed one of those ropes all the way up to the top, and then rappelled their way, hand over hand, across the I-beam, and down the second rope. They deserved their scolding about safety, when the teacher found out.

Wesley did not like the public showers after gym class. Most of the young boys found it repulsive to be seen in the nude. Once, during showers, one of the boys noticed a woman teacher was in the office, talking with the school coach, and she could see through the window, watching the boys taking showers. How disgusting! As some of the boys scurried for clothes, Wesley's friend flipped his towel up over his head, as he headed for his locker saying, "she's not going to see who I am!"

In one school term, the public school system tried to undermine the keen sense of shame and modesty Aaron and Amanda lovingly instilled into their children. Seeing grown-up children undressed, seemed shockingly indecent to them.

Aaron's girls found no use for algebra, gymnastics, famous composers, or prehistoric history They would have gladly deleted what they learned about Zinjanthropus and the Stone Age and filled that spot with worthwhile things.

With a sigh of relief, high school ended. They learned how others acted and dressed, and told dirty jokes they did not "get", but they had many good times also.

In seventh grade, some of Wesley's school friends enjoyed Boy Scout activities. Four of those boys came along home with him on a Friday night, and they headed for the woods, roughing it. Frank Angelo, Mike Klassen, and Dick Hurst discussed camping and fishing and sleeping out. They placed hay bales beneath each tent because the temperature in the night dipped to 17°, well below freezing and they needed the hay for insulation. They actually caught a few fish and ate them. They came in the house and enjoyed supper with the rest of the family. Amanda served a common meal of pork and sauerkraut, and the boys considered it a special feast. Awesome! They realized that Wesley lived a different culture. They all admired the woods, the creek, the pond and even the swamp, plus the big barn with animals. Every child should have a privilege like that, but not many had the chance.

Amanda knew why she chose a small farm, rather than a small business. Early Americans survived by hunting. In Peter Brubacher's generation, wild game was scarce and they did not hunt wild animals. They preferred the homegrown meat. Only the city people survived without butchering meat and those people lost their connections with the soil and raising animals. The schoolbooks started teaching children where milk and eggs come from. Any time children did not learn how to dress a rooster and how to raise their own food, they grew up deprived. Amanda lived to see those problems compounded when children learned that animals have rights.

Mandy, the youngest in the family, actually enjoyed school, and fit in better than the rest. Most of the time, Mandy combed her hair in two pigtails. She started them pretty far front on the ears, but sometimes she wore her long hair in a bun and tied a ribbon around it. Amanda retied the ribbon!"If you are going to wear it anyway, it might as well be neat, "she said. Mandy wished to go through high school. Math and spelling were her favorite subjects, and it made her sad to quit after eighth grade. School days were happy days!

Mandy begged to attend a Halloween party. She did not see anything wrong with attending and Amanda nearly gave her permission. Friends were important in life, but what entertainment did they have at such a party? Halloween used to be innocent foolishness in the past, but every year the holiday became more sinister. People tried to add some good to an evil holiday, but the evil multiplied rapidly.

After putting 15 children through eight grades, Aaron and Amanda had their fill, and Mandy stayed home. Years later, as Mandy grew up and looked back over her teenage years; she thankfully appreciated her parents firm" No" about going through 12th grade. She had a wonderful education helping others and worked at an assortment of occupations before marriage. She had learned all the reading, writing and arithmetic she ever needed for her lifetime.

27

Leaving Home

Daniel enjoyed music of all kinds, especially country tunes. Eventually he bought a fiddle and spent many evening hours practicing, mostly in his bedroom that he shared with Walter. He had the bright idea of getting Walter to play the guitar along with him. He even bought a guitar and learned to play it, just so he could teach Walter and get him to make tunes. It was not Walter's thing! He never made any serious effort to learn. Eventually; Daniel came to the conclusion that Walter was not going to play any musical interest, not even if his life was threatened with a gun at his back.

Daniel kept on practicing like he really had his heart in it. In the evening when Daniel was finally ready for bed, [or so he thought] and partly undressed, he thought of one more detail he wanted to practice. And then, according to Walter, Daniel stood there in shirttails and shorts and practiced until late in the night while Walter wanted to sleep. Aaron and Amanda slept in the next room and seldom complained; neither did the rest as Daniel sang and fiddled everyone to sleep.

Daniel found decent friends with Chet,'Glay' and the fiddle gang. .. boys that arrived to help Daniel sing along with musical instruments. Amanda appreciated his choice of friends and she wrote in her diary 'fiddle gang here'. Daniel enjoyed going to Green Dragon to look at all the records, listen to the music, and to notice pretty girls.

Aaron and Amanda attended a household auction and saw the auctioneer trying to get a bid on the real estate. When Amanda saw how he begged for a ridiculous low offer, she went over to Aaron and asked, 'Are you going to let them sell the place for that?"Aaron started bidding and bought the place for $4,325. The five-acre property had

an ideal location at the top of Turkey Hill, but it needed some tender loving care.

Aaron came home with no idea what he wanted with the place. He asked Daniel if he wanted the place? After thinking it over, he took it, and Aaron helped him get a loan at the Blue Ball bank. With a loan from the bank, advice from Uncle Menno living close by, help from his brothers and a lot of effort and sweat of his own, they made the house livable. After hanging the last wallpaper, Daniel rented it out and made bank payments. Perhaps someday he could live there, but he was only nineteen years old.

Aaron and Amanda were greatly concerned, when Daniel got a draft notice! In 1961, World War II was long gone, but many young men received draft notices for the Vietnam War overseas. Amanda did not understand what the war was all about, but neither did she understand what all happened when Joshua disappeared out of her life in wartime.

In 1940, the government started the Selective Service drafting system, requiring all young men to register at the age of 19. The drafting increased after the bombing of Pearl Harbor. During World War II, people could get a draft exemption, by working for the department of agriculture without pay. The government provided the transportation and the work, but the churches controlled the CPS camps, [Civilian Public Service]. The churches provided food and healthcare. Mennonite Central Committee had started twenty years earlier in 1920, to help feed starving people overseas. They reached out and helped support the hungry servicemen at the CPS camps. Those camps ended in 1947. The government allowed all Conscientious Objectors of war, to apply for 1W status.

Therefore, instead of serving in the military, Daniel applied for 1 -W service as a conscientious objector, and so did other young Mennonite boys. The government allowed them to serve time elsewhere, and Daniel chose to serve his two years, at the Good Shepherd Home in Allentown, caring for crippled boys and young men.

Daniel and Edna in 1 W service

In February, at the age of twenty-two, Daniel passed his physical exam at Harrisburg. A few weeks later, Amanda helped Daniel pack his clothes to leave home for always. It was a sad day in her life, and she cried at the thought of it all. The children watched their mother shed tears and couldn't understand why." What was so alarming about Daniel going to Allentown?"

Everything looked different to Amanda, because she keenly remembered how Joshua went to serve his country, but Daniel was not going to war and it was not at all the same thing. Yet, Amanda understood that Daniel knew very little about city life, and all the evils that a person could meet there. He learned farm safety, gun safety, near drowning, and dangerously felling trees, etc., but how could he fend for himself alone in a city?

Daniel had learned a lot of common sense, and his parents trusted him. It was a big help in knowing he had a steady girlfriend, Edna Horst, and he was not interested in all the things a city offered. Sarah Ann missed Daniel, because she was closer to him than any of the other siblings. It hurt to see him leave! Sarah Ann and Ruth felt sad when they stood on the cement porch with Amanda and watched his car go out the lane, until they could not see him anymore. Amanda missed Daniel more than the others did, and worst of all, was the thought of a child leaving home for always! Did they teach their children enough?

At the Good Shepherd Home, Daniel lived in an apartment by himself, quite a culture shock. The home provided room, board and laundry for single I-W boys. He played the fiddle after work and did some woodworking. He even learned typing! After he was married, Daniel and Edna lived half a block away in a second floor apartment. He worked as an orderly, doing all sorts of odd jobs and cleaning up messes. He mostly worked second shift and spent his time feeding handicapped children, bathing them and getting them to bed. He helped the crippled boys and he gave them haircuts. For the most part, the children were a lively and cheerful set. There was rarely a dull moment!

Several times Aaron and Amanda came to Allentown to see where Daniel lived and what he worked. He gladly gave them a tour of the home for crippled children. As he introduced his family to co-workers and patients, he said, "These are some of my brothers and sisters." They marveled at such a big family!" Are they all healthy and are they all normal?"

Amanda made sure that all their children had a turn to go along and visit Daniel, and see where he worked. When Wesley, Lydia, RoseAnna and Mandy went along, they hinted for soft ice cream on the way home, and Aaron wanted to buy some. Amanda hesitated and said, "This we didn't do for the rest of the children!" All her life, she tried her best to keep every child equal. ..she felt guilty of splurging... and was it fair?

Aaron paused enough to consider Amanda's point of view, but he liked ice cream as much as any of them, and he could almost taste the cone already. Aaron said, "We cannot help that we were poorer then... this is now... how big a cone do you want?"

Aaron said, "Make them large," and he spread his hands wide, showing the merchant how big she should make them..."as big as you can!" RoseAnna and Mandy could barely eat all of theirs, but the ice cream was delicious. With bellies full of ice cream and many thoughts about crippled children being penned-up like that, they found a deep contentment. They all felt richer than they ever dreamed possible...able to work and play... close to nature...with parents. ..not cooped –up in a pitiful place like that!

When Daniel came home, with a few days off in November, he brought along a crippled boy, named Harold. The handicapped boy responded to love and enjoyed the outing. Some of those children were not badly lacking, but their parents admitted them into the institution, so they could go their own way. They even considered Down's syndrome children a burden to their parents. No public schools had special-education teachers for them.

At Christmas and Easter time, the crippled children received more candy than they could eat. When Daniel came home, he brought along some stale candy for his younger brothers and sisters. One time he even came home with a pet parakeet, complete with a cage. Someone did not want it anymore at the children's home, and Daniel found a good home for the bird named Peter. Peter surprised everyone when" she" laid eggs. After several years, the parakeet became egg-bound, and Amanda could not tolerate its suffering. Without telling the younger children, she took the parakeet out to the woodshed, where she bravely and quickly pulled off its head and tossed it to the cat!

In his spare time at the children's home, Daniel made a purple martin house, with his woodworking tools. He presented it as a gift to his parents. The farm pond and open spaces created an ideal location for it, close to the house and barn. Louise liked birds and she was mighty proud of a brother like Daniel, even if the purple martins never moved in.

When Daniel came home from Allentown for the weekend, he wanted to help Ruth and Rhoda learn to drive, with their new learners permit. He gave them instructions where to go..." now turn here. Follow this road awhile... now turn there." They had no idea where they were or where they were going, until Daniel said; "Now we are in Maryland! See that sign, Welcome to the state of Maryland!"

Daniel lived alone in Allentown for one whole year and then he married Edna at the home of her parents, Michael and Mary Horst, in Lebanon County, close to Millbach. On a cold, damp, drizzly day, the big limestone farmhouse filled with about 150 guests. Bishop Milo Lehman united them in marriage while Preacher Abe Zimmerman and preacher Banks Horning also had part in the services.

Amanda remembered in detail who gave what at their wedding twenty -five years ago. She made sure each child had something to give as a remembrance and every one of her girls wore a new dress for such a grand occasion.

RoseAnna had just turned eight years old and felt a bit nervous. She had plenty of orders of how to act at a wedding, and what to do and not to do. When Amanda showed her that she is supposed to sit beside Edna's parents during the services, RoseAnna felt humiliated and cheated. Worse yet, she discovered her chair was between Mike Horst and the wall, out of the sight of her parents. She did not think it was fair, but she was too big to cry.

After a big meal, everyone admired the useful wedding gifts. In a mood of celebration, the bride's friends watched for a chance to turn the bride upside down. "To shake the mischief out of you!" they said. "You are now a married lady!"

Daniels younger sisters were puzzled and amazed at such doings and someone teasingly said "We might turn you upside down too!" Louise was not going to let that happen, and with a sister beside her, both girls hid under a bed upstairs. While hiding there, they marveled at the cleanliness, because under their beds at home were bed woollies, maybe some boxes and pumpkins at wintertime. No one found them hiding beneath the bed, but neither was anyone looking for them.

After a short trip to the New England states and

Canada, Edna started working at the Good Shepherd home, and they moved into a second-floor apartment. Edna did things like give pills to patients and also worked at the laundry and ironing.

In April, Aaron and Amanda had an "infare" or reception dinner at their home, for Daniel and Edna. They started in advance, getting ready for such a special occasion. Dick painted the old kitchen ceiling, and Walter made a porch railing. Many things needed repairs and Rhoda painted the outhouse. The cellar -way got whitewashed with a combination of slaked lime and water. Martha painted the screen door. Amanda repaired her old chairs and painted them blue.

The guests that arrived for the wedding reception at Aarons were mostly Daniel's aunts, uncles, and cousins, those not invited to the wedding. Thirty-four people ate in the house, for a full course meal while 46 children ate a picnic lunch back in the woods. In the afternoon, those children enjoyed a game of baseball in the hayfield.

Sarah Ann had the privilege of going to Longwood Gardens with her friends. She enjoyed the beautiful gardens so much that she wanted to share them with the rest of her family. She went again and met her friends; Maggie Burkholder, Anna, Mary, Elva, and Irene High there, on the day she brought along her own mother and sisters, for such a special outing. Louise worked too far away in Lebanon County, and they had more people than they could comfortably crowd into the station wagon for a long drive, so they went without her.

Sarah Ann picked up Rhoda at Ivan Zimmerman's on a lovely Wednesday after work, and Rhoda remembers which voile dresses the twins wore. Eleven people packed into the station wagon with Sarah Ann at the steering wheel and Amanda in the front seat, plus a few younger ones.

Lydia remembered hearing the cardinal whistle in a treetop, on a wind still evening, just before a rain, marveling at the beauty and wondering what heaven is really like. They enjoyed the display of colored lights on the water fountains and topped off the memorable evening by stopping for soft ice cream on the way home. While driving home, it rained so heavily that Sarah Ann could hardly see

to drive, but they had wonderful memories and did not want to tell Louise much about it. Life is not fair in many ways. After the long drive, they came home about 11:30PM.

On July 10, Aaron and Wesley returned from Eli Huber's sawmill with the Farmall Super C tractor and a trailer load of slab wood, to cut up into firewood lengths. RoseAnna and Mandy saw Aaron coming on the road towards home, while they were on the way home from getting the mail. Both roads ran parallel and they said, "Let's race Dad home!", as they took off running at top speed! Panting, they rushed towards the house and triumphantly thought, "We beat, we beat!"

They soon realized something went wrong. The tractor, partway in the lane, lay tilted at a strange angle, with Amanda and some children around it. What happened? They met Ruth running to open a car trunk, looking for a jack. She wore a pale alarmed look on her face and panted, short of breath. Aaron lay on the ground beneath the hub of the rear tractor wheel. The hitch on the tractor looked as if it might snap at any time and crush Aaron completely. With trembling hands, she grabbed the car jack and her little sisters followed.

Amanda said,"Doppah kumm unnah rouse, epps ols-nugh runnah folt! Doppah! [Quick get out from underneath before it falls down yet! Quick! Aaron could not move and neither could anyone pull him.

Aaron's tractor had a clutch on the left and two brake pedals on the right. Most of the time, he connected both brakes together with a bar across the top. The only time he needed to brake each wheel individually was when he wished to make a sharp turn at the end of a row in the field as [ZTR] zero turning radius. Aaron made the careless mistake of coming down the lane with too much speed and then hit one brake only. He thought he had the brakes connected as one, and he instantly jackknifed the tractor and trailer.

Wesley had been riding on the load of wood, and saw his dad thrown off when the tractor tipped. He fell also, but blithely leapt off unhurt and the slab-wood stayed on the trailer. Scrambling to his feet, Wesley ran to help Aaron, and he was

terrified to see his father moaning and gasping for breath while pinned beneath the big tractor wheel. He tried his best to pull him away, but he could not. Panic stricken, he ran across the wheat stubble, to the house. Martha panicked, too scared to look, and she stayed indoors. The rest rushed out to help, but all the big boys were at work, and several girls worked away, such as Rhoda, Mary and Louise.

Amanda demanded and ordered, "Ruth... someone... go find a jack!"Children scattered quickly looking for a jack, and they could not find any, except for a car jack. Wesley knew more about a jack and where Aaron had it last. Some of the younger children were crying. Was Dad dying?

Amanda and Wesley tried to get the handyman jack positioned under the wheel, a most dangerous position for such a Jack, and their efforts did not succeed. The wheel did not budge.

Frantically, Amanda said, "Let's push!" With supernatural powers, Ruth and Amanda pushed against the wheel, while Wesley tried to operate the jack handle. Their combined efforts, with God's help, were just enough to free Aaron.

He appeared dead, but he soon regained consciousness and started breathing, to their tremendous relief. After a while, his strength returned, and he dazedly stood up and walked to the house with the help of Ruth and Amanda. He lay down in bed, and begged to have his shoes removed.

"Ruth," Amanda requested, "take the car and drive to Clem Leinbachs to call Dr. Lauria. "I must stay with Aaron." "But Mom," protested Ruth, "I can't, I don't know how to shift gears!" Amanda said, "Sure you can!" Therefore, Ruth, taking the younger children with her, started out the lane in the old Chevy. Somehow, she drove one mile out and back without shifting any gears. Wesley repeatedly asked, "Will Dad be dead when we get home?" Each time, Ruth answered, "We don't know yet."

At home again, Ruth swept and cleaned up around Aaron. Thankfully, Dr. Lauria arrived and other than some chest and neck pain, Aaron seemed to be fine. He was bruised and sore. Wesley did not trust leaving the bedside of his father for the rest of the afternoon. At the age of 10, He was greatly concerned and worried. Imagining life without his father was far beyond his comprehension.

RoseAnna asked," Wesley, How could you run in that field barefooted, in all that sharp wheat stubble?" Wesley replied, "I didn't feel a thing. I just ran!" Wesley had nightmares and flashbacks about the accident for a long time afterwards.

While pinned beneath the tractor wheel, Aaron had a vision... He was taken towards heaven, and when he was almost there... he was called back to stay on earth after all...! Amanda knew it was not by their own strength that they lifted that tractor. God did! Aaron was still needed!

Aaron often wished for a silo when fattening steers and those dreams became reality in May of 1962. The girls enjoyed singing in the brand-new silo, as their voices echoed and rang under the new dome, high above them. The Fickes silo company from TerreHill erected a 10'x40 ', stave silo. Aaron put in some silage with not enough moisture and thought he could add some water with the garden hose. When the boys maneuvered the hose all the way to the top, Aaron turned the water on and wondered why it would not come through. With one half pound of pressure per foot of elevation, Aaron did not have enough pressure in the garden hose to push the water that high up.

Later, Aaron bought a 420 John Deere tractor for $1100 from Ed Hurst at Adamstown equipment. Dick felt highly honored when he had the privilege of driving that John Deere tractor home all the way from Adam.

∾

Walter bought a 1959 Plymouth. He started working for Victor Weaver, dressing rabbits and chickens at home in his garage. Victor added an assembly line, and expanded several times, opening as a business in 1959. Many young people started working there. Walter took along Mary Ann Kilmer and Manuals Martha. Walter started about a month before his seventeenth birthday and Pete started soon after he turned sixteen. Using a sharp knife and a scissors, each person removed one part from a chicken, as the chickens on assembly line moved on. With people on both sides, the assembly line moved fast enough to process one hundred and twenty chickens a minute all day long. One person could cut twenty hens per minute. In the short time Pete worked there, he earned four pay raises, from $1.05 to $1.20 per hour.

Walter met Marian there, as she worked for her Uncle Victor Weaver. It was not love at first sight, but included some gizzard throwing first! They were not with the same church, but ran around together weekends. Marian's parents were the Elmer J.Martin family and Marian could tell many stories about living in South America for two years. Walter's sister's looked like a skinny bunch of girls when she first saw them.

After several years of dating, Marian and Walter planned their wedding date for November 3, 1962. About five weeks before that, Walter joined the Lancaster Conference Mennonite church, where Marian attended.

Walter kept on working at Wickes lumber company and Marian kept her job at Victor Weaver's. Aaron did not forget how he lost money on chickens and he told his sons to ask a girl on the first date if she likes raising chickens. If she does, then quit her! None of the boys thought that was necessary.

Walter and Marian did not plan a big wedding, and they married at Bishop Mahlon Witmer's house, in New Holland. The wedding reception was at Marian's brother Chesters farm, on a snowy winter day. After the wedding, Walters did not go on a wedding trip,but promptly moved to Schoeneck, where they had bought a house on ten acres for $5500.Quite a bargain!

Two weeks later on a Saturday, Aaron and Amanda had a wedding reception dinner for Walter and Marian. Fifty two guests ate a big meal. Since the next day was Sunday, with the cleaning all finished, Aaron and Amanda again had fifty-two guests invited for Sunday dinner, just for anyhow.

Weddings were special in Amanda's life, and she did not get her fill in her youth. When Sarah Ann informed Amanda that she was planning on a March wedding, Amanda got busy, and so did everyone else!

Mahlon Zimmerman

Mahlon Zimmerman turned twenty-two years old before he had his first sled ride, because his parents lived in Florida. He worked at the Lancaster General Hospital, as an orderly in 1W service. He wore white uniforms at work, leaving them there, and wearing his regular clothes otherwise. He worked on the ambulance crew, and he saw some gory things. With his parents, Mahlon Zimmerman Seniors, far away in Florida, Mahlon mostly ate at the hospital cafeteria.

Mahlon and Sarah Ann dated long enough that Amanda knew it was time to finish Sarah Ann's quilts. On a snowy New Year's Day, with some roads closed, Walter and Marian managed to come through, and stayed for the day. Aaron and the boys stripped tobacco, while the house buzzed with activity. The factory closed for the holiday, so the big girls set up four card tables and two sewing machines plus the ironing board, for enjoying the day off.

Amanda worked at a velvet comfort top for Sarah Ann's hope chest. She had saved an assortment of velvet scraps and cut up garments from the Reading mission. After everyone returned to work, Amanda quilted a wool batt. In her 7'x8'quilt frame, she pinned a sheet of cheesecloth -type, curtain material, from the mission. On top of that, she carefully pulled and stretched 2 pounds of raw wool, distributing it as evenly as possible, before carefully adding a top sheet of the same sheer curtain material. With a C—clamp in each corner to hold the frame together, all was ready for quilting the comfort batt. Children of all ages helped Amanda with big needles and long stitches, as they practiced stitching and bonded the batt together with love.

The next day Amanda was ready to make the comfort. With long straight- pins, she secured the backing of soft cuddly cotton to two sides of the wooden quilt frame. She clamped a C -clamp in each corner and pinned the two remaining sides to the frame. Then she added the quilted wool batt, and on top of that, the colorful patchwork of the velvet top. With colorful yarn, everyone that wanted to help, tied together all three layers with durable square knots. The warm cover lasted a lifetime, and Amanda taught all her daughters that bedcovers should never touch the floor. This one especially, was not washable; therefore, Amanda made a huge slipcover, like a big washable pillowcase over the entire cover. "Don't wear your quilts and comforts out in the wash ", she repeated many times. All the lush velvet in bright colors, crafted with care, remained hidden beneath the slip- cover.

Amanda said, "Mother told us that the border of a quilt needs more quilting than the rest of the quilt, because that is where people jerk to pull the covers straight. They also stress the border, when they hang the quilt on the laundry line."

Sarah Ann had several finished quilts from home, including one made with the latest puckered nylon, in assorted dress scraps. Nylon was in style and never needed ironing, but the worst part was that it was cold in winter, and uncomfortably hot in summer. The durable fabric did not wear out easily and Amanda used some as a quilt back. Sadly, the quilt did not stay on a bed with such a slippery backing.

Mahlon and Sarah Ann could not have the spring wedding they wanted because the bishop had those days already promised for other weddings. Mahlon had poor living quarters at Lancaster and he needed a home, so they chose an earlier date.

Looking around the house, Amanda saw what all should be done before a wedding at home, and she put some gears in motion. Pete and Dick, two talented handymen, worked at Wickes lumber company and brought home supplies for repair work. Money was not so scarce anymore, as their growing children paid money home and room and board rent to their parents.

This was Amanda's chance to give her daughter a wedding, as she herself had dreamed of, nearly 25 years ago. A wedding at home, created a lot of work, especially for the oldest girl in a family. On January 8, Mary and Martha started painting the woodwork in the hallway upstairs. Aaron and Amanda's bedroom needed two coats of paint on the ceiling, and one coat on the walls.

It took two days to wallpaper Sarah Ann's bedroom, where she planned to display all the wedding gifts. Amanda wanted each piece of wallpaper hung to match perfectly to the next one, with no offset in the pattern. The finished wallpaper looked so fresh and clean, that the next day they removed the old wallpaper in the northwest bedroom. Dick, at 6'2"tall, painted the stairway walls and the ceiling, without using a ladder. Pete and Dick replaced the floorboards on the well-worn stairway. Sarah Ann, Dick and Amanda went to Musser's in Goodville and purchased a new carpet and linoleum. They laid it by themselves, such as most others did. Emptying the room was half the job. They worked hard to roll up the sheet of linoleum from the parlor floor, and laid that piece in the boy's bedroom upstairs. Shuffling all the furniture took time, and they worked long at getting everything in its proper place again, in time to sleep that night at bedtime.

Pete and Dick put up five large four by eight sheets of plywood, to make sliding closet doors along the entire north wall of the girl's big bedroom. A pipe held all the dresses on hangers and even concealed the unsightly brick chimney.

Girls painted the parlor woodwork while the floor was bare and then Pete and Dick laid the new carpet. They replaced all the trim boards and put the furniture back where it belonged. Among all the other work, it took a dozen new dresses for the wedding.

Sarah Ann and Mahlon were published at church on February 17, for their March 2 wedding. After that, no one tried to keep anything a secret, but most people already" knew "the secret, but perhaps not the exact date. The next day Mahlon and Sarah Ann went to Claude Beam, the local justice of the peace, for their marriage license.

Aaron kept busy, running errands and paying for the wedding. More important to him, was the new telephone line coming their way. After paying for an entire mile of electric poles earlier, the telephone wires now shared those same utility poles. The telephone arrived on February first, just in time for the fuss and commotion of getting ready for a wedding. Aaron eagerly told every businessperson about his new telephone number. Dr Lauria removed the number of Hartranfts and Clement Leinbachs on Aarons file cards, and listed HI5-2323. All of Terre hill started with HI5 [445].

Aaron could call anyone he pleased now...but there was a catch. He could only call the people that owned a telephone and none of his close brothers and sisters had any, neither did his parents. Only Aaron's brother in Indiana had a phone on his side of the family and only Amanda's sister Ketty and Dan Martin in Indiana, on her side. The wall-mounted telephone hung on the south kitchen wall, beside the door to the porch. Any person talking on the phone, stood on the porch to talk, as they tried to escape all the noise of a big family.

A telephone was nothing new and Amanda remembered in detail, how she talked on a phone at Evans. In Michigan, Amanda worked one and a half years for Dan and Adele Evans. They lived in the rear of Lin Wagglys general store. Adele as an only child, inherited the store and Amanda helped take care of their two little girls, Mary, age 3 and Jill, a one year old. While the parents tended the store, Amanda did the housework. She cleaned, cooked and pumped water by hand to do the laundry. In the back part of the store, they had an electric refrigerator and Amanda went into the store when she needed something from the refrigerator. When the phone rang, they expected Amanda to answer it. She learned to speak on the telephone, but at the age of nineteen, she did not dial any numbers.

Telephone or not, the next weeks disappeared rapidly while the girls painted woodwork in another bedroom and Dick and Rhoda came down sick.

Rhoda had a tooth pulled five days earlier, and it bled all night, until 4:30 AM. Aaron and Amanda were alarmed when Rhoda fainted and they called Dr, Halsey in the night. No longer, did they run to the neighbors to make a telephone call and the dentist told them to bring Rhoda to his office.

Amanda helped organize the new closet in the girl's bedroom. All the many dolls had a place where they belonged, on the big long shelf inside the closet. Mary and Martha kept right on painting chairs and the battered wood box and then they varnished the new stairway boards, clearly showing the wood grain. Walter and Marian came home one day to work, and they helped Dick wash off the smoky kitchen ceiling.

Sarah Ann spent most of a day baking cookies for the freezer, to serve with wine at the wedding. Amanda spent a whole day cleaning the dirt in the damp cellar. Under the old part of the house, was the dirtiest spot around, with a ground floor, where the potato bin and jar shelves stood. They tried their best to have everything clean enough for food preparation and refrigeration down there. None of the serving dishes would fit into Amanda's full refrigerator.

Among all this activity, Amanda still had to take care of her own routine work. She baked two cakes, ten pies and a big batch of cinnamon rolls one day, while Aaron fetched a load of potatoes to share with Menno's, Jesse's and Dawdy Shirks.

Pete and Dick took time out for canning meat at Akron for MCC (Mennonite Central committee). Even Sarah Ann looked forward to that occasion, and took a load of girls in the evening.

Sarah Ann got her own set of China dishes just in time. She used them on the bridal table at her own wedding, three days after the dishes arrived in the mail. Mahlon came before the wedding day and helped Aaron, Pete and Dick move all the furniture from the first floor of the house, onto the tobacco wagon, and over to Jesses. They needed all that room for many chairs and guests. Then the men fetched the folding chairs at Bowmansville fire hall, and set them up for the wedding services. Everyone scurried with the last-minute preparations and Lydi-Jes-sey came in her helpful way, taking orders how to cook for the wedding. Several waitresses also showed up for directions.

On March 2, 1963, Sarah Ann and Mahlon's wedding day dawned on a silvery spectacle of ice-coated trees. On icy and slippery roads, Mahlon went to the bakery in Leola and picked up the wedding cakes. Sarah Ann paid for the cakes, to save some last minute work. They had no way to freeze them if they made them in advance.

As the guests arrived, they stopped at the walk, where half a dozen hostlers waited to park their cars in the frozen hayfield. The hostlers numbered the horses and carriages with matching chalk numbers before they put the horses in the barn. Not many horses came. After the guests gathered upstairs, a chosen young couple served cookies and wine to anyone that wanted some. It was an honor to serve cake and wine, just as it was an honor to be a gift receiver. None of those guests wore special dresses, but both of the attendants had matching dresses.

Bishop Joe Weaver united them in marriage in the afternoon, because he had another wedding that morning. One hundred and thirty guests ate supper. The wedding was nothing out of the ordinary, except at suppertime; when it was time to serve the ice cream, the cooks discovered a dripping gooey mess of melted ice cream. Whoever cleaned the refrigerator, forgot to plug it in again. There was no time to go to a store for more ice cream, and so the guests ate pretty squares of bought cake without ice cream. Jake Burkholder reminded them many times over the years, that they didn't serve the ice cream.

Sarah Ann owned a five-dollar camera, but no one thought of taking pictures of the bride and groom, until the next morning. They posed on the front porch steps then, squinting towards the bright sun, for a picture. Sarah Ann and Mahlon never did find out who set all the alarm clocks that went off in their bedroom at all hours of the night.

At the wedding, D. Walter Martin said to Mahlon, "You made the start here now." Aaron and Amanda could see there were nine more girls to go. The three oldest children married within a year's time, and Amanda said, "They are leaving faster then they came!"

Daniel had purchased a home on five acres, on top of the Turkey Hill. He did not move there and

sold the Turkey Hill place to Mahlon and Sarah Ann for $7,500. They lived there seven years and sold the place for $12,000 after they sold off a $3,000.00 building lot.

Amanda was pleased to have her daughter live barely 3 miles away! That is what Amanda would have enjoyed for the first year of her married life, when her parents lived over a thousand miles away. Mahlon and Sarah Ann waited until he could have vacation, and then they took a trip to Nova Scotia.

Sarah Ann continued her job at the Walter W. Moyer Company. She earned $2.16 an hour, on piecework, depending on how much she got done, by the piece. That was considered good wages for a girl at that time and her checks were bigger than Mahlons, as an orderly. After he fulfilled his two years of service, he got a better job.

After the wedding was over, Amanda had time to stop and think for herself, and took time for a garden seed order and a Sears order. Aaron and Amanda, with many helpers, butchered three pigs and a beef, because each of their three married children received one-half a pig from home, BW Shirks had canned meat for Aaron and Amanda back in 1937, but thankfully, Amanda could save all that work and the meat went in the freezers.

Daniel finished serving two years in Allentown, and moved home to the place where Edna grew up. Since she was an only child, and her parents retired from the dairy farm, Daniel bought the home farm and Edna stayed at the only home she had ever known.

With three children married, and the next two going steady, Amanda saw how rapidly things were changing. Pete was courting Naomi Martin, daughter of Henry and Emma Martin, and Dick was seeing Ruth Zimmerman, daughter of John and Sadie Zimmerman. The twins also started with the youth group, and boyfriends brought them home faster than Amanda could keep track.

Just a few weeks after Daniels moved home from the city of Allentown, they had a baby girl named Susan! It did not really seem possible, but time moved rapidly, and Aaron and Amanda were first time grandparents! Martha stayed with Daniel and Edna several weeks, as a maid for the new baby.

Two married brothers and one married sister added new dimensions to the younger children's lives. Wesley spent two weeks helping Daniel around the farm, and they both enjoyed it. Mahlon and Sarah Ann took Lydia, RoseAnna and Mandy along to the Philadelphia zoo. They were simply delighted, because they remembered very little of the family day spent there, when they were quite young.

Aaron and Amanda announced a singing for the youth group at their place. Everyone pitched in to help clean up for such a special occasion; it really did not take much, when everyone put his or her own things away. Amanda could get a close -up look at what other girls wore, because she was still in favor of plainer clothing.

28

After three children left home in one year's time, Amanda saw a need to make more quilts. She wanted each daughter to have an assortment of quilts from home because she considered them a bare necessity. She enjoyed quilts and quilt making, as a lifetime hobby, but Amanda did not want to hand over ready-made quilts. She preferred that each daughter made her own. She wanted them to learn the creative aspect of choosing colors, while saving scraps and studying patterns. Amanda provided the inspiration and the push needed for each daughter to make her own quilts and find her own patterns.

Seldom did Amanda have a ready-made pattern given to her. With ingenuity, she cut up a corn flakes box and made an accurate pattern on her own, from an idea she saw at a quilting. Mary's pineapple quilt turned out to be the only major flop, with a pattern problem. After all the pieces had already been cut, you can be sure Amanda did not want to throw them out, and the quilt proceeded until it was finished. She added enough quilting stitches to flatten the project, and most people never noticed. One other time she tangled with a faulty diamond that did not lay flat where the eight points met. After that she always wanted to sew one sample block first, before she cut the rest of the pieces.

Amanda enjoyed all the intricate patterns of quilts, but when it came time for making every day quilts to use on her own beds, she discovered the joy of making a broken star quilt without so many tiny pieces. Instead of putting 25 pieces, or more together into one large diamond, she used one colorful piece of print fabric to make that big diamond. She called it her 'foulah shtonnuh' quilt[lazy star quilt], and she made many of them in a short time. She made those to give away, and some were a heavy comforter top for knotting. By combining attractive color-combinations, Amanda used nearly

fifteen- hundred less pieces per quilt top and still made nice covers.

When Jesse's gave a piece of fine purple print material to baby Louisa, Amanda saved the fabric until her daughter grew big enough to fit that size of yardage. Disgustedly, Amanda saw that she waited a little too long and Louisa could not wear such a small dress. She did not bother cutting into the material and saved it for a lovely fan quilt for her daughter. The wide purple border matched the center of each patchwork fan. Amanda wanted to use up every inch of the fabric, but she goofed in her arithmetic and again the purple print fabric came out short. She had already cut the borders and did not have anything that even closely matched. She fretted a while, but her face broke into a triumphant smile, when she noticed that she could add a patchwork fan in each corner of the quilt to make the border reach. The finished quilt pleased her, and the four extra fans made attractive curved corners on the quilt, with no one ever guessing her dilemma. She had successfully used up nearly every inch of the purple print. She passed on to the next generation, her ability to figure patterns and seams in detail, even without exact patterns. Many times the backside of her quilt had one corner of a different color, where the fabric 'almost' reached. That was her signature!

Every one of her 10 daughters started hand piecing her first quilt as a four -patch or a nine -patch. Amanda had some favorite patterns but she enjoyed the challenge of trying something different. She tried patterns such as, Aunt Lydia's favorite, log cabin, maple leaf, bear paw, monkey wrench, pineapple, Dresden plate, broken star, endless stairs, lone star, and trip around the world. Sarah Ann made a lovely appliquéd tulip quilt, and so did Ruth. Rhoda tried appliquéd roses. The hearts

Martha appliquéd on her quilt top went much faster. One of the girls appliquéd maple leaves. Irene made a brick quilt, and Louise tried a colonial star, all with Amanda's oversight. She wanted each daughter to embroider a quilt, but not all of them did. Sarah Ann finished a detailed state bird and flower quilt but along came Tri-chem fabric paints and saved some tedious stitching for Louise. Amanda made May Basket quilts for Pete and Dick and some of her patterns had no names.

When Aaron planned to have a raising for an extension to his barn, he gathered lumber and supplies while Amanda's thoughts promptly turned to quilts and food preparation. Not many people considered paying for professional help of any kind, because they depended on doing things on their own, or asking neighbors. In March of 1964, when Aaron and Amanda had the barn raising, Amanda framed the two May Basket quilts and many women came along with forty volunteer farmer-carpenters. While their husbands hammered, the women came for 'the quilting'. When it was chore time, and the guests departed, both quilts remained unfinished. Some men returned the next day to finish the roof and Lydi-Jes-sey walked over to help quilt. Sarah Ann brought mommy Shirk along, but even then, the quilts remained unfinished and Amanda rolled them up and put them both away. They stayed that way awhile, rolled onto the wooden boards of the frame, due to all her other work. June arrived! Her father, Peter Brubacher spent 10 days in the hospital to remove a tumor on his bladder. Two months later, he was back in the hospital for a second tumor surgery.

No one thought about quilts when Pete worked hard helping Aaron and Amanda lay new linoleum in the kitchen. The first linoleum squares in 9-inch tiles, lasted nearly 20 years, with rugged wear. On his day off, Pete laid three sheets of hardwood subfloor, and two days later, he finished the project with Amanda and the girls helping until past 10 PM. Later, he helped put a small porch roof above the parlor steps, and those tall parlor -steps finally got a railing and a walkway. Sarah Ann had often wished for a parlor walk, but she married before the walk happened.

Amanda ordered a brand-new couch for $40, from Alden's mail order catalog. It was a tan plastic—covered sofa -bed without arms. In one flip, the couch flattened into a bed. Before buying a couch, Amanda would have preferred to sit on it first, touch it, and check it out, but she could not. The new soft vinyl couch did not disappoint her. The washable surface had many years of hard wear in the kitchen among many children and even young grandchildren bouncing on it at the window. The mailman could not deliver such a large package to the mailbox, and someone fetched the couch at the Narvon station, where it arrived by train.

Time brought many changes, and Amanda, with the entire community missed shopping at Sam Rubinsons Store. It burned to the ground on Feb 4, 1964. Two months later, they tried to start up the Rubinsons Store again in the old Wright's Bakery building. Amanda bought clothes and many pieces of fabric at Rubinsons over the years. When she returned from shopping at Rubinsons, she trashed her receipts but cherished the S&H green stamps that came with every purchase. The more she spent the more points she collected. When she gathered enough to fill many stamp books full, she redeemed the points for something pictured in the "redemption catalog." The most exciting thing about redeeming those points was the fact that she could not spend her credit for paying bills and buying groceries. She tried to choose practical gifts and she bought a Cosco high chair for a baby gift one time. Years earlier, she bought Sarah Ann a new doll with those points. Giving to others brought her such great delight!

Amanda enjoyed shopping in the evening at Harry goods store, because her daughters with drivers license enjoyed the shopping more than Aaron did. He did not like Harry's auction either, when he had to wait there on a boring day. One Saturday morning Aaron took Jesse Brubacher's and Amanda to the auction and left them there until evening, pleasing everyone.

Amanda heard of the modern invention of electric blankets. She was quite sure she never desired to sleep beneath one. It was not a surprise to her, when Harry Goods store sold many scorched electric blankets. Some of them actually had a hole burned into the blanket and others had a minor brown scorched spot. She was amazed at the quality of the warm plush blankets at $1.50 apiece. She bought 15 of them and carefully removed the plastic wiring, with the help of her children. She returned to Goods Store for twenty more blankets when she saw the practical, cuddly softness.

Aaron and Amanda could have used many of those blankets in the past 25 years, and all their children remembered taking a jar of hot water along to bed to warm their feet in the coldest wintertime. If the jar rolled out from beneath the covers at night, it froze by morning in the unheated upstairs. Amanda saved one blanket for each of her children, plus several to give away. She appliquéd patches where a hole burned through the blanket. She did not want to throw away the heap of plastic wiring, and showed her children how to braid the wiring into durable jump ropes.

Caretaker

When Aaron was chilly during church services, he went out to the anteroom and came back in wearing his long trench coat with the collar turned up, very noticeable! That made quite a show and so did his habit of watching the thermometer, and stretching over to read it better. When Bowmansville Church needed a new caretaker, guess who got the job? Aaron did!

On May 23, 1963, Aaron Shirk started tending church at Bowmansville. Deacon, D. Walter Martin, paid him $125 a year to tend the furnace, and ventilate the building just right, by opening and closing the windows during services. That also included sweeping the church after every use. On alternate Sundays, the horse and buggy group used that church house.

Aaron felt honored with his new responsibility, but his children did not. Sweeping the empty church house seemed to come around much more often than twice a month. The worst part of all was the embarrassment of having their father walk around opening and closing windows during services. When he walked past the big floor register

above the furnace, he held out his outstretched hand to feel the heat. Much worse, he asked the teenage girls along the back wall if they were cold or felt a draft from the windows. Later, when Mandy sat inside the window, he opened the window from the outside, just to ask, "Is the temperature okay?" The big girls cringed and thought, "Please Dad, please don't do it that way." It was okay for someone else to do it, but not their own father.

Aaron had a lot to learn about keeping the temperature just right. He soon found out he could not please everyone. He commented, "If Mabel Halligan goes out to get her sweater, at the same time that Pauline Martin is fanning, then it is just right!" Sometimes he had trouble with too much heat in the coal furnace, and then he poured water on the hot fire, slowing it down and wasting some coal. A crowded church-house compounded the problem. Aaron said, "we do not need more room in the front, just in the back of the church!

Aaron had no pride in clothes, and he wore whatever was in his reach. Amanda had a hard time keeping Sunday clothes separated from the patched up everyday things. Sometimes he would helplessly ask, "What do you want me to wear?"

He went to church early one Sunday morning to start the coal furnace, and he did not come home again as he had planned. Instead, he just stayed for the services, sitting up front near the center of the church; wearing a blue flannel plaid shirt beneath his Sunday suit coat! The grown daughters had a hard time keeping their mind on the services, but Aaron did not see anything wrong with that shirt.

He was a caretaker for fifteen years, until Aaron and Amanda ran out of children to sweep the church and then D Walter Martins girls swept church over the years. They were not impressed either. Eventually the church community started taking turns to sweep.

Any time during the week, when Aaron had cold ears, he pulled out a big red hanky from his pocket and used it as a bandanna, wearing his black felt hat on top. Looks did not matter to him! Underneath it all, Aaron had a warm heart! There were not many things he enjoyed more in life, than visiting and meeting people. A handshake and a word of encouragement went a long way, as he liked to chat anywhere he went. When Aaron knew that the feed man would be coming his way, he had the barn doors open and waiting. Sometimes he even brought out some coffee and cookies for a snack. Many years later, the man from Troops mill said, "That's what I remember best when I hear the name of Aaron Shirk... a warm welcome with coffee and cookies, and the barn door opened in advance."

Twice a year, the Horning church and the Joe Wenger church met for spring and fall housecleaning. Aaron wanted to be among the first ones there, but he never made it. Amanda was not ready that early. John Leinbach and Noah Leid, among others had the butcher furnace set up heating water, before Aaron arrived. The big iron kettle next to the water pump, served just fine as a water heater.

Church members arrived bringing buckets and cleaning supplies, scrubbing with a passion. Walls, floors, benches, and the whole works. First, the cobwebs came down, and the window blinds for cleaning. Using tall ladders, the men washed windows outside. Twice a year, at feet washing time, the congregation used a dozen antique wooden foot tubs, held together with metal bands. Those were scrubbed too. Even the songbooks were carefully wiped and taped if necessary. Everyone worked together, and finished long before noon. 'Many hands made light work!

∾

Peter Brubacher's brother Isaac came to visit Aaron's from Seattle Washington. Amanda's uncle Isaac remained a highly honored guest. He was a minister. When they came and stayed long enough, Pete and a few of his sisters took Uncle Isaac Brubacher deep-sea fishing. Martha wished she could go along, to eat the cookies she helped put in the lunchbox. The fishermen came home with three lard cans full of fish, pleasing Amanda because they seldom got their fill of seafood.

Just last month, a neighbor brought them forty-four crappie fish to clean and eat. Aaron loved to eat oysters and occasionally they even had fresh clams.

In the backyard set an empty brooder house, no longer needed. Wesley had it fixed up for raising guinea pigs and rabbits at one time, but now it stood empty, with a leaking roof. It could be a playhouse, but they had a nicer one. It was just the right size for a cabin at the edge of the woods, but Aaron did not want it there. The girls asked, "Mom, may we sleep out in the brooder house tonight?" Amanda did not see any harm in sleeping in the backyard, but Dawdy Brubacher did not approve of such shenanigans, if he should notice. Since Amanda's father was staying with Aarons at the time, Amanda said, "Dawdy would think it's wrong to sleep outside when people should be thankful for their own beds." Eventually, Amanda consented, and the girls carried pillows and bedding outside unnoticed. Louise, Irene and Lydia tossed and turned on the hard wooden floor, listening to the night sounds, as they eventually drifted off to sleep.

In the night, rain dripped on them through the leaking roof. After discussing the situation, they made a dash for the house, and dumped all the damp covers in a heap on the kitchen floor, thankfully finishing the night in clean soft beds. The next morning, Amanda frowned at the pile of bedding and asked her daughters to hang it on the clothesline.

With a tent from the dump, Louise, Irene and Lydia tried sleeping out at the edge of the woods. First, they mended the tent, and scrubbed it with pine oil. They worked hard for a poor night's sleep. Lydia was scared in the pitch-black night, among many strange night sounds, and even her flashlight made spooky shadows. Louise said to Irene, "I wish Lydia would have stayed in the house."

Aaron and Amanda enjoyed the call of the Whippoorwill for twenty-five years, and then the Whippoorwills dwindled. Lydia remembered one spring night when Amanda came over to the girl's bedroom and asked, "Is anyone still awake? I hear a whippoorwill!" That night the whippoorwill sang long and loud.

Every one of the family stepped out of the house on a rare occasion, to see a huge helium filled blimp follow the turnpike. What keeps it up there and just how does that work? In the evening, they saw it again! Some blimps had Goodyear written on the side.

Aaron's family lived in this secluded and peaceful spot,but unrest and concerns about nuclear bombs made the newspaper headlines. What would happen if enemies dropped bombs on America? The Walter W. Moyer Company expanded one more time and built a huge fallout shelter beneath the new parking area. Several other businesses also displayed fallout shelter signs, to alert people where to hide, if the need arises. They stored water and survival items there, just in case. No remote area was safe from destructive atomic bombs, and those thoughts were disturbing.

In the mail, Aaron and Amanda received a notice about Civil Defense Preparedness Signals: A steady blasting siren signal of three to five minutes means an attack alert. Take action as directed by your local government. A wailing tone or short blasts for three minutes means ATTACK, take cover immediately! Tune your radio to 640 or 1240. Do not use your telephone. If you are in a building, go to the basement. If you cannot reach shelter, lay face down, flat on the ground or crouch on the floor of your car.

The "unknown" was bad enough, but the rioting and looting amid civil unrest in the 60s, was more disturbing. Why do black people clash with white people and burn cars as close to home as Reading, only thirteen miles away? Vietnam War stories abounded, while the hippies and university students were saying, "God is dead! Do as you please! "The "flower power" generation was doing drugs, and surely the world cannot last much longer like that. Philadelphia was just an hour away, with curfews and rioting.

Worry would not help, and always just borrowed more trouble. What are equal rights? Aaron and Amanda put their trust in God and the Bible promises, not into the government." If these young people do not dig in and work, what will become of America? "wondered Amanda. The styles were disgusting among the hippie movement, and even among church people. Amanda saw too much pride and vanity in her own teenage daughters, wearing shorter skirts, as they puffed and waved their hair

in front of the mirror. She did not like the style of her daughter's coverings hanging down on the back of the neck and said, "*It fits like a loaded diaper. Why do girls want to follow trends, and not put the hair up higher on the head? I hope you will all someday be busy enough that you won't spend so much time at the mirror combing your hair.*"

Amanda knew life would never be all roses without some thorns, and she thanked God for all the good things they enjoyed. Life seemed simpler in Michigan, when people had lived at a slower pace. She often thought back to many details. Her mother taught her that wool dresses wear clean. They wore the same Sunday dress all winter in Michigan, without washing it. When springtime arrived, her mother washed those dresses gently by hand and hung them on the line dripping wet. The weight of the water helped pull on the fabric and keep it from shrinking. Anything woolen had a higher value to Amanda. Perhaps she understood how hard her grandmother worked at washing, carding, spinning, and weaving the wool they gathered. She knew it added extra warmth in cold Michigan winters, on their beds, in her dresses, and in a cold sleigh ride.

Amanda bought dress shields to catch the perspiration under the arms of her teenage daughters, to save on unnecessary washing. They also discovered deodorant. Amanda said, 'Surely you do not expect to wash that dress after every time you wear it. "You will wear it out in the wash!"Amanda lost out and her daughters washed many more garments than she thought necessary, and so did her sons. "Who ever heard of changing underwear every day? She preferred the simplicity of wearing everything until she could see or smell the dirt. Before that, the boys each owned two union suits and that reached just right. They wore one pair all week while the other one was in the wash. The boys over summertime had no underwear and neither did their neighbors. None of them had any pajamas and thought those were for fancy people in town.

After so many years of wrinkled cotton dresses, along came perma –press! My what an improvement! Suddenly her daughter's dresses needed very little ironing. Amanda soon learned how to crumple a corner of new fabric, testing for fiber content with less wrinkles. The new fabric came in 45" widths, instead of 36 inches and it stayed so crisp and dressed –up. She could also buy slinky jersey that did not wrinkle, or the puckered nylon that soon lost out, because it was hot in summer and they had to wear full slips beneath the semi-sheer fabric.

Cooking Improvements

Amanda never heard of casseroles! She might have enjoyed using up every left -over scrap of food, but she seldom mixed food together, because Aaron preferred things separate. He even propped a table knife beneath one side of his plate to keep thin, runny food away from other food on his plate. He ate one thing at a time, not mixing anything, unless it was a tried and true idea the way his mother cooked, such as soup.

Aaron liked tomato soup and nearly every Saturday evening the family sat down to a supper of tomato soup and grilled cheese sandwiches. They ate a bigger dinner that day and the teenagers had plans to quick eat and leave. Cleaning and washing the floors allowed less time for cooking.

Aaron always enjoyed fried potatoes and sometimes Amanda stretched them to reach around for everyone. After the potatoes fried in butter, she added a dozen raw eggs, stirring and frying them gently, to make enough to fill the serving dish. Cubed stale bread, also helped extend that dish, when she fried bread pieces with potatoes and eggs.

Back during the Depression years, Amanda learned to save every scrap or drop of food in a container. Thirty years later, the catsup bottle was not empty, until she rinsed it clean. She could not waste the last of the juice in a fruit jar, nor anything else. Modern technology changed things at an amazingly rapid rate. Amanda had no use for the jets that flew overhead, or the latest technology such as television, but the invention of a rubber scraper, as a spatula to empty jars was important to her. Even when they could afford to spend more, food was a sacred gift, and she felt accountable, down to the last drop.

Sugar was rationed in wartime, and as soon as there was no limit, folks dumped more sugar in their food than necessary. Amanda had a cookbook by Mary Emma Showalter, printed in 1950. Mary Emma gathered most of those recipes in the 1940s. People splurged on sugar, making up for the lack of sugar allowed to them during world war two. Some of the sickeningly sweet recipes, improved with less sugar added, but Aaron brought home sugar in one hundred pound sacks. They did not realize they were addicted to sugar and many times, they drank sweetened drinks between meals. Amanda made gallons of tea from the mint plants that grew against the house. Aaron did not want water between meals if he could find cold tea in the refrigerator. If Amanda did not make the tea fast enough, Aaron and the rest of the family wanted peppermint water. He sometimes made his own! They bought peppermint oil for making peppermint drink. Aaron filled a pitcher with water and added a generous scoop of sugar. The tricky part was to add only a fraction of a drop of the oil. A whole drop, flavored nearly two gallons.

The new product of Miracle Whip or salad dressing pleased the taste buds of Amanda. It was a miracle in improvements over the slightly moldy sour cream that Amanda sometimes skimmed, and then used it to make salad dressings, by adding sugar and vinegar with a pinch of salt. They enjoyed bought dressing on sandwiches and even on raw dandelion salad. Salad dressings came in Ball canning jars, and impressed Amanda with the extra canning jars for her to use.

Crisco was another new word for their vocabulary. The factory girls first heard about it from a recipe shared at work. When Sarah Ann walked into the grocery store and bravely asked for Crisco, the merchant asked, "Do you want liquid or solid?"She was stumped! She had no idea what the product was, and she went home without any. After asking more questions at the factory, she needed the solid kind, for making fluffy frosting.

Amanda did not want or need many new inventions. She had no desire to keep up with everyone else. When she got hold of her first seam ripper. ..that was a different story. Now they were talking her language! Before this, her sharply pointed buttonhole scissors had been the best tool for ripping. Even a child could rip a seam with such a handy new gadget, and she soon had more than one seam ripper.

Amanda's grocery lists lengthened. They could afford to buy saltine crackers for soup instead of using dried bread cubes. She could buy such luxury items as band aids, Kleenex tissues, tape and even paper towels, (used sparingly), and plastic bags. ..what is the world coming to. ..plastic this. ..and plastic that. The first plastic bag Amanda had, came in the mail as a promonotional gift from the Pioneer seed company.   The large flat bag said 'Pioneer' in bold letters. Amanda found so many uses for that bag that she wished she could buy some like it.

The latest parlor curtains came in sheer lightweight plastic with floral patterns. Some people had plastic doilies and plastic bureau scarves. Toys in brittle plastic did not last long, but the plastic rubber pants were a big improvement over the rubber ones. Amanda preferred the plastic tablecloth on her extension table, over the oilcloth ones. When she discovered plastic bags, she used them a lot. She happily sewed elastic around a large circle of clear plastic to make bowl covers. She could see through it and spent time stacking and organizing her refrigerator.

Amanda cooked most of her lifetime with inferior cookware. The lightweight aluminum kettles scorched her supper many times when the range was hot. She learned to move the kettles to the cooler end of the stove, but she had many girls that learned by experience. The latest stainless steel kettles were an improvement, but she named the flimsiest stainless kettle,"Oh-bren kessle" [meaning scorch- kettle].. Aaron bought a sturdy stainless steel milk bucket and he used it twice a day at milking time for many years.

Seasoned salt was a new product that pleased Amanda. One time in particular, they had a large group of Sunday dinner guests. When the men reached for their hats to go home, Aaron and Amanda automatically invited some folks for leftovers and a simple supper. Occasionally teenagers needed a place to eat supper before going to a singing. Amanda trimmed the chicken meat from the bones and added more water to the soup if necessary. Everyone liked the seasoning of seasoned salt in the thin watered –down chicken noodle soup.

Aaron liked to try new products such as shaving cream in a can, but he still preferred the shaving mug with a round piece of soap fitted in the bottom. With a big puffy brush, he made a lovely lather for shaving himself and Josie. The only shaver he had was a straight razor which always got sharpened on a strap, [called a strop.]The razor was dangerously sharp and he handled it carefully.

Along came the safety razor. Aaron opened that shaver and put in a new razor blade for nearly every shave.

The toilet paper at the grocery store came in lovely pastel colors. Style- conscious people planned the soft tissue to match their room colors. Next, came softly printed floral patterns in many colors, almost too pretty to flush down the pot.

The Leewards catalog came in the mail, full of beautiful craft items and things to make. Even Amanda enjoyed browsing through the embroidery items, patchwork pillows, paint by numbers set, quilts and much more. She bought some stamped pillowcases ready to embroider, and some punch work pillow tops, one for each girl. Using colorful yarn and a needle punch, they followed the pattern punching up and down, creating a velvety soft picture of colorful flowers sculpted on a black background.

Aunt Eva showed her nieces how to make hairnets, with durable thread. It was an age-old craft, much like the fishermen made their nets in Bible times

Any time a child came to Amanda and said, 'I am cold!"She checked out what they wore and bluntly said, "Do setsht kolt sie. Gay do may glaydah owe!" [You should be cold. Go put more clothes on!]In Michigan, people dressed warmer and did not depend on a thermostat on the wall. There was no such thing as bad weather, only unprepared people." We stayed home in adverse weather and prepared for such occasions in advance, "Amanda said.

Time changed rapidly, and it was hard to comprehend all the changes Amanda saw around her.

When she was a child, she learned the art of knitting, because her parents needed more stockings and mittens for their family. She knitted a mitten for herself and poked around too long, in making the second one, and then she discovered her hands had grown bigger. She could not wear those mittens and gave them to her younger brother Joshua.

Hand knitting no longer paid, because the yarn cost more than the ready-made product. Knitting, spinning and weaving fell by the wayside and Amanda did not teach her daughters how to knit, unless they wanted to know, simply out of curiosity. She saw no use in crocheting lace and tatting hankies, because it was not necessary. She showed her daughters the fancy feather stitching on comfort tops, but Amanda considered that a frivolous decoration, barely worth the bother. She had her hands full teaching sewing, making buttonholes, quilting, and the more useful arts in fabric.

When every one of Aaron and Amanda's grown daughters took along between five and 10 quilts from home, those were of utmost importance for practical reasons. Quilts were the best way to use leftover scraps, and it taught her girls how to make a useful necessity, creating with their hands. Louise's first quilt took coaxing and encouragement every step of the way, when Amanda insisted half of it must be sewed by hand.

After completing a first quilt, Amanda helped her daughters to choose which simple patterns appealed to them, and she cut the pieces precisely, making sure, they fit. When Louise pieced the blocks of her nine- patch quilt, Amanda enjoyed setting the completed blocks together. She added the borders, marked the lines for quilting, and framed the quilt. She used a yardstick every time, making sure one side of the quilt was not a bit longer than the other side.

It did not take much cajoling to teach her daughters to notice patterns and find inspiration to start another quilt. None of the quilts fell by the wayside, half finished, not with Amanda in the house! She completed them herself if there was any problem, and encouraged her daughter to start again on a different pattern.

Amanda wanted her daughters to know how to make homemade soap. Her mother in Michigan always made her own. Her parents saved the wood ashes in a wooden barrel, and that is how they burned down their new house before Amanda was born. The old timers knew how to make homemade lye. By trial and error, they learned how to leach rainwater over wood ashes, but sometimes their soap got mushy. Wood ashes from oak, hickory and ash trees made a different strength of lye, than that leached from pine and such. Grandma wanted the lye strong enough to eat a goose feather when she swirled it through the liquid. As soon as the storekeepers sold sodium hydroxide lye, made from salt, many pioneers stopped making lye, because the bought lye made a better and more consistent soap.

Sometimes Amanda bought soap from the store, but when she had more time and fewer children underfoot, she made more homemade soap. She used it to wash Josie's wash, and she saw how well it cleaned their rugs and overalls. Most of the children had a turn at grating bars of homemade soap, by shredding it on Amanda's box grater. Then she soaked the grated soap with boiling hot water until the lumps dissolved, and everything turned into a slimy mess. That was the way she wanted it, so that it dissolved faster in the water. Louise carved a fish from a block of fresh homemade soap. The soft soap shavings curled neatly on a pile. Amanda did not mind, because she wanted those crumbled shavings. Any time a batch of soap flopped, Amanda had the option of a do over. She grated it, melted it, and mixed it again.

During the depression years, Amanda's mother, Sarah Ann Brubacher, often sat up on a Saturday evening mending stockings and underwear, so that everyone had clean clothes to wear on Sunday for church. They also wore that same pair all week. Clothing was scarce and Amanda did not have Sunday shoes or a Sunday coat in her childhood. They wore what they had for school and the same to church. Each of the children had two sets of everyday clothes, so they could wear a clean outfit when the other one was in the laundry. For Sunday, they each needed only one dress, and they did not see a need to launder those unnecessarily.

Amanda spent many hours mending.

Before the 1920s, people seldom noticed stockings because they remained hidden beneath long skirts or pant legs, and no one saw them except in the laundry. The most common stockings were black. As styles changed, women wore shorter dresses and stockings became a fashion statement. Suddenly the stores sold them in assorted colors. That was when Mennonite church leaders asked their members not to follow the latest fashions. Serviceable black stockings showed conservative unity and less pride. They knew that the Bible did not require any one to wear black stockings to get to heaven, but the Bible plainly taught meekness, humility and modesty.

Rather than working in a factory to earn money, Peter Brubacher's sister Barbara bought a knitting machine to make stockings at home. She encouraged her brother to try knitting stockings in their home, with the help of their growing children. After thinking about that, and wanting to keep their children occupied, Peter bought a big clumsy knitting machine in 1922. The Gehrhart knitting company supplied them with yarn and Peter's family knitted men's stockings by the dozen, according to their orders. Peter did not have much work over the coldest part of winter, and he helped make some stockings to sell. The girls and Silas helped crank the handle to make the tube style stockings. Mary and Betsy helped their mother close up the toes, stitching by hand. Their mother pressed them on a form. Peter sold them, but it was not a paying proposition. The yarn cost nearly as much as the finished product, with not enough margin for a profit.

On the day Peter bought the knitting machine, it was already outdated. Newer electric models worked faster and used thinner threads for softer better stockings. Amanda did not know if her father ever earned enough money to pay off the knitting machine.

Peter kept the machine, just in case someone wanted to earn money working at home, and maybe he did not want to admit defeat. He knew that no one would pay much for it, so when he moved his possessions from Michigan to Pennsylvania, the big heavy knitting machine came along. They lugged it up the stairs to Aaron and Amanda's attic where the obsolete piece stayed for nearly 70 years, never needed again! Amanda occasionally demonstrated how it worked, reviving nostalgic memories of her childhood. My, how times changed! None of them liked to wear stockings made with bulky yarn.

29

Amanda enjoyed singing more than listening to any records and music. She also wanted to uphold the church standards, and she was keenly disappointment when her daughters brought home a record player. They parted with their own money and put the record player in the parlor. Aaron did not care. After listening to the old Victrola in the stripping room all those years, what was the difference?

In the church council and guidelines, cameras were forbidden as "making an image". Most teenagers had cameras anyway and Amanda did not scold about them, neither did Aaron. The few poor photos Aaron and Amanda had of their school days grew more special, as time went on.

Amanda saw that a camera could be used in a decent way, but she also saw the down side of taking pictures foolishly. She did not say much about all the photos her daughters had from their friends. In her memory, the faces of her own classmates faded and she wished she could remember them. Perhaps that was why she encouraged her oldest children to trade name cards the size of business cards as keepsakes from friends. Amanda had two autograph books filled to capacity. She collected verses and best wishes from a wide assortment of people, some from Canada, Michigan, PA, Ohio and Indiana.

Skrudland Photo Company had a lot of trade developing films by mail for her daughters and the girls waited eagerly for the snapshots that came in the mailbox. They saved their photos in scrapbooks such as Amanda never could. None in their group owned a camera in Michigan, nor did they have the money for developing films. All the years when Amanda was slim and Daniel was young they had no pictures. Amanda never faced the camera as' posing 'because that bothered her, but she often repeated to her children, "I just wish I had a picture to show you what this farm looked like when we first arrived. You would not recognize it!"

"You look out and see the open pasture around the pond, next to a white board fence. That was all one tangled thicket where the bootleggers could hide and that land did not belong to us. The house and barn are still here because they were built to last! Between the house and barn, you now see a well-kept lawn and shrubs, where a tangled overgrown garden once grew inside a fenced area. Most people had fences back then to protect their valuable food plot from an escaped farm animal or chickens scratching in the dirt. The mucky swampland is dry. You cannot imagine the pristine quiet before the Turnpike arrived and the public road resembled a rutted field lane, and the rocks jutted ruggedly in our much longer lane. Forget the power line, that is modern and so is the pond and our favorite Norway maple tree. We planted that tree as a tiny sapling in 1938. Aaron's mother helped water it carefully. As it grew taller, Aaron tied the horse to it and the horse nearly killed the tree, by chewing off a large patch of bark.

The horses needed to rest in that bit of shade when Aaron came in to eat. The hitching post Aaron put there, made a useful improvement and saved our only dense shade tree, even if you teenage girls did not like the ancient looking hitching post where the boyfriend stopped at the parlor walk. " Aaron and Amanda's children could not comprehend what Amanda talked about and the hitching post had to go, because no one used it anyway.

RoseAnna and Mandy never remembered riding with their parents in a horse and carriage anywhere. Lydia remembered faintly. They had no way of knowing what their older siblings endured as hardships and neither did they have the privileges that accompanied those hardships. Nothing in life is divided equally! Amanda could plainly see that luxury did not create happiness. She found a deep joy in reading her Bible, cuddling babies, and saving every bit of food. Joy radiated in doing the best with what God gave to her, and in sharing and giving all she could. 'All you have is all you need!'

∽

Peter Brubacher moved in with Aaron and Amanda, while taking turns among his children. His health was declining, and he had a bladder tumor removed in January. Three months later, he had a second surgery, for another tumor. Aaron and Amanda cared for him the best they could, but they still kept on inviting company on a weekend.

Four days after Peter came home from the St. Joseph Hospital, he stayed at Jesse Brubacher's for less commotion and a chance to get a nap. It was Ascension Day, 46 guests came to Aaron and Amanda for dinner, and afterwards the guests enjoyed touring Dick Ziemer's lovely flower garden and ponds, just one mile east of Aarons.

When Dawdy Brubacher lived with Aarons, Amanda asked Martha to drive Pete's 58 Chevy with a stick shift, to a doctor appointment in TerreHill. Martha never drove a straight shift before, and repeatedly choked off. Amanda desperately wanted to get Peter Brubacher to Dr. Lauria and kept coaxing Martha to keep going, and somehow she made it all the way there and back again.

Life was varied and full of surprises. Amanda packed a Sunday lunch for a picnic in the woods, on a nice day in June. At the age of 49, she donated blood for the first time. Children were active all around her, with never a dull moment! Lydia and RoseAnna slept out in a tent in the woods with Jesse Brubacher's Eva and Naomi, talking half the night. Mary got a drivers license, and four short months later, Amanda trusted her to drive in the city of Reading, getting eyeglasses.

Irene started in Goods one-room school, for three hours each Friday, fulfilling the law. Uncle Elias Shirk taught, helping out at school one day a week, assisting the regular teacher. He was not a teacher by nature, and he had a problem pronouncing all the vocabulary words, but Elias could keep order!

He asked the students, "What is the abbreviation for empty?" Everyone looked puzzled and someone said, "There is no abbreviation for that word!" Elias said, "Sure, at Wickes when a box is empty, we mark it M T. When Elias gave the spelling word of "angshetty", a student whispered to Irene, "What was that?" Irene whispered back, "I think he means anxiety," The girls explained their problem, when Elias asked, "Why are you whispering?"He said, "Let's get a dictionary", and sure enough, the girls were right!Elias pronounced, the capital, Lima, Peru, the same as lima bean, because no one had taught him better, but he was still eager to learn.

When Aaron and Amanda went on a trip to Canada, the girls at home decided that was their chance to have their kitchen "nice". They made the table small by taking out all the table boards, and for dinner, they set out some snack-foods, for something special. When Pete and Dick came home for supper, they scolded the girls for not making a cooked meal. They were hungry for meat and potatoes, not snacks!

On the weekend, when the young folks left for youth group activities, Martha, Mary and Louise stayed home alone. After dark, they went to bed early so as not to get scared, with their parents far away in Canada. Before they fell asleep, the dog started barking and they could see car lights turning in their lane. Sitting up in bed, they saw the headlights snap off. Fear gripped their hearts !Straining their ears, the girls heard the south kitchen door open and someone bumped against the bench in the dark. After more bumping noises, the girls were shaking with fright. Someone sneaked into their house and not just maybe!

Headlines in the Lancaster daily paper had announced, "Timmons", a wanted criminal was loose, and believed to be hiding in their area. After a while, the intruders left, but the girls could not sleep. Real fear was something they rarely dealt with. In the night, Aaron and Amanda came home from their trip and noticed some wet towels hanging around. No one could explain what happened, until a long time later. Some young boys admitted driving through the area, and they stopped in at Aarons, looking for something to clean up a carsickness mess.

Lydia had heard enough of grownup conversations about Timmons, to know that he was a dangerous criminal. She was afraid that he would get them. Amanda put her children at ease by saying, "What would anyone want with us?" That comforted Lydia and the others, and so did the story that someone found Timmons in a mountainous area of Pennsylvania and locked him up somewhere. They trusted everyone they met.

On another occasion, Ruth awoke during the night and heard someone knocking on the kitchen door. Rap, rap, rap...there it was again ! Quickly she went to her parents' bedroom, and said, "Someone is knocking on the door!" Amanda was not excited, but got up and put on a long flannel robe, over her nightgown. Then she went downstairs to the unlocked door, and standing there in the dark, was a big colored man. "I'm out of gas on the Turnpike," He said. "I climbed over the fence and walked for help, would you have some gas I could buy?" Amanda woke two sleeping boys and sent them out to get some gas for the stranger. She explained to her children, "I wasn't scared. Surely people need help when they knock on your door at night."

A stranger arrived at Aaron and Amanda's house in the daytime. The newspaper reporter had no way to telephone and call ahead to let them know he was coming. Irene knew she won a prize in a Cappy Dick contest, but she had no idea how she would receive that prize.

Every day, when the Lancaster Intelligencer Journal newspaper arrived in the mail, Amanda skimmed over the births and deaths. Aaron studied farming and beef prices and the children enjoyed the comic page. Perhaps Aaron didn't admit it, but he enjoyed Alley Oop in the comic strips as well as Dagwood, Blondie and Maggie and Jiggs.

Once a week, Cappy Dick had a puzzle, quiz, or a color contest for children. Every now and then, one of Aaron's children submitted an entry. Everyone marveled when Irene won more than a plastic trinket! A man with a camera came to take a picture of Irene. He also brought her prize, a set of eleven classical books, with titles such as

Black Beauty, Treasure Island, Heidi, Tom Sawyer etc. Quickly Irene changed into a clean dress, and someone combed her long braided hair, while the man waited. There was no clean spot anywhere in the house except in the parlor, and the stranger ducked beneath drying laundry, strung crisscross everywhere, trying to get to the parlor. The next day, Irene had her picture in the newspaper, beside the stack of books she won. Aaron's children appreciated the books and spent many hours reading them.

⁓

Aaron and Amanda entertained the youth with occasional singings at their place. Amanda noticed the dress styles and saw that her girls had room for improvements. Not everyone dressed the same and some in the group still had the simplicity she admired. Aaron did not notice clothing and he had more of an interest in entertaining and talking to the youth. Some of them watched him swallow a raw egg and bring it back up again, without breaking the egg yolk, and then again several more times with the same egg, out in the stripping room. The boys never saw the likes and Aaron liked the attention. Amanda greatly appreciated the youth group and their decent conduct, especially the wonderful Christian hymns they sang with their blended voices. She knew many of the songs from her youth and she enjoyed any new song.

For a singing, Amanda bought candy for the dish in the middle of the table and she distinctly remembered a singing at her parents in Michigan. Without buying candy, they elegantly served real wintergreen berries in a dish for their treat. She had helped to gather the red berries in the woods.

Amanda appreciated animals, but she was not big on pets in the house. Louise had an aquarium in the parlor awhile, with real bought aquarium fish. Later when the fish died, she filled the aquarium with fish and things she caught in the creek. Grandchildren eventually pounded the aquarium and cracked the glass to put an end to the extra bother. In winter time,the parlor was only warmed for the weekend.

The parakeet Daniel brought home from Allentown got much more attention and Amanda allowed it to fly around in the kitchen. One day the children excitedly rushed indoors saying,"Look what we found!"On the meadow fence, they found an exhausted parakeet. It was easy to catch and obviously, it flew a long way to come way out back to Aarons. None of the neighbors lost a parakeet or ever owned one, and so they gave it a good home in the same birdcage with the other parakeet..

Rose Anna played with cute little opossums and she wanted to keep them. She found out they do not make good pets. They have exceedingly sharp teeth, they want to sleep in the daytime, and they are not very intelligent.

Amanda showed her children how to make a deck of' donkey 'cards with cardboard from empty corn flakes boxes. Several stacks of the homemade cards each numbered from one to twelve. Each of the players, rapidly tried to stack their cards in the center pile, starting the pile with number one and ending it with number twelve, before starting the next pile. Whoever used up their cards first won. The younger children all wished for a chance to help entertain their sister's beaus with a game of donkey on a Saturday evening. With nothing planned for the evening date, Ruth and Carl even helped the younger children swatting flies. Rook games rated near the top, on such occasions.

Ever since Amanda quit school, she occasionally sang and hummed the tunes of the songs she learned forty years ago. Many words eluded her. She forgot what came next and that bugged her. She always wished she knew where to get a copy of the old school songs. Then Daniels planned a trip back to her childhood home, and they took Amanda along. Aaron preferred to stay at home and he did. That is why they did not return to Michigan more often.

The highlight of the trip was meeting up with a former classmate and finding a songbook with all the words that evaded Amanda. They obtained permission to take the book along home, and returned it later. Amanda took the out —of- print booklet to a print shop and made a copy for each of her children plus anyone else that wanted one. She sang cheerfully!

In 1964, Pete purchased a 24-foot house trailer for $750. He went to Indiana looking for a place to park his trailer, where he might find a place to serve 2 years of 1W. service. When Pete went to Indiana, Amanda eagerly went along, spending some time with her sister Katie. RoseAnna age ten and Mandy, eight years old, also went along. Aaron was more than happy to stay at home and work.

Cousin Joe Martin helped Pete with job- hunting one day and Cousin Ben Shirk went with him the next day. They found a place close to South Bend Indiana, only 25 miles away from Uncle Ben Shirks and Uncle Dan Martin's. He planned to serve at the Northern Indiana Children's Hospital. Most of the children in the home were retarded and many were completely helpless, needing special care and a lot of love.

When Amanda came back home, she rapidly gathered household basics for Pete's house trailer. She made a cover for a box spring, to save him some money. Pete quit his job at Wickes Lumber Company and on May 26, he left home for Indiana. Goodbye to their fourth child leaving home!

With his 1958, six-cylinder Chevy car, Pete towed his 24-foot house trailer. He had one flat tire in Ohio, but he made it. In South Bend, it cost $22 a month to park his trailer. He worked the evening shift, from 2:30 to 11 PM, as an orderly.

One month after Pete left home, Uncle Ben's oldest daughter Bertha, married Melvin Zimmerman. A wedding invitation to a cousin getting married out of state, was exciting enough, and the thought of visiting Pete in Indiana, made it a high priority. Ruth, Rhoda, and Martha along with their special friends, Carl Weiler, Mervin Brubaker, and Mervin High, went together in one carload and had an enjoyable trip. They started at four o'clock in the morning and the boys slept at Pete's, while the girls went to Dan's for the night.

Aaron did not wish to go and he allowed Dick to drive the 1962 Ford sedan, taking along Dick's girlfriend Ruth, and Pete's girlfriend Naomi, as well as Aaron's parents, BW and Annie Shirk. With room for one more person, they took along Mary Ann

Zimmerman, also invited to the wedding. That was an interesting combination of people, and a trip to remember. Dawdy Shirk was a talker! They went to Lake Michigan and saw the Michigan sand dunes.

Weddings in Pennsylvania, served a full course meal, and this wedding was different. Bishop Will Ramer officiated at the Sunday evening services held outdoors under the shade trees on the front lawn. Instead of a full course meal, they served only refreshments, and Pete drank down his punch in one gulp and said rather quietly, "The sample was good!"It was a warm day and the boys were thirsty. The punch was delicious but the cups were too small. Dick said, "I wish it was only half as good and twice as much!"The beautiful tiered cake, mints and nuts served with the punch, were not a full course meal like the one they had imagined.

When Pete and Naomi had their names published in church, for their upcoming wedding, Aaron and Amanda got busy cleaning up, because they planned to have a reception on the day after the wedding, quick, before Pete's go to Indiana.

All the guests sang outdoors, before the sermon started at Pete and Naomi's wedding, in the big farmhouse, on August 8, 1964. One hundred and seventy-one guests ate supper at Henry Martins after the wedding ceremony by Bishop Milo Lehman. Aaron Horning was the preacher from Naomi's side and Paul R. Martin from Pete's side, plus Deacon Walter Martin.

The next day Aaron and Amanda had 80 guests at their farm for the" infare" (reception). They served a full course meal for the aunts, uncles, and Shirk cousins not invited to the wedding. Amanda and four daughters skipped church that morning and worked to get ready, after attending the wedding the day before.

Most people tried to attend every wedding they could, if they had an invitation. One year later, after Bertha and Melvin's wedding, Bertha's sister Anna Mary, married Melvin's brother Roy, on November 28, 1965. Martha was invited as a server, and a group of girls went for the wedding. Ruth, Rhoda, Martha, and Mary went with Ada Zimmerman and Margaret Martin for a memorable trip. The girls had time to make calls with their cousins in Indi-

ana. They visited married cousins, Fannie, Nancy, Katie and Naomi' Kilmer', living in Indiana. After seeing the cousins, they slept at Uncle Dan's and went to Yellow Creek Church on Sunday morning.

Aaron and Amanda had no desire to take all the children on a trip at the same time, but they saw that all their children had a turn to go to Indiana while Petes lived there. "We are going to Indiana,"raised high expectations! Amanda baked cookies in advance and bought some snacks. A trip that far, always included a picnic beside the road. Picnic tables dotted the turnpike, every so often, all the way there. Aaron admired those rest areas to get out and stretch. Amanda packed plenty of sandwiches and cold drink, usually homemade spearmint tea.

Howard Johnsons had places along the turnpike to stop and buy food; mostly for the rich people. Aaron and Amanda didn't mind a picnic lunch and wanted to save that money. A trip to Indiana cost more than a trip to Canada, because it was farther and they drove their own vehicle after they arrived. The county roads were easy to understand, in neatly numbered squares. When the Indiana young folks came to Pennsylvania they commented, "The layout, confusion and hazards of such poor roads look like children made them and did not know any better."

Only the newest vehicles had air conditioning and most people drove with 4-60 AC...Four windows open. ..at 60 miles an hour... with the side wings turned inward, to blast a maximum amount of air. The July heat dried everyone out and whipped the girls' long hair into their faces. Sunglasses shielded their eyes from the harsh light and helped keep the hair out of the eyes. The bored children, wrote down all the different states from the license plates they could see on the other vehicles. Aaron allowed them to wave at truckers and the children motioned them to honk their horns. He thought the road was long.

Louise was but a baby when the turnpike cut through Lancaster County, and she waited fifteen years to drive on the big highway. "So that is what the bridges looked like, racing along and looking up from the bottom, "she mused. Everyone seemed to be in a hurry and so were Aaron and Amanda.

When Aaron came along to Indiana, Pete made sure he took his parents to the O- hare airport and to the stockyards in Chicago. He knew his dad would marvel at the way steers moved on such a large scale, dwarfing the largest sale barns in the east. With younger children along, they also spent time at Deerland Park, and fed some tame deer that ate food from their hands.

At Uncle Bens for breakfast the next morning, Aunt Grace stretched open her extension table and served her guests as royalty, using her Sunday tablecloth. She served Cheerios in her best china dishes, to show appreciation. Louise innocently thought these relatives lived so far above them in class, that they served food in style like that every day, to their own children. Only much later did she discover, they usually ate in a small breakfast nook on a regular day.

Life in general, kept Amanda so busy that it was four months before she sent her first letter to Pete and Naomi in Indiana. When Mahlon and Sarah Ann's first baby arrived, Aaron and Amanda had a second granddaughter. The name of Wanda was a strange name, and Dick said "Vonda, budda, ceiling!" (Walls, floor, ceiling). It took a while to get used to the name, but everyone enjoyed a new baby close to home.

The third grandchild, arrived right on Amanda's birthday, February 22. Walter's chose the name of Clydine. Mandy was only eight years older than the oldest grandchild and those granddaughters loved coming home to Aunt Mandy. She took the children outside and showed them the new kittens and Wesley's bunnies. Lydia, RoseAnna and Mandy, finally had babies in the family to cuddle and to entertain.

Amanda remembered the birthdays of those first grandchildren. She enjoyed memorizing poems in school and she still liked memory work. She rattled off the names and their birthdates so many times that she had them all down pat, until she had over seventy grandchildren.

Great Event

In January 1965, Walter came home and started making a much-needed bathroom for Aaron and Amanda. For practical reasons, they chose the smallest room upstairs, the hall- room, for the new luxury. Lydia, RoseAnna and Amanda slept in that bedroom. They moved that bed and crowded it into the big girl's bedroom, and then they had four beds and nine girls in one oversized room. No one complained! The extravagance of having an indoor bathroom made up for any inconvenience otherwise.

Crowding in with sisters made many happy memories. Add a stray bat in the middle of the night or a giggle fit, and other people just did not know what they missed! More than once, Amanda came over to the girl's room and said, "You better settle down so everyone can get some sleep!"The many happy memories they garnered, seemed as if they slept nine in one room for all their lives. It was actually only for seventeen months, until another daughter left home.

Lydia, Rose Anna and Mandy slept together in one regular sized bed. As they kept growing, they crowded more and all slept on their sides with their knees bending the same way. If one of them wanted to turn over, everyone else had to turn over, but no one complained. That was part of growing up in a big family, and Amanda told them how she slept four in a bed in Michigan, with two heads at each end.

Rose Anna slept in the middle and that was the worst spot. She had a problem in the summertime when she sweated and could not cool off. Wintertime was just as bad, because Lydia and Mandy tucked the covers around the edge of the bed tightly and the taught center of the covers did not touch her, like the roof of a tent.

When Lydia, RoseAnna and Mandy slept three in a bed, they had an occasional dispute over covers, coughs and not enough room. On one such evening, Lydia argued that RoseAnna has bad breath. Mandy smelled it also and insisted it must be from RoseAnna in the middle, because Rose Anna did not smell it. This went on for several evenings until Amanda came to the scene and assured RoseAnna that it was not her breath. Upon further investigation, she discovered a rotten pumpkin beneath the bed. She stored pumpkins there each fall and soon used them. This one was put away out of sight and forgotten, but RoseAnna never forgot!

No one could imagine the luxury of having a new bathroom! Just suppose... no one needs to go out back alone in the dark... or look for a sister to go with her...won't it be wonderful? One time Mandy stepped out in the dark, and discovered a skunk at the cat dish at her feet. She quickly decided she did not need the out-house after all! Just imagine a real bathroom indoors... no more bathing in the cold cellar... in the galvanized washtub...

The septic system came first, and then the work started indoors. It progressed slowly, because Walter did the carpenter work and he no longer lived at home. He worked many hours as opportunity afforded and Pete helped him. It took a lot of patience until Walter and Pete completed the bathroom. After that, the bathroom was a high-traffic area, with many girls combing their hair. No one managed to put a mirror and the washbowl on the outside.

As the children used the new bathroom, they sometimes still shared the same warm soapy bath water, asking, "Does anyone want to take a bath before I let the water down?" They never knew a water shortage, but they sometimes waited to flush until several of them went, because that seemed wasteful.

Amanda made all her homemade quilts six foot square and so did most others. That size did not allow much room for anyone hogging the covers. As Dick kept right on growing to six feet two inches, she saw the need for bigger quilts.

When Amanda heard about Dick's choice of a girlfriend, she was impressed! Ruth Zimmerman, who was a former schoolteacher, could fill in where Dick might need help with reading comprehension. If anyone needed a schoolteacher for a wife, it was Dick, and that worked out just fine. All his life, Dick never had a problem finding work, because he enjoyed working, and he never found a job he did not like. From helping Amanda with the laundry, to forking manure until his hands blistered, work fascinated him. He was sharp with numbers, and a capable manager. With a willing mind and a gentle disposition, he never ran out of things to do.

The same lad with such a rough start, made some good choices. Before he could walk, Ruth and Rhoda rudely pushed him off his mother's lap. He lived at Dawdy Shirks until he felt he belonged there, with more attention than one child needed. When they returned him to his parents, he cried with homesickness for the quiet luxury he craved. He adjusted to the commotion, but he was at the wrong place at the wrong time when Rhoda fell out the window, right on him. He cried long!

Dick ended up in a school with an incompetent teacher that had no desire to teach him to read in first, second, and third grades. It was only Dick, out of the fifteen children, that needed a tonsillectomy. He did not ask questions and seriously thought the doctors were trying to kill him. Dick craved home life and he was required to go work for others, against his wishes, until homesickness overwhelmed him, and he could not eat anymore. Dick happened to be the first of the bunch to attend high school, where he was mocked to tears, and forced to continue. All the trials he suffered helped shape him into a caring and compassionate person.

[A psychologist that studied children who survived war and serious atrocities, noticed that those who conquered life with a positive attitude, had certain qualities that helped them cope. Successful survivors almost always enjoyed the affection of an extended family. They took on themselves important responsibilities that boosted their self-confidence. They were encouraged to practice a special talent or skill. Child survivors never lost hope, despite the odds. Their formal religion convinced them that things would somehow transcend their current pain.]

Dick worked at Wickes lumber company for five years and enjoyed his work, but when given the new job opportunity of working on a dairy at Philhaven Farms, he took that job and quit at Wickes, even taking a pay cut. Dick and Ruth had wedding plans, and Dick preferred a stay at home job, that he considered a better occupation for a married man and perhaps it would keep him from getting drafted. In March of 1965, Dick moved away from home, living alone in half of a huge double house, 36 miles away. Living alone, even just four months, was a major adjustment for him, after leaving a big family. Mark and Verna Martin lived in the other half of the big farmhouse and he ate meals with them. Marks, newlywed, started working one week before Dick arrived but Mark was manager number one and Dick was his assistant, until Mark and Verna moved away.

On July 17, 1965, Bishop Milo Lehman married Dick (Aaron Shirk Junior) and Ruth Zimmerman, at the home of the bride with 171 guests present. John and Sadie Zimmerman lived at Route 2 Lebanon, on Mount Zion Road. Ruth Shirk and Carl Weiler had the honor as attendants on Dick's side, while Edna Zimmerman, sister of the bride, and Raymond Zimmerman, cousin of the bride served as attendants on her side.

The menu for the supper was bread with butter and pineapple jelly, cold sliced ham and beef, new potatoes, noodles, beef gravy, peas, coleslaw, pickles and olives, cheese and crackers, coffee, cornstarch pudding with graham cracker crumbs and bananas, apricot tapioca, angel food cake, chocolate sheet cake, fruit salad, plus mint candies and Hershey kisses. The angel food cakes had no icing, and the Shirks thought that rather strange for a wedding, but that is how Ruth's family always ate them. She hardly even realized that other people put icing on angel food cake!

Dick's sisters wore alike dresses for the wedding, all made of pink taffeta. Amanda bought a bolt of the durable fabric at Frank IX in new Holland. That was the only time the girls ever owned matching dresses. The tightly woven fabric was hot in summer and cold in winter and did not wear out easily. It resembled plastic, and was most likely designed for making jackets, such as windbreakers. Everyone became tired of the same hand-me-down dresses, and poor Mandy at the end of the row, complained about so many identical dresses that never wore out. Mandy asked, "Whose big idea was it anyway?" As soon as she outgrew one dress there was always another one right like it, because they were all made the same, with the same uncomfortable material.

Not long after Dick and Ruth married, they received a notice from the draft board. Oh, no, they thought their plans were smashed! After Dick called his boss, Noah Kreider the farm board chairman, he had no problem. Noah Kreider said, "Give me that letter, I know those fellows in Lancaster!" Noah had one of the secretaries at the hospital type up a letter of appeal, stating how desperately they needed this young man to continue working on the dairy farm at the Phillhaven mental hospital. They soon had a deferment for Dick. They arranged for him to stay, because the Phillhaven Farm was also set up for IW service, even if it would be less than 60 miles from home... a major requirement.

Dick and Ruth waited six weeks before they went on a wedding trip to the West Coast, and then they travelled together with Pete and Naomi. In late August, Dick and Ruth drove to South Bend, Indiana, and packed their belongings in Pete's new Volkswagen bug. They spent the next three weeks looking at the western half of the USA and some of Canada. It was more of a sightseeing tour, combined with a camping trip, but they all enjoyed it very much. Most nights they slept in two-man tents and cooked their own breakfasts and suppers. Then they bought their lunch if they could find a 25 cent hamburger place. This was before the days of McDonald's and other fast food places started.

They stopped to see Great Uncle Isaac Brubachers in Seattle, Washington, staying there for one night. Amanda's Aunt Ruth accommodated them well, even if she put Pete and Dick together in one bedroom with Naomi and Ruth together in another!

Both couples spent a grand total of $251.52 on their wedding trip. They traveled over 9000 miles and saw 21 states plus British Columbia in Canada. Gas was priced around $.35 per gallon and the VW bug ran cheap, even when they had every corner packed tightly.

Palm Sunday tornadoes ripped through northern Indiana when Pete and Naomi lived there, on April 10, 1965. They had attended church in the morning and then they went to Lloyd Martins for dinner that Sunday. In the afternoon, the sky turned into an unusual color and turbulence, looking dark and stormy. Lloyds and their guests watched the clouds and showed concerns about tornadoes! They soon heard about the twisters close by. When Petes headed for home, the farther they drove the more damage they noticed. Massive destruction loomed everywhere, among miles of downed power lines, and roofs missing among unbelievable damage. It was not just one tornado, but what a relief to see that South Bend had been spared.

Aaron and Amanda anxiously wondered about the headlines! Are Petes okay? What about Uncle Ben's at Goshen and Uncle Dan's at Nappanee? Pete did not have a telephone and Aaron and Amanda thanked God heartily, when they finally received word, that the Indiana relatives were all safe.

Aaron took his Ford car to Paul K. Oberholtzer's garage for repairs, a few days after Christmas. He planned to take it with the gas tank empty, but Wesley did not understand, and he filled the tank from Aaron's large gas tank at home. While draining the full tank at the garage, the fumes ignited and the explosion burned down the entire shop, including Aaron's car, for a total loss of $20,000. Aaron repeated the unusual story many times, to all who listened.

In 1965, Aaron bought a red, 1952 Chevy pickup truck. It was the only pickup truck he ever owned, and he did not keep it long. Everyone in the entire neighborhood needed him to haul bigger items." Would you go fetch more two by four lumber for the raising tomorrow. .. if you go to the sale barn, bring me some hay. ..would you bring the truck to help us move... my wife bought a bedroom suite at the auction..".and so it went.

Everyone that needed Aaron's truck also needed a licensed driver and his time. Aaron did not want the job! It did not take him long to see that gas was cheap, but keeping vehicles on the road was not. When a relative or a neighbor went along somewhere, they laid a quarter on the seat and asked,"Lunked un fottle?"[Is a quarter enough?] Perhaps it covered their share of the gas, leaving nothing for license, insurance, repairs, new tires and time. One neighbor that rode along to work every day said, "I hope you have good snow tires, because at $.50 a day, I don't intend to push." All too often, one person said."I would pay too, but I don't have my wallet along!"

Aaron bought a 1967 Chevy with a 327 engine and more power. He said ", It's a wild one!"Aaron put up with accidents and dents on his vehicles, but he had a hard time overcoming the awful accident of spilled milk in his car. When he no longer had a cow on the farm, he found it more convenient to fetch fresh milk at the neighbors. On the way home, he braked hard and spilled a whole gallon of milk in the carpet. No matter how hard they tried Aaron and Amanda never got rid of the stench of spoiled milk. It happened in July and the car soon smelled as bad as Josie's sour milk bucket used to. No one told Aaron to add a lot of soapy water, right after sopping up the milk, and then use a shop- vac. {He never heard of a shop-vac anyway.]

All this time, even after five children left home, Aaron still talked about mineral rights and mining. Herb Kohl didn't give up on Aaron's ideas, and Amanda mentioned a 'prospector ' in her diary. Aaron bought more land, east of his property. The place had a house and a small barn, with road frontage along the blacktop. The house on the' Styer place', had an unusual shape. One tall section towered over the lower half, and the children nicknamed it,' the giraffe house'. Aaron did not want the buildings, he wanted the land. Several years later, arsonists lit the barn and the house was not worth fixing up.

Amanda appreciated the large patch of asparagus in the field. She greatly enjoyed eating asparagus and had nine girls at home yet to help pick it. At one time, Aaron and Amanda had tried starting such a patch for selling produce, but that grew up in weeds. When springtime arrived in 1966, the children all had their fill of picking asparagus. Girls walked side by side, combing a large area in one sweep. They had no problems finding the first tender shoots, and they gathered enough that Amanda had plenty for the freezer, and some to give away to her others. She took a bunch of asparagus as a gift; to anyone they went to visit.

Amanda's mother taught her that people should pick asparagus until the longest day of the year. When June arrived, her daughters had a hard time finding asparagus among the weeds and grass, with no weed control. Aaron disked the patch but

Aaron's truck as a snowball fort.

the weeds grew back rapidly. Mandy walked along and saw a dead pheasant. "Look what I found," She exclaimed as she reached over and picked it up by the tail. The flapping and squealing and shock that followed, cannot be described in words! The hen pheasant, alive and well had depended on camouflage to hide her, as she remained sitting on her nest of eggs. When the explosion ended, Mandy stood in shocked disbelief, still holding some tail feathers! It took a while until her heart beat normally again! The memories remained vividly for the rest of her lifetime, and for those that stood laughing at her.

Wesley

Wesley grew up in the middle of a row of nine sisters, and he never knew what he missed by not having a brother his size. With a sense of humor, he made the best of what he had. Sisters were fun to tease and it did not take much to make them squeal. All he had to do was look at them, and they went tattling to mom. Amanda said, "Well, just don't look at him!", but that was hard to do. Wesley knew how to get attention! Wesley even threatened to bite a fish worm in half, trying to get attention from his sisters.

Wesley did not need to work for others, because Aaron needed another son around the farm. Wesley teased his younger sisters unmercifully at times. All he had to do was say, 'Mice un rottuh greeyah dich," [Mice and rats will get you] and the

trouble started.

When the children went out the door to school, someone hollered," Bus!"That was not unusual and they hit high gear running as fast as they could, and then Wesley said,"April fool!"It was the first day of April. Once, Irene forgot her lunch. Rather than go back and get it, she hollered to her sister coming out the kitchen door,"Ich hop my lunch fa-gess-uh! [I forgot my lunch]The sister misunderstood and thought she said,"De bus iss uns Jess-uh". [The bus is at Jesses].Every one RAN!

Wesley grew up among long hair everywhere! One long hair did not bother him much and he laid it aside, thankful that he did not need to shampoo and comb a mess of hair like that on his head. Short hair bothered him much more. When he needed a haircut, he straddled a kitchen chair and wore Amanda's faded old half apron across his back. He guarded the neckline carefully, making sure no hair slid down his back to make him itchy, because he did not want a bath.

One girl after the next, learned how to give haircuts by practicing on Wesley. The hand -held hair clippers had a way of pinching the skin and cutting visible notches in his dark straight hair. Wesley cringed and pulled his shoulders up to his ears, even before his hair started falling around him. He panicked, because in his younger years, he found nothing on earth more terrorizing!

Haircuts on a Saturday night, meant going to church with a botched-up hair cut. One sister frantically took a black crayon and colored the white gap of skin shining through his straight dark hair. Another time he walked around with a tuft of dark hair taped in place sincerely meaning, "Im sorry!" Nearly drowning and drinking kerosene, plus all the trouble that found Wesley, did not alarm him as much as yet another beginner trying to cut his hair!

His older brothers had some inferior haircuts from beginners and they sometimes spent seventy-five cents for a haircut at the barber in Bowmansville. The big boys got so modern that they saved money and went to the barber in Bowmansville for a haircut. It cost 75 cents each!

Lydia, RoseAnna and Mandy helped Wesley act out the story of "The Three Billy Goats Gruff" after they read the story in their school reading books. They propped up one end of the long bench beside the table, and used it as a bridge. RoseAnna pretended to be the troll under the bridge, while Lydia, Mandy and Wesley acted out the part where the goats walked across the bridge. RoseAnna called out, "Who goes tripping across my bridge?"

The billy-goats got too rough, and the pretending halted when the bench crashed on RoseAnna's finger, causing her great pain. She cried all the way to the doctor's office. "I'm sorry," could not fix the bloody, mangled fingertip, and neither could the doctor. Without numbing it first, he stitched it together carefully with four stitches, and wrapped it up. Disfigured scars remained on the flattened fingertip for the rest of Rose Anna's life.

When Wesley wished to catch some banties, three sisters worked just fine to go along out and help. While Wesley crawled high up among the empty tobacco rails, Lydia age 12, shown the flashlight for him. "Be very quiet," Wesley instructed. "We don't want to scare the chickens." Then he added, "Watch out for the hay hole."

"What?" said Lydia, but he was too late, as she plunged down the dark opening in the barn floor of the hayloft, designed for tossing down the straw bales. She fell eight feet down, onto the newly cemented floor of the steer stable below. With horror, RoseAnna and Mandy saw what happened and Mandy hollered down to the steer pen, "Bisht dote?" (Are you dead?) Lydia did not answer, as she lay unconscious! As a flashlight shone down on her, someone asked, "Are you okay?" She heard the question, and tried to answer, but only a moan escaped her lips. By the time Wesley came down to help her, Lydia struggled to her feet, and even walked to the house without assistance. The rest were shook up more than Lydia was. Her back hurt, but otherwise, she was okay.

Aaron appreciated all the help he could get. He often reminded Amanda how much help she had around the house and he had only one son remaining to help him. When Aaron did not keep his son busy, Wesley found things to do, such as trimming the cat's whiskers. To make both sides even; he kept on trimming until the whiskers were all gone.

Life on the farm was wonderful, but so was going along to the Reading mission. It rated higher than Christmas Day, and Louise wished for glasses, just so she could go along. Amanda had no favorites, but when Ruth, Mary, and Irene, needed glasses, Louise seldom went along, and she worked away summers.

The Reading mission operated as an outreach to help the needy. They had a huge amount of rumpled clothes in big boxes for digging, like at yard sales, before anyone heard of yard sales. The children wanted to know what secrets lay in the bottom of each big box, and so did Amanda, while searching for clothes to alter. Amanda had a strongly inherited desire to make something from nothing, or was it learned? Scrounging was about saving money, but it was also a mental therapy, even if she were a millionaire.

Everywhere in Reading, Amanda watched sharply all around her, like a mother hen with a brood of chicks. As they walked along the sidewalks, children turned to stare at colored people, something they seldom saw anywhere else. "Look at those women dressed in black and white, almost like Amish! "Amanda said, "Please don't stare at them," but the children did anyway. .. what a bonnet...and why like that?. Those stiffly starched outfits looked uncomfortable. Amanda explained, "Those are Catholic nuns."

Amanda relaxed a bit at Rogers while waiting to have Mary and Lydia's eyes tested. The Kresge's Store often had bargains and the children eagerly wanted an escalator ride. Stepping onto that moving stairway felt just the same as stepping on the moving drag, out in the fields when gathering rocks. When Amanda returned home from Reading and unpacked her belongings, she had reason to have a headache, and need a good night's sleep. The smell of the city smog, the loud pounding music, the roar of traffic and the stress of crossing streets made their remote farm feel like a haven of rest, as it truly was! Who would choose to live anywhere else?

∽

When the boys were younger, they bought a kite with their pooled savings. 'This brand-new kite should really fly grand!" said Walter." Do you think we can put it up high enough that Jesse's boys can see it? Just think how it might sail!"Walter, Pete and Dick could hardly wait to try it out. Saturday kept them busy and they needed a stronger breeze. On Sunday, they did not concentrate on the sermon, when they saw a perfect wind rippling the treetops outside the church windows.

After church they dashed upstairs and changed into overalls, and started knotting together all the feedbag strings they could find, the only string they had on the farm strong enough to hold a kite. Right from the dinner table, the boys raced out to try the rare beauty of a new kite. Tension mounted as the kite gently lifted off the ground, as perfect as their dreams come true. The wind lifted it up higher and higher amid youthful elation. One knot of the many did not hold and suddenly the runaway kite swooped and sailed at the mercy of the breeze. The boys watched helplessly as it dived towards the woods, and "oh no," right into a tall poplar tree...the tallest tree in the area! There it hung while all three brothers schemed how they could possibly retrieve their brand-new kite. They certainly had no intentions of giving up and letting it there! Climbing the tall tree proved futile. Three brothers pondered the situation glumly."Well," they agreed," The only way we can get our kite back, is to cut down the tree."

With time to spare, Walter, Pete and Dick found two hatchets. They started chipping and chopping the stately poplar tree, eighteen inches in diameter. The soft wood of poplar chopped much easier than beech wood or an oak tree. They knew how to fell a tree in the direction they wanted it to fall, and they knew to stay away from any falling tree. "I'll take another turn"...chip...chip...chip...Timber-rrrrr...there she goes. .."After the crash, they hurried to the treetop to get their kite, but the flimsy paper kite lay smashed, never to fly again. Chalk it up as education!"

"Now what? Let's go stack some straw bales into a complicated tunnel, "the boys agreed. "We could make many steep steps up and down, to make them appear as dead ends, to anyone following our tunnel in the haymow..."That happened awhile back, but Aaron and Amanda saw all kinds of action, even if they never attended a circus in their life. The closest they ever got to such frivolous entertainment, was to observe their children growing up.

Children of all ages enjoyed playing with the hand -cranked corn sheller. The flywheel picked up enough speed that it shelled several more ears of corn before coasting to a stop. Whoomp...whoomp. ..whoomp. Perhaps the guardian angels kept all the children's hands undamaged from the dangerous toy. Walter shelled some ear corn and quickly wrote his name with the shelled corn, in 6-foot tall letters on the ground. When the many chickens came pecking, they outlined his name in chickens, at least until the corn disappeared.

Homemade stilts created pastime and laughter, as children waited their turn to try them out. That was easy, compared to riding the unicycle the boys made. When the new tricycle from Sears finally wore out, after many years of taking turns, the boys salvaged the front wheel and drilled a hole through a short log, to put the 5-inch long shaft through the log. Then, with four nails, they fastened a 2 x 6 board as a seat, and several of the boys practiced until they learned to ride on their single-wheeled contraption. They had a hard time riding on gravel, but it went down the barn hill, and on the long new cement walk. The seat wobbled loose occasionally, and it did not work well on uneven ground, but the unicycle was a challenge and provided entertainment in the form of showing off.

Teenaged boys gathered in Aaron's barn, to make confetti for an upcoming wedding. They shredded newspapers with the lawnmower, and shoved the paper through several times, until the size of the pieces suited them. The boys gleefully stuffed the chopped newspaper into sacks, and hid them in a car trunk until Saturday.

Daniel was one of the hostlers at Luke Horst and Fannie Leinbachs wedding, just one mile out the road. The fun began after the wedding dinner ended. The rowdy combination of boys had some from the Joe Wenger church and some from the

Horning group. Daniel thought the rambunctious boys could have done much better, but the day had a happy ending when Clement Leinbach gave the hostlers a generous tip for their good behavior. Clement was the father of the bride!

If watching their children grow up, compared to a circus, Aaron and Amanda's lives compared to a three-ring circus, when five daughters were dating at the same time. There was no way Aaron and Amanda could know all that happened around them, and they did not try to keep track. They did not know the parents of their children's friends, when many came from Lebanon County. If a daughter said,"William Brubaker's have a singing on Saturday night,"Aaron and Amanda had no idea where that might be. She wished to know how they spelled that, Brubaker or Brubacher? Might they be relatives? Girls got advice and opinions from each other and their older siblings. They did not confide in their parents as much.

When the older children started running around with the youth group, they felt shy and insecure. Amanda begged Sarah Ann to attend youth gatherings, and some of the others also struggled to fit in after changing churches, and making new friends.

When Ruth and Rhoda turned 17, that changed. They were bashful slim girls, at the legal age for dating but not interested in boyfriends at all. Their brothers advised them, "Do not spoil your names by turning down boyfriends without giving them a chance first! "Therefore, Ruth and Rhoda said "yes" every time boys asked them for a date.

Two boys chose two sisters for a double date, not worrying about "nothing to say", as they traveled together. The boyfriends came together and went home together, after both couples went to a singing together. It was twice as much fun as going alone. When boys asked the twins for a date, they did not care which name goes with whom, because they did not know each other. The twins asked questions like, "Who are your parents? Where do you live? Where did you go to school?"Ruth and Rhoda schemed among each other, ditching the boyfriends at the same time. They really did not want any boyfriends! They were scared to go

steady, so after three or four weekends they broke up before the young men had thoughts about going steady. As soon as the twins were blank, other boys asked them. Many boyfriends found their way to Aaron Shirks place over the years, for those first six girls. From there on down, the younger set found a better system of making more serious decisions, before asking a girl, and they only dated one partner.

For several months, five sisters were dating at the same time, in the same house, before Ruth and Carl's wedding. Amanda could see all the importance of romance that she missed with their courtship by mail. At Easter time, and on Valentine's Day, the couples exchanged fancy packages of candy, such as a ruffled heart box with assorted chocolates. The boys dressed up with long neckties, and opened the car door for the girl to scoot in, beneath the steering wheel, across a wide bench seat. The girl did not always slide all the way over to the other side, but sat in the middle. The boyfriends later admitted to intentionally sitting on a wide skirt, or the flared coattails, for an excuse to sit closer, although they were bashfully reserved most of the time. Ruth and Rhoda had identical coats and named them "turkey tails". The widely flared skirt of the coat fanned out, due to the many gores, wide at the bottom and snugly fitted at the waist. The long coattails that draped across the seat were easy to sit on intentionally or otherwise. Their wide dress-skirts measured approximately a hundred inches wide at the hemlines, sometimes more.

Aaron and Amanda's many girls made many new dresses and they had the fun of trading dresses, just to hear the compliment at a singing, "Is that a new dress?" Their basic dress patterns stayed the same, tightly fitted with a short zipper down the side at the waist —line. With both arms straight up, a girl squirmed and wriggled to pull on the tight dress over her head. They worked to remove it the same way, because dresses with zippers down the back were not common yet. Those teenagers tried every conceivable way to style the cape, which they wore separately, overtop the dress. Every now and then, some even tried lace, against Amanda's wishes. Their skirts contained plenty of material, to make them wide and swishy to swing out a bit in a big four game. Box pleats and double box pleats came into style.

Wearing look alike matching dress and shirts, were the 'in' thing for couples. Girls that never sewed a shirt in their life, soon learned how. Then, when a boyfriend arrived wearing his homemade shirt to match her dress, unplanned, she made him wait a few minutes while she went upstairs to change into her dress to match.

Every birthday and Christmas brought wrapped gifts such as Aaron and Amanda never had the privilege of exchanging. Amanda saw her daughters receive nice gifts such as a dresser set, a chenille spread, a pole light or a lighted picture, a mixer or last of all a chime clock as an engagement gift. Aaron and Amanda didn't have any chime clock. In fact, they never exchanged any gifts in their courtship.

On laundry day, Amanda put all the big girls' underwear into the same drawers, as first come, first serve. It was common for someone to come checking, "What slip are you wearing, is it mine?" Amanda was horrified at how many nylon stockings her girls bought. "Such flimsy stockings, why don't you buy better ones," she asked. Garter belts held up the thigh-high stockings, and it took a lot of fuss to keep the seams straight in the back. Last thing before leaving, it was common to hear, "Are my seams straight?" Even the best nylons did not wear long. Any little snag soon made a long runner. Amanda did not discard nylon stockings with runners or holes. She saved them to make a sturdy rug someday [, but she never did.] The best polish for patent plastic shoes was mayonnaise or a bit of cream for a fabulous luster.

When Aaron and Amanda went to bed on a Saturday or Sunday evening, it wasn't long until they heard cars coming and going, scouters coming and people talking. Scouters were other youth from their group dropping by unannounced, often hinting or begging for treat before they leave. The girls went to the kitchen to find treat for them, such as pretzels and drink hoping the scouters take the hint and leave soon. Sometimes the kitchen turned

into a real grand party, as three or four couples met for treat.

"Duh vie-duh duh vake, duh shennah de mate," was an old-time saying meaning, "the farther the road-the nicer the girls." That of course, was not true, but it helped make new friends where people did not know about each other and their personal shortcomings. Half of the singing group came from Lebanon County, and Aaron Shirks lived far out of the way. Friends asked, "How do you get there?" "After driving south through Bowmansville, you turn left at Levi Leinbachs big red barn, out beside the 625, and then it is the last place before the wooded hills." (Just don't paint that barn white, Levi!)Nine of Aaron and Amanda's children married partners from Lebanon County, a group of Horning church people, that started buying farms there in 1931.

With so many teenage girls, came many invitations and gatherings. Tupperware and Stanley parties were popular and Aaron's allowed their girls to attend those parties, and even buy things, but they were not supposed to book any party for themselves." A pyramid scheme is a racket," Amanda said, "and not for people that believe in the Golden Rule. Why obligate your friends for your own selfish gain?"None of their children ever booked a party.

Aaron and Amanda's children attended many singings as the most common form of social gatherings. They also attended watermelon parties, ice cream parties and skating parties, in season. Occasionally, they had a ballgame in the summer time, as a highlight, after a farmer gave permission to use his newly mown hayfield. Not only the skilled players helped, but everyone joined in the fun.

With no special plans, the couples sometimes stayed at home and played a game of Rook, Crokinole or Chinese checkers with their younger siblings, who greatly enjoyed helping. They sometimes went deer spotting locally, with three or four couples crowded together in one car. With a good spotlight, they scanned the field edges and roadsides for deer at night. Once a year Bernville displayed an extravagant amount of Christmas lights. Christmas caroling came annually, and so did hayrides. Spelling bees were popular, and Amanda was pleased if any of their children won. She remembered the thrill of spelling bees in her childhood. The Golden Valley Boys drew a crowd at the local fire halls where they entertained with string instruments and singing.

Aaron and Amanda desired to know the young people better, and even invited the parents for a Sunday dinner, to be acquainted. The best chance Aaron found to meet these young men, was at seven o'clock when they arrived for a date. Aaron had an uncanny way of standing beside the barn with a milk bucket, doing chores, at precisely the moment the boyfriends came around the turn. The boys did not mind to stop and talk with Aaron, because he did most of the talking, but the girls did not like it at all. They were embarrassed, wondering," What might Aaron be telling him?"

After things settled down, Ruth was seeing Carl Weiler, and Rhoda went with Mervin Brubaker, son of George Brubaker. At the same time that Martha dated Mervin High, son of Melvin High, Mary was going steady with Carl's younger brother Roland Weiler Junior. Those four couples spent a lot of time together in the kitchen, with enough commotion, to make the younger children curiously watch down the register through the kitchen ceiling occasionally.

The big girls did not want the home-place to look sloppy. They polished the philodendron leaves with butter to make them gleam. They cleaned up the outside more than ever before. They could not move the dump at the edge of the woods, no matter how much they wished to hide some old rusted vehicles. When Carl Weiler asked,"Where is Dick?"Ruth said,"Back at the dump!"When Carl went back there to talk to Dick, he was impressed with the graveyard of usable vehicle parts. To the girls surprise; the boyfriends thought the dump was just all right and even attractive.

Teenagers only called their partners on the phone in a dire necessity, maybe once or twice in a year. They dreaded the thought of a parent answering the call. Mervin High and Mervin Brubaker together, decided to surprise their girls during the week, and dropped in unannounced, on a Wednesday evening. The girls were drying their

hair after a shampoo and they were embarrassed. They thought the house looked a mess! The worst thing by far, was the dirty milk bucket setting in a puddle of milk right inside the door. Some manure stuck to the bottom of the bucket! The fresh milk was in the refrigerator but no one had cleaned the bucket, and there was no time to do that before both Mervins saw it! Both of them grew up on dairy farms!

When recalling the incident in later years, Rhoda said, "They wanted to surprise us, and see how it really made for real, and they certainly succeeded! What good did it do them if they married us anyway?"

After Louise turned seventeen, girls wanted a parlor at the same time, the youngest one got the best parlor. With only four rooms on the first floor, they did not each have a couch to sit on. The twins and their boyfriends shared the kitchen, with Ruth and Carl Weiler sitting on the wood chest. It was March and there was no other place to stay warm. With a lot of laughing and commotion, one boyfriend took the yardstick and poked it under the parlor door saying, "It's time for the next shift to have the parlor!"

After two months of this, Ruth and Carl announced their wedding day for May 21, 1966, after that, the secret was out, and plans progressed rapidly. Ruth took two weeks off from working in the factory to help clean up inside, and outside, doing a very thorough job. She sewed six dresses for the younger children in advance and her own wedding dress hung finished and waiting. Amanda said, "Wait to put the hems in the skirts, until closer to the deadline, because growing girls might still grow taller."

Ruth purchased navy whipped cream poly material for Amanda, and sewed that dress, even when Amanda enjoyed sewing, as much as Ruth did. Ruth fashioned a dozen fluffy white half aprons as gifts for their 12 waitresses whom wore navy blue dresses. On each ruffled heart shaped pocket, she pinned a bow, on which she wrote the words "Ruth", and "Carl" on the streamer ends of the ribbons. She first saw that idea in Indiana, and it was not hard to copy

Amanda did not like to see any fancy dresses and frills. She wanted her daughters to dress as she did fifty years ago. In Michigan, young people made changes when they married, and the bride and groom dressed like their parents from the wedding day on. When Ruth bought pale blue brocaded taffeta for a wedding dress, Amanda was disappointed with her choice, for such a solemn occasion. The dress was plenty short and the shoes too fancy to suit her. The bodice fit as tight as an onionskin, and the tightly fitted sleeves, had darts at the elbows so they could fit tighter, like the bought pattern Ruth used. Amanda was convinced that when the young people did not make changes on their wedding day, the church drifted faster in dress standards. Amanda let some things slide, knowing Carl's parents were not from the same church as Aaron and Amanda were.

Amanda talked the talk, and walked the walk, hoping her daughters would someday understand.

Ruth and Carl had a beautiful wedding day, with the outdoors of springtime lush and green, splashed with the color of irises and perfumed with peonies. Pete walked around with papers, closely examining the seating arrangement for calling the names at mealtime. Ruth and Carl with their attendants, sat upstairs in the girls big bedroom, watching the gift receivers opening beautiful packages. When the services began with the song of "Tread Softly", Ruth, Carl, and the two couples as attendants, came down the stairs and found their seats. Ruth's twin sister Rhoda, and Mervin, served as attendants on her side with Carl's brother Leon and Marian on his side.

Banks Horning, Aaron's home preacher, cleared his throat and spoke about a mother and daughter working side-by-side. Ruth was suspicious that he knew she would not work away from home due to homesickness. Bishop Joe Weaver married them.

After the full course meal, nobody skimped on photography, saving memories for years to come. Ruth held a crocheted hankie in her hands when she posed for pictures. Later on, the waitresses showered the bride and groom with homemade newspaper confetti, and even the young nieces and nephews enjoyed the party atmosphere.

Carl's father lay in a coma at the Ephrata hospital, recuperating from brain tumor surgery and he

was not among the 165 guests present that day. He never knew they were married, at least they don't think he knew, and he died six weeks later. Amanda packed some leftover food for Ruth and Carl, to eat as they traveled to the New England states, for one week. They did not want to go any farther, in case his father died suddenly, and they needed to hurry home. The newlyweds resided in their own house trailer, at the Bluebell trailer court along 322, and Ruth continued working in the factory, where she met her sisters every day.

Aaron and Amanda worked long after the honeymooners left on their trip. They returned the borrowed dishes, songbooks and fire hall chairs. The peas and strawberries ripening in the garden were highly perishable. Everyone kept busy!

In June of 1966, the Bowmansville congregation needed a new preacher, a miracle of choosing by the lot. Without training or campaigning to be a minister, one man of the laity would be chosen to preach. Many travelers came from a distance for the special occasion, and someone needed to open their home for a crowd of guests. Since Aaron and Amanda cleaned so thoroughly for a wedding, they offered to host the ordination dinner, with other volunteers bringing food and serving the meal.

When the votes were taken at church, it had nothing to do with voting. Any man in church could go into the ante-room alone and give one name in secret, of whom he thought might be qualified for the work of preaching. When the bishop announced seven candidates in church that Sunday, Sarah Ann and Mahlon were shocked to hear their name among the rest...surely not them... how could they?

In church, three days later, on a Wednesday, Bishop Joseph Weaver found the slip of paper in the randomly chosen book of Titus and Florence Martin, and he was the new preacher, to the great relief of Sarah Ann and Mahlon. After the church services, all the travelers and ministry came to Aaron Shirks for dinner. They served 150 guests, with many volunteer helpers, on June 28.

Amanda served large amounts of food and raised a big garden. The twins and Martha eagerly hoped to garner some vegetables for their winter food supplies also. 1966 turned out to be an exceptionally poor gardening year and Amanda barely got enough put up for her own family. The girls bought their vegetables from the store that first winter.

In July, Martha and Mervin announced their wedding date for August 6. Mervin was already working in 1W service in Allentown, Pennsylvania, and Martha was only 19. The girls gave their money home to their parents and kept only 10% until they turned twenty and then they were of age, but Amanda said, "Circumstances alter the situation". Martha did not have to give money home after they were married, and Amanda tried to help them find used furniture. Martha had saved all the money she could, but had only collected $750, and gone were the days with prices like Amanda had, when she filled her house with $100. Mervins skimped and saved, even doing without a telephone in service for two years. Their co-workers occasionally brought them a message.

Martha had help trimming the yard and waxing the floors. 151 guests arrived on a nice day for their wedding. Martha's two grandfather's and Mervin's two grandfathers were present at the wedding, performed by Bishop Joe Weaver. Mary and Roland were attendants, even when Roland had a broken foot due to a running gear of a wagon dropping on his foot at Edwin and Erma Hoover where he worked. The bridal party stood behind the bed full of gifts when they posed for pictures, to conceal Roland's cast and the crutches on the floor beside him, out of sight. The gift receivers helped pack the wedding gifts in Mervin's 1959 4-door Ford. At Allentown, Mervin and Martha lugged all those gifts up 40 steps to their third-floor apartment without ehlp.

On the same day, one hundred & twenty five miles away, another wedding took place with a lot more "ado", than the simple wedding of Martha and Mervin. At the White House in Washington DC, the President's daughter, Lucy Baines Johnson, married Patrick Nugent.

Martha and Mervin took a one-week wedding trip to the Smoky Mountains. One motel in Tennessee cost $7.50. Mervin served two years at the Allentown State Hospital, as a farm hand. Mental patients greatly rejoiced to help work outdoors on the farm, a highlight of their day.

Moving furniture in and out of the house for a wedding was a lot of work, but Aaron and Amanda were not finished, for the year. Two days after Martha's wedding, Rhoda sewed at her own wedding dress. Rhoda could hardly wait until after Mervin and Martha's wedding, so she could start with plans for her own wedding. After she finished her wedding dress, she did not like it and started over. The first one felt like raincoat material and Rhoda later cut it up to make a bathroom curtain that lasted for forty-five years. She bought dress material of brocaded taffeta such as Ruth had for their wedding. All of the new brides made a second best dress, and they displayed those dress samples beside the wedding dress samples, as souvenirs at the wedding. No one ever came up with a logical explanation what a second -best dress was. It perhaps could serve as a spare in case of emergency, but no one saw that second- best dress on the wedding day.

The fastest way to damage a new dress was by standing too close to the stove in the kitchen. Sometimes the girls unknowingly melted a hole in their skirts! The new polyester fabric melted easier than cotton.

Rhoda and Mervin Brubaker planned a wedding for December 3, 1966, and no one seemed to be excited at all! Where Rhoda had worked so hard, helping her sisters get ready for weddings, they were no longer at home to help with hers. No one bothered painting anything, and the lawn did not need any care in December. The week before the wedding, Rhoda came down with the mumps, and everything looked "fer-late-lich !"[bleak]. Amanda wore the same dress she had for Ruth and Martha's weddings.

With such apathy, Rhoda suggested that when the last girl in the family gets married, the rest of the family might only brush back their hair a bit, with no excitement remaining. Two days before the wedding, Martha helped bake eight sheet cakes at Mahlon and Sarah Ann's house. The night before the wedding, Aaron, Mervin High, Mahlon and Wesley helped peel three bucketfuls of potatoes. They were ready for the big day when 160 guests arrived on Saturday morning, on a very cold day. Mary and Roland served as attendants on Rhoda's side. On Mervin's side his younger sister Joann and Reuben Martin were attendants. Guests wore their coats in the unheated upstairs of the farmhouse, and that night the temperature dropped to 4°. Rhoda and Mervin drove away to a happy home of their own, after a trip to Florida.

On a Sunday afternoon while driving through Myerstown, a car full of girls stopped at a stop sign. Boys in an oncoming car, pulled up beside them and asked Louise for a date with Ivan Martin. They were blocking the road and it did not take long to say yes.

Ivan had no idea Rhoda and Mervin had wedding plans a few weeks after that. Ivan and Mervin were first cousins because their mothers were sisters. When Louise timidly asked Ivan if he wants to be gift receiver at the wedding, he said, "No way!" She regretted she gave him a choice, because it was the first time anyone had given her the honor of being gift receiver. Someone else got that highly rated job, while Louise and Ivan were just guests.

The next year Irene started dating Marlin Brubaker, who was also Ivan's cousin, but on the Martin's side. Ivan and Marlin lived neighbors at Mount Zion, near Myerstown, and often came together to Aaron Shirks.

After three weddings in six months time, Amanda kept stepping to stay ahead of making quilts for the next girls. Martha appliqued a lavender orchid quilt top from Leewards. To keep her busy in their apartment, she quilted the entire top by herself. Louise invited twenty-five girls to a quilting with three quilting frames set up at one time in separate rooms. Some of the girls were just learning to quilt and some ended up on the floor beneath the quilts, writing a journal of sorts, about who's who. They needed a break when they had sore fingers. Amanda was pleased with all the quilting the girls did that day, while she prepared dinner and a treat. Social events like that were missing in her teen years, with not many friends remaining in their group in Michigan.

At one time, others knew Aaron and Amanda as, "De shloppich-ey Aaron Sharickuh" (the slop-py Aaron Shirks). Times certainly changed and the teenage friends did not seem to mind, thus pleasing Aaron and Amanda. They had many unexpected guests overnight when their children brought friends along home without asking first." Hush, not so loud. We have extra guests upstairs!"

After singing a parting hymn, walk a mile was a popular social game at singings, after the dating couples left. Randomly paired couples walked side by side, in a long line along the edge of a back road, getting acquainted. The line kept shifting and rearranging, as extra boys and girls walked along splitting couples and telling one or the other to move several spots forward or backward in the lineup. It was a fun way to become acquainted, and some couples held hands, while others did not. Some people walked along behind the game, chatting and not helping, just walking.

All the teenagers wore polished church shoes for every social event. Sometimes those dress shoes were uncomfortable for walking. No one dared to be seen in everyday shoes, such as canvas shoes. In 1969, a new game of volleyball showed up. Anyone wanting to jump around in a game like that, brought along comfortable shoes to wear. Eventually they did not want to carry along extra shoes, and more people wore casual shoes for comfort.

After several vehicle accidents in a game of walk a mile, those games faded out." Come as you are" parties made a big hit among the youth group during the week, even if not everyone found out about the short notice party. Several people drove around gathering up friends unprepared to go away. They were told to come as you are, in everyday clothes, chore boots, blue jeans, aprons and all, with no chance to change or comb hair first. It was strange seeing boys wearing denim pants at a gathering.

When enough parents disapproved of their children's excuses for casual meetings during the week, in a laid-back atmosphere, those parties ended.

Anytime teenage girls planned a trip to Canada, Amanda encouraged her daughters to go. Martha went to Canada with girls her age and so did Mary. Louise and four other girls took Irene Brubaker over to Canada to be attendance at a wedding with Edgar Gingrich. Aaron said, "Yes, you may have our car." Amanda talked about all the relatives in Canada. They were distant to the younger generation and total strangers. "Try to make sure you get to Peter Brubacher's sister Barbara that is still living!"Amanda said. Barbara was just another senior citizen in a teenager's point of view, but Barbara considered it a real honor that the girls stopped by for a short call. She gave Louise a handmade pincushion as a keepsake of remembrance. It was twenty years earlier, when Irene and Louise had been to Canada with Aaron and Amanda for this same Aunt Barbara's second wedding.

As soon as the travelers arrived from Pennsylvania to Canada, they parked their vehicle until it was time to leave for home. Canadians arranged meals and beds for them, everywhere they desired to visit. They made many new friends. They could choose sightseeing, social events or whatever they wished, all with good food and elegant Sunday dishes, and hospitality beyond what most 'shtatesahs'[people from the states] gave in return. Canadians would not think of giving travelers a map and asking them to drive on their own. Friends could stay as long as they wished without spending a dime.

Amanda did not think that any of her girls should get married without learning the essential art of baking bread, but she lost out. Amanda could look back in life and she saw that many things rated higher than bread. Other people ate bought bread in Michigan, but the Peter Brubacher family made their own. Amanda's mother used a "bock mauled", a wooden dough tray; about 15" x 30" and 10 inches deep, with dovetailed corners and a well fitting lid. In the evening, her mother started some yeast in potato water in a gallon-sized crock. She brought the dough tray to the warm kitchen overnight and her father added 25 pounds of flour early the next morning. Mommy Brubacher mixed the bread dough in the shallow end of the tray, carefully not allowing the yeast mixture to touch the wooden boards. She worked a ball of dough to the right consistency and carefully used all the flour

she dampened. She cut and shaped each lump into a loaf; and placed the dough balls into her bread pans to rise and then bake. She scraped the wooden tray with a broken knife and covered the remaining flour with the well fitting lid, for next time. They had no problem with bugs and moths getting in their flour. Sometimes they used all the remaining flour in the bin for pies.

In Pennsylvania, Amanda and many others cut corners with bought bread. She heard the common saying, "Duh bakkah bokt my brote, ovvah ah flikt net my shtrimp!" [The baker bakes my bread, but he does not mend my stockings.] Every housekeeper had to mend their own stockings, but they had no problem finding a baker.

When Amanda thought back to those years, she saw a tremendous change since then. Their own children grew up faster than she imagined possible. As the girls got drivers license, they applied for jobs with a higher income. Any girl wishing to"hire out", as a household servant, cold find all sorts of jobs. Some of those jobs did not pay much in monetary value, but most of them paid in learning how to run a home. The poorer the management, the more the helpers learned, thinking,"Not like that!"

Ruth and Rhoda each had the opportunity to step into a one-room school and be a teacher. None of them accepted the job and they preferred the factory. Factories had better pay and the luxury of going home each evening, all finished for the day!

The Walter W. Moyer Company treated their workers as one big family. They needed promptness and dependability to keep the assembly lines running smoothly. Rhoda got stacks of freshly cut garments straight from the cutting room, where busy workers cut out the underwear. After Rhoda sewed the gussets in the ladies panties, she stacked them for Louise.

Louise sewed the elastic around both legs, and returned each bundle of two dozen garments into the next bin. The next worker closed one side seam, and the next person added waste elastic.

After closing the last side seam, the next worker securely tacked three spots where the elastic ends met. The size tag completed the garment, displaying the name of a company such as Sears Roebuck or Penny's.

The floor lady, with the job of overseer, had to keep the lines running smoothly. Workers could not take off without her permission, and if one person were sick for a while, it would throw off the whole line. It took skills in public relations, to understand the workers and their needs. Every time someone had a birthday, the company went all out to honor her with a corsage of real live flowers, usually orchids, straight from the florist, matching the color of the dress she wore that day. The company did not want people to take off from work for a birthday event, and helped create a festive day. Everyone treated others when it was their own birthday. Moyers announced the birthday names over the loud speaker each morning.

All of Aaron's girls worked at the factory over the years, and some of them stayed long enough to earn a five-year service award. Martha and Mary at one time worked on the assembly line that made the ruffled rubber pants for babies. A few times, they salvaged some scraps and sewed deluxe rubber pants for the dollies at home, with rows of ruffled lace. RoseAnna sewed waist elastic on rubber pants, and Irene started on circular waist elastic. Factory work was not enjoyable work for people that liked action, but jobs were valuable with not many choices available. Sisters had each other and always a family supper, with the evening together at home.

In 1966, the Ephrata Review had all the factory workers pictured for an anniversary celebration, at a time when Ruth, Rhoda, Martha, Mary, and Louise worked at Moyers. People toured the factory for five days of open house in June. The Walter W Moyers factory started on a small piece of land from Ephrata Cloisters, and kept expanding until it became one of the best knitting mills anywhere. The fabric was knit right there, then sewed and shipped to many different companies such as Gerbers, Sears and Penny's.

Hundreds of sewing machines hummed and clacked loudly until noon, and then a switch turned off the power for one hour. That was when the fun began, as the girls gathered with their friends. The one hour of fellowship and fun together, attracted many young Mennonite girls to work at Moyers, even more than the paychecks did. With up to a dozen friends in a group, some walked to the local stores in downtown Ephrata, to Newberry's, Harris's, Silco, the bank, the music store or the bookstore. With one eye on the clock, they ate a packed lunch, as they walked. Mary entered her name in a door prize drawing at Harris's and she won $25 worth of merchandise. She divided those riches in many ways and bought gifts for her younger siblings and Mom.

When not in a mood for shopping, the girls sat on stairways in a secluded spot, or walked out back to sit beside the Cocalico Creek. Workers had the opportunity to buy seconds and bargains occasionally. The most attractive things for sale were the ruffled rubber panties for babies, with three rows of ruffled lace across the back.

Any new mother -to –be received an astonishing gift of a complete layette, including diapers, pins, rubber pants, blankets, undershirts and all, when a new baby was the reason for quitting. At Christmas time, each employee received a ten to twelve pound turkey as a generous gift, after attending their Christmas program.

Minimum wage at $1.60 an hour was not all roses! Employees worked when they were half-sick, and some had to work beside people using foul language amid dirty jokes. Sarah Ann and Louise both spent years beside a greedy worker. The small, medium, and large sizes averaged out, when shared equally. When the girls left on lunch break, the greedy worker rearranged bins, grabbing the best moneymaking sizes. She was an elderly lady that did not need the money, but enjoyed stashing her treasures here below, buying stocks and bonds. It was evident that she did not have Amanda for her mother, where the golden rule was put into action. The floor lady could see what happened, but as long as the work was done without squabbles, she let it go.

Rose Anna worked beside a grouchy old lady

at Moyers and one morning she tried showing her the optimistic side,by cheerfully saying, "Good morning!"The grouch replied, "What is so good about it?" In the 1970s, the Walter W Moyer factory closed and moved overseas, all in the name of progress.

28 Photo of 9 wallet size sisters Place this wherever it fits best. No caption necessary

When big girls worked in the factory, Aaron and Amanda had a steady income with more money to spend. Auctions rated highly on Amanda's list of hobbies all her life, even back to the age of four in Michigan. When Amanda was tied down with many little children and no money, auctions were out of the question, but now she could go to many of them. Amanda bought each of the boys a used cedar chest from home and tried to find a used bedroom suite for each daughter, but could not find bargains fast enough and therefore paid $100 towards a new one a few times. The latest Formica topped extension cables cost $100 at David Hoover.

Harry's Auction in New Holland sold things on evenings or on Saturdays, when the factory girls could take Amanda. She loved to help fill any empty house; fondly remembering the help, they appreciated in filling their first home. Prices were much higher now, but so was the income. She also noticed that the next generation was harder to please, wanting things matched and pretty. In the 1960s, kitchen appliances were popular in green and gold colors, instead of just plain white. Melmac dishes, made of plastic, came in printed patterns of floral designs. Ruth had a set with lovely blue flowers, and the dishes did not break.

Amanda had a strange delight in buying feather pillows for her children. Each child received one set with their cedar chest, and yet she kept on buying pillows at bargain prices. Perhaps it was something she wished for, and had a shortage when she needed them, or perhaps she had fond memories of how hard people worked in Michigan, plucking the fowl and making pillows with a sense of accomplishment. Polyester pillows replaced feather pillows, and Amanda did not understand why her children snubbed bargain pillows. It was easy for

her to see the difference in one generation's time, how rich these people were choosing to live. Did she help spoil them?

Beneath the table at Harry's Auction, hidden in a box, Amanda discovered a set of dishes for sale. For $2.50, she bought the service for 12, china set in good condition, for Louise. After watching her sisters choose the latest patterns, Louise wanted a modern set, and more plates. Reluctantly she accepted the set of dishes, thinking that some day she might replace them. Twenty -five years later, her friends commented on the beautiful antiques, unlike anyone else's. She was pleased with those dishes after all, and the cast-iron frying pan in constant use for 35 years, and the baloney slicer Amanda bought for her over auction.

Diabetes

At the age of fifty-one, Amanda's blood sugar levels showed diabetes. Dr. Lauria tried to explain carbohydrates, but that was hard for her to comprehend. Amanda understood that sugar and sweets such as candy, jelly and pastries, caused problems, but every year she filled the freezer with sweet corn, lima beans and peas. She did not understand carbohydrates. Beyond eggs, meat and dairy products, almost everything she ate was on her list of starches to eat sparingly, balanced with protein. Amanda had a hard time considering bread, noodles, cereal, pretzels, crackers and potatoes as something to limit. Those staples were the mainstay of their diet. All the fruit in her huge supply of canned goods should be limited, and so was ice cream! Green beans, lettuce and cabbage, remained among her favorite vegetables to eat in abundance. She did not plant spinich, brussel sprouts, cauliflower or greens. She had a hard time avoiding white flour and so did her father.

Peter Brubacher stayed with Aaron and Amanda, and he had diabetes. It was time to learn to cook all over again in a different style. She could buy produce at the store, even out of season. Looking back over her grocery list for the past quarter century, Amanda could see how the carbohydrates caught up with her. She hardly ever cooked with- out flour, sugar, cornstarch, and tapioca. She wanted cheap food to fill her large family. Every year they bought sugar by the hundred pound bags for canning, and white flour in abundance. Back in Michigan, they also had white flour as a basic staple. In the century before that, people could not sift flour and remove the bran, because the screens had not been invented. Whole-wheat flour turned rancid and did not store well, therefore when Dawdy Brubacher had a choice, he preferred the white flour because it kept much longer. They soon preferred the softer, fluffier bread.

White flour became readily available about the same time refined sugar was plentiful, and the combination of using both in abundance, was not good. Aaron and Amanda had no idea that those basic foods were not health foods, and they ate them in large amounts. Gradually, snack foods and soda pop arrived in the local stores and some people called them" junkfood". Amanda did not like that word, because all food was a gift from God and none was junk, but she had much to learn about nutrition, and the need to make choices. Gone were the days when they hungrily and thankfully ate whatever they found or gathered.

Things changed drastically all around, and Amanda pushed a modern grocery cart in a well-lit store, with money in her purse, even choosing out of season foods and things ready-to-eat. More variety was available in the local stores. It used to be that only kings could afford to live in such luxury, eating exotic foods from faraway places!

After accepting charity many years, Aaron and Amanda wanted to share with the poor and the needy because they could better afford to be on the giving end. They did not forget how many hired helpers they had, and they remembered the joy of finding outgrown clothes in a box beside their mailbox, given anonymously. "Use it up, wear it out, make it do, or do without", was still a common way of life. Amanda was no longer poor, but she automatically pinched pennies for the rest of her life.

She was disappointed to observe the people in front of her at the grocery- store checkout, while she waited in line. She could not help but notice the loud and bold children with a "me first" attitude, as the mother paid with food stamps for expensive items and ready to eat luxuries. Welfare started out as a good idea to help the needy, but things went wrong and Amanda knew more was caught, than taught in raising children. Who would teach that daughter to make pies from scratch, and teach the children how to mend clothes and raise a garden and make do with less? Was the problem from too much TV, or just a lack of common sense? Amanda did not have any answers but she could not help but wonder what those children might grow up to be. Were they from a broken home, or did their parents mix up important priorities?

Nothing in life was free, unless someone else paid for it, not even those food stamps. No matter if it was a free pen or a calendar, or something as valuable as the plan of salvation, someone else struggled to pay for it! Hard working people paid for the welfare program and all the government handouts!

Closer to home, Amanda could see the effects of a broken home. Just across the Turnpike lived Herb Kohl, with a wife and two children. Aaron became friends with Herb Kohl and arranged for him to drill with a well driller, on Aaron's land, looking for iron ore. Aaron still dreamed about mining. The heavy old well drilling rig arrived in the woods in 1960, in the beauty of springtime. Aaron kept on buying woodland, and bought some from Ivan M in 1970.

The diamond studded drill bit pounded through layers of rocks and soil. In one day the drill went 8 feet deep, and four days later, Aaron bailed Herb out of jail. By the next month, they had drilled 101 feet deep, while Aaron walked out many times, checking in high hopes of finding iron ore. With a good strong magnet, he wanted to find bits of iron among the dirt, but he was disappointed. They chose a second spot and tried another well, but the project was a failure. All they found was good drinking water! Aaron went to visit Herb Kohl when he ended up in jail for "unjust reasons".

Meanwhile, Herb Kohl's wife left him and their young children... how sad! Donna and Carl, the size of RoseAnna and Wesley, came along with their father when he returned, drilling for iron ore. They automatically became friends and hung around more than necessary, especially after their mother was gone. They had nothing of a home life, and craved family life. When Carl came along, Aaron put him to work as a son and Carl helped Wesley plant tobacco and work on the farm.

When Stauffer's Orchard donated cherries for charity, Aaron took four of his own children plus Donna and Carl, to pick cherries for the poor people, donated through Mennonite Central Committee. The next day they returned to pick some cherries for Amanda's winter supply.

Donna and Carl were at Aarons all day on a Saturday, when their father did not show up to fetch them like usual. He was drunk! That night Donna slept between RoseAnna and Mandy, weeping softly into their pillow. "What if Dad doesn't come back?"She sobbed. On Sunday morning, Aaron and Amanda took Donna along to church. Herb Kohl became more stressed without a wife.

The Kohl's were upset and scared at home, when they saw something like a meteor, and they feared atomic bombs and atomic fallout. They had other concerns also, and one morning Carl Kohl arrived saying, "Mr. Shirk, what are we going to do if Amanda leaves you?"

The Kohl's had no idea how solid a marriage could be! Aaron had many problems and concerns over the years, with health problems, in-law stress, money problems, amid church decisions and school problems, with fifteen children to raise. Things did not always go smoothly, and yes, feelings were hurt many times, but divorce was not an option. Having Amanda leave him, was not at all a fear to him, ever! Aaron truly found a wife like the Bible says in Proverbs 31; 11.The heart of her husband doth safely trust in her, so that he shall have no need of spoil.

Amanda claimed that any wife should be able to get along with any husband, providing he was not a drunk or a hoodlum. She saw firsthand, that she could not change Aaron and she had to accept him as he was.

Running down the lane with hair and pigtails flying, was the closest thing to heaven on earth for Aaron's young children. It was not about the lane or the pigtails, it was not the lovely day or about winning a race, but it was the warmth of love. No matter how humble the setting, the love and security of a close-knit family drew them together. It was about gathering at the table, and silently bowing their heads, three times a day, no matter what the food, while sharing bits of conversation and bonding for a lifetime. It was about parents that worked together through thick and thin, and children needing them both! Aaron did a good job of providing for his large family, but the love of a mother was the hub of family ties. A mother that would never leave, "until death do us part." Children could not understand the security of a complete family until they were grown and looked back. Aaron and Amanda prayed many, many prayers for faith and strength, but always in secret and never for a show. No one said, "I love you," to the children, but they felt the strongest force on earth, love!

Broken homes were nothing new, as Satan tried his best to get between man and wife. Back in Michigan when Amanda was a child, her mother's brother, John Brenneman and his wife Alzina Rufford, had major problems. They lived on a 10-acre clearing, with a tarpaper shack, formerly an Indian dwelling near Burt Lake. Amanda remembered her cousins Walter, Arthur, and Norma, living two miles east of Peter Brubacher's. They had a stove there, but hardly any furniture.

When autumn came, they moved in with Aaron Kilmer's, a few miles south of Brutus, where another son, Raymond, was born. Then they moved into the town of Brutus, where they had a baby named Eleanor but she died with pneumonia. After a while, they moved to Petoskey, the Emmet County seat, where baby Erma joined the family. One year later, they moved to the city of Grand Rapids, Michigan.

John Brenneman worked on a night shift, and his problems multiplied. Eventually John and Alzina seperated, with five young children, and they struggled to cope. John realized his children needed good homes and a better upbringing, so the oldest son, Walter, went to live with Dawdy Brenneman's, as a hired hand. Arthur, the second boy moved in with his single aunt and single uncle, Joe and Salome Brenneman, one mile away. At school age, he was an able worker.

Peter Brubacher had the best place for the youngest three, where Norma, Raymond and Erma fit in among first cousins. Norma was the oldest, about eight years old, the same age as Katie. She keenly remembered the love showered upon them, and how three motherless children cried into their Aunt SarahAnn's apron. After living in the city, Norma knew nothing about gardening, and when her aunt asked her to weed the carrot row, she innocently pulled the weeds, and every one of the carrots also. The children kept in touch with their real mother and knew she loved them.

Norma formed a lifetime bond with her cousins and considered them as sisters. "Stuck on sisters, " [in Dutch, she said," Oh-ga-bopt a shvestah!"]Amanda and Norma remained closer than ordinary first cousins did, even eighty years later. Words cannot describe the powerful love of motherhood, and those willing to stay at home raising children, as the Bible says, in Titus chapter two, verse five "Keepers at home. " Fathers also had a tremendous responsibility.

∽

Aaron's brother Elias lived just across the Turnpike, barely a mile away. They raised a big family of seventeen children and remained with the horse and buggy church, using steel wheels on the farm equipment. Their oldest children remained faithful to the church rules, but one son bought a car against his parents' wishes. That created problems at home, because Elias and Nancy did not want their other children to follow such an example. They kindly explained the situation to Benjie and asked him to leave home, as long as he owned a car.

Aaron had a soft spot in his heart, for his seventeen-year-old nephew. He did not like to see him turned out like that, even if he understood the reasoning why. Half of Aaron and Amanda's children already married and moved out, and they certainly had room for one more. Benjie moved in and shared the boy's bedroom, where Wesley had two beds in one room, and Amanda barely noticed another plate at the table.

Taking in Benjie was no problem, except for the hurt between Elias and Aaron. Benjie soon bought a record player and musical instruments that his parents had forbidden. He enjoyed all kinds of music and especially the banjo. He joined the Weaverland Conference Church, and associated with their young people.

Benjie dug in to help work, as any son would help his parents. He worked hard in the tobacco fields and made himself at home. Wesley enjoyed Benjie as a brother, and Benjie needed that, while he missed his own brothers. Benjie stayed with Aaron and Amanda for about one year until the draft board caught up with him. He went for a physical and served two years of 1W service at Williamsport, Pennsylvania. He married Elsie Martin.

All of Aaron and Amanda's children learned to drive and get drivers license without even a doctor bill, but they kept some guardian angels extra busy. On Sunday afternoon, Wesley and Lydia headed towards Churchtown and met some of their friends coming towards them. With too much speed and not minding his business, Wesley started fishtailing and lost control of the vehicle. He ran off the road onto a grassy strip and laid the car over on its side. Their friends stopped to help, and together they righted the car and drove on, only bruised. The next week, Aaron wondered how the mud got on the door latch and his teenage children were not sure if he really wanted to know.

Wesley spent time with his cousins around the neighborhood, plus Noah Martin and Johnny Martin. Noah had no brothers and his mother was a widow, Mrs. Rube Martin. Johnny was an only child, the son of preacher Paul Martins. Wesley, Noah and Johnny [the three Musketeers] spent a lot of time together as "brothers" without a brother. It happened often, that Aaron and Amanda traded Wesley after church for two girls. He went home with Noah, while Noah's two sisters; Ruthie and Mary came along with Aaron and Amanda to play with Lydia, RoseAnna, and Mandy, or vice versa, with Lydia, RoseAnna and Mandy staying at Rube Martins place. It kept the younger children happy on a boring Sunday afternoon, and they all met somewhere in the evening to trade back again.

Johnny's mother Pauline, Mrs. Paul Martin, was the daughter of Eli Martins, and Pauline married her father's hired hand, Emerson Ringler. When Emerson died at the age of 33, Pauline married their hired hand, named Paul Martin. They had no children besides Johnny, and they were good friends of Aaron and Amanda over the years. Wesley and Johnny were quite a combination!

Aaron and Amanda did not lie awake at night concerned about their children, but trusted them to a higher power. At 3:30 AM, Benjie knocked on Aaron and Amanda's bedroom door, concerned that Wesley did not come home yet. Amanda could not shake her thoughts of concern. Children came home with all kinds of excuses for being late, but not this late! She could not sleep again, and woke the girls and asked, "Does anyone know where Wesley went?" One of them said, "Oh, yes I forgot, Wesley said he plans to sleep out with Johnny and Noah."

On a Sunday afternoon, the neighborhood boys knew how to find each other, even without telephones, but finding entertainment took imagination. One cousin said, "Those big dark cherries are ripening over at Lamberts, let's take a look!" Therefore, they biked over, and noticed cherries dropping down onto the roadway, where the massive cherry tree hung across the blacktop, like public property.

Wesley climbed way up to the top of the tree for the best and the most of the luscious fruit, while half a dozen boys all helped themselves eating cherries. To their surprise, Paul Lambert stepped out of the house with a gun and ordered, "You better leave! "They did not think he would shoot anyone, but they preferred not to wait and see if he was serious, or if the gun actually worked. The boys scrambled onto their bikes and left in a hurry, abandoning Wesley at the top of the tree. The bikes all disappeared, because Wesley had been riding double with someone else, due to a bike shortage. He was too scared to say, "Wait for me!" Without a sound, he flattened himself against the big tree trunk, like a scared wild animal. After he was sure the coast was clear, he descended branch by branch to the lowest one, about 8 foot up. He carefully

dropped down and hit the ground running for the 2 miles home.

In younger years when Wesley was bored, among so many girls, he enjoyed playing with the telephone. Everyone shared a party line, with each home a different ring. Four short rings meant it was for Aaron Shirks. Aaron enjoyed picking up the receiver first, deciding who the caller might be. "Do you want big Mandy or little Mandy?"He asked. No one else had a father like that, and he embarrassed 'little Mandy' when the phone call was from one of her friends.

Nobody had any secrets, on such a telephone system! When certain ladies hung onto the phone lines chatting, with not much to say, Wesley enjoyed listening in on their conversation. As they paused in a discussion of what they could make for supper that night, Wesley quickly said, "Oatmeal". Then he hung up. He enjoyed the telephone as a past time, only when his parents were not watching, because he knew they did not approve. One of his favorites, was munching big hard pretzels close to the receiver, and listening for comments. He enjoyed making all kinds of unmannerly grunts and animal sounds, all unknown to his parents.

Many times neighbors butted in on a telephone conversation, asking, "May I please use the telephone?" A busy party line was only half of a telephone, because many times people could not get through, no matter how urgent, when the line at the other end was busy. As soon as private lines became available, most people gladly paid a little more for a personal telephone.

The old number of 445-2323 changed to 445-6591 and stayed that way nearly half a century. Other people came to Aaron Shirks to use the closest telephone now, such as Jesse Brubacher's and Ike Zooks. Mabel depended on Amanda dialing the number for her and she did not know how to dial when she was alone."Do I start at that number or end at that number? "She started her finger at the zero and turned the dial until it came to the number she wanted, but she had it all wrong. She was supposed to start at her chosen number and spin the dial to the right all the way to the end, before removing her finger.

Benny playing a banjo

As young as six years old, Wesley learned to drive the Farmall tractor for planting tobacco, because he was too small to be planting the plants. He practiced making straight rows and when someone complimented Aaron on the straight field rows, Aaron said, "I can't drive that straight, Wesley did it" and that was a real compliment!

Amos Ringler asked Aaron to bring his tractor to haul grain to the barn. Aaron sent Wesley and Amos did not trust a youngster backing into his barn, but Aaron said, "Wesley can back up better than I can. "Driving tractor was easier than other strenuous farm work, but Aaron never really enjoyed it, he preferred driving horses, and he would rather work harder and let Wesley drive the tractor.

A homemade raft on Aaron's farm pond served as a boat. It consisted of a wooden frame, with six large empty metal barrels beneath it. With an anchor, the children could stop to fish in the middle of the pond, but they did not have an anchor. Ru-

ben and Benny Brubacher helped Wesley rig up a bucket of rocks, much heavier than necessary. After they lowered the bucket to the bottom of the pond, it took two people to retrieve it. When two boys stood on the same side of the raft to lift that bucket of rocks, all their combined weight tipped Wesley into the cold water with his clothes on. The law of gravity was alive and well on that day, and the anchor remained at the bottom of the pond. Chalk it up to education!

Looking down in the murky water of the farm pond, anyone could dream about big fish and snapper turtles down there. No one knew for sure. One day in December, Wesley found a 21-inch, large-mouth bass frozen in the clear ice. It weighed five ½ pounds, but it was not fit to eat. No one ever caught such a whopper at Aaron's farm pond.

Wesley did not have a brother to help shoot target or sight in a gun. He asked Mandy to shoot at a tin can on the fence post. She innocently knew she could do that, but Wesley did not tell his sister that his new gun kicks hard. She refused to try that a second time and Wesley got the biggest 'kick', in watching her get kicked. The bruise turned black and blue!

Wesley had a good sense of humor and he could make people laugh. He used his talents in making many new friends everywhere he went. As an 'only boy at home', Aaron took him along more often to places such as the Lancaster stockyards, and sometimes he treated him with a soda. They spent more time together, as father and son, than the older boys ever could among a group of them. The same thing happened at BW Shirk. When boys came in a group, they did not get to know their grandfather as well as Wesley did, all by himself.

He came to his grandfather quite often, because Aaron supplied his father with neat 12-inch chunks of locust wood, used for making handmade pegs for mortise and tenon joints. BW Shirk made every wooden peg individually, by first splitting the log into large splinters, nearly 2 inches in diameter. With a wooden mallet, he then pounded each square peg into a rounded hole to trim and shape it just right for the next barn raising. With hand tools, he whittled a point on one end of each peg, until it resembled a huge wooden nail. Locust wood did not rot easily. He needed a straight grain for added strength, but slightly curved pegs soon straightened out, when put into use like a big wooden nail, into pre-drilled holes. BW Shirk closely guarded his sharpened tool for pounding out the pegs, because the blades did not work when youngsters pounded and ruined the cutting edges. Over the years, he made many of those wooden pegs and it took perhaps 100 pegs (more or less) in building a barn, every time someone announced another barn raising.

Many tobacco farmers allowed a dozen tobacco stalks to bloom and ripen into seed-heads. They harvested the tiny round seeds for starting next year's crop. Those prime -quality leaves matured, and remained in the field longer than the rest of the crop. Wesley was pleased to have those perfect leaves for his own, as a gift from his grandfather. He dried them and sold them, with Aaron's tobacco crop.

The favors Wesley received from the close fellowship of his grandfather, taught him to cherish his own grandchildren many years later. Love must be taught and passed on to the next generation with gentleness and kindness.

B W Shirk enjoyed his grandchildren, and he talked with them. He delighted in handing out chewing gum to help children remember him. And warts. .. if he knew anyone had warts, he bought them."If I give you one penny for each wart, they will disappear, "B W Shirk said. He knew the virus problem would disappear on its own, but Louise felt rich with fourteen pennies without working for them. BW Shirk's father Benjamin Horning Shirk, with a surly, stern personality, seldom said a word to his grandchildren. Back then,' children should be seen and not heard'.

Amanda had happy memories of her grandparents in Michigan and she told her children all about those days. *Lydia and I took turns helping grandmother Brenneman with her Saturday work. We washed the kitchen chairs. Then we helped wash dishes and the cream separator. Grandmother Brenneman added a little cream to the dishwater for sparkling dishes. We gathered and washed the eggs and I remember making whipped cream with a fork. She gave me a shallow dish with cream and a fork to whip it, when I was about twelve years old. I worked awhile at whipping that cream but it turned out fine.*

Grandmother mopped up the bedroom, living room and kitchen. Then she scrubbed the shanty walk, pump bed and board walks to the outhouse. She scrubbed vigorously every Saturday morning, sometimes whistling while she worked. After a delicious dinner I helped her in the garden in the afternoon. Then grandmother put on a clean apron and treated me with a piece of candy. Those big pink wintergreen lozenges made a lifetime impression. My mother did the same thing, but you younger children did not get the privilege of helping her clean. They were never sloppy people and they did not raise so many children, so close together.

The Peter Brubacher family rested every Sunday afternoon, or else they visited neighbors in Michigan. Children liked action and we considered our grandparent's farm a boring place on Sunday afternoon, while the grownups sat and talked. We found things to play like hide and seek outside, or quietly played something indoors such as hide the thimble. Instead of hiding a person, we quietly took turns hiding grandmothers thimble. All the guests piled their winter wraps on grandmother's bed and we made dolls with them. We wrapped up mother's black shawl and put the smallest child's coat and cap on that bundle after we tucked a white hanky across the face area first.

In wintertime us younger girls always wore cloaks or capes [like Little Red Riding Hood pictures, but not red], over our winter coats to keep us warmer in an open carriage or in a sleigh. Mother made those cloaks with three layers of wool material to keep us warm. We used those hoods to make more pretend dolls.

We enjoyed going to Grandpa's because we got such a good dinner. One time grandma cooked some soft taffy and gave us each a fork to roll the taffy and eat it. Amanda loved to reminisce and so did her father.

Peter Brubacher often longed for Canada and the relatives that lived there. Not much remained, the way he remembered things when he grew up there, but he went to Canada for a whole month in 1968. Dicks took Amanda to bring him home again after he wished to return. Aaron preferred to stay at home.

Grape Nuts

Any time Wesley and his friends roamed the neighborhood on a Sunday afternoon, they knew they were welcome in Amanda's kitchen and in the summerhouse, snooping for a snack. Nothing was off- limits, unless Amanda had some freshly prepared special food for invited guests. On a Sunday afternoon, teenage boys met up with a cake, and tried to cut a piece. It was so tough that they could not cut it with the sharpest knife, and they went to get the hatchet. They still could not make pieces and gave up; not knowing what went wrong with that recipe.

Perhaps it looked like a cake, but they found Amanda's dried out Grape-Nuts. She made them for a breakfast cereal and she dried them out completely before grinding them. The recipe had nothing to do with grapes, or nuts. Amanda used whole-wheat flour, shortening, salt and sugar, mixed with buttermilk and baking soda to make a thick batter. After baking it like a cake, she dried it out and she sometimes grated it on her box grater or hand cranked it through their food grinder.

In summertime, Amanda skimped on making eggs for breakfast, because the only way she could heat the eggs was to heat the house with a fire in the cook stove. Cold cereal, served with milk and fruit, saved time.

Wesley enjoyed Reuben and Benny Brubacher right next door, first cousins a little older than him. They went rabbit hunting over at Titus's but didn't see anything to shoot. With a sense of humor, Wesley tossed a clod of dirt in Reuben's direction and said, "Rabbit coming your way!" Reuben shot instantly and thought he killed a rabbit, but he could not find any. Amidst all the laughter, he discovered he had been tricked.

With time to spare, Wesley made a noise contraption to see if he could scare Josie. He laid a log chain lengthwise on a tobacco rail in the upper barn scaffolding. With a long piece of twine, he fastened one end to the chain and the other end went down through a crack in the barn floor, attached to the stripping room door. When anyone opened the door, the big heavy chain fell fifteen feet and rattled to the floor above. Wesley saw Josie coming and knew he would go get oil for his wagon wheels first, so he waited at the corncrib in high hopes it would work. Josie jumped a little and said,"De boo-vuh!"![These boys!]

One Sunday morning Wesley found himself seated between two unruly boys in church. He kept ducking to get out of the way between them. When the commotion caught Aaron's attention, he did not know what was going on, but he fetched Wesley and made him sit up front, where Wesley was humiliated and felt he was innocent.

In 1960, Amanda's Uncle Arthur Brenneman suffered serious burns, while working beneath the hood of his truck. Gas ignited and he was admitted to a hospital in Virginia for extensive skin grafting. He barely survived! Arthur had a disfigured face for the rest of his life and one ear had nearly burned off. Aaron and Amanda wished to help the family. The best assistance they could give was to keep their son, Butch Brenneman. He temporarily moved in with Aaron and Amanda over that time.

Butch and Wesley were quite a combination, and full of action. In the big boy's bedroom, they played with Daniels violin and guitar. They spent a lot of time at the farm pond, and Butch said, "If I drown in the pond I will blame Wesley for not waiting on me". Wesley joked about that, because he knew Butch would not blame anyone after he died. They had such a good time together, that when Butch needed to return home, he was hiding at the next farm, over at Jesse's, hoping no one could find him. That didn't work, and he went home.

Wesley learned to like gardening, perhaps not the weeding, but picking things like beans and strawberries, and husking corn. He enjoyed riding the big tame horse named Tony, to shovel harrow the soil. It worked better that way, than the new garden tiller because the harrow did not grab or damage the plants that hung into the row. The front-tine tiller often balked and bounced on the rocky soil.

On a wet dewy morning, Wesley helped take off a large amount of sweet corn, and he used the station wagon to haul it to the shade tree. Sweet corn day was a lot of work for everyone and Wesley enjoyed the party of husking corn. After blanching, Wesley skillfully used the long wooden corn cutter with a metal blade, swiftly cutting and scraping to remove the kernels from the cob. Sweet corn in the freezer, tasted so much better and saved a lot of work! Wesley learned to make applesauce with the wooden stomper in Amanda's colander. He also kept busy any time he could help his parents dress some chickens. Wesley had a homemade bow and arrow, deadly enough to kill a banty, but that was no big loss, because the bantam went into the soup.

Dressing chickens was a common occurrence. First Amanda put water in her canners to heat. Aaron removed the heads and children were allowed to watch. The chickens flopped around with their heads off and splattered blood. After they were scalded, everyone pitched in to remove the feathers. Sometimes the hot water cooked the chicken skin enough that it came off with the feathers. Amanda complained about that, because she wanted to save all the skin. She knew the skin made a good flavor and a nice yellow color in chicken soup. {Too bad, nobody told them that the water needs to reach one hundred and fifty degrees and then the skin stays on if the hen is dipped for one minute.}After the feathers all came off, Amanda singed the hair off the chicken skin by holding the hen by the feet over a bonfire. The bonfire smoked Amanda and singed her hands a bit. Sometimes she rolled up a thick newspaper and with flames at one end; she quickly used it as a torch.

Then Amanda sat on a chair and scrubbed those plucked hens with a scrubbing brush and lava soap. She carefully picked tiny pinfeathers a long time. The white hens looked much cleaner than those with tiny dark pinfeathers beneath the skin. That is why commercial grown turkeys are mostly white.

Amanda wanted all her children to learn how to dress poultry, and encouraged them to help. Aaron enjoyed cutting up chickens after Amanda finished scrubbing them. With a sharp knife, he butchered a hen in a few minutes. He butchered faster, when he tried to impress a child. Louise stood by and watched! The whole thing fascinated her as Aaron tossed the good meaty parts in the cold water. "See the chicken heart", he said, "the piece some of you children like the best. Here is the liver. After I cut this gizzard partway, you may peel out the contents." The smell did not deter Louise as she mar-

veled at the grass and stones inside the gizzard.

Mary kept out of the way as much as she dared. She folded the clean laundry and even preferred the low- down job of washing heaps of dried-up dishes. She did not want to butcher chickens nor dress wild game! Between the two of them, both sisters worked at what they preferred.

Amanda cooked a huge canner full of meat, and saved eight drumsticks for packing lunches the next day. When eight scholars came to school with so many chicken legs, a cousin said, "our chickens only have two legs, how many do yours have?"Amanda served cooked chicken with potatoes and such, on the first day, fried chicken on the next day, and the rest went into the soup. She wasted nothing, not even a tail or the wing tips. The half-grown eggs from inside a hen, simmered on the wood stove for a tasty treat, or maybe a between meal snack. Aaron taught the children to enjoy the egg stalk, the part inside a hen where the eggs traveled through, and the children nearly fought for it. Amanda was not so sure about that!

Many years later, Mary called Louise on the phone, with her twenty five foot telephone cord swaying from the phone on the wall, to the receiver in her hand at the kitchen table."Now where did you say that I should cut next? I have the legs and the wings off...now what?"

Louise said, "Grab the heart and rake out all the organs. ..carefully cut around the behind without cutting the entrails... remove the green gall from the liver and carefully peel the lining from the gizzard...isn't it amazing how the gravel in there grinds all the grass and corn they eat ?Clean up the mess! Oh, fuh-guess nets fet heffly! [Forget not the fat gland].Remove that miraculous oil gland that God planned for waterproofing all our feathered friends."

Neighborhood boys went fishing to Elias's, and took along a burlap sack, to bring home the fish they caught. They did not get any fish that day, and on the way home, while crossing the turnpike bridge, they paused to watch the traffic. With an empty sack in one hand, and a fishing line in the other hand, they put the two together and lowered the sack over the side of the bridge. They had no idea how dangerous it might be, dangling an empty sack in the traffic.

When Wesley was not teasing his many sisters, he entertained or pestered poor old Skip, lying on the porch in the sunshine. One time Wesley took a magnifying glass and directed the sunshine through it, onto skips ear as the dog slept. After the third yelp, Amanda found out what happened, and put an end to that, but not before Skip carried a slight scar on his ear for the rest of his life.

Aaron and Amanda received a wedding invitation to Peter Brubacher's youngest brothers, youngest son's wedding. George Walter Brubacher and Lynda from Colorado invited them to a wedding out west. George was Amanda's youngest cousin, born after she was grown and married. She did not know him well, but a wedding invitation to a first cousin rated highly. She knew that for practical reasons, she could not attend a wedding so many miles away. Aaron did not like to travel and they hardly knew the people. None of her sisters could afford or wish for such a trip. Amanda willingly stayed at home and sent a handmade quilt as a gift. She did not have the time to make a quilt, so she gift-wrapped one that Louise had recently made for her hope chest. She mailed the quilt, and replaced it later.

30

When Mary turned seventeen, Ruth Ann Martin surprised her with a birthday party, on a Sunday afternoon. Many friends arrived, bringing brightly wrapped gifts just for Mary. Not all the girls had a party, and Mary was honored. She felt obligated to return the favor, and she held a birthday party for Ruthann, when Ruthann turned seventeen.

Most of the youth group stayed at home or went with their parents until they turned 17, old enough to go to singings and start dating, all at the same time. Mary, like her older sisters, was almost too bashful to enjoy social life at first.

She saw Roland Weiler at Green Dragon, when she was 16, and she knew he was Carl Weiler's younger brother, and not from the same church that she was. It took a while until they actually met, because Mary dated others first, and so did Roland. All five of the Weiler boys eventually joined the Weaverland Conference Church.

One evening during the week, Roland's friends picked him up, and only then suggested they ask a girl for him. When he hopped in their car he didn't bother grabbing a coat or his shoes, not knowing of their plans, and he ended up nearly at Aaron Shirk's farm, stocking footed. The other boys dropped him off just before the end of the lane, and then they went to ask Mary if she would accept a date with Roland. The answer was yes! Meanwhile, in the short time Roland stood there alone, in stocking feet; Aaron and Amanda came home from somewhere and saw Roland, standing there in early March, looking cold. Aaron and Amanda soon heard the rest of the story. Mary had a date for Saturday night!

Roland Weiler Senior, at the age of 57, had surgery for a brain tumor, and spent the rest of his life in a coma. Sometimes his eyes followed Mary and Roland when they stopped at the Lancaster hospital, for a visit, and they often wondered what all went through his mind as he lay there, for one half year, unable to speak.

In 1966, Mary had a wonderful opportunity to go to Canada with three girlfriends, but she did not trust going along in case Roland's father might die while she was gone. The girls assured her that he lived one half year like this and they would bring her back if necessary. Three days later Amanda called over to Canada, trying to locate Mary to let her know that Roland Weiler Senior passed away. All four of the girls, cut their trip short and left Canada; arriving at the Harrisburg depot at 6 PM. Aaron and Amanda met Mary and took her to the Strattling funeral home in Ephrata for the visitation. Roland Weiler brought Mary home afterwards.

Mary and Roland had several years of getting to know each other, while the twins and Martha were still at home. It did not seem long to Amanda, until they were getting ready for another wedding. Mary went with Roland to order a suit at Hagers in Ephrata. They went to Dr. Bender for a six-dollar blood test, before applying for a marriage license. On a Saturday night, Aaron drove to Deacon Walter Martin with a secret, telling him to publish another daughter's wedding plans, at church the next morning, for a wedding three weeks later.

When Walter Martin came in the house and lifted up the calendar page, his daughters knew the secret, without a doubt! They saw he talked with Aaron outside. After several years of dating, not many people were surprised anyway. Those' secrets 'were eventually replaced with engagement announcements.

Mary had cut dress samples to give away as keepsakes, from the leftover scraps of her finished wedding dress. She took a week off from the factory and everyone dug in to help for a wedding. It was a year and a half since Rhoda left home and thought no one cared about another wedding.

On May 25, 1968, one hundred and seventy eight guests helped celebrate Mary and Roland's wedding on a lovely spring afternoon. They hoped most guests overlooked the un-mowed yard! That was supposed to happen at the last minute and then it rained all day. The lovely peony bushes and Irises, in bloom decorated the lawn.

Roland painted his car bumpers black and the strip of chrome on the side of his car. He bought a hat to dress like the other men at church. They moved to 1841 W. Main St. Ephrata, along the 322, on a steer and tobacco farm.

Aaron and Amanda tried their best to get everything returned to its proper place, before the peas and strawberries ripened in the garden. After every wedding at home, they needed time to recover.

Mary doctored for a goiter problem a few months before their wedding and then she needed surgery a few months after they married. Thyroid problems ran in the family on the Brubacher side. Aunt Betsy had problems and so did Rhoda later on.

Any time Amanda heard a strange bird call; she stopped and listened, because she knew the majority of their calls. By doing so, she automatically taught her children the art of bird watching, even without binoculars and keeping records of bird lists. She bought her first paperback bird book, and memorized all she could, and in wintertime she sent a child to the barn for some "shroat," [cattle feed], to sprinkle on the deep snow for the birds outside the kitchen window. All of nature was dear to her, even way back as a child in Michigan. Back then, they did not have much wildlife, besides an abundance of plants and birds. As the children grew up, Amanda had more time for a walk in the woods and she did not just see trees, but she studied all the plants as she went, naming those she knew. For in knowing the true name of something, we tend to feel closer to it.

The girls at the factory talked about a jack in the pulpit. One innocent friend asked, "Do you mean the thing that jumps out of a box?" She never had the privilege of observing a jack in the pulpit plant in her childhood.

Among the Jack in the pulpit, adder tongues, pipsissewa, trailing arbutus, bloodroots, crows foot, skunk cabbage and the wintergreen berries, Amanda found many plants that puzzled her, because she had no reference books to look things up. Amanda remembered Jerusalem artichokes growing wild in Michigan, but she was not sure if the plants that grew along the bank beside the garden were the same or not, therefore she did not cook and serve the roots.

Amanda pointed out the plants she knew, and repeated the names she learned in her native tongue; burdock/gletta, thyme/gwendle, Yarrow/shoaf ribba, mullein/wool-kraut, catnip/katza-kraut, sage/solvei, stinging nettle/brenn-asel, yellow dock/holwa-gaul, plantain/sie-orrah, dandelion/pissabet, chickweed/hinkle-darm, mallow or cheese plant/kase boppla, boneset/darich-vox, comfrey/shwatz-votzel, elder/hullah, Drake/mai-epple, purslane/sie-botzel, parsley/patah-ley, currents /cons drouva.

Amanda remembered how Uncle Joe Brenneman and Aunt Salome cooked and ate fern fronds when the fiddleheads curled up tightly in spring. Amanda never tried them.

Amanda talked about the' cons drouva' [current bushes] beside her mother's garden in Michigan. The red ones made a lovely jelly, the nearly black ones looked good in homemade wine and her mother used the white currents in pies. Two or three government men came one day and made them dig up and destroy all their black current bushes for medical malpractice reasons. Aaron and Amanda knew that many plants had medicinal value, but no one taught her how to use them. After doctors learned about penicillin and other 'miracles', people did not pass those valuable home remedies on to the next generation, because they trusted doctors to fix anything! Amanda missed out on herbal lore.

As a novelty, Amanda showed her children how the plantain leaves resembled pig ears in the grass, and the leaves of the yarrow plant, resembled the rib cage of a sheep. She showed them how the burdock seeds stuck to the screen door, much like Velcro. They could spell out letters with burdock seeds on the screen. The thick jelled leaves of the sedum plants, she called 'turtle bellies'. Amanda squeezed or pinched a leaf just right, without ripping the membranes and blew it up like a tiny balloon.

When it came to home remedies like comfrey, burdock, plantain and such, they ignored them all and put more confidence in Dr. Lauria. He could cure all that they ever wished for... even pneumonia and dreadfully broken bones. Not long ago, anyone with a broken bone poking through the skin, might as well start planning for a funeral, because there was nothing a doctor could do to fix it, except maybe amputation. Every cut scratch, or puncture wound was serious business, before antibiotics.

Aaron learned to enjoy raw dandelion greens and he gathered many, but Amanda did the hard part of cleaning the leaves. Amanda's favorite, needed repeated washings, to suit her inspection, because Aaron brought dandelion to the kitchen with mud and a fish worm or two. She liked dandelion with hard-boiled eggs and bacon dressing. Some people even canned dandelion to preserve it for wintertime. Watercress remained among Aaron's favorite salad foods, but it did not grow in their section of the Black Creek. Every chance he had, Aaron ate watercress in a sandwich.

The fallen logs and rotten wood on the forest floor seemed just right for morel mushrooms in springtime, but Amanda could not find any in Pennsylvania, as Michigan had. The mushrooms grew from a mycelium below the ground, a vast network of tiny roots that thrived on rotting logs and fallen leaves, and the rootlets remained there all year. As the soil warmed up and spring rains arrived, mushrooms flourished. It happened every year about the same time that asparagus started growing, and the oak leaves grew as big as squirrel's ears. Searching for the elusive fungi brought people to the woods, in the beauty of springtime. Even without finding any mushrooms, they found a peaceful contentment and closeness to God among such an elaborate creation. As soon as a canopy of leaves shaded the forest floor, the mushroom season ended.

Among the peat bogs of Michigan and Wisconsin, it is possible that a mycelium is the largest living thing on earth, even weighing more than a redwood tree, or a blue whale. It remains hard to prove, hidden away out of sight. When conditions are right, mushrooms pop up unexpectedly in all sorts of places. Love is like that, with a network of friends and family connected with a powerful unseen bond.

Drivers License

Aaron and Amanda both knew that she needed a driver's license, but Aaron was the one that pushed to see it become a reality. If he should die first, what would Amanda do without transportation? Nobody happened to drive by such an outback location to pick her up and take her along. In 1968, he bought a 1966 Ford with an automatic transmission, just in case Amanda ever wanted to learn to drive. He wanted her to have easier driving, for fear she would never manage shifting while driving.

Eventually Amanda consented to try for a driver's license, because she wanted to go many places. When Lydia turned sixteen, she took her mother along to try for a learners permit. They both went for a physical before they could drive. Perhaps Amanda had been a skinny bride, but she now weighed 195 pounds at 5' 4".Mother and daughter practiced driving in the wide-open hayfield beside the house, backing up and turning around many times.

A four-year-old granddaughter went along on a trial run, when Amanda accidently slammed on the gas instead of the brakes while turning sharply. This tossed Wanda and really scared her, especially when her grandmother panicked and just pushed the gas pedal harder and harder, before finding the brake, while going in circles. Wesley and Johnny Martin, age seventeen, laughed until their sides hurt, from watching a grandma doing donuts in the hayfield. They took their car out there and did the same thing, but Amanda parked hers!

She remembered the first car ride of her life. Amanda said, at the age of 16, I worked for a neighbor and he gave me a car ride. 'The model T had curtain sides and a roof like a top buggy.

In my mother's childhood, they ran up the bank, and off the road every time a car came, which did not happen often. They came back down and studied the neat pattern the tires made in the dust."

Aaron and Amanda could scarcely comprehend all the changes since then. Amanda never dreamed back then, that she might someday drive a car by herself!

At the age of fifty-four, Amanda passed her driver's test... on the third try. Her father still lived and saw what she did, but Peter depended on those wheels to go everywhere. He feebly, could no longer step into a carriage. Amanda used her own wheels for quiltings, sewing circles, and auctions, and helping others every chance she had. She soon became the manager of sewing circle at the Fairmont home, and she loved it! The Fairmont home had started only five years earlier.

Amanda did not like when a quilt had one side longer than the other. At home, she carefully measured with a tape measure to make the sides even, as her mother had taught her. She had access to modern soft knit fabric donated to charity. She frowned on using a stretchy back on a patchwork comfort. She said," When the back stretches more than the top of the finished cover, the seams in the patchwork top will pull apart. At sewing circle, she learned to cut corners a bit, when quantity counted more than her precise neatness. The group of women that met every month, made many covers for the needy.

Amanda could not find the dimmer switch on her car, and drove to TerreHill with her headlights on high beam. When a Rissler boy parked beside her, she asked, "Please help me find the dimmer switch." It was on the steering column and not on the floorboard where she had searched.

Amanda helped cook chicken and pick the meat off the bones for a soup supper at the firehall. No one wanted the chicken wings, the skin and the backs so she took those scraps home. She saved every bit of skin on the necks and tails or whatever looked edible, especially the chicken wings. Amanda rolled the cooked wings in cracker crumbs and gently fried them in butter. Every one of the children enjoyed the golden crunchy delicacy. Only the bones remained for the cats and the dog.

When Aaron came to the barn and found his biggest fattest steer dead from no apparent cause, he was puzzled, and two weeks later, he found a big hog died mysteriously. Upon investigating, they discovered a bare electrical wire touched a back rub, used by the cattle. Aaron's time was not yet up... he could easily have been a casualty of electrocution. Maybe it helped that he wore rubber boots. Even Amanda, with all her frugal ways did not want to eat meat that did not bleed first. The huge pile of corn- fed meat; all went to the scavenger at TerreHill.

Amanda often wished to attend funerals in Canada, but she could not. Now she had a driver's license, and when Aunt Selina's funeral announcement came, Aaron allowed her to go without him. He serviced the car for her and he was pleased to stay at home. Amanda was good at map reading, and she knew most of the roads from her former trips to Canada. She planned a trip with Martin Kilmer's and Christian Kilmer's, taking along Lydia age 16, for a second driver, both of them beginners.

Amanda never drove on a four- lane highway before, and the other traffic bothered her. When a vehicle followed her closely, she drove in the left passing lane and Lydia asked, "Why"? Amanda said, "I want the car behind us to get past us!" God was with them, and they had a safe trip and a wonderful fellowship.

Eight weeks later, they received another funeral announcement from Canada, when Uncle Amos Brubacher died. This time Walter and Marian took Amanda, Silas and Lydia, the same three siblings that traveled together to Canada in 1937, looking for partners. So much happened since then... enough to fill a book. Silas and Lydia had married, and both were widowed.

Walter was driving north through Pennsylvania and he thought Silas was fast asleep in the backseat, when Silas spoke up and said, "Up here you want to make a right turn." Silas was right, and he knew the way exactly, even if many people did not notice how bright he was.

Amanda enjoyed her newfound freedom in coming and going as she pleased. She did not mind staying until the end of an auction, finding more bargains, when she knew nobody else waited on her. She spent more time with her sisters, and took them for doctor appointments, as they stopped many places along the road to make calls wherever they pleased.

She still had many teenage activities around her and many people with schedules, coming and going. When Irene came home at bedtime, Amanda said, "Oh, so you were away?" Irene had been at sewing circle, and when her friends heard such a story, they marveled, because their mothers were overly concerned until they came home again. Scouters on the weekends made commotion, and sometimes a carload of girls giggled outside their screened bedroom windows, or loud boys clamored for a treat.

A thief would have had a hard time avoiding people among all the activities. Occasionally Aaron became suspicious about stolen fuel, but he could not prove anything and he had children using more gas from that tank than he might realize. Years ago, Aaron's cows were missing one morning. He looked around the neighborhood and declared them stolen! Aaron came over to Titus and said,"I am sure that so -and -so stole my cows and sold them at the Allegheny Auction. " Titus told him to look at Weaver Martins on the other side of the hill. Sure enough! He found them all, very much alive and well.

Aaron and Amanda had reasons to trust everybody that drove in their long lane, but their children excitedly planned to catch a thief! One night they slept in the barn waiting, and sure enough, lights turned in the lane, raising their blood pressure in excitement !The thief turned out to be no thief at all, just Benjie. One weekend a group of girls seeking adventure, slept out in the barn, just for fun, when they could have had proper beds.

Aaron and Amanda's children attended many local spelling bees like the one at Martindale fire hall, Hinkletown, Crossroads, and Bowmansville. Amanda enjoyed spelling bees all her life, and allowed her children to attend if they helped in the spelling class. Mandy often came home with a prize, sometimes   just a game or a dollar. When she won

first prize she received $1.50. Third prize might be simply a candy bar, but the honor of winning was worth the most. Irene won second prize in a Dutch class, translating English words into the Pennsylvania Dutch language.

When the girls came home from sewing circle, late on a Wednesday evening, Aaron sat up canning beans for Amanda. She cooked each canner nearly three hours and he took the last ones out of the canner at one o'clock in the morning. He helped Amanda in the garden many times when his back was better. He crawled on hands and knees to pick the strawberries, and Wesley helped him pick the pickles and the green beans.

Aaron asked Amanda to cook sheep meat and let the children guess what they are eating. They guessed all sorts of things, but not one of them thought of a sheep.

As Peter Brubacher aged, he did not like the noise and commotion around him. Amanda discussed distant relatives and things in the past with her dear father. They mentioned Michigan and faraway places the children never saw. When Amanda talked about "de, I-o-way pik-ah" [Iowa piker], her children knew nothing about the May City group and they did not want to know.

Peter had diabetes and Amanda did not want the children to eat ice cream when he was there, so the four youngest children sneaked a box of ice cream and a handful of spoons for an ice cream party on the girl's bedroom floor. Upstairs, out of sight, Wesley, Lydia Roseanna and Mandy, sat on the floor, squaw- style, and all dug in, to empty a box of ice cream. Amid laughing and giggling, they had a real party.

Peter had diabetes, but he kept on eating bread three times a day, as the staff of life. He grew up eating bread with every meal, and sometimes more than one slice. He started every meal with a slice or two; of buttered bread topped with jelly or apple butter. For dessert, he ate another slice, with any fruit or applesauce on top. Even with diabetes and a lifetime of smoking the pipe, Peter lived to a ripe old age of eighty-nine. He had low blood pressure and so did Amanda. Most of their children inherited that.

Aaron's girls felt sorry for their tired looking grandpa, and one time they helpfully turned on some music for him, playing records to cheer him up. He did not appreciate it one little bit, and complained to Amanda, who scolded her children and told them, 'Please keep all the music away when Grandpa is here!"

When boys are little, they wish to grow up and do bigger things. When they are fathers, burdened with cares and responsibilities, they envy the lifestyle of grandpa in retirement. Grandpa looks back on his entire life and thinks, "If I could be a boy again...!" He saw how short life really was, and what it was all about. He could see things differently now, and truly, life is but a vapor! Once to live... and once to die...

Peter Brubacher got sick and died at Christian Kilmer's on May 6, 1969. They held the visitation and the funeral dinner there, with burial at the Bowmansville Mennonite Church. He had outlived most of his friends and people of his generation, and he was ready to move on. His obituary in the newspaper said, "P M Brubacher dies, 144 kin. 'Only four of his children had children, but they brought him forty nine grand children. Not one of them carried the Brubacher name.

Ivan

Aaron and Amanda needed a desk for many years. Since the girls brought home so many factory checks, she ordered a new desk for one hundred dollars. George Zimmerman made it from solid cherry wood, with a bookcase top section. Amanda did not fill the top with books; she stacked it full with dishes and such. Louise admired the desk and ordered one just like it, for their future home.

When Louise and Ivan's wedding came along, it was routine to know which fire hall had the narrow chairs, and where to order what. Irene enjoyed the planning and ordering, so she helped a lot. On March 7, 1970, Louise turned 21, on their wedding day. One hundred and sixty three people crowded into the house as tightly as possible. Less than half the guests could see the bride and groom, even after eliminating many names on the guest list, con-

densing it as much as possible. They could invite only two of Ivan's many aunts and uncles and very few cousins.

In the afternoon, some guests stepped out on the porch to watch the solar eclipse. Amanda's sister Lydia heard that the newlyweds planned to travel to the West Coast, and possibly stop in for a call at Great Uncle Isaac Brubachers, where Pete's and Dick's had such a warm welcome. Lydia seriously considered going along, because she saw the car was not full. She did not seem to understand that she did not have a chance and she was not welcome! Louise and Ivan sighed with relief when Lydia remembered she had other plans that interfered, and she needed to stay at home.

Ivan and Louise first lived at Newmanstown, in Lebanon County, working for a dairy farmer. Ivan lost his farm deferment. Selective service letters arrived in the mail later that year, and they moved to a trailer park near the Norristown State Mental Hospital. There Ivan spent two years milking cows for the hospital. The 600-acre farm had a dairy, pigs and a farm to raise their own food for 2,600 mental patients. Other Mennonite Concientious Objectors worked for the same Hospital. Some worked among the patients as orderlies. After 1972, the drafting ended and the dairy closed due to a lack of skilled help. Town boys without a dairy background had a hard time learning all the detail and many were not dependable.

Aunt Lydia had the privilege of planning her second wedding! Perhaps she already knew that 'secret' when she attended Ivan's wedding. After Eli Stauffer died, she remained a member of the Pike Mennonite Church for twenty years. Then she joined the Joe Wenger Church again. Several years later, she married Christ Shirk. [Christ is pronounced Krist] Eli had 11 grown children and Christ had 12 grown children, therefore Lydia had 23 grown stepchildren in all, but none of them to call her own. She still claimed her nieces and nephews as her close blood relatives. She chose Lydia and Carl Hoover as usher, while Irene and Marlin served as waitress and hostler after the services at Churchtown Church, on a Sunday morning. They planned a simple wedding, but 89 people attended the wedding dinner. His children plus her stepchildren included many families besides her nieces and nephews. Sixty people stayed for supper, on November 22, 1970.

Uncle Christ, as everyone called him, had some serious back problems and went for surgery in Ephrata. He walked into the hospital by himself but the doctor made a wrong cut and Christ spent the rest of his life on a wheelchair. He was paralyzed soon after their wedding, and spent time at the Reading Rehab Center. Lydia spent the rest of her life, caring for a wheelchair patient as long as she was able.

Christ Shirks first wife, Esther Ruth Beery died in 1966, and he remained single four years, until he married Lydia. He was the same Christ Shirk whom Lydia dated back in 1937, on the same night when Aaron and Amanda had their first date. After both Lydia and Christ went their own way, they met again to share their golden years together.

Aaron put up a wooden board fence, all along the pasture, visible from the house. It turned out to be a high maintenance project, with occasional loose boards, and most of all it needed paint repeatedly. Ruth, Rhoda, and Martha brushed on gallons of paint on the new fence and so did Mary, Louise, and Irene. As the girls married and left home, the fence still needed more paint. Wesley, Lydia, RoseAnna and Amanda added many more gallons of white paint.

As the children painted the fence, they discussed how people know when they date the right person. Irene said, "I want a man that loves children, sings and will listen to my complaints and still love me." Lydia said,"I want a smart man with money for a new house. 'Roseanna said,"I want a particular man!" [their dreams came true.]

Wesley liked horses, but he settled for a pony. He bought Queenie from Henry High, with a cute new colt named Trixie by its mother's side. Wesley had a pony cart and he used it as

Martha, Rose Anna, Rhoda, and Mandy painting fence

his transportation before he had driver's license. Many children had a ride on the pony cart, as adventurous entertainment.

Mandy put a saddle on the pony and went to get the mail. She carefully put the mail in a plastic bag that hung at the pony's side, like the pony express. The pony started running, and the bag started slapping him on the side. The pony ran faster... slapping the bag harder... and Mandy hung on! She did not have the saddle fastened properly, and it slid upside down. Mandy found herself beneath the pony and the she let go of the saddle. The pony ran home and left Mandy in the dirt, unhurt, but scared and bruised.

At Martin Kilmer's sale, Aaron bought another pony for $35 and Wesley walked it home for the two and one half miles, because it was too young to ride. He named that one Stormy, because he enjoyed reading about the horses on Chincoteague Island and when Stormy had a colt, he named it Misty. Wesley bought ponies at Henry High; about three miles out the road, and Henry had a daughter that he admired quite awhile already.

When coming home from Bowmansville, one tire on Wesley's pony cart had a blowout, right in front of Henry High's farm. Wesley could hardly believe his good fortune, because it gave him a chance to borrow a pony cart and talk to Janie. He noticed her ever since the age of 14, when they went to school together. When Wesley's ponies were not securely fenced in, Queenie walked back home again, the three miles to Henry High's farm where she grew up, and he fetched her there. When it happened a second time, Aaron suspiciously accused Wesley of letting the pony go intentionally.

On April 19, 1970, Aaron and Amanda went to Bowmansville Lancaster Conference Church to see Wesley baptized. In June, Wesley and Janie announced their engagement, and they were married on a cold and windy Saturday, November 14, 1970. Bishop Luke Horst married them, as the first wedding he officiated. Lydia and Carl Hoover served as attendants on his side and Benny Brubacher with Ruth Ann on the other side. After the wedding, Wesley and Janie headed to Florida for a short trip. They enjoyed camping and took along a Cole-

man gas stove and sleeping bags, but they did not find attractive campgrounds as those that they had imagined. One night they spent seven dollars for a motel, but agreed it was not worth that much.

.After the wedding, Queenie returned to the barn she preferred, because Wesleys now lived there. Queenie lived to be 20 years old. Henry High's attended Lancaster Conference Church, and Wesley was concerned about what Janie might think of his common parents, from Weaver land conference, but he worried about the wrong thing. They accepted each other well and Janie liked his parents. She said Wesley inherited his mother's disposition. No one degraded another's church, not his parents or hers.

Four months after the wedding, Wesley received a letter from the draft board. He served two years in Beltsville Maryland and they lived in an apartment there. He worked at an animal research center. The government studied cow's digestive systems in the department where Wesley started working. Each cow had a four-inch opening in the side, where a flexible, four inch in diameter clear plastic hose protruded from the stomach. They removed the plug at the end, to observe partly digested food. They could reach inside!

For his last eight months, Wesley worked with chimpanzees and monkeys. The government was also studying a brain disease called' kuru' and tried to find a cure. Kuru was a problem among the primitive people of British Guinea and New Guinea. Some of the research they did on mice and injected the disease right into the brain, through the skull.

Wesley noticed how smart the chimps were when he fed them bananas. One greedy one always wanted more. Wesley did his own research and checked to see how many that one could eat. The chimpanzee greedily ate 39 bananas and the remaining bananas in his hands did not go down anymore. His belly was stuffed! Wesley did not have enough work to keep going, at the rate he was taught to work. [That is where trouble starts].

Sometimes he mowed lawn and such. When he came across a big black snake, he wondered what a chimp would do with a snake because they lived in captivity and never saw a snake. He put the snake's head through the hole where he fed them bananas and oranges and the chimps were terrified. They howled fiercely, starting at one end of the building, rippling all the way down the row!

One hundred and twenty five monkeys and chimpanzees, in one long building made a tremendous rackey! One day Wesley tossed an icicle on the tin roof and he was surprised! When he came inside, they were deathly quiet. Some instinct warned them. When the veterinarian was doing his routine work, Wesley asked if he should make all the noise die down. The vet grinned and said,"Good luck!"He did not think Wesley could do any such thing. Wesley tossed another icicle on the roof and the vet certainly wanted to know what he did, because he never heard such quiet in there before.

The chimps were all very curious and liked to spit. They picked on Wesley! [Is there any wonder?] He wore cover-alls with a white triangle of his t-shirt showing at the neck, and that is what they aimed at. The veterinarian said,"You can make them quit. Squirt them in the face with rubbing alcohol from a syringe, after they spit on you." That was the end of the problem. After that, all Wesley had to do was carry an empty syringe displayed in his pocket.

Wesley and Janie returned home, after their two years, and they lived about three miles from Aaron and Amanda. They raised four children and Wesleys were there for them, when Aaron and Amanda needed help. Janie was a kind, soft-spoken", keeper at home ", type of person. No one had any problems getting along with her.

They lived neighbors to Josey, the tramp that still strolled the neighborhood, and patrolled traffic at Green Dragon. Without a housekeeper, his brand-new house soon became a sorry mess.. Josey had a collection of six flashlights, three police whistles, 28 police badges, two radios, four alarm clocks, three guns, and a tea kettle.

Things did not go well for Josey and he ended up in jail for molesting young boys. Aaron took neighbors along in to visit Josey, and he took Josey to see the guidance counselor at Lancaster. He was there for the court trial, because most other people had a hard time understanding Josey's mumbled speech. When the judge asked Josey, "Who is your attorney?" Josey said, "Why, Shirkey!"The judge then turned toward Aaron and asked, "Are you Shirkey?""Yes," replied Aaron. "What do you suggest we do with him?" the judge asked.

The trial did not last long because both sides agreed Josey should be put into the County home. The judge wanted to leave Josey in Aaron's custody until they made arrangements. Aaron refused and they put Josey into jail for one week, waiting on the paperwork. When Aaron came to visit him in the county home, Josey said, "I liked it better in jail than I do in here, because there I could chew tobacco. "Later on, Josey was allowed to have his favorite pastime of chewing tobacco.

Aaron did not forget Josie. On a nice day; he took Josie out of the county home and gave him a tour of all his old jaunts. Josie met many people and saw the familiar roads. After awhile Josie wanted to go' home'. Aaron knew that Josie was at the right place! He watched TV most of the days until he went blind, just as his mother had. Josey learned to enjoy the county home so much that he did not want to leave. He died there. None of his relatives showed up for the funeral, but about fifty local Mennonites and three or four others attended his funeral at the Center Church, on January 4, 1986.

31

In 1970, Aaron and Amanda had one last child going to school. Mandy enjoyed all parts of every school she ever attended and had no problems at Garden Spot High School, among many friends.

Mandy was through eighth grade at the age of fourteen and the law required her to attend school until fifteen. She ended up walking to school one day a week, to the new Black Creek Parochial School, which Aaron and Amanda would have appreciated years earlier, just one mile away. Mandy could have attended eighth grade there also, but she chose to stay with her friends at Garden Spot.

Mandy never before attended a one-room school, but she soon learned how a one-room school operated. Mary Kilmer as the teacher had eight grades in one room. At first, the commotion bothered Mandy as she tried to blot out other classes. She practiced selective hearing! Every week she wrote a diary describing what she worked, instead of going to school. She handed in her diary, and spent time learning by doing. Vocational classes lasted three hours a week and gave her more time at home and time for helping her married sisters. Her time was well spent as she accumulated education in all sorts of hands- on learning during that school term.

Over the years, the teachers learned from each other and the one-room schools kept improving with a better curriculum.

The school systems started in colonial times to help students become productive and useful members of society, and so that children might learn to get along better with others. The richest people paid private tutors or sent their children to private schools, and the poor children did not have the opportunity to read and write. They practiced obedience and religious beliefs, housekeeping and food preservation among other useful skills of farming.

Tax supported school systems started so that all children could be more useful and learn to read the Bible. The leaders knew that deprived children crippled a society and would create more low-income families. Somewhere along the line, the entire system ran amok. The Bible, supposedly the reason for starting the public schools, was removed from the public schools entirely. Children were more deprived of the important things in life than ever before. They had less secure home lives, and watching their mothers working at home did not appear important.

When both parents worked away, many school-aged children came home to empty houses and watched TV, with more time for mischief. Better, give them more homework to keep them occupied! Aaron and Amanda wondered why their younger children brought home so much homework. "Were they not able to keep up at school?" she asked. Children had less time for farm life and family time, with long hours spent over books in the evening. Aaron and Amanda were thankful when all the school years ended. The many changes they witnessed in their lifetime were not all for the better.

Officials of the school system declared that a country that has the schools, holds the nation, and the world. Build more and better schools, with longer hours! The sad truth was, "the hand that rocks the cradle, rules the nation"! No country was stronger than its families, because homes are the foundation of all the schools, churches and the government. Building schools was much easier than building good homes.

In 1972, the Supreme Court ruled in favor of allowing the Amish and Mennonites to have their own schools and teach vocational education, rather than higher education. They did not need more than an eighth grade education to become productive citizens. They preferred a life of doing good and teaching children to work, with time left to enjoy nature.

∽

The Pennsylvania Game Commission stocked trout in the mountain stream on Aaron's property. The Black Creek started less than a mile away, where strong springs continually pushed clear water from beneath the ground. The crystal-clear water flowed over dark ironstone rocks, creating the appearance of a black creek. Most of the fish were no bigger than aquarium size, unless the state stocked more trout. Aaron's children loved to splash and wade in the cool shallow water in summertime. Trout had very few places to hide, so close to the mouth of the river. The girls saw a 12-inch rainbow trout, soon after trout season opened. With nothing along to use for catching a fish, Louise desperately scooped it up with her skirt, and eagerly took it home for the frying pan.

On a Sunday afternoon, if the children did not hike to the woods or to the dump, it was to the Turnpike Bridge. Other children gathered there, and it became a neighborhood hangout. Sometimes the children pumped an arm up and down, and the truckers blew their horns. Leaning across the thick concrete sides, many a child tried to spit on a passing car, but seldom could they manage, due to the precise timing needed, and also because they ran out of spit. Among peer pressure, some got into trouble by dropping things onto vehicles. Occasionally, a policeman stopped and scolded them. The older boys remembered daring one boy to walk the full length of the bridge railing, from one side to the other, across all four lanes and he did, on that 6-inch wide concrete ledge! They were too innocent to understand how easily a child could splat down on the roadway without another chance. For safety reasons, the Turnpike secured all the overhead bridges with mesh fencing.

One mile farther east, the children had just as much fun, gathering beneath the Turnpike and slopping in the water. The dark damp tunnel had an arched ceiling and walls covered with moss and lichen. Singing inside the arch echoed beautifully, and so did hollering. Amanda allowed no shrieking or screaming unless it was a call for help. Beneath the arch, they could scream for all they were worth and no one told them to be quiet, because no one could hear them.

The water at the outgoing edge tumbled a few feet to make a lovely waterfall! At times when the sun hit the falls just right, the mist and sunshine made a perfect rainbow, serenely beautiful.

The arch below the turnpike did not change over the years, except for the graffiti.

Elias Shirk's mulberry tree also attracted children of all sizes, when the mulberries ripened in the warm sunshine. Aaron and Amanda did not own a mulberry tree. Climbing and raiding that tree was worth a scolding when the children came home with stains on their clothes and even the soles of their feet turned purple.

Louise still enjoyed the woods and all the detailed beauty therein. She watched a yellow-shafted flicker hide inside its perfect round hole. The hole happened to be inside the creosoted power line pole. Aaron reported it to the power line company, and PP&L asked for the number on the pole. They came out and replaced it.

Thick ice covered everything in January 1969. No school! Aaron and Amanda had only two scholars left. RoseAnna and Mandy rejoiced with a day of vacation, and started skating. With their ice skates, they skated on the walk, and then almost anywhere else they pleased, because the icy crust did not break through.

When Mandy hung up the wash, on a different occasion, her basket kept sliding away. Suddenly, with a bright idea she went sledding in a plastic laundry basket. It worked grand! She also remembered tying a pillow to her behind one time when she went skating, so it would not hurt so much when she fell. She needed more practice skating, and Amanda suggested, "You should have tied the pillow on to your head!"

A stray cat arrived at Aaron Shirks, and wanted to come indoors. Amanda did not want a house cat, but she finally gave in, because the cat was well trained. The cat wanted to sleep upstairs in the girl's bedroom closet, but they carefully latched the stairway door at night. On a lovely night in April, Missy managed to come inside and sneak upstairs to the girl's bedroom when they were sleeping. She meowed so desperately in the night, that Mandy reached over and opened the closet door. She gave the cat what she wanted, so they could get some sleep. Before daylight, the girls heard brand-new kittens. Mandy was delighted! Amanda was not so sure about that.

The huge closet in the girl's bedroom held many dresses for many girls over the years. Sometimes Amanda washed them separately, and waited two weeks before setting up the wringer washer just for permanent pressed clothes. When Ivan and Harvey Hoover worked at painting the trim on Aaron and Amanda's house, they could not help but notice so many dresses on the clothesline. They asked Mandy, "How many dresses do you wear in one week?"

On e time during the night, the weather turned cooler and Lydia got up for more covers. Irene heard someone was getting covers, and decided to get some covers for her own bed also. Lydia did not hear Irene get out of bed, and suddenly she saw a tall white form coming right towards her! She yelled, "Who is it? Who is it?" Irene reached out to her, and said, "Shhhh! It's just me." When those hands reached out towards Lydia in a corner, she hysterically woke up everyone else. All the girls in the room thought it was funny, except Lydia. When they settled down, and were almost sleeping again, Lydia started laughing… suddenly it looked funny to her also. Then a genuine giggle fit started.

On a blue Monday evening, Amanda asked RoseAnna, "What's wrong?" RoseAnna said, "Ach Mom you wouldn't understand!" Amanda said, "You mean we could raise fifteen children and not understand?" In a different situation, Amanda told one of her teenaged children, "There are more pebbles on the beach!"

Amanda required that all her 10 daughters learned to sew their own coverings. Sometimes the coverings did not turn out just right. Mandy asked, "Why can't RoseAnna just make mine also?" Amanda said, "A covering is a sign of submission and humility, and we are not to have pride in how it fits." Case closed! Every one of the girls sewed their own dresses and coverings and eventually learned how, without regrets. At one time Ruth and Rhoda brought girls along home to teach them how to make coverings.

At the age of 54, Amanda still helped to unload tobacco. She helped her youngest children practice playing baseball, mostly pitching and catching, but she still took her turn at bat. She could pitch quoits and enjoyed fishing. She broke her rod, while trying to bring in a bass at 5 AM on a beautiful April morning.

Every one of Aaron and Amanda's fifteen children had a unique story about getting drivers license. Mandy learned to drive, on a 66 Ford straight shift car, often dirty and used as a farm truck. The keychain was a large safety pin or at one time, a piece of baler twine. The big girls drove the good car to work in the factory every day, but when Mandy took her driver's test, Aaron wanted her to take the good car. It looked so much better, and it smelled better because the straight shift car still had an awful odor since Aaron had spilled a gallon of milk when he braked too hard.

Mandy's heart pounded as she waited on her turn for her driver's test. Then up stepped a great big black man to give her the road test. She seldom saw any black people and she quivered and shook down into her shoes! As soon as she started driving, it began to rain and she could not find the wipers. After searching for the wipers, she noticed she had crossed over the yellow line on the road. She saw the stop sign but forgot she was driving an automatic car. She landed both her feet on the brakes at the same time and stopped rather suddenly, explaining, "I don't usually drive this car." When she tried parallel parking, the instructor said, "The tire is touching the curb."

Mandy knew she failed by now, and suddenly relaxed. The rest went fine. At the end, her instructor said, "I'll let you pass, but you should stick to the back roads for a little while longer." Mandy's happiness and elation overflowed! That was one really nice Negro man!

When Amanda bought a cedar chest for RoseAnna, she purchased the last one also, for Mandy. The girls crowded bedroom did not have room for four cedar chests, therefore Amanda stacked two on top of each other, until Irene married and left home.

The youngest children led different lives than the older ones in the family. At the age of sixteen, Rose Anna asked her parents for permission to go away on Good Friday afternoon. Aaron said."If you water the tobacco beds first, you may go. "Rose Anna was pleased and her friends were astonished at her parent's leniency. Rose Anna had no idea how Daniel and Sarah Ann had it, when they were sixteen! .

Rose Anna and Mandy sometimes tried to clean up and make the place look nice. Amanda said.""I gave up on that long already! I wanted things clean and orderly, but that is not the most important thing in life."

When the grand children came home, Amanda said to her own children, 'Don't let your scissors and thimbles lay on the sewing machine! There's many a child lying in a grave, with a thimble in the throat."

None of the back roads had names until April of 1969. Suddenly Aaron and Amanda had a street address; of 492 Laurel Road, instead of rural route one, Narvon PA. Many things changed! Canada geese arrived on the pond and made a nest for the first time, in 1972. Up until then, they all migrated and kept on moving.

Irene

In 1971, Kurtzy brought salvaged pudding by the truckload to Aaron and Amanda's barn floor. Amanda had a hard time throwing out anything usable, and she could not tolerate such a tremendous amount of food going to waste. The cases of individual serving sized, snack puddings came sealed with pull- top lids. Amanda helped sort the damaged sticky mess of smelly, split- open tin cans of rotting trash, to salvage the top quality smooth Vanilla, chocolate, and butterscotch pudding sealed and worth saving.

Amanda set up the wringer washer and the rinse tub in the basement, and presoaked one batch at a time, saving everything that was not spoiled. She still had four girls at home, and kept them busy. Many neighbors came to buy the pudding as well as the durable large plastic buckets with tight fitting lids. Amanda never before, had plastic buckets with tight fitting lids and considered them a modern luxury, with many uses, such as rustproof, mouse proof storage.

At first, everyone enjoyed the cases of pudding, as delectable and smooth as ice cream! Week after week, and month after month, made a difference until no one liked it, especially the girls involved in cleaning sticky messes of the cans, among some with broken seals. The paper labels fell off the cans when they washed the pudding, but each can had a printed code and flavor name stamped on the bottom.

Amanda's Aunt Salome Brenneman needed a place to stay, in her old age, and she took turns staying with her nieces, nephews and stepchildren. Salome was a sister to Amanda's mother, living together with her brother Joe Brenneman as his housekeeper in Michigan, in a three-room tar papered house, just a mile down the road from Peter and Sarah Ann Brubacher, years ago. Amanda remembered their kitchen floor with a trap door leading into a small cellar, with a ladder down into it. Amanda helped Salome with odd jobs, sometimes staying there a week at a time, when she was young.

Joe and Salome Brenneman both stayed in Michigan until the church disintegrated. Then, in 1938, at the age of 43, Salome married Aaron Martin, who had been widowed twice, and had 12 children. Aaron Martin and his grown daughter had wedding plans at the same time, so to make less work; they had a double wedding with father and daughter marrying on the same day.

After living in Pennsylvania several years, Aaron and Salome Martin with their five youngest children, moved to Mexico. They met up with many hardships while living there, among malaria and typhoid fever, and Aaron died there. As a sickly widow, Salome returned to Pennsylvania, barely able to return, nothing but skin and bones. Walking with a cane, she resembled a witch, with her sunken facial features, but she recovered again, and spent her time among her married stepchildren.

In July, she moved in with Aaron and Amanda, after staying awhile with Martin Kilmers. Salome had no children of her own, but had 12 stepchildren. Amanda had a hard time understanding Salome, who had mental problems. Some days she just walked the floor, and she did not eat her dinner. Her stepson Levi Martin came and talked to her and her brother Joe Brenneman came to visit her. Aunt Salome had funny ideas and Amanda told her to stop acting so dumb! Amanda and Salome battled about the problem of Salome not wanting to take her prescribed medication. She slyly spit it out, and Amanda noticed. Deacon John Martin came to see her, and so did her sister Alsina Brenneman. Amanda helped occupy her mind, by taking Salome to visit at Martin Kilmer's and to see Silas. She took Salome along to Enos Sauders barn raising.

Amanda tried her best to keep Salome's hands busy, and one thing Salome enjoyed working, was hemming flannel diapers by hand. In her old age, Salome still fantasized about having a baby of her own. Amanda asked her girls to keep away all the big dolls that might offend her, because Salome did not like dolls as an image of something God created.

When Aunt Salome went upstairs to bed at 9 PM she did not go to sleep, and at 3:30 AM Amanda found her on the bathroom floor. She helped her to bed after what appeared to be a possible overdose of pills. Dr. Lauria came out to the farm,

and said Salome might have had a light stroke."Do not move her to another residence, until she is feeling better. "She had been at Embreville Mental Hospital several times. In 1972, Amanda found Salome with four long stockings knotted together, threatening suicide.

Her false teeth clattered when the family sat down to eat at the table and nearly took away the appetite of those at the table.

Amanda wanted to attend a funeral in Indiana for Roy Zimmerman's two-year-old Galen, who died in a farm accident. The mother of the child was Aaron's niece, Ben Shirk's daughter Anna Mary. Many travelers from Pennsylvania attended the funeral on July 30, 1971. Dawdy Shirks, Jesse's, Aunt Eva, Pete's, Carl Weiler's and Walters among others had the privilege of going, but Amanda stayed at home with Aunt Salome, who was still in bed. The next week Salome had another stroke, or whatever it was, and Amanda thought Salome lay dying! She told Irene to call Dr. Hess and Levi Martin. The situation looked alarming to Amanda, but the doctor did not bother coming out, and gradually Salome improved again. She improved enough that she came to the table to eat again, and the next week Aaron and Amanda moved her to Christian Kilmers.

Irene sighed with relief, because only four weeks remained for all the details of her and Marlin's wedding. Amanda went to Priscilla Brubacher's funeral in Maryland and she was not at home when a salesman came to the door selling Cutco knife sets. Some of Irene's friends bought knives such as this, and Irene paid for a set of her own, for $123.81. Amanda was horrified and said, "Why, that is more than I spent for all our furniture and house wares together!"

When Aaron bought his farm, the bootleggers supplied him with whiskey, to stay on his good side, although Aaron never had a craving for alcohol. He considered whiskey as a medicine and it stayed in the stripping room a long time. Aaron and Amanda occasionally made homemade wine as a medicine. Amanda wanted to make the dandelion wine as they did in Michigan and she tried grape wine and wild cherry wine, because the wild cherries grew in abundance along the stone fences.

Aaron made pokeberry wine with the common purple inkberries. He battled rheumatism, and someone said the toxic wine of inkberries would help him. He clearly labeled the bottle as poison and even displayed a hand-drawn picture of skull and crossbones. 'Take 1 tablespoon a day as medicine!'

When it came to making wine for a wedding at home, Aaron and Amanda did not care to try. They bought Mogan David grape wine, the same kind the deacons bought for communion at church. Their homemade wine often did not get right, and they had plenty of other work.

Ruth came on Thursday and helped Irene scrub the kitchen floor and even the outhouse! Sarah Ann made the wedding cakes like usual and kept that mess out of Amanda's kitchen. She had bought wedding cakes for her own wedding but made cakes for some of her younger sisters.

Amanda picked lima beans and set them in the cellar in advance for making succotash. The evening before the wedding, they husked the corn and cut it off, shelled the beans and peeled the potatoes, for 180 guests. Amanda cooked the hams and they carefully sliced that after it cooled. After all of them had baths, none went to bed early.

Irene was a skinny bride weighing 93 pounds, with a 23-inch waistline, but that was no problem. Amanda was about that size, on her wedding day back in 1937.

Irene and Marlin's wedding day on September 11, 1971, turned out not much different from the past six weddings before hers, except, there were no hostlers and that was a first! The people parked their own cars in the field next to the house. When Banks Horning and his wife arrived, he parked his car at the end of the walk and they came to the house, thinking hostlers would move the car. Someone noticed, and kindly moved the preacher's car to the newly cut hayfield.

Lydi-Jes-sey came as head cook like usual, and Irene helped with the last-minute details, of moving throw rugs and washing a few more dishes, until Lydi-Jes-sey said, "Just go now", as people started arriving. Ivan's came at 7:05, to make sure

he had all the instructions about seating people for the services and the dinner. He announced names for seating people in four rooms and even some on the south porch with the windows open, so they could hear the services. Most people seated in the back parlor could not see the bride and groom, and neither could those seated in the kitchen.

Irene scurried around skipping breakfast and she felt half sick, so concerned about details that she didn't bother looking in the mirror again, and she forgot to add straight pins to her covering. Bishop Joseph Weaver, Bangs Horning and Lloyd Burkholder preached a wonderful sermon. All of her young nieces and nephews in the congregation remained quiet. Marlin was the oldest child in his family of four children, therefore she invited all thirty-six of her nieces and nephews. The sun came out, and it was a nice day after all, despite the rain and thunder in the morning. 180 people ate dinner. For some reason, the ice cream melted in the basement refrigerator freezer, and the waitresses hurried to Martindale, and came back with" homemade ice cream." It was good! [Aaron paid them for it.] In the afternoon girls sang beautifully, upstairs and most people admired the wedding gifts on display.

"You did a good job, Lydia! Thank you for everything you did for us, 'said Amanda, as Jesse and Lydia left the kitchen to walk home, tired to the bone." We do not deserve any praise,"said Lydi-Jes-sey,"We just cooked what you gave us and you had everything well prepared for us."

Most of the cooks did not accept compliments well, no matter how hard they worked, because all praise belonged to God !The men set up the tables and chairs in crowed quarters and they all had a long day on their feet. After they cleaned up the last dishes and dried up kettles, they hardly had time to sit down. They did not bring a wedding gift for the bride and groom, like everyone else did. They also did not receive a thank you gift, because they considered all the hard work they did, as their gift to the newlyweds.

After the guests departed, Marlin donned work clothes and helped move furniture back into the house and returned chairs to the Bowmansville fire hall, to help Aaron and Amanda with all the extra work. Then they headed to Texas on their wedding trip. They borrowed uncle Willies VW, putting on almost 4000 miles in one week, and spent a total of $229.04.

Aaron went to Sammy Hursts and bought a new chime clock as a gift to Amanda for their 36th wedding anniversary. They could not afford a chime clock at first and simply did without one. Over the years, their children gave or received chime clocks as engagement gifts, and Aaron and Amanda's clock was just about as special even now!

The youngest girls at home bought Amanda a beautiful poinsettia plant for Christmas, something she never had. When Amanda discovered the price tag, she scolded a bit,"Such extravagance just for me?"

Amanda enjoyed flowers all her life and noticed the beauty God scattered around her. She enjoyed gifts and gift giving just as much, but bought cut flowers seemed wasteful to her. Those brought less cheer to her than the flowers gathered out-doors, even weeds. She thought spending money for cut flowers that soon die, was a waste of money that should have been spent for food or worthwhile things. Her parents taught Amanda to give all she could, all her life, but not like that.

The married children noticed that Amanda should have an automatic washer for her laundry, and together they gave their parents one for Christmas. All fifteen children helped pay for it, even the youngest ones still at home. She seldom used the newfangled contraption and did not consider it necessary, now that all the diapers and baby clothes belonged to the next generation.

All her life Amanda carefully sorted laundry into many piles. She did not wash things mixed together and now she could hardly find a load of things she wanted to launder together. No one could convince her to mix dark colors and light colors. And furthermore,"Do you people think it is right to waste an entire tub full of warm soapy water for one load of wash? That is extravagant! We worked hard to carry and heat our wash water." At first, Amanda washed a few pieces and fished them out of the water, then washed a few more pieces and wrung them out, before she washed the

dirtiest things and completed the cycle. She still washed her good dresses by hand. It took quite a while until she learned to use and appreciate the new washer, but eventually she did.

Every year the family gathered for Amanda's birthday celebration and she suggested they forget all the wrapped packages and gifts because she needed so little. Much more, she cherished singing together as a family. Every year the family had a wonderful fellowship of singing, with even the youngest schoolchildren helping to sing. The children still enjoyed giving their mother gifts of appreciation and one year they gave a scrapbook of family photos, another year a tablecloth of friendship patches, with each of the fifteen children's names embroidered among decorations. One year, Amanda unwrapped twenty-six gifts, one for each letter of the alphabet, to open one each day. She received a birthday calendar with photos. They made a unique clothes pin rack and each of the fifteen clothespins held a paper diaper loaded with small gifts of appreciation. They made a framed wall hanging with each of the children's names on a heart in the picture. Everyone helped stitch a family history, apple tree quilt, with a name on each of over one hundred apples. She had three more grand children after the quilt, so those last three names went on a throw pillow.

In a letter, Amanda wrote; many thanks to all of you for the big gift for my birthday! I do feel I am being honored too much, more than I deserve. Give all honor and thanks to the father in heaven where all praise, honor and thanks belong. All our blessings come from him and it is through God's grace and mercy that we are what we are and where all our help comes from.

Aaron and Amanda's parents did such a thorough job of teaching these thoughts, to the extent that their children and grand children seldom heard a compliment in their childhood, besides saying Thank You!

Aunt Salome returned to stay with Aaron and Amanda indefinitely. After some struggles about not taking medications, she settled in for nearly a year and a half. Amanda stayed home more and made six quilts and comforters as a mental therapy

for Salome and herself. One comfort at a relief sale brought $80 for charity, to warm Amanda's heart. In her spare time, Amanda sewed many slips, shirts, nightgowns, sheets and pillowcases for MCC, and she spent many days on the road driving horse and buggy neighbors as necessary. She commented, "I am happiest when helping others."

Over the years, Amanda enjoyed shopping at Harry Good's store. It was the best place around, shopping for shoes in decent styles. Teenagers searched first in the reduced bin, looking for shoes to their liking, and the store always had a cheerful helper available to help fit proper sizes. Amanda used to say, "It's not so hard to find shoes that fit the feet, but it seems they must fit the head also!"

Aaron and Amanda did a lot of shopping at Harry Good's and Mandy remembers the day her sisters paid at the check-out and left without her, as she admired shiny watches in the glass showcase. Next thing she knew, she looked around frantically up and down every aisle hoping to find just one sis-

ter. She realized they actually did leave without her and Mandy was on the verge of tears, when Irene came rushing back in and said, "We did not go very far before we missed you and turned around!"

In 1973, Harry Good's Store moved over to a big brand-new store, and Amanda had to learn all over again, where to find things in such a huge store. She enjoyed the sale at the old store in December and bought much more fabric then what she needed for herself. For only five dollars, she bought 22 yards of black corduroy and 37 years later, her daughters donated that roll of corduroy material to charity, unused! Amanda no longer needed to sew homemade coats, and the fabric was too heavy for her garments and lightweight covers. One month after the fabric sale, she helped neighbor ladies clean out the old Good's Store, getting ready for an ordination dinner there.

On January 8, 1974, Amanda helped serve the noon meal to 150 people for Ezra Martin's ordination. The new preacher was only 23 years old!

1972 Floods

Aaron and Amanda's family scattered to homes of their own and they missed hearing from each other. Walter's moved to Tipton, Missouri on November 4, 1972. They were the first to move so far away. Walter and Carl Weiler came up with the suggestion of circle letters as a clever idea to keep in touch. Amanda wrote a letter and sent it to one of her children, that one added a letter and sent it on to the next one, all the way around the circle, until the envelope contained 16 letters, one from each family member. After that, everyone removed their old letter as it returned to them, and then added the latest update, quickly mailing it on to the next person. Everyone enjoyed hearing the interesting details about life beyond headlines.

In 1972, floods created a disaster area needing all available help for cleaning up in June. Aaron wrote in the family circle letter as follows:

"We are setting high and dry after our recent floods, which we praise the Lord for and also for the strength He gave us to help others. The massive cleanup is being pushed hard by the plain people, as we go up the river to Harrisburg and beyond.

The outside people don't understand how such a movement is organized. I have been helping at Birdsorough with the helicopter rescue from the national defense, as I was driving the emergency vehicle on the ground, checking out calls. We would see people sitting on porches, doing nothing, while neighbors to those flooded out needing help. The officials were ashamed of their people, while we make ourselves useful. Lancaster TV was after me two times in one day to get on the TV for the rescue workers. I tried to explain that the plain people want work, not publicity. They finally settled for me to answer questions, but every time I answered a question, one of the TV team would push a mike in front of my mouth. So I guess they got what they wanted, some of the questions were when and from where did the plain people come from? [answer]Mostly from Switzerland at about the time, William Penn took over Pennsylvania. [question] How are these people able to work together on free labor and with such a good cooperation? [answer] "They are taught this from their parents", I said, "as they grow up in their country homes." I don't remember all the questions but if I would have gone on TV, I certainly would have brought attention to the world, of the fact that the rescue workers had no more than 8 years of education in one-room country schools! PS, I guess the next time I'll go into some basement, cleaning where the TV people can't find me."

Aaron had a way of enjoying all the publicity he received and then some more!

Amanda eagerly devoured the entire circle letter and enjoyed listening to the cute sayings of innocent little children. Amanda remembered how Daniel threw stones into the air as high as he could, when he was young. When he came to the house, he said, "I threw a stone up so high that it didn't come down again!" "Oh, I don't think so," said Amanda doubtfully. "Vell ovvah net sellah dauk," said Daniel, meaning (well, but not that day anymore!)

Those years were long gone but the memories remained. When she was five, Rhoda showed her sore thumb to Amanda and said "Mom, press on my thumb." When Amanda did, Rhoda said, "Ain't it hurts?

Some children had an uncanny way of understanding things backwards, and as she looked back, Amanda remembered having problems understanding things, even the 23rd Psalm, when she was a child. 'The Lord is my shepherd I shall not want'...took her many years until she understood the full meaning. In her childhood, she did not understand a comma after the word shepherd. She thought it said that the Lord was a shepherd that she should not want.

Aaron enjoyed the circle letters, but some were hard to read and not about the things, he wanted to hear. He preferred that Amanda would scan them and read aloud only the topics that appealed to him, even when he had just as much time to read them. Amanda kindly tried to explain that maybe some parts of his letters are not interesting to everybody else.

When it was his turn to write he cut it short and wrote: *"I won't have much to write now, for one reason it's raining on the first day of hunting season, second reason, I just heard that my letters are junk, so to keep out the junk I will play safe. A clear sheet is worth more than junk", Aaron*

Later in a different letter, he wrote:" Dear family, from one end to the other, wishing you just the very same I wish to ourselves, eternal rest and tax exempt, all at the time when Christ our Savior returns again for us."

32

Missouri, 1973

When BW Shirk looked down across the valley, he saw no vacancies for his children and his grandchildren. Where could they live? Gradually farms became scarcer, and the prices went higher. Aaron and Amanda also wondered what would happen with all their children, and where would they find homes? Aaron saw that they could not all find homes at Bowmansville.

They had a surprise when their children wanted to move far away, across the Mississippi River, all the way to Missouri. Walter and Marian were the first of Aaron Shirk's children to move there. They bought land in the Versailles area, in 1972. Preacher Titus Martin and Allen Fox searched in that area for more available farmland. After talking with Amos Horst, they headed north to Edina and Memphis, Missouri, looking for land. They discovered 180 different farms listed for sale among several real estate agents in northeast Missouri. Older farmers retired and the next generation no longer desired to farm where the old people quit. That was before the government program of CRP, paying farmers for not working.

In 1973, fourteen families from Pennsylvania moved to Missouri for the privilege of buying their own farms. Mahlon and Sarah Ann, Roland and Mary, and Ivan and Louise moved that year. All three families unloaded in three days time, in a strange new land of weather extremes. At the time they moved, in the beginning of March, it was extremely muddy! The soil in Pennsylvania contained enough rocks to keep people from sinking deeply into the topsoil, but Missouri didn't. All of them had a lot to learn about Missouri mud... mud. ..everywhere... even children stuck in the mud while trying to walk.

Any young people that wished to farm, had a tough time starting out on their own in Pennsylvania...Aaron wrote, *"As land gets sold for $2000 per acre, there is no hope for replacements around here. Complete farms sell at $3000 per acre. We can't hate anyone to move where farms can be bought. I am getting too fat, weighing 200 pounds with my teeth out. If the grandchildren in Missouri see something odd looking, move around out west, don't shoot, it is Grand pa!".*

Amanda wrote, "People certainly move around a lot, but we can't all live on our home place. I suppose this is God's way of spreading the gospel, so we should all let our light shine wherever we are. Try to be an example, safe for the younger generation to follow,"

Beneath it all, Amanda remembered all the problems of starting a church group in May City, Iowa and in Brutus, Michigan. She wished them well in Missouri and knew they could change their minds, and come back.

Titus Martin moved to Missouri in November 1972, and therefore the newly started church had a preacher. Amanda could hardly wait to see the new territory, and she hitched a ride helping Mahlon and Sarah Ann move. They attended church at Hedge City, with thirty-two adults and sixty children present, at the small community church, formerly unused and standing empty. Amanda saw the advantages of starting a new community and she wanted to see it prosper.

She returned home from her trip, just in time for Mandy's seventeenth birthday party. Before Mandy was old enough to date, it was no secret that she was interested in Henry Martin. Her girlfriends planned an elaborate O Henry party! Her friends arrived with the biggest box they could find, all wrapped up in surprises. Mandy tore off many layers of wrapping paper and newspapers and between the layers, fell out more O-Henry Candy bars.

Mandy and Henry started dating soon after she turned 17, and the home place nearly shook with noise among more teenagers. Occasionally some boys rearranged the furniture in the parlor and messed up just enough to get attention. Eventually one back leg on the sofa had problems and the couch was propped on a tin can of pineapples, and nobody seemed to care.

A surge of travelers and tourists swarmed to Missouri that first summer, checking out farmland and prices. The fourteen families living there had many travelers, friends and neighbors dropping in. They were much too busy to get homesick. Aaron encouraged the next generation to keep farming and he was not opposed to them moving far away, but he preferred to stay at home, and he said, "Old trees have deep roots and should not be transplanted."

Aaron's brother Elias Shirk and most of his children moved to the Versailles area, in the southern half, two hundred miles away from the Memphis area. Martin and Christian Kilmers also moved there, with the horse and buggy group.

Carl and Ruth Weiler moved to northern Missouri the next year, and later, in December 1979, Mervin and Martha High joined the crowd. They started a dairy farm in Iowa, just north of the Missouri line, but still part of the same church community as the others. Aaron and Amanda traveled back and forth many times over the years, and always arrived with packages of food or quilts or something to share. At first, they brought along some of the salvaged tin can pudding, and Amanda put forth efforts to bring home -canned fruit, or frozen food.

In 1973, Aaron farmed his last tobacco crop. He no longer wished to smoke or raise tobacco, and together Aaron and Amanda hoped to travel more to their married children. Tobacco was more work than Aaron could handle after all his boys left home, at the same time when he no longer needed to depend on tobacco as an income. He quit smoking and encouraged others to quit. His parents tried their best to keep him from starting the low-down habit, back in the 1930's. It took Aaron

nearly forty years and at a high cost, to see how right they were.

In July, Aaron and Amanda made an 18-day trip to Missouri. Aaron was sure they did not want to drive nonstop, so they paid for a $13 motel, something they rarely did all their life. They filled their vehicle with things like canned goods and baloney for their children in Missouri. Food was a big gift, not that their children were going hungry, but they fed many "tourists." Amanda keenly remembered how she moved 1000 miles away from her parents, and how she missed them at first.

Preacher Titus Martin, had been ordained at Bowmansville, but now preached in MO. Sometimes he preached all alone with no other minister or deacon present. On those occasions, he randomly chose a man from the laity to read the text for him, and then also to give testimony. One Sunday morning he chose Aaron Shirk without any advance notice. Aaron felt a little nervous standing at the pulpit and yet highly honored. He served as a deacon that day.

After reading the text, Aaron took his seat and Titus stood up to preach." Dearly beloved, may the grace and the peace and the love of God the father, be here with us in this morning's hour. We are spared and privileged to be assembled here together, undisturbed with unlocked doors and windows to worship in spirit and in truth. By grace are we saved by faith and not of ourselves..."

After Titus talked for nearly an hour, he took his seat and Aaron gave a testimony. Services usually started with two songs and closed with two songs. After the services, no one seemed to be in a hurry to leave. They all stood around and talked awhile.

Aaron enjoyed his trip to Missouri, but traveling several weeks like that and sleeping in strange beds hurt his back all over again. When he came home, he went to bed in pain. Eventually he went to Dr. Berberian in Lancaster, for an injection, and later on, a second one. Aaron suggested that maybe a train ride might be easier on his back, for the next trip to Missouri. He claimed he had some of his mother's desires to 'simply stay at home', because he gets "shipping fever".

Amanda dug in to work when she returned home. Lydia, Roseanna and Mandy had kept the house well, and had a singing planned for the youth group at Aarons the weekend they returned. Amanda found work stacked everywhere she looked, and August was crowded with things to do for yet another wedding in September, besides preserving food for winter.

Aaron dreaded all the work, when he heard Lydia and Carl had wedding plans. He said,"If I had known how much work weddings were, I would have built a wedding hall for the first daughter's wedding! " He asked the ministry, "Why don't we allow weddings at our church house?" They explained to him that they are allowed to marry at church, if the bride and groom quietly marry in the anteroom before regular church services, with no fuss of any kind, not even the bride and groom sitting closely side by side during the regular services that day. The men belonged to one side in church, and the ladies on the other!" Lydia did not want such a wedding, even if the reception and the gifts could all be at the home farm.

Aaron was puzzled and said, " I still cannot understand that! Church is the first place we take our babies when they are old enough to go away and baptism vows are made there, why not marriage vows at church also? RoseAnna overheard the discussion and she secretly wished for a garage pretty soon.

On Sept 1, 1973, Lydia and Carl Hoover got married at home in extremely crowded quarters! By now, her family alone nearly filled the entire house, and Carl came from a big family. Nieces and nephews, cousins galore and many aunts and uncles names could not remain on the guest list. That was understandable, but when it came to crossing off names of close friends, that hurt feelings.

When Walter and Marian arrived from Missouri, they brought along two special guests, neighbors that traveled with them. Lydia was not pleased to see two total strangers crowded into the limited seating arrangement. Never the less, they had a happy wedding day, and Bishop Joe Weaver again said as he did at all the previous weddings, "May you have just enough clouds in your life, to make a beautiful sunset."

In the past year, Lydia had helped scrub more tin- can pudding than she cared to admit, and it certainly did not look appealing to her. Amanda mixed some tin can pudding, in with homemade cornstarch and most people thought it was just fine, hidden under whipped cream, and graham cracker crumbs.

The guests that came with Walter and Marian, commented that Lydia and Carl's wedding was as close to a Catholic wedding as they ever saw any. Walters enjoyed taking their Missouri neighbors on a tour through Pennsylvania Dutch country, stopping in among relatives and quaint places of interest. The Missouri guests marveled at the water pumps working like well drilling contraptions, such as they never saw before.

Aaron and Amanda got busy planning a nice big garage before another wedding came along, so the last two weddings might have more room and less work.

Missouri, 1974

When Carl Weilers moved to Missouri on March 25, 1974, Amanda went along. Baby Clair was only three weeks old, and Carl's wanted to be in Missouri in time for spring farming. Amanda stayed three weeks in Missouri without Aaron, but he did not mind and said he felt sorry for people that have to travel. Three short months later, Amanda was back in Missouri with Aaron along.

In southern Missouri, Aaron and Amanda walked in at Walter's Tipton farm, surprising them! Aaron helped Walter disk land without rocks in the deep rich topsoil. Later Aaron and Amanda came to the Memphis area where they had five married daughters. They divided their time equally among their children.

The girls called ahead, telling each other when their parents were coming, "Hurry up and clean your refrigerator, because Mom and Pop are coming tomorrow!"With so many travelers coming and going, Aaron and Amanda did not care if the sheets in their beds were not quite clean since the last guests just left, or if toys littered the floor. They wanted to help work and shared with the farming, gardening, canning, cooking, baking, and whatever they could help. They also enjoyed eating. After a leisurely meal, other guests promptly helped wash the dishes, but Amanda always preferred to put away the leftover food, saltshakers, dishes, and especially things in the refrigerator. She rummaged around and scolded. 'Why is some of this food uncovered? This should have been on the table...!"She complained anytime something was growing a beard, hidden away in a back corner of the refrigerator...forgotten. She did not like to see wasted food, and maybe she felt it her duty to keep on teaching her daughters. She could see instantly if someone was living on 'ready to eat' luxury items, or if their shelves were nearly bare.

Amanda saw crumbs on the floor after dinner and cheerfully swept the room. Her nimble fingers automatically sifted through the pile in the dustpan. She removed a valuable penny, a puzzle piece and a rubber band. Then she put the paper scraps in the waste can, but she made sure the crumbs and the three spilled Cheerios went out the door. "If your cats will not find the crumbs then surely the birds might," she said. "Never destroy food!"

Amanda quickly forgot how it made with their fifteen children at home...and she said, "Don't let your children stand on the chairs, they could get hurt. Are they always this loud?. ..No, don't do it like that! If you snap those string beans by hand instead of cutting them with a knife, you would not cut apart and lose those tiny seeds inside each bean... When you hang up the wash, do not hang my nightgown upside down... And do not let the baby cry... surely it wants something! Are the rubber pants uncomfortable?. ..Don't your children help with the dishes...?" Amanda asked. She did not realize how much the children helped around the house when she was not around. She was in their way when she fed the cats and helped clear the table. Any company around the house created an unnatural tension until they left again. Aaron and Amanda were always welcome, but it was also nice to see them move on.

When watching Amanda pack a suitcase, one of her children marveled. 'I did not know there were so many ways to fold a nightgown!" She folded and refolded, to use up the last bit of space. In a home, in a room, in a refrigerator, or in a suitcase, Amanda always found room for one more, even

in her heart; even when others declared it was full. She was among the world's best at utilizing space.

Aaron and Amanda moved on to Indiana, spending four days with Aaron's brother Ben and Grace Shirk, and Amanda's sister Katie and Dan Martin.

Arriving back in Pennsylvania, after several weeks away from home, Amanda found plenty of weeds to pull. RoseAnna and Mandy helped pull nine wheelbarrows full of weeds and they froze 56 quart of sweet corn for the next trip to Missouri. Amanda also dried four dish pans full of cut corn which shrank down to one and one half gallon after she dried it. Aaron went to the doctor at Lancaster for another injection for his hurting back. He simply did not travel well!

Amanda kept right on preserving food for her extended family, and filled five boxes of home canned food plus six pumpkins and one half bucket of red beets for Missouri. She found a way to travel without Aaron for her third trip to Missouri in 1974. Willis and John Z. Martins took her along for two ordinations planned for Missouri. Aaron Weaver was ordained to preach and Ivan High was the new deacon.

Back home again, Aaron and Amanda were busy inviting Sunday dinner guests or making calls of some sort every Sunday, and sometimes more than one stop in an afternoon. The younger children at home played tetherball and the older children never heard of such a game. For five dollars, they bought a helicopter ride from the Green Dragon parking lot. Amazing! The girls slept out on the top porch balcony and the mosquitoes nearly ate them up.

Amanda kept saying, about different things, "Oh didn't you know that?" She repeated things many times to many ages of their children until she thought they all knew, but the youngest ones didn't. Rose Anna and Mandy kept finding things in the attic while cleaning, that they did not know they had. The older children had different circumstances, but all fifteen, had happy memories of skating and swimming at the pond. In wintertime, RoseAnna and Mandy made a huge snowman at the end of the lane.. Amanda remembered powdery snow that squeaked when she walked in Michigan and then they seldom had a wet snow that packed.

Laurel Scribe

In 1974, Aaron started writing letters in the " Budget ".The Amish newspaper welcomed scribes interested in writing a column every week about their home community. As pay, they received their subscription free of charge. Someone commented about Aaron quitting his smoking habit and he wrote" *the cigars just didn't taste good anymore, so I quit. I think the quality is much poorer than it used* to be, *but please, no one give me honor as all honor belongs to the Lord. Being a writer, I never know when some other writer will bump into me and then my clothing would stink like tobacco.*

Some people think you just sit down and write the news for the Budget column, but it don't work that way. As we look to the Lord for guidance and at times this can be as heavy as carrying a vote for the ministry which I did four times now, three times for preacher and one time for Bishop.I would like to make something clear, that I am just a writer, and that you pray for me, A.M. Shirk

Our earthly chores are, looking after 28 head of heifers, and we now have three surveyors working on 25 building lots, and are building Laurel Lake number two at this time. Bootleg run comes in from the side that is the good strong spring area where the bootleggers made their brew in 1937.

Aaron spent most of his life dreaming about mineral rights and mining riches. He happened to be doing the right thing at the right time for altogether the wrong reasons. Gradually he saw his dreams come true in a way far beyond his wildest imagination. All the rocky wooded hillsides in his possession, turned into riches, as land prices soared. Many people preferred a building lot in the woods, as a secluded peaceful location for a new house.

For the past years, Pete had been in the building development business and he helped his father design a new blacktop through the woodland, as well as locating pond sites. The building permits, zoning laws, sewer systems, government taxes and regulations, were sometimes beyond Aarons understanding.

Someone talking with Aaron said, "I don't smoke, I don't drink, and I don't read the Budget!" Aaron wrote in reply; *we cannot agree with those who call the Budget a gossip line. When our family is scattered half way across the United States, we long for news from them. The moments are precious as we gaze up and down the columns in the Budget for news from loved ones far away.*

March 13, 1975, Aaron writes: The state of Pennsylvania and the United States government is conducting a Dylox spray by helicopter this spring in our area, which is listed as a populated and high public use area. Thy spray is to kill the gypsy moths, which are killing our oak trees. We are asked to remain inside while the spray is applied, as there could be some stains on clothes and wash lines. It is not poisonous to humans or animals.

Two weeks later, he wrote; we have very little wind going the last few days, which makes it ideal for spraying oak trees for gypsy moths. There were two helicopters with booms, spraying Laurel Hill. We were fortunate to qualify for this service by the United States government, and they parked the helicopter here overnight. I had a study on gypsy moths with BenTtresselt, the tree specialist. The US government will be looking into this situation also, for possible spraying plans to take place in springtime. Efforts are being made to save the Oak trees. The gypsy moths have now quit eating, and have discarded their outer skin with their caterpillar fur coat. From a worm, they are now in a dark hard-shelled cocoon in some sheltered hiding place. In two weeks, they will hatch into moths. The male is brown with a 1 ½ inch wing span: eggs can remain attached to where they are layed until next May when they hatch into caterpillars the size of pinheads They can float along with the wind for 30 to 40 miles, then as they start eating, the whole process starts over.

We are finally on a diet, and it is all my wife's fault that she is just too good a cook.

My wife runs the window fan, blowing the kitchen air out, while I turned it around and bring the shady side of the house inside. We wonder which one is right.

We had just finished eating dinner, when the telephone rang, it was a call for eight pints of type O positive blood, needed immediately at the Ephrata hospital for preacher Ben Martin's wife. I have been chairman of the blood drives for a number of years, but usually we are given several days time. Mrs. Martin was very low and so was the blood bank. We want to thank the donors for meeting this need.

Sometimes I feel like Alley Musser. When a customer in his store asked,"Do you have a floating head?"Alley said,"Sometimes!"The customer wanted an electric razor.

I have been complaining about our high taxes here in the US. Today I met a middle-aged couple from Sweden where taxes are 60% on everything they buy, with free doc-

tors, dentists, hospital and schooling. An hourly wage earner gets the same wages as a college student gets for their time. However, they don't know how long this method will last.

∽

At the Blue Ball bank, Aaron met Mr. and Mrs. Kurut, strangers from India. He made friends with Dave and Evelyn Kurut, and brought them home to spend two nights with Aaron and Amanda. They cooked four meals for them and Aaron took them the next day to MCC at Akron, canning meat for the needy and meeting people. They sat up talking until nearly midnight… Eight months later, the Kuruts came back to Aarons several days and overnight, showing slides of India and taking Aaron and Amanda out to eat dinner at Zinn's Diner. Strangers to Aaron were just friends that he never met.

Amanda helped put seven quilts in frame at the Bowmansville fire hall and she spent the next three days helping to quilt them. She wrote in a letter, "I'm expected to pretty much manage Bowmansville fire hall quilting week, and someone takes them home to finish binding them. The Ladies Auxiliary make the lunch and the treat for three days straight." Amanda's picture appeared in the newspaper and Aaron wrote in the Budget, "The plain people are making quilts for the Bowmansville fire company. This was our first try on public auction with the top going price on their golden eagle quilt, with golden stars, selling for one thousand dollars. People who can afford such covers on their beds are helping our fire company along with their expenses and I do hope to get the ladies stirred up about quilting for next year's season."

"I was on my knees for news, when Ervie suggested I put the snapper soup in the Budget. He dragged a fifteen-pounder home from the mountains last week. Then Ervie's wife cooked the thing for three hours until the meat came off the bones. The meat was cut short, with noodles, corn and water added. A few of their Amish neighbors showed up this week for snapper soup. Some took a second serving! It is our turn for a Sunday dinner visit at Ervies, but not until we are sure that, the snapper soup has all disappeared. To me the

snappers appear too much in the snake family. We like to think of something else when we see a long neck sticking up out of a meat platter in front of us at a friend's table. Thanks just the same!

Besides all her other work, Amanda was the best transportation for all the ladies in the neighborhood of the horse and buggy church. She took them to doctor appointments, dentist, groceries," quilting's of all kinds, plus other charities. She gladly helped quilt at all the fire halls around, including Fivepointville, Goodville, Churchtown, Bowmansville, and at the Fairmont home. Amanda enjoyed the freedom of coming and going without a driver's inconvenience or impatience.

In the twinkle of an eye

Amanda wrote," *In the twinkle of an eye, God can take all that we have. I often feel myself very slack in being thankful enough for our many blessings. We were at Dick's on Sunday evening and watched them milk cows in a modern dairy barn. It sure goes different than it did by hand".* Amanda could still remember back to the age of four years old, when she watched her grandfather milk a row of cows by hand, and her dad helped. At the end of the row stood a bull tied in a stanchion. Amanda and her sister Betsy watched intently, and when the bull turned his head to look at them, Betsy panicked and backed up quickly, accidentally sitting squarely into a bucket of fresh warm milk."

"*I sometimes wonder what some of the old pioneers would think of this modern world, if they could see how fast everything goes, I can't help but think the end is coming fast. My daily wish and prayer is that we may live, to all meet together in an unbroken family in that beautiful home beyond the skies, and that non-need to be left behind. May God be with us all, until we meet again. From mother and grandmother"*

House fire

Lydia and Carl Hoover moved to Missouri, and lived on nice farmland, with a small worn out house. They did not know if they should build a new house and tear down the old one, or try to repair what they had. God answered those prayers with a house fire in the middle of the night, and not at all, what they wanted. On a cold night in February, they escaped with their three-month-old baby Charlene and the clothes on their backs. The cause of the fire might have been the old wiring. When they first smelled smoke, the flames already leaped through the wall of the house, where the wind caught and spread the fire rapidly. Lydia, wearing bedroom slippers, grabbed her coat and a quilt to wrap up baby Charlene. Their telephone lines burned, so she went to the closest neighbors, Ivan Highs to call for help. A few people driving past, saw the flames and helped grab several things from the living room end of the house, including the desk, with its paperwork and a couch. Everything else was gone before the firemen arrived. Lydia had purchased some fine old antiques at a family- only auction, including a unique sewing machine dated in 1897, and a wooden- tub, wringer washer. Those possessions were merely treasures here below, and so was Carl's coin collection.

They spent the rest of that night with their neighbors, Mary and Ivan High, where baby Randy was only four days old. After spending a week living at Roland Weiler's, Preacher Titus Martins spared their used house trailer, as a temporary dwelling for Carl and Lydia so they could live on their own place among the action of building. Many people volunteered to help build a big new house in a hurry, with not many detailed extras.

Aaron and Amanda replaced the cedar chest Lydia had received from home, and you can be sure that it arrived tightly packed with necessities. Amanda made a fan quilt from Lydia's dress scraps, still in her possession. She added a blanket and a fuzzy bed-sheet for the cold Missouri nights. She sent a new dark green, double knit dress that Mandy and RoseAnna sewed in a hurry. Lydia also received a walnut extension table, made from trees cut down on Aaron's farm. The boards had not been dry enough to make a table before Lydia and Carl moved to Missouri.

Mandy took time off from her job, and traveled to Missouri with some teachers. They needed another driver when Mary Edna Hoover and Becky Hoover moved to Missouri to teach one room schools. Sharon and Sandy Stauffer also went along. Mandy enjoyed the one-way trip and helped to work at Carl Hoover's after their house

fire. They appreciated her help, very much. Mandy did not know how she would get back home, and she ended up bravely flying on a jet.

Carl Hoover's took her to the St. Louis airport, 200 miles away. They arrived five minutes before the plane planned to leave. Lydia and Carl had a great concern that Mandy might miss her flight. Mandy had no worries, until she saw how far she had to walk to get there, after they were at the airport. The corridors were empty and Mandy RAN! She was out of breath and rejoiced to plop in her seat just in time, as they waited a few more minutes on another man. She did not mind the two-hour layover in Chicago. Mandy wrote a letter and visited with a Catholic nun. She enjoyed the flight. When the plane landed, it bumped and she was alarmed. ..what was that? None of the other people showed any fear, so she kept on reading. Aaron and Amanda fetched Mandy at the Harrisburg airport and they all arrived home in time for supper. It was good to be home, a wonderful place!

Aaron and Amanda made many trips to Missouri and Mandy ended up at home alone sometimes. On one such evening, Mandy hung on the phone talking to a good friend, when an old rattle trap with a loud muffler came driving in the lane. A young man with real long hair came to the kitchen door. Mandy had missed her chance to run and hide because the kitchen light was on. She was scared and told her friend, Esther Mae Martin,"Do not hang up! I will lay the phone down and go to the door. If I holler... I need help!" The stranger asked,"May I speak with Mr. Shirk?" Mandy did not like to answer that question but she said,"He is not here right now." The stranger said, "I am seeking permission to set traps down at the creek. When would be a good time to come back?" Mandy thought rapidly. She did not want to tell him she would be alone for another week. She said, "Dad always says those who ask permission are all right, so I'm sure it's okay to set traps." He said, "thank you," as he went on his way. Giving a stranger permission to trap, brought him back every evening to check those traps, but thankfully he never came to the door again.

33

The younger girls, spent many hours of time brushing on many more gallons of white paint on the board fence. They also spent a lot of time trimming flowerbeds and trimming the walk. They never heard of Round-up and edged the walk with salt. Mandy picked up what she thought was black plastic and a snake wrapped around her arm tightly. She screamed in panic! She was not seriously scared of snakes but this was too much, as she struggled to get rid of it. On another occasion, Mandy picked up a snake in a bucket after RoseAnna convinced her it was dead, but it was not. She screamed and threw it for all she was worth, as the snake slithered off, although damaged. She had just wanted to check out the snake and make sure it was not a copperhead, and she never found out. All the snakes with a small round pupil in the eyes, such as people have, are not poisonous, other than the brightly colored coral snake, living far away. The snakes with a pupil slit up and down, like cat eyes are the dangerous ones. The big fat brown mottled water snakes only appeared to be harmful.

None of Aaron and Amanda's family ever got hurt from a snake, even working among them. Both seemed to respect each other's territory, and the large black snakes were the best mousers around, rarely seen.

RoseAnna and Lewis Nolt started dating in early March of 1973. He asked her for a date at the Martindale spelling bee. Many young people gathered there and Aaron and Amanda knew their children did not just go for the spelling contest. When Lewis arrived for his first date, he got stuck in a snowdrift in the lane. RoseAnna had worried about the deep snow in the lane, but Aaron did not think the snow mattered. RoseAnna felt her blood pressure rising and Lewis was embarrassed. Wesley helped get them out of the drifted snow.

Aaron apologized to RoseAnna later and said," I did not realize that Lewis's 1968 Camaro was lower than Marlin's '65 GTO and Carl Hoover's '68 Chevy Nova." Some cars were jacked up to the legal limit, back then, even if they rode rough and bumpy.

Amanda saw a wedding approaching, even before anyone told her. She could see how fast her other girls disappeared and she was busy getting quilt-tops quilted all winter. RoseAnna had five quilts for her hope chest, a Lone Star, Four Patch, Log Cabin, Goose on the Pond and a tan one without a name, made from factory patches. Using up the leftover blocks, she made a matching crib quilt.

Beneath the south porch was a spot to store the push mower, gardening tools and any such thing that had no proper place. It was a catch all for junk! The teenage girls made sure the latticework cover stayed in place to conceal the embarrassing things. When the dog had a litter of puppies under the porch, so close to the parlor walk, Rose Anna resented it. To her amazement, Lewis liked the frolicking puppies that scattered bones and miscellaneous clutter in the yard. Lewis had the pick of the litter to keep for himself and the puppy grew into a fine farm dog on their dairy.

Time moved rapidly and RoseAnna and Lewis Nolt announced their wedding plans for May 31, 1975. That was a jolting thought to Aaron. If at all possible, he wanted a garage built before then, because he did not forget about all the hard work from the previous eight weddings.

Pete was a carpenter and he understood all about blueprints, so Aaron had him draw up plans for a new garage and a laundry. Six weeks before the wedding day, a crew demolished the old summerhouse, making way for the garage. The carpenters worked fast and five days before the wedding, Harold Hoover, the plumber, hooked up the water supply yet,before the wedding.

Pete installed a half bath in the old part of the house, eliminating the need to race upstairs to the bathroom.

Travelers for the wedding started coming from Missouri, five days in advance and kept Amanda too busy to write her own diary. Mahlons slept at Aarons on Tuesday evening, and all the families from Missouri came for the wedding, all six of them. Walter's, Carl Hoover's, Ivan's, Roland's and Carl Weiler's all came for beds or meals in one week's time.

Lydi-Jes-sey came again as head cook and Jessie's Mabel came for directions. Janie showed up and helped scrape the new potatoes. They worked ahead all that they could, and they even had the space available to set up chairs three days before the wedding. On the wedding day morning, the bride and groom dusted all the chairs before the guests arrived, on a warm sunny day.

Lewis came from a smaller family. He had no brother and four sisters, and one of those was unable to attend due to a miscarriage. Sonny Ivan came without Mary Kathryn, but RoseAnna's family filled in and made up for his smaller side. Out of the two hundred guests invited, one hundred and eighty came, with a total of thirty-two grandchildren attending. Most of the guests sat down to eat at the same time. The menu consisted of Rolls, cold sliced ham, potatoes with browned butter, peas, gravy, macaroni salad, fruit salad, pudding, marble cake and ice cream.

Lewis's brother-in-law, Abner Oberholtzer had the text. He was newly ordained to preach, just a month earlier. Joe Weaver married the first eight daughters at Aaron and Amanda's farm, but since Bishop Willis Martin was ordained and lived closer, Aaron chose him this time.

Aaron and Amanda had a family reunion of sorts, and the children took many pictures. They gathered at Pete Shirks the next day, except RoseAnna and Lewis, who headed to the New England states on a one-week wedding trip. They returned for a special friend's wedding on the next Saturday.

Times changed rapidly. Aaron and Amanda delighted in watching their children and wonderful grandchildren come home, but they rejoiced to see them leave again. The rambunctious young children had too much noise and commotion.

Mandy

Mandy took turns helping her married sisters, and even got homesick, but she cried into into her pillow and got over it. RoseAnna could not handle homesickness when she lived at home, and she did not work away as much. Amanda said, "RoseAnna was like Ruth. " Gradually, RoseAnna got used to helping her sisters. She worked at Daniels, Mahlon's Walter's, Ruth, Rhoda, Martha, Mary and Irene. She stayed only one week at a time, or less. She helped at Mahlon's a few days at a time.

It was Mandy that helped at Roland's, when she slept on the couch one night, with big trucks roaring past all night, right beside the 322. She also helped at Wesley's when they had a new baby Janetta and later for baby Juanita. She remembered distinctly, how Wesley and Janie left for a doctor appointment and Mandy stayed alone a few hours at Beltsville, Maryland. She walked to the post office to mail a letter, and when she stepped out, the door locked behind her. She had no key, and she was used to country life. She managed to climb in a window.

Mandy could hardly wait another week to go home from Carl Weilers one time. She missed the remodeling job of new paneling in the parlor, and she was counting the days until it was time to go home, when Mervin Brubaker broke his back from a falling branch. She bypassed going home because Mervins needed her help right away, and she was sooooooooooooooooo disappointed. Mervin and Rhoda raised calves to sell and they needed Mandy for a whole month, because they had children and Rhoda had to help in the barn. The last one of Aaron and Amanda's ten girls, did not reach around to everywhere they needed her. She took a week of paid vacation from her job, to help Mervin Highs with their new baby Kathy in January 1974.

Mandy thought her life compared to a piece

of furniture moved many times, wherever others pleased!

When Mandy had worked at Daniels, the rooster terrified her! She carried a scoop of grain to the hen house and she used the empty grain scoop to carry the eggs. When the mean rooster startled her, she instinctively wheeled around and threw the whole works at him! Oops! There lay the cracked and broken eggs among a few whole ones, and the chickens quickly started eating them! Mandy gathered up the scoop and the best eggs and hurried out the door. She apologized about the loss, and felt badly, until her big brother smiled and said," They are only bent!"

One of the girls working at Daniels broke a dish while working there and Edna said,"''Now iss sell moll ouse um vake!''[Now that is out of the way.]No one scolded about a broken dish.

Besides helping her sisters, Mandy's first job after age sixteen, was at the Moyers factory where her sisters worked. She discovered another job more to her liking and applied at Conestoga Wood Products. She could not start there until September and worked temporarily at Miller's Store in Bowmansville.

She learned to work the old-fashioned cash register, and cut meat for the customers. Mandy pumped gas and unload supplies, or whatever. One day she could not find the gas cap on a vehicle until the owner showed her that it was hidden beneath the license plate.

Mandy liked her woodworking job at Conestoga Wood Products. It was much closer to home with better pay and better working conditions. She gave her paychecks to her parents and only kept ten percent until age twenty. Many things changed over the years, but Aaron and Amanda tried their best to keep all their children as equal as possible.

RoseAnna had many dates on the old worn couch. She wanted a better couch and bought her own new living room furniture, including new end tables. She took it along when she left home one year later, but Mandy made do with an Afghan covering the worn —out fabric on the sofa. The can of pineapples still propped up the one leg that was missing on the couch, and it had a way of flopping flat into a sofa bed, when someone moved it. With

the last girl dating, Amanda did not see a need to replace that old couch, and a pretty couch is not what boyfriends came to see.

After the O Henry party, Aaron knew Mandy had her eyes on Henry Martin, but he did not know who he was. They were not dating yet. Mandy was not at home on a Sunday afternoon, when a load of boys came to Aaron's, and he invited them in for supper. They obliged, and stood around the kitchen while Amanda instantly prepared food for more than the two of them, as she had planned. Aaron enjoyed talking with the boys and had a good time getting their names out of them.

Amanda had no company fare planned, and made a simple supper of pretzel soup. Aaron liked it and the children didn't. When Aaron talked to the boys he figured- out which one was Henry, because he shied back and nearly slipped in the narrow crack between the refrigerator and the cupboard. When Mandy returned and heard the details about 'pretzel soup', she hardly believed the story. It had been years since Aaron and Amanda served pretzel soup.

Teenage girls worked hard at landscaping the flowerbeds and painting every detail. One time Mandy held the flashlight, while Lydia finished painting the flowerbed rings, those big wide metal steel wheel rings that once belonged with the steamer for steaming tobacco beds. Mandy nearly froze her fingertips in March, trimming the walk precisely before her first date with Henry...and guess what... he did not even notice!

Planning a tenth wedding at home, in thirteen years time should have been easy, but it was not. When Mandy and Henry tried choosing a wedding date, they could not please them all, because eleven of her brothers and sisters were expecting babies that year. One of them could not come to the wedding, even after they changed the date once. Aaron and Amanda had a dozen new grandchildren in 1976.

Aunt Salome moved in with Aaron and Amanda and stayed there quite a while. Amanda sewed her a new flannel nightgown and took her to see her doctor. Aunt Salome complained about sore feet and a sore back. They moved the couch into the sewing room so that she could sleep downstairs. Salome was not so good and vomited blood in the night. Amanda took her to Ephrata for chest x-rays and to Dr. Hess at TerreHill. It was a relief to move her on to Deacon John Martin's, because only five weeks remained until Mandy's upcoming wedding at home.

It was time to concentrate on another wedding, but meanwhile Silas was in the hospital with a heart attack, also needing some of Amanda's time. Sarah Ann gave Mandy a beautiful appliquéd quilt top as a gift of appreciation, because she helped her big sister many times with babysitting. Amanda knew the quilt would look better finished, so among all her other work, she put the quilt in frame just 3 ½ weeks before the wedding. Quilting relaxed Amanda, and she had no problem finishing the quilt.

Any young people that married in Pennsylvania, before the age of twenty-one, could not get a marriage license without the signature of their parents. Not many of Aaron's children waited long enough for that. Aaron and Amanda went along to the Justice of the Peace one more time, to sign for their last child.

A group of girls had a party for painting the board fence, because Aaron and Amanda no longer had a row of girls to help. Amanda started defrosting two freezers and thoroughly cleaned the house from top to bottom. The cellar stairs needed scrubbing and they mowed the yard twice that week. Travelers arrived for the wedding about the same time that Aaron's started setting up the fire hall chairs. Two Canadian couples stayed with Aaron and Amanda overnight on the evening before the wedding. Wanda, a granddaughter from Missouri, came to help work and she slept there on Thursday night.

For the final wedding, even with the new garage and much more room, Aaron helped move some furniture out of the house to make room for displaying the wedding gifts on the tables in the old kitchen. Lewis offered to mow the lawn for the wedding and he mowed in circles like a hay field, with his riding mower. Mandy thought it looked worse than their every day neat mowing, but the wedding went on.

Mandy's mind overflowed with last-minute details about her wedding, when Aaron walked in smiling and said, "I bet you can't guess what I have in my pocket?"When all eyes turned upon Aaron, he pulled out three little skunks, saying, "I saw the mother dead on the road, so I picked up these little orphans." The cute little stinkers were adorable, but "Please pop," said Mandy, "Take them out of here! That coat must stay out in the stripping room until the wedding is over, I smell skunk!"

There were times in the past thirty-five years, when children would have squealed with delight at the thought of a pet skunk, but the timing was all wrong! The last child planned to leave home, and who wants a skunk? Aaron gave them to Davis Ziemer, the man that trapped snapper turtles at the pond. He planned to de-scent them for a pet shop dealer.

Aaron's extended family kept expanding, and Henry came from a large family. With a limit of only two nieces or nephews per family, they still had too many people. The bridal party and both families combined numbered ninety people. Only ninety-two chairs fit at the tables for the noon meal and many special friends had to wait for the second setting. Amanda insisted that Silas had to be in the first setting because he had diabetes and should not wait so long until mealtime.

With such a big family, they had more people than the garage could comfortably hold, and they opened the overhead doors, to seat more guests and some people were too cool. Two hundred and ten people attended the wedding.

Travelers lingered from Missouri, after Mandy and Henry left for their trip to Nova Scotia. Carl Hoover's came for dinner and Mahlons stayed for the night. Roland's came the next day and Amanda had help to shell peas and return some borrowed rugs and dishes. They had a lot of work to recover from a wedding. A day after the wedding, Marty Reeds brought Aunt Alzina [Norma's mother, the one that had her children grow up with Peter Brubacher's children] to Aaron and Amanda for a three-day stay. Amanda's Sister Katie stayed overnight and so did Lavina and Larry Kaufman from Indiana, who came for the wedding.

Aaron and Amanda sorted through tables and chairs from two different fire halls. Since Mervin Highs lived close by, they used his pickup truck and then returned it after supper. Amanda took time out to pick the sugar peas. It was a bittersweet moment, to see the last child leave the nest. They saw it coming... but could it really be true?

From Sarah Ann's first date in June of 1959, to Mandy's wedding, wedding on June 5, 1976 all the parties and teenagers disappeared. Aaron did not get his wish to have a girl left over. There was no one left to mow the lawn anymore, and no one to run for the telephone. Aaron and Amanda soon put an extension phone upstairs to save their health, instead of rushing down the stairs before the phone stopped ringing.

As long as the boyfriends kept coming, Aaron and Amanda had no problem getting the lawn mowed neatly. One time when the grass was extra long, Mandy and RoseAnna used a bushel basket with one of them walking along beside the mower, catching the grass clippings that blew out the side, for a neater lawn. When they were in a hurry to finish mowing, RoseAnna and Mandy pushed the lawnmower downhill rapidly beside the long lane, and loaded the mower into the car trunk, drove it up to the top, and mowed downhill again fast. It took four trips of driving the lawnmower uphill in the car trunk, but it went faster and easier than pushing up that hill.

Amanda remembered how her father mowed the yard in Michigan. Peter Brubacher with a scythe, chopped down the tallest growth only one time in the summer, and the area was small. Aaron and Amanda's older children mostly grew up pushing a reel- type mower in the small yard around the house, until they purchased a newfangled contraption, a power mower, and they mowed much more than necessary.

Before Mandy and Henry returned from their wedding trip, Aaron bought a nice new riding lawnmower, because he saw it was now his job to mow the yard. Aaron and Amanda had the long sloping lane blacktopped. It was too late for their children to play on it, but the grandchildren loved coasting down on wheeler toys, and trikes. The rainwater no longer washed away the gravel.

Aaron and Amanda had no more children and no more weekend fuss. No more singings, scouters nor weddings. It all happened so suddenly! In less than forty years, Aaron and Amanda lived alone again. They both enjoyed the quiet solitude and yet they missed the noise and activity, until the grandchildren came home...

Aaron and Amanda were suddenly in the autumn of their lives. Abundance lay everywhere. ..more than they could use or gather. Gone was the weight and responsibility of raising their large family, and gone was the financial stress and the school problems. Around them fluttered colored leaves and luxury, they never imagined possible. They often wondered what would happen to their many children. Thankfully they all grew up and had it better than their parents had in the past.

Aaron and Amanda stayed as busy as ever, just in a different way. Canadians came overnight, and when they left, Amanda worked fast to do a bit of cleaning and packed for another trip to Missouri. She went to bed at 11 PM and left home the next morning at 4:30 AM, taking along many packages.

In July of 1977, Aaron and Amanda hosted another large Shirk reunion. It was eight years since the last one. Over 200 guests arrived and many from far away could not attend. Every one enjoyed meeting relatives and talking so much that they called their gathering 'The National Shirk Convention' and planned more such gatherings in the future, once every five years.

After a good Sunday dinner at Christ Shirk's, Christ called Aaron and asked,"Aaron, do you have your suit coat?" Aaron double -checked and said "Yes I do!" Christ then said, 'There is only one suit coat here and it isn't mine. It has false teeth in the pocket!"That settled it, Aaron's teeth were missing, but he did not miss them much. They did not fit properly and he put them in his pocket when he ate.

Aaron and Amanda kept right on going, inviting company for dinner and canning pears until late in the evening. They both helped at the Fairmont home where 100 people gathered to can 1,392-quarts of pears in one day, for the old people's home. Later Amanda returned there to can green beans and more pears for charity.

Amanda occasionally she did babysitting for three-year-old Jason Milner living on Laurel Hill. She wrote,"Whoever calls this baby sitting, doesn't know how little I sit when children come."Mrs. Milner came to Amanda, to learn how to quilt and to sew. That was something that no one bothered teaching her. She helped Amanda put a quilt in frame and was fascinated with the entire process, of stitching all three layers together in tediously tiny stitches. Amanda taught many people how to sew and she still taught patiently. For Christmas, she sewed fifteen durable cloth shopping bags as gifts for her married children. She used her own shopping bag, just like it, as a travel tote. Not so long ago, a shopping bag was something she needed while shopping in Reading, and traveling on the bus.

Amanda sewed Aaron a new blanket –lined coat for every day. She usually wore a shawl, but she cut out and sewed a short coat for herself with a lining and a blanket interlining. She had no pattern. She said,"My heavy shawl is not convenient for driving, when I sit at the steering wheel. It gets in the way when I turn sharply."

Budget clippings

Aaron writes in the Budget:

We are overburdened with sightseers from the big cities, like we are animals in a zoo. Last week a New York couple asked to watch a funeral procession of all horse and buggy people, but their interests were much like watching a parade. At Churchtown, right on time, a policeman was needed along the many sightseers on the public highway so the horse and buggies had a chance to get out of the churchyard without being blocked in. Yesterday Mr. Will wrote an article in the Washington Post about the Amish in the Gap Area, and their way of life.

Some people thought the Mennonites were a cult, because they followed the teachings of Menno Simons. Menno was a Catholic priest that led a group of people away from the Roman Catholic Church in the 1530's. They studied the Bible and agreed it was not right to baptize infants. The Mennonite followers never worshipped Menno or his opinions. They followed the Bible and especially the Sermon on the Mount where Jesus taught against going to war, swearing and holding offices that required the use of force. They belonged to a Protestant group that was persecuted for their Anabaptist religion in the Netherlands and northern

Germany among other places. William Penn offered them religious liberty. Aaron wrote," We are happy to live in a country where we can worship free and at will."

"Here on Laurel Hill, two more houses are being started this week, with an awful lot of interest lately to move into the woods."An older couple from Long Island New York was looking to buy two acres of land in our community to build their retirement house. They want to get away from the high crime area. An Army general of West Virginia is looking to buy a new house on Laurel Hill, we discovered that some of these people feel safe when they move in among the plain people, thinking God would protect them.

After living in Missouri several years, and returning to Lancaster County Pennsylvania, Aaron's children noticed a vast change, with more traffic and more tourists. With their high-tech cameras, city people and strangers drove close to horse and buggies, taking pictures through open car windows. Why all the fuss? Where there had been no difference, just one generation ago, there was a widening gap in dress standards, simply because Mennonites and Amish lived what they believed. They wanted the Biblical truths, honest hard work, helping others and simplicity. They got more attention every year, because they did not believe in bold and gaudy clothes, with indecent exposure.

Aaron wrote in the budget; Elmina Yoder and Lillian Beiler, teachers of the Weaver land Mennonite school, were arrested last week on charges of aggravated assault, by whipping a child in their school. The child was Stephen Force, age 7, son of Gary Force. The teachers are free on bail.

(Four months later): Stephen Force has gained nationwide publicity about a whipping in school. I have reason to believe the parents are doing their best to teach a problem child the proper way. If the same medicine was used today that was used fifty years ago, many teenagers would have a sure cure coming their way. Our dad had an old apple switch behind the wood stove, with long dried out knots on it, we boys all knew where the knots were, especially in the summer when we had thin pants on. Taking the Bible and the switch out of the schools is saying, 'Go and do what you want". If that is what America wants, that is what she will get. Written by A.M. Shirk.

Aaron and Amanda saw a distinct downward spiral of the school system. The school houses and the teachers were not so much to blame as the laws. With no Bible reading and no spankings teachers lost respect and order! Some good teachers quit.

Aaron wrote, "We are receiving numerous requests for a life story in a book form, about the writer and his family. We have talked this over and decided a book is not only costly but time-consuming."I am hoping to bring out a few happenings as time goes on and space permits in our Budget column!"

Today 40 years ago, me and Mandie were published in church to get married. The 40 years have passed over us like a shadow that has already gone down. It was like a dream. We grew up together. She was 22 and I was 23. Then we goofed, we forgot to sign our marriage license until sixteen years later. I learned to eat raw dandelions with dressing. She had to learn to like oysters. We butchered our first beef, a big bull under the forebay. Neither one of us knew much about butchering. We hung it up with a pulley and tackle. I stood up on a stepladder then skinned the thing like a rabbit.

When gathering scraps for the slop bucket, I accidently dumped the week's collection of cream from the kitchen stove into the bucket. We didn't get any butter made, but we might be eating good ham next winter.

Forty-four years ago, I was driving two horses in a log sleigh with a wagon box on it, loaded with young couples on a cold windy evening in drifting snow. I was the only one without a girlfriend, automatically making me the driver. They all seemed too cozy, wrapped in blankets while I was up front, cold through and through. How I wished for my warm bed. Snow banks were drifting higher and higher closer and closer home. We decided we better leave the road and take a field and hunt for more shallow snow. While crossing the ditch the couples and blankets dumped clear, the horses ran home and the sleigh was demolished, leaving the couples hitchhiking the rest of the way home. I never did like sleigh rides ever since!

Aaron wrote; "I had been planning on a jet plane out of Philadelphia, but couldn't get my wife in the plane. She wanted to travel on the ground, so we greased the old Ford and patched the trunk, and then took off on the Turnpike westbound, spending several weeks in Indiana and Missouri. At Lydia and Carl Hoover's place, we were taken up like king and queen. Even my Sunday suit was put in a clothes closet. Getting ready for church the next morning was a problem. I just couldn't get my pants on until I discovered I was trying on Carl's pants and he is 50 pounds lighter than I. We went to the new church called Northview, ten miles south of the Iowa state line. This is the fourth year

I am trying to hear Levi Zimmerman preach. We missed him again, as Levi was at Hedge City. We went to visit them at their Rutledge farm, where I was greeted with a left handshake, his right hand being neatly wrapped. Now what shall I put in the Budget? Levi said; do not make a big long story about the short piece of my long finger that went in with the silage. Levi reached in the running machine to clean out some clogged up corn when it caught. If you have to reach in when the machine is running Levi, put a paint mark around your arm to know how far you can go without getting caught!"

We hit a bad time to visit in Missouri, right in the middle of soybean harvest. Some combines were running day and night. I went along to the grain elevators in Unionville, Missouri, where beans were put up in big round metal bins, grain bins."

As Aaron stood around with pencil and paper, asking many questions, he told everyone, "I am a news reporter!"Aaron's son-in-law tried his best to conceal the identity of the strange reporter, and preferred that no one knew it was his father-in-law. Aaron enjoyed watching the action of loading soybeans onto barges at the Mississippi River.

On Sunday, while driving from Millport Church to Carl Weilers, Aaron and Amanda met 40 wild turkeys on the narrow dirt road. In their childhood, wild turkeys were scarce. He was pleased to see three deer cross the road in front of them and they were fascinated with the delay of the freight train, crossing in Rutledge. Aaron liked to hear the coyotes, because they did not hear them in the East.

I know that most people do not believe in dreams, he wrote, but the last night in Missouri, I dreamed the cops got me on the way home, and then before we got to St. Louis we ran into a speed trap. We had pushed the cruise button at 60 and the cops got me for 66, which is 11 miles over. I don't know what color I was, but the policeman was black. After thanking him for stopping us and deciding our new car was having a mechanical failure, he told us to set the speed at 53 and let us free, telling us we could have gotten a ticket. What a relief!

Our neighbors, Ike Martin's are moving to Wisconsin the last week in October. It always gives us a chilling feeling when we think of a good neighbor moving far away. There is a "roomer "floating around here that Mandy and I are moving to Missouri. Just don't believe that story!

Two weeks ago, one of our neighbors had his farm tractor stolen and no thief has been caught yet. If they catch the thief, the law might smack him on his fingers and tell him not to do it again. I am in favor of going back to the" wipping post" for all stealing, with ten strokes to every $100 value stolen.

There is an east wind picking up moisture as it comes in over the Atlantic. When God makes it rain on our hills, it's all spotless, pure. We can see it in the raindrops on the window. This alone would make us believe that there is a God in heaven. A M. Shirk

"Our beautiful mountain is all leafed up with green, red, pink, yellow, and brown. I brought a new poem along in from the woods; Autumn all trimmed with gold, with the beauty of God untold. Summer days are all but lost, now covered with a winter frost. If we live on to next spring, we'll start over and again begin." A.m. Shirk

"We paid $4550 for a 2 acre triangle of wood land between our home and the public road right in our frontage with about half in trees and the balance in blacktop. I had bought the same land back in 1937 for ten dollars an acre when my dad, BW Shirk, was furnishing the money and starting us off. He was so disappointed to find that I would pay such an exorbitant price for worthless land that he made me go back and cancel the sale. He always said,"Do not buy things unless you have the money!"Now, 39 years later the price of $4550 is cheap, according to our sons, Daniel and Pete."

A nest of killdeer escaped unhurt from the cutter bar of the mower while I was mowing weeds in our pastureland. Our mockingbirds kept some of our Canadian visitors awake last night.

"November four, election day with a light turnout at the Bowmansville fire company where I voted to try and keep the Spring Grove School open. It is rather new and centrally located. If this school goes on the auction block, there will be a new addition added to the city school and our scholars hauled off to town where there is more corruption and higher taxes for all." Aaron and Amanda no longer had any schoolchildren, but they cared deeply about the next generation, and they paid many school taxes.

I was down myself with the grip last week. By using home remedies, I dragged around with the bug for a whole week. Those who went to the doctor for medicine got through in only seven days. To fight the colds off, I eat raw onions every day. Mandie says the smell is enough to keep

the colds away from her also. She enjoys watching the snow come down...and remembers the scenes of her childhood. I enjoy watching the snow leave!

"A woodpecker is pecking on our steel pasture gate every morning to wake us up at six o'clock!"

"We again helped pack clothing at the MCC [Mennonite Central Committee] Center at Ephrata for overseas shipment to help clothe people in need with not enough to cover their bodies because of poverty. I wonder when some other country will start shipping clothing to this country for those who have too little clothing on."

"Our dinner invitation was at my sister Annie's place, Reuben Weavers, and was the dinner ever good, just like my mother used to make. I offered to do the dishes and guess what, I got the job! Stacks of dishes to wash for a house full of visitors, but my sister Eva did follow up on the dishwashing with instructions for me, to do the job right. My brother Elias from Barnett, Missouri, was a weekend visitor for the first time in six years. Two of my brothers and two of my sisters hadn't seen each other for six years and it was nice to get together to review the good times we had when we were boys."

When Amanda traveled to Missouri without Aaron, he wrote; I have been batching all week long, with cats, dogs and ducks. I was making my own meals until the good stuff got all, out of the refrigerator. Everything was a leftover mess including myself. When it finally got to me, I slammed the refrigerator door, grabbed a gallon of milk and traded it in at the neighbors for a cup of hot coffee. I never knew before how necessary an old man needs a cook. Even the cake that had burned four months ago, would taste good about now. The girls came home and washed up the floors that I did not even know were dirty, for mom's homecoming.

Mandie came in from the garden the other day with a 10-pound cabbage head, that immediately went into sauerkraut and we are having a sweet time together because she added sugar instead of salt.

William Kilmer's with their five children, from California, Missouri, came along home for dinner. I am his uncle and advised them to try to make a go of farming out there on $300 an acre farmland with 10% rains, while we are trying to make a go at $3000 an acre with 100% rains. Many people ask me when we will be moving to Missouri. I am the kind that's chicken about getting homesick and very hard to get out of our nest."

About the only news around Laurel Hill is that Mom spilled the floor wax on our kitchen linoleum, and I keep spinning around in circles when carrying in the firewood.

Our plans were to eat a chicken soup lunch in the churchyard after the people go home, but instead we went along home with Eli Zimmermann's to a real chicken dinner with lots of extras on the table. I lost 10 pounds on our new diet, but feel like having gained 11 pounds back.

"On our way home at supper time many cars stopped along the road where Christmas trees were being sold. People seem to sidetrack from the real meaning of Christmas, with Santa Claus for their Savior and presents for all under a cut off tree that soon will perish. May we look to Jesus with thankful hearts this holiday season?"

This week's story is entitled, "God wants both hands." Soon after our engagement back in 1937, we bought our present home consisting of 42 acres for $2000. To make a living, I was growing and smoking tobacco to the gills. Dad bought me a watch if I would not smoke until I turned 18. It never did keep good time for me, and I smoked. This seemed to be the way of life till I became a writer with a pen in my right hand and a burning cigar in my left. Soon I lost the taste for tobacco and temptations never came. Instead of a good smell, they just stink! Yes, God wants both hands, but I will never be a testimony to the people here. They remember me in the East, with a cigar in my mouth and in the West; they remember the smell of my Sunday suit. However, it does seem strange when I meet someone that is smoking, holding a cigar to his back that soon disappears. Yes, God wants both hands, yours and mine."

As time went on, Aaron had more regrets about smoking. He wrote in the Budget: *We earnestly plead with everyone who smokes to quit the habit, and to those that did not start yet, to look to your future years to preserve your health-habits and be a light to others!*

Mandie and I, with Martin Kilmer's, spent a weekend in Maryland to visit our wives' relatives. We had the Budget on the front seat, and as we passed Washington DC, we checked for Les Troyer's address for a short stop-off. Of course, we did not find it, then thinking about our President Jimmy Carter being nearby, in honor of him, I ate a pack of salted peanuts, while filling our gas tank.

The dogwoods are in bloom once more in our land, bear-

ing the nail marks of our Lord on every flower, even the one that's there for me, signifying Christ's crucifixion on the cross-shaped flower. The Dogwood tree with its twisted top shall no more rise high like the oaks and popular, but bare a flower every year in reach of me.

Aaron spent time writing poetry. He enjoyed rhyming words, but he lacked the rhythm. Aaron sometimes wrote a poem in Dutch and sent it to Richard Beam for printing. All the compliments he got, went to his head! Aaron kept on writing.

Es Pennsilfaanisch Deitsch Eck

Editor: C. Richard Beam
406 Spring Drive, Millersville, Penna. 17551

MICH UN DIE MANDIE

Mich un die Mandie sin uscht alt,
Iwwerall wu mir hiegehn is es kalt.
Mir hocke in unserm Haus
Un gucke iwwerall uscht naus.
Es hot awwer e deel Schnee,
Der Wind bloost uns noch meh.

Mich un die Mandie hocke bei em Offe,
Dreimol der Daag dien mir koche.
Es nemmt uscht so bissli,
Alles datt uns in unser Schissli.
Mir dien unser Gscharr verschmiere
Un dien abwexle fer sie wesche.

Mich un die Mandie hen Kinner ghat:
Sie sin all gheiert un ziege fatt.
Wu sie all waare noch deheem,
Waare mir beinanner in e lange Lehn.
Mir waare ganzi aarmi Leit
Un doch waare mir sadde gscheit.

Mich un die Mandie drieb un sunnich,
Unser Leben waar siesser denn Hunnich.
Die Zeide awwer waare sadde hatt,
Doch hen mir blendi Gleeder ghat.
Sie waare ganz ausgewohre
Un doch hen mir sie ghat fer Yaahre.

Mich un die Mandie in der Schpreierseck
Hen gschatt bis es nemmt schier kee Deck.
Datt hen mir gschlofe wie en Block,
Mer hett's mache kenne fer en ganzi Woch!
Es waar so hatt fer uch (uff) Schtee
Fer der nei Daag griege fer geh!

Mich un die Mandie hen awwer ghat
En Drupp Kinner zu fiedre awwer en Latt.
Alles waar gessen un nix meh datt.
Es waar alles so gut wie en hot gebatt,
Welschkannmosch un Kiehschtallmillich,
Unser ganze Drupp waar doch so willich!

Before spring has entirely engulfed us we want to print MICH UN DIE MANDIE, which was mailed to us on February 28. This is the first column we're writing since MICH UN DIE MANDIE reached us.

A. M. Shirk, the author of MICH UN DIE MANDIE, writes as follows:

"It took me about one hour to write this poem while taking my noon rest here at Laurel Hill, Pa. on February 27, 1980, while looking out the window and waiting on spring to come our way. Snowflakes are passing our kitchen outside in a softly blowing March wind. The little cracks around our farmhouse door keep us well supplied with fresh air. Neither one of us is taking up chalking here on our little ranch. Mandie just turned 65 on Washington's Birthday and I was 66 the night before Christmas. I still feel stalled with my poor spelling, but Mandie was a top speller in a Woodland, Michigan, school, and with Bischli-Gnippli a top speller in Pennsylvania. I hope by these two helping me we can get this poem going about how we used to live years ago when we were poor and did not even know it."

We are again indebted from our poet friend from Laurel Hill. His letter expresses beautifully the genesis of the poem. Let's hope we'll hear from him again as soon as those spring breezes thaw him out.

April 16, 1980   Es Bischli-Gnippli

Translated:

Me and de Mandie are but old ,
Everywhere we go it is cold
We sit in our house
And look everywhere just out
It had although some snow
The wind blows us some more
Me and de Mandie sit by the stove
three times a day do we cook
it takes but so little
all that's there in our dish
we do our dishes smear
and we take turns for to wash them
me and de Mandy had children
they are all married and moved away
when they all were still at home
were we together in a long lane
we were totally poor people
and yet were we rather decent
me and de Mandie dreary and sunny
our love was sweeter than honey
the times were rather hard
yet we plenty clothes had
they were all worn out
and yet had we them for years
me and de Mandie in the straw tick
had dug until took hardly any covers
there had we slept like a log
we could make it for a whole week
it was so hard to stand up
for the new day get to go
me and de Mandie had though had
a group of children to feed although a lot
all was eaten and nothing more left
it was all so good and had enough
corn mush and cow barn milk
our whole group was yet so willing

34

Aaron and Amanda had 34 grandchildren with the oldest one merely ten years old. They had many lively gatherings, and most of the children came home often. The loud grandchildren filled in where Rose Anna and Mandy thought they never had a baby in the family years ago. Those toddlers got into things and messed up things, almost like revenge, for the way Sarah Ann remembered her things messed up by her little sisters years ago.

By the time Aaron turned 65 years old, his children showered him with 65 grandchildren. The first ones were a lot more special and Amanda remembered their birthdays. They fit in well with the younger children at home, and Amanda knew them personally. Aaron and Amanda kept right on teaching.

. The numbers kept on adding up, until they had 103 living grandchildren, many in Missouri. Daniel commented, "Mom has enough grandchildren now for a wedding every ninety days for the next twenty years" and he was right!

Amanda tried to remember all her descendants, and she recorded each new baby's name and birth date. Irene made a huge rotating chart resembling a turning pinwheel so Amanda could see how many children each family had. In the center of the wheel, she recorded Aaron and Amanda's names and wedding date. Around that, she added the fifteen children and beyond that, spiraled their children as Aaron and Amanda's grandchildren, with enough space to record the wedding dates and the grandchildren's children.

In 1985 on Irene's 35th birthday, Marlin and Irene had a stillborn son named Matthew.

When Mahlon and Sarah Ann Zimmerman lived on the Turkey Hill, three miles close to home, they came back and forth to Aaron and Amanda often.

All the aunts and uncles at home adored Wanda, Willard and Roseann, and got to know them well. Sarah Ann could easily come home to her parents and Amanda sent a child over to help at Mahlons, as one big extended family. Sometimes Aaron went right past to BW Shirks and the girls came along back home for the night. Mandy washed the dishes for her big sister and picked some tea for her. She did a bit of cleaning and washed out buckets full of soiled diapers. When she was young, Sarah Ann washed out hundreds of diapers.

Mahlon and Sarah Ann rejoiced with a second son. Now they had two boys and two girls, but baby Dean had health problems. Their fourth child was born with clubfeet, and the doctor put both feet into casts. Dean was a weaker child, and he died in his mother's arms, on the way home from a doctor visit, while they stopped in the parking lot at Harry Good's Store. Mahlons lived in a daze awhile! They had no idea baby Dean had such major problems. He was buried without an autopsy or any genetic testing, because he definitely died from natural causes, at the age of two months.

Three years later in Missouri, Mary and Roland had a third child with major problems, after having two healthy children. Baby Roland Weiler, the fourth, had the doctors puzzled. They did many tests and admitted him to the hospital, eventually calling it I-cell or Hurlers disease. Such children had a genetic problem inherited from both parents. All the aunts, uncles and cousins on both sides of Mary and Roland's family tree appeared normal, with no clue as to where the problem originated. The doctors insisted that some relatives somewhere, passed on a genetic defect on Roland's side, as well as on Mary's side of the family. Meanwhile, when baby Roland was two years old, they sadly

Angel children and the spiraled name chart.

lowered him into the grave, among the support of family and friends.

Aaron wrote in the Budget about his trip to Missouri for the funeral of his grandson." We arrived at Edina, at our daughter Ruth and Carl Weiler's place for dinner and in time for the funeral. Preacher Allen Martin had the services at the home of Roland Weilers, before the funeral procession arrived at Millport church. Four teenage boys carried the casket over the hill to the final resting place of little Roland. The plot of 4 acres is the same place Grace Kurtz was buried, due to her complications from appendicitis. The plot for a cemetery is being acquired free, by a city doctor's donation. A new church is likely in the future, located on the west side of the native Millport Church that is getting to be much too small for special occasions.

Preacher Titus Martin, the founder of our church in Missouri, had the last rites at the graveside. Levi Zimmerman of Missouri and Elam Ray Martin of Pennsylvania held services in the church house. After the services, we had supper in Carl Hoover's new house that had not been lived in yet. That too, was full of people not having too much room for the cooks to get around. We mostly visited our five daughters and their families with a Sunday Shirk gathering around the Carl Weiler table, also an evening singing at Paul Zimmerman's to our honor which we enjoyed very much. "

After Mary and Roland Weiler had two more healthy children, they had three more that died young. Where did the problem originate? Mucolipidoses (ML) are rare genetic disorders caused by the body's inability to produce certain enzymes, causing progressive damage. Roland's children inherited I –cell disease, which is a type of ML or mucolipidoses. The occurrence is estimated at one in 25,000 births. Both parents are carriers of a recessive gene that causes enzyme deficiency in a child. With both parents being carriers, each child has one chance in four of having the disorder. Incompletely broken down carbohydrates remain stored in the body causing progressive damage. The cells filled with storage material are known as "inclusion cells," hence the name "I-cell" disorder. Children with I-cell problems usually stop growing by the age of three and are seldom taller than three-foot. Roland and Mary's I-cell children did not talk, but certainly understood much about their surroundings and the facial expression of people, far be-

yond ordinary speech. They were prone to chest and ear infections and runny noses. They were not potty trained and could not feed themselves. Swollen gums and troublesome teeth were a prominent characteristic, and they preferred liquid food. With weak lungs and a weak heart, most such children died before the age of three or four, with a peaceful death during sickness or a hearts gradual failure. The newborn babies weighed less and were floppy, with lower muscle tone. The children could smile, laugh and show pleasure.

Regina and Faith lived to be almost four years old. They could communicate with grunts and motions without using words. Most of the times they wore cloth diapers because they had sensitive skin. When Mary asked them which diaper they wanted to wear, they chose the cloth ones every time, no matter how deluxe with the latest improvements on Luvs' and Pampers and such.

The children brought much joy to those around them, and were loved and spoiled by all. The older children in the family helped their parents cuddle and love them to the very end.. .."They have learned, in nurturing... these children so frail and sweet; the place...a strange and sacred spot... where joy and sorrow meet! "Sadness and happiness cannot be the same, but this was truly a place where joy [greater than happiness] and sorrow [deeper then sadness] met! Half of Roland and Mary's children entered the pearly gates, home free, without spot or blemish. Junior, Cheryl, Regina and Faith reside in eternity among the angels.

In later years, Roland's discovered health problems on his mother's side, from the Rutt linage. On Mary's family tree, it became evident that Amanda might be a carrier, but Aaron was not, therefore, Aaron and Amanda's children had no problems. Back in Michigan, where Peter and Sarah Ann buried three small boys, no one had a clue about genetic problems. They simply buried them without modern testing, like so many other young children of their generation. "When a child is born, it is ripe onto death."

Just across the road from Peter, lived his brother Henry M Brubacher married to Katie Gehman, and they buried seven young children, trusting God in all his wisdom, and thanking him for their many blessings. From a family of fourteen children, they buried babies named Titus, Peter, Mary, Amos, and Phares. When they moved from Michigan to Snyder County Pennsylvania in 1919, they buried two more very young children, named Elizabeth and Lucy. Among all of Aaron and Amanda's many descendents, the next generation might see more such problems; depending on how many might be carriers.

Mommy Brubacher's sister, [Amanda's Aunt Mertie], married Solomon Reist and they buried two young children. Their first son, Elias died around the age of two or three. After three healthy sons, baby Titus lived only a few days. A few weeks later Mertie died also and Solomon remarried, to Mae Babcock, of the Funk church. They had five more children without health problems, and no one can prove anything.

Amanda's mother, Sarah Ann Brenneman, married Peter Brubacher. Sarah Ann's grandmother was Elizabeth Ann Miller, born March 9, 1835. They were not of the Mennonite faith and had a tradition that when a daughter turned 21 years old, she went walking to earn her own living. The story goes that Peter Wayne Selner (born May 7, 1872- died October 27, 1868), came riding by on horseback and took Elizabeth along to be his wife! Their daughter, Mary Isura Selner joined the Mennonite church and married Henry Brenneman (born 1863-died 1943). In 1906, Henry was ordained as a minister at the Maple River Mennonite Church in Brutus, Michigan. He was Amanda's grandfather. The Peter Wayne Selner genealogy is hard to trace, with no records available.

Amanda wrote in a letter, "life is very uncertain, we must not dwell too much in the past and not try to think too far into the future. Sufficient unto the day is the evil thereof: Matthew 6:34. We must remember that the dark days are needful also, to bring us closer to heaven. Yes, time does move on swiftly, but I doubt that I will see the year 2000. I do not expect to ever have it nicer here on earth than what I have it now."

Amanda went with Aaron for his first back treatment at Boyd Clinic in York, Pennsylvania, and a second treatment three days later. Two weeks later, he went for a third treatment, while Amanda packed suitcases for a 10-day trip to Canada, in November 1975. Aaron and Amanda did not take a map along to Canada and Amanda wrote in her diary, "We stopped often to ask the way." They received a warm welcome at cousin Norman Brubachers. All The names listed in Amanda's diary appeared as though they met everyone they knew in Canada and then some more. They stayed over two Sunday's and attended a German singing. Aaron and Amanda started for home in a snow blizzard and they endured three hours of driving in heavy traffic with the sun in Aarons face, for miserable driving conditions.

Amanda wrote, "Thankful to God for a safe trip home!" Canada had a mail strike and Aaron brought a pile of mail along home to drop off in the US Post Office. Many people that wrote in the Budget preferred to write news about births, deaths, weddings, and such. Aaron embarrassed others with some of his opinions and unusual thoughts.

His column in the Budget said, "If you plan a trip to Canada in the winter time, take the stud or spiked tires off your car. They are prohibited on Canadian roads. The reason for us to make this trip was for a visit with my wife's relatives. Her father was born in Canada and it was like going home for her. As we drove in the driveway at David Brubacher's we developed car trouble. We left our car at the Elmira garage for repairs and then took David's car to go visiting. Sixteen years ago, they were stranded over at our place, and took our car to go visiting. We spent a day visiting with Aaron Webers, the Canadian Budget writers. We made a morning call at their neighbor's mink ranch (or mink farm) where a number of the church boys worked skinning mink. They had 11,000 prime black furs. I checked prices for a mink coat for Mandie, my wife. It would take 15 mink skins at $20 each to make one fur coat. All finished, the bill would be $2000 for a mink coat. That is what we paid for our 42-acre place in 1937. She will be wearing her three cornered shawl, with a big saving and we are both happy this way. I would rather smell the mothballs on her winter shawl, than those stink'n mink.

Aaron tried to find unusual topics for his Budget columns, and commented that he writes the Alley Oop [a far-out comic strip] of the Budget. Many people followed his columns, no matter how unusual. Aaron spelled poorly, but he still found a delight in writing, because no one interrupted before he finished his point of view. He did not want Amanda to correct his spelling, for fear she might censor or correct things. Ruth did not appreciate seeing Carl Weiler's name spelled as Carol...just the way it sounded to Aaron.

Amanda stayed up until nearly midnight, making many popcorn balls and wrapping Christmas gifts for the grandchildren. She still made treat and candy because that is what Christmas meant in her childhood. Amanda quit wrapping gifts for each child individually, because she could not please them all. They already had more toys than they needed. She could not keep them equal and she had no idea if they already had that book? Amanda still wanted to give something for the joy of giving, so she gave each child a 50-cent coin to buy what they wanted. Some of them saved the coin as a trophy, just to admire and dream upon.

At the Blue Ball bank, Aaron met Mr. and Mrs. Kurut, strangers from India. He made friends with Dave and Evelyn Kurut, and brought them home to spend two nights with Aaron and Amanda. They cooked four meals for them and Aaron took them the next day to MCC at Akron, canning meat for the needy and meeting people. They sat up talking until nearly midnight... Eight months later, the Kuruts came back to Aarons several days and overnight, showing slides of India and taking Aaron and Amanda out to eat dinner at Zinn's Diner. Strangers to Aaron were just friends that he never met.

Amanda helped put seven quilts in frame at the Bowmansville fire hall and she spent the next three days helping to quilt them. She wrote in a letter, "I'm expected to pretty much manage Bowmansville fire hall quilting week, and someone takes them home to finish binding them. The Ladies Auxiliary make the lunch and the treat for three

days straight." Amanda's picture appeared in the newspaper and Aaron wrote in the Budget, "The plain people are making quilts for the Bowmansville fire company. This was our first try on public auction with the top going price on their golden eagle quilt, with golden stars, selling for one thousand dollars. People who can afford such covers on their beds are helping our fire company along with their expenses and I do hope to get the ladies stirred up about quilting for next year's season."

"I was on my knees for news, when Ervie suggested I put the snapper soup in the Budget. He dragged a fifteen-pounder home from the mountains last week. Then Ervies wife cooked the thing for three hours until the meat came off the bones. The meat was cut short, with noodles, corn and water added. A few of their Amish neighbors showed up this week for snapper soup. Some took a second serving! It is our turn for a Sunday dinner visit at Ervies, but not until we are sure that, the snapper soup has all disappeared. To me the snappers appear too much in the snake family. We like to think of something else when we see a long neck sticking up out of a meat platter in front of us at a friend's table. Thanks just the same!

Aunt Barbara

Amanda had an Aunt Barbara far away in Canada, the daughter of Notion Jecky Brubacher. Aaron also had a single Aunt; named Barbara, living much closer home.BW Shirk's Sister Barbara remained single all her life. Aaron and Amanda's children hardly noticed meek and quiet, great Aunt Barbara, until they were older and found history fascinating. She became an inspiration to many of her great-nieces. When Aaron and Amanda's children and grandchildren came to Pennsylvania from Missouri, they enjoyed meeting 95-year-old great-aunt Barbara, a piece of living history. She industriously kept her hands busy weaving straw baskets and hats for many years. She did not wear eyeglasses ever, even to the age of 100 years old. In a stooped manner, she pulled weeds and gathered rhubarb to sell. She knew a lot about plants, and brewed tea from the common mallow weeds. When Ruth Weiler asked her what health foods she recommended for longevity, she suggested possibly some mallow tea and such, among other healthy living.

Only twice in a century, in the last twenty years of her life, did Barbara need a doctor. Once due to a buggy accident and the other time she had pneumonia. As Barbara lived on, she outlived her friends and relatives, and everyone her age. "Did God forget me?" She pondered as the years went on, and she was ready to move to eternity. She went to church when she was almost deaf and could hardly see. She humbly said," I got a blessing just being there. "She died at the age of 100.

Perhaps Barbara lived longer because she did not have the stress of raising a family. Amanda and Barbara were not related. What they both had in common, was a strong Christian faith and contentment with their lot in life.

Years ago, Barbara taught some of her nieces how to sew by hand. She showed Lydi-Jes-sey and her sister Eva, how they could sew faster, if the garment they sewed stayed taut. With a sturdy safety pin, she showed both the young girls how to pin their sewing to the cuff of the long bloomers they wore, by pinning the hand sewing securely through the dress, to the bloomers. That way they learned to sew neater and faster.

History became fascinating as young children grew older. They discovered several more interesting characters in their family tree.

The best-known one was Aaron's great grandfather, Joseph Shirk, the inventor, born in 1820. He had very little formal education, but he taught school for a short time. He studied Greek, Latin, and geometry etc. and he could read in several languages. Joseph was a printer and exceptionally good in math. He studied books he borrowed from others who went to college. He greatly improved the grain cradle, made a transit compass, the first one to use spider webs for crosshairs, and he possibly invented the colt revolver. He showed his idea of five or six shots in a revolving gun to other people and he did not apply for a patent. That way it was hard to prove if the idea was first his. Joseph Shirk made his revolver before the Colt revolver patent in 1836. In later years, Joseph Shirk's son Peter, went to the Colt revolver factory and asked

to see the original one and they refused to show it. On his deathbed, Mr. Colt told his sons to offer Joseph Shirk several thousand dollars, but Joseph declined it. He did not want honor and never patented anything. It did not matter to him that over thirty million sold.

Joseph Shirk designed the revolver for hunting squirrels, or animals to eat, and he never dreamed people would use something like that during wartime for killing people. He was a peace-loving conscientious objector and he opposed war. He was an ardent abolitionist and opposed slavery. He spent much time in prayer and Bible reading and paid the government an exacted amount, to be excused from military duty during the Civil War.

Joseph was an expert in surveying, by studying the stars. He helped figure the disputed boundary line between Berks County and Lancaster County. No one argued his decisions. He was a legend in his lifetime, and he had a patient and hard-working wife, Esther [Horning] Shirk. Shirks are persistently stubborn!

He lived at the time when people were hurt and killed while connecting train cars together with a pin and clevis. He totally designed the train coupler, and it has not been improved since then, except for size. His son sold that idea for $500, as the highest price they got for anything he made.

Joseph Shirk studied herb books and served as a doctor during an epidemic of malaria or yellow fever. He knew which medicinal plants worked for which ailments. He made special pliers to pull teeth and he used them when necessary. When Joseph was exposed to a contagious epidemic, he treated the sick with herbs, and came home and hung his clothes inside the smokehouse to kill the germs.

Joseph Shirk had twin sons named Joseph and Benjamin. He made twin highchairs for his twin sons and Aaron and Amanda bought one of those highchairs, at a family auction. The hand- made sturdy highchair never saw paint, and the oiled wood worked just fine for the hard use of raising many children. He built it to last many more generations. [Twin Benjamin was the father of BW Shirk and B W Shirk bought his farm from twin

Ben through his sister Mary.]

Joseph enjoyed astronomy and its celestial mysteries. To him, the solar system was like an open book. He wrote to those that printed the almanac, and told them, "The eclipse is figured wrong in your almanac!"He spent many hours sitting up late working and tinkering with ideas and he said to his children," be quiet or else go to bed." Visionary people are either rich or poor and seldom in between, or average. His wife and children lived like poor people and neighbors felt sorry for those thirteen children and their parents.

Joseph made a rhyme or jingle about their five sons; Patah and Mosey, Ben and Josey, Grishtly hinnah nogh-sey.[Peter and Moses, Ben and Joseph, Christian on behind them].

There was a time when Aaron Shirk had eight children and he thought he would try that too. He said, "Daniel, Dolly, Walter Pete and Dick, tzwilling and chick!"[Daniel, Sarah Ann, Walter, Pete and Dick, twins and chick.]Martha had the nickname of chick or chickly when she timidly hung around her mother's skirts, too bashful to allow others to hold her. She followed as closely as a chick to a mother hen.

On the Shirk side, Ulrich Shirk [born March 9, 1663] came to America from Sumiswald Switzerland. He was the son of Peter, born October 16, 1639, who was the son of Ulrich, born June 19, 1614, the son of Casper, the son of Hans Shirk.

Amanda bought a big fat Zimmerman history book for each one of her children, as a Christmas gift, because she knew eventually most people desired to know their roots.

Abraham Herr Brubacher 1731 to 1811 came to America in 1750 from Switzerland.

Melchoir Brenneman from about 1631 was also born in Switzerland. He was imprisoned there for his religious beliefs in the castle of Thun in 1659. He fled to Griesheim Germany in 1671. Two of his sons Christian and Melchoir emigrated to America in about 1717. Many Mennonite descendents that came to America from Germany actually descended from Switzerland.

Amanda's mother, Sarah Ann Brenneman, had a grandmother named Veronica Miller. Her mother was a Hochstetler, a direct descendent from the Hochstetler massacre story, written in a reading book at school;

Over 250 years ago, many Indians lived in America, and they were not all friendly ones. In Berks County, close to what is now Roadside America, young people gathered at the Jacob Hochstetler home, paring apples for drying, on Sept 19, 1757. [In 1738, Jacob came to America from Switzerland for religious freedom]. After the guests all went home and the family went to bed, their dog gave a warning that something was wrong, and young Jacob Jr opened the door of their log cabin. He was shot in the leg and sounded an alarm that woke the whole family.

Three French scouts and seven Indians stood near the outdoor oven. His first instinct was to grab the gun and shoot to defend his family, but his father believed in nonresistance and kept them from firing at the enemy.

Joseph always claimed the family could have been saved had the father given his consent to fire, because they were all good marksmen. The family hid beneath the house where they stored their apples and potatoes. The Indians set the house on fire, and the family remained hidden until they thought the Indians left. As things got too hot, the family tried to escape out the basement window. The last Indian happened to turn around and see them, and he called the others back. Three of them were killed and scalped and the rest taken prisoners.

A son John and his family lived nearby, and left their home, helplessly watching the entire attack, while hidden among heavy undergrowth. The mother was killed as she struggled, trying to get through the small opening of the cellar window.

Jacob and his two sons Christian and Joseph lived with the Indians several years after they were taken as prisoners. One of the first things the Indians did was to pluck the beards of the white man, because everyone knew that Indians could not grow beards.

Eventually Joseph escaped and returned to the white people. He was a great, great, great, great, great, great grandfather to Amanda. Veronica

Hochstetler was a grandmother to Henry Brenneman, Amanda's grandfather. No matter what happens, it is better to turn the other cheek also,. Matt 5; 39

Any of Aaron and Amanda's descendants that studied genealogy, could agree with the Bible verse, "the lines are fallen onto me in pleasant places; yea I have a goodly heritage. Psalms 16; 6

Pete's development

After leaving home, Daniel and Dick started out on dairy farms, and Walter and Pete "grew into" building houses, after learning about lumber from the bottom on up.

They first learned about wood grain and knotholes in the boards, as they unloaded the train cars at Wickes. After that, they sold lumber and other building supplies to eager customers and learned much about quality and do-it-yourself. With Mahlon, Walter and Pete together, they started building houses as "Shirk and Zimmerman ". "In 1968, they successfully purchased and developed a subdivision named "Whispering Pines." Later on, their business name changed to, "Shirk Builders", Titus Shirk and Ed High worked for Walter and Pete.

Aaron sometimes took workers to help clear off trees for making a lake and some roads at Whispering Pines. At the edge of the field, Aaron cut down a large tree with branches spreading wide. When the tree fell, the wide spreading limbs hit the ground and the butt end of the trunk bounced off the ground and caught Aaron below the chin, and threw him back. He had no chance to get away due to the tangle of thorns and green briars all around him. Titus watched it happen and dreaded to go look for Aaron. He thought he might find his brother dead! Aaron was alive and well, other than a slight cut and some nasty scratches where the tree tossed him in the briar patch, for a cushioned landing.

Titus quit in 1969 and started developing building lots in his own neighborhood, on land he owned. Ed High quit and so did Walter when he moved to Missouri, but Pete kept on building ever since May 1, 1967. He continued expanding and he

borrowed a large sum of money. When the interest at the bank rose from 7% to 18% percent, in a short time, Pete nearly lost everything, but he hung in there.

Aaron and Titus worked together discussing building lots, and Aaron saw the possibilities of developing his woodland, the land he planned to mine someday. Together they planned the road, "Laurel Top Circle." They schemed many plans among themselves, after Titus's own building lots all sold. Aaron and Titus with the help of Jesse Brubacher and his bulldozer started a road through the woods, thoughtfully turning left here, and right there as they followed the curve of the land. The township had not approved of what they were doing, but it was Aaron's land. The major problem they faced was one owner with a parcel of land not for sale, where they wanted their road.

A M Shirk enjoyed some of the legal battles, working with people at the top. They designed two cul-de-sacs; one from the top down the hill, while the other one came towards it from the bottom up. One woman opposed their project and created a tremendous amount of trouble suggesting "possible hazardous waste!"

Someone offered Aaron one half million dollars for his property, but he turned down the offer, because he saw the prices kept on going up on building lots in the woods. He enjoyed the action! The land he bought from Henry Burkholder in 1955, for $13.50 per acre, prospered from the power line, and then he sold it at $7000 per acre, twenty some years later. Aaron finally realized that he did the right thing at the right time when he bought all the woodland, albeit for the wrong reasons.

The 'American dream 'worked for Aaron. He started out with nothing and he made it to the top. It took everything he had to get there, including a network of neighbors and friends to help him. Without Amanda's help. .. who knows... behind every successful man, there stands a woman. She trusted and believed in him.

When Aaron got wound- up about anything, he had a one -track mind. People around him heard the same topics repeatedly and could not turn him off. When he started selling land for new houses, perk tests discovered hazardous waste.

Aaron had given Mr. Kurtz permission to dump garbage on his land, but Aaron did not know Kurtz started dumping harmful chemicals illegally. When he needed perk tests to sell buildings, he met obstacles.

Aaron wrote in a circle letter:

After four years of illegal dumping, 29 poisons assayed by the Lancaster County laboratories are now going into the public's stream, and on to Lancaster where they drink the stuff. Local homes are in danger of serious chemical damages in their well water. All levels of government are now in the area, township, county, state and federal. Kurtzy got himself a big bulldozer to cover up quick, but the law already has the samples and pictures of the place. Everything must be dug up, and hauled off! Four men from Harrisburg with two state police had a search warrant, with local officers looking in with field glasses for 3 ½ hours on our property. Our congressman, Bob Walker, is coming here soon. The Lancaster County commissioners called and are coming. There are scores of others such as our popular state congressman, Noah Wenger on the job too, including the governor's office at Harrisburg and EPA in Washington. What takes so long, is to find out how many Harrisburg men are involved in this scandal and pay off? They told me to stay out of it.

Later;

"We are finally getting attention from the US government; EPA is taking action at our neighbors up on the hill. Nine officers with badges had been on the Kurtz property with search warrants, three were federal marshals loaded with guns, four were core drilling for test samples, two were taking water samples from area springs and wells, and we hope to hear the test results in the next 10 days.

The person that suggested "hazardous-waste" wanted the pond Aaron and Titus had built, plus 25 acres of land to go with it, real cheap. Eventually they offered it to her for nothing, if she lets the road go through, but she did not. Pete told the Township people that she will not give up, but they could buy it for $40,000 and that was turned down! Aaron sold it over auction then, and it fetched $240,000. They needed that money to keep going,

creating a road and several ponds, they fixed up Aaron's barn and the house. The money from those 25 acres kept them going for the next 30 years.

Aaron was pleased with the money value of his property, as he smiled about broken dreams of mineral rights and iron ore, all in the past. He never went deep into debt, but he never accumulated a pile of money. When he could afford it, he bought a brand-new 1980 Oldsmobile car, and he saw more money coming. He wrote, *'Our new car is late in arriving, or Mom would have the biggest Christmas present that I ever bought for her. Well she deserves it! I know she skimped along with little or nothing when you were kids.*

Aaron always wanted to share and invite others to his farm, from a single stray person, to large groups. When he heard a wagon train from Arizona was headed to Lancaster County, he gave them a hearty invitation.

Aaron wrote in the Budget; *the wagon train from Arizona came here and stayed two days, with one hundred and forty people, eighty-five horses, and ten covered wagons. They had a water tanker truck, cattle truck, trailer, campers, for the lead men, a school bus with bags of clothing and a hay truck. Then they had this odd-looking thing on four wheels, with three doors on each side. When I asked, 'what is that?" They said, "That is what we call our potty shack!"*

Four big Wigwam tents were set up for the night with ten covered wagons out around, unhitched. They had a wood fire in the middle of our ten-acre field, with our wooded hills on three sides.

We want to thank all the kind people for all the good food they donated. They appreciated the fresh homemade bread and donuts from Shady Maple, shoofly pie from Hartings Bakery and fresh eggs from Phares Hurst's chicken house.

Wagons, horses and tepees from the VisionQuest wagon train form a circle Thursday on the Caernarvon Township property of Aaron Shirk. A Lancaster County youth is ber of the train, which is destined for Erie.

About half the wagon train consisted of their leaders; teachers, office manager, a nurse, horse shoer, and a vet. The prisoners on this wagon train ranged in ages from thirteen to twenty years old. They had brushes with the law and then the court gave them a choice. They could go to jail or an institution or on the wagon train for a year, working together with their leaders.

Each prisoner is to express their feelings so they can be helped.""What if a prisoner gets stubborn and does not obey orders?"I asked. "We put them down and sit on their chest until they give up."

The first horses that came here were tied under our spruce trees along the fencerow. Two horses started kicking at each other like the end was near. A big hornet nest was hanging nearby! A colored boy cut the tie rope and no one was stung but the horses.

I had the idea to stand back and write notes for The Budget for the next day or two, but I soon had other jobs, like putting stone on the muddy field entrance. I took Titus to Green Dragon where he bought a load of hay, delivered to our farm from Green Dragon. He came back with the load, and the wagon train people paid cash for five and a half ton of timothy hay. They were well pleased with the semi —truckload at $101.00 a ton. This event was open to the public and all those interested. We must have had several thousand visitors and regret we could not meet them all.

My brother Menno came to see the caravan, and he saw a man he took for the leader or frontier marshal. He went to talk with him and discovered it was neighbor Sam Martin, blending in well with his boots and a black hat. The cowboys and scenery matched in like the American west.

The most outstanding event took place the last evening, when a group from Conestoga Wood products came and sang. It rained too much for the singers around the campfire to use songbooks so everyone sang by heart. Although it was not perfect, it made a perfect hit with the prisoners or 'kids'. After each song, the prisoners clapped their hands and then a colored boy from Mississippi would call out in a southern accent, for more" Mo-uh, mo-uh!"

After thirty minutes of singing, I announced time for visitation. Each prisoner was to visit with one of our young folks. I doubt that we had enough of our group to go around, but this program was planned by one of the wagon group leaders and myself, to help teach the prisoners how young folks go straight and free. I do not know how long this took, but some had skipped supper. I left and went to the house

soaked to the skin! I heard the next morning that one of the prisoners had accepted the Lord and said, 'I want Jesus to come into my heart."

I picked out two prisoners to be questioned for Budget news. A small for her age, white girl named Dee Dee Anderson from St Paul MN. At age thirteen years old, she spent six months on the wagon train and has six to go. She told me she just kept getting herself in trouble, shoplifting and stealing till the cops got her and brought her to court. She chose the wagon train and is not sorry. She wants to go straight when she returns home. Her home court must pay the wagon train what it would cost to keep her in the institution out there.

I picked a white eighteen-year-old Clifford C Fenstermaker of Allentown. He is thirty days near the end of his term. The wagon train plans to make a run to our place next year, and Clifford is looking to be a group leader when he meets me again at our place.

This wagon train plans to end at Erie PA on November 1, 1980. There, the wagon trains will be dismantled, loaded onto trucks, and hauled to Arizona, to start over next spring. Perhaps the train will double to twenty wagons with so many kids needing help. They spend several hours a day teaching school lessons to those that should be in school.

Then there is a smaller train starting at Oil City PA, just for PA prisoners. It is coming here some time next summer.

35

Cancer

On April 30, 1981, Amanda wrote in a circle letter; I am sorry to say that Aaron has not been so well and in bed most of the time for the past six weeks. At first, he had sort of a flu bug and lay around most of the time and still done his barn work and sometimes short road errands for neighbors. Since April 5, he was not out of the house except to go to the hospital, and yesterday, the ambulance took him to Reading Hospital, with such severe chest pains in his rib cage and sometimes in the heart area the last days of March. On April 5, I took him to the Reading Hospital for heart a gram, chest x-rays and blood tests and they found nothing serious and decided it's arthritis and put him on pain pills, but he had to take so many until they even took a hold. Finally, in the middle of April, his pain subsided and he could rest and sleep better again, so one by one the pills were discontinued. The doctor had checked him here at home three times in the past two weeks. Most of that time, Aaron came to the table and he went to the bathroom by himself, until last Saturday the 25th, he could not stand on his feet anymore. He had a tingling, itching feeling in his legs. Last evening at the hospital, they took more x-rays and a mile o gram etc. and found a cancerous tumor pressing on his spine, and if not operated on, he could never walk again and maybe not anyway. He had surgery on April 30 between his shoulder blade and spine, but nothing inside the rib cage. He is as good as can be expected, we just have to wait and see.

Our family is well as far as we know, except for Mary and Roland having another little girl that is not normal. They named her Cheryl and Pete's have a baby James, born on the 22nd. He is doing fine but he is a Down's syndrome, as his youngest sister Ruthanne is, at age 18-month-old. We also had three normal grandchildren.

It is time I get ready to go to the hospital. Mandy will take me to Reading and Wesley's will fetch me in the evening. Aaron is still in intensive care and we can only be in 10 minutes at a time every hour. Wishing you all what we wish for ourselves, Gods almighty guiding hand to lead us all to that beautiful home above, where partings are no more and all is peace, joy and love without pain and sorrow for evermore. Love to all, Amanda and Aaron Shirk"

Aaron's brother Titus came to cheer him up after he returned home. Aaron said, "I have arthritis!" His legs gave him so much trouble, that Aaron tied two baler- twine strings to his feet so that he could pull the strings to make his legs move like puppets. Dr. Bender said, "There is so little difference between cancer and arthritis that it is very hard to detect." That thought comforted Aaron.

Some days he wished for company and said, 'Now where are all these people that we visited? '' Visiting the sick was one thing Aaron and Amanda had not neglected. They both enjoyed it!

Aaron had problems with cancer back in 1979 when the doctors removed a thyroid tumor, at the West Reading hospital. He stayed there two weeks and two days and he came home on the day that Banks Horning died. D Walter Martin brought him that message, and Aaron wished he could attend the huge funeral of their home church preacher, with many guests from out of state. That was out of the question. He had a slow recovery after he came home. Aaron was convinced that his battle with cancer started with smoking tobacco. He boldly spoke out against using tobacco, to anyone that listened.

Aaron related, "I had a serious problem of homesickness when I was fourteen years old and worked for Aunt Barbara. Now I am 65 and have cancer. I can tell you that homesickness is by far the worst of the two!

Aaron missed church for nine weeks in a row, and he was glad to go away again. He took a neighbor to New Holland on business, and to the hay sale, but that was too much for him. He had pain and swelling on his bladder with a fever and he felt miserable. Aaron wrote in the Budget, "Some of my friends think I should retire now at age 65, while recovering from my hospital stay, but that's not for me. That is for the birds! Many people are already retiring and living off the government. People with a healthy body should remain active and still do a little light work."

Aaron felt much worse, when he wrote the next letter. "This leaves me a shut-in again, with infection from a prostate operation. I went out in the damp and cold too soon and had to learn the hard way. I suffered more pain in the past week from swellings, then what I suffered from all my operations together at the hospital. A man of 65 should know better, and Mandie must watch the outside doors so I don't sneak out when she is not looking."

Aaron improved gradually and he had the privilege of a last trip west to see his children and

grandchildren in Missouri. Deep in thought on his own land, Aaron carved names on a beech tree, showing how much he still loved his wife, even at a distant part of the woods, where most people did not know it was there for another thirty years.

The lump from the side of Aaron's neck was treated with radiation, and not much later, he was diagnosed with prostate cancer. Aaron said, "I would like to give all my children and grandchildren a great big hug." He wrote a thank you column in the Budget, *"Through the Budget, many friends and loved ones showed concern and especially with their prayers for the writer of this column to be able to get back to writing again. We never knew our column was that important and thanks for the many kind visitors that came to our house when the days were long and the shadows were deep. May God bless all of them?"*

When the cancer returned, Aaron had surgery to remove a tumor on his spine, which left him paralyzed from the waist on down. He spent the month of May admitted to the hospital and the doctors had nothing more they could do for Aaron. They planned to send him home to die.

Aaron had a lot of time to think about death, as he lay in the hospital week after week. He thought maybe his cancer came from smoking, even if he hadn't smoked for the past ten years. Many thoughts drifted through his mind about all of life's happenings. He picked up the telephone and called his children one at a time, sincerely and tearfully, asking for forgiveness of his mistakes and shortcomings.

Aaron and Amanda had a day brightener when his brother Ben came from Indiana, to see Aaron. Ben and Grace stayed overnight, and Amanda made breakfast for them. Aaron was losing out, even after his last radiation treatment. Lydia came from Missouri to see her father for the last time. Aaron was restless and begging to come home from the hospital. He spent all his life in a very small radius of the area where his father was born, raised, married and died. He preferred to die there also. He was concerned about the huge hospital bill, using the money that Amanda might need after he was gone.

Amanda rested on Sunday morning while Lydia went to church, and then Aaron called at

11 AM asking what takes so long. They packed a quick lunch and took it along to share with him at the hospital. Amanda brought Aaron's shoes and clothing along because the doctors planned to release him in the morning, even if Amanda didn't know how she could care for him at home, so helpless. Aaron begged Amanda not to leave him...but she needed a break and wanted to go home and pick the peas. No one suspected that he was so near to the end. Many times when Amanda left his bedside, Aaron said, "Pray for me." or "See you in heaven!" He often asked forgiveness for his many faults and shortcomings.

Lydia started home to Missouri and Amanda worked out in the garden picking peas, when Janie kindly brought Amanda an unexpected message. "The hospital has been trying to reach you, because Aaron has died! Amanda could hardly comprehend the thought... "How shocking!... Why didn't I stay overnight? I never knew if Aaron exaggerated things or if he really felt that bad..." Janie finished picking the peas, while Amanda got ready to go to the hospital. Wesley was not available, so Janie took Amanda to West Reading. Aaron died suddenly with a blood clot. God in his mercy spared Aaron and Amanda from the pain and suffering that lay ahead, because Aaron would never have walked again.

The immediate cause of death...1 pulmonary embolism, due to . ..2 paraplegia, due to. ..3-metastic carcinoma of spine.

The visitation at Aaron and Amanda's house resembled a boisterous happy reunion and nobody was mourning. The children sat by age and those in the front row shook hands until they had enough, while those crowded in the back row could not shake hands nor talk with anyone going through the line. They rejoiced to see their school friends, neighbors and relatives they had not seen in a long time. The noise was almost embarrassing. They tried to keep it down a bit, out of respect, but "Oh look, there comes Dale Stamm with her mother Mary...and is that Linda Weinhold...is it really?. ..I did not see her since we went to school!"Among each other, the children agreed their father would have loved it. Aaron's second cousin looked just

like Aaron, and Amanda's sister Betsy from Missouri, gave Amanda a great big sisterly hug. Friends became dearer, as time moved on.

On June 19, 1981, all of Aaron's children, and all but one of the75 grandchildren gathered around the coffin for one last farewell. (One toddler stayed in Missouri at a babysitter.) Most of the 15 children really did not think they needed to shed any tears, but one by one as the tears started, they sympathized with each other, until there was probably not one dry eye left.

Grandchildren of all sizes gathered around the grave with their parents. Some smaller ones got so close to the open grave that their parents pulled them back a little, to make sure that none falls in. Their parents answered many questions afterwards.

Bishop Willis Martin explained how sometimes a twig or a branch is broken from a family tree, but now the trunk has split down the middle. He also commented that Aaron was always ready to make peace, no matter what. A large crowd of guests ate a soup and sandwich dinner in Aaron and Amanda's garage.

Amanda's mind numbed and her diary remained blank for the next week. Wesley offered to stay with Mom and sleep there overnight for the first night alone. She did not ask for more assistance, and Wesley commented, "She is one tough cookie!" She had a strong faith in the Bible and knew that God would not forsake her now! She had no fears, day or night.

Amanda wrote, *"Aaron is gone now to his reward and we would not wish him back in his painful condition. I believe it was God's will to have it so, but why didn't the doctor see his tumor three weeks earlier when he was in the hospital? Why did they keep on with treatments when he was losing out? Why didn't we get to see the x rays? Why didn't they let him go home earlier? We all know Aaron was not perfect, but the good outshines the other. May we all try to live, so that we will get to meet in that beautiful home above."*

Amanda had wished to outlive Aaron someday. .. but not so soon...! She knew he was not good at finding his own things or cooking for himself. He would be keenly handicapped without her, and she knew that no one else would understand his ways. Aarons own sister Lydi-Jess-sey once commented,"Who but Amanda could get along with Aaron?"

Gradually, Amanda got on with her life after the guests all returned to their homes. She missed Aaron in many ways. He no longer wrote columns for the Budget, so after awhile she did, starting two months after the funeral. *"I will finally try to write a letter for all you readers, as I know my husband; A.M. Shirk's letters are missed. I also want to thank you for all the letters and cards we've received during his illness and death. I received over 200 cards and letters since his death, and we also had close to 200 cards before his death."*

After writing details about Aaron's sickness, Amanda wrote, "His departure was so gradual we all had time to prepare for it. I believe Aaron repented of all his shortcomings and was very ready to leave this world, a chance not everybody has, or will get."

Amanda went with Dicks to Indiana to attend a minister ordination on June 30, in which Aaron's brother Ben shared the lot. The lot fell on Roy Ramer the Deacon, and therefore they needed to ordain a new Deacon. Amanda came home and ten days later she went with Mandy and Henry Martin and their three little boys to Missouri for another minister ordination in which son-in-law Mervin High shared the lot. Raymond Zimmerman was ordained as a preacher."

Amanda wrote, "Maybe after school starts I can get some widow lady friend to stay or live with me for a while, until I know or decide what to do with the farm. So far, our youngest son Wesley, two and a half miles out the road, is looking after the cattle."

Mandy came home often and Amanda *depended on her youngest daughter.*

Wesley and Janie took care of the farm and mowed the yard, and spent a lot of time with Amanda whenever she needed them. Mandy and Henry lived at Terrehill and came home to help often. Amanda agreed that both families should choose one item of her many belongings, as pay. Wesley chose Aarons good chain saw as a practical gift, and Mandy picked her mother's old solid china-cupboard that cost $5.50 at an auction in1938, where Amanda first learned to bid.

Amanda did not want to move to any other location, but neither did she want to live all alone. The house was too big and too quiet. She fulfilled all her wedding vows, and she could now do as she pleased. She could cook the green beans with bacon again, but it was hardly worth cooking just for herself. Even her favorite wheat mush like they ate in Michigan, did not tempt her. The house stayed clean most of the time, and she did not need to mind the clock. She had a newfound freedom, but nobody would miss her. She did not need to go to the church of Aarons choice anymore.

Amanda reminisced about church issues: As a child, she followed her parent's instructions without hesitation. After she left home, Aaron was the head of their home, 'as long as they both shall live. 'Since she outlived Aaron and her parents, she had the privilege to decide things for herself now for the first time. She looked around and saw many different church groups, some as plainly dressed as her parents had been and some fancy groups with no plain church rules remaining.

Amanda never went to church or to school without wearing an apron. Her parents said," An apron is a sign of service!". Amanda's mother braided her girl's hair to the ends and then wrapped both pigtails in a neat figure eight, using hairpins to hold them up for church. At the age of twelve, Amanda started wearing a prayer veil to church, and at fifteen, she put her large volume of hair, up in a bob [or bun],and no longer wore pigtails. At that age, she also wore a cape on her dresses and no longer buttoned the dress down the back. In winter, her mother made heavy woolen dresses and those had a matching piece of bought ribbon for a belt, due to the bulky fabric, otherwise they allowed nothing fancy.

No matter what. .. Amanda never attended church wearing a short-sleeved dress and she never saw her father in a short -sleeved shirt, for the sake of modesty and respect. That was fancy and too revealing! Sometimes they wore out some dresses with the sleeves cut off for everyday, but her mother patched the elbows many times.

Amanda went to church with her parents, in a horse and buggy, Peter Brubacher hitched up the horse to the carriage and then everyone in the family met him at the walk. Sarah Ann [mommy Brubacher] wore her shawl and a big black bonnet, while her daughters wore their starched sunbonnets. The men folks wore black hats and off they went.

Every other Sunday, the horse and carriage group alternated with the "Funk 'church group in using the Maple River Mennonite meeting- house. The 'funk' Mennonites allowed a more stylish dress code and they owned cars.

On the alternate Sunday, the congregation gathered at the schoolhouse for church services, more centrally located. They drove six or seven miles to go to church, but they conveniently walked to the schoolhouse, only half a mile away. They held communion services at the church house twice a year, but Amanda was baptized at school.

The public school teachers had a higher education and none of them were Mennonites. Therefore, they had a problem with a Christmas tree at school when they used the schoolhouse for church services. The teacher's desk served as a pulpit for the preacher and the congregation sat in the school desks. The biggest people sat along the front where the fold -up seats had no desk in front of them. The preacher did not want a decorated tree beside him for the services and one time the church people moved it out, and disappointed the teacher. They also had a problem with a flag up front, but that was easier to move. They wanted God first, and none of the members wanted to pledge allegiance to a country.

Jesse Brubacher Senior tended the woodstove and he brought along two chairs for the ministers. He sometimes brought in extra benches as needed. Jesse as caretaker swept the schoolroom after every use. The school desks had wrought iron sides with a fancy design, and a wooden writing surface. The wooden table space folded up for people to kneel during prayer. The children sat with their parents until second or third grade size. The teenagers sat along the back and anybody that whispered during church services was too young to sit away from his parents. The same shelves that held lunch boxes during the week, held rows of hats and bonnets on Sunday morning.

The songs and sermons were all in German. Amanda never went to German school, but she learned how to read it, by following along in the songbooks. The German that Amanda's parents spoke in their everyday home life, had less English words included, than the Pennsylvania Dutch dialect had, and that helped Amanda learn more German words.

Daniel Brubacher served as Bishop and Amanda's grandfather, Henry Brenneman was the preacher. Christ Leinbach was the deacon until he moved to Pennsylvania and Henry Martin replaced him. Henry stayed until the church dissolved. Those that did not move away joined the 'funk' group. Bishop Daniel Brubacher moved to Canada and Grandpa Brenneman died.

Amanda listed the names of those she remembered in Michigan." Only Cyrus Ebys and their son Jeremiah Ebys, plus Manesseh Kulps and Henry Martins lived near the big church house, two miles west of Brutus. Menno Shantzs and Abe Ringlers lived near Pellston, about five miles north of Brutus.

Grandfather Henry Brenneman, Abe Sauders, Eli Burkharts, Harvey and Jesse Brubachers, Christ Leinbachs, Isaac Kilmers, Elias Newswengers, Noah Brubachers, William Martins, Wilson Reeds, William and Daniel Brubachers plus the Gregory's; Isaiah, Elis, Franks, Henrys, and Amos and us lived in the Woodland settlement around the schoolhouse, several miles north and east of Brutus.

Amanda worked for others every summer until she turned seventeen. That year she stayed home because she was in the instruction class to join church. They did not have class meeting every summer, so eight youths applied for church membership at one time. Lydia Ann Martin, Elsie Ringler, Sidney and Jesse Brubacher, Christian Kilmer, Betsy, Silas and Amanda gathered with the ministry on Sunday afternoons for instruction meeting. Amanda made her first black dress for baptismal services, and the plain- colored calico cost nine cents a yard. Before God and many witnesses, Amanda and the other youths promised to remain faithful. The preachers talked about searching for the pearl of great price in Matthew 13 verse 46. Amanda found it in her youth and she was not about to let go.

The straight and narrow road looked brighter all the time, and she realized that all the shadows and trials in her past had a bright light behind them all. She still held on to the teachings she learned long ago. The biblical truths about Christianity were not for just one church, but to all who believed and obeyed. She still held on to the basic simplicity of love, honesty, respect, modesty and doing unto others as you would have them do unto you. Amanda realized that she and Aaron lived as poor weak mortals struggling with sin, and yet God worked through their lives.

The church Aaron chose was now Amanda's choice, because she used her driver's license nearly every day. She missed Aaron many times, but she found plenty to keep her busy. Money was not a problem, thanks to Aaron's wild imaginations about mining iron ore. Amanda marveled at the turn of events in her lifetime. Many things looked so different when she could look back. Her main regret was, "I wish I had been nicer to Aaron and let him have his own way more."

Amanda enjoyed the outdoors and the woodland. "In quietness and solitude, shall be thy strength!" She found a solace as she spent time outdoors alone. Early in the morning, she went fishing just before a rain. It was perfect out there and she ate fish for breakfast! She ate all she wanted and did not need to remove any bones for children's plates.

Amanda learned to associate with the widows in the area, and they planned a trip to Virginia, helping clean up after a damaging flood. She spent most of her time in the kitchen while there, because she was the only cook that could peel onions without crying. Onions did not irritate her eyes, or many of her children's eyes.

For half a century, Amanda used up fabric scraps and made practical covers. She enjoyed arranging colors and prints from her scrap pile. By attending every quilting possible, and designing quilts for her daughters, Amanda worked on hundreds of quilts. She used feedbags, auction fabric, and whatever she found reduced at Sam Rubinsons. Not once, did she enter a fabric store, selecting the latest coordinated colors and styles at top dollar. That was too extravagant!

A friend brought some material to Amanda and asked her to sew a log cabin quilt. The matched colors turned into a lovely pattern, and Amanda got paid for her hobby. That was fun! She made several more quilts to sell, because her children were grown and gone. Amanda pieced some quilt tops for other people, and later she sewed a dark-colored nine patch, with an antique look. The finished quilt brought her $495! Why would anyone pay such outrageous prices for a cover to sleep beneath? Amanda went on to earn over $1000 for her hobby in one year. The arthritis in her gnarled fingers slowed her down as time went on. Handmade quilts became a big business, until the imports with less quality, sold for much lower prices.

With careful planning and consideration, Pete helped Amanda plan a new retirement house built against the farmhouse with a large garage connecting the two houses. Not only did Pete help Amanda with plans for the new house, he also saw her tremendous need for help in planning and developing land for building permits. He was not looking for more work, but no one else understood the business end better than he did, with all the land he bought and sold in building new houses.

A new house

After living in the same spot for 55 years, Amanda planned to move, from one end of the house, over to the new edition, her retirement home. It was time to get rid of quite a collection of clutter. She did not need many of her things and started to sort through the old yellow cupboard that held her Sunday dishes. "This one was mothers, and that one was from Canada, the salt dish was used before salt shakers were invented, and some of the things were treasures from auctions." With patience and help from others, she labeled dishes so that each grandchild received a piece, and some would be sold over auction.

In years gone by, Aaron and Amanda hung their home cured hams in this cool dry area. Amanda dried pop corn braids up here and stored a box of love letters Aaron sent to her in 1937. The attic was a wonderful place for children to snoop on a rainy day, with the sound of rain on the tin roof!

Rhoda spent time helping Amanda sort barrels in the attic. The secondary chimney near the center of this snapshot shows how it was designed with removable bricks. That way the entire attic could be converted into a huge smokehouse, but Aaron and Amanda used the attic for storage and did not want things all smoky. Up here is where the knitting machine stayed for seventy years. The window on the left is where Mary and Martha peeped out from beneath a row of coats and saw Josie leave over towards Jesse Brubachers. Louise removed the bricks in the chimney occasionally to observe the chimney swift nest inside the chimney.

Here in the attic, it was much harder to decide what was trash and what was treasure. Antique dealers sometimes bid high on junk, but what was junk? Wesley came home often to help in many ways where he could. It was a lot of work to keep the place going with no man around. His wife, Janie was dependable when Amanda needed help, and just three miles away.

Amanda's married children came to help her with all the work of getting ready for an auction. The women cleaned out the southeast room and started in the attic, digging through barrels of old coats and clothes packed in mothballs. The men that arrived to help brought in firewood and cleaned up the stripping room. Paul Hurst and Daniel came to make a list of possessions

to print on a sale bill. It was hard for Amanda to part with some sentimental items, so she kept some of them.

Amanda drove to church all alone, and gone were all the years of getting children ready for church in a hurry, and helping Aaron find his hat. Amanda commented, "I wish I had spent more time cooking when there were many mouths to feed. It was much more fun to cook when a table full of people enjoyed eating." When frost threatened, Amanda could not tolerate losing any green tomatoes. She gathered them all and canned them for green tomato pies, even though she had few people interested in eating them. She felt it her duty to preserve all the food God trusted to her.

When the temperature dropped below zero on a windy day, the water pump froze in the springhouse, an unusual happening. That was when Amanda really missed not having a man around the house. Phares Martin came and couldn't fix it. Then Joe Wenger took the pump to Martindale for repairs, and he worked until dark to get it working. When it snowed, Wesley and Jevon came and plowed the lane for Amanda. The roads were bad enough that Amanda could not drive, and Clement Leinbach kindly fetched her and the other ladies in the neighborhood, for the Terre-Hill Fire Co. quilting.

Some things didn't change much. Children full of energy still kept skating on the old farm pond! The schoolchildren came from Black Creek School to skate for one long recess. Many skaters turned up on a Sunday, bringing 11 buggies and a dozen bicycles from the Joe Wenger and 35er groups. Ever since Walter hooked up electric lights at the farm pond, more neighbors gathered for skating after dark. The lights attracted them, among all the ponds in the neighborhood, and they knew they were welcome any time.

In January, the electricians came, hooking up the wires for Amanda's new house and the dry wallers kept busy. Amanda had the fun of choosing floor coverings of her choice. In February, the new kitchen cabinets arrived and her house had heaters with thermostats, now won't that be a wonderful luxury!

With the excitement of a new house came financial decisions and estate planning. A trip to Menno Shirk to file income taxes was something Aaron always took care of, until now. Amanda keenly missed Aaron when she called Wesley for help about a disabled cow. They sent two more cows to market. She had a wonderful warm feeling to have such a big family working together as volunteers came to help her. The kitchen linoleum arrived just in time for the auction day. Uncle Titus came in the evening to help line up equipment for auction. The entire neighborhood helped as needed. Janie spent half the day cleaning upstairs and scrubbed the old kitchen range for Amanda. Alice Shirk biked over to help.

When Sunday came, Amanda rejoiced for a day of rest, and she was more than pleased to have company in the evening. Norma Reed and Christ Shirks came, with Elam Martin's bringing them, and fetching them again. Lydia, Amanda and Norma had a good time reminiscing about growing up in Michigan, as they had lived together in the same house and shared everything. How times have changed! Lydia and Christ Shirk would have loved to move in with Amanda to stay, and Amanda considered that possibility, but Christ needed special care and a special lift for his wheelchair and handicapped problems. Amanda could have handled Lydia maybe, but not the combination of both of them.

Walters came from Missouri and so did Rolands. The day of the auction arrived on March 6, 1982. Five of Aaron and Amanda's married children and their families living in Missouri could not attend. Farmers had several poor years in a row, and they had no money to spend for traveling and auctions. 18% interest rates at the bank hurt them financially.

The usual crowd of family and neighbors chatted among others, such as antique dealers and strangers. When the auctioneer held up moth eaten union suits, Amanda was embarrassed, wondering why they were not trashed, but they sold at a high price. Amanda had purchased pillows at the 1950 family auction of B W Shirks personal belongings. They had ordinary, striped feather -ticking covers. As the auctioneer held them up, Amanda commented, "Those two pillows are stuffed with cork stuffing! "The auction paused as two antique dealers checked out the pillows and paid $100 apiece...cork stuffing meant they were wartime pillows and older than WWII.

Paul Hurst did the auctioneering and Menno Shirk's family did the clerking. Every auction around the neighborhood had a "penny man." When no one wanted the item for a penny, it went on a 'no sale 'pile. The penny man moved the pile of leftovers and took what he wanted after he paid. At some auctions, the penny man had bargains, but at Amanda's auction, they did not charge the penny man a full price because Amanda had saved too many trashy things. Other people did not save so much useless junk, such as empty tin cans. She was definitely a pack rat by nature and the family was not quite sure what antique dealers all collected.

In March of 1983, Henry and Mandy with their three little boys, moved into the old farmhouse where Aaron and Amanda had raised fifteen children. Amanda loved children all her life, and now the house rang again with the noise and laughter of children, after 5 years of quiet.

Many helpers carried many belongings and Amanda served the noon meal for Henery's moving day. After a long busy day, they made the beds and tucked their boys in for the night. Grandson's Cleason, Lyndon, and Kevin brought new life and action to the old farmhouse. Mandy was now at home again, sleeping in the same bedroom where she grew up, but now with a husband and not a room full of sisters. It almost seemed as if Henry intruded in the girl's bedroom, with Mandy's vivid memories of years gone by. The sounds at night, outside the windows were still the same, and so was the noise of spring peepers calling. The maple tree outside the window seemed like home and so did the song of the katydids and the bullfrog's.

The living arrangement so close to Amanda, created a need for many adjustments for everyone involved. Amanda went to church with Henry's, and there was a man around the house for chores and breakdowns.

Amanda came and went as she pleased, but mostly she "went. "She took Eva Shirk to Ruben Weavers for a call and Lydi-Jes-sey to quilt at Christ Shirks, and a call at Harry Troups, where Eva worked. They stopped at Shady Maple. Amanda drove to Lebanon County for a call at Mikesy and went to visit Rhoda, RoseAnna, and their families. She took Dora Krieder along to visit Silas. She took Irvin Brubaker to Blue Ball twice for manure spreader parts, and she picked up Adin Kilmer's and Melvin Sauders from Missouri and made calls all day with those travelers. Later she drove "taxi "to Bareville auction. Amanda took Mommy Shirk and Annie along to visit Uncle John and Aunt Barbara Shirk. She took her sister Lydia to her foot doctor and to Weaver Shirks for new shoes for Amanda and Christ. Amanda spent a day with widows and took along Mrs. Banks Horning, also a widow. She took Clemensy and Esther Ringler along to a big quilting at Fairmont. She attended

the Smoketown school reunion where Aaron went to school when he was a boy. Aaron's brother Ben's came from Indiana for that occasion and Amanda took along Eva, Jesse, Lydia, Clemensy, and Davy Newswengers. Living among horse and buggy people Amanda remained busy, running a neighborhood taxi, but she thrived on the fellowship, and feeling needed.

On a lovely spring evening in May, Amanda went fishing with Henry's little boys and returned with 29 bluegills to clean and eat. She enjoyed every minute. She still cleaned fish, slowly and carefully by removing the scales and the fins. She watched people in Missouri fillet fish, but that looked wasteful to her, even if she had to admit, she could not get more meat off the bones with a knife. She still saw bits of meat wasted.

Amanda enjoyed babies and watched her chance to help babysit the little boys at the other end of the house. Amanda offered to keep at least one twin, when Mandy went grocery shopping so she would not have her hands so full. When Mandy returned, Amanda said, "next time I want both of the twins or none! The lonely twin whimpered and hunted for his brother and crawled down the hall and back, looking for his other half, until you returned."

Henry had a full-time job at Conestoga wood products, and he farmed on the weekends, and evenings. Sometimes Mandy helped him by driving the tractor for making hay, even occasionally driving with a baby on her lap. Amanda did not like to see little boys so close to the farm equipment and offered to keep children.

Wesley and Vernon spent time grading and seeding a new lawn for Amanda and she was pleased when they came in for dinner at her table, when they worked at making the walks and the porches. Amanda rejoiced with each new day and cheerfully looked on the bright side. On a rare occasion, she wrote in her diary, " had a frustrating day, trying to make a real estate settlement with Wentz and Weaver," she complained," I'm searching out old deeds and the maps that Aaron had about woodland and Kurtz's dump, for selling more building lots. In June, Amanda received 16,000 dollars for a one ½-acre building lot settlement.

Amanda did not need to worry about money, as she packed her suitcase for a 22-day trip to Missouri. She started on a Trail ways bus with Ruth Brubaker headed for Tipton where Walter's wife Marian, met them. Amanda rejoiced to spend time with her sisters, Mary and Betsy and shared the same church bench with them for the last time in their lives. Christian Kilmer's drove her places in the horse and carriage to make several calls. Amanda reveled in the fond memories! The next day a niece, Annetta, took Amanda visiting wherever she pleased, and Suetta, a great-niece, drove her the next day.

Walters took Amanda 200 miles north to the Memphis area, where Amanda spent two weeks with six married daughters. She enjoyed a glimpse into their homes and helped them work. She was there for a Bar-B-Q, she helped quilt, made a tractor seat cover and mended, she shelled peas, made noodles and canned red beets.

She attended the ordination where a new preacher replaced Abner Oberholtzer, after Abner became the Bishop. "The lot is cast into the lap of Carl Hoover!" Amanda's son-in-law was ordained to preach at the age of 29 years old. 200 people ate dinner at Earl Weilers, but Aaron was not among them. She missed him! She knew Aaron would be honored to hear a son-in law preach.

When Henry's went on a short trip to Canada, Amanda had time all alone again. She stopped at Shady Maple for groceries, and noticed some reduced cherries that urgently needed canning. She really didn't need many cherries but they needed her! Nobody should dump food and she could can those cherries that touched her heart! Amanda wanted to salvage them and bought two boxes full at $10 a box, with no one at home to help her do them. She worked long and late 'trimming 'the bad spots and canning those cherries, even without time to spare.

After three days at home, Amanda packed for another trip, to the funeral of Manasseh Kulp in Indiana. Spending time with her sister in Indiana was worth the trip, and Manasseh Kulps were people dear to Amanda. That was where she had worked when she was a teenager... long ago in Michigan.

The other travelers in Amanda's group, returned to Pennsylvania without her, while she spent 10 wonderful days with friends and relatives. She knew she was not needed at home. She saw where Ben Shirks and Dan Martin's children lived and then Ben Shirks took Amanda along to the thumb part of Michigan where three of Ben's married children lived. Melvin Zimmerman's, Weldon Zimmerman's, and Donald Martin's had a pea shelling party when they arrived, and shelled eighty quarts by hand.

When Amanda returned to Indiana to spend a night with her sister, they made many calls the next day, to Elsie Gregory, and the new widow Mrs. Manasseh Kulp. Uncle Joe Brenneman came in the evening, and all these people had roots in Michigan years ago.

When Amanda returned home, she enjoyed showing her grandsons how to braid the onions together to hang them up. She spent time reading, writing and singing. It was frustrating when she could not find things she knew she had, and there was no one to blame except herself. After spending a long time looking for a white pencil to mark off a dark quilt border, she gave up and used a sliver of bar soap, like her mother taught her.

Sewing and quilting rated near the top of Amanda's long list of hobbies, therefore at the age of 70, she started making one quilt top for each grandchild as a wedding gift. She kept right on sewing for the next 20 years but did not quite complete her project. The younger grandchildren had their mothers help sewing together the four patches that Amanda pieced precisely. The older grandchildren had nicer tops in a variety of patterns. Amanda did not quilt any of them.

Amanda picked two big buckets of elderberries and spent time making jelly. She was 68 years old and did not need to save the money, but she still had vivid memories of a huge elderberry bush in the corner of her mother's spaded garden in Michigan, and the joys of sharing and gathering wild fruit in her childhood. Memories sweetened the flavor of the elderberry jelly.

Amanda occasionally received a card or a gift from a secret pal to keep her curious who it might be. Once a year, In August, they revealed all the secrets at a supper gathering. RoseneMartin picked up Amanda and drove her there, where she discovered Lavina Weaver had been her secret pal in 1983.

Amanda still enjoyed guests at her house. Carl Weilers came from Missouri and slept there two nights with children along and two days later Mervin Highs came from Iowa and spent the night there with their children. Eli Kilmer's and seven children came for a call from Missouri. Daniels brought Silas for dinner and Uncle Joe for supper. Nine widows gathered at Amanda's place for a covered dish dinner. Later, cousin David Brubachers from Canada came for the wedding of Eunice Huber and Virgil Martin. They spent four nights in Amanda's beds and Amanda gladly accommodated such honored guests that had done so much for them in Canada.

Carl Hoover's spent three nights with Amanda. They came for church conference and Lydia planned a sister's day, while the men attended to church business, an annual event. All the PA sisters gathered at mom, for a jovial time while working something for Amanda. Five widows came to Amanda for Sunday dinner and enjoyed a leisurely stroll through the woods, gathering moss and plants to make winter gardens. In a glass container, they arranged plants to grow as a terrarium.

Every day was a gift, the" present! "Amanda had many things to learn and to discover. Henry's took her deer spotting after dark, since deer became more plentiful than ever before. Many times, she saw her teenage children go deer spotting in years gone by, but no one had ever taken her and shown her how the eyes glow in the spotlight. Amanda enjoyed the fluorescent eyes and so did Henry's little boys.

Amanda stopped at the butcher shop for smoked turkey breast, at one dollar a pound, a bargain she enjoyed. She also purchased a 40-pound box of deer bones for the dogs, but that seemed wasteful to her and she cooked them first. After she picked all the meat scraps from the bones and saved the broth, then the dogs could have the bones. She ate some meat and cooked some into scrapple, by cooking cornmeal in the meat broth until it thickened. Saving the meat was not so much about pinching pennies, but about saving food!

Amanda attended the first cookie exchange in her life, at Marlin Brubaker's, where her Pennsylvania daughters each brought Christmas cookies to trade for more varieties. Everyone brought two kinds of cookies and took along home 12 kinds.

When another building lot sold on Laurel Top Rd., Amanda received, $22,000.Pete helped Amanda with her finances at the Blue Ball bank and started her very first savings account ever, after paying off her last loan.

She had money to spend on birdseed and even bought cat food! Her barn cats still preferred food that Amanda cooked for them. No matter how much money Amanda had, she detested waste in any form, and she took her shoes to Weaver Shirk to have them fixed, rather than buy new ones for herself.

When the mail came, she spent a lot of time looking at the births and deaths in the obituary column of the Lancaster intelligencer Journal. She did not appreciate the sweepstakes folders that came in the mail. "'Reader's Digest should manage that money to help the needy", she commented. Amanda said, "I feel guilty when I read about the hardship of others, and about people going hungry." She had everything she wished for! She sent more greeting cards to more people than what she received. Get-well cards, sympathy cards, anniversary cards, and birthday cards all had a letter tucked inside. Each grandchild received a birthday card in the mail, including many colorful stickers, such as Amanda would have enjoyed in her childhood, and still did! Amanda copied a line," What lies behind us, and what lies before us, are tiny matters compared to what lies within us."

Amanda gathered black walnuts, and picked up persimmons, to prevent waste. She took a dish full of ripe persimmons along as a covered dish to sewing circle. Amanda sewed many charity items such as shirts, pants, underwear, and dresses for Haiti. She still enjoyed recycled clothing, altered to fit, and she ripped apart older dresses to cut them up. The scraps made comfort tops, for charity. When Rubinsons store had a closeout sale, Amanda bought a huge pile of fabric, and waited one hour at the checkout. It was such a big event that some people waited two hours to pay. Any time when Amanda did not feel like cleaning, she called at Titus Shirks and Laura biked over, doing a good job for her Aunt Amanda.

Amanda had more than she could wish for, when God blessed Henry and Mandy with another son Bryan and later, identical twin sons, Matthew and Mark, at the old farmhouse on the other side of her garage. Amanda greatly enjoyed children, even at the age of 72, but she noticed that things were not done the way she would do it. When Henry and Mandy raised watermelons in the garden, they tasted bland, like a cross of raw cucumbers. Henry allowed the boys to eat the heart out of each one and then put the rest in the slop bucket for the chickens. They did not preserve watermelons for wintertime, and they were not good enough to give away. Amanda went through the garbage bucket and ate some watermelon, telling her daughter to be less wasteful.

Amanda found some green beans that Mandy tossed out in the garden, and she scolded, 'These are not too old!" [she gathered them and ate them]. .."Are you cleaning again?". .."Are you washing that already?. ..Wear things until they are dirty or you will wear it out in the wash!" When Mandy scolded a child, Amanda thought she was too harsh with the children but at other times she asked,"Are you just going to let them go and get by with that?"

Mother and daughter had no major clashes and Henry understood Amandas saving ways. They really appreciated her occasional babysitting. When Mandy left to fetch the schoolchildren, with a sleeping child at home for ten minutes, she told Amanda to be in charge.

Amanda made new friends with neighbors in the new houses on Laurel Hill. Carol Munzenberger admired Amanda's skill in sewing and asked if she could alter the shoulder straps on her daughter's sundresses, to wear to the Caribbean Sea on her honeymoon? Amanda did! She made and gave a dahlia pillow as a wedding gift, neatly wrapped in recycled, used wrapping paper that she ironed first, to remove the wrinkles.

Sarah Ann and daughter Wanda bravely flew from St. Louis to Philadelphia for the wedding of Pete's Loretta and Jeff Mellinger. Wesley picked them up at the airport. They happened to be in Pennsylvania for the funeral of Jesse Brubacher Junior's 18-year-old son Marlin, who died suddenly in a bicycle accident. Amanda took them along to the funeral, and someone asked Sarah Ann, "Was your first airplane ride scary?" Without hesitating, Sarah Ann said, "It was not nearly as scary as going with mom to the funeral and passing buggies on those narrow roads and sharp turns!

Amanda's driving became a hazard on the road. She could not always think fast enough and her reflexes were slower. Walters Clydine went with her grandmother and said, "Not again, grandma nearly cleaned out the ditches!" She was alarmed about her grandmother's driving.

Some neighbors realized Amanda had a problem driving safely, but everyone appreciated her generosity and her driver's license. No one wanted to see Amanda cause an accident, and perhaps kill someone, and yet no one wanted to "clip her wings "by taking her driver's license away.

36

Silas

After more than ten years of looking, Silas found a wife! When he first came from Michigan to Pennsylvania, he asked many girls, but there did not seem to be any for him. Silas just did not fit in anywhere with a speech problem and his clumsy ways. Grandma always said, "sis ken heffly so shep es net un dekkel aw fit." (There is no pottery so crooked that a lid won't fit). God had a wife for him after all, but Sarah Hawk was already forty-eight years old, ten years older than Silas, and he had to forget his dreams of raising a family.

Silas found a kind and patient companion to live with, someone to do the housework in a home of their own. She was a bit slow and so was he. Love cannot be explained, and age was no barrier.

Sarah's father, William Hawk was an alcoholic father, with a row of children to raise, including cute little Sarah. When Weaver and Maggie (Auker) Hurst went to Altoona to visit Maggie's sister Fannie, they were appalled at the condition that Fannie faced, with a husband like William. Weaver Hursts had three sons but no daughters, and they offered to care for the dark curly haired two-year old. Therefore, they took her along home and never gave her back! Maggie bonded to lovable placid young Sarah as she helped her with the housework.

Sarah and Silas had a simple wedding on September 3, 1949, at the Lancaster Conference Mennonite Church. Aaron and Amanda were not sure if they could attend the wedding or not, due to the ailing health of Aaron's mother, but she lived one more week after all.

Silas sold Mc Ness products as a door-to-door salesman. Many people felt sorry for him, and bought just enough to keep him happy. While trying to explain what he was selling, he showed his book to a customer. They noticed the price list and Silas said, "Now muss ich sell nugh duppla." (Now I must double that.)

Silas, precise and neat, enjoyed singing and he learned all the notes in music, but he had a voice problem. He also enjoyed visiting with people, but many avoided him when they could not understand him. Most people did the best they could and perhaps Silas, in his limited ability, got closer to perfection than many others did.

Silas was happily married to Sarah Hawk for about nineteen years. After she died, he became lonesome and dissatisfied, searching for companionship. He found a decent housekeeper when Emma Ennis moved in with him. She said, "Silas, you look cute when you are cross!" She soon had him chuckling again. When they visited at Aaron and Amanda's table, they agreed, 'we do not need sugar in our coffee, we are sweet enough". The Eastern Church group did not approve of a live-in arrangement, and they did not marry, so she moved out and Silas kept looking.

When Flossie Wealand met Silas in 1973, it was love at first sight. Flossie wrote a letter to Silas;"*I am a little older than you are, almost 69 years. Here is my phone number, if you want to call me. Thank you for your nice letter. I saw you a few times at Dohner's and at Richland Church. The Lord was leading since. I have been praying the Lord will lead us to be happy. I have not had no happy life in the pass. I had nine children, three died. The oldest, Norman Junior, don't come see me. None go to church, I pray for them. Time goes slow when you are not here"*

Later Flossie wrote, "*Did your housekeeper, Emma, move her things out yet? My sister might come to my wedding. Let me know what your "neeses" (nieces) think of it. If God wants us together, no one can stop it. From Flossie.*"

Forty guests attended the wedding of Silas and

Flossie on October 18, 1973 at 6 PM, near Mount Zion. Aaron and Amanda were among those guests, and truly wished her brother and his wife contentment and happiness. Eight months later Amanda went to visit Flossie at the Phil Haven Hospital, due to mental problems. Three years later, Flossie spent six weeks recovering from a heart attack at the Lebanon Valley Hospital. Amanda spent 10 days helping her brother Silas, in his apartment at Lebanon Valley, when his wife was in the hospital. The place needed a housekeeper and Amanda felt needed as she scrubbed and cleaned where she could see a major difference. Silas needed her help very much, but Amanda could not see the sunrise, nor the moon set at night. She felt cooped up and missed the farm and the great outdoors.

A slow death was heartbreaking, as Silas sat beside his wife in the hospital and did not see her improving. Flossy Brubacher died at the age of 78, on December 10, 1982. The funeral took place at the Shirkville Mennonite Church.

Silas had a light heart attack and spent nine days in the hospital. The doctor would not release him to an empty house, due to his many dizzy headaches. Amanda looked around at all the luxury around her. She wrote, 'I feel at home in my new home. The less I need to work, the lazier I get. I no longer need to take out the wood ashes with the new furnace. Only my seven farm cats depend on me." She cooked extra for them and spoiled them. Since Aaron was gone, she saw no reason why her brother should not move in with her, because he did not want to live in an old people's home. He had no children, and not many options.

In a letter Amanda wrote, *"I feel it my rightful duty to give my brother a home here, even if I have to crowd myself together a little more. Reducing my belongings to fit into five rooms is quite a job, and the pioneers that moved west, had all their possessions in one wagon. I still enjoy piecing and quilting and I have mountains of things I want to do, but I am still the happiest when I can do something for others."*

Poem; OTHERS

Lord let me live from day to day,

That when I kneel to pray, my prayer will be for others.

Others Lord, yes others, Let this my motto be.

That while I live for others, I will have lived for thee!

Daniel's and Mervin Brubacher's moved Silas's possessions to Amanda's house, in January, 1983, after Amanda lived alone in her new house for a year. She hesitated to give up her only guest room that she had planned for travelers. Family and friends came anyway and some of them slept in the basement, with a dehumidifier running.

Silas brought along his compact antique desk full of personal letters and papers. He collected old books and he had many boxes of other things to unpack. He was a pack rat! He kept his belongings in good condition and never had children touching his things. He also brought along a small mini barn that was his.

When Silas lived with Amanda, Henry and Mandy Martin lived in the farmhouse. Silas enjoyed the children as much as Amanda did, and he finally found little boys that were not scared of him. He bounced the twins on his knee and played rough with them, among peals of laughter and "Do it again!". He enjoyed Amanda's grandsons as though they were his own. Even in his senior years, Silas sometimes got down on his hands and knees to talk to the baby on the floor.

After Silas had a stroke, he could not drive for a while, and his driver's license expired. He wrote a letter to the Pennsylvania Department of Transportation saying," I need my driver's license, because I want to ask a girlfriend." They returned his driver's license!

Among the letters and treasures in his desk, Silas kept letters from the 1930's and 1940's. He saved some rejection letters from girls he had asked;

'One girl wrote; 'I sent

the table linen back, not because it was not good enough. I think you did good at choosing gifts but I did not want you as a boyfriend. Thanks for the birthday present. I do not mean to insult you, but I still do not want your company as a boyfriend or a lover....

Another girl wrote; 'The candy was very good, and I think the table linen is nice. I do not wish to correspond so I think I will return it."

Another letter from Salem Ohio stated," Dear sir, Greetings in Jesus holy name. Well I shall write a few lines tonight to answer your letter I received. You are five years on behind. I am married and have a very nice married life. I do not know much to write, but I am sure there are still other fish in the pan to be fried..."

" Another excerpt from the state of Virginia; "Not that I think myself better than you or anyone else, but I am not interested!"Silas worked hard at keeping track of which girls he asked, and he kept on trying.

As long as Silas had a driver's license, he was a salesman selling McNess products, door to door, or selling trees for Stark Brothers. At one time, he sold Mason shoes. He could do a fair job, because he could handle the money and he did precise and honest bookkeeping. People felt sorry for him, and they purchased enough to keep him going.

Silas and Flossie had been married nine years, and he still wished for a third wife when he was 78, even with Amanda as a dependable housekeeper. Amanda tried to reason with him and she asked, "What do you have to offer a wife?" Silas no longer had a home or a driver's license, and no way to earn money.

Silas enjoyed traveling all his life. When he heard that Dicks went to Indiana, without the car being full, he regretted he could not go along to see his sister Katie, and just to travel. He said "Luss uss net vittah happen-ah," (let it not happen again), he warned, shaking his finger at his nephew.

Silas moved in low gear, neat and precise. He needed patience all day long. Amanda helped him fill his prescriptions and keep his doctor appointments. He had diabetes, a pacemaker and a hearing aid. Amanda understood him better, than anyone else on earth did. They reminisced about Michigan,

Canada and childhood things, about his brother Joshua, and life in general.

Silas held his big red handkerchief by one corner, then held his arm out with the hanky dangling in the breeze, as an indicator of which way the wind blew.

More than anything else, Silas enjoyed putting together puzzles. Amanda and Silas had quite a collection and they glued them together as soon as they finished a puzzle. Amanda had many other things needing her attention, but she said, "A puzzle spread out on the card table, pulls me like iron to a magnet."Silas had an eye for shapes, Amanda went by color, and together they worked like a team. Sometimes Mandy and Henry's boys from the other end of the house came over to join in the puzzle fun. Cleason, Lyndon, Kevin, and Brian watched Silas put the puzzles together and helped him.

With a shaky hand, Silas signed each completed puzzle with his wiggly handwriting. Amanda gave one finished puzzle to each of her 15 children, so Silas could keep on finishing and gluing together more puzzles.

Silas did not get all of Amanda's attention, her sister; Aunt Lydia claimed every bit she could, even more so after Aaron died. When Amanda dropped off the Brubacher family circle letter at Lydia and Christ on October 24, it remained unwritten until Amanda came back in December, and read it to Lydia! Her eyes were not the best anymore. Amanda took Lydia to most of her doctor appointments, and sometimes Silas stayed there with Christ until the sisters returned. Silas cracked English walnuts for them.

At the age of 68, Amanda had her picture taken for her driver's license for the first time, and cleaning the inside of the car was now her job. Every day brought new things to try. Amanda drove alone to Bowmansville church, and got a flat tire just as she arrived. Thankfully, Adin Leinbach changed the flat tire for her.

She kept forgetting the garage door opener, and backed her car into the closed garage door at home. It happened more than once! When she mangled the door badly enough so that she could not get out and go to sewing circle, she borrowed Mandy and Henry's vehicle. She had no problem driving that car, but she claimed it needed more pep. She preferred more power beneath the hood.

Spring arrived bringing thousands of geese flying north, a lovely time of year. Amanda and Silas found time to go fishing together, and they enjoyed blackberry picking in the meadow with Henry's family, when summer arrived. Amanda was busy as ever, helping can peaches and pears and peeling potatoes and cleaning up. She still enjoyed inviting company for Sunday dinner. Some things never changed, and Amanda still enjoyed making feather pillows, as she did in her childhood. She made a pair of pillows with new duck down as a baby gift for a grandchild.

Amanda pieced a dozen nine patches before breakfast and had her heart into sewing circle, helping the needy. She taught Silas how to cut quilt patches into 6-inch squares, for charity. Amanda never ran out of things to do and still enjoyed nailing together a birdhouse or a small bench. She liked woodworking.

Amanda enjoyed an 8 day trip to Missouri for her granddaughter, Cheryl Weiler's funeral and home again. She also had the privilege of taking a twelve-day trip to see Michigan and relatives in Indiana. Marty Reed drove, and took along Jesse Brubacher's, mommy Shirk, Leah and Barbara, Harvey Kilmer's and Leah Hursh. Amanda visited the old home place where she grew up at Brutus Michigan. She met people by the name of Gregory, Eby, Babcock, Newswenger, Burkhart, Bushkirk and Sauders. She again saw Burt Lake and went to Mackinac Island. Amanda was pleased with the privilege of going along for a round trip price of $95. Looking back to her childhood, brought many happy memories and amazing changes in 75 years.

This was the third house Amanda's father had built when he was young. The first one burned to the ground in the night and the second one was a quick log cabin. Amanda remembered how they lived in this house many years before the inside was finished. She remembered open beams on the ceiling and the studs exposed along the walls. Amanda and her sisters pretended the walls were cow stanchions. She was a teenager before her father plastered the walls!

Amanda looking at her former home in Michigan

The floors wore unevenly without linoleum and everywhere a nail protected the pine flooring, it formed ridges. Amanda was born here and married here. She did not wish to stay here when the church disintegrated and she wanted a home of her own. All the fond memories of childhood overwhelmed her. "To think how little we got by with, in growing up, and we were just as happy then as now, with all our extras," said Amanda.

∞

Silas lived to fetch the mail, and every day he walked or drove to the mailbox, as the highlight of his day. His walking cane had a small seat attached, where Silas could sit and rest to get his breath halfway up the hill. The biggest problem was when Henry came home from work and Silas met him first, preventing Henry from entering the house to his eagerly waiting wife and children. Silas stood holding Henry's mail, and craved Henry's attention, as the only man around to talk to. Mandy did not like to share Henry with Silas, when the little boys could hardly wait for their daddy and supper was waiting.

With a shaky hand, Silas handed over one piece of mail at a time, longingly wishing Mandy and Henry would share the contents, such as a letter from friends in Canada, or a package he knew contained snapshots.

Eventually they put an end to that idea and Silas just laid their mail on the counter. Living with Silas took an extreme amount of patience. Mandy and Henry took him along to many places. He wanted to see everyone else ready to leave first, before he got ready. No matter how much those little boys adored their great uncle, the twins howled in protest, all bundled -up and strapped in their car seats while Silas slowly put on his rubbers, on a sunny day, no matter what the weather. With shaking hands, he buttoned every last button just right, no matter who was waiting, or crying. Silas was slow, and hard of hearing, but a perfectionist! One morning he was late for church, because he needed to open a new tube of toothpaste!

A favorite quote of Silas' was; "Shoff net tzoo hot, ovvah blipe droe un ouse de bose-hite."(Don't work too hard but stay busy and out of mischief). In parting, he often said, "God be with you till we meet again."

Every time Silas saw yet another new house in the making, he said, "You'd think people would all have houses by now!" Amanda noticed and commented, People years ago lived together, even in crowed quarters. Why do all these people want so much to themselves without sharing?" Many nice big houses had only one or two people living there. It used to be that people shared homes with their extended families.

Silas lacked in driving skills and he had a way of bumping his car against the barn every time before he parked it. The barn boards splintered and Henry stacked pallets there. He could still feel a bump when he was nearby when Silas came home. In the cold weather, Silas had a hard time warming up his car. He revved the engine and a cloud of exhaust rose up high. Neighbor Ervin Brubaker called and asked", is everything ok over there? From here, it looks like the barn might be burning!"

In 1989, Henry and Mandy, with six sons, moved away from Amanda's house onto a dairy farm. Walter and Marian moved in to help take care of Amanda. Marian had a green thumb, and did most of the gardening, and Amanda enjoyed picking fresh vegetables or digging new potatoes as she pleased. They shared the same garden, but lived at opposite ends of the garage, in separate homes.

Walters noticed Amanda and Silas aging rapidly. Amanda helped Silas with business matters, straightened out his checkbook and wrote a check for this State Farm insurance and his delinquent taxes. When Silas's car did not pass inspection, he went car shopping at different places. Amanda went with him to the Blue Ball bank to help understand financial details. When Silas was shopping at Horning Dodge for a new vehicle, he had a" heart spell", and the ambulance took him to Ephrata Hospital ICU. Silas came home with a pacemaker and Amanda managed many Dr. Appointments and prescription drugs for him. He had a 24-hour heart monitor and he had it checked via the telephone. Silas had a hard time turning in his driver's license, and sadly got them ready to send in the mail. He would miss his license very much, but he understood that others could take him where he needed to go.

His church gave Silas a most beautiful scrapbook and Amanda enjoyed it also. Amanda kept busy every moment of the day, and she did the grocery shopping for Silas, Lydia and herself. She took her sister Lydia delivering Amway products, at 14 different locations, plus stopping here and there. Lydia claimed Amanda's grandchildren as though they were her own, and she insisted they come and see her, every time someone came from Missouri.

On a Saturday evening, Mrs.Gid Reil took Amanda along on a wonderful sleigh ride in the snow, with precious memories of Michigan...and Canada...in the crisp white snow. Amanda did not have a cutter ride like that since the day she married and left Michigan.

Amanda enjoyed a trip to Kentucky to see Aaron's brother Elias Shirks and their grown children. She had the privilege to ride in a horse and carriage, while making calls at Noah Shirks, Weavers, Johns and Jason's, with dinner at Sams, and to Elias's for the night. She underlined the fact that she had an unforgettable rough, stony, hilly, trip on back road hills, making memories.

Wesley had serious back problems and ended up with surgery, about the same time, a chiroprac-

tor in Missouri commented that Sarah Ann, Ruth, Martha and Lydia's x-rays showed they are sisters. They all inherited an extra vertebrae! Perhaps Aaron had the same problem. The extra vertebrae fused to a next one, and did not bend, creating problems in the lower back as they aged.

When Jesse Brubacher died, on Sept.18, 1996, he was not just another uncle, and every one of Aaron and Amanda's children desired to meet Jesse Brubacher's children. Walter, Sarah Ann, Ruth, Martha, Mary, Louise and Lydia came together in one van from Missouri without bringing their partners along. That made a lively trip, and when they packed up to return home again, Jesse's Mabel [Brubacher] Martin looked inside the van and said, "that looks juicy!" She had many fond memories of living next door.

Amanda plainly understood that the old must die, and the young can die. She saw her parents and her husband lowered into the grave, and many others, but nothing prepared her for the shock of finding her brother dead in her own house! She knew he was wearing out, but he had no complaints or discomforts lately. When Silas went to the bathroom at 2 AM, he rested his head on his arm, propped on the vanity, and went to sleep while sitting on the commode. Amanda unlocked the bathroom door the next

morning and found him there, when he did not answer her call.

Marian helped Amanda by calling the doctor, and then the undertaker. It was nine years since Aaron passed away, and Amanda went through the same routines, choosing songs and planning a funeral, with the help of many friends and neighbors. Silas had no children to notify, but a few remaining sisters and many nieces and nephews. Amanda had the visitation at her house, where Silas had resided. Aaron and Amanda's nieces and nephews sat in the second row, next of kin.

On the day of the funeral, the ministry held a fifteen-minute church service at Amanda's home, before the funeral procession headed out the long lane to Bowmansville church, (Lancaster Conference Mennonite Church) beside his first wife Sarah. His church served a light lunch, and Silas did not have a big funeral.

After the people went home, Amanda returned to a quiet house. She had many sewing projects and things to do. When her spare room stood empty awhile, Mahlon's Jolene moved in from Missouri and boarded there for four years. That way Jolene made many new friends and attended a larger youth group on the weekend while Amanda benefitted from her presence.

Taking driver's license

Christian Kilmer's Naomi died in Indiana, and Amanda really desired to attend that funeral of her niece married to Lester Martin, and maybe see her own sister Katie again. Marian and Naomi, (two daughters-in-law) went out of their way to take Amanda on a memorable trip. Naomi drove several hours, and asked, "Marian do you want to take a turn driving?" Marian hesitated, not quite trusting to drive such a new minivan, so Naomi kept driving and fell asleep on the Turnpike in western Pennsylvania. She was jolted wide-awake when the wheels left the pavement! She kept repeating, "oh my, oh my, I can't stop, what can we do?" The vehicle was out of her control and going fast, and for a while it appeared that they would stay upright and just go for it wild bumpy ride across the turf in the median. They began to slow down, when Bam, the front end of the van hit a solid concrete culvert.

The van stopped on its side with the driver's side up! Naomi somehow climbed over Marian, and got out the window. A stranger stopped and asked Marian if they could help her, "yes, open my seatbelt!" Marion was hurt the most, and her leg appeared to be broken. Below the knee, her foot turned sideways.

An ambulance soon arrived and took them all to the closest hospital, at New Stanton, PA. Amanda had been calmly relaxed, sleeping in the back seat. She had a cut on her forehead that bled profusely, but she was not hurt much otherwise, neither was Naomi. Walter and Pete came to take everyone back home, so Naomi, Marion and Amanda did not get to see Indiana and the relatives at the funeral.

Marion refused to sign admission papers at the hospital, even if they begged her three times pleadingly. One nurse even said, "You are in the way in the ER if someone else should arrive!" The hospital admitted Amanda and she stayed overnight. Before Walter and Pete arrived on the scene, the nurses gave Marian morphine, and put her into Amanda's room. Walter and Pete took Marian and Naomi along home in Pete's motor home, and returned the next day for Amanda. She was badly bruised, black and blue in the face, but okay otherwise.

Marian's leg was badly twisted but actually not broken, beneath a nasty cut. She went home wearing a removable Velcro leg brace, after the doctor straightened her bone. Marian was a slim person but she was hard to move with her very awkward straight leg.

Naomi asked Pete to take them in the first place, but he was much too busy. He regretted that decision because he found plenty of time to go bring them back home and buy a new vehicle. Naomi felt responsible, as though the accident was all her fault, and she felt bad about it. She took Amanda into their home and cared for her in every way she could. Marian felt it was her fault, because she should have been taking a turn to drive. Be that as it may, it was all hindsight. God moved in a mysterious way, and that is what it took to get Amanda

to stop driving. She never sat behind a steering wheel again, after seeing how quickly something could happen. She was never in a traffic accident before! Pete's new minivan was demolished, but that was as nothing compared to letting Amanda drive until she kills someone on the road.

∽

Herman Vogt from Germany read Amanda's letters in the Budget. He was a political scientist, ordained as a Lutheran minister, writing a book about alternative cultures in the United States. He wanted to study the Amish in Pennsylvania, the Church of Jesus Christ of Latter-day Saints in Utah, the Pueblo Indians of New Mexico, and the Hispanic Society in Arizona. Herman wrote a letter to Amanda, asking permission to spend several weeks in their neighborhood. Amanda enjoyed German reading and writing, and she said, "Yes".

Herman Vogt arrived at Amanda's residence in August and boarded there. Wesley and Walter helped show him around, and he slept at different places. He attended Churchtown church with Amanda and Henry's, and he attended the Amish church at Honey Brook, as well as the Bowmansville Joe Wenger church. Amanda made many meals for him and she was too busy to write in her diary. She took him over to Jesse Brubacher's for supper and Petes had a chicken barbeque for all of Aaron and Amanda's children and grandchildren that wanted to meet Herman. Walters took Herman and Amanda to the Ephrata Cloisters and to the open market at Green Dragon,. He was keenly interested in the Black Creek one-room school where Alice Shirk taught. He met many other people in the area, and he took along home a small quilted wall hanging. He enjoyed his tour and Wesley took him to York, for a bus to go to Washington DC, and then he flew home to Germany.

Amanda felt rich when she made a new friend, no matter if it was the lowest waif in society, or someone near the top. Amanda knew that Aaron would have loved meeting these people. Herman enjoyed his trip to Lancaster County Pennsylvania so much, that his daughter Dorothy came along the next time.

⁓

Amanda kept busy, even without her driver's license. She had time to sew sleeves into two dresses for Aunt Lydia. Amanda went looking for mushrooms and walked her Budget letter to the mailbox. She enjoyed the Christmas carolers that came to her door; children came from Black Creek School! She spent many hours on the telephone talking to her children and her many friends. She enjoyed the deer hunting stories from Missouri, as much as though they happened at her doorsteps. Amanda pieced several quilt tops for pay, for Daniel's wife Edna, and she appliquéd several tops for Ruth Weiler in Missouri. She still had time for travelers, and serving dinner guests. She did not forget the hospitality of inviting newlyweds for Sunday dinner, such as people invited Aaron and Amanda in their first year of married life.

Anytime Amanda wished to go away, she depended heavily on other people. Walters took her many places such as to a German singing, canning fruit at the Fairmont home, going to Aunt Lydia and all the grocery shopping and such. Marian took Amanda to the Lancaster Courthouse, to the Ephrata hospital for stomach x-rays and to dinner invitations. Henry and Rachel Van Zee kindly took Amanda along to church many times.

Without drivers license, Amanda still went traveling. Wesley took Amanda to Maryland to meet her cousin Lena, and two others. Together those four traveled to Niagara Falls and Canada by bus. They had a three-day bus tour around the falls. Amanda first saw Niagara Falls in 1937, but she still pondered the magnitude of such a miracle in God's creation. Fifty years later after seeing the falls countless times, the powerful waterfalls still tumbled with no end in sight. One drop of water is such a great miracle, and how can anyone resist the truth of the creation story?

After spending time with relatives in Ontario, they took another bus to Detroit with beautiful scenery all day, and arrived at Petoskey Michigan. Friends and relatives took them to Burt Lake and the Mackinac Bridge, for a four-hour boat ride. They later returned by bus to Pittsburgh where Walter and Marian fetched Amanda again.

Aaron had often said, "These Michigan people should have been born with wheels beneath them!" Nancy and Anna Mary Kilmer took Amanda to see the Strasberg Railroad Museum, when they came traveling to PA from Missouri. Wesley lived close by, and Janie took her mother-in-law many places.

Amanda enjoyed many trips to Missouri. She took a leisurely six-week trip in 1992, staying for two weddings. Travis and Anna Mary Martin married on May 23, and Amanda stayed for Fay Elaine and Shannon Weiler's wedding on June 27. She spent one day with each of her daughters. The married children in PA said, "You sisters in Missouri see more of mom than we do, because she does not come to spend a day at a time with us." At Roland's, Amanda watched Faith enjoy a bath and she helped her little handicapped granddaughter put stickers in her sticker collection, a fun thing because they both enjoyed stickers so much.

She toured Oakwood Industries where a grandson helped make oak furniture and she toured the Country Cooked Potato Chip factory, where Ivan worked. Her descendants in MO enjoyed a chicken BBQ in her honor, and Mahlons had a picnic at Lake Show Me, where they watched Willard, a grandson, give sailboat rides. Amanda did not want a ride!

In between the weddings, she met her sisters in central Missouri. Daniels came from PA to take Amanda home again, but they went to Wisconsin first and met Jim and Clydine Sauder, Amanda's granddaughter. Aaron's nephew, Eli Shirk made a good tour guide to locate the rest of the nieces and nephews in Wisconsin. After a forty-five minute boat ride at Wisconsin Dells, they bought a 40-pound block of good cheese and headed home again.

Amanda never complained about loneliness at home. She found the simple secret of happiness... and there was nothing complicated about it. Anytime she made others happy, she was happy. Meeting friends and helping others left no room for self-pity. She made seven phone calls in one evening, keeping in touch. She was not forgotten; even president and Hillary Clinton sent her a birthday card when she turned 81.

Amanda enjoyed traveling, but she also appreciated the close-up wonders at her doorstep, such as the 16 little ducklings that hatched in the east end of the barn, as well as the birds at her feeders. Marian brought a cleaned and dressed chicken to Amanda's kitchen. Amanda realized how much she depended on Marian for every little thing, even more so, on the day that Marian stepped on a bee. Being highly allergic to the bee sting, Marian had a serious reaction! The ambulance came screaming to Amanda's residence and took Marian to the hospital for two nights. She nearly died!

Thankfully, Marian recovered, and still took Amanda shopping, and elsewhere. At the grocery store, Amanda had trouble reading labels, and so did her sister Lydia. Both of them were slow and choicy, preferring certain brands of groceries. Amanda tired of her sister Lydia's fussy shopping many times, but soon Amanda tried Marian's patience, in the grocery store.

Amanda told her visitors that she still did her own cooking and sewing, and housework. She did not know that the electric kitchen range was turned off at the breaker switch every night for safety reasons. Amanda's hearing was really keen, often too keen, when she heard things talked about her in the next room. It was true that she could still sew, but not her own clothes. She spent lots of time in her "shpeel shtoop" (play room), her sewing room. Amanda learned to sew by hand, at the age of four, and 90 years later, she sewed nearly every day on her electric sewing machine, for the sheer joy of it! Others cut the 3-inch square patches in assorted colors, and she had the fun of arranging them into four patches, creating wedding gifts for her 103 grandchildren. She also made a crib quilt for the first-born great-grandchild in each family. That kept her busy until her gnarled fingers bent with arthritis could no longer quilt or use a thimble.

Rhoda's granddaughter said, "You are the oldest person I know! "Amanda cherished that thought.

When Amanda had a slight stroke, the doctor put her on blood thinner at the hospital, where she spent two days. Janie took Amanda to her many doctor appointments. Amanda was aging, and she was not eating properly. Walter and Marian saw a need for a special helper for Amanda.

Rosene Martin lived close by and worked three days a week at a pretzel bakery, making hand twisted pretzels. She also had a job at Green Dragon one day a week. On her days off, Rosene helped Amanda, two days a week. That was all the help Amanda needed at the time, and Rosene kindly caught up on Amanda's housekeeping.

Amanda still enjoyed sweets when her sense of taste was nearly gone. Rosene baked cookies and Daniel sometimes stopped in at Harding's bakery and brought along some goodies, as Aaron used to.

Amanda repeated stories over and over again. Everyone tired of the same stories! She enjoyed reminiscing about the past and often repeated how that people thought Aaron and Amanda might lose some children, so close to the wooded hills. After listening to the same story one time too often, Marlin Brubaker said, "Maybe you had more than 15 children and one did get lost!" "Ach, no!" Amanda insisted.

Amanda was seventy-nine years old when her youngest grandchild was born. She did not recognize those youngest ones as her grandchildren and they fit in better with the dozens of great-grandchildren. Her memory had filled to capacity... like one of those tacky fly ribbons she hung on the kitchen ceiling. It was full and there was no room for more, and the glue was no longer sticky.

Her memory no longer recorded current happenings, but she could still accurately say where the horses and the cows stood in the barn in Michigan, and she still knew their names. She said: *The first horses my father had that I remember, were Tom, a black horse and Jerry, a brown one. Later I remember Molly the buggy horse, she was quote old. Then we had Flora, she had several colts...big heavy farm chunks. We bought a dappled gray mare from Uncle Joe Brenneman, named Bertie. She was a partner for Laura, Flora's first colt born at our place. We found Bertie dead in the pasture one morning, bloated with colic!" We lived so far north that our corn did not fully ripen, so we cut it for silage. Our wooden silo had only boards across the top for a roof."*

Amanda memorized many poems; Katrina comes to our school, her seat is next to mine. She used to live in Germany beside the river Rhine. Her cheeks are pink as cherry bloom, her lips ten times as a red. But none of us could understand a word Katrina said. She always comes to school on time, her desk is just as neat, I'm sure I'm twice as careful, since Katrina shares my seat. She makes me have some new thoughts, some kinder thoughts to know. But though I cannot speak to her, I love Katrina so.

Without skipping a word, Amanda could recite the poem: Twenty froggies went to school...down beside the rushing pool...! She also remembered the poem about the Barefoot Boy with cheeks of tan, and she recited the Village Blacksmith, as well as many other poems and the names of the people in her school and in her childhood. When her young children came sobbing to her, years ago, Amanda often said, "Suppose my little lady, your doll should break her head. ..would you make it well by crying, till your eyes and nose are red?"After Amanda recited the entire poem, her daughter usually forgot the hurt. Amanda still knew all the words.

Amanda had conveniences at her fingertips, like never before. Instead of a wood stove, she had a thermostat on the wall for heating and cooling. She had the latest electric appliances, even a microwave. The automatic washer, and dryer nearby, needed very little of her time for doing the laundry, but gone were the huge piles of dirty wash. She no longer needed to preserve food. Pete said, "If mom had all these conveniences years ago, she could have raised thirty children!"

Amanda did not like to use a window fan, and possessively said "Des iss my house!" (This is my house). She wanted to keep the windows closed in summer time to keep the warm air out. Pete installed an air conditioner that she learned to appreciate, without knowing it. When guests arrived from out of state, Amanda greatly enjoyed giving them a small gift or souvenir, such as people in Canada always did. At times, she opened her hutch and gave away Blue Willow dishes and antiques, not knowing better. She enjoyed giving!

Every year she was harder to please. She wanted her undershirt hung up by the straps, not upside down! Her sister Lydia was even harder to please, and when Marian kindly helped Lydia with laundry, she took it along home to dry, where Lydia could

not see how it hung. Lydia got upset when a helper put dishes in the wrong place on the shelf, and her canning was not done right if others did it for her. Davy Hoover's kept Lydia and Christ out of the nursing home as long as possible, but eventually they could not handle them at home.

When Lydia and Christ both moved to the Fairmont home, their personal items sold over family auction at Davy Hoover on Sept 2, 2000. Since Lydia and Christ both married twice, more families were represented. Several days before the auction, Rhoda, Irene, Naomi, and Ruth obtained permission to take Amanda to see the auction things, and mark what Amanda remembered. Amanda, like a child, wanted everything she saw! It jolted her memory into vivid recall of years gone by. "This stuff means more to me than to anyone else, 'she said. Amanda knew which things from Lydia's glass- front cupboard came from Michigan.

Rhoda said, "This old broken off table knife is junk." Amanda said, "Geps mol haoh" [give it here] then they marked the knife as grandma Sarah Ann Brenneman's Sunday table knife and it brought nearly $17 on the sale day.

Amanda pointed out Joshua's extra long baby dress and baby cup. Many items brought back loving memories of home, as she held them close. "Oh, Joshua!" Oh how times have changed... Michigan... the sweet innocence of childhood... Amanda wanted it all, and oh, the memories that went with Joshua's set of double dominoes!

Her children explained to her," We may not take anything now, because it is all set up for the auction day and we will buy it then." They had to watch their mother, because Amanda slipped into her pocket, a hand-made wooden chain she knew her Uncle Isaac had carved. He also made a horse –hair, pocket -watch chain. Amanda keenly remembered watching Uncle Isaac make one and she never quite figured out how he did that. "Oh no mom, you must let it here and we will buy it at the sale, just for you," Irene said. They bought the wooden chain for $50!

Amanda's sister Katie bought Joshua's baby cup and his Church and Sunday School Hymnal book. Rhoda bought a glass jar full of soil from

Michigan and one from May City Iowa...souvenirs that held memories to the people that had lived there. For $115, Amanda purchased the tiny iron with a removable handle that her mother had used to iron coverings. It had come in a cupboard her parents bought at an auction in Michigan... the sweet memories overwhelmed Amanda. .. her mother... yes, her mother ironing a covering... oh for a mother's love! Amanda got a lump in her throat and tears in her eyes.

37

Walters moved to Missouri in 2002 and Duane and Sylvia Leinbach moved to the home place. Amanda enjoyed the privilege of watching their young children, her great grandchildren.

Rosene was a good helper, and she had drivers license to take Amanda many places, but Amanda needed more help on other days. Jesse Brubacher's Annie lived just across the field, and came as needed. She skillfully coaxed Amanda to take a bath, and helped shampoo her hair.

Annie had a talented way of painting beautiful saw blades and milk cans and everything anyone asked her to paint. She painted many horse and buggy scenes, because they sold well. Annie became a hero, when she painted a damaged spot on the linoleum where Sylvia had quickly set down a hot pan on the floor, after the hot pan burned her hand. No one would ever notice the scar anymore!

Amanda's daughter Ruth, married Carl Weiler and lived in Missouri. She had breast cancer, and lost all her hair with chemo treatments. When Pete's Lucille sent wedding invitations to everyone, for July 1996, Ruth felt unable to attend. With some coaxing and a plane ticket given to them, Carl and Ruth came to the wedding, even if she wore a wig. All the fifteen children rejoiced to be together for the first time in fifteen years. They had not been together since Aaron's funeral in 1981. Time brought many changes and that was the last time Carl saw his mother before she died.

Several years later, Ruth's cancer returned. She sent Amanda many letters by mail, but her neat hand -writing turned shaky, when she was dying with cancer. With a Mother's Day card to Amanda, Ruth wrote, *"oh how I begged the Lord for good health, but I need to resign and say Thy will be done! It makes me sad to see my sisters able to travel, and to work, but God has a good place ready for me, and I just thank him for forgiving my sins. I pray that I could hold out faithful to such a happy end in heaven."*

Ruth was anointed with oil, and felt at peace. She was the first of the fifteen children to enter eternity. She died on July 3, 2001. Ruth and Carl Weiler had nine children, with three still at home. Kenny married the following month, but Marlene, the youngest, was only seventeen. Amanda wanted to attend the funeral and everyone thought she should. Petes brought Amanda to MO in their motor home, and Annie came along as a helper. Amanda understood that Ruth died, but she soon forgot!

Within the next year, five more of Amanda's close relatives died. On February 11, 2002, Aaron's brother Ben M. Shirk, died in Indiana, and three weeks later, Christ Shirk died, leaving Amanda's sister Lydia a widow at the Fairmont home. Amanda went to visit Lydia regularly, still fulfilling the nearly 70-year-old promise, "I would do most anything I could for you!" Lydia craved Amanda's attention more than ever!

Amanda and her sister Lydia

When senior citizens died, Amanda understood that their allotted time of three score and ten years, was spent, but death was harder to understand, when Wesley's wife Janie died from cancer, on March 17, 2002, at the age of 50. She struggled with a tumor on her brain, and cheerfully looked forward to heaven, saying," The best is yet to come!" After the funeral, The Shirks had a family get-together at the Fairview reception Center, where 225 people attended. Fifty-five people came from Missouri for Janie's funeral. The parting hymn had new meaning, when the family sang together, "farewell brethren, farewell sisters, till we all shall meet again."

Wesley Shirk and Carl Weiler were both widowers, in less than eight months time. They formed a bond of understanding.

Amanda's stepmother -in- law died, four weeks later, on April 19, 2002. That same year, Amanda's sister Lydia died at the nursing home on August 30.

When Amanda turned 90, Martha said, 'Mom, just think, you are 90 years old!" Amanda said "Ach mainshts? Sell vorah duch olls olde lite! [Do you mean that? those used to be old people!]

Sunsets

For 65 years, Amanda could look out of her west kitchen window and see the most gorgeous sunsets. Perhaps the sun did rise an hour or so later, behind the shadow of Laurel Hill, but the sunsets in Amanda's life were most glorious, with Jesse Brubacher's farm buildings silhouetted in lavish color and also the lone black walnut tree, on the line fence between them. Amanda often paused with a thank you prayer for God's goodness, and for the food she prepared for her family as she stood working by the stove, admiring God's vivid handiwork while making supper. 'There is no diamond in the world as beautiful as a sunset!'

The sun was setting in Amanda's colorful life, and one of her favorite songs was, "We are going down the valley one by one... human comrades you or I will there have none..." Her sisters Mary and Betsy had died and so did their husbands and Amanda's brother Silas. Since Lydia and Christ

died, Amanda had only one sister remaining on earth, and both Katie and Amanda had out- lived their husbands.

Duane Leinbach's had a fourth daughter born at home, soon after they moved on the farm. Amanda was delighted with a brand new baby, to rock and to cuddle. She came over and looked at baby Sara, and held her... and asked, 'What is her name..., and how much did she weigh? The next day, the baby was new all over again, because Amanda forgot, and the next day again...and again....

Duane's took Amanda one square meal a day, but she forgot to eat, as she read the paper and the food turned cold an hour later. They kept tabs on grandma, with an intercom.

Duane Leinbach fixed up the old bank barn, as a shop for his electrical business. They enjoyed raising their family on the farm, close to the pond and the woods. Their children had fun riding trikes and bikes on the long blacktopped lane. Amanda enjoyed watching children and all the action around her, as her lovable great granddaughters came singing to her and spoke in her native language of Pennsylvania Dutch.

Duane enjoyed hunting for spring mushrooms, and cutting firewood. He tried tapping trees for maple syrup, and enjoyed the wild geese, deer, turkey and the fox. He successfully planted watercress to eat, such as Aaron had often wished for and he did not think he could raise any. Duanes considered it a real privilege to live close to nature, and he built a small cabin in the woods, with a bridge across the creek. His cattle in the pasture kept the meadow attractive for walking the trails.

Every fall when the leaves turned color, the Shirk family converged at the home farm for a winter garden day. Dozens of people headed to the woods, collecting any moss or plants of interest for a winter terrarium. Amanda enjoyed the leisurely walk into the woods, although rather slowly. Eventually her family took her along on a wheelchair, and she leaned over admiring pipsissewa, wintergreen berries, crowsfoot. ..look at this...and that! Through the creek and up the slope, a trail turned right, across the powerline. The old road remained as part of the' bootleg trail 'and the history of moonshine, seventy years ago.

In pleasant weather, Annie lured Amanda outdoors for a walk around the circle drive, by carrying along baby Sara. Amanda scolded that the baby needs a cap or stockings, even in the heat of August. Any time a baby cried, she still checked for diaper pins accidentally opened, but she found none, because the babies wore disposable diapers! The elastic in the rubber pants was not too tight either, because they did not wear any, so Amanda insisted that the Pampers might be uncomfortable. All her life, she did not want to hear a baby cry, and said, "Uss vill dugh eppus!" (It wants something.) She remembered those years when her own babies wore safety pins and sometimes one popped open. Each diaper had four pins back then, two big ones at the top and two more that held up the stockings.

Amanda no longer walked to her mailbox and seldom used the stairs. She barely did any work anymore, and did not need to work. She often got her days mixed up after a nap. She still enjoyed every new day as a gift from God, and found contentment in all that she did. When talking to a daughter on the telephone, Amanda said, "I never had it so good!"

Sylvia was used to grandma and her ways, and scarcely noticed how bad Amanda's memory really was. Eventually, they hired Pauline Weaver to stay with Amanda day and night. Amanda did not think anyone needed to take care of her, because she could do it herself! It was not hard to convince Amanda to let someone move in with her, by asking, "Would you have room to take in Pauline Weaver, as a lady that needs a place to stay?" It was true that Pauline wanted a job and a place to stay, and Amanda never turned down a needy or a homeless person all her life.

The arrangement worked better than anyone had dared to hope, as both learned to live together in peace. When Amanda became defiant or possessive of her belongings, she soon forgot. She could not hold grudges, when she could not remember, and the two became friends.

Remarriage

Carl Weiler missed Ruth more than words could tell. After three lonely years, he married her first cousin, Ida Martin. She was the daughter of Dan and Katie Martin from Indiana, living in Canada, as a missionary among the Indians at Red Lake. She had remained single, among her many friends from the deep North Woods.

On their wedding day, June 12, 2004, the mother of the bride, and the mother of the groom were sisters, Amanda and Katie. Amanda was not a mother to Carl Weiler, but he treated her as such, the only mother remaining and the grandmother to his children. The sisters wore alike new dresses, and sat side by side in their wheelchairs, enjoying the moment, but not remembering why.

Four months later on October 16, 2004, Wesley also remarried. He found a wonderful wife that resembled Janie, and had remained single all her life, seemingly just for him. He was a truck driver, and Wanda worked on a night shift at a bakery, but their time together was well spent, as they each kept their individuality.

Amanda enjoyed traveling but she could not remember that she was there, even for the moment. At the age of 91, she went along in Pete's motor home to Indiana one last time, to the funeral of Dan Martin, her sister Katie's husband. She did not know why she came, nor did she recognize her Indiana relatives. On the way home, a dark-haired young man held the door open for her at a rest area. Amanda asked him, "Are you Johnny Kilmer?" Everyone grinned!

When Amanda needed cataract surgery, two of her daughters went along, to make sure they know what the doctor said. He commented on, "bringing the family along today. "The girls smiled and said they were two out of the 15 children. "My, my, such a big family... and grandchildren... and great grandchildren may I ask?" He was amazed with the numbers of 103 living grandchildren, and 275 great-grandchildren, what a family!

When the doctor asked, "Amanda, how are you feeling today?" she said," I have much more to be thankful for, than to complain about." He smiled and said, "Make sure you teach that to your 400 children!"

Those numbers rapidly increased, and soon Amanda had 500 descendents. In Missouri, a grandson had twins, Lavon and Martha High named their babies, Aaron and Amanda! Amanda was pleased when she heard the names, and when she saw the twins, but she couldn't remember them.

Current schoolbooks taught in 1990; " the number of people living today is greater than the total number who ever lived and died before us. Five billion people live on the earth, and if the present growth rate continues, another 5 billion will be added in the next 40 years. Can the planet support that many people? Will the coal and oil be exhausted? "Those numbers might sound alarming, until a person understands the power of God, natural disasters and diseases.

Amanda had no concerns about overpopulation, because she understood that a swarm of hard working people helping each other did not pose a problem. The low moral standards in America concerned her much more. She said, "The educated and the rich people are having less and less children, while in the slums they still have so many. The world will become unbalanced, with not enough honest hard working people." Lloyd Burkholder's sermon mirrored her thoughts, when he preached and said, "The world is in dire need of good Christian homes!"

America was becoming an abomination, long before Obama ruled the nation! A democracy is always temporary in nature, and not a permanent form of government. It will only exist until the voters start voting themselves generous gifts from the public treasury, and then it will collapse, due to selfish and dishonest people near the top. Headlines in the local papers revealed corruption and spiritual wickedness in high places.

Amanda wrote, "It is later than we think and we should have our lamps filled and ready! God's guardian angels are over the little ones, but we must still do all in our power to protect them, and not forget to thank God for their and our safekeeping."

America was comparable to a rugged old gas-guzzling vehicle with very loose steering! With The check- engine light on, rusted metal, cracked windshield, chipped paint, patched tires, leaking oil, and the muffler dragging loudly, it kept on going. Who would ever wish to be the president of America? Pray for all the leaders, they need help!

More and better schools cannot fix the problem of broken homes, and corruption within the hearts. No country is stronger than its homes...and that appeared alarming, but Amanda had no more worries in her life, because she kept forgetting.

Long ago, on November 16, 1937, Aaron and Amanda married in Michigan, on the same day as Aaron and Ada Leinbach married in Pennsylvania. Both couples lived close together near Bowmansville and enjoyed visiting together. In their senile years, Amanda and Ada had much in common. As they sat side-by-side chatting happily, both widows kept repeating the same question to each other, "Vaasht do ess meah khiat hen duh same dauk?" (Do you know that we got married the same day?)

Amanda came up with some unusual sayings, stuck in her mind from many years ago. She memorized a vast amount of poetry and much of it remained. She also quoted, "I wish I was at home and the dog was here!" She said it many times, and still remembered her dog at home in Michigan, named Nellie. Another quote, "so gates in de shtates, un in Canadah ken bassah!" (So it goes in the states and in Canada no better.) See you later alligator! Among all the childish things, Amanda knew the words to many nice songs. She sang, 'My faith looks up to thee..."many times over.

She still enjoyed a sense of humor. Rhoda's daughter came to visit, and Amanda asked," How far did you come? "When Lisa said "thirty miles", Amanda quickly said ", that is how far I have to your house!"Amanda knew she was born in 1915, but she did not know her age. If anyone asked, she fondly said,"As old as my tongue and a little older than my teeth!"

Amanda wished to go home... home to Michigan... Any time when Amanda thought she was not at home, Annie Brubacher reminded her of the song, "This world is not my home, I'm just a passing through."Amanda talked fondly of Michigan and the people that lived there... especially the Gregory's...William... Rhoda... and Magdalene, from their church. Martha asked her mother, "Do you think those people are still there?" "Why yes!" Amanda insisted. In her mind, those things never changed in 70 years.

Amanda seldom sewed patches anymore, and no one laid out blocks for her at the sewing machine. With a sudden desire to sew, she cut and sewed together neat squares of toilet paper, when no one was watching. She still had a love of sewing, and so did all her daughters... and many granddaughters. Amanda passed on her uncanny skill of using every inch of fabric. One thousand miles away, a merchant noticed that some of Amanda's granddaughters used considerably less fabric to make the same dress pattern others made. If they laid each pattern piece precisely the right way, the dress could be pieced beneath the cape if necessary. Some of the ladies enjoyed the challenge and the satisfaction of skimping, even when money was not an issue. Perhaps it all started back when Amanda had to make do, with her limited feedbag fabric, or the dresses she altered.

When Amanda had a grouchy day, Irene made her happy, by reminding her to recite the poem about the leaves; Come little leaves said the wind one day,...come over in the meadow with me and play...Amanda finished all the verses, and sweetly forgot everything else.

Pauline

Pauline Weaver spent several weeks at Green Pastures and suddenly everyone understood how important she really was! Amanda needed her! Pauline had a choice, "Do you want to resume your job taking care of Amanda, or would you prefer to move in with your sister, where you had lived?"

Pauline had lived as the plainest Piker, using the outhouse in the middle of winter and living without electric or telephone. She returned to help Amanda. Pauline adapted well and learned to appreciate the microwave, air-conditioning and all the modern conveniences. Everyone rejoiced to see her come back. When she first started working, she did not want to take care of Amanda's personal

care, but it all happened so gradually and she was a perfect fit for the job. Annie Brubacher came several days a week and Pauline could take a day off. Amanda needed them both!

Annie and Pauline

Amanda's descendants added up rapidly with new great grand children every month. Pauline recorded each new addition on the chart on the wall. Some of the four hundred great grands had names she could barely pronounce. "Don't they like their children?" she asked.

Amanda still enjoyed going to church, and she did not want to miss communion. When Henrys came, and took her to Churchtown, they arrived late on purpose, to make the occasion less tiresome. Bishop Amos Martin passed out bread to each person individually as he said,"This is my body, which is broken for you... this do in remembrance of me...". Amanda wanted to share her communion bread with her daughter. The day was long enough, because Amanda had a hard time keeping her mind on the services. The babies got all her attention! She talked rather loudly, clucking, cooing, and gently whistling at every baby she met. Babies were still the most precious thing on earth !The bishop reminded everyone that some have taken communion for the first time and maybe some for the last time... It is not always the old ones that are taken...

After church dismissal, Amanda asked other people repeatedly, "Who are you? And who are your parents?" She had nothing to discuss, but kept repeating, "It was good to be here!"

Amanda's lungs were too weak for much singing, but she still enjoyed to listen, and quietly sang along. She had no use for any more earthly possessions, gifts, or keepsakes. The biggest gift her children could give at Christmas time or at any time was singing. Wesley and Wanda took Amanda to the Fairview reception center for a huge Shirk gathering and a singing in her honor. They told Amanda repeatedly where they were taking her and why. When they arrived she wondered, "Why do you bring me here where I hardly know anyone?" It was true. Amanda heard a lot of noise and commotion from her 301 descendents, that gathered to sing for her that day, but she did not recognize the many faces that called her mom or grandma, let alone the dozens of great grands, and a great, great, grandchild.

It was harder taking Amanda anywhere, and instead of doctor appointments, they opted for hospice. When the hospice nurse arrived, she first noticed and discussed things with Pauline, and checked Pauline's pulse and blood pressure. The nurse understood the value of taking care of the caretaker.

The hospice nurse met Amanda at her worst, as they were trying to change her into clean clothes. Amanda contrarily said, "I'm moving out tomorrow!" Everyone grinned and understood, knowing she was not able to do that, as she shuffled slowly with her walker. The hospice nurse helped straighten out what pills Amanda should take and which ones she could drop. She offered sedatives if necessary. Otherwise, everyone realized that Amanda really did not need to have so many checkups. After reevaluating her case, the nurse said, "Amanda's prognosis was for more than one year to live. " Therefore, hospice quit coming.

Amanda still kept her hands busy, and sometimes she measured things with the skirt of her apron, as though it were a yardstick. Over the years, Amanda used her apron in many different ways. In the garden, she used her apron as a bushel basket, and at the stove, it was her hot pad. While holding a baby on her lap, she used her apron as a blanket many times. The apron wiped away tears and she used it as a tape measure. Most of her aprons measured thirty-six inches wide.

One time in Michigan, Silas opened a banana with a worm in the center, and 80 years later those memories obsessed Amanda's mind, and she did not forget. Before eating any banana, she split it into three sections and inspected each piece carefully, although she never found a worm. Those memories lay dormant when Amanda had more important things to do, but in old age, she could hardly eat a banana properly.

Thankfully, Amanda could not see all the food that America wasted. As for dumping clothes, America was just as wasteful with their leftovers and out of style things. Young people threw away rather than mended clothes. Not many learned to wear things out as Peter Brubachers taught Amanda. Darning socks and mending went the way of the spinning wheel... outdated and unneeded. Amanda still insisted that "willful waste makes woeful want."

⁓

After Titus's funeral on July 14, 2009, Amanda asked Wesley, "Who are your parents?" Wesley gave her a big hug and said, "you are my mom... you changed my diapers!" Amanda did not recognize Louise, and thought she belonged to the Christian Kilmer family... perhaps Ada. Many years ago when the Brubacher families gathered, Aaron said, "if all of you take your children, I will take the rest!" Louise resembled those Kilmer cousins. With so many children playing together, do you think she got in the wrong carriage?

Wesley came to visit Amanda, and later he said, "I have to go home now mom!" Amanda said "I want to go home too! Wes spoke gently until his mother had tears in her eyes, "Yes mom, when the angels come, you may go home with them."

Was the best time of Amanda's life, her childhood in Michigan, or was the best time when she rocked and cuddled and taught her lively young children with Aaron at her side or perhaps the years of traveling as she pleased? She treasured her abundance of friends everywhere she went. Each step of the way, had advantages and disadvantages. As she looked back, Amanda felt fulfilled with a satisfaction of knowing she tried her best, even when she made many mistakes. Every day was the best day!

President and Michelle Obama sent Amanda a birthday card for her ninety fifth birthday. (A family member found an address where anyone with a thirty day notice, could ask for a birthday card for anyone over eighty years old.) Amanda added her card to the one from George and Laura Bush and the one from Bill and Hilary Clinton.

Life was short and winter came next! Amanda had white hair and her mind was numbed, like the cold of wintertime. She shuffled along slowly, after her mind was mostly gone and her book was closed. She still kept her gnarled twisted fingers busy holding a book, or twisting the trim of her blanket with the hands that cooked thousands of meals, for perhaps thousands of people, stitched millions of stitches and gave unselfishly to all she met. Love, the strongest force on earth is a natural affection, only when it is passed on and taught to others. Amanda did what she could, with what she had. Everything God gave to her was worn out. She tried her best in passing the torch to the next generation.

God be with you 'till we meet again!

With a weak voice, Amanda still sang, "Christ is all... all in all." Every time her children or any guests said goodbye, Amanda replied, "God be with you till we meet again."

When Amanda saw her Sunday tablecloth that she used so many times, she asked "did you bring that along?" While driving along familiar roads she said, 'I don't know where I am...I never want this way before! She said,"Hivvel nuch un hivvel noonah, oom de eck-a room!"[uphill, downhill and around the corners] She counted silos and asked repeatedly, 'Where are we going? Do the people know we are coming?"

Annie and Pauline could hardly manage Amanda's care anymore, at the same time that Duane Leinbach's planned to move into their new house on Yellow Hill, leaving Aaron and Amanda's farmhouse empty.

Who will take Grandma?

Who will take Grandma? Who will it be? All of us WANT her- I'm sure you'll agree!

Let's call a meeting- let's gather the clan. Let's get it settled as soon as we can.

In such a big family, there'll certainly be one, Willing to give her a place in the sun!

Strange how we thought that she'd never wear out, But see how she walks...it's arthritis, no doubt.

Her eyesight is faded, her memory is dim. She's apt to insist on the silliest whim.

When people get older, they become such a care! She must have a home, but the question is where?

Remember the days when she used to be spry? Baked her own cookies and made her own pie.

Helped us with lessons and mended our seams. Kissed away troubles and mended our dreams.

Wonderful Grandma! We all loved her so! Isn't it dreadful, she has no place to go?

One little corner is all she would need. A shoulder to cry on...her Bible to read.

A chair by the window with the sun coming through, Some pretty spring flowers still covered with dew.

Who'll warm her with love so she won't mind the cold? Oh, who will take grandma now that she is old?

What! nobody wants her! Oh, yes, there is One, Willing to give her a place in the sun.

Where she won't have to worry or wonder or doubt, And she won't be our problem to worry about.

Pretty soon now, God will give her a bed, But who'll dry our tears when dear grandma is dead?

Selected

. Irene and Marlin generously offered to take

Amanda into their home. In by-gone years, Irene thought she could care for the handicapped, because she was used to playing with broken dolls. Amanda took in needy people all her life and taught her children to do the same. Marlins converted a room just for Amanda and moved her in, on August 30, 2010. The bedroom suited Amanda, as she looked around and asked, "How did you manage to get such a big house?

Amanda's hearing remained sharp. She heard traffic on the road...the clip clop of horses feet... she heard a cell phone singing and many beeping, buzzing sounds that her generation grew up without. She heard someone walking upstairs, and the washer vibrating. She heard a hair dryer whirring and asked. "Do I hear the threshers?"She slept well. Irene said,"We are not going away today..."Oh yes!. ..going to Michigan"! Marlin's two young girls, Lovina and Louise helped care for grandma with a lot of work and sacrifice. "

Amanda was not at her daughter's home long, before she scolded Irene and said,"Des iss my house!"She did not remember she moved! She enjoyed any children that came and especially babies! Is it mine? I like her more than anyone else does!

Amanda's sons spent countless hours getting the home farm ready for auction. The girls put in long days emptying closets and corners full of trash and treasures. None of the children wanted to buy the farm at the current value. The well- kept, eighty-six acre farm, held untold memories, but the time came to say goodbye. On September 24, 2010, Tracy Jones the auctioneer never saw such a crowd of people arrive for a real estate sale. All of Aaron and Amanda's children came; and their friends and neighbors gathered to meet them. The farm sold for over a million dollars!" My, what would Aaron say?"

Time does strange things! All the children recalled vivid memories everywhere. Looking back can be enlightening and sobering, but it gladdened their hearts. Among this farm they found security and a sense of belonging. The riches they shared were satisfying and fulfilling in a way they never dreamed possible as they reflected on how things turned out. While growing up, they were easily embarrassed and not aware of their good fortune.

Amanda holding baby Amanda

Parents had loved them and taught them not to fear people.

The next day, Tracy Jones auctioned Aaron and Amanda's remaining personal family possessions at Pete's garage. Touching keepsakes stirred up deep memories...such as Aaron's shaving brush and the pan that he hung a cake in, on the wall...the wedding dress and history galore. Some things came from Michigan such as the knitting machine, a slate blackboard, dishes, quilts, dolls, Joshua's ball and much more. .. The spouts for tapping maple syrup still worked as good as new. Words cannot describe the auction from 9am to 4:45pm.

Amanda the millionaire! Such a title she never sought and never dreamed possible. She had no need for it. Why didn't God give the money to Aaron and Amanda when they needed to rely so much on others? He certainly could have, but perhaps he wanted them to feel poverty. How else could they understand the plight of others? How else could they blindly trust God and not money? His strength is made perfect in our weakness. Aaron and Amanda certainly had many weaknesses and serious struggles in their life and even so did the children of Israel back in Bible times. That is what life on earth is all about, a proving ground, a battle-ground for whatever comes your way.

None of the children ever quite realized how deeply Amanda's childhood affected them. She taught the next generation the best she knew and she wanted them to pass on the important things to their children. No matter how humble, it was a valued gift to have parents like Aaron and Amanda. The inheritance money distributed to their children was not nearly as big a gift to them, as that of teaching them right from wrong.

Amanda's health declined. In her last days, she talked about eng-el [angels]. RoseAnna talked to Amanda about Jesus and Heaven and asked, 'Did you see angels? As Amanda gazed heavenward, beyond Lewis and RoseAnna she smiled and softly said 'Yes'. She died in her sleep on December 28, 2010.

The news travelled fast and many travelers started packing and planning, because Amanda had 555 living descendants, besides all the in-laws. The family tree had turned into a forest! The great grandchildren numbered four hundred and thirty two. Amanda was twenty-three years old when she had her first child and Daniel was twenty-four at the time of their first child and so were their oldest daughters, or else those numbers could have stacked up faster yet. Amanda had six great- great-grandchildren.

All the 103 grandchildren wanted to be at their grandmother's funeral, but some could not come. Rhoda's Lisa and Leroy Hoover had a new baby girl on the day of the viewing, and some from Missouri did not come. Many of the younger great-grandchildren were not present.

Marlin Lauver stood up to speak at the Martindale Reception Center for short services before the funeral procession lined up a dozen cars, not including any grandchildren. The young preacher was only four years old when Aaron died. He summed up the life of Aaron and Amanda in one sentence when he said, *'Hardships, toil and poverty do not degrade society."* Aaron and Amanda understood that clearly, as they had looked back over their lifetime. The preacher went on to say, "Sin and wrongdoing are the downfall of mankind. Make righteousness your priority! Modern thinking has no room or time for a big family. Fifteen were dear to her !The family chose Psalms 34; 19 Many are the afflictions of the righteous, but the Lord delivereth him out of them all.* They sang, Shall we gather at the River.

Wild geese flew overhead on a brisk winter day as the family gathered at the graveyard; on January 3, 2011,. Preacher Leon Zimmerman reminded everyone that the battlefront is continually shifting. Amanda's testimony of faith has been handed down. Your assignment is to follow her as she followed Christ. At the closing of the grave they all sang," If you love your mother, meet her in the skies."

Bishop Amos Martin and John Martin preached inside the church." *Parents have no greater joy than to see their children walk in truth. Amanda's life book is closed, never to be opened again in this life. But at the great judgment day, her book, your book, my book will be opened, and our lives will be revealed and we will be judged according to our work. We cannot earn salvation, but "as ye did it unto the least of these my brethern, you did it unto me." John Martin went on to point out the impact of parent's choices; how many times those decisions multiplied in a big family. Time represents opportunity! What do you have time for? We were given this new year, and we are accountable and responsible for how we use it, if we will waste it or use it for service to Him. When a new year is gone, you can never recall it. It will fade into the past. You cannot depend on saying; My parents were Mennonite or Amish because that will not get us there. You and I will have to give an account of ourselves. Ye must be born again! Today is the day of opportunity, not yesterday or tomorrow. What really matters is, "Do I have Jesus in my heart? "*

He said,"When we went to visit Amanda, she repeated her children's names so often, until we left, we could almost repeat them ourselves. Her family was important to her". Among many more good thoughts, Amos read in Psalms 90, "we spend our years as a tale that is told." Amanda's tale had many pages! God put a period at the end of Amanda's book of life. Teach us to number our days, that we may apply our hearts unto wisdom. We are inclined *to heap to ourselves lots of information. Knowledge can be good and right, but it is so sad, when in the accumulation of knowledge, we fail to apply it. Wisdom is the application of knowledge! Are your choices a reflection of wisdom? Every day, as we are given a new day, put forth a little extra effort to include someone else in your plans. Begin by listening! We tend not to listen too well. Be willing to hear the struggles of others. Your mother often shared this German song. Entlich, Entlich [At last, at last !] Entlich has become real to her now.*

Finally, this old world will come to a close, and open into eternity.

Finally, finally there must be an end to all necessity

Finally ends the heavy yoke wrath and fear will then be broke

Finally turns the stumbling block into a precious golden rock. Entlich, entlich, Kumt ga-viss

Our responsibility is to conduct ourselves in a way to leave an impact on future generations. Today we have the opportunity to be vitruous men and women. Teach your children to say as Amanda did, 'God be with you 'till we meet again. 'If each of you will keep that comment, and use it as a mantle of her faith, how far will it spread?" The family sang, "Farewell brethren farewell sisters, till we all shall meet at home.

Nearly five hundred people gathered at the Martindale Reception Center for a soup and sandwich lunch, with the atmosphere of a reunion, before the crowd dispersed.

The half has not been told, but thank you, Aaron and Amanda for the choices you made... in choosing Christianity...simplicity...honesty and contentment in your living example, by appreciating God's creation on a small farm in God's country... not forsaken!

The World Book Encyclopedia says, 'Homemakers are the backbone of society!" Aaron and Amanda knew that and so did their parents as they passed on the important tools of, faith, hope and love. Never in their wildest imaginations could they have guessed how far their children might go.

No other generation before Aaron and Amanda saw so many changes in a lifetime...from frugal farming to space age technology and the computer generation. One of Amanda's children toured the holy lands at the same time a grandson flew to Spain and England on a business trip. Many things changed, but the Bible did not!

Aaron wanted to tell you that God wants your two hands and two feet! Amanda found the way to happiness was in helping others. Both are the same thing, as you put Christ first in everything you do. Live for Him each day and meet again in eternity. Nothing else matters! God be with you, 'till we meet again.

ABOUT THE AUTHOR

Louisa, the 10th child of Aaron and Amanda, married Ivan Martin and moved to Missouri in 1973, on a farm of their own. They raised nine children, Travis, Talmon, Troy, Timothy, Katrina, Sterling, Kermit, Mandy and Shane and have a growing number of grandchildren close by.

As a child, Louise enjoyed the out -doors, and nature in every aspect, from picking up a small snake to climbing a tree. In school, she learned drawing, something Amanda excelled in, but did not promote. In third grade Mrs. Zimmerman, favorably commented about Louise's lopsided freehanded Chickadee, in front of the class and boosted her confidence. When paint by number sets came in style, Amanda ordered some from Lee Wards. With those leftover paints, Louise doodled in art, and later acquired better supplies. As a bird lover, many of her projects included a bird.

She did not have painting lessons, and quilts were more fun. Creating income with her hands, while staying home with her family, formed a lifetime hobby.

Louise wrote a weekly nature column, at an elementary level for three years, working up the nerve to see her words printed. With that confidence, she desired to finish this book. A quilt is a work of art for one private home, and a book reaches out to many people.

One of the Shirks lost a cordless telephone and found it inside the deep freeze. What a surprise! As she repeated the story, an in-law said, "other people do things like that also, but it takes a Shirk to tell everyone about it!" Perhaps there is too much truth in that, but all the little details, even the embarrassing ones, are the facts that complete the picture of fifteen children and the life they lived.

They say, 'only the hunter, has the fun of telling the story, 'and it has been enjoyable digging up family history. People that helped proof read this said, 'Much could be said about the Aaron Shirk that we knew.' When a second person stated the same thought provoking comment, Louise realized that she only saw the inside story. She did not try to conceal the rest. If anyone out there has accurate information or memories of Aaron, please share them so she can better answer the next generation that keeps wondering, "Who was this A M Shirk?" Every time they ask that question, the other person chuckles and smiles and cannot explain. We would like to hear the rest of the story, even about eccentric, outspoken opinions. Send them to Louise Martin Route 3 Box 253, Memphis MO 63555.

More people need to write for their enjoyment and for God's honor. Everyone has a story to tell, no matter what the circumstances. Start by collecting bits of history and stories about the characters that you want the next generation to remember. Perhaps some -day your grandchildren want to know the details after you are gone. Now is the time to gather those memories and jot them down, even if you have no desire to write a book. Children cherish the past, mostly when they get older. Your memories can be gold nuggets of treasures for them. Take advantage of our freedom of the press! There are more publishers available than ever and books are not out of style, even in the computer generation. With the help of God, you never know what can happen to five loaves and two small fishes. All the mistakes in this book belong to Louise, and if there be any praise, it all belongs to God.

Let them praise the name of the Lord: for he commanded, and they were created. Psalms 148:5